WILD FLOWERS

SARAH RAVEN

PHOTOGRAPHY BY
JONATHAN BUCKLEY

B L O O M S B U R Y
LONDON · NEW DELHI · NEW YORK · SYDNEY

For Alexandra Chaldecott and Kate Hubbard,
who both encouraged me to write this book.

And in memory of my father, who first set me
on the wild flower path.

All my life, I have been in love with wild flowers. In the 1970s, as a girl, I used to go botanising with my father, John Raven, who was a classics don at Cambridge. From when I was seven or eight, we would go on trips together in his Morris Minor (later replaced by a mustard Mini Clubman), with a couple of ham rolls, a bottle of fizzy apple juice and a large bar of Fruit & Nut. We would see pasqueflowers on Therfield Heath in Hertfordshire, oxlips in Hayley Wood in Cambridgeshire, fritillaries in Magdalen Meadow, Oxford. On expeditions further afield, we would find Mountain Avens tucked into the limestone pavements of the Burren in Ireland, spreads of sea-lavender on the salt marshes of the Norfolk coast and exquisite miniature alpine plants high on the hills of Argyll.

My father was an expert amateur botanist with an incredible grasp of everything that made up a place: its geology, soil, altitude, the way it faced in relation to wind and sun, and the plants that were likely to grow there. He inherited his love of the natural world from his father, Charles Raven. Between them, astonishingly, they painted almost every plant in the British flora. On their expeditions, whenever they found a new example, they would get out their paints and record it that night in their lodgings or, if it was too rare a specimen to pick, in situ. I still have eighteen volumes of their watercolours.

I have less patience than my father ever did, but he taught me how to look with an eagle eye and, even more usefully, how to botanise at twenty miles an hour. We used to drive along lanes together – not too fast and not too slow – me looking out of the window at one verge, him at the other, shouting out whenever we spotted a cracker.

Getting to know wild flowers adds a new layer to the way you experience the world. An ordinary walk is suddenly full of a new cast of characters. Some you will know already, plants that appear reassuringly in the same places year after year: Primrose, Bluebell and Dog-rose. These will become old friends. But you will also gather your favourite rarities, high-glamour creatures, such as Frog Orchid, Fly Orchid, White Water-lily and the perfect single flowers of Grass-of-Parnassus, each stem exquisite and strange.

Of course, there are bores, as at any party. I do not love Dog's Mercury, and I can take or leave Dandelions. But if you look, you will find their more intriguing relatives, hawkbits, just round the corner, some pale and modest, others a bit racy – a touch of orange here, a splash of lemon yellow there. Even the thugs are interesting: Indian Balsam, Butterfly-bush and Japanese Knotweed, all shockingly brutal in their way. The point is that a party where you know half the guests is always going to be more fun. What was just background before suddenly becomes a world in itself.

My father died when I was seventeen, and that was the end of my formal botanising trips for twenty years. I did not stop loving wild flowers; I just stopped hunting them. Particularly on trips abroad, I would still find myself wandering down a lane just to see what wild flowers were there. Then, recently, it struck me that this was how I was spending my most absorbed, relaxed and happy times. That moment of realisation is what lies behind this book.

When I took up botanising again in earnest to begin my research, I worried that most of the interesting wild flowers would have gone. The facts and figures certainly made uncomfortable reading. During the second half of the twentieth century, we ploughed, drained and 'improved' – with fertilisers or herbicides – almost all of our ancient meadows; others were abandoned and grasslands became rank and dominated by Bracken. The UK Biodiversity Steering Group estimated that 97 per cent of lowland semi-natural grassland in England and Wales disappeared during the fifty years to 1984, and the surviving meadows are fragmented and often degraded. Almost all our meadow plants are rarer as a result, with Green-winged Orchid, for example, now vanished from half its historical range and in many counties reduced to a handful of sites.

It is not just our meadows that have changed. In the four decades after the 1940s, most semi-natural habitats were drastically altered. Following the food shortages of the Second World War, ploughing grants were introduced, leading to the loss of unimproved grassland. New farming machinery enabled steeper slopes to be ploughed, and the myxomatosis outbreak of the 1950s, which decimated rabbit populations, further reduced the amount of chalk and limestone grassland, with vast stretches quickly reverting to scrub. Surveys of unimproved chalk grassland suggested a 20 per cent loss between 1966 and 1980.

Our roadsides have fared little better. Until the mid twentieth century, a lengthman carrying a scythe was employed to cut back the vegetation along every road and lane. The cut material was raked and stacked for a week or so, leaving time for the seeds to drop into the sward, encouraging wild flowers. Now, our roadsides are cut by toppers and the cuttings left where they fall, over-enriching the environment and adding to the effects of fertilisers and herbicides from adjoining farmland. This has vastly increased the growth of grasses and tall, strong growers such as Hogweed and Common Nettle.

That is not the half of it. We have stopped managing most of our woods and coppices; only plants that thrive in shade, such as Bluebell and Early-purple Orchid, are doing well in these neglected woods. We have drained many of our marshes and wetlands for agriculture and, as a result, the previously common Early Marsh-orchid has disappeared from 45 per cent of Britain and 40 per cent of Ireland. Thousands of miles of hedgerow have also gone, hugely decreasing plant numbers. According to one survey by the Institute of Terrestrial Ecology, the total length of hedgerows declined by a fifth in England and a quarter in Wales between 1984 and 1990.

The good news is that our wild flowers are – here and there – on the up again. Conservation organisations are reversing these downward trends, and grant aid has encouraged habitat restoration during the past twenty years. The flowers are more restricted in range than they once were, but far from extinct.

So, while there is no room for complacency, all is not lost. In researching this book, I have had a revelatory couple of years finding one life-enriching flower after another. Inevitably, I had to make some tough choices when choosing which plants to put in, and which to leave out. I decided to profile the species that you are most likely to see when going about your daily life, as well as a few that are rare but extraordinary. I included well-established escapes from cultivation as well as true natives, as you are just as likely to see these when out for a walk and want to know what they are.

Then, I needed to come up with some kind of principle by which to organise them. Being part of nature, and therefore by definition unruly, the plants would not fall into neat categories, so I made up my own. I divided them between eight habitats: wood; lane, wall and hedge; meadow; chalk down and limestone dale; arable and wasteland; water and wetlands; heath, moor and mountain; and coast. These overlap, so, for instance, there are many plants that grow in a wood that will also flourish on a dappled, shady lane. I have indicated these plants at the beginning of each habitat section.

Jonathan Buckley and I travelled to more than a hundred different sites to track down the flowers, from the Outer Hebrides to the southernmost tip of England, from far western Ireland to East Anglian beaches. Sometimes I would find twenty or thirty plants in one place, and Jonathan would then lie on his stomach for hours at a stretch photographing them. We both agreed that his pictures should not take the usual botanical specimen approach, which always seems to involve standing above the plant and photographing it like a shot rabbit. Only when you get down to a plant's own level can you see it for what it is, as well as every aspect of its environment, which make a great show for its crucial reproductive moment.

My greatest hope is that this book might encourage you to look at wild flowers with fresh eyes. If you feel inspired to go on an expedition of your own, the best starting point is your county's Wildlife Trust website; most counties have nature reserves. But do not get too hung up on finding the perfect location – where you go should not matter hugely. Even if you are stuck in a traffic jam on the motorway, or sitting on a train staring out of the window, once you are tuned in to this way of looking at the world, it is extraordinary what lovely things you will find right under your nose.

We all need to fall in love with wild flowers, and those who have loved them in the past must rekindle their affections. It is not just about appreciating biodiversity and all that implies for a rich and healthy environment. It is also about us, our connection to nature and the deepest possible delight that can be derived from feeling at home in a spectacularly flowery world.

Wood

The wood is where wild flowers start their year. They have to get out early to beat the shade of the leaves on deciduous trees, which close over to create deep shadow by mid May.

The tapestry usually starts in early March with Lesser Celandine, Ground-ivy and Primrose, and if you are lucky the odd patch of Sweet Violet, usually in a deep, voluptuous purple with the odd albino form. This is gradually added to by Wood Anemone, white and pink in carpets that can cover the whole woodland floor.

These plants merge together against a sea of green: Dog's Mercury, the glossy dark leaves of Bluebell and the odd spathe of Lords-and-Ladies. It is worth a special trip to chalky woods to find the green-flowered, shrubby Spurge-laurel and the Green and Stinking Hellebore.

I look forward to trips to Betty Dawes Wood in Gloucestershire for the mass of wild Daffodils and to Hayley Wood in Cambridgeshire for its Oxlips. They are both places that I visited as a child with my father in spring.

Bluebells are the dominant theme in the next wave of flowers, with the occasional Early-purple Orchid, splotch of Yellow Archangel and white stars of Greater Stitchwort scattered among them. Swathes of Ramsons colonise the lower, damper ground.

There is incredible scent in a wood at this time of year. At first it is very soft, unless you lie down and put your nose in a Primrose or Sweet Violet. Then it is vast and wafting, as the Bluebells emerge into flower. It is one of our most delicious and life-enriching flower moments.

Once the leaf canopy closes over, the range of wild flowers is much reduced. The same few plants appear again and again: Foxgloves, Wood Sage, Enchanter's-nightshade, red-berried Lords-and-Ladies, long-flowering Yellow Pimpernel and Wood Avens and the richly coloured Red Campion. Ferns are there, too, lush and green: Male-fern, Broad Buckler-fern and, the most elegant of all, Lady-fern.

Even these shade-tolerant plants seek out what light they can and spring up in larger numbers on the edges of sunny rides and woodland margins. That is where you will find curtains of Honeysuckle in June, filling the air with its incredible spicy fragrance, strongest at dawn and dusk. It is when an area has been coppiced and strong light reaches the floor that the summer wood is most colourful. Then Red Campion and Foxglove appear not by the hundred, but the thousand.

If you are lucky, in open woodland with reasonable levels of light you will find some rarities in the late spring and summer wood. Fly Orchid and Greater Butterfly-orchid in May or June; Broad-leaved Helleborine a few weeks later. These stand like beacons, conspicuous from metres away, appearing in similar spots from one year to the next. There is also the pretty Nettle-leaved Bellflower, which flowers all summer long, and the purple-belled, fat-fruited Deadly Nightshade, sometimes appearing in a good clump on the sunnier side of a wide path through a wood.

Woodland flowers diminish in autumn, save for the yellow-green flowers of Common Ivy. Before the golden Hazel catkins that will herald the start of the growing year in January, the only colour in a wood comes from evergreen leaves and Holly berries. In deep winter, when all the dried, stalky and seedy remains of the year's flowers are outlined in hoar frost, the woodland floor becomes a sparkling re-enactment of its springtime beauty.

You may also see Bell Heather (p.349), Bilberry (p.349), Bittersweet (p.393), Bracken (p.351), Bugle (p.68), Bramble (p.66), Common Figwort (p.72), Common Gromwell (p.72), Common Ivy (p.73), Cow Parsley (p.77), Crab Apple (p.77), Creeping Buttercup (p.149), Cuckooflower (p.297), Dogwood (p.79), Elder (p.80), False Oxlip (p.81), Field Forget-me-not (p.248), Germander Speedwell (p.85), Goat Willow (p.86), Golden-saxifrage (p.302), Gorse (p.355), Greater Knapweed (p.201), Greater Stitchwort (p.87), Herb-Robert (p.91), Hairy Violet (p.201), Hawthorn (p.89), Marsh-marigold (p.311), Oak (p.101), Pendulous Sedge (p.316), Perforate St John's-wort (p.209), Primrose (p.103), Rosebay Willowherb (p.258), Sheep's Sorrel (p.366), Sweet Violet (p.111), Timothy (p.166), Traveller's-joy (p.112), Tufted Vetch (p.166), Water Avens (p.318), Wild Angelica (p.324), Wild Strawberry (p.120) and Wood Crane's-bill (p.121).

Bird's-nest Orchid
(Neottia nidus-avis)

A plant from another world, this is always fun to find. It is one of three British orchids that have no green leaves. Instead of photosynthesising to make food, it gets what it needs from a mycorrhizal fungus. It can therefore survive in deep shade. The fungus absorbs carbohydrate from tree roots, providing minerals for the tree in exchange. The orchid gets its carbohydrates from the fungus, but does not provide anything in return. If you come across a Bird's-nest Orchid, you are likely to discover other interesting plants, as this grows in traditionally managed woods; the particular fungi that the orchid relies on, Sebacina, are associated with beech. The name Bird's-nest refers to its roots, which are a great untidy mass. Its flowers have a nice, slightly sickly honey scent.

Plant type Orchid family, Orchidaceae. *Flowers* May–June. *Height* 20–40cm. *Description* Erect saprophytic herb. Leaves are brownish, scale-like, sheathing the stem. Inflorescence is a dense spike of honey-coloured flowers. Each flower has perianth segments that form a hood, except the lower petal, which forms a diverging, two-lobed lip. It is most likely to be confused with unrelated species, such as broomrapes (p.421), rather than other orchids. *Companion species* Beech, although it may be found in mixed woodland and overgrown hazel coppice. *Distribution* Native. Found throughout Britain and Ireland, although rare in most regions. It is locally common in parts of southern England, becoming increasingly scarce to the north. It is very rare in northern Scotland. A significant decline in its distribution since 1945 is due largely to the replanting of semi-natural ancient woodland with conifers. *Habitat* Deep shade in broadleaved woodland on calcareous soils. It is most abundant on the chalk and limestone of southern England.

Bluebell
(Hyacinthoides non-scripta)

If we did not have bluebell woods, we would travel across the world to see them. They are unique to the Atlantic seaboard of Europe, so only we know what it is like to walk through a wood in April and May and get that incredible smell: a soft, sweet, almost indefinable scent. This perfume is oddly equivalent to the colour: a combination of so many different blues (and sometimes whites and soft pinks) that when you see them en masse you cannot quite define it. We resist the temptation to pick bluebells, but cutting them in fact does no harm. It is tramping across the foliage, or pulling out the bulb centre, which kills them. If you have picked a handful, sear the stem ends (2–3cm) for fifteen seconds in boiling water and they will look good for a week in water.

Plant type Asparagus family, Asparagaceae. *Flowers* April–May. *Height* 20–50cm. *Description* This hairless, perennial bulb has glossy, narrow leaves with hooded tips, which pierce the soil like missiles in early March. Flowers are cylindrical and bell-shaped, full of yellow stamens, with two blue-purple bracts at the base. Six perianth segments each curl up separately at the tip, like pigs' tails. It is easily confused with Spanish Bluebell (p.107) and the hybrid between the two (opposite). *Companion species* Bugle (p.68), Greater Stitchwort (p.87), Lesser Celandine (p.18), Ramsons (p.23), Wild Strawberry (p.120) and Wood Anemone (p.30). It also thrives in the shade of cliff-slope bracken. *Distribution* Native, very common across the British Isles, except high mountains and fens. Absent in Orkney and Shetland. *Habitat* Wide variety, including deciduous woodland, hedge banks and meadows. It prefers neutral to acid soils. Forms extensive carpets, especially under a closed canopy, where it often co-habits with Ramsons.

Bluebell (Native-Spanish Hybrid)
(Hyacinthoides x *massartiana)*

This fertile hybrid of the native Bluebell (opposite) and Spanish Bluebell (p.107) is the commonest cultivated bluebell in gardens and increasingly common in the wild. Discarded bulbs readily naturalise and then cross-fertilise with *H. non-scripta.* The danger with this hybrid (unlike the Spanish form) is that it thrives in a shady woodland setting and, with its hybrid vigour, is a more robust plant than the native. If numbers are not monitored and controlled, big hybrid colonies could form, which will slowly muddy the genetics of our own plant.

Plant type Asparagus family, Asparagaceae. *Flowers* April– May. *Height* 30–50cm. *Description* Depending on how many times it has crossed, its appearance varies across the spectrum between the native and Spanish forms. Hybrid plants tend to be a bit taller and broader than natives. Unlike the native Bluebell, which has curved stem tips that hang slightly, the hybrid has vertical stems, leaning but not curved over, and flowers that are more densely packed, with a slightly wider bell shape. This mimics the Spanish form, but like the native Bluebell, the hybrid has flowers with the perianth segments curled back. It also has a lesser scent. *Companion species* Greater Stitchwort (p.87), Ramsons (p.23) and Wood Anemone (p.30). *Distribution* The hybrid was first recorded in the wild in 1963 and its range and frequency are increasing. It is relatively widespread in woodland and woodland margins, particularly close to urban areas where the Spanish Bluebell is prevalent. In more remote regions, the hybrid is proportionately rarer or even absent. *Habitat* Like our native Bluebell, this now occurs in a wide variety of habitats – deciduous woodland, hedge banks and meadows. It has a greater pH and heat tolerance than the native, so it also does well on chalk and on sunny banks and roadsides.

Broad Buckler-fern
(Dryopteris dilatata)

Walking through the wood at Sissinghurst, Kent, last spring, just as the sun was falling, I came across a stand of Broad Buckler-fern on the far side of the small stream. Normally unnoticeable in a dark, damp part of the valley, every plant was spotlit, like a burning bush in the spring dusk (pp.42–3). The fronds of Broad Buckler-fern are arranged in dense crowns, and there were twenty or thirty plants scattered quite evenly through this patch of wood, each with leaves arching elegantly outwards, with every scale on the stem, every part of every frond, bronze-gold and haloed. This is one of the most delicately arranged ferns, its pinnae widely spaced, the stem standing out in strong contrast to the lush, bright green leaves. It typically has a bearded, scaly stem of a dark chocolate-brown colour, with a deep brown-black central zone. It grows in similar places to Male-fern (p.19), but the overall impression of Broad Buckler is brighter, lighter and more elegant. It has more highly cut, three-pinnate fronds, whereas Male-fern is mainly once pinnate, sometimes twice pinnate near the main stem.

Plant type Buckler-fern family, Dryopteridaceae. *Height* 30–150cm. *Description* Fronds are triangular, varying in colour from olive green to darker, bluish green. They are clustered in a dense 'shuttlecock' crown that arches outwards. The frond stalk is normally shorter than the blade and is densely covered with pointed scales, each of which has a dark brown centre and pale edges. *Companion species* Bluebell (opposite), Elder (p.80), Pendulous Sedge (p.316) and Wood-sorrel (p.33). *Distribution* Native. Common throughout Britain and Ireland, absent only from the area surrounding the Wash. *Habitat* Shady places on neutral to very acidic soils, including deciduous and coniferous woodland, hedgerows, ditches, open moorland, rocky slopes, boulder scree and rock fissures.

Broad-leaved Helleborine
(Epipactis helleborine)

It may not have the smoky beauty of its relative Marsh Helleborine (p.309), but in its own way this has a touch of glamour, looking more like an orchid from a Malaysian rainforest than a plant of English deciduous woodland. Each flower spike is tall and substantial, with thirty to a hundred flowers on each spike. The hearts of the flowers are pink, with jutting-out green wings and a chocolate-brown throat, although the colours are variable. In shady places, they tend to be greener, developing the pinky-purplish tinge in the sunnier spots on the edge of a wood. You will normally find them in groups of one to three rather than the big family drifts associated with Marsh Helleborine.

Plant type Orchid family, Orchidaceae. *Flowers* July–August. *Height* 25–80cm. *Description* Robust, erect perennial herb. Stem is downy towards the top; stems are sometimes clumped, with several arising together. Leaves are dull green, broad, oval and spirally arranged up the stem, becoming narrower towards the top but reduced to scales at the base. The largest leaves are 5–17cm long and 2.5–10cm wide. Inflorescence is a dense, one-sided raceme. Each flower has three oval, greenish purplish sepals and three petals, the lowermost forming a cup-like structure with a projecting, heart-shaped lip. *Companion species* Enchanter's-nightshade (p.9), Wood Sage (p.32) and Yellow Pimpernel (p.35). *Distribution* Native. Occurs throughout the British Isles. Quite frequent in southern England and Wales, it becomes more localised to the north and is very rare in northern Scotland. It is also localised in Ireland. *Habitat* Deciduous woodlands, particularly beech woods. It is also found along disused railway lines, hedgerows, roadsides and, in northern and western Britain, limestone pavement, scree and grasslands.

Columbine
(Aquilegia vulgaris)

We have become so used to seeing this plant – or one of its hybrids – in our gardens that we may not at first appreciate those rare and marvellous occasions when it appears in the wild. The British common name comes from the Latin *columba* meaning 'dove'; the Latin name from *aquila* meaning 'eagle'. Each flower does indeed look like a cluster of birds, and its odd shape makes it insect specific. The nectar is secreted at the base of the long spur, or hollow horn, that tops every petal, and is accessible only to long-tongued bumblebees. Also known as Granny's Bonnet, the Columbine used to be common: it often appears in church carvings, such as the misericord supports at Ripon Cathedral in Yorkshire.

Plant type Buttercup family, Ranunculaceae. *Flowers* May–June. *Height* 50–90cm. *Description* Tall, hairless perennial with hanging blue or violet-blue layered flowers. Each flower has five interior spurred petals contained by five spurless sepals in a flounced, layered skirt. They have dark crimson-purple stems, the colour extending into the midrib of the leaf. Leaves are greyish green, often washed purple, arranged in three parts, each one with three lobes. The ones that rise from the root rather than the stem are prettily crenellated, giving them the shape of Maidenhair Fern (p.404). *Companion species* Deadly Nightshade (p.6) and Tufted Vetch (p.166). *Distribution* Native, rare. Local and decreasing in the wild. It occurs as a native or alien throughout the British Isles, but it is a little less rare in southern England and south-west Wales. *Habitat* Native colonies occur in calcareous woods, scrub and fen, as well as stream sides, damp grassland and on scree slopes. Garden escapes naturalise in quarries, and on roadsides and railway banks, and tend to be a mix of colours, including pink and white, which rarely occur in native species.

Common Cow-wheat
(Melampyrum pratense)

The flowers of this unusual-looking plant remind me of the fingers of a rubber glove. They are long and tubular in a pretty primrose yellow, arranged in pairs and held straight out from the stem. The plants make quite scraggy, loose, sprawling domes in the grass, covered in flowers right through the summer. A hemiparasite on grasses, it was once a prized plant, because cows are very keen on it and it was thought that it produced higher-quality butter. The generic name is Greek and comes from the words *melas* ('black') and *pyros* ('wheat'), because of the black, wheat-like seeds. The specific name, *pratense*, means 'growing in meadows', although it is usually a plant of woodland, moorland and hedgerows. Common Cow-wheat is a larval food plant of the Heath Fritillary butterfly, one of our rarest butterflies.

Plant type Broomrape family, Orobanchaceae. *Flowers* May–September. *Height* 8–40cm. *Description* This is an unusual plant to find in a woodland setting, because it is an annual. It is erect and hairless, its leaves oval-lanceolate, almost stalkless and untoothed, 1.5–8cm long. Inflorescence is a loose spike with flowers arranged in opposite pairs in the axils of leaf-like bracts. Flowers are 1–2cm long and much longer than the calyx. Calyx teeth are curled upright. *Companion species* Bilberry (p.349) and Gorse (p.355). *Distribution* Native. Found throughout the British Isles and common in southern England, Wales and the Highlands of Scotland. It is rare in parts of central-eastern England. It is also quite localised in Ireland, being most common in the north. *Habitat* Woods, scrub, heaths and upland moorlands on well-drained, nutrient-poor, acidic soils (more rarely on chalk and limestone). In woodlands, it is usually found in clearings, rides and on the edge. It is an ancient woodland indicator species.

Common Dog-violet
(Viola riviniana)

This is an exceptional flower, but because it is not quite as exquisite as the Sweet Violet (p.111), it is known as the Dog. One of our prettiest wild flowers, it dresses the floor of a newly coppiced wood, shady lane or roadside bank with mauve, purple and even white flowers right through the spring. It can grow in huge, spreading, straggly clumps with twenty or thirty flowers per plant, and as a semi-evergreen it often has a presence all year. Bees love it, too, and it is among the violets (including Early Dog-violet, p.8, Sweet Violet, p.111 and Hairy Violet, p.201) that are the crucial larval food plants for five of Britain's most threatened and declining butterflies: Pearl-bordered Fritillary, Small Pearl-bordered Fritillary, High Brown Fritillary, Silver-washed Fritillary and Dark Green Fritillary. The adult butterflies also feed on nectar from violet flowers, but they are not restricted to them, visiting other spring flowers, such as Bugle (p.68) and Primrose (p.103).

Plant type Violet family, Violaceae. *Flowers* April–June. *Height* 3–20cm. *Description* Perennial with five-petalled flowers in pale to deeper purple (and every shade in between) on stems with neat, heart-shaped leaves. Freely branched from the base, with flowers and leaves on the same stems. Sepals are pointed; spur is notched (at the tip) and paler than the petals. Easy to confuse with Early Dog-violet and Sweet Violet; Dog-violet is not scented. *Companion species* Bluebell (p.2), Bugle, Lesser Celandine (p.18), Lords-and-Ladies (p.19) and Wood Anemone (p.30). *Distribution* Native and widespread throughout the British Isles. *Habitat* A marker plant for ancient woodland, found in deciduous woods and hedge banks, usually in light shade; it also occurs on lane sides more in the open. It can really romp away in a coppiced wood when the light is first let in, sparking off mass germination and carpeting huge areas very quickly.

Daffodil

(Narcissus pseudonarcissus)

It is easy to feel blasé about Daffodils. We have become so overfamiliar with the cultivated displays that blanket our gardens and parks each spring that when we come across a carpet of wild Daffodils on the floor of a wood, we may not appreciate its magic. No man planted these beautiful flowers, whose common names include Lent Lily and Easter Lily. The bulb colonies settled by themselves and gradually extended over hundreds of years. Cultivated hybrids often lack the grace and prettiness of our bi-colour form, its strong central yellow leaking out into cream, the blunted and irregular trumpet resembling the pattern left by a burnt-out fluted candle. The interlopers, planted widely on our roadsides, are a slight danger to natives: like Bluebells (p.2), they are hybridising, with the risk that the pure genes of the native form might become muddied.

Plant type Onion family, Alliaceae. *Flowers* March–April. *Height* 20–35cm. *Description* Hairless, perennial, bulbous herb with solitary flowers turned to one side on flattened stalks. Flower is 5–6cm wide, composed of an outer whorl of six pale yellow perianth segments and an inner golden yellow, trumpet-shaped tube, 25–30mm long. Leaves are 12–35cm long and 5–12mm wide, erect, linear and grey-green. *Companion species* Cuckooflower (p.297), Lesser Celandine (p.18), Lords-and-Ladies (p.19) and Wood Anemone (p.30). *Distribution* Native, rare, but locally abundant, scattered throughout England and Wales, more frequent in the south and west. It is regarded as introduced in Scotland, Ireland and eastern England, and has been in decline since the mid nineteenth century. Where it still hangs on, the pattern of eradication is often clear to see: a solid sweeping carpet in a wood creeps out under a hedge, then stops abruptly, the bulbs destroyed by repeated ploughing. *Habitat* Damp open woodland (often with ash, oak and bracken) as well as heathland, commons and meadows, usually on mildly acid soils.

Deadly Nightshade

(Atropa belladonna)

I remember this from my childhood as something exciting and sinister. It is one of our most poisonous plants – my father said I should not even touch it. The flowers are sultry, a velvety, veined purple on the inside with a wash of green straw on the outside, and the berries have an air of danger about them, too: juicy and shiny, too good to be true. Every part of the plant is poisonous, with the roots and seeds the most lethal, fatal even if you eat a tiny quantity. The plant contains alkaloids that attack the nervous system, making the heart race, the pulse weaken and the pupils dilate. The specific name *belladonna* probably originates from its use in the sixteenth century by fashionable ladies, who dropped dilutions of its juice straight into their eyes to dilate their pupils to make them look more beautiful. It is not poisonous to birds and reproduction is mainly by bird-distributed seed.

Plant type Nightshade family, Solanaceae. *Flowers* June–September. *Height* Up to 150cm. *Description* Erect, bushy, branched perennial herb. Leaves are oval, ribbed and pointed to 20cm long. Drooping, bell-shaped flowers are usually single or in pairs, situated in the leaf axils or in the forks of branches – they have a faint but unpleasant scent. Berries form inside the flowers, green at first, then shiny black. It is often confused with the less poisonous and much commoner Bittersweet (p.393), also known as Woody Nightshade. *Companion species* Common Figwort (p.72), Dogwood (p.79), Greater Knapweed (p.201), Ground-ivy (p.14) and Perforate St John's-wort (p.209). *Distribution* Native. Occasional to locally frequent in southern and eastern England but rare elsewhere. It also exists as an introduction or garden escape. It has declined because of agricultural improvement and, in some cases, eradication. *Habitat* Woodlands and scrub on calcareous soils, where it thrives on dry, disturbed ground and often flourishes following coppicing or scrub clearance. As a native, it occurs solely on calcareous soils, but it tolerates a wider range of soils as an alien.

Dog's Mercury

(Mercurialis perennis)

A ubiquitous woodland plant with dull matt-green leaves and even duller, dock-like flowers, Dog's Mercury is particularly common on chalk and can form extensive carpets to the almost total exclusion of anything else. However, it often indicates that there might be more interesting plants about. In beech woodland or hazel coppice with abundant Dog's Mercury as ground cover, you may find Common Twayblade (p.148), Early-purple Orchid (p.9) and Lady Orchid (p.17). It has always been considered inferior to annual Mercury (which is poisonous, but in small doses was used as an emetic), hence the Dog part of its common name. Every part of the plant is poisonous. Nicholas Culpeper said 'there is not a more fatal plant, native of our country than this'. It smells nasty, too, the scent attracting midges to pollinate the flowers.

Plant type Spurge family, Euphorbiaceae. *Flowers* March–April. *Height* 15–40cm. *Description* Dioecious perennial herb. Stems are unbranched, with pairs of oval-elliptical leaves, each 3–8cm long. Male flowers resemble miniature catkins, small and green, arranged in spikes rising from the leaf axils. Female flowers are in long-stalked clusters of one to three. *Companion species* Hazel and beech woodlands and coppice. *Distribution* Native and common throughout most of Britain, it spreads underground by its creeping rhizomes (at an amazing three feet per year). Absent only from the far north of Scotland and the area surrounding the Wash. In Ireland it is native at one site in the Burren and elsewhere it is a rare alien. *Habitat* An ancient woodland indicator species. In lowland areas it is largely restricted to shaded sites, including ancient woodland, older planted woodland, hedgerows and shaded banks, but in the uplands it occurs on unshaded basic crags, scree, cliff ledges and in ravines.

Early Dog-violet

(Viola reichenbachiana)

Also known as Woodland Violet, this forms beautiful scattered carpets on spring wood floors. Mixed with Lesser Celandine (p.18), Bugle (p.68) and Primrose (p.103), this and Common Dog-violet (p.5) create a mixed tapestry, like the flower-studded grass in Botticelli's *Primavera*. Bees love it and, like Common Dog-violet, it is a key food source for five of Britain's most threatened and declining butterflies: Pearl-bordered Fritillary, Small Pearl-bordered Fritillary, High Brown Fritillary, Silver-washed Fritillary and Dark Green Fritillary. This is fussier than Common Dog-violet, preferring to grow in chalk woodlands and hedge banks. It used to be called Pale Wood Violet, and the flowers do tend to be paler in colour than those of the Common form.

Plant type Violet family, Violaceae. *Flowers* April–May. *Height* 3–20cm. *Description* Five-petalled flowers in pale to deeper purple (and every shade in between) on stems with neat, heart-shaped leaves. This perennial is easily confused with Common Dog-violet and it is similar in that it is not scented, it is freely branched from the base with quite a sprawling habit, and it has flowers and leaves on the same stems. Early Dog-violet's sepals are also pointed, but it flowers a little earlier than Common Dog-violet and has narrower leaves. The spur is long and not notched and is darker than its petals. It also has narrower upper petals with purple veins on the lower petal. *Companion species* Bugle, Bluebell (p.2), Lesser Celandine, Lords-and-Ladies (p.19) and Wood Anemone (p.30). *Distribution* Native. Slightly less common than Common Dog-violet, confined largely to England and Wales. *Habitat* This is a marker plant for ancient woodland, found in deciduous woods and hedge banks, usually in light shade, and on lane sides, more in the open.

Early-purple Orchid
(Orchis mascula)

We have these in our wood at Perch Hill, a good dusting of them in an ancient ash coppice on a shady but south-facing slope. They are spread in groups of ten or twelve, each group spaced about ten feet apart in an area where one of the ashes has fallen, allowing light to get in and spark germination of the seed bank. The flower spikes vary so much: you get the odd white one and some pale pink, as well as the classic deep, rich magenta. Some are very tall with crimson-black stems – these seem to be the strongest and most successful. The paler ones are slimmer, more wan – they may be the weaker strain. This is one of the earliest-flowering orchids; only the Early Spider-orchid (p.198) flowers sooner. It has a distinctive scent – similar to Lily-of-the-valley at first, soon tinged with black currant, eventually reeking of tomcat as it goes over, particularly strong at night.

Plant type Orchid family, Orchidaceae. *Flowers* April–June. *Height* 30–60cm. *Description* Erect, hairless, perennial herb with shiny green leaves – often with dark purple blotches – forming a basal rosette and sheathing up the stem. Bright magenta-purple flowers are loose, widely spaced on the stem. Similar to Green-winged Orchid (p.154), but easy to tell apart by its spotted leaves, larger flower spike and absence of green veins on the sepals. *Companion species* Bluebell (p.2), Dog's Mercury (opposite), Lady-fern (p.17), Lesser Celandine (p.18), Lords-and-Ladies (p.19) and Male-fern (p.19). *Distribution* Native. Widespread across Britain and Ireland, although it has declined in some areas of central England and Scotland during the past century. It is absent from Shetland. *Habitat* Grows in any soil; most frequent in woodland coppices. Also occurs in calcareous grassland, hedgerows, scrub, roadsides and railway banks and on limestone pavement and moist ledges.

Enchanter's-nightshade
(Circaea lutetiana)

Enchanter's-nightshade is not a show-stopper, but it has pretty, deep crimson calyces enclosing the buds, which split open to provide a zap of colour contrasting with the pale white flowers. The individual flowers have an odd shape, apparently four symmetrical petals in a rectangle, which are in fact two petals each divided into two, with prominent anthers sticking out of the centre. This is one of the commonest plants of the summer wood, and you will see it in sprinklings even in darker corners. The leaves are out of scale with the flowers, chunky and solid beneath the delicate flower spires. It has a rhizomatous, persistent root system, which can colonise an area quickly. The rhizomes are long and brittle to aid its spread. This is a member of the willowherb family, but, unlike most of its relatives, it does not produce vast amounts of wind-scattered seed, looking like a snowstorm on a windy day. Instead, its fruits are covered in small hooks, which latch on to animals. It is not related to Deadly Nightshade (p.6) and is not poisonous. The origins of its name are obscure.

Plant type Willowherb family, Onagraceae. *Flowers* June–August. *Height* 20–70cm. *Description* Erect, perennial herb with creeping roots. Inflorescence is a loose spike held well above the leaves. Flowers are white or pale rose in colour, each with two petals divided to halfway, 2–4mm long, two stamens and two stigma lobes. Leaves are oval, tapering to the tip, with rounded bases. *Companion species* Hart's-tongue (p.15), Wood Sage (p.32) and Yellow Pimpernel (p.35). *Distribution* Native. Very common throughout the British Isles except in the north of Scotland and the Scottish Islands, where it is rare. *Habitat* Moist, usually limey, shaded habitats, including both ancient and secondary woodland, hedgerows, scrub, stream- and riverbanks. It is also a weed of cultivation.

Fly Orchid
(Ophrys insectifera)

Often small in full sun with just two or three flowers, in dappled shade the Fly Orchid can become a giraffe, its legginess lifting it above the grass and woodland flowers around it. A spike can reach 60cm, with five or six flowers on a stem, but the spikes are always slender, delicate and elegant. This is an exciting orchid to find, each flower a black and conker-brown fly. It has, in fact, evolved to resemble a small female wasp, and emits pheromones to attract male wasps. As the wasp attempts to mate with the flower, its head becomes coated with pollen, which it carries from plant to plant. This is not very successful: pollination rates are low, with less than 20 per cent of flowers setting seed.

Plant type Orchid family, Orchidaceae. *Flowers* Late April to early July. *Height* 15–60cm. *Description* Erect, perennial herb. Between one and ten flowers are widely spaced up the stem. Leaves are shiny, dark green, narrow, strap-shaped and flaccid. Sepals form a small hood and a pair of green wings, 6–12mm long. Upper petals are dark purplish brown and narrow, resembling the antennae of an insect; the lip is up to 15mm long, also dark purplish brown with a shiny blue patch in the centre. It has two wing-like side lobes and a deeply notched mid lobe, velvety in texture at its extremities. *Companion species* Bugle (p.68), Lesser Celandine (p.18) and Wood Anemone (p.30). *Distribution* Native, widespread but in localised patches. In southern England, it is largely confined to chalk and limestone. It also occurs on limestone in the Morecambe Bay area, Yorkshire Dales, North York Moors and White Peak, Derbyshire. It has declined by half during the last hundred years because of scrub encroachment, woodland clearance and a decline in coppicing. *Habitat* Limey soils, usually in open grassland or open woods (particularly beech woods).

Foxglove
(Digitalis purpurea)

The sweeps of Foxgloves that appear in coppiced wood and felled (or burnt) forestry plantations can be on such a scale that you might imagine you could see them from the moon. They spring up suddenly where the ground is disturbed for the first time in years and the sunlight hits the wood floor, sparking a mass germination. Almost all the flowers are the same deep pink, with the odd spike of glowing white; very rarely you will see a rich, dark apricot one, a few tones darker than the seed strain 'Sutton's Apricot'. Foxgloves appear in hundreds and thousands because of their prolific seed production. There are twenty to eighty seed heads on each spike, each seed head containing thousands of seeds, which can germinate decades after being spread. Foxgloves are poisonous, particularly the leaves, which contain digoxin. This compound is used widely in very small doses to combat heart failure.

Plant type Speedwell family, Veronicaceae. *Flowers* June–August. *Height* Up to 150cm. *Description* Downy biennial or short-lived perennial with an unbranched stem. Alternate leaves are green, 15–30cm long, oval-lanceolate and bluntly toothed. Inflorescence is a raceme of pinkish-purple flowers, each with a tubular-bell-shaped flower, 40–50mm long, which is white on the inside with dark purple spots. Calyx is much shorter with pointed teeth, and fruit is an oval capsule. *Companion species* Broad Buckler-fern (p.3), Hart's-tongue (p.15), Male-fern (p.19), Rosebay Willowherb (p.258) and Wood Sage (p.32). *Distribution* Very common throughout the British Isles, except in the Fens and on chalk. It is scarce in Cambridgeshire and Lincolnshire. It may occur as a garden escape outside its native range. *Habitat* Open woods, woodland clearings, heath and moorland margins, riverbanks, sea cliffs, walls and waste places, and railway embankments.

Goldilocks Buttercup
(Ranunculus auricomus)

A drift of buttercups in the middle of a wood in dappled shade is a surprising sight. We usually associate buttercups with meadows, out in full sun. But this is more delicate than the rest of its clan and cannot survive with the competition of all the other plants out in the open. It flowers a good month earlier than the others, before the leaf canopy closes, in deciduous woods, wood edges and shady hedge banks, and tends to form quite definite groups in the slightly brighter, clearer areas of a wood. It is a shambolic-looking plant, its flowers often missing petals, even when they are freshly opened, so they rarely have the neat, ordered shape of other buttercups. The other telltale sign that this is Goldilocks is the shape of the leaves. The base leaves are vaguely kidney-shaped and usually, but not always, three-lobed – not hugely different to other members of the genus. But those attached to the flowering stems look like the whirling blades of a helicopter.

Plant type Buttercup family, Ranunculaceae. *Flowers* April–June. *Height* 30–40cm. *Description* Erect, more or less hairless perennial herb. Yellow flowers are 1–2.5cm across, smaller than those of the three common sunny meadow buttercups (pp.144, 149 and 158). *Companion species* Greater Stitchwort (p.87), Solomon's-seal (p.26), Timothy (p.166), Wood Avens (p.31) and Yellow Pimpernel (p.35). *Distribution* Native. Widespread throughout Britain and Ireland, although rare in parts of Wales, Scotland and less wooded parts of England. *Habitat* An ancient woodland indicator species, characteristic of deciduous woodland on chalk, limestone and basic soils, as well as heavier and more fertile soils. It also occurs in scrub, on roadsides and in churchyards, and rarely on moorlands and mountain ledges sheltered by boulders.

Gooseberry
(Ribes uva-crispa)

Gooseberries have been grown in British gardens since the thirteenth century. The Victorian botanical illustrator Anne Pratt wrote: 'The earliest notice of the gooseberry which I have found is in the fourth year of Edward I, 1276, when plants of this genus were purchased for the king's garden at Westminster.' They were not recorded in the wild until 1763, and there is much debate as to whether or not they are true natives. Whatever their origins, a bush of them is a nice surprise to come across on a walk. They are unmistakable, with their prominent brown spines at the leaf bases, dangly flowers and then, in June and July, hairy, hot-air-balloon-shaped fruits – magpies and jays particularly love these. Gooseberries are delicious cooked with honey, with a few heads of elderflower added for the last couple of minutes. The bushes are quite short-lived, as the stems and main branches are very brittle and can easily break off to ground level in a storm.

Plant type Gooseberry family, Grossulariaceae. *Flowers* March–May. *Height* 1.5m. *Description* Densely branched, spiny shrub. Leaves are small, deeply palmately lobed with spines at the leaf bases. Flowers are pale, pinkish green often edged with purple, with reflexed sepals, usually only one to three flowers together. Fruit is oval, 10–20mm long, bristly, yellow-green, sometimes tinged with red or purple. *Companion species* Cuckooflower (p.297), Hazel (p.15), Water Avens (p.318) and Woodruff (p.32). *Distribution* It is not clear if this is native or introduced, but wild gooseberries are found throughout Great Britain, the seeds dispersed by birds. It is common in many areas, although absent from much of the Scottish Highlands. It is also less frequent in the area surrounding the Wash and in Ireland. *Habitat* It grows in many deciduous woods, hedges and scrub. It also occurs as a relic of cultivation, near and around habitation.

Greater Butterfly-orchid

(Platanthera chlorantha)

This is a magnificent flower, tall and stately. Its pale lime-white colour and luminosity, as well as its sweet night scent, help to draw in pollinating moths. Each individual bloom has a long tongue, which guides the moths in towards the pollen and nectar. Lesser Butterfly-orchid (p.359) is similar, but while the Greater is a beacon that you can see at 30 metres, the Lesser is smaller and more delicate, generally found in small clusters rather than solitary splendour. The way to tell them apart is by looking at the yellowish-green pollen sacs (pollinia) in the centre of each flower. In Greater Butterfly-orchid, these are close together at the top and wider apart (4mm) at the bottom. In the Lesser, they are parallel all the way down.

Plant type Orchid family, Orchidaceae. *Flowers* Late May–July. *Height* Up to 40cm. *Description* Erect, hairless orchid with two, sometimes three elliptical, green, unspotted leaves. Creamy-white flowers form a cylindrical spike. It has large leaves (10–15cm long) compared with those of Lesser Butterfly-orchid (5–8cm long). *Companion species* Dog's Mercury (p.8), Early-purple Orchid (p.9) and Herb-Paris (p.16). *Distribution* Native. Found locally throughout mainland Britain and Ireland, with a distinctly southern bias. It has declined during the twentieth century because of the felling, disturbance and coniferisation of woodland and the agricultural improvement of pasture and scrub. It has been lost from nearly half its historical range in England and more than half in Ireland. *Habitat* Usually found on well-drained calcareous soils in scrub, woodland and young plantations, as well as more open downland, rough pasture and hay meadows. It occurs sometimes on sand dunes and railway banks, and rarely upon mildly acidic soils in moorland and wet, heathy pasture. It is tolerant of both dry and wet conditions, but on chalk it may have a preference for heavier and wetter soils. It can vanish from woodland if it becomes too intensely shaded, but may reappear if the canopy is opened.

Green Hellebore

(Helleborus viridis)

One of our earliest spring flowers, rare and often quite well camouflaged, tucked underneath the trees, this is always thrilling to find. Its rich green flowers, clustered at the top of slim stems, turn to seed pods by the middle of spring, but look handsome into early summer. We are so used to seeing its relations in the garden that it is easy to think of Green Hellebore as a garden escape. But it is almost certainly a British native. Some say that it may have escaped from medieval gardens, where it is recorded as having been grown, but given its abundance in many ancient woodlands, well away from human habitation, it is more likely to be native. All parts of the plant are extremely poisonous.

Plant type Buttercup family, Ranunculaceae. *Flowers* March–April. *Height* Up to 40cm. *Description* More or less hairless, bushy perennial herb. Leaves are long-stalked, digitate, up to 15cm across, with seven to eleven leaflets rising from a central point. Flowers are green, with five spreading green sepals. It could be confused with the evergreen Stinking Hellebore (p.27), but that has flowers and leaves together on 70–80cm-tall stems, while Green Hellebore has flower stems separate from the basal clumps of leaves. *Companion species* Early Dog-violet (p.8), Lesser Celandine (p.18), Moschatel (p.20), Ramsons (p.23), Sweet Violet (p.111) and Toothwort (p.29). *Distribution* Native or alien. Scattered throughout Great Britain, although not found further north than southern Scotland. Native populations are confined to England and eastern Wales. It is never common as a native and in many areas it is very rare – it is largely absent from central eastern England. The most significant concentrations are on the limestone and chalk of southern England. It is found in Northern Ireland as a rare alien. *Habitat* Rather shady habitats, usually on chalk or limestone. It is found in woodland glades, rocky dingles and old hedge banks. It is an ancient woodland indicator species and sometimes occurs in places that old maps show as relics of much larger woods.

Ground-ivy

(Glechoma hederacea)

Not a great beauty, but noticeable for its early-flowering, light-purple carpets from the end of February, even in quite dense shade. This makes it invaluable for bees, providing one of their earliest reliable sources of food. It is also evergreen, like ivy – hence its name. One of its characteristics is the production of lots of over-ground runners, or creeping stems, which can root. This gives it a ramping habit and has earned it its other common name of Runaway Jack. Before the cultivation of hops in the sixteenth century, the leaves of Ground-ivy, which is also known as Gill, were the chief source of bitter flavouring for beer. Even after hops had become widespread, alcohol flavoured with Ground-ivy was sold as a beer alternative: Jonathan Swift once wrote that he 'was forced to . . . dine for ten-pence upon gill-ale, bad broth and three chops of mutton'. It can be used to make a slightly minty-tasting herbal tea.

Plant type Dead-nettle family, Lamiaceae. *Flowers* Late February–May. *Height* 10–30cm. *Description* Evergreen perennial with both creeping and climbing leafy flower stems up to 20cm tall. Leaves are green at the top, vivid purple behind, matching the stem. Pale purple flowers – arranged in whorls of two to four, where the leaf meets the main stem – have deeper purple spots in the heart, dribbling out onto the lower lip. It can be confused with Bugle (p.68) and Selfheal (p.163), but Ground-ivy is smaller than both and has paler purple flowers than Bugle, while Selfheal flowers in full sun in summer. *Companion species* Bluebell (p.2), Bugle, Lesser Celandine (p.18) and Lords-and-Ladies (p.19). *Distribution* Native and very common across the British Isles, except parts of northern Scotland. *Habitat* Woodland rides, recent coppice, scrub, hedgerows, permanent grassland, waste ground and shady places in gardens – basically everywhere with shade.

Hard-fern

(Blechnum spicant)

If a child drew a fern, this is what they might come up with: a red-brown stem with scalloped green ears coming off both sides, like the blunt teeth of a saw. This simple shape makes Hard-fern easy to recognise. It is at its loveliest as new fronds unfurl early in the year, each one a tightly wound spring that gradually relaxes until it stands vertical above the crown of the plant. It is one of the few woodland plants that remains green throughout the year, giving shape and structure to the woodland floor. It has two types of fronds: the outer fronds are sterile and evergreen, the inner fronds fertile and less persistent. The sterile fronds are slightly shorter than the fertile ones, which have sori on their undersides. You will see this in woods and shady hedge banks on acid soils, but also – particularly in colder, wetter climates – growing out of drystone walls and rocky hillsides.

Plant type Hard-fern family, Blechnaceae. *Height* 10–60cm. *Description* Short, erect, densely scaly rhizome, bearing a tufted crown of several once-pinnate fronds. *Companion species* Bluebell (p.2), Hart's-tongue (p.15), Male-fern (p.19) and Wood Melick (p.31). *Distribution* Native. Common in Wales, Scotland and northern and western England. It is also common south of the river Thames and in south-western England. However, it is rare in much of the Midlands and East Anglia apart from a small concentration in Norfolk. In Ireland, it is common in most areas apart from the centre. *Habitat* This hates lime, growing on damp peaty or loamy soils in deciduous and coniferous woodland. In wet climates it extends onto open moorland, stream sides and hedgerows. It is a classic indicator species of acidic soils in southern England.

Hart's-tongue
(Asplenium scolopendrium)

Hart's-tongue is impossible to mistake for anything else, its leaves not frilly, or delicately cut, but shaped like dug-out canoes with curly bowsprits when they first emerge in spring. Later they flatten out to look like tongues, straight-edged, glossy and brilliant green. This was one of the four or five key species of the Victorian fern craze, during which more than five hundred books were written about ferns and fern collecting. The fashion brought a number of rarer species, such as Forked Spleenwort (*A. septentrionale*), Killarney Fern (*Trichomanes speciosum*) and Royal Fern (*Osmunda regalis*), near to extinction – indeed they did become extinct in parts of their range. As the craze continued, nurserymen joined the bandwagon and the cognoscenti started to favour a new multitude of cultivars. Interesting mutants of Hart's-tongue were either found in the wild or raised from spores. These can be frilled and crisped, lacerated, narrow, crested, arrow-shaped and so on. Hart's-tongue, as an evergreen, is one of the beauties of a winter wood, still looking shiny, bright and healthy.

Plant type Spleenwort family, Aspleniaceae. *Height* 10–75cm. *Description* Crown-forming fern with strap-shaped, evergreen, leathery leaves, undivided and lobed at the base. Stem is black-purple. Sori are linear, in pairs along the veins on the underside of the fronds. Its specific name, *scolopendrium*, is Latin for 'centipede', a reference to the sori, which resemble the legs of a centipede, its body the main vein. *Companion species* Bluebell (p.2), Common Ivy (p.73) and Wood Anemone (p.30). *Distribution* Native. Common throughout the British Isles apart from the Highlands of Scotland, where it is mostly absent. Absent now also in some intensely agricultural parts of East Anglia. *Habitat* Shaded, sheltered, humid places, such as rocky woodlands, stream and hedge banks, where it often forms large drifts. Also found in grikes in limestone pavement and on brickwork, where it often grows in a stunted form.

Hazel
(Corylus avellana)

Hazel usually provides the first real colour in a wood or hedge, the yellow tassels on its bare, silvery-brown branches trumpeting the start of the growing year. When I had our daughter Molly early in the spring, my husband, Adam, decked our bed with boughs of Hazel picked from the woods, and we spent the first few days of Molly's life in a catkin-strewn bower, the midwives horrified by the abundance of pollen. The pendulous catkins are the male flower heads, a crucial food for early foraging bees. The female flowers are harder to see: little lumps on the branch, like leaf buds, with protruding crimson tentacles. In summer and autumn, the branches are covered with swelling green cobnuts in a velvety whorl of bracts, the nuts gradually ripening to a warm brown. The oak standard and hazel coppice of the lowland clays and loams that surround the Kent/Sussex border is an archetypal habitat, full of quick-growing ground flora, such as Sweet Violet (p.111), Wood Anemone (p.30) and Primrose (p.103) – a critical plant combination for woodland butterflies.

Plant type Birch family, Betulaceae. *Flowers* January–March; fruits September–October. *Height* Up to 8m. *Description* Many-stemmed deciduous shrub. Rounded, oval leaves are 5–12cm long. It has separate male and female flowers on the same plant. Male catkins are 2– 8cm long; female catkins 5mm long. Male catkins appear before the leaves. *Companion species* Common Dog-violet (p.5), Oak (p.101), Primrose, Ramsons (p.23) and Red Campion (p.24). *Distribution* Native. Widespread and common. *Habitat* Woodland, scrub and hedge banks on less acid soils. It is native in the understorey of many woods, scrub, hedgerows, riverbanks, limestone pavement, cliffs and gullies, but is also widely planted in copses and hedgerows.

Herb-Paris
(Paris quadrifolia)

The symmetry of this plant gives it its beauty and its name: four equally placed, large green leaves create a kind of dish out of which a single, spider-like flower springs on a perfectly upright stalk. The generic name *Paris* is derived from the Latin *par*, which means 'equal'. It is often found in a sea of Dog's Mercury (p.8) – both like half-lit shade – and yet the two plants could not be more different. Dog's Mercury is rather dull and ubiquitous, whereas Herb-Paris has a strangeness and exoticism that is always thrilling. The closer you look, the stranger it becomes, with a dark purple, fly-like dome at the centre of the flower, a spreading skirt of four wide sepals alternating with four narrower green petals, and an upper crown of eight long, narrow stamens that look as if they belong to a marine creature.

Plant type The only British member of the trillium family, Melanthiaceae. *Flowers* May–July. *Height* 15–40cm. *Description* Erect, hairless, perennial herb with a whorl of usually four (but sometimes three, five or more) flat, dark green leaves with a flower emerging from their middle on a long stalk. Blade-like leaves are green, net-veined, 6–12cm long. The flower produces a poisonous, single black berry. *Companion species* Bluebell (p.2), Dog's Mercury and Hazel (p.15). *Distribution* Native, locally frequent but not common, yet widely spread across the British Isles. Absent or rare in much of Scotland, the west coast of Wales, the area around the Wash and the far south-west of England. Not found in Ireland. Many sites were lost in northern England and central Scotland before 1930, and there has since been a decline in the south east, largely due to the destruction and coniferisation of woodland. *Habitat* This ancient woodland indicator species likes moist, calcareous soil and occasionally grikes in open limestone pavement. It prefers the open stages of the coppice cycle but can persist in deep shade for prolonged periods. Regeneration is mainly by vegetative spread, not seed, so it is slow to colonise.

Holly
(Ilex aquifolium)

It is not for its flowers but for its glossy, spiny, dark green leaves and red berries that we notice holly. Some years are noticeably more berried than others; these are the winters that follow good long summers, with sun and plenty of rain, in which Holly bushes flower for longer than usual. The berries are loved by thrushes, fieldfares and redwings, and its leaves and flower buds, together with those of Common Ivy (p.73), are one of the principal larval foods of the Holly Blue butterfly. The dense foliage also provides good nesting sites for birds. You will often see Holly next to Oak (p.101). Its prickly leaves protect the Oak seedling, keeping grazing deer and rabbits at bay. Holly is itself susceptible to browsing when still at the seedling stage, but once the plant is a year or so old, it forms the fiercely spiny leaves that protect it. As it matures, the leaves near the top often become unspiny again, as they grow beyond the reach of grazing animals.

Plant type Holly family, Aquifoliaceae. *Flowers* May–August; fruits in winter. *Height* 3–15m. *Description* Dioecious, small, slow-growing evergreen tree or large shrub. Bark is smooth. Leaves are wavy, spiny-edged, dark glossy green, leathery and arranged alternately. Separate male and female flowers are 5–7mm across with four white (sometimes purple-tinged) petals, arranged in clusters. Male flowers have four stamens. *Companion species* Enchanter's-nightshade (p.9), Hart's-tongue (p.15), Male-fern (p.19) and Oak. *Distribution* Native. Holly is our commonest native evergreen, absent only from the most remote parts of the Scottish Highlands. *Habitat* Abundant in oak and beech woodlands on acidic soils, where it often forms a shrub layer. It is characteristic of grazed wood pasture in places such as the New Forest, where it forms local pure stands – holms – and was formerly pollarded.

Lady-fern
(*Athyrium filix-femina*)

One of Britain's most elegant ferns, this is named for the prettiness of its highly serrated leaves, which are a pale, fresh green. Their pinnules are delicate and deeply cut into segments, which are themselves also finely toothed, creating an overall look that is more refined and interesting than that of the coarser Male-fern (p.19). To really appreciate the fineness of the leaves, lay a frond out on a piece of white paper. They remind me of the intricate ironwork that you used to get in the walkways and grills of Victorian glasshouses, which could have been inspired by the patterned effect of Lady-fern's leaves. This was one of the most popular ferns collected by the Victorians at the height of their fern craze, and the true wild form has since produced hundreds of varieties as a result of selection by nurserymen.

Plant type Lady-fern family, Woodsiaceae. *Height* 20–120cm. *Description* Similar in appearance to Male-fern (p.19), but smaller and strongly deciduous, dying down rapidly in the autumn. Fronds are yellow-green, twice pinnate, the petiole between a third and a quarter as long as the blade. Pinnules are 3–20mm long, deeply lobed, with the lobes toothed. *Companion species* Bluebell (p.2), Broad Buckler-fern (p.3) and Wood Anemone (p.30). *Distribution* Native and common throughout Britain, although absent from much of Suffolk and the area surrounding the Wash. It is common in Ireland, except in central Ireland. *Habitat* Moist but well-drained acidic soils, usually more acidic than those favoured by Male-fern. Lady-fern is particularly frequent in deciduous woodland, especially on stream banks and in moist, rocky habitats. It is also found in hedgerows and drainage ditches, and is one of the few species able to colonise metalliferous lead and tin mine deposits.

Lady Orchid
(*Orchis purpurea*)

Its name makes it sound like a delicate beauty, but second to Lizard Orchid (p.404), Lady Orchid is the biggest orchid we have in Britain. A good specimen is hard to trump. You can spot the best spikes from a hundred yards away, each one a lighthouse of colour amid the short, chalk grassland on the half-shady edge of a wood. Each flower has a dark crimson-scarfed head and a sparkly white-edged and freckled pink dress with a rouched skirt and matching sleeves. The plant can stand a good 45cm high, the flower section a fifth or sixth of the total height, with up to forty ladies, each just bigger than a thumbnail, partying at the top. The stem has basal leaves, more like those of a lush green hosta than an orchid.

Plant type Orchid family, Orchidaceae. *Flowers* Late April to late May/early June. *Height* 25–45cm. *Description* Erect, hairless herb with a cylindrical lower spike that comes to a point. Flowers are vanilla-scented, three sepals forming a dark purple helmet. The lip is 12–18mm long and white, often flushed with rose and sprinkled with tiny crimson hairs, divided into several lobes. Leaves are oval-oblong, up to 15cm long and 5cm wide, shiny green and flaccid. The shape and colour of the flowers are similar to those of Burnt Orchid (p.192), but that species is much smaller, flowers later and grows in closely grazed, calcareous grassland, where Lady Orchid is rarely found. *Companion species* It typically grows through a carpet of Dog's Mercury (p.8) or scrubby grass. *Distribution* Native and nationally scarce, now almost confined to Kent, where it is not uncommon in woods on the North Downs. *Habitat* An ancient woodland indicator species, it occurs in open woods (particularly beech), coppice woodland, scrub and grassland (not heavily grazed) on calcareous soils. It is also found in secondary woods.

Lesser Celandine
(Ranunculus ficaria)

The buttercup of spring, Lesser Celandine flowers in scattered carpets in woods and along the sides of streams and lanes from the end of winter. Its leaves are elegant, like a shiny, bright green version of a cyclamen leaf, often but not always with soft dappled blotching around the outer surface. Because it is everywhere, in great numbers, it may be underappreciated. This is a shame, because it is friendly, sunny and simple, with pure-yellow insides to its flowers, washed green or bronze on the outer surface. Lesser Celandine is an invaluable early-season source of pollen and nectar for many insects. It is less popular with gardeners, who tend to hate this plant because it is a romper, spreading quickly in disturbed ground, its tuberous roots breaking off and re-rooting readily. On some plants, tiny bulbils form where the leaves join the stem, and if these are cut or broken off, they can root too. Those with immaculate lawns dig this out on sight – a few plants chopped up and scattered by a mower quickly become many more.

Plant type Buttercup family, Ranunculaceae. *Flowers* February–May. *Height* 5–15cm. *Description* Invasive tuberous perennial with glossy, hairless, heart-shaped leaves, which form a rosette. Each leaf is on a stalk, not hugging the ground. Flower has usually three sepals and eight to twelve narrow, oval, brilliant yellow petals, with matching yellow anthers and centre. Sometimes confused with Greater Celandine (p.87), but despite its name it is unrelated and at most a third of the size. *Companion species* Bluebell (p.2), Bugle (p.68) and Ground-ivy (p.14). *Distribution* Native and very widespread almost everywhere in Britain. *Habitat* Grows in slightly shady, slightly damp places, such as woods, damp meadows, hedge banks and roadsides. It also grows in maritime grasslands, riverbanks and shaded waste ground.

Lily-of-the-valley
(Convallaria majalis)

The tiny, almost bashful Lily-of-the-valley lives in shady woodland and is a miracle to come upon. Delicate, graceful and spare, like the bridesmaid to a virgin queen, its restrained display is worth crossing the country to see. No more than six or seven white flower bells appear fully out at one time on every dropping stalk, luminous against the flat, green background of its own matt foliage. Its vanilla honey scent is by far the sweetest of any British native – a pure gift. In a good drift, few of the plants will be in flower and, when there are large areas of leaves only, it can look like Ramsons (p.23). Take care: as with many bulbs, if you trample the foliage, you kill the rhizome.

Plant type Asparagus family, Asparagaceae. *Flowers* May–June. *Height* 15–20cm. *Description* Hairless perennial with creeping rhizomes. Fragile, curving stems are hung with six or seven small, creamy-green pearls on one side, which gradually open, lowest first, into purest-white rounded bells. Leaves are stalked, oval-elliptical, untoothed and parallel-veined, 8–20cm long by 3–5cm wide. Fruit is a red berry. All parts of the plant are poisonous. *Companion species* Bluebell (p.2), Lesser Celandine (p.18) and Wood Anemone (p.30). *Distribution* Native, rare, but abundant locally across Wales, England and Scotland. Absent from Ireland. Native distribution is obscured by garden escapes. It favours ancient woodlands. *Habitat* It thrives in two distinct habitats in the British Isles – ancient woods on sandy, acidic soils in the lowland south and east of England, and limestone woods. In both, it requires dry, freely drained, nutrient-poor soils. It tends to grow in dry woodlands, on base-rich soils. Fruits are not often produced, and the plant spreads mainly by sending out new shoots from its rapidly creeping rootstock.

Lords-and-Ladies
(Arum maculatum)

The owl midge, which spends much of its life in a cowpat, pollinates Lords-and-Ladies (also known as Cuckoo Pint and Parson in the Pulpit), which has a cunning physiology to draw the insect in. The spadix (the spike at the centre of the 'flower') is packed full of carbohydrate and, when ripe, it warms up. The slight heat and cowpat smell that it emits deceives the midge and draws it in. The midge enters the floral chamber at the base of the spadix, passing a ring of stiff bristles, which prevents it from escaping, and pollinates the female flower positioned at the deepest point of the chamber. The stamens then ripen on the male flowers, also hidden within the chamber in a ring just above the female flowers, dusting the midges with pollen as they try to escape. The midge is released as the pollinated spadix quickly dies and the ring of bristles wilts.

Plant type Lords-and-Ladies family, Araceae. *Flowers* April–June, fruiting July–August. *Height* 30–45cm. *Description* The most prominent feature is the dense, spiked inflorescence – the spadix – which is cylindrical, club-shaped and green, ripening to a dark chocolate-brown to purple, and enclosed in a large sheathing bract (the spathe), which usually has a claret-purple rim and subtle purple pinstripes on the soft green. Leaves are arrow-shaped on long stalks, bright green with a purple-spotted stem. Leaves are sometimes splotched with black. Bright red berried fruits, 5mm across, are poisonous to us, but loved by birds. *Companion species* Bluebell (p.2), Ground-ivy (p.14), Primrose (p.103), violets and Wood Anemone (p.30). *Distribution* Native and common across Britain, but populations north of southern Northumberland and Cumbria are considered alien. *Habitat* Woodlands, shady banks and hedgerows, on moist, well-drained and reasonably fertile, mildly acid, base-rich or calcareous soils.

Male-fern
(Dryopteris filix-mas)

Probably the most common 'crown-forming' fern of woodlands and one of the first ferns that beginners are likely to come across, Male-fern is tall, upright, bushy and quite elegant. The fronds are not as intricate as those of Lady-fern (p.17) or Broad Buckler-fern (p.3), but more so than Bracken. They look at their best when just unfurling, the tips uncoiling like a spring. The fronds persist right through the year into winter, when they usually get beaten down by wind, rain and snow, and often remain shaggy and messy at the base of the plant as the new fronds unfurl. Male-fern is slightly more tolerant of basic (alkaline) soils than Lady-fern or Broad Buckler-fern, so it occurs in all parts of the British Isles.

Plant type Buckler-fern family, Dryopteridaceae. *Height* 75cm. *Description* Deciduous fern with a short, stout, erect rhizome bearing a single crown. Fronds are four times as long as they are broad, oblong-lanceolate in shape, once pinnate with 15–30 narrow, triangular pinnae on each side of the frond. Frond stalks are covered in sparse, pale brown scales. The less common Golden-scaled Male-fern (*D. affinis*) can be distinguished by the black spot at the base of each pinnae and by its longer fronds, which have a firmer, more leathery texture than those of Male-fern. *Companion species* On higher, dryer ground: Bluebell (p.2), Foxglove (p.10), Wood Anemone (p.30) and Wood Sage (p.32). On lower ground: Marsh-marigold (p.311) and Ramsons (p.23). *Distribution* Native. One of the most common and widespread ferns throughout the British Isles. *Habitat* Woodlands, hedgerows, ditches, roadside verges, stream banks, rocky hillsides, cliff ledges and scree slopes. It prefers light, well-drained but moist soils that are mostly acid to neutral. It is found in urban habitats too, including railway banks, bridges and walls.

Mistletoe
(Viscum album)

You can spot Mistletoe immediately in poplars, limes and willows, as well as hawthorns and craggy fruit trees in old orchards. At a distance, you can see only the berries, white and slightly shiny, scattered over what look like two massive stork's nests. The mistletoe clouds are usually spaced evenly through the tree, growing straight out of the bark. To begin with, they look like growths erupting from the inside of the tree, stretching the bark, before breaking through to form their own green twigs and pairs of leaves. The berries look like dull pearls or white currants, blue-white rather than creamy green. If you squeeze one between finger and thumb and then try to drop it, you cannot – they are as tacky as chewing gum when you are trying to put it in the bin. That is how it spreads: after eating the sticky berries, birds wipe their beaks on tree branches, depositing the seeds.

Plant type Bastard-toadflax family, Santalaceae. *Flowers* February–April; fruits November–December. *Height* Forms clumps up to 1m across. *Description* Dioecious, woody, hemiparasitic shrub. Stems are repeatedly branched with pairs of yellow-green, narrow-elliptical, leathery leaves. Flowers are very small, four-petalled, in a compact green-white, three-to-five-flowered inflorescence. Fruit is 6–10mm across. *Companion species* Crab Apple (p.77), Hawthorn (p.89) and Goat Willow (p.86). Contrary to the legend, it is rarely found on Oak (p.101). *Distribution* Native. It is mostly confined to England and Wales, most frequent in south-east England and the West Midlands. A nineteenth-century study found that it grew on 34 per cent of apple trees in Herefordshire orchards. It has been gradually increasing during the past twenty years – despite the heavy harvest at Christmas – perhaps as a result of global warming. It is quite scarce in south-west England and west Wales, and very rare north of the Humber Estuary. In Ireland, it is found only in the north, where it is very rare. *Habitat* Hemiparasitic on a variety of trees in orchards, parkland, hedgerows and gardens.

Moschatel
(Adoxa moschatellina)

This very early spring flower dies back soon after flowering, so you can easily miss it, but keep your eyes peeled for it because its flowers are extraordinary. Its other common name, Townhall Clock, makes it easy to recognise. The small green flowers on top of delicate thin stems have five distinct faces, four arranged as if on the surface of a cube, the fifth facing upwards. It is miniature and endearing, and there is no mistaking it – the only member of the Moschatel family, which numbers 150–200 species worldwide, that is native to Britain. If you get your nose right in among them, the flowers have a faint smell of musk – hence its common name – or perhaps elder blossom with a bit of almond.

Plant type Moschatel family, Adoxaceae. *Flowers* March–May. *Height* 5–15 cm. *Description* Erect, hairless, rhizomatous perennial herb. Basal leaves are long-stalked, pale green and trifoliate, each leaflet 5–10mm long with two to three blunt lobes. Stem leaves are similar but smaller and arranged in opposite pairs. Inflorescence is a head of five pale, yellow-green flowers. The four outward-facing flowers each have a three-lobed calyx, five-lobed corolla and ten golden stamens. The skywards-facing flower has a two-lobed calyx, four-lobed corolla and eight stamens. *Companion species* Dog's Mercury (p.8), Early Dog-violet (p.8), Lesser Celandine (p.18), Primrose (p.103) and Sweet Violet (p.111). *Distribution* Found throughout most of Great Britain, although it is quite rare in parts of eastern England and absent from far north-west Scotland. It is also confined to just a few sites in Ireland and may not be native there. *Habitat* Damp, shady places, particularly deciduous woodland, hedge banks, river and stream banks and shaded grassland sites in uplands. It prefers base-rich soils.

Nettle-leaved Bellflower
(Campanula trachelium)

Many of us grow bellflowers in our gardens because they flower from midsummer until autumn and the individual flower stems last for ages. Nettle-leaved Bellflower has purple-blue, bell-shaped flowers spread out between the leaves in the top section of stem. Its characteristic leaves are pointed, with a jagged edge and deeply indented veins, like those of Common Nettle (p.241). This is an increasingly rare and localised plant, so picking it is not a good idea, but it used to be eaten in spring, the new shoots harvested like nettles for wilted greens or soups. Nettle-leaved Bellflower and its larger relative Giant Bellflower (*C. latifolia*) are both excellent garden species, with double blue and white forms available.

Plant type Bellflower family, Campanulaceae. *Flowers* July–September. *Height* 50–100 cm. *Description* Robust, erect, bristly perennial herb. Leaves are oval-triangular, cordate, up to 10cm long, long-stalked at the base, shorter-stalked above. Inflorescence is a leafy panicle with flowers in groups of one to four on short branches. Each flower is pale to deep purplish blue, 25–35mm long and pointed, with green calyx teeth up to 1cm long. *Companion species* Broad Buckler-fern (p.3), Foxglove (p.10), Lady-fern (p.17) and Wood Sage (p.32). *Distribution* Native. Restricted to England and Wales south of a line from the Humber Estuary to the Mersey. Within this range it is quite common in many areas, particularly the West Midlands and the chalk and limestone outcrops of southern England. However, it is absent from much of south-west England and Wales. In northern England and Scotland, it is found only as a naturalised alien. It is native in a few places in south-east Ireland. *Habitat* As a native on dry, base-rich, usually calcareous soils in woodland, scrubby grassland and hedge banks.

Oxlip
(Primula elatior)

The Oxlip's flat, pretty flowers are like those of a Primrose (p.103), only a little smaller. But they are held up high above the plant, lots of flowers together in a cluster (or umbel), similar to those of a Cowslip (p.195). It is a subtle creature making a flamboyant display; that is why it was used in the breeding of so many of the showy polyanthus now seen in classic spring bedding schemes. However, its flowers are a pure, creamy vanilla (Cowslip's are a deeper yellow with orange streaks), a glamorous delicacy that is a universe away from its often coarse modern bedding equivalents. If you ever want to convince anybody that a wild flower is more beautiful than its cultivated descendants, show them one of these. Get them to smell it, too – it has a sweet, almost freesia-like scent.

Plant type Primrose family, Primulaceae. *Flowers* March–May. *Height* 20–30cm. *Description* Oxlip can be distinguished from Primrose and Cowslip by its less wrinkled and gently furry leaves, which taper abruptly to a long, winged stalk (Primrose has no stalk and Cowslip's leaves taper gently). Primrose flowers are arranged singly on a woolly stalk, not in an umbel. Oxlip has downy stalks, less woolly than those of Primrose. False Oxlip (p.81), a hybrid between Primrose and Cowslip, tends to be bigger and chunkier. It is found only where both parents grow, which tends to be in lighter, better-drained soils and situations. *Companion species* Bluebell (p.2), Early Dog-violet (p.8), Lesser Celandine (p.18) and Wood Anemone (p.30). *Distribution* Native, confined to parts of Essex, Suffolk, Cambridgeshire and Huntingdonshire. *Habitat* Ancient woods, particularly those dominated by field maple, hazel, ash and oak on damp, chalky boulder, poorly drained clay soils – especially where seasonal flooding occurs. Occasionally found in wet alder woods and damp meadows.

Purple Toothwort
(Lathraea clandestina)

When you come across this in a dank, wet wood, it looks as if someone has been through on a paper chase, scattering purple tissue at the base of the trees. This exotic toothwort is a parasite, mainly on willow and hazel, and grows around their roots in light shade on the edges of a wood. I have seen it near Perch Hill, appearing every few hundred yards as a small, brilliant-coloured patch on the steep banks of the stream. Everything around it is in muted earth colours, and then there is this intense chemical splash with more blue in the purple than in any other plant I know. Bits break off when the water is in flood and implant themselves further downstream. Like a glimpse of a kingfisher, it is intense, exciting and otherworldly. There is something a bit witchy, too, about the way it has no stems and clusters, fungus-like, around the trunks.

Plant type Broomrape family, Orobanchaceae. *Flowers* April–May. *Height* 3–8cm. *Description* A low, parasitic perennial herb, easily distinguished from Toothwort (p.29) by its larger purple flowers (40–50mm long) with a hooded upper lip. Leaves are reduced to scales and are alternate or opposite, kidney-shaped, clasping the stem. Stems are wholly subterranean, so the clusters of large, colourful flowers appear to arise directly from the soil. *Companion species* Alder (p.348), Hazel (p.15), poplar, sallow and willow. *Distribution* Introduced. A native of Belgium, France, northern Spain and central and southern Italy, it was introduced to cultivation in Britain in 1888 and first reported in the wild in 1908 at Coe Fen in Cambridgeshire, where it still survives. It is now sparsely scattered across the British Isles, especially in the southern half of England. *Habitat* Usually found in damp, shady places within open woodland, coppice and hedgerows. It favours stream and river margins, where dispersal may be assisted by floodwaters in damp woods and stream banks. It is also grown as a garden curiosity.

Ramsons
(Allium ursinum)

One year at Perch Hill the cows got into the garlic wood and their milk had to be thrown away for a week because the lush, oniony smell of the garlic was so persistent that the milk was unsellable. If you have ever walked in woods where Ramsons, or Wild Garlic, is in bloom, just looking at a photograph of it may be enough to bring its pungent scent to mind. You may or may not like the smell, but en masse, Ramsons – like Bluebell (p.2) – gives us spectacular carpets in damp woods in spring. Its flowers are typical of an allium: pretty, pure white stars at the end of short stems, resembling a compact sparkler. I love the fact that the leaves are up so early, too, often pushing their way through the ground before anything else in February. Ramsons is delicious to eat – the flowers look and taste lovely scattered over a bowl of soup or a salad, and the young leaves (in March and April) make an excellent, strong-flavoured soup by themselves. The roots can cause stomach upsets, however, so be sure to stick to the stuff above ground when you forage.

Plant type Onion family, Alliaceae. *Flowers* April–June. *Height* 45cm. *Description* Perennial herb with white, star-shaped flowers in open domed umbels above soft, spear-shaped, bright green leaves that smell strongly of garlic when bruised. *Companion species* Ramsons often grows in the same woods as Bluebells, but seldom intermixes. It usually forms dense colonies that wipe out all competition, favouring the damper regions of ancient woods. *Distribution* Native. Common and very widespread, except in some areas of the Scottish Highlands. *Habitat* A common plant of damp woodlands, scrubland, hedgerows and shady banks on rich, loamy, mildly acid to calcareous soils, often forming extensive carpets.

Red Campion

(Silene dioica)

I have always been keen on Red Campion. When I started gardening, I planted a drift of it combined with the biennial Caper Spurge (p.237). The contrast of shape and colour was brilliant, and they flowered for weeks together, with me cutting them back every so often to keep them going longer. But as a prolific self-sower, Red Campion was not the ideal thing for a small garden and I ended up weeding all its children away. In the wild, however, it is a wonderful spring-flowering plant of woods and lane sides. Its solid blotch of colour is oddly muted, not pale, but not bright either, and that modesty is beautiful. The specific name *dioica* refers to each plant having flowers of one sex only, so you need at least two to achieve reproduction.

Plant type Pink family, Caryophyllaceae. *Flowers* Mostly May–June, but can flower March–October. *Height* 60–90cm. *Description* Hairy dioecious perennial herb with creeping rhizomes. Rose-pink flowers have deeply forked petals. Leaves are in the shape of a lance blade, tapering from a rounded base to a point, 3–10cm long. Hybrids with White Campion (p.115) are common and fertile; they will cross with the parent plant, producing all shades of pink and red. Unlike White Campion, Red Campion is scentless. *Companion species* Bluebell (p.2), Greater Stitchwort (p.87), Lady-fern (p.17), Male-fern (p.19) and Ramsons (p.23). *Distribution* Native, widespread and common in Britain, although a little less frequent in East Anglia and the Scottish Highlands. *Habitat* An ancient woodland indicator species, most frequent in lightly shaded habitats, such as hedgerows, woodland clearings, rides and coppice, where mass germination can be sparked by increased light. It can survive in deep shade in a non-flowering form. It is also found on mountainside scree and cliffs, as well as coastal environments, where it occurs in sheltered cliff-top grassland and scrub, stabilised shingle, sea-bird rocks (where it can become huge, as in the Outer Hebrides) and rock crevices. It thrives on fertile, base-rich or calcareous soils.

Red Currant

(Ribes rubrum)

The wild Red Currant is a prettier and more delicate plant than the domesticated form, which is thought to be a hybrid between this and Downy Currant (*R. spicatum*). Flat, fresh, hand-shaped leaves are held out on long green stalks, which sprout from the tips of the woody stems of the previous year to catch the light. From the point where those stems emerge, gently flexing flower bracts fall away, each of them holding ten or twelve half green, half apricot-pink flowers, the whole effect open, airy and feminine. In the summer, it has small, shiny red berries, which are quickly stripped by birds. At Sissinghurst, they grow all along the edge of the stream in the main wood, where the water has carried the fallen fruits. Scrunch one of the hairy leaves in your hand and you might expect it to release a currant-like scent, but Red Currant leaves are unscented. Both Black Currant (*R. nigrum*) and Flowering Currant (*R. sanguineum*) – likely to be garden escapes – have a distinct smell of tomcat.

Plant type Gooseberry family, Grossulariaceae. *Flowers* April–May, fruiting from July. *Height* 1–2m tall. *Description* Small deciduous shrub with alternate, five-lobed downy leaves. Flowers have five petals and five sepals. Berries are globular, 6–10mm across (smaller than in the cultivated form), usually red, although they can be pale, or even translucent white. *Companion species* Bugle (p.68), Cuckooflower (p.297), Golden-saxifrage (p.302), Pendulous Sedge (p.316) and Wild Angelica (p.324). *Distribution* Native, widespread and common, although rare in northern Scotland. It is often found as a garden escape. It is considered alien in Ireland. *Habitat* An ancient woodland indicator species, it occurs in moist woods, hedges, shady stream sides, wet alder and willow scrub and carr.

Sanicle
(Sanicula europaea)

Sanicle is not a stop-you-in-your-tracks plant but one that grows on you. It is not light and floaty like most umbellifers but tightly clumped and solid, like a molecular model in a chemistry lab. Its pale pink flower heads are on the end of thin red-green stems, its oval fruits covered with hooked bristles so that they can latch on well to passing animals to guarantee wide seed dispersal. It was once a popular and effective wound herb, long associated with skin healing, and was said to relieve chest infections. The common name Sanicle comes from the Latin *sanus*, meaning 'healthy'.

Plant type Carrot family, Apiaceae. *Flowers* May–August. *Height* 20–60cm. *Description* Hairless perennial with white or pink flowers. Umbels do not have many rays – or stems – and the stems are quite short, so they a look a little clumpy. Basal leaves are up to 6cm wide, long-stalked and similar to those of Wood Anemone (p.30), but more leathery. They are very shiny below. Fruit is oval, 3mm long and covered with hooked bristles. *Companion species* Common Gromwell (p.72), Dog's Mercury (p.8), Early-purple Orchid (p.9), Hard-fern (p.14), Hart's-tongue (p.15) and Male-fern (p.19). *Distribution* Native and widespread across the British Isles, but absent from Shetland and scarce in parts of northern Scotland, East Anglia and the area around the Wash. In some areas there has been a decline in recent years due to lack of coppicing and woodland destruction. *Habitat* This ancient woodland indicator species favours deciduous woodlands, especially ash and beech woods, on moist, calcareous soils. It may also occur in hedge banks and shaded roadsides. In the north and west of its range, it is occasionally found in relict woodland in gorges and in sheltered stream ravines. It may also grow on neutral or mildly acidic soils.

Soft Shield-fern
(Polystichum setiferum)

This is easiest to identify in the spring as it unravels differently from the other common ferns. Rather than emerging as a spike with a coil at its tip, it comes out bent over, like a shepherd's crook, with the coiled spring hanging down, straightening and unfolding from there. Once fully unravelled, it is tall and stately, much like Male-fern (p.19), in a mix of beautiful colours – a softer green and a greyish, smoky copper – all the way down the central stem. This is shaggier, however: more densely scaly and hairy all along the stem from the tip to the base of the frond, whereas Male-fern and most of the other common ferns have scales only over the lowest section of stem, the so-called stipe. This can be evergreen in a sheltered spot.

Plant type Buckler-fern family, Dryopteridaceae. *Height* 150cm. *Description* Tufted perennial fern with twice-pinnate fronds in dense 'shuttlecock' crowns. Fronds are soft, bright green, lanceolate, with many well-spaced, linear-lanceolate pinnae, each of which is 5–10cm long. Petiole is a quarter as long as the blade and is densely scaly and hairy. Sharp, bristle-tipped pinnules distinguish this species from Buckler-, Male- and Lady-ferns. The lowest pinnule of each pinna on the top/upper side is larger than all the others, making a prominent upward-facing line towards the tip of each frond. *Companion species* Common Ivy (p.73), Lesser Celandine (p.18) and Male-fern. *Distribution* Native. Common in southern England, Wales and the Welsh Marches and throughout Ireland. It is more localised in the rest of Britain and quite rare in north to east Scotland. There are concentrations in Norfolk, the North York Moors and around Morecambe Bay. *Habitat* Shaded deciduous woodland, hedgerows, lane banks, sheltered stream sides and the peaty bottoms of grikes in limestone pavement. It prefers sloping or well-drained ground.

Solomon's-seal
(Polygonatum multiflorum)

The most beautiful thing about Solomon's-seal is its grand architectural form. The stem makes a loose arch from which the buds and then the flowers are suspended, like seals from the bottom of a medieval document. That is one possible origin of its name, although some say that the word 'seal' came from the old leaf base scars on the rhizome. The whole plant is in a wonderfully reduced colour range: pale-green stem, slightly darker, greyish-green leaves, buds green-tipped and gradually whitening into flowers as they emerge. It is worth having a close look at the undersides of the leaves, where the rib structures at the base look exactly like Gothic fan vaulting.

Plant type Asparagus family, Asparagaceae. *Flowers* May–June. *Height* 30–80cm. *Description* Hairless perennial herb. White, tubular flowers are 9–15mm long, located in stalked clusters of two to four, which hang down from the leaf axils. Stalkless, alternate leaves are oval-elliptical, pointed and spreading on each side of the stem. Flower produces a blue-black berry in late spring, which can persist until autumn. Two rarer native species of Solomon's-seal, *P. odoratum* and *P. verticillatum*, have angular stems, not round ones, as this one does. *Companion species* Greater Stitchwort (p.87) and Red Currant (p.24). *Distribution* Native and locally frequent throughout the British Isles, with a distribution centred on Hampshire, Wiltshire, south Berkshire and Somerset. It is scattered elsewhere in south-east Wales and on the limestone in Derbyshire, Yorkshire, Lancashire and Cumbria. It is much planted, and its native status is now difficult to determine. *Habitat* Dry woodlands, especially on chalk and limestone but occasionally on more acid soils in ash and field-maple woods. In Hampshire, it is surprisingly common on stiff clay-with-flint soils overlying chalk.

Snowdrop
(Galanthus nivalis)

In some woods, especially in south-west England, snowdrops turn the ground white – you can see this at 'Snowdrop Valley' near Timberscombe in Somerset. They are almost certainly not native, but have been growing here for a long time – there are records of them in the wild dating back at least 250 years. Our commonest British wild form is a simple single, small and elegant, although lots of the double form occur naturally, too. We have now created hundreds of hybrids from cross-breeding these two with natives from other countries and chance variations. The flowers have a faint honey scent and provide an early feast for bees, which in turn pollinate the flowers. Seed set and production is usually low, however, and thus Snowdrop reproduces mainly by bulb proliferation and distribution (especially the double form, which cannot produce seed). The bulbs get spread around by animals, or eroded from stream banks and carried downstream.

Plant type Onion family, Alliaceae. *Flowers* January–March. *Height* 15–25cm. *Description* Bulbous perennial. Leaves are basal, linear, keeled, grey-green and 4mm wide. Flowers are solitary, drooping and have a green spathe that is notched at the tip. Each flower has three white outer perianth segments, 14–17mm long, and three smaller, notched inner perianth segments. Inner perianth segments have a green spot at the tip. Fruit is an oval capsule. *Companion species* Ground-ivy (p.14), Hart's-tongue (p.15), Lesser Celandine (p.18) and Winter Aconite (p.30). *Distribution* Probably introduced, although it is sometimes considered to be native in the Welsh Borders. It is frequent throughout much of Great Britain but rare in north-west Scotland. It is also rare in Ireland, confined to scattered colonies in the north and east. *Habitat* Shaded places, especially moist woodlands and churchyards.

Spurge-laurel
(Daphne laureola)

I am mad for any green-flowered plant, and Spurge-laurel is no exception. It gets its common name from the colour of its flowers, which recalls the acid green of the euphorbia, or spurge, family (the second part of its name comes from the fact that its leaves look similar to those of the shining Laurel tree). This evergreen shrub grows on woodland edges on thin chalk and limestone soils. It reproduces by self-layering and by seed. However, because it flowers in early spring and requires cross-pollination by early flying butterflies (such as the Orange-tip) and bumblebees, seed set is poor. This explains why it has always been quite rare. Daphnes are famed for their highly scented flowers. Those of this species have a faint smell of musk, which gets stronger in the evenings to draw in early flying moths and bees. My parents grew it in their garden on chalk, where it filled the shadiest corners. They also grew the strong-scented, deep-pink-flowered Mezereon (*D. mezereum*), another British native, which is now extremely rare in the wild.

Plant type Mezereon family, Thymelaeaceae. *Flowers* February–April. *Height* Up to 1m in height and spread. *Description* Erect, hairless, evergreen shrub with leathery lanceolate leaves, which are collected together at the tops of branches. Four-lobed green flowers are situated in clusters in the leaf axils. It produces small, black, oval fruit, 12mm long, which are poisonous. *Companion species* Hairy Violet (p.201), Stinking Hellebore (p.27), Traveller's-joy (p.112) and Wood Spurge (p.33). *Distribution* Native. It is restricted as a native to England and Wales, where it is rare, although it is more common in south-west England. Elsewhere, it is introduced. *Habitat* Woodlands, woodside scrub and glades, situated on heavy, neutral to basic soils, often in quite deep shade. It occurs most often in beech woodlands.

Stinking Hellebore
(Helleborus foetidus)

The nice thing about this green-flowered plant is the crimson rim on its flowers, which is subtle and heraldic. I love the demureness of the hanging bell-shaped flowers, each of which is like a piece of Arts and Crafts jewellery, or a wood carving. The finger-like leaves are handsome, too, but the overall habit is a mess; the stems are somehow too tall for their weight, so they often collapse sideways and the plant as a whole looks a shambles. Pollinated by honeybees and bumblebees, Stinking Hellebore's seeds are dispersed by snails. Each seed has a white ridge along its side that produces an oil, which is attractive to snails. They eat the oil, and the seed sticks to their slime to be carried off to a new site to germinate. All hellebores are poisonous, with an acrid, but not foetid smell.

Plant type Buttercup family, Ranunculaceae. *Flowers* January–April. *Height* 80cm. *Description* Evergreen, bushy perennial herb. Cup-like, green flowers are edged with crimson-purple. Flowers have no stipules, five petals, five sepals, many stamens and many unfused carpels. Stiff, leathery, evergreen leaves are very dark, spread out like palm fronds, each individual leaflet (there may be three to nine) serrated. *Companion species* Hairy Violet (p.201), Hazel (p.15), Holly (p.16) and Spurge-laurel (left). *Distribution* Native. Rare, but very locally frequent in southern England and Wales, particularly in yew and beech woods. It also occurs on the chalk of the North and South Downs, the oolitic limestone of the Cotswolds and Northamptonshire, the magnesian limestone of Yorkshire and the Carboniferous limestone of the Mendips, north Wales and Lancashire. It is very rare in Scotland and Ireland. *Habitat* Shallow, calcareous soils. It likes some, but not deep shade, so it is usually found in small colonies in woodland glades or open scrub, on scree slopes, rock ledges, hedge banks and as an introduction in churchyards. It often occurs along woodland edges or paths, on disturbed ground, coming up – often in abundance – from buried seed.

Stinking Iris
(Iris foetidissima)

It is not for the summer flowers that you notice Stinking Iris but for the brilliant scarlet-orange seeds in their fleshy bright green seed pods, which top the plant right through late summer and autumn. They are the reason why this is a popular garden plant, brightening up shady corners late in the year. The flowers, looked at closely, are weirdly beautiful, typically iris-like in shape with three petals and three sepals. The white petals are washed purple at the tip and coppery bronze at the base, and purple-veined all over – clear tram lines directing insects to the nectar at the centre of the flower. Its name comes from the scent of its leaves, which when crushed smell rather meaty and strong, supposedly like roast beef. Stinking Iris is widely naturalised in churchyards, probably as a result of birds feasting on graveside flowers and arrangements from the church that have been chucked on the compost heap.

Plant type Iris family, Iridaceae. *Flowers* Late May–July. *Height* 30–80cm. *Description* Perennial herb with clumps of sword-shaped evergreen leaves, 10–20mm wide, held upright. Flowers are grey-purple, 6–8cm across, usually two or three together. Falls are obovate-lanceolate, grey-purple at the fringes, yellow-brown in the centre; standards are spoon-shaped and brown-yellow. Styles are the same colour as standards. Fruit is a green, club-shaped capsule, 4–5cm long, which splits to reveal orange-red seeds. *Companion species* Common Ivy (p.73), Ground-ivy (p.14), Stinking Hellebore (p.27) and Wild Madder (p.426). *Distribution* Native. Common in the south of England and Wales, rare in the north. In Ireland and Scotland, it is absent but occasional as an introduction. Its native range is much obscured by garden escapes. *Habitat* It is a locally abundant plant of hedge banks, open woods, scrub and sea cliffs, usually on well-drained calcareous or base-rich soils. It is highly tolerant of drought and shade.

Toothwort
(Lathraea squamaria)

Finding Toothwort is like meeting some crabby old stranger in a wood. It is one of our weirdest native plants, with no chlorophyll (green pigment) in any of its parts. It is parasitic on trees and absorbs its nutrients from them, so it does not need chlorophyll to make its own food. Instead, it has small, pad-like suckers, which attach to the roots of the host plant. These dissolve the tissue until the main feeding elements in the root are reached. The sap is then diverted from the root to the Toothwort. There must be some kind of finely balanced relationship: the removal of too many nutrients would cause the host to die, but this never seems to happen.

Plant type Broomrape family, Orobanchaceae. *Flowers* Late March–mid April. *Height* 8–30cm. *Description* Toothwort is often confused with other broomrapes, but this stout herb differs in several ways. It has a creeping rhizome, an equally four-lobed calyx and a more or less tubular corolla with non-spreading, parallel lips. Broomrapes, by contrast, have no rhizomes, a two-lipped calyx and a corolla with two spreading lips: the lower lip is three-lobed and the upper lip is two-lobed. Toothwort flowers are arranged in a one-sided spike with scaly bracts. The sticky hairy calyx is a yellowish-white colour, while the corolla is pink. Leaves are reduced to tooth-shaped scales. *Companion species* Bluebell (p.2), Early-purple Orchid (p.9), English Elm (p.80) and Hazel (p.15). *Distribution* Native and widespread across the British Isles. It is absent or very rare in much of northern Scotland, East Anglia and Cornwall. *Habitat* A parasite of trees (usually elm and hazel), it is found in woods where these species thrive.

White Helleborine
(Cephalanthera damasonium)

Not quite a beauty, but an impressive, slightly ghostly flower, which appears in good-sized colonies in the dappled shade of deciduous woods. It can be a whopper, with chunky, ribbed leaves and large creamy-white flowers, which look rather like a shell that never fully opens. It is mostly self-pollinated, which explains why the flowers do not have to open to let pollinator insects in. The absence of the need to attract anything else for its continued survival makes it weirdly self-absorbed. If a strait-laced librarian was going to become a flower, she might look like this, but that is no reason to be down on it. This is a plant living a very private life – a spinster who turns herself out neatly in public.

Plant type Orchid family, Orchidaceae. *Flowers* Late May–June. *Height* 15–60cm. *Description* Erect perennial herb. Greyish-green, unspotted leaves are elliptical-lanceolate, placed alternately in two opposite ranks and held at 45 degrees to the stem. Leaves become narrower and more bract-like further up the stem. There are one to twelve flowers in the spike, each pointing upwards. *Companion species* Broad-leaved Helleborine (p.4), Common Gromwell (p.72), Deadly Nightshade (p.6) and Wood Spurge (p.33). *Distribution* Native. Plentiful in its core range of southern England. Its distribution closely follows the southern England chalk formation and it is found on limestone in the Cotswolds. Within these areas it is locally frequent. However, it has been lost from 40 per cent of its historical range and is extinct in many counties where it was once found, largely because of woodland clearance and replanting. *Habitat* Principally a plant of woodlands on well-drained calcareous soils on chalk and limestone. Its favourite habitat is beech woodland.

Winter Aconite
(Eranthis hyemalis)

Together with Snowdrop (p.26) and Hazel (p.15), Winter Aconites are the first flowers of the year to appear, and you cannot miss them. They carpet the ground with brilliant yellow-gold saucers, held on short stems like miniature yellow buttercups among the moss and leaf litter in the shade of shrubs and trees. Their generic name refers to this early flowering: *Eranthis* is derived from the Greek *er*, meaning 'spring', and *anthis*, meaning 'flower.' The specific name *hyemalis* is a Latin word, meaning 'pertaining to winter'. This is not a British native, but it has long been a popular garden plant, first recorded in cultivation in 1596. A native of southern Europe, where it grows in open woods on well-drained soil, it was recorded in the wild here in 1838. The leaves die back quickly once the flowers have gone over. Aconites usually appear in such abundance where you find them that you can pick them to arrange in an egg cup or shallow bowl as an early celebration of spring. If you sear their delicate stems in boiling water for fifteen seconds, they will last almost a week in water.

Plant type Buttercup family, Ranunculaceae. *Flowers* January–March. *Height* Up to 15cm. *Description* Low, erect, hairless perennial herb. Basal leaves are glossy green and palmately lobed. Flowers are solitary, 2–3cm across, with six yellow, petal-like sepals and three deeply lobed, leaf-like bracts that form a ruff beneath. *Companion species* Lesser Celandine (p.18), Primrose (p.103), Snowdrop and Sweet Violet (p.111). *Distribution* Introduced. It is mostly found in central and eastern England, becoming increasingly rare north and west of here. However, scattered colonies occur as far north as Moray and Banffshire in Scotland and as far west as Wales. It is not found in Ireland or on the Isle of Man. *Habitat* It grows best in the sparse grass beneath trees. It is found naturalised in large numbers in open woodland, grassland, scrubland and churchyards and on road verges.

Wood Anemone
(Anemone nemorosa)

A clump of these is like a group of five-year-old girls in their tutus, going off to their first ballet lesson: pure, pretty and cheerful. Finding anemones in a wood at the beginning of spring fills me with optimism. They reassure me that their place has not been too much mucked around, a symbol of renewal on ancient roots. They are very slow colonisers: the seed is rarely fertile, so they spread by root growth 'at a snail's pace – no more than six feet each hundred years', as Richard Mabey puts it. That is what makes them such a reliable ancient woodland indicator species. The flowers do not produce nectar, but they are an invaluable early-season source of pollen, particularly for honeybees.

Plant type Buttercup family, Ranunculaceae. *Flowers* March into April, before the leaf canopy closes in deciduous woods, usually a few weeks earlier than Bluebell (p.2), but they may overlap by a week or two. *Height* 5–20cm. *Description* An easy-to-identify white-flowered perennial herb. At least six sepals and six petals are arranged around egg-yolk-yellow anthers and a green heart. The outer three petals are often dusted deep pink. Leaves are palmate and in whorls of three, making a mid-green halo halfway up the stem. Stems are flushed purple-crimson, often changing to green as they reach the flower. *Companion species* Forms quite uniform carpets through moss, but you may see Bluebell, Bugle (p.68), Ground-ivy (p.14), Lesser Celandine (p.18), violets and sometimes Bramble (p.66) near by. *Distribution* Native and common throughout the British Isles. *Habitat* Mainly woodlands, but also hedge banks (particularly in the West Country) and less often in heathy grassland, moorland and limestone pavements. It is more abundant in recently coppiced woods, largely replaced by other species (such as Bluebell) in woods where the shade is constant. It thrives on the slightly higher, better-drained ground with some light and has a wide pH tolerance, occurring both on chalk and clay.

Wood Avens
(Geum urbanum)

This rather insignificant-looking plant is so common in woods and shady hedgerows, and flowers for so long, that you are bound to see it on a walk. Once you have noticed it, you will see it again and again throughout late spring and summer. It looks like a small-flowered and scraggy buttercup or a yellow Wild Strawberry (p.120), with flowers on a much taller stem. During the fifteenth century, the whole plant of Wood Avens (including the roots, which give off the smell of cloves) was hung over doors to keep the Devil away. Despite its ordinary appearance, it was considered to be one of the most magically powerful of all herbs; its other common name, Herb Bennet, originates from the Latin *herba benedicta* or 'blessed herb'. Its achenes are burr-like, with a hooked tip, distributed readily via animals' fur and human clothing.

Plant type Rose family, Rosaceae. *Flowers* May–August. *Height* Up to 60cm. *Description* Downy perennial herb. Basal leaves are pinnate with a large, bluntly three-lobed terminal leaflet and two to three pairs of smaller, unequal leaflets. Flowers have five petals and five green sepals, on long stalks with leafy stipules at the base. Fruit heads are globular, made up of many achenes, with the styles persisting as hooks to assist animal dispersal – this is unusual and characteristic. Goldilocks Buttercup (p.11) is sometimes found alongside this plant in southern English woods and can be confused with it, but that has kidney-shaped basal leaves. *Companion species* Water Avens (p.31), Wood Sage (p.32), Wood-sorrel (p.33) and Yellow Pimpernel (p.35). *Distribution* Native. Everywhere except the Scottish Highlands. *Habitat* Woodlands and shady places in hedgerows, gardens and scrub on mildly acidic to calcareous soils. It prefers damp soils, but also appears as a street or garden weed, self-sowing along urban walls.

Wood Melick
(Melica uniflora)

Many sedges, rushes and grasses look like little brown blobs, not attention-seeking enough to be of interest to the non-botanist out on a walk. But this one I cannot resist. It is a delicate spray of a plant, one of the most elegant common woodland finds, particularly when back- or side-lit by the sun. You will see it en masse in a wood or a shady bank beside the road, with hundreds of plants in series, all catching the light. It keeps going through most of the year, but it is at its prettiest and most delicate when freshly unfurled in the spring. The leaves come first, a bright, clean green, remaining alone for about a month. Then, in May, the little pill capsules of the flower buds emerge, arranged along the stalk-like grains of dark, purplish rice. It resembles a necklace that you might give to a young girl – modest and restrained, the flower heads standing out clearly against the leaves.

Plant type Grass family, Poaceae. *Flowers* May–July. *Height* 30–70cm. *Description* Slender, curving perennial grass with soft, flat, bright green leaves and a loose, spreading, little branched panicle. Flower spikelets have two layers of flowers. Leaves have scattered hairs on their upper surface and are rough and hairy on their lower surface. *Companion species* Bluebell (p.2), Hard-fern (p.14), Hart's-tongue (p.15) and Primrose (p.103). *Distribution* Native and widespread across the British Isles, although less frequent in Ireland and Scotland. *Habitat* An ancient woodland indicator species, which occurs in woodland rides and margins, and in shady hedge banks and rock ledges, usually on free-draining, base-rich soils. It favours the edges of clearings and stream banks within dense woodland. It is one of the few grasses that will grow in beech woods, although it is usually confined to less sun-starved areas.

Woodruff

(Galium odoratum)

The Latin name *odoratum* had always puzzled me, as I had smelt this plant in flower and could not find a whiff of perfume. But the name refers to the scent once dry: the flowers and leaves combine to produce a sweet smell of freshly mown hay (due to a chemical called coumarin) and they keep their scent for months. As lavender is today, dried bunches of Woodruff were made into garlands and bundles to scent a room, hung in wardrobes to deter moths and layered with stored linen to keep it smelling sweet. It also makes a delicious tisane. You can tell this little plant is a member of the bedstraw family because of its tiny star-shaped flowers, which emerge from the leaf axils of the whorls of narrow leaves. Have a close look at the leaves and you will see that each one is edged with small, forward-pointing prickles.

Plant type Bedstraw family, Rubiaceae. *Flowers* April–May. *Height* Up to 30cm. *Description* Erect, rhizomatous perennial herb with bright green, fine leaves in a lush carpet. Small white flowers in umbel-like heads form a light mist over the top. It has unbranched, four-angled stems, with elliptical-lanceolate leaves in whorls of six to eight. Corollas are four-lobed and 4–6mm long. *Companion species* Bluebell (p.2), Lesser Celandine (p.18) and Wood Avens (p.31). *Distribution* Native and relatively common throughout the British Isles, although occasional in East Anglia and occasional to rare in northern Scotland. It has declined during the past thirty years and is now a little rarer in the wild, but many of us will recognise it from shady borders and shrubberies in the garden, where it is planted as a popular spring shade ground cover. *Habitat* An ancient woodland indicator species, it is found in deciduous woods, scrub and shaded hedge banks on calcareous or richer, base-rich or neutral, often damp soils.

Wood Sage

(Teucrium scorodonia)

This is a busy little plant, with twenty or thirty flower bobbles scattered along its flower spikes, and crinkled leaves, like a Savoy cabbage crossed with nettle and sage. As a whole, the plant is not tightly bunched but open and airy in form. It crops up all over the place in early summer. You will see it in the lighter patches of a wood, and in nooks and crannies on hillsides and heaths, poking out between the rocks and boulders. In my part of the world, it also grows all over the shingle at Dungeness in Kent. Its flowers are a soft lemon-lime, its leaves as deeply creased as an old Greek face. Unlike most dead-nettles, the leaves have little scent. It has elegant seed heads, the skeletons of which are one of the loveliest things to be seen in a wood during the winter, often holding on into the following spring. In their one-sided clusters, they remind me of the many feet of a long, thin millipede.

Plant type Dead-nettle family, Lamiaceae. *Flowers* June–September. *Height* 15–60cm. *Description* Downy, erect perennial herb. Inflorescence is a loosely branched, leafless spike. Flowers are pale yellow-green with corollas 5–6mm long; the uppermost tooth of the calyx is broader than the others. Leaves are 3–7cm long, oval and cordate-based. *Companion species* Bell Heather (p.349), Bracken (p.351), Oak (p.101) and Sheep's Sorrel (p.366). *Distribution* Native. It is found throughout Britain and Ireland, although it is largely absent from some parts of central and eastern England and also much of central Ireland. *Habitat* Well-drained, acidic to mildly calcareous mineral soils, occurring in a wide range of habitats, including woodland (particularly dry, acidic open woodland), hedgerows, scrub, heaths, limestone grassland and pavement and mountain ledges, to an altitude of 600m, as well as coastal dunes and shingle.

Wood-sorrel
(Oxalis acetosella)

There are two good things to know when you find this pretty woodland plant, with its pure white, lilac-veined flowers above bright green, clover-shaped leaves. The first is that Wood-sorrel is a weather vane: the leaves fold up before and during rain, and when it gets dark. The other is that it is edible and delicious, with a sharp lemon taste like Sheep's Sorrel (p.366) or Common Sorrel (p.147), giving it its common name. Add a few leaves to the top of a salad, but do not eat handfuls of it – too many can be poisonous. The taste comes from oxalic acid, hence its Latin name, *Oxalis*. This has its first flush of flowers in spring, producing very little seed, followed by a second flowering on shorter stalks in the middle of summer. These never open and are self-pollinated, but they are the source of most of Wood-sorrel's all-important seed.

Plant type Wood-sorrel family, Oxalidaceae. *Flowers* April–May and sometimes a second time in summer. *Height* 3–20cm. *Description* Creeping perennial herb with long-stalked, trefoil-shaped leaves. Flowers are solitary, 10–25mm across with white, lilac-veined petals, on 5–10cm stalks. Grass-of-Parnassus (p.302) has similarly delicate white-veined flowers, but this is a bigger all-round plant and grows in heathland, not in shade. It can be confused with the alien Pink-sorrel (*O. articulata*), which has umbels of pink flowers and leaves that are edged with orange spots on the underside. *Companion species* Primrose (p.103), Wild Strawberry (p.120) and Wood Sage (p.32). *Distribution* Native and widespread throughout the British Isles. *Habitat* Often found on mossy banks around fallen trees and on stream sides in a wood. It thrives in shady, dryish woods, too, avoiding wet or very chalky soils. It is one of the few species able to survive in the deep shade of conifer plantations.

Wood Spurge
(Euphorbia amygdaloides)

The brightness and fullness of its flowers makes Wood Spurge a cheering sight, its acid-green wands retaining their splendour for at least three months in dappled shade. I grow lots of this plant under the hedges and trees at Perch Hill. I pick it, searing the stem ends in boiling water for thirty seconds to seal in the poisonous sap, and it lasts nearly two weeks in a vase. Mixed with Wild Cherry (p.117), its woody stems also seared, it makes a bright and fluffy fresh spring display. If you find lots of it – and you often will – picking the odd stem is fine. It is the larval food plant of the scarce Drab Looper moth.

Plant type Spurge family, Euphorbiaceae. *Flowers* March–May. *Height* 45cm. *Description* Rhizomatous, downy, almost evergreen perennial herb with red-tinged, often branched stems. Leaves are oblong, untoothed and usually broadest above the middle. Flowers are greenish yellow, arranged in five-to-ten-rayed umbels that grow from overwintering rosettes at the top of the previous year's stem. Wood Spurge is easily distinguished from other euphorbias by its downy stem. *Companion species* Dog's Mercury (p.8), Early-purple Orchid (p.9) and Primrose (p.103). *Distribution* Native only in southern Britain, where it is common. It stretches as far north as the area surrounding the Wash, and is rare in Wales but common in the south west. The alien *E. a.* var. *robbiae* was first cultivated in Britain in 1891 and is now naturalised in many places, such as shaded banks, roadsides and woodland. This can become a weed in gardens; its leaves are dark green and broader with a strongly rounded tip. *Habitat* This ancient woodland indicator species occurs in broadleaved woods and shady banks on basic to mildly acid soils. It often flourishes in newly cut coppice. It is also found in scrub, hedge banks and occasionally rocky outcrops.

Yellow Archangel

(Lamiastrum galeobdolon ssp. *montanum)*

This may seem ordinary when you pass it on a walk, a dead-nettle with primrose-yellow flowers. But seen close to, it is exotic and extraordinary. Each individual flower is shaped like an angel. The leopard-skin lip draws in pollinating bees, and a thin crimson line directs them down the back of the hood towards to the nectar, where – as they drink – they deposit pollen on the flower stigma and fertilise it. Archangel is edible: Richard Mabey suggests using it like Common Chickweed (p.239), adding its young tops and leaves to salad, or stir-fries.

Plant type Dead-nettle family, Lamiaceae. *Flowers* May–June. *Height* 20–60cm. *Description* Like any dead-nettle, this perennial herb resembles a nettle in its overall shape, habit and leaf, but it does not sting. Unlike the Common Nettle (p.240), it has colourful, two-lipped flowers. The upper lip is helmet-shaped, the lower made from three equal-sized lobes, the lowest of which is strongly marked like leopard skin. It also has a dead-nettle's characteristic round bubble buds. Flowers and bruised leaves give off an acrid smell. If the plant has strongly silvered leaves, it is likely to be the non-native *Lamiastrum galeobdolon* ssp. *argentatum,* possibly a cultivated variant of *montanum.* This was first recorded in the wild in 1974 and is now considered a potential threat to native woodland vegetation in Cornwall and other counties. *Companion species* Bluebell (p.2), Greater Stitchwort (p.87), Lesser Celandine (p.18), Ramsons (p.23), Red Campion (p.24) and Wood Anemone (p.30). *Distribution* Native, common in the south, rarer in the far north of England towards the Scottish Border. It is native only in England and Wales and the east coast of Ireland. *L. g.* ssp. *argentatum* is now more frequent than the native *montanum* in Scotland. *Habitat* Damp woods, hedges, roadsides and the grikes of limestone pavement, commoner on heavy acid soils in England and Wales, particularly in the east. It likes part, not total shade, thriving on the edges of woods, and is more abundant following coppicing. It is an ancient woodland indicator species, spreading slowly by seed and with long, creeping, leafy runners, which root.

Yellow Pimpernel

(Lysimachia nemorum)

A cousin of the well-known annual wild flower of arable field margins and gardens, Scarlet Pimpernel (p.259), this version is strongly perennial (like another cousin, Creeping-Jenny, *L. nummularia*). A little more straggly and sprawling than Scarlet Pimpernel, it is pretty and bright against the woodland floor and continues flowering away from the middle of spring until the autumn. One plant can form a ground-clinging splotch of brilliant colour; its leaves and flowers create carpets where a bit more light gets into the wood beside paths and rides. The flowers turn towards the light, all facing in the same direction and, like sunflowers, tracking the path of the light across the leaves and mosses on the wood floor. You can tell this apart from Creeping-Jenny, which is similar but bigger, because Yellow Pimpernel's flowers open right out, whereas Creeping-Jenny's remain partly closed and bell-shaped. When Yellow Pimpernel is not in flower, the leaves and habit can lead to confusion with Common Chickweed (p.239), so you need to take care if you are foraging for salad leaves. Chickweed is delicious, Pimpernel is not – the leaves are bitter and slightly poisonous.

Plant type Primrose family, Primulaceae. *Flowers* May–September. *Height* It sprawls, so it is width, not height, that you measure: 40cm. *Description* Prostrate, hairless, sprawling perennial herb with shiny, pointed oval leaves, 2–4cm long, arranged in pairs opposite one another on short stalks and deeply veined. Yellow (1–2cm across) flowers are solitary, situated on stalks as long as the leaves in the leaf axils. Each flower has five petals with long, pointed sepals behind. *Companion species* Lily-of-the-valley (p.18), Red Campion (p.24) and Wood Melick (p.31). *Distribution* Native and common throughout Britain and Ireland, although less frequent or absent in parts of the East Midlands and central Ireland. *Habitat* Deciduous woodland, old hedges, glades, damp grassland, fens and marshes, shaded gullies and cliffs in upland areas. It thrives particularly on heavy clay soils.

Snowdrops (p.26), Kingscote Wood, near Horsley, Gloucestershire, 11 February.

Daffodil (p.6), Betty Dawes Wood, Newent, Gloucestershire, 31 March.

Oxlip (p.21), Wood Anemone (p.30) and dog-violets (pp.5 and 8), Hayley Wood, near Longstowe, Cambridgeshire, 19 April.

Broad Buckler-fern (p.3), Sissinghurst, Kent, 26 April.

Early-purple Orchid (p.9) and Bluebell (p.2), Perch Hill, East Sussex, 3 May.

Bluebell (p.2), Sissinghurst, Kent, 4 May.

Ramsons (p.23), Three Groves Wood, Chalford, Gloucestershire, 15 May.

Lady Orchid (p.17), Denge Wood, Garlinge Green, Kent, 7 June.

Foxglove (p.10), Mayfield, East Sussex, 4 July.

Holly (p.16), Warkleigh, Devon, 7 November.

Mistletoe (p.20), Eastham Bridge, near Tenbury Wells, Worcestershire, 30 November.

Birdlip, Gloucestershire, 1 December.

Lane, Wall & Hedge

You don't even have to get out of your car to botanise in a lane or hedgerow. I know this from my father, who used to drive along at twenty miles an hour as soon as he came off the major roads, often veering onto the verge when he spotted something a bit unusual. It used to irritate us as children, but now I find myself doing the same thing, trying to recognise wild flowers as I whisk past – though of course this is slightly safer if you are the passenger. Even when bored in a traffic jam on a motorway, rather than playing I-spy, you can get everyone engrossed in a game of 'name-that-plant'.

In no other habitat in the British Isles is the region so immediately recognisable as in a lane. Not only are the fencing and wall materials very different from one area to another, but the flowers on the roadside are distinctive, too.

In my part of the world in the south east of England, and through much of East Anglia and the Midlands – the main food-producing areas of Great Britain – we have a dominance of umbellifers in spring and summer. This starts with white clouds of Cow Parsley and creamier-coloured Hogweed, then great burgeoning hummocks of the delicate and lacy leaves and flowers of lethal Hemlock. We have plenty of docks and thistles, as well as brilliant blue Alkanet and Common Nettle, all plants that thrive on the highly nitrogenated overspill from artificially fertilised fields.

Near the coast, other plants start appearing: fleshy acid-green clumps of Alexanders, red and pink splotches of Red Valerian, and the odd scattering of exciting plants such as Wild Onion.

In the West Country, the lanes are often deeper and narrower, with drystone walls studded with the rubbery leaves of Navelwort. The invasive Three-cornered Garlic creeps in everywhere.

Up in Yorkshire and further north, there will be lots of Lady's-mantle, which is hardly ever seen down south, and Sweet Cicely, Melancholy Thistle, Montbretia and Water Avens. I had an exhilarating find in Yorkshire last summer – a huge, long-established clump of Pyrenean Lily in full bloom. As a species, this has been found in the wild for 150 years in the north of England, and the elderly lady who lived in a cottage opposite remembered the clump being there all her life. It might not be a true British native, but it still felt thrilling to find a lily in the wild.

If you are lucky, wherever you are, you may catch a glimpse of sudden brilliant patches of orchids: big magenta splotches of Early-purples in spring, followed by Common Spotted and Heath Spotted-orchids in early summer. In the north, you can find the chunky spires of Northern Marsh-orchid, and on chalk, drifts of Chalk Fragrant and Pyramidal Orchids.

I was staying on the South Downs last summer and found a magnificent patch of Pyramidal Orchid just outside the village of Alfriston. One day, on the way down to the sea, there were forty or fifty perfect flower spikes. The next day, the group was down to ten, the others cut off by a roadside flail before their seed had ripened. When lane and roadside grass cutting is done too early, it favours early seeders and more brutish plants, reducing the flowery richness of all our lanes and roadsides. If verge cutting is left until late in the season, and the cuttings are raked off, the resulting wild flowers can be stunning.

Alexanders
(*Smyrnium olusatrum*)

This is one of the first plants to be seen, fresh and bold, emerging in hedgerows and lane sides at the beginning of spring. Everything about Alexanders is robust and juicy. The stems have the feel of rhubarb, the leaves are like a shiny Angelica and the umbellifer flowers resemble those of a carrot or Wild Parsnip in soft green. It all looks – and is – supremely edible, with a flavour a bit like celery, parsley or chervil: it was almost certainly introduced by the Romans for that reason. The stems were cooked and eaten like cardoons or celery and, as with those plants, the best-tasting bit comes from the centre, blanched naturally by the outer layers of leaves. Just as we eat purple-sprouting broccoli, so you can eat the young flower buds of Alexanders. Cut and steam them, ideally just before the flowers have opened.

Plant type Carrot family, Apiaceae. *Flowers* April–June. *Height* 50–150cm. *Description* Biennial herb with basal leaves that are thrice trifoliate, the upper leaves less divided. Leaf stems have no stipules and are alternate, sheathing the stem, with inflated bases to the leaf stalks. Individual leaflets are oval to diamond-shaped. Flowers have many rayed umbels, each individual flower 1–5 mm across, usually with five petals, five sepals (although these are often absent) and inferior ovaries. Seeds are large, ribbed and black when ripe. *Companion species* Bugle (p.68), Common Comfrey (p.71), Red Campion (p.24) and White Campion (p.115). *Distribution* Introduced in Roman times and now widespread. It freely self-sows, thriving near the coast and spreading inland on roadsides and lanes. It can form blankets that cause problems for rare natives. Rare or absent away from the coast and in north and west Scotland, except in or near monastic gardens. *Habitat* Hedge banks, cliffs, bases of walls, grassy roadsides, path sides and waste ground.

Barren Strawberry
(*Potentilla sterilis*)

If you find a patch of this on a hedge bank or on the edge of a wood and expect to enjoy a sweet foraged feast, you will be disappointed. It looks similar to Wild Strawberry (p.120), and it is indeed related, but its fruits are yellow and never fleshy. It comes into flower much earlier too, so if you see strawberry flowers before April, they are almost certainly those of the Barren form. The gaps between the petals are much wider than in Wild Strawberry, so you can see clearly the green calyx between them. Another way to tell them apart is by the leaves: those of Barren Strawberry are a greyer green. In Wild Strawberry, the terminal tooth of the trifoliate leaf is longer than the teeth on either side; in the Barren form it is always shorter, so three more bluntly rounded lobes make up every leaf.

Plant type Rose family, Rosaceae. *Flowers* February–May. *Height* 5–15cm. *Description* Low perennial herb. Leaves are trifoliate, toothed, bluish green, with spreading hairs beneath. The lowest tooth is shorter than those of either side. Flowers are white, 5–15mm across, with five petals and five sepals. Sepals are longer than or the same length as the petals, and visible between them. Fruit is a group of achenes on a hemispheric or conical hairy receptacle. *Companion species* Primrose (p.103), Sweet Violet (p.111) and Wood Anemone (p.30). *Distribution* Native. Common throughout the British Isles apart from the area surrounding the Wash, the far north of Scotland and the west coast of Ireland, where it is local or rare. *Habitat* Usually found on dry, well-drained, calcareous or sandy soils, where it may occupy a variety of habitats, such as hedge banks, meadows woodlands (particularly in rides and coppiced areas), scrub, rocky screes and crevices, roadside verges and old walls.

Bird Cherry
(*Prunus padus*)

It is relatively rare to see this frothy, small-flowered cherry in a hedge. The individual flowers are grouped together into miniature candelabras, light, white and airy, and there is always a mass of them on the plant. They also have a delicious almond scent, and the peeling bark has a distinctive smell, too. My parents used to have one of these in their garden in Cambridgeshire, so I know that if you cut the stems quite short and sear the ends in boiling water for thirty seconds, they last well and are lovely to have in a small vase by your bed. The black August fruits are too sharp and mean to make good eating, but in eastern Europe they are used to flavour brandy, in the same way that we use sloes in vodka or gin. John Gerard wrote in 1597 that it 'groweth very plentifully in the north of England . . . in Lancashire in almost everie hedge', and this north/south divide still exists.

Plant type Rose family, Rosaceae. *Flowers* May. *Height* 3–15m. *Description* Deciduous tree, which forms a substantial shrub in the hedge if clipped. Elliptical, toothed leaves are 5–10cm long. Small white flowers are arranged in long erect or drooping racemes, usually ten to forty together. *Companion species* Cow Parsley (p.77), Red Campion (p.24) and White Campion (p.115). *Distribution* Native, most widespread in east Yorkshire and Wales. There are also native populations in Norfolk and Suffolk, but elsewhere it is introduced. It is much planted both within and outside its native range. *Habitat* Moist woodland and scrub, stream sides and shaded rocky places; also in carr in East Anglia. It may be found on a wide range of soil types, but is most frequent on damp calcareous and base-rich substrates, avoiding very dry or very acidic conditions. It spreads by suckers and often forms thickets.

Black Bryony
(*Tamus communis*)

There are three highpoints to Black Bryony's year. The first is when it comes streaking out of the top of a hedge in spring, with so much oomph in its growth that it bends and swirls above the hedge line as if out of control. Through the summer its glossy, slightly snaky, heart-shaped leaves decorate the hedge banks like something on a William Morris wallpaper, with cascades of tiny, lime-white flowers. Then, in the autumn, its berries form in a brilliant red. These tend to hang on longer than most hedge berries, bright and shiny like mini Christmas baubles on a chain. They provide good late food for birds but are very poisonous to us and other animals, containing a toxic glycoside called saponin. If eaten, they cause blistering of the skin and burning of the mouth, and in large quantities they can be fatal. Bryony derives from a Greek word meaning 'to grow luxuriantly', which it certainly does at the early stage. It is a British oddity, the only wild plant in the yam family.

Plant type Black Bryony family, Dioscoreaceae. *Flowers* May–July. *Height* 120–360cm. *Description* Twining perennial herb with dark, pointed, heart-shaped leaves up to 15cm long with palmate veins. Coiling stems can be up to 5m long. Small, yellow-green, bell-shaped flowers have six perianth lobes and are arranged in racemes. They are dioecious: the male flowers are stalked, the female stalkless. *Companion species* Blackthorn (p.64), Burnet Rose (p.68), Dog-rose (p.79), Hawthorn (p.89) and Hop (p.92). *Distribution* Native. Confined to England and Wales. *Habitat* An ancient woodland indicator species, which grows on neutral to calcareous, well-drained soils, particularly those overlying chalk and limestone, but also on clay. It can be luxuriant in hedgerows, woodland edges, along paths and in wasteland, but is often found in a non-flowering state in woodland.

Black Medick
(Medicago lupulina)

With its small, yellow pompom flowers and three-part leaves, Black Medick looks like a clover. The bobbles are not, in fact, one flower but up to forty individual florets. The seed pods are a distinguishing feature: black when ripe, coiled and 2mm across, they remind me of a miniature pomander studded with black cloves, although they are oval in shape, not round. It grows in all sorts of grasslands – on moderately fertile clay as well as limestone and chalk – and because it is one of the few plants that thrive on a regular mowing regime, its numbers are ever increasing on verges and lane sides. Another widespread member of this family is Spotted Medick (*M. arabica*), which has fewer flower heads and a clear black dot at the centre of each leaf, as well as larger, spiny, spirally coiled pods.

Plant type Pea family, Fabaceae. *Flowers* April–August. *Height* 5–25cm. *Description* Downy, spreading, prostrate, annual or short-lived perennial herb. Leaves are trifoliate with rounded leaflets, 5–20mm long. Flower heads are compact, 3–8mm across, with twenty to forty yellow flowers each. Easy to confuse with Hop Trefoil (*Trifolium campestre*) and Lesser Trefoil (p.157), but Hop Trefoil has larger flower heads, 10–25 mm across, while Lesser Trefoil is almost hairless (not downy), and both of these have straight (not coiled) pods. You can muddle them up with clovers, too, but all the clovers' seed pods are short and straight and none of the genus has yellow flowers. *Companion species* Bulbous Buttercup (p.144), Creeping Buttercup (p.149), Dandelions (p.246), Meadow Buttercup (p.158) and Wild Strawberry (p.120). *Distribution* Native. Very common throughout England and Wales and common throughout most of Ireland, although more local in the north west. In Scotland, it is confined to the lowlands and coastal regions and absent from the Highlands. *Habitat* Frequent on mown grassland, such as lawns and roadside verges, as well as dry grassland and disturbed places on relatively infertile neutral or calcareous soils. It prefers a sunny site.

Blackthorn
(Prunus spinosa)

Blackthorn is one of the first plants to flower in huge abundance, starting at the end of winter when it is often freezing. People confuse it with Hawthorn (p.89), but that flowers later and has flowers and leaves on the stem at the same time. The black stems of Blackthorn, or Sloe, break out in white flowers before the leaves emerge, each flower smaller and scraggier than other *Prunus* blossoms, but hugely welcome. It is marvellous for hedging, but you need good gauntlets if you are going to handle it – if you are pricked by one of its thick, menacing thorns, it takes ages to heal. Blackthorn spreads partly by seed and partly by suckers, which is why it often grows in solid, dense thickets. It is the food plant of the Brown-tail moth, whose caterpillars often cover the branches in conspicuous webs or tents. The caterpillars are covered in hairs that easily break off and can cause terrible itching and rashes when you touch them. Blackthorn's sour, damson-like fruit is classically harvested in the autumn to flavour gin.

Plant type Rose family, Rosaceae. *Flowers* March–April. *Height* 1–4m. *Description* Thorny shrub with white-petalled flowers, several together, 5–8mm across. Leaves are elliptical-lanceolate. Twigs are dark grey-brown when young, blackening as they age, and covered in straight-sided thorns. Fruits (sloes) are globular, blue-black, 10–15mm across and bitter-tasting. *Companion species* Black Bryony (p.63), Bramble (p.66), Hawthorn and White Bryony (p.115). *Distribution* Native. Common throughout the British Isles except the far north of Scotland, where it is more local. It is frequently planted on new road sidings, and the planted varieties are often imported forms that flower up to a month later than the native. *Habitat* Open woodlands, woodland edges, hedgerows and scrubland. It may also grow on screes and cliff slopes and in a prostrate form on shingle beaches. In some habitats it is considered invasive, particularly on chalk grassland, where it may quickly colonise areas that are not grazed regularly.

Bladder Campion
(Silene vulgaris)

You will rarely go for a summer drive in the Scottish Borders and not see regular white splotches of Bladder Campion beside the road. I cannot remember ever seeing it in my south-easterly, Wealden part of the world, with its soil of heavy clay. Bladder Campion has five-petalled flowers, similar to those of its relatives Red Campion (p.24) and White Campion (p.115), but the petals are faintly veined with a network of purple-brown and the flower is backed by a blown-up balloon or bladder-like calyx. This is its defining feature, shared with the much smaller Sea Campion (p.411). The stems are often covered with cuckoo spit: it is a favourite plant of froghoppers, whose nymphs produce the white puffs of frothy bubbles. Like White Campion, this is mainly pollinated by long-tongued bees and night-flying moths. It has a clove-like scent to draw them in, emitted only in the evening. It is also edible and said to taste like peas – the young shoots and leaves are good in a spring salad or as quickly wilted greens.

Plant type Pink family, Caryophyllaceae. *Flowers* June–August. *Height* 25–90cm. *Description* Perennial herb. It is usually waxy and (more or less) hairless, although it is sometimes hairy. Flowers are white, 18–20mm across. Petals are bifid. The distinctive calyx tubes are inflated and strongly ribbed, 10–12mm long, resembling oval bladders. Leaves are oval, pointed and greyish green. *Companion species* Common Figwort (p.72), Elder (p.80) and Sweet Cicely (p.110). *Distribution* Widespread throughout the British Isles, less frequent in south-west and south-east England, central Wales, northern Scotland and Ireland. *Habitat* A wide range of soils, especially chalk and sand. Its habitats are usually open and grassy, such as roadside verges, arable field edges, fallow land, rough pasture, railway banks, waste ground and quarries.

Bramble
(Rubus fruticosus)

Gardeners and walkers tend to hate Brambles, because they lacerate your hands when you are weeding and can catch your ankles on a walk. If you can forget the thorns, you can enjoy their beautiful flowers, white to deep pink, with a bundle of pinkish-white anthers forming a hazy cushion around a green style filling two thirds of the flower. The flowers are typical of the rose family: big, flat, open saucers emerging from a small, round calyx and thorny stems. The leaves are pretty, too, deeply indented with veins and slightly crinkled like a fan, the other edge often pencilled with crimson. The fruit, of course, is one of the most delicious hedge harvests of late summer and autumn. Bramble is actually an aggregate of microspecies, which are all slightly different in their leaf shape, flower colour, distribution of hairs or fruit – there are at least 2,000 across Europe. This is because Bramble can produce seed without pollination, so new seed carries mutations, leading to the production of new species. The flowers are a good nectar source for insects, including butterflies, and later the fruit is a valuable food supply for small mammals, such as dormice.

Plant type Rose family, Rosaceae. *Flowers* June–September. *Height* Up to 3m. *Description* Scrambling shrub. Stems are arching, angled and covered in hooked spines, prickles and hairs. Leaves have three to seven oval, palmately arranged leaflets. White or pink flowers are situated on panicles at the end of the previous year's stems. *Companion species* Blackthorn (p.64), Elder (p.80), Hawthorn (p.89) and Traveller's-joy (p.112). *Distribution* Native. It is found throughout the British Isles, absent only from parts of the Scottish Highlands and Shetland. *Habitat* Anywhere not heavily grazed or mown. It reaches maximum vigour and diversity on acidic soils.

Broad-leaved Everlasting-pea
(Lathyrus latifolius)

The flowers of Broad-leaved Everlasting-pea are an incredible colour, similar to that of the famously spectacular Sea Pea (p.413), but a little more cleanly magenta and without Sea Pea's addition of purple. Each flower is at least twice the size of Sea Pea. It is known as 'everlasting' because it is perennial (many of the pea family are annual) and it flowers through summer into autumn. This is the introduced relative of our native, similar-looking Narrow-leaved Everlasting-pea (*L. sylvestris*), which has flowers with a cream base, richly flushed with pink, and much narrower leaves. Neither is scented, but they are closely related to sweet peas. Broad-leaved Everlasting-pea has been grown in our gardens for hundreds of years and was first recorded in the wild in 1670. You can tell the difference between the Narrow-leaved and Broad-leaved forms by the stipules, which are like little wings at the base of the leaves. Those of the native species are less than half as wide as the stem, while those of this species are more than half as wide.

Plant type Pea family, Fabaceae. *Flowers* June–September. *Height* Up to 3m. *Description* Climbing or scrambling perennial herb. Leaves are in solitary pairs and are broad and oval, 7–15cm long, with branching tendrils. Stem is broadly winged. Flowers are magenta-pink, 15–30mm long, in racemes of three to eight flowers. Pod is hairless, 5–7cm long. *Companion species* Bramble (p.66), Dog-rose (p.79), Honeysuckle (p.91) and White Bryony (p.115). *Distribution* Introduced. It is mostly confined to southern England and Wales, although it is never particularly common and is rare in many regions. It is very rare in northern England and Scotland. In the West Country, its distribution is largely coastal. *Habitat* Hedges, wood borders and scrub, and on rough banks and sheltered sea cliffs. It sometimes occurs as a garden escape.

Broad-leaved Willowherb
(Epilobium montanum)

You are likely to recognise the Broad-leaved Willowherb from your garden, because it is a very common garden weed, germinating like mustard and cress as soon as the soil warms up in April. Its creeping stems also root separately, so when you weed it out, these separate roots often remain in the ground and quickly regrow – be sure to root it out properly with a trowel before it takes hold. It is one of the smallest-flowered and most insignificant members of the willowherb family, with its flowers rarely opening out fully. The flower buds hang their heads, straightening up only when in full bloom. After flowering, it forms fluffy white seed heads, which waft about the garden finding bare ground to settle on. The generic name *Epilobium* is derived from the Greek words *epi*, 'upon', and *lobos*, 'pod', and refers to the flowers, which sit at the end of a long, thin pod.

Plant type Willowherb family, Onagraceae. *Flowers* June–August. *Height* 20–60cm. *Description* Slender, erect perennial herb. Stem is round, almost hairless. Leaves are oval to lanceolate, short-stalked, toothed and arranged in opposite pairs. Flowers are 6–9mm across with rosy-pink, notched petals and arranged in terminal racemes. Stigma has four lobes. *Companion species* Common Chickweed (p.239), Garlic Mustard (p.84), Hairy Bitter-cress (p.251) and Small Toadflax (p.260). *Distribution* Native. Very common throughout the British Isles. *Habitat* Usually grows in hedge banks, ditches and woodland and also on waste ground and as a weed in gardens. It prefers base-rich or calcareous soils. It may also be found growing on rock ledges and in gullies.

Bugle
(Ajuga reptans)

Bugle is one of my favourite common wild flowers, its stems and leaf bracts stained and veined with purple, warmer and richer in colour than the paler mauve of its flowers, with their protuberant bottom lip. If you look at it close to, it has a very narrow red margin and central vein to each of its leaves; the whole plant has a smoky elegance, always looking young and healthy, its colour and shape standing out from the fresh spring grass. Bugle spreads by creeping, rooting stems – hence its tendency to grow in patches of prominent purple, which repeat themselves a few hundred yards down the lane. The settled places where it tends to occur are lovely to be in: hidden grassy slopes beside streams, or in churchyards, which have a minimal mowing regime. Bumblebees love it, and you can sit and watch a bumblebee working a patch for a good half-hour.

Plant type Dead-nettle family, Lamiaceae. *Flowers* April–June. *Height* Up to 30cm. *Description* Upright perennial. Obovate leaves are 4–7cm long with a sheen of purplish crimson over dark green. Inflorescence is a spike of mauve-blue (rarely pink or white) flowers arranged in whorls. Flower has two lips (upper and lower), as well as a square stem like other dead-nettles, but the upper lip is very short, so it is hardly seen. The lower lip has white streaks. It is sometimes confused with Selfheal (p.163), but the flowers of that are arranged more tightly in a purple blob at the top of the stem. *Companion species* Bluebell (p.2), Common Dog-violet (p.5), Early Dog-violet (p.8), Germander Speedwell (p.85), Sweet Violet (p.111) and Wild Strawberry (p.120). *Distribution* Native. Common across almost all of Britain and Ireland. *Habitat* Damp, deciduous woodland and woodland rides and damp patches on lane sides and churchyards. Also shaded places and unimproved grassland on neutral or acidic soils.

Burnet Rose
(Rosa pimpinellifolia)

The earliest wild rose to flower, this has perfect, pure white single flowers with a whorl of yellow anthers at their heart and a good sweet scent. The young buds are intensely red, turning green as they age. The stems are always dark brown or even black and totally encrusted on all sides with thorns. The hips are purple-black as well, which immediately identifies it later in the year. All other common wild rose hips – Field-rose (p.82), Dog-rose (p.79) and Sweet-briar (p.109) – are bright red. It can look hugely different, depending on where it grows. I have seen it in a thicket in Cumbria forming an impenetrable mass like Blackthorn (p.64), and I have seen it pygmied on the wind-blasted grasslands of the Lizard coast in Cornwall, where it clings to the ground like a spiky starfish hunkered down in the grass, each plant less than a foot across. Once the flowers are over – by early summer – it is more noticeable for the brilliant scarlet galls that burst through the stems. This is probably called Burnet Rose because it has small, neat, oval leaflets, which look similar to those of Salad Burnet (p.213).

Plant type Rose family, Rosaceae. *Flowers* May–July. *Height* 15–60cm. *Description* Low, suckering, patch-forming shrub with prickly stems and straight, narrow, stiff thorns. Flowers are white, solitary, 20–40mm across and produce a globose purple-black fruit. Leaves have three to five pairs of small oval leaflets, 0.5–1.5cm long, often purple-flushed. *Companion species* Honeysuckle (p.91), Meadow Crane's-bill (p.96) and Wood Crane's-bill (p.121). *Distribution* Native. Widespread in Britain and Ireland, mostly confined to the coast. It is more common on the west coast than the east coast. *Habitat* Most often found on sand dunes and sea cliffs, but also inland on sandy and less acidic heaths, in scrub and hedgerows on chalk and limestone, and on basic cliff ledges in upland areas.

Bush Vetch

(Vicia sepium)

The flowers of this muddy-coloured vetch are clear purple when they first open, but they quickly fade as they age to a pale mauve. Individual flowers often brown before they drop, and the result is a dowdy mix of colours. When mixed on a lane side with the clear white flowers of Greater Stitchwort (p.87), or pale yellow Primroses (p.103), however, it looks beautiful. This species is easy to tell apart from Bitter-vetch (p.144) because its terminal leaflet is replaced by a branched tendril. This turns Bush Vetch into a scrambler and a sprawler, which spreads up into hedges and envelopes other lane-side plants as the months go on. Like many vetches, it is pretty indestructible.

Plant type Pea family, Fabaceae. *Flowers* Sometimes in March, usually April–August. *Height* 10–50cm. *Description* Low climbing or spreading hairless perennial herb. Leaflets are widest at the base, blunt-tipped, each 10–30mm long, arranged in pairs. Its leaf width is a telltale sign, as most other vetch species have narrower leaves. Flowers are 12–15mm long, in racemes of two to six, on very short stalks. The lower calyx teeth are longer than the upper; the pod is 20–25mm long. If it was not yet in flower, you might confuse it with Wood Vetch, which has similar leaves and tendrils, but the latter is easily distinguished by its incredible flowers, white with purple veins. *Companion species* Greater Stitchwort, Red Campion (p.24), Sweet Vernal-grass (p.110) and White Campion (p.115). *Distribution* Native. Ubiquitous in the British Isles. It is absent only from the area around the Wash and parts of the Scottish Highlands and Shetland. *Habitat* Mildly acid to neutral or calcareous soils in hedge banks, waysides, wood borders and lightly grazed grasslands. In upland areas, it favours more open, ungrazed situations.

Cherry Plum

(Prunus cerasifera)

From a distance, when you see a puff of Cherry Plum in full bloom in the hedgerow, you may think that it is Blackthorn (p.64). The flowers look much the same – slightly scraggy, pretty, simple and white – but there is a big difference: the leaves are beginning to emerge with the flowers (Blackthorn flowers appear on bare branches). You might also mistake it for Wild Plum (p.119) but, like Blackthorn, that has slightly hairy, grey or brown young twigs, whereas Cherry Plum's new wood is hairless, green or reddish. Wild Plum flowers a good month later, too. In the autumn, it is easy to distinguish Cherry Plum, as its small round fruits are yellow or red (or a mixture of the two), not blue-black like sloes and damsons. From the outside, they look like cherries, but they have smooth, flattened stones, like plums – hence its name. They are sweet and delicious when ripe, and make excellent jam. If the fruits are at the right stage, you can use the Mediterranean olive technique for harvesting. Lay a large sheet or net on the ground below the tree and then give the branches a shake to dislodge the fruit. You will have bucketloads within minutes.

Plant type Rose family, Rosaceae. *Flowers* Late February–April. *Height* Up to 8m. *Description* Occasionally thorny, deciduous shrub or small tree. Young twigs are not usually spiny: the thorns develop on older wood. Leaves are oval, hairless, glossy on the upper sides, 3–7cm long. Flowers appear at the same time as the leaves and have five white petals. Fruits are 2–2.5cm across. *Companion species* Blackthorn, Dog-rose (p.79), Field-rose (p.82) and Hawthorn (p.89). *Distribution* Introduced. It is common in southern England but rare in the north and west. It was often planted as a shelter belt for orchards and has spread from there. *Habitat* Roadsides, hedges, woods, copses and ornamental plantings.

Chicory
(Cichorium intybus)

The blue flowers of chicory will jump out at you, even if you are tearing past in a car at fifty miles an hour. They are a sudden flash of colour, but they open only in the morning. By lunchtime, the flowers close and they stay closed until dawn the next day. There are many cultivated garden varieties, which can be harvested through the winter, and this hardy plant will survive outside almost whatever the weather. Once the plants flower, the leaves become exceptionally bitter, but before that the basal leaves are delicious and crunchy. Without the flowers, they are not easy to recognise, so you need to know where your plants flowered last year so that you can go back and pick some leaves. You can harvest the petals from the flowers, too, for scattering over salads. It has declined in the wild during the twentieth century, probably because it is no longer widely cultivated. The wild population was in the past reinforced by escapes from gardens. I still grow lots of it in my vegetable garden at Perch Hill.

Plant type Daisy family, Asteraceae. *Flowers* July–August. *Height* 30–100cm. *Description* Perennial herb. Stems are tough, hairy, grooved and branched. Leaves are pinnately lobed. Bright blue flower heads are 2.5–4cm across, situated in clusters in the leaf axils. You could confuse Chicory with the rarer Common Blue-sowthistle (*Cicerbita macrophylla*), but that tends to have paler flowers and its leaves have cordate end lobes. *Companion species* Common Figwort (p.72), Common Nettle (p.241) and Common Toadflax (p.74). *Distribution* Introduced, probably as an edible crop by the Romans; also grown as a fodder crop. It is frequent to locally common throughout England, but rare to locally frequent in the rest of the British Isles. *Habitat* Roadsides, field margins and rough grassland on a broad range of soil types.

Common Bistort
(Persicaria bistorta)

This may look modest in ones and twos, but it seldom grows like that, usually appearing in carpets in damp patches beside the road. It has neat, cylindrical, pale pink flowers, each one like a bottlebrush on the top of a long stem, always straight and unbranched, with dock-like leaves (but with silvery undersides) at the base and two or three smaller leaves running up the stem. Its many common names – Easter Ledger, Pudding Grass, Pudding Dock – all refer to the fact that it is used to make the savoury Easterledge pudding, also known as Dock Pudding, in the north of England. This cleansing, bitter dish is traditionally made around Easter time as a post-winter detoxifier. There are many different recipes, which all include wild collected greens, such as Common Nettle (p.241), Dandelions (p.246), Lady's-mantle (p.156), Watercress (p.320), one or two Black Currant leaves and Bistort. In Yorkshire, there are pudding-making competitions.

Plant type Knotweed family, Polygonaceae. *Flowers* May–August. *Height* 30–100cm. *Description* Perennial herb. Basal leaves are oval, blunt with cordate bases; upper leaves are triangular, pointed. Inflorescence is a dense spike of pink flowers, 4–5mm across. Each flower has three stigmas. *Companion species* Dame's-violet (p.298), Globeflower (p.301), Meadow Buttercup (p.158) and Pignut (p.161). *Distribution* Native. Widespread throughout the British Isles, but common only in northern England. It is rare in much of eastern England, and has declined in the lowlands of south and eastern England. It was introduced into Ireland. Its native range is obscured by alien populations, as it is widely grown in gardens. *Habitat* Base-poor soils in damp roadsides, damp pastures, hay meadows and river banks, tall-herb communities in river valleys and mountain ledges.

Common Comfrey
(*Symphytum officinale*)

A rough, hairy plant with leaves that are sandpapery to the touch, Common Comfrey has many useful properties. Like its cousin Borage (*Borago officinalis*), its leaves are edible. They are popular in Italy, boiled and served as a wilted green (the furry texture disappears on cooking). Bavarians make a party dish by dipping the small, tender leaves in batter and frying them. The leaves also contain a substance called allantoin, which promotes healing in connective tissue – a poultice of pulverised Comfrey leaves was historically used on war wounds. The roots were also lifted in spring and grated to produce a sludge, which was packed around broken limbs like plaster of Paris. Comfrey is a rich source of potash, and is often grown specifically for this reason. A mush made from Comfrey leaves (one third leaves to two thirds water), left to stew for three weeks and then diluted with a little water, can be used to feed potash-hungry sweet peas, tomatoes and beans. I introduced Comfrey to my herb garden for this reason and later regretted it, as on heavy soil it quickly becomes invasive.

Plant type Borage family, Boraginaceae. *Flowers* April–July. *Height* Up to 1.5m. *Description* Erect perennial herb, well-branched, with white flowers arranged in a coiled spray (a cyme) with tubular-bell-shaped corollas, 14–18mm long. It hybridises with purple Russian Comfrey (p.105); you may also see plants with creamy-yellow, purple or pinkish flowers. Calyx teeth are less than half the length of the corolla, the stems much branched and unwinged. Leaves are hairy, pale green, oval, slightly cordate at the base. *Companion species* Garlic Mustard (p.84), Greater Celandine (p.87) and Horseradish (p.93). *Distribution* Native and widespread. *Habitat* Hedgerows and copses, lane sides, by roads and railways, and waste ground. It also lines streams and rivers.

Common Cornsalad
(*Valerianella locusta*)

Cornsalads are well known for fragrant, edible leaves, their basal rosettes widely cultivated in winter and early spring for adding to salads. This species is a native annual, which germinates in colder weather and grows through early spring. It is also quite delicious. It flowers as soon as the weather warms up, each miniature pale-blue posy cupped in a dainty nest of bright green. The cup is made from the flower bracts, not the leaves. The Cornsalad's other common name is Lamb's Lettuce, which may have come from the fact that the plant appears at lambing time, or because it is a favourite food of lambs – tender and sweet. There is another common species (also edible), Keeled-fruited Cornsalad (*V. carinata*). Its fruit is more or less square in cross section, with a groove down one side, whereas the fruit of Common Cornsalad is flattened on two sides, making it rather like a squashed chestnut.

Plant type Valerian family, Valerianaceae. *Flowers* April–June. *Height* 7–30cm. *Description* Slender, more or less hairless annual. Leaves are untoothed; the lower are spoon-shaped, the upper oblong. It has pale blue-mauve flowers, which are five-lobed, 1–2mm across, arranged in dense terminal heads on dichotomous forking branches, highly distinctive in this genus. Fruit is a nutlet, 2.5mm long by 2mm wide. *Companion species* Ivy-leaved Toadflax (p.93) in walls; Bugle (p.68), Lesser Celandine (p.18) and Wood Anemone (p.30) at the base of walls. *Distribution* Frequent to locally common in the British Isles, except in northern Scotland and north-west Ireland, where it is rare. *Habitat* Grows on a wide range of disturbed habitats – walls, gravel paths, railway tracks, paving, gardens and, rarely, arable land. It also grows on thin soils with other annuals, and on rock outcrops, scree, sand dunes and coastal shingle.

Common Figwort
(Scrophularia nodosa)

Once seen, this is never forgotten – nothing else looks like it. Its flowers always seem oddly small in relation to the rest of such a tall-growing plant. All the petals are fused into a tube. Its top surface is crimson, with two curved horns, and the base is creamy yellow, so the whole thing looks a little like a bee. In fact, it is wasps and not bees that flock to it, attracted by its strong smell, which resembles the acrid pong of Elder (p.80), particularly if you crush any part of it. If you stand and watch a plant on a sunny day, there will be a multitude of wasps feasting on the nectar at the base of the petal tubes – you can plant it as a wasp magnet, away from where you want to sit out in the garden and eat. 'Fig' is an old word for piles, which the globular red flower buds, seed pods and root protuberances were all thought to resemble. As a result, an extract made from the leaves of Figwort was recommended to treat piles and tubercular swellings. The Latin generic name also originates from its use for treating scrofulous swellings.

Plant type Figwort family, Scrophulariaceae. *Flowers* June–September. *Height* 40–80cm. *Description* Erect, mostly hairless perennial herb. Leaves are green, oval, pointed and toothed and situated on short stalks opposite one another. Stem is square but unwinged. There are five blunt green sepals. The corolla is up to 1cm long with two red-brown upper lobes and three green lower lobes. *Companion species* Common Gromwell (right), Common Toadflax (p.74), Common Valerian (p.74), Corn Mint (p.245) and Great Mullein (p.250). *Distribution* Native. It is found throughout the British Isles, except in the Highlands and northern Scotland. *Habitat* Woodland rides and margins, as well as hedgerows and other shaded habitats on moist, fertile soils. It also occurs in ditches, on riversides and sometimes on waste ground.

Common Gromwell
(Lithospermum officinale)

Common Gromwell is a bottlebrush of a plant, with lots of long, thin leaves and flower stems emerging almost at right angles from the main stem. On the roadside or in a clearing in a wood, its overall impact is greater than the sum of its parts. It is tall, upstanding and precise in its habit, with insignificant small white flowers that have a hint of green, It is famed for its incredibly hard seeds – hence the genus name: *litho* (stone) *spermum* (seed). 'These little nut-like fruits are at first of a dull, greenish white, but afterwards become of a greyish colour, slightly tinged with brown, and are bright and glossy like porcelain, and so hard that it is difficult to break them,' Anne Pratt wrote. In winter, when the green portion of the plant has died away, its skeleton remains, decked from top to toe in these elegant, pearl-like seeds.

Plant type Borage family, Boraginaceae. *Flowers* May–August. *Height* Up to 60cm. *Description* Erect, downy, perennial herb with lanceolate, pointed and stalkless leaves up to 7cm long. Inflorescences are situated in the leaf axils. Flowers have creamy-yellow corollas, 3–6mm long, and five narrow calyx teeth. There is also a similar, rare and fast-declining annual arable weed member of this family, Field Gromwell (*L. arvense*). *Companion species* Lesser Celandine (p.18) and Wood Spurge (p.33). *Distribution* Native. Frequent to locally common in the south and east of England and Wales, but rare in Scotland and Ireland. In Kent and Sussex it is largely confined to the chalk downs, but in parts of south central England (such as Hampshire and Wiltshire) it seems to be more widespread. *Habitat* Grassland, hedgerows, dry lane banks and wood margins, almost always on calcareous or base-rich soils. Many plants often germinate freely following the coppicing or clearing of trees and bushes on a stony, chalky slope.

Common Ivy
(Hedera helix)

This is an excellent wildlife plant – probably one of the most important you can have in a garden – because its autumn flowers are a key food source for many hoverflies, butterflies and, most of all, bees. There is not a lot for these insects to feed on in the countryside and woods later in the year: the Sussex University bee laboratory has found that our honeybees fly further to forage in July, August and September than in earlier months because there are many fewer flowers in the landscape. That is where late-flowering ivy comes in, stacked full of nectar and pollen. In the spring, it is also the food plant of the Holly Blue butterfly, the only blue found in urban gardens. Its black berries are a valuable food source for birds during harsh winters, and the foliage provides cover for nesting birds and mammals in winter and spring.

Plant type Ivy family, Araliaceae. *Flowers* August–November. *Height* Climbs to 30m. *Description* Evergreen, woody, perennial climber. It may also form carpets on the ground. Stems have adhesive roots and downy young twigs. Leaves (4–10cm long) are glossy, dark green and hairless, with undersides covered in whitish hairs. Leaves on non-flowering shoots are palmate with three to five triangular lobes, while those on flowering shoots are elliptical and unlobed. Flowers are borne in umbels and each flower has five sepals, five yellow-green petals and five stamens. *Companion species* Bramble (p.66), Dog-rose (p.79), Field-rose (p.82) and Honeysuckle (p.91). *Distribution* Native. Very common except in the most remote parts of the Scottish Highlands and Outer Hebrides. It is becoming hugely common in woodlands – probably because of increased organic matter and decreased management – where it tends to smother ground flora. *Habitat* Hedgerows, woodland, scrub, rocky outcrops, cliffs and walls.

Common Mallow
(Malva sylvestris)

Common Mallow can look moth-eaten from a distance, its leaves blighted by rust and peppered with little pinprick holes. Close to, each flower is a rather coarse, over-made-up beauty, with little subtlety – a pale geranium pink with bold, strong purple markings over every petal, thick seams of colour that direct insects in. Once the flowers are over, you can see the seed pods, which are shaped like old-fashioned pork pies, crimped at the top. The Greeks and Romans ate young mallow shoots as a vegetable, sometimes to excess. The orator Cicero complained that the dish gave him indigestion, but the naturalist Pliny found that mallow sap mixed with water would give him day-long protection against aches and pains. Italians still use mallow for a wild-collected tempura; the buds and stem tips are harvested, dipped in batter and fried.

Plant type Mallow family, Malvaceae. *Flowers* June–September. *Height* 45–90cm. *Description* Perennial herb, spreading or erect. Leaves are palmately lobed, sparsely hairy and toothed. Flowers are situated on stalks in the leaf axils, with petals 15–30mm long, usually between twice and four times the length of the sepals. *Companion species* Alexanders (p.62), Broad-leaved Dock (p.236), Common Knapweed (p.146), Common Toadflax (p.74) and Mugwort (p.99). *Distribution* Introduced, probably by the Romans. It is common in England and Wales except in the Pennines and Cumbria. In Scotland, it is mostly restricted to the east coast and absent from the far north west. In Ireland, it is more frequent in the south east and rare in the north west. *Habitat* Well-drained, often nutrient-enriched soils in unshaded situations. It is found on roadsides, railway banks, waste ground and field borders, often near settlements, around farms and near the shelter of walls, and occasionally on sea cliffs.

Common Toadflax
(*Linaria vulgaris*)

The pale yellow and orange flowers of Common Toadflax are stalwarts of the roadside and meadow, flowering right through summer but coming into their own in autumn, when there is much less around to compete. Toadflax carries on looking fresh and colourful until the winter cold hits. A late summer verge cutting may even produce a second flowering well into November. More of us should grow this in our gardens for that reason alone – it provides a succession of flowers for a four-month stretch and it forms dense, upright, prominent patches of slightly greyish, healthy-looking leaves. I love the Toadflax's flower shape: its endearing, snapdragon-like, two-lipped flowers have a long, Columbine-like spur at the back of each one. Only a heavy insect, such as a bee, can depress the palate (the bottom lip of the flower) to get access to the tube and nectar within it. Its common name comes from the belief that this plant had no therapeutic uses and was fit only for toads.

Plant type Speedwell family, Veronicaceae. *Flowers* July–October (November if grass verges are cut late). *Height* 30–80cm. *Description* Erect perennial. Linear-lanceolate leaves are 3–8cm long, in whorls near the base but alternate above. Flowers are arranged in a dense raceme. Each flower is yellow with an orange palate, a long, straight spur and two-lipped flower tube, 15–25mm long. *Companion species* Chicory (p.70), Common Mallow (p.73), Cypress Spurge (p.78) and Wild Parsnip (p.119). *Distribution* Native. Common throughout most of the British Isles, but rare or absent in north-west Scotland. In Ireland, it is mostly confined to a few scattered populations on the east coast. *Habitat* Open grassy places, stony and waste ground, hedge banks, road verges, railway banks and cultivated land, especially on calcareous soils.

Common Valerian
(*Valeriana officinalis*)

More of us should grow Common Valerian. It fulfils the same role as the ever-fashionable *Verbena bonariensis* in the garden: tall, airy and elegant, flowering for months on end and providing food for many insects. As the flowers fade, finches move in to eat the seed. It also has a nice vanilla scent when the flowers are newly opened. The genus name derives from the Latin *valere*, 'to be healthy', and the plant has many therapeutic properties. Culpeper recommended it for a wide variety of nervous afflictions, and it was also used to treat epilepsy. Common Valerian is said to be hallucinogenic and the roots are believed to have a sedative effect. It was given to civilians during the First World War to calm their nerves during air raids, and an extract from the roots is still added to many herbal tranquillisers.

Plant type Valerian family, Valerianaceae. *Flowers* June–August. *Height* 30–120cm. *Description* Erect perennial herb. Leaves are pinnate, oppositely arranged, up to 20cm long, with lanceolate, bluntly toothed leaflets. Lower leaves are stalked and upper leaves are stalkless. Inflorescence is an umbel-like head (5–12cm across) of pinkish-white flowers, each with a funnel-shaped, five-lobed corolla with three protruding stamens. Red Valerian (p.407) is easily distinguished from this by its red flowers and undivided, oval-lanceolate leaves. Marsh Valerian (p.313) has undivided, elliptical basal leaves and stem leaves that are not divided all the way to the midrib, with narrower leaflets. *Companion species* Common Spotted-orchid (p.148), Common Twayblade (p.148) and Wood Spurge (p.33). *Distribution* Native. Found throughout the British Isles, although absent from Shetland, rare in the Hebrides and quite local in Kent, where it has declined. *Habitat* There are two distinct habitats. Ssp. *collina* is found in dry, calcareous grassland and rough grassland and roadsides. Ssp. *sambucifolia* is found among tall vegetation in fens, marshes, water margins, damp woodland, alpine meadows and ditches.

Common Vetch
(Vicia sativa)

The flowers of Common Vetch are a lovely bi-colour, with a deep crimson-purple nose and paler magenta-pink wings, which fade as they age. It reminds me of a small-flowered version of my favourite sweet pea, 'Matucana'. Until the invention of nitrogen fertilisers in the twentieth century, Common Vetch was extensively sown for its nitrogen-fixing properties. It is an effective soil enricher for pastures, and had high nutrient value above ground, too, in pasture grass and hay. This is why there are three subspecies of Common Vetch established in the British Isles, only one of which, ssp. *nigra*, is considered to be native. Both ssp. *segetalis* and ssp. *sativa* are aliens, probably introduced by the Romans as animal feed.

Plant type Pea family, Fabaceae. *Flowers* May–September. *Height* Up to 40cm. *Description* Erect, trailing or scrambling annual herb with leaves divided into leaflets, four to eight pairs terminating in a tendril. Leaflets are variable, either linear or narrow, but widest at the middle or above. Flowers are bright pink or purple, 10–30mm long, two to three together in the leaf axils. Calyx teeth are almost equal. Common Vetch may be quickly distinguished from other vetch species by the two black-blotched stipules at the base of each leaf. *Companion species* Bulbous Buttercup (p.144), Creeping Buttercup (p.149), Hairy Tare (p.252), Hemlock (p.304) and Meadow Buttercup (p.158). *Distribution* Native (*V. sativa* ssp. *nigra* only). Despite its name, this is not the most abundant of British vetches. It occurs throughout Great Britain but is absent from much of north-west Scotland and most of central Ireland. In many parts of England, it is quite local or rare. *Habitat* Grassy and wayside places, particularly dry and sandy sites. Ssp. *nigra* is particularly found in dunes, shingle, sea cliffs and heathlands.

Cotton Thistle
(Onopordum acanthium)

The most statuesque of our wild thistles stands up more than two metres high, with the whole plant reaching almost as wide. It has huge flowers, too: brilliant purple pincushions that are lethally spiny below. The flowers are always crawling with insects, each tiny tuft hiding nectar deep within its flower tube. Once the flowers are over, finches devour their seed, goldfinches in particular. I grow this in my garden as a windbreak – it is one of my favourite instant-height plants – but you will see it in the wild most commonly on the freely drained soils of East Anglia. The Latin specific name comes from the leaves, which are similar in form to those of acanthus. On the Continent, where it comes from, cotton fibres collected from this plant were used to stuff mattresses and pillows – hence its common name. An oil acquired from the seeds was also used for cooking and lamp fuel. Its other common name is Scottish Thistle, and it is the heraldic emblem of the Scots.

Plant type Daisy family, Asteraceae. *Flowers* July–September. *Height* Up to 250cm. *Description* Erect biennial. Leaves are oblong, stalkless, wavy-lobed and spiny, white and cottony on both sides. Stem is spiny-winged, cottony and branched above the base. Flower heads are solitary, 3–5cm across, with purplish pink florets. *Companion species* Common Toadflax (p.74), Mugwort (p.99) and Viper's-bugloss (p.214). *Distribution* Introduced. It is frequent in the east and south of Great Britain (most frequent in East Anglia), although becoming rare in the north. It is very rare in Ireland. *Habitat* Like most thistles, it has a preference for disturbed ground, growing in fields, hedgerows, rubbish tips and other waste places, often near market gardens and farm buildings, perhaps dispersed to new sites in manure or contaminated straw. It grows on well-drained acid to calcareous soils.

Cow Parsley
(Anthriscus sylvestris)

With Hawthorn blossom (p.89) and the occasional pink splotch of the flowers of Crab Apple (p.77), Cow Parsley creates the defining look of our lane sides in May. It froths upwards, the odd river of bluebells running through it, a splash of Red Campion (p.24) and Greater Stitchwort (p.87) adding a shorter, denser white to the party. Several umbellifers grow in our lanes throughout spring and summer, and it is useful to know which is which. Cow Parsley has unmarked green stems, which distinguishes it from the very poisonous Hemlock (p.304). That is an important difference, because Cow Parsley is edible (though if in doubt, don't go there). Cow Parsley tastes like chervil and its young leaves are good in a salad. Its fruits are smooth and oblong, distinguishing it from Bur Chervil (also edible), which has fruits covered in hooked spines. Rough Chervil (which is poisonous) has similar smooth fruits to those of Cow Parsley, but has purple-spotted stems.

Plant type Carrot family, Apiaceae. *Flowers* April–June. *Height* 60–100cm. *Description* Tall, erect, downy perennial herb. White flowers are 3–4mm across, arranged in umbels that are four- to ten-rayed and up to 6cm across. Fresh green, fern-like leaves are two to three times pinnate, scarcely downy with pointed leaflets. Stems are hollow, furrowed, downy below and unspotted. *Companion species* Crab Apple, Greater Stitchwort, Hawthorn and Red Campion. *Distribution* Widespread and very common across the British Isles, although rare in parts of north-west Scotland and the Shetland Isles. Cow Parsley has become more common in the last fifty years, thriving on the increased nitrogen in the soil and able to withstand roadside cutting, which often comes after it has sown its seeds. Its canopy effect has been detrimental to more delicate roadside species such as Early-purple Orchid (p.9) and Common Spotted-orchid (p.148). *Habitat* Characteristic of roadsides and hedgerows, but it also occurs in woodland rides and edges, abandoned pasture and unmanaged hay meadows, and on railway banks, waste ground and cultivated ground. It avoids very wet and very dry ground.

Crab Apple
(Malus sylvestris)

Any apple blossom is beautiful, and the Crab Apple's all the more so because you find it growing wild. Its plump pink buds open to clear white saucers, retaining a flush of pink on the outside. This is the last fruit blossom to flower in our hedgerows, only starting to bloom in late April and on through May. Then come the miniature apples, higher in pectin than most domestic fruit varieties and brilliant for helping to set any autumn jelly or jam. Harvest lots when you see them and make them into jellies flavoured with mint, sage, rosemary

or juniper berries – delicious with meat or game. Crab Apples also make an excellent pudding, baked with honey and apple juice and served with vanilla ice cream – they have the taste of an apply quince. The domesticated apple is far more widespread in the wild than our native Crab. It is difficult to tell them apart from a distance, but Crab Apple's branches are thorny and its mature leaves are hairless, while the mature leaves of domesticated apple are hairy on their undersides and its fruit is larger. Crab Apple regularly hybridises with domesticated apple, creating lots of intermediates.

Plant type Rose family, Rosaceae. *Flowers* Late April and May. *Height* Up to 10m. *Description* Small, rounded, deciduous, thorny tree. Bisexual flowers, 2.5–4cm wide, are located on umbel-like heads; they are usually pink in bud and white when fully open, although some are flushed pink. Leaves are oval-pointed, toothed and hairless when mature. Bark is brown and scaly. Fruit is a yellow-red apple, 2cm across. *Companion species* Dog-rose (p.79), Elder (p.80), Hawthorn (p.89), Honeysuckle (p.91) and Hop (p.92). *Distribution* Native. Widespread across the British Isles, although local in Scotland. It is rarely cultivated, but is undoubtedly a parent of orchard apples. *Habitat* Hedgerows, scrubs, copses, roadsides and rough ground, usually occurring as single trees and native in old oak woods.

Cypress Spurge
(Euphorbia cyparissias)

You will see Cypress Spurge on acid sandy soils in southern England, and on chalk downland in Kent beside the road as you whizz past, an unusual splotch of bright, sharp green. This and many other euphorbias have been popular for centuries in gardens, and that is almost certainly where it originally escaped from, but it now grows happily in the wild. The common name spurge is from the Old French *espurge*, meaning 'to purge', and relates to the plant's traditional use as a purgative. Like all euphorbias, its leaves and stems contain a toxic milky latex, which, if it comes into contact with your skin, can cause burns and blistering. The reaction is strongest on hot, sunny days, when the sap must be more distilled. The specific name, *cyparissias*, is Latin for 'like a cypress', and refers to the shape and pine-like arrangement of the thin leaves on its youngest shoots.

Plant type Spurge family, Euphorbiaceae. *Flowers* June–August. *Height* 10–30cm. *Description* Erect, hairless perennial herb. Stem is branched with many alternate, narrow-linear, toothless leaves up to 3cm long and 2mm wide. Inflorescence is a nine- to fifteen-rayed umbel with many oblong bracts at the base. Upper bracts are yellow (turning red later) and triangular; glands are crescent-shaped. *Companion species* Common Mallow (p.73), Common Toadflax (p.74) and Yarrow (p.167). *Distribution* Probably introduced, although some authorities suggest that it may be native on chalk downland in south-east England. It is naturalised in scattered localities throughout Britain, but absent from Scotland and Ireland. *Habitat* Chalk grassland and scrub; also a casual of waste ground and roadsides. It can colonise arable margins and may become established on sand dunes. It grows on some racecourses, often introduced with horse feed or bedding.

Danish Scurvygrass
(Cochlearia danica)

Driving on a main road or motorway early in the year, you may notice this by the roadside and in the central reservation, the grass turned white with its flowers. On roads inland from the coast these patches can go on for tens of kilometres. This is a relatively new phenomenon. Until the 1980s, Danish Scurvygrass occurred only on the coast, but it has undergone a spectacular increase and moved inland. The seeds are probably carried by cars and lorries, then dropped along the way. With the increase of winter gritting during the past twenty years, the residual concentration of salt in the soil on major roads has increased sufficiently to enable these seeds to germinate and thrive. The stone ballast used in road-building creates a similar habitat to its native cliff top, so it romps away, while the turbulence created by fast-moving traffic transports seed from the new colonies even further inland. Danish Scurvygrass is edible: picked from the coast (not beside the road), its leaves or flowers add a punchy, mustardy taste to salads, mayonnaise and French dressing.

Plant type Cabbage family, Brassicaceae. *Flowers* February–June. *Height* Up to 20cm. *Description* Overwintering annual hairless herb with shiny, dark green, ivy-shaped basal leaves. Stem leaves are stalked and oval. Small, lilac-white, cabbage-like flowers are 4–5mm across. *Companion species* On roadsides, it forms colonising carpets on its own. *Distribution* Native. Occurs on the coastlines of England and Wales, although it is more local in Scotland and Ireland. It is increasingly common. The distribution map shows it heading inland in streaks that closely correspond to the trunk road network; it is spreading at a rate of 15–25km per year. In future, we will see it turning off onto the side roads, but it is restricted to the roadside by its need for salt. *Habitat* A species of cliff tops and sand dunes, as well as pavements and sea walls in coastal towns. A very hardy species, it survives well in the hot, dry, salty edges of roads and motorways.

Dog-rose
(Rosa canina)

This is the epitome of what a flower should be: single, simple, pale pink petals with a green stigma and a halo of anthers making a fluffy golden dome in the centre. The petals bleach to white at their heart and the leaves are pretty too, strong-textured and chiselled in outline, a deep rich green. Dog-rose is not one single species. Rather, it is a variable aggregate of similar subspecies, which explains the variation in the depth of pinkness of the flowers and the shape and size of the hips. It clambers through hedges from front to back like Honeysuckle (p.91), preferring the sunny side, while Honeysuckle favours the side with more shade. The flowers have a mild but sweet scent. The bright red hips that form in late summer have traditionally been foraged to make rose-hip syrup and tea.

Plant type Rose family, Rosaceae. *Flowers* June–July. *Height* Up to 3m. *Description* Shrub with arching stems and broad-based, strongly hooked prickles. Leaves have two to three pairs of toothed leaflets, which may be hairless or slightly hairy. Flowers are pink (sometimes white), spread flat (not cup-shaped, like those of Field-rose, p.82), 4–5cm across and arranged in groups of one to four. Although it is extremely variable, Dog-rose can be distinguished from Sweet-briar (p.109) by its more vigorous and taller habit. Also, Sweet-briar has leaflets and flower stalks that are covered with brownish, sticky, apple-scented hairs. *Companion species* Bramble (p.66), Elder (p.80) and Hawthorn (p.89). *Distribution* Native. This is the commonest wild rose in many places, common throughout most of England, although it is more local in parts of Yorkshire and East Anglia. Similarly, its distribution in Scotland is quite scattered, but it is generally more common in the lowlands. In Ireland, its distribution has two clusters, one in the north east and the other in the far south. *Habitat* Well-drained calcareous to moderately acidic soils. Habitats include roadsides, railways, waste ground, woodland, scrub, hedgerows, cliffs, riverbanks and rock outcrops. It can rapidly colonise disturbed sites.

Dogwood
(Cornus sanguinea)

Dogwood, like rhododendron, is a marker plant for soil pH, but it tells you that you are on alkaline, not acid, soil. We do not see this plant in our hedgerows in the Weald of Kent or Sussex on heavy acid clay, but in east Kent or Plantlife's Ranscombe Farm Reserve in north Kent, both on chalk, it is as common as Elder (p.80). It is among the first bushes to come into leaf – pale green in early March, a brilliant contrast to the red stems. Then come the pretty flowers in creamy-white, flat umbels, like elderflower but more densely clumped, less lacy and airy. In autumn, the leaves turn to match the red stems and it has black, globular berry fruit. The only other member of the dogwood family that is native to the British Isles is Dwarf Cornel (*Cornus suecica*), a rare and dissimilar plant of the Scottish Highlands, but there are two other species you might confuse it with: Red-osier Dogwood (*C. sericea*) and Cornelian-cherry (*C. mas*). Both are occasionally found naturalised as garden escapes.

Plant type Dogwood family, Cornaceae. *Flowers* Mid May–July. *Height* Up to 4m. *Description* Deciduous shrub with purplish-red twigs. Leaves are oval, pointed, untoothed and without stipules, 4–8cm long, opposite one another. Three to five main veins are curved towards the apex of the stem. Flowers are creamy-white, four-petalled, arranged in a flat-topped umbel. *Companion species* Wood Spurge (p.33) on the woodland edge. *Distribution* Native and locally frequent throughout Britain, although rare in Scotland and considered to be alien there. It is quite common in most of England, but becoming scarce in the far south west and north west. In Wales, it is largely absent from the most remote districts. Rare in Ireland. *Habitat* Hedgerows and shelter belts, woodland and scrub on limestone soils or base-rich clays, sometimes dominant in hedges and scrub on chalk. It is frequently planted in landscape schemes and is introduced sporadically, or occurs as an escape, outside its native range.

Elder
(Sambucus nigra)

Second to Hawthorn (p.89), Elderflower is the commonest hedgerow blossom in the British Isles. You can see it clearly from a distance, its creamy-white lace handkerchiefs laid out above the leaves, the umbels a mixture of heavy looseness, like the head on a pint of beer. The cream colouring comes mainly from the pollen-laden anthers, which give the flowers their characteristic scent and flavour, now so fashionable in a sugar-syrup cordial. To get the best taste, harvest the flowers when fully open from plants in full sun. If it's raining or if they are going over, or are harvested from branches in the shade, they can have a faint hint of cat's pee. From late summer, the bushes will be covered in shiny black berries, which are excellent for making drinks and chutneys and have a very high concentration of Vitamin C. The flavourful fungus Jew's Ear (*Auricularia auricula-judae*) is often found on the root masses and dead branches of this tree.

Plant type Honeysuckle family, Caprifoliaceae. *Flowers* May–June. *Height* 10m. *Description* Suckering shrub or small tree. It has deeply furrowed bark and pinnate leaves with oval-elliptical, toothed leaflets, 3–9cm long. These have a very acrid smell when you crush them. Inflorescence is like an umbel, 10–20cm across, much branched with many creamy white flowers that are 5mm across. Fruit is a small black berry, again arranged in umbels, each 6–8mm wide. *Companion species* Common Nettle (p.241) and Hogweed (p.156) in places that have been enriched by nitrogen, such as house ruins, churchyards and badger sets. *Distribution* Native. Very common throughout the British Isles except the Scottish Highlands. It is thought to have been introduced to Orkney and Shetland. *Habitat* Fertile soils in woodland, hedgerows, grassland, scrub, waste ground, roadsides and railway banks.

English Elm
(Ulmus procera)

Mature English Elms in a hedge are a rare sight thanks to Dutch Elm Disease. Their magnificent, lime-green seed pods in spring are reminiscent of hops in a hedge in autumn. They do grow to about six metres, but then, with the disease, they die. The current outbreak of Dutch Elm Disease began in 1965, caused by a fungus, *Certocystis ulmi*, carried by elm-bark beetles. This damages the trees by blocking their water-conducting channels. Elm flowers appear early in the year, followed by papery seed pods. The leaves come in April or May. Patches of the foliage turn golden yellow in late summer, but the autumn leaves are among the last to fall. Elm wood has great strength and is resistant to water; it has been used for boat building, furniture and, famously, beach groins. Elm is the food plant of the White-letter Hairstreak butterfly, which has declined hugely since the outbreak of the disease.

Plant type Elm family, Ulmaceae. *Flowers* February–March; seed pods March–June. *Height* Up to 30m. *Description* Tree with erect trunk and oblong outline, with many suckers produced from the base (making it well adapted for growing in hedgerows). Rounded to oval leaves, 4–9cm long, have a toothed margin and sharp point and their upper surface is roughened by short hairs. The other British member of the family, Wych Elm (*U. glabra*), has a broader, more spreading outline with suckers absent or few, so it does not grow in hedgerows. *Companion species* Hawthorn (p.89), Hazel (p.15) and Oak (p.101). *Distribution* Native. Its natural distribution is difficult to distinguish because of planting, but it probably does not extend beyond England and Wales. *Habitat* More confined to hedgerows and field borders than Wych Elm and rare in woodland, although it may form small copses. It loves a deep and moist soil.

False Oxlip

(Primula x *polyantha)*

This hybrid between Primrose (p.103) and Cowslip (p.195) looks like something you would buy in a garden centre, not find growing wild at the base of a hedge. Big, lush and covered in large, showy, sunny yellow flowers, it looks similar to the true Oxlip (p.21) but is more chunky and floriferous, the plants making big clumps often twice the size of Oxlip, but as single one-offs, not swathes. It spreads only by vegetative growth. Like many hybrids, it is sterile. Oxlip, by contrast, forms carpeting drifts on the woodland floor, but each plant is more subtle and delicate. The two grow in different places. Oxlip likes heavier, wetter ground and grows mainly in deciduous old woods with more shade, whereas False Oxlip appears anywhere that the parents grow quite close together, in hedges, shady banks and meadows.

Plant type Primrose family, Primulaceae. *Flowers* March–May. *Height* 30–40cm. *Description* Perennial herb. There is considerable variation in the hybrids depending on which parent is the mother or father (offspring typically resemble the mother). Flowers are always smaller than those of Primrose but with a richer colour, and usually larger than those of Cowslip. It is easy to confuse with true Oxlip, but the corolla tube of False Oxlip has folds (true Oxlip has none) and its flowers are a deeper, more golden yellow than those of true Oxlips, and usually streaked with orange. *Companion species* Bugle (p.68), Cowslip, Dog-rose (p.79), Lesser Celandine (p.18), Primrose and Sweet-briar (p.109). *Distribution* More local than its parents, with distribution becoming increasingly scattered towards the north of England. Rare in Scotland and Ireland. *Habitat* Calcareous soils, grassland banks (where Cowslips are common), deciduous woodland and hedgerows (where Primroses are common).

Fennel

(Foeniculum vulgare)

Most of us know what Fennel looks like because it is grown so widely in our gardens as a kitchen herb. The leaves have a gentle aniseedy taste and the flowers are an excellent addition to salads. The seeds have a similar taste and have been used to aid digestion since the Middle Ages – they are still eaten after meals in posh Indian restaurants. Fennel is one of the last wild flowers to come into bloom, its brilliant golden plateaux opening as summer ends and staying fresh and bright through the autumn. It grows on disturbed ground beside the road and in big colonies in waste places and on railways. It has a deep taproot that enables it to survive in drought-prone places, such as baking hot lay-bys, where there is little else to compete. Its hollow stems are important over-wintering habitats for invertebrates.

Plant type Carrot family, Apiaceae. *Flowers* July–October. *Height* Up to 2m. *Description* Erect, hairless perennial herb. Leaves are pinnate, repeatedly divided into thread-like, waxy green leaflets. Umbels are many-rayed, 4–8cm across, with bright yellow flowers, 1–2mm across. Fruit is oval and rounded, with broad ridges. *Companion species* Common Nettle (p.241), Red Valerian (p.407) and Viper's-bugloss (p.214). *Distribution* Introduced, probably by the Romans, as a medicinal and culinary herb. It is frequent throughout Britain as far north as Yorkshire, but scarce and casual further north. It is rare in Ireland. *Habitat* Open ground and waste places, especially near the coast. Typical localities include roadsides, sand dunes and sea walls. Inland, it is usually found on disturbed ground, such as wasteland and rough grassland near habitation, as well as gravel pits and rubbish tips.

Field-rose
(Rosa arvensis)

In early summer the hedgerows round Perch Hill are thick with Field-rose, which is commoner on our heavy soil and thickly wooded land than the Dog-rose (p.79). Contrary to its name, it appears more on woodland edges and in well-established hedges than it does in fields. It clambers up and over other shrubby plants and makes good long runs in hedges, where it in turn provides a climbing frame for the leaves and vines of plants such as Black Bryony (p.63). The flowers are short-lived, but perfect while they last, bright white and faintly veined, giving them an ethereal translucence. The yellow anthers at their heart turn gold as they ripen. You might expect the flowers to smell delicious, but they are almost scentless.

Plant type Rose family, Rosaceae. *Flowers* June–July. *Height* Up to 1m. *Description* Low, scrambling or trailing deciduous shrub. Flowers are white, cup-shaped, 3–5cm across, in clusters of one to six. Leaves are hairless, divided into two to three pairs of leaflets, each of which is 1–3.5cm long. Red fruit have weak green stems. Roses are difficult to identify from their flowers alone: rose hips are normally required to be certain. Burnet Rose (p.68) has white flowers, but these are solitary and produce purplish black hips. Dog-rose (whose flowers can be pink or white) is also easy to confuse with Field-rose. You can tell the difference between them by looking at the styles. In Field-rose, the styles are united into a column surrounded by the anthers, whereas Dog-rose has multiple, short, separate styles at the centre of the flower. Field-rose has curved thorns, whereas those of Dog-rose are straight. *Companion species* Black Bryony, Blackthorn (p.64), Elder (p.80), Hawthorn (p.89) and Hornbeam (p.92). *Distribution* Native. It is widely distributed throughout England and Wales but becoming scarcer in the north, parts of west Wales and the East Anglian Fens. It is absent from Scotland, except where introduced, but present throughout Ireland, where it is most common in the south east. *Habitat* Roadsides and railway banks, scrub and hedgerows, woodland edges, clearings and rides, on a wide variety of soils. It avoids very acidic sites.

Fox-and-cubs
(Pilosella aurantiaca)

When my children were younger, I would pass a huge drift of Fox-and-cubs while driving them to school every day, about thirty plants studding a steep grassy bank in a housing estate on the edge of Robertsbridge. It was an incongruous place to see this plant, which is much more common in the north of England and borders of Scotland, but typically appears in distinct colonies such as this, spreading by leafy runners. I love its cheerful colour – the origin of its common name – with fully open flowers and smaller buds collected together on tall, slim stems. The orange stands out clearly against the unopened buds, which are in a fuzz of short black hairs, and the tassel flowers look good whether fully open or going over. That seems to be the case with all orange-tinged garden plants, such as the darker-coloured English marigolds – they age with elegance. Fox-and-cubs is an ornamental hawkweed, native to France, Germany and Scandinavia, that has been grown in gardens since at least 1629. It was first recorded in 1793 in the wild, where it tends to colonise roadsides on heavier soils.

Plant type Daisy family, Asteraceae. *Flowers* June–July. *Height* 20–40cm. *Description* Perennial herb with leaves in a basal rosette and on the flower stem. Orange florets vary in their depth of colour in different situations, some flowers being red or deep orange, more rarely pale yellow, with dark brown styles. *Companion species* Common Sorrel (p.147), Oxeye Daisy (p.159), Rough Hawkbit (p.162) and Sheep's Sorrel (p.366). *Distribution* Introduced; native to central and northern Europe. It is now found throughout the British Isles and is common in many regions, although it is absent or rare in some areas, such as the Scottish Highlands. Introduced to North America and Australasia, it is considered a noxious weed in many US states. *Habitat* Railway embankments, roadsides, walls, churchyards and other waste places.

Fuchsia

(Fuchsia magellanica var. *macrostema)*

We tend to be blasé about seeing this exotic plant growing abundantly in the wild, so used have we become to seeing it in gardens. It is one of our genuine wild flowers now, growing in hedges in coastal areas of Cornwall, the west coast of Ireland and some parts of Scotland. You will rarely see it as a single plant, because reproduction is usually by suckering, and one bush will gradually form a thicket. The gnarled, weather-beaten bushes often stand two metres high, each one decked from soil to sky with intricate flowers, literally thousands of them on a decent-sized bush, hanging below the branches. Every one is a ball gown, with red outer skirts and a purple shift below, a fringe of pink-red anthers and a single stigma on the hemline. The caterpillar of the Elephant Hawk-moth feeds on the leaves, and the thick bushes are popular with nesting birds, such as bullfinch and dunnock.

Plant type Willowherb family, Onagraceae. *Flowers* June–October. *Height* Up to 3m. *Description* Low shrub. Leaves are opposite, elliptical and toothed, 25–55mm long. Flowers are drooping and have four bright red-pink sepals, four violet petals and eight stamens. Fruit is a black berry. *Companion species* Bramble (p.66), Honeysuckle (p.91), Montbretia (p.98), Raspberry (p.104) and Three-cornered Garlic (p.112). *Distribution* Introduced from South America in 1823. Locally frequent on the west coast of Britain, especially in Devon, Cornwall and Argyll. It is cut to the ground by hard frosts, which is why it prefers warmer coastal districts. Fuchsia is common along much of the Irish coast (especially in the west) and also in some inland areas. It is also found on the Isle of Man, Orkney and Shetland. *Habitat* Principally found as a planted hedge or in the gardens of abandoned cottages, it is also naturalised in hedgerows and scrub, by streams, among rocks and on walls.

Garlic Mustard

(Alliaria petiolata)

One of those plants that you see en masse, carpeting the shady base of a hedge along a lane or roadside, Garlic Mustard does not appear as the odd plant here and there, but by the fifty or the hundred. Each plant in isolation has a straightforward handsomeness – the way the leaves come out so flat from the stem, the bright freshness of the leaf's green and the good clean contrast between its colour and the bleached white flower. Known also as Jack-by-the-Hedge, Garlic Mustard is, like all brassicas, edible. You can add a few of its mildly garlicky-tasting leaves to a salad; they used to be picked to make a green sauce to serve with fish or lamb. This is a very common plant, which you can harvest without anxiety. Pick the small and tender leaves in the first year. As a biennial, it flowers in its second year, and you can pick the leaves and flower buds at that point, too. They can be harvested as early as February if there has been a mild winter, and there is often a second crop of leaves in the autumn. This, together with another roadside plant, Cuckooflower (p.297), is the principal larval food plant of the Orange-tip butterfly.

Plant type Cabbage family, Brassicaceae. *Flowers* April–July. *Height* 20–120cm. *Description* Hairless, erect, biennial herb with white flowers (6mm across) arranged in a raceme. Leaves are cordate, toothed and glossy, smelling of garlic when bruised. *Companion species* Bluebell (p.2), Cuckooflower, Lesser Celandine (p.18) and Wood Anemone (p.30). *Distribution* Widespread and very common in England and Wales, less so in Scotland and Ireland. Rare or absent in north-west Scotland and western Ireland. *Habitat* Shaded hedge banks, riverbanks, disturbed woodland, woodland edges and clearings, walls, road verges and waste ground. It grows well on relatively fertile, moist soils, avoiding only the most acidic sites.

Germander Speedwell
(Veronica chamaedrys)

As a child, I loved this plant and always knew it by its other common name of Bird's-eye Speedwell. It might be small, but it is beautiful – perfect upright flower spikes with smoky crimson stems and several saucer-like flowers in the clearest blue. Look at one closely and you will see that it is exquisite. Two stamens emerge from a pure white centre, the white continuing as a narrow band into the main face of the flower. The white is then edged by a deep indigo-blue line, which flares out with dark veins into the main blue of the petal. Speedwells love the disturbed, clear ground of the anthill. One of the best spring wild-flower sights I have ever seen was on anthills on chalk downland, where Germander Speedwell was growing with Crosswort (p.196) and Ground-ivy (p.14), creating a chance combination of brilliant blue, purple and acid green that was as good as any planned garden scheme.

Plant type Speedwell family, Veronicaceae. *Flowers* March–July. *Height* 10–30cm. *Description* Annual, creeping and ascending herb. Flowers are bright blue with a white eye, 1cm wide. Leaves are oval-triangular, stalkless, 1–2.5cm long. Stem has two opposite rows of long white hairs. Fruit is heart-shaped and shorter than the calyx teeth. *Companion species* Ground-ivy, Hairy Bitter-cress (p.251), Scarlet Pimpernel (p.259) and – on chalk – Crosswort. *Distribution* Native. Found throughout the British Isles, where it is very common in most areas, although it is rare in Shetland. It spreads vegetatively by prostrate stems, which root at the nodes; reproduction from seed is apparently rare. *Habitat* More or less ubiquitous, growing on hedge banks and grassland and in woods, as well as on rock outcrops, upland scree, road verges, railway banks and waste ground. It is found on most soil types, except the most impoverished.

Giant Hogweed
(Heracleum mantegazzianum)

This statuesque plant is one of Britain's largest herbaceous perennial wildflowers, standing as tall as a man, with flower heads the size of dinner plates and leaves the length of my arm. I love to see it growing beside the road, but it should be treated with caution. Its stems, if touched, can cause serious blistering burns, thanks to chemicals within its sap that are known as furocoumarins. The reaction is at its strongest on hot, sunny days, when the sap must be more concentrated. It is a garden escape that became a problem in the second half of the twentieth century, when the huge increase in road building provided it with an ideal linear habitat in which to spread. Like many invasive plants, it is difficult to eradicate, susceptible to weedkillers only when young. Each plant may produce up to five thousand seeds, so it can really romp away, often growing beside streams and rivers, the water spreading the seeds over a huge distance. It is now legislated against in the 1981 Wildlife and Countryside Act, which makes it illegal to plant or cause it to grow in the wild.

Plant type Carrot family, Apiaceae. *Flowers* June–July. *Height* Up to 5.5m. *Description* Large perennial herb. Stem is hollow, red-spotted, slightly hairy and up to 10cm across. Leaves are pinnate, sharply toothed and up to 1m long. Umbels are up to 50cm across, each flower bearing white petals that may be up to 12mm long. Fruit is oval, very flattened, hairless or slightly hairy. *Companion species* Hedge Bindweed (p.90), Indian Balsam (p.305), Rosebay Willowherb (p.258) and Russian Comfrey (p.105). *Distribution* Introduced as an ornamental plant in gardens, native to the Caucasus mountains and south-west Asia. It is now naturalised in many parts of the British Isles. *Habitat* Roadsides, waste ground, open wet woodland and near rivers.

Goat's-rue
(Galega officinalis)

Goat's-rue is an abundant motorway plant, which forms big, bushy domes in huge bands beside the road, completely colonising patches of slope or siding. Its flower colour is variable, from pale, soft mauve to almost white. If you look at the mauve plants carefully, homing in on each pea flower, it looks as though white outer wings have sucked up a soft purple pigment into their veins, which contrasts with the paler, almost white of the lower keel petal. From a distance all these elements merge into one pale mauve. As a quick-growing legume, Goat's-rue was introduced into cultivation for fodder and as a medicinal herb in 1568, and first recorded in the wild in 1640. Then everyone saw how lovely it was in flower, so it made its way into people's gardens. Its name probably comes from the leaves, which are slightly smelly when bruised.

Plant type Pea family, Fabaceae. *Flowers* July–September. *Height* Up to 100cm. *Description* Erect, hairless perennial herb. Leaves are pinnate with four to eight pairs of oblong-lanceolate leaflets, each leaflet up to 1cm across. Flowers are white to pale purplish lilac, 10–15mm long, in oblong racemes. Pods are cylindrical, 20–50mm long. *Companion species* Common Ragwort (p.242) and Oxford Ragwort (p.101). *Distribution* Introduced. A native of eastern and southern Europe and western Asia. Its spread is very recent. It is now recorded in three quarters of areas in and around London. It is also common in south-east England, and occasional to locally frequent elsewhere. There are clusters of populations in the Midlands and northern England and a few scattered colonies in Scotland and south-west England. Until recently, it has been predominantly an urban plant, but it is now spreading into rural areas. *Habitat* Roadsides, railway banks, rubbish tips, waste places and gravel pits.

Goat Willow
(Salix caprea)

Early in the spring, Goat Willow looks like a light bulb in the hedge, its bright white-yellow catkins shining out while everything around it is still bare-branched and grey. Different boughs are often at different stages in their flower progression, one branch fluffy with yellow anthers while another is at the tight-grey, velvety rabbit-paw stage. Even within one bough, you sometimes get different degrees of flower development, from fresh and tight to going over. Where I live in Kent, older people call this the Palm Tree, because it was once used widely to decorate the church on Palm Sunday. It is also known as Pussy Willow or Great Sallow, and its bark contains the drug salicylic acid, which is the original source of aspirin. Goat Willow is an invaluable early source of pollen for foraging insects.

Plant type Willow family, Salicaceae. *Flowers* March–April. *Height* Up to 10m. *Description* Shrub or small tree. The catkins appear before the leaves and are unstalked and erect. Male catkins are 2–4cm long, while the female are 3–7cm long. Both are covered in silvery white hairs, the male with two golden stamens per flower, the female with two green stigmas. Leaves are oval. It can be confused with the less showy Grey Willow (*S. cinerea*), but this has obovate leaves, and the raised ridges under the bark of second-year twigs, which are characteristic of Goat Willow, are absent. *Companion species* Bugle (p.68), Common Sedge (p.296) and Lesser Celandine (p.18). *Distribution* Native. Frequent throughout the British Isles, although rare in the far north of Britain, the Shetland Isles and the west coast of Ireland. *Habitat* Hedgerows and open woodland, woodland margins, scrub and around rocky lake and stream sides. It may grow in waste ground and can tolerate drier and more base-rich soils than Grey Willow. It has also become increasingly abundant along disused railways.

Greater Celandine
(Chelidonium majus)

Whenever I see Greater Celandine I think of warts, as there is a widespread claim that the bright orange sap from this plant is the one and only effective treatment for them. This is a large but quite delicate plant with an open, airy structure and custard-yellow, papery-looking flowers, like a smaller version of the seaside Yellow Horned-poppy (p.427). It is in the poppy family and has that characteristic, slightly ethereal feel; it is, in fact, only distantly related to its namesake Lesser Celandine (p.18), which is a member of the buttercup, not the poppy, family. In both cases the genus name originates from the time of year when it flowers – the Greek *chelidon* means 'swallow', a signature bird of spring.

Plant type Poppy family, Papaveraceae. *Flowers* May–August. *Height* Up to 90cm. *Description* Branched, hairy perennial herb, with flowers just larger than those of a buttercup (20–25mm across) in clusters, each with two sepals and four petals. Leaves are almost hairless and blue-grey-green beneath. They consist of rounded leaflets, the terminal one being three-lobed. *Companion species* Horseradish (p.93), Red Campion (p.24), Russian Comfrey (p.105) and White Campion (p.115). *Distribution* It is unclear whether this is a native or was introduced by the Romans, who knew it to be a therapeutic plant. It is common throughout England and Wales, but much less frequent in Scotland. *Habitat* It grows by roadsides and paths at the bottom of a hedge or out in grass, particularly near habitation in the crevices of old walls, in paving and on waste ground.

Greater Stitchwort
(Stellaria holostea)

Greater Stitchwort is one of the most ubiquitous plants of the spring lane. You will see it everywhere and it flowers for months – it is one of my real favourites. To see it for what it is, you need to lie down and put your head flat on the ground. It is pretty enough until you do, with simple, pure-white flowers on spidery, hair-thin stems with grass-like leaves. But with your eyes right down among them you can see the elegance of the matt, greyish-green, paired leaves and the ten-lobed petals (which are, in fact, five petals divided to halfway or less) with their pretty halo of anthers in between.

Plant type Pink family, Caryophyllaceae. *Flowers* March–June. *Height* 15–60cm. *Description* Perennial herb with weak, brittle, more or less erect stems, with leaves arranged in pairs, each narrow and lance shaped. White flowers are 20–30mm across, making it easy to tell apart from Lesser Stitchwort (p.157), which has smaller flowers (5–18mm across) with petals split more than halfway, so that you can see the green calyx behind. Marsh Stitchwort (*S. palustris*) can also cause confusion, but this looks more like Lesser Stitchwort, with the petals similarly divided, and grows only in damp and marshy spots. The colours of the leaves differ, too: Greater Stitchwort's are not as glaucous as Marsh Stitchwort's, nor the fresh bright green of Lesser Stitchwort. *Companion species* Bluebell (p.2), Cow Parsley (p.77) and Yellow Archangel (p.35). *Distribution* Native. Common throughout the British Isles except on very acid soils. Absent from areas surrounding the Wash, parts of northern Scotland and western Ireland. *Habitat* Hedgerows and woodland – it is an ancient woodland indicator species. It is also common on unmanaged grassy roadsides. Tolerant of a wide range of soils, but does best on those that are moist, mildly acid and infertile. It avoids permanently wet conditions.

Green Alkanet
(Pentaglottis sempervirens)

Some people think of this as a terrible garden weed, but I like its vibrant blue. Green Alkanet is the coarser, hardier, shorter and stouter equivalent of the May-flowering Mediterranean plant anchusa, which many of us grow in our gardens. When it is at its newest and best, Alkanet provides the same intense colour. The flowers look a little like those of a speedwell, but they are bigger. They are also edible – they do not taste of much, but they look good. Freeze them in an ice cube, float them in a drink or a bowl of soup or scatter them over a salad. Bizarrely, being blue, this plant gives out a red dye, which has been used in the past for tinting oils and – in southern Europe, where it comes from – to deepen the colour of cheap red wine. Like Sweet Cicely (p.110) and Alexanders (p.62), it is often found growing near medieval abbeys, where it was once cultivated for this dye.

Plant type Borage family, Boraginaceae. _Flowers_ April–July. _Height_ 30–60cm. _Description_ Erect, bristly perennial. Leaves are undivided, oval, untoothed, flat, up to 20cm long and so hairy that they are almost spiny. They are alternately arranged up the stem, without stipules. Bright blue flowers are on long stalks, five-petalled, 10mm wide, arranged in dense inflorescences with a bract below each flower. _Companion species_ Cleavers (p.238), Common Nettle (p.241) and Red Dead-nettle (p.257). _Distribution_ Introduced. A native of south-west Europe, it is now widespread across the British Isles, although absent from much of northern England, western Scotland, Wales and Ireland. _Habitat_ Mostly found near habitation in lightly shaded places at the base of hedges, on roadside banks, scrub, woodland and riversides. It also grows in waste ground. Beware of it in the garden – it reproduces prolifically from seed and can be invasive.

Guelder-rose
(Viburnum opulus)

The flowers of Guelder-rose are reminiscent of garden lacecap hydrangeas, although they are just a bit less showy. A full circle of flat, creamy-white flowers around the edge encloses as many little Elder-like flowers at the centre. The leaves are pretty, too. They are palmately lobed, which distinguishes Guelder-rose from the other members of the family with umbels of white flowers, such as Elder (p.80). We notice it most for its berries – which are poisonous – and rich crimson and scarlet leaves in late summer and autumn. The Guelder part of its common name comes from Gueldres, or Guelderland, on the border of Holland and Germany, where many unusual varieties have been cultivated. It is planted in parks and gardens, and plants that spread from these sites to the wild sometimes include yellow-fruited cultivars. This is also the wild ancestor of the Snowball Tree, _Viburnum opulus_ 'Sterile', in which more sterile flowers replace the smaller central fertile flowers to make full, greeny-white globes.

Plant type Honeysuckle family, Caprifoliaceae. _Flowers_ May–June, fruiting July–October. _Height_ 2–4m. _Description_ Deciduous shrub with greyish twigs that are hairless and angled with scaly buds. Leaves are dark green, palmately lobed, sharply toothed, downy on their undersides, 5–8cm long. Flowers are white and appear in flat, umbel-like inflorescences. Only the smaller, inner flowers (6mm across) are fertile. Outer flowers (15–20mm across) have no stamens or stigmas. Fruit is a globular red berry. _Companion species_ Alder (p.348) and Goat Willow (p.86). _Distribution_ Native. An ancient woodland indicator species, which occurs throughout Britain. Common in England and Wales but more local in Scotland and scarce in upland areas. It is quite frequent in Ireland. _Habitat_ Woodland, scrub and hedgerows, especially on damp, calcareous soils and on stream banks. It favours damp places, but is also found in dry habitats.

Harsh Downy-rose
(Rosa tomentosa)

Why this is called Harsh I have no idea. Its leaves are soft and fluffy on both sides, as are its flower stems, giving rise to its species name – *tomentum* being the Latin word for a soft, fine wool used to stuff cushions. This general furriness distinguishes Harsh Downy-rose from other pale pink- to white-flowered single roses. Its flowers are some of the largest of our native roses, up to 5cm across, simple and pretty against a slightly grey-green leaf. Its overall habit is different to that of other wild roses, too, with stout, long (up to 3m) shoots that arch away from the centre of the plant and longer flower stems (2–3.5cm), making a laxer, taller-growing shrub. Unlike briar roses, such as Sweet-briar (p.109), the leaves of Harsh Downy-rose are not apple-scented.

Plant type Rose family, Rosaceae. *Flowers* June–July. *Height* Up to 3m. *Description* Scrambling deciduous shrub. Leaflets are 1.5–4cm long, densely covered with soft fine hairs on both sides, with glandular hairs on the undersides. Stems have stout, almost straight but sometimes curved prickles. Hip is ovoid, 1–2cm long and covered in glandular hairs (although it is sometimes smooth). Sepals usually fall off before the fruit ripens. Soft Downy-rose (*R. mollis*) also has furry leaves, but it has deep pink flowers and short flower stalks (0.5–1cm long). *Companion species* Dogwood (p.79), Hawthorn (p.89), Hedge Bindweed (p.90) and Honeysuckle (p.91). *Distribution* Native. It is largely confined to central and southern England and Wales, with a handful of outlying populations in northern England and Scotland and central and southern Ireland. It is often rather localised and never particularly common, except in a few areas, such as the Weald of Kent and Sussex, the Chilterns and the West Midlands. *Habitat* This hedgerow climber usually prefers calcareous to mildly acidic soils and is found on woodland edges and in hedgerows, where it appears to thrive in relatively shady conditions. It also occurs in more open habitats, including scrub, rough grassland, disused quarries and less acidic heaths.

Hawthorn
(Crataegus monogyna)

Hawthorn blossom reminds me of those classic Japanese ink drawings: each flower neat, the crimson-tipped stamens radiating over five white petals, their buds perfect, milky and spherical, like doublet buttons. The leaves, flowers and berries of the hawthorn, which is also known by the names of May-tree and Quickthorn, are all edible; the berries, in sealing-wax red, continue into winter on the branch and are an invaluable source of food for birds in snow and hard frosts, so it's good not to cut hedges in the autumn. Our most famous individual thorn tree is the Glastonbury Holy Thorn, said to have been brought to the town by Joseph of Arimathea, Jesus's great-uncle, when he visited England during his mission to spread the word of Christianity after the Crucifixion. The Glastonbury thorn is unusual in that it flowers twice a year, once as normal on old wood in spring, and once on new wood (the current season's matured new growth) around Christmas. This is when you might expect a tree from Palestine to bloom, which gives the myth some resonance.

Plant type Rose family, Rosaceae. *Flowers* May–mid June. Hawthorn is famously erratic as to when exactly it starts to flower, influenced by how long winter continues. *Height* Up to 10m. *Description* Thorny, deciduous shrub with distinctive deeply three-to-five-lobed leaves. Flowers are white, sometimes pink and (like most members of the rose family) with five petals. Fruit is an 8–10mm oval berry. *Companion species* Elder (p.80), Goat Willow (p.86), Holly (p.16) and Oak (p.101). *Distribution* Native. Common throughout the British Isles, apart from the far north west of Scotland, where it is less frequent. Because it has been widely planted as a hedging plant for many centuries, the limits of its native distribution are unclear. In northern Scotland, it is often confined to areas near habitation, perhaps suggesting that it is not native there. *Habitat* Occurs in hedgerows, scrub and woodland borders. It may also be found as an understorey within woodland. It may persist as scattered shrubs in grazed sites, spreading rapidly once grazing subsides. It is found on a wide range of soils.

Hedge Bindweed
(Calystegia sepium)

There are few of us who do not recognise the clean white trumpets of Hedge Bindweed. This is one of the gardener's hated plants, a perennial weed that has a very deep and breakable root system and can form a new plant from only a small section of root. It is also a choker of other more delicate things, forming huge curtain canopies over garden or hedge plants, excluding their light and starving them by making photosynthesis impossible. When I moved to Perch Hill, the garden was thick with Hedge Bindweed and I lost lots of interesting plants by failing to keep on top of its triffid-like growth. Having said all that, its large bell flowers are impressive, their clear whiteness luminous at dusk. Unlike morning-glories, to which it is related, Hedge Bindweed stays open into the night and sometimes all night if there is a full moon.

Plant type Bindweed family, Convolvulaceae. *Flowers* July–September. *Height* Up to 3m. *Description* Creeping, climbing perennial herb. Flowers are white (rarely pale pink), 3–7cm across. Leaves are arrow-shaped, up to 15cm long. Epicalyx has two bracteoles, which are longer than the calyx but not overlapping. *Companion species* Black Bryony (p.63), Blackthorn (p.64), Hawthorn (p.89) and Honeysuckle (p.91). *Distribution* Native. It is found throughout Britain and Ireland and is very common in most areas, becoming local only in upland areas and the north of Scotland. It is absent from most of the Scottish Highlands. *Habitat* Hedges, scrub, woodland edges, railway banks and waste ground. It also occurs in artificial habitats in built-up areas and near habitation, and is a serious and persistent weed of arable crops and gardens.

Hedge Woundwort
(Stachys sylvatica)

Hedge Woundwort is a hairy, tough old plant, which grows out of the bottom of hedges in early summer. It has square stems, large woolly leaves and smoky-crimson tubular flowers, each divided into a top and bottom lip. All these characteristics place it in the dead-nettle family, and it looks like a less ornamental version of its relations, garden salvias. It fools me in my garden and I fail to remove it, thinking its lush, full young leaves promise something exciting, but it can behave like a thug, spreading rapidly by rooting runners and creeping rhizomatous roots, killing more delicate plants in its path. You will know it immediately when you weed it out, as its crushed leaves have a pungent and unpleasant smell. In its favour, it is a valuable nectar source for bumblebees, and it has long been used – as its common name implies – to treat wounds and stem bleeding. Modern experiments have shown it to have antiseptic qualities.

Plant type Dead-nettle family, Lamiaceae. *Flowers* July–September. *Height* 30–80cm. *Description* Bristly perennial herb with creeping rhizomes and erect stem. Leaves are oval-cordate, 4–9cm long. Inflorescence is a loose spike of beetroot-red flowers with a white pattern on the lip. *Companion species* Bramble (p.66), Hawthorn (p.89), Hedge Bindweed (left) and Wild Privet (p.120). *Distribution* Native and ubiquitous. It is very common throughout the British Isles, apart from Skye, the Scottish Highlands and the west coast of Ireland, where it is local or rare. *Habitat* Typically hedgerows and woods, but it may also be found on the banks of rivers and streams, in rough grassland and waste places and, locally, as a persistent garden weed. It usually grows in light or moderately shaded localities on moist, fertile, mildly acid to basic soils.

Herb-Robert
(Geranium robertianum)

The fronds of Herb-Robert are like pretty little trees, each of the branches bright green, with the leaves outlined distinctly in red on their outer edges. It tends to hold its leaves out proud from the heart of the plant, so you can usually see the outline of each individual leaf. It is also known by names such as Stinking Crane's-bill and Stinking Bob, because of the acrid pong that its leaves emit when you crush them. Due to tannin, this is so powerful and distinctive that I can smell it instantly in my head. Another characteristic feature is the rich-red wash that often covers the whole plant, particularly when it is dry. The redness, due to anthocyanins or red pigments, also tints many autumn tree leaves and is typical of several crane's-bills. The red may have given it its common name of Robert, thought to be a corruption of the Latin *ruber*, meaning 'red'. It appears to be dainty, but that's deceptive as it can rapidly become invasive.

Plant type Geranium family, Geraniaceae. *Flowers* Almost any month of the year. *Height* 10–40cm. *Description* Annual or biennial herb with palmate leaves, cut to the base, with leaflets that are also highly cut. Stem and leaves are often flushed with red. Petals are 8–14mm long, pink and un-notched. A white-flowered form is not uncommon in the Yorkshire Dales, Derbyshire and Upper Teesdale. *Companion species* Germander Speedwell (p.85), Ivy-leaved Toadflax (p.93) and Lords-and-Ladies (p.19). *Distribution* Native. Widespread and very common across the British Isles. It is less common in parts of the Scottish Highlands. *Habitat* Frequent in urban and rural areas. It grows in a wide range of habitats and soil types, including woods, hedgerows, walls, shaded banks, limestone pavements, coastal shingle and disturbed artificial habitats, such as brownfield land. Absent from strongly acidic soils.

Honeysuckle
(Lonicera periclymenum)

If wild flowers had a beauty parade, Honeysuckle could win Miss British Isles. Its deep crimson buds give a jewel-like richness to late-spring hedges, fading to a dusky coral-pink just before they bloom. The open flowers are a random mixture of yellow and white in the petals and the anthers, backed by fresh green, coin-shaped leaves. The overall shape is winning, too, with the flowers held up bold and strong on long crimson stems, often out and above the line of the hedge. It is no wonder that William Morris used it to decorate his furniture and wallpapers. Honeysuckle's intoxicating, sweet scent is particularly strong at night – pollinating moths may detect it from a quarter of a mile away. The plant is early to come into leaf, one of the first hedge plants to gain some flesh after the winter. If you were to design a flower, would it not look and smell much like Honeysuckle?

Plant type Honeysuckle family, Caprifoliaceae. *Flowers* June–September. *Height* Up to 6m. *Description* Twining, climbing shrub. It may creep along the ground, but seldom flowers when this is the case. Leaves are oval to elliptical, untoothed, downy, grey-green and opposite one another, 3–7cm long. Flowers have trumpet-shaped, two-lipped corollas, 4–5cm long, creamy yellow on the inside, sometimes tinged with purple on the outside, with protruding stamens and style. They are arranged in terminal whorls. Fruit is a red berry, which looks poisonous but is not. *Companion species* Black Bryony (p.63), Dog-rose (p.79), Field-rose (p.82), Sweet-briar (p.109) and White Bryony (p.115). *Distribution* Native. It is very common throughout the British Isles, absent only from the area surrounding the Wash and a few parts of the Scottish Highlands. *Habitat* Hedgerows, scrub and woodland and shaded rocks. It prefers freely drained, moderately basic to acidic soils, but also grows on poorly drained base-rich clays, avoiding waterlogged conditions.

Hop
(Humulus lupulus)

Where I live, on the Kent/Sussex border, Hops are triffids in the hedges, romping up in the first few weeks of spring, emerging from the top in a mass of twining vines and bright green, vein-indented leaves. That is one of their high moments, when you catch sight of their spaghetti stems backlit as a silhouette breaking the line of the hedge. Hooked prickles on the stem help them climb. You can harvest and eat the tips at this tender stage. Boil for just a minute and serve with hollandaise, like forager's asparagus; they are also excellent in an omelette. Next come their flowers, the males insignificant, almost invisible in contrast to the females' layered ra-ra skirts, which enlarge through the summer and dry and endure as the seed pods. That is the other great moment: spotting the hedges with a fresh, light green when everything else is turning old and brown through the autumn. Harvest a vine or two and bring them indoors. They smell heady and acrid – deliciously strong. This is the stage at which they are used to clarify, preserve and flavour beer.

Plant type Hop family, Cannabaceae. *Flowers* July–August. *Height* Up to 6m. *Description* Rough, hairy, square-stemmed, clockwise-twining herb. Leaves are palmate, long-stalked, toothed, 10–15cm long. Male and female flowers are on separate plants. The male flowers are in lax lateral panicles, while the female flowers are pale green in rounded clusters. The only other member of the hop family found in the wild in Britain, Hemp (*Cannabis sativa*) is easily distinguished from Hop by its non-twining growth and more deeply lobed leaves. *Companion species* Black Bryony (p.63), Hawthorn (p.89) and White Bryony (p.115). *Distribution* Native. Common in England, occasional in Wales and Ireland and rare in Scotland. It is thought that many populations in southern England are relics from cultivation. *Habitat* It likes to scramble along hedges and up telegraph poles, but it also grows in moist, open woods and frequently as an escape from cultivation.

Hornbeam
(Carpinus betulus)

This hedge plant is close to my heart because it grows quickly and easily on heavy clay – the soil we have at Perch Hill. I planted lots as windbreaks when we first moved in. It is bright and elegant in leaf: the leaves are brilliant green and slightly pleated with a sawtooth edge. It flowers through the spring, with green and crimson catkins, but it is in the summer that it really shines. The seed pods are extraordinary, like miniature pagodas, with layer upon layer of narrow, papery pods in a pale, washed-out green. The timber of hornbeam is one of the hardest of any British tree. It has traditionally been burnt to make charcoal, which is why there is so much of it in our part of the world: when the Weald of Kent and Sussex was the industrial heart of England, charcoal was made to smelt iron. Hornbeam has also been used to make cogs, mallets and butchers' blocks.

Plant type Birch family, Betulaceae. *Flowers* April–May. *Height* 15–25m. *Description* Long-lived deciduous tree. Trunk is often fluted, with bark that is smooth and grey. Twigs are sparsely hairy. Leaves are bright green, oval, toothed, 3–10cm long, hairless on the upper side, slightly hairy on the veins on the underside. Male and female flowers are on separate catkins. Fruit is a small seed within a three-lobed, leafy bract. *Companion species* Oak (p.101). *Distribution* Native and very common in south-east England, where it is often the dominant species in woodlands. It is thought to have been introduced in the north and west, where it is increasingly local, although it is still quite frequent in northern England and Wales. It is rare in Ireland and very rare in northern Scotland. It is also extensively planted. *Habitat* Deciduous woodland on a broad range of soils. It is frequent in hedgerows, where it was often layered to make a stock-proof fence.

Horseradish
(Armoracia rusticana)

It is the leaves of Horseradish that you will notice most of the year beside the road: large, leathery and deep green like a dock, but with an elegant sawtooth edge and prominent veins. The leaves often seem puckered, as if they have been threaded on the outer surface and gathered, and they can sometimes be huge – almost a metre long. Horseradish flowers in spring, with white single flowers, typical of the brassica family, but its point for us is neither its flowers nor its leaves (which are both edible, although they taste more of cabbage than Horseradish) but its intense, mustardy taproot. To make sure you have Horseradish, not dock, before you start to dig, crush a leaf and you will be hit by a waft of that characteristic smell. The root's flavour is at its most intense after flowering in late summer and autumn, and is particularly delicious with beef – of course – and smoked fish, and also beetroot. This native of Russia and the eastern Ukraine was introduced before 1500, initially as a medicinal herb. It was later used as a vegetable. It is incredibly invasive, so do not be tempted to dig up a bit and plant it in your garden.

Plant type Cabbage family, Brassicaceae. *Flowers* May–August. *Height* Up to 1.5m. *Description* Tall hairless perennial with large basal leaves (30–100cm long), oval-oblong, toothed, shiny dark green and long stalked. Flower stems are branched with white flowers, 8–9mm across, in white panicles. *Companion species* Common Comfrey (p.71) and Greater Celandine (p.87). *Distribution* Introduced. It is frequent to locally common in England, less so in Wales and Scotland. *Habitat* Roadsides, waste ground, railways, sandy seashores and riverbanks. The rougher the ground, the more Horseradish seems to relish it. It spreads by root fragments, for instance from allotments and old gardens.

Ivy-leaved Toadflax
(Cymbalaria muralis)

One of my favourite wild flowers, Ivy-leaved Toadflax looks like a miniature purple snapdragon, cladding walls and steps wherever you look. At its best, in full flower in late spring and summer, it reminds me of wisteria: it has the same tumbling, purple bubbles but is a fraction of the size. It also looks good for most of the year. It is thought to have been introduced when its seeds were brought in with some marble sculptures from Italy to Oxford around 1630. This self-sows very freely and germinates well in brick and stone mortar, its roots creeping into all the nooks and crannies. It can also root from fragments or from nodes. When the flowers go over, the seed heads bend away from the light so that they are more likely to be shed into cracks in the stones. The seeds have ridges that wedge them in place, while the developing rootlet forces its way further into the crevice. The Latin genus name *Cymbalaria* refers to the shape of the leaf, which is depressed in the middle to look a bit like a cymbal. This feature easily distinguishes it from other small-flowered members of the Toadflax family, such as Small Toadflax (p.260). The edible leaves have a warm, pungent flavour, like those of Watercress (p.320).

Plant type Speedwell family, Veronicaceae. *Flowers* May– September. *Height* 10–70cm. *Description* Small, sprawling, hairless perennial herb. Leaves are palmate, 2.5cm long, rather like those of ivy and quite succulent. Flowers are lilac or white (pp.124–5) with corollas 8–10mm long, solitary in the leaf axils. *Companion species* Maidenhair Spleenwort (p.95) and Wall-rue (p.114). *Distribution* Alien. A neophyte, introduced in the early seventeenth century from southern Europe and recorded in the wild from 1640. Very common throughout most of the British Isles, although rare and absent in much of Scotland, especially the Highlands. It is also more localised in parts of western Ireland. *Habitat* Most frequently found on old walls, bridges and pavements, but also in other well-drained rocky, stony places, usually near habitation. Large, prostrate patches also often grow on shingle beaches.

Japanese Rose

(Rosa rugosa)

Better known to gardeners by its Latin name, Japanese Rose has become widespread in the British Isles, and naturalised in many places, particularly beside the coast. This native of China and Japan was introduced into cultivation in 1796, but not successfully grown until 1845, and first recorded in the wild in 1927. It is grown in gardens for its incredible disease resistance – it almost never suffers the scourges of mildew or black spot, the bane of the rose-grower's life – and for its fat, ornamental hips, which stay on the plant into winter. It has pretty, highly fragrant flowers, single and crinkly, the texture of the petals more like that of a poppy than a rose. Its tolerance of saline conditions makes it a popular plant in gardens by the coast, too – hence its increased occurrence there in the wild. It is also very spiny: Richard Mabey writes that it was planted in anti-thief barriers by Essex Police in 1993.

Plant type Rose family, Rosaceae. *Flowers* June–September. *Height* 2m. *Description* Dense, suckering shrub. Leaves are divided into two to three pairs of leaflets, which are glossy green, wrinkled and hairy. Stem is covered in a mixture of hairy, broad-based and thin prickles. Flowers are large, bright pink (occasionally white), 6–9cm across. Fruit is large, up to 3cm in diameter, bright red and pumpkin-shaped. *Companion species* Honeysuckle (p.91), Marram (p.405), Montbretia (p.98) and Silverweed (p.418). *Distribution* Introduced. Its distribution is quite scattered and is most dense near major urban areas. It is often planted on roadsides and roundabouts and in urban places, and in traditional mixed hedging to attract wildlife. It is less common in upland and remote areas, but is quite common on the coast in the Hebrides. Its distribution continues to increase. *Habitat* Found as a garden escape, in hedgerows, sand dunes, sea cliffs, road verges and waste ground.

Large Bindweed

(Calystegia silvatica)

This is even more rampant than Hedge Bindweed (p.90), but its flowers are beautiful. They sit upright above a hedge, huge, perfect white trumpets emerging from a green calyx, washed over with crimson. They stay open on bright, clear nights, reflecting moonlight and studding the hedge with beacons. Their leaves are elegant, too – a heraldic shield shape. For years, this was thought to be same species as our native Hedge Bindweed, but it was recognised as a separate species in the latter half of the nineteenth century. It has invasive roots – every small section a potential new plant – but both this and Hedge Bindweed have slightly shallower roots than Field Bindweed (p.248) and are therefore a little easier to manage. If you are absolutely determined, you can dig them out.

Plant type Bindweed family, Convolvulaceae. *Flowers* June–September. *Height* Up to 5m. *Description* Hairless creeping or climbing perennial herb. Flowers have trumpet-shaped corollas, 6–9cm across, which are usually white but sometimes have faint pink stripes. Five sepals are concealed by two large, overlapping, inflated bracteoles, which are typically strongly pouched, like the baggy protuberances on cavalry officers' jodhpurs, and measure 18–45mm across when flattened out. Flower stalks are hairless. *Companion species* Blackthorn (p.64), Bramble (p.66), Hawthorn (p.89) and Wild Privet (p.120). *Distribution* Introduced from southern Europe. First cultivated in 1815, collected from the wild in 1863. It is common throughout England and Wales (except in upland districts), but confined to lowland and coastal regions in Scotland. It is quite frequent in Ireland, slightly more common in the east than in the west. *Habitat* Gardens, hedgerows, fences and waste ground. Seed set is low, but it compensates for this by spreading from root fragments.

Lucerne
(Medicago sativa ssp. *sativa)*

From a distance, you could confuse this with Tufted Vetch (p.166). The flowers are the same purple and they form quite dense patches of colour beside roads. They are both members of the pea family, but Lucerne has a more pompom-like arrangement of small individual flowers, rather than the column-like inflorescences of Tufted Vetch, and when you get closer, you can see that Tufted Vetch does not have trifoliate leaves. Lucerne was first cultivated in Britain during the seventeenth century. It is a valuable and nutritious fodder crop, its seeds and leaves rich in proteins and vitamins – it was widely grown during a period of world protein shortage in the 1950s. Like all legumes, Lucerne fixes nitrogen from the air through nodules in its roots. Since its introduction, 'improved' strains have been developed and imported from the United States and Europe, so a wide degree of variation in leaf size and flower colour occurs in the wild as a result of hybridisation. Lucerne is one of the favourite larval food plants of the migrant Clouded Yellow butterfly.

Plant type Pea family, Fabaceae. *Flowers* June–September. *Height* 30–90cm. *Description* Erect perennial herb with racemes of purple to lilac flowers. Fruit is a spiralling pod with two to three turns. *Companion species* Bulbous Buttercup (p.144), Creeping Buttercup (p.149), Goat's-rue (p.86), Meadow Buttercup (p.158) and Perforate St John's-wort (p.209). *Distribution* Introduced from southern Europe. Some relic populations are very persistent and long-lived. Lucerne is most frequent as a wild plant in the east and Midlands of England, becoming scarce towards the north and west and absent from nearly all of Scotland and Ireland. *Habitat* Naturalised on field margins, roadsides, rough grassland and waste ground.

Maidenhair Spleenwort
(Asplenium trichomanes)

One of the commonest plants you will see spotting village walls, Maidenhair Spleenwort is evergreen and ever-present. The whole plant is at its brightest in the spring, when the new fronds unfurl. Looked at closely, each frond is made up of paired leaflets (or pinnae), laid out like a set of dinner plates, half stacked one on top of the other, from giant platters at the base to coffee-cup saucers at the tip. The spleenwort family contains many well-known wall and rock ferns, most common in the wetter climates and rocky landscapes of the north and west of the British Isles, but some – like this one – have been long known for colonising artificial, man-made habitats in the south and east. The construction of the railways, creating lots of damp, shady, sheltered wall habitats in cuttings and railway tunnels, helped their spread. You can tell Maidenhair Spleenwort from the other much less common species Green Spleenwort (*A. viride*) because it has strongly contrasting glossy, ebony-like stems.

Plant type Spleenwort family, Aspleniaceae. *Height* 4–20cm. *Description* Small, tufted fern. Fronds are linear, evergreen, hairless, once pinnate, 4–20cm long, with blackish stalks and midribs. Pinnae are oblong, slightly toothed, blunt, 3–7mm long, clearly stalked. Sori are 1–2mm long on veins on the underside of the pinnae. *Companion species* Ivy-leaved Toadflax (p.93), Rustyback (p.105) and Wall-rue (p.114). *Distribution* Native. Found throughout Britain and Ireland and common in many areas, especially in the west, including Wales. It is quite local and scarce in parts of East Anglia. *Habitat* Grows in a range of rocky habitats, including cliffs, rock faces, screes, mine waste and, perhaps now most commonly, on walls, especially railway walls and sidings.

Meadow Crane's-bill

(Geranium pratense)

This is one of our showiest road-verge plants, and the largest flowered of our native crane's-bills. It flowers for ages and, like many hardy geraniums, it is extremely valuable to insects, the paler, radiating veins on the petals guiding bees to the nectar within. It has a mighty rootstock that enables it to force its way up through the mulch of flailed grass on the roadside, and its spring-loaded seeds can be catapulted six feet away in a good breeze. With the right mowing regime, it can appear in a pretty, light dusting of plants along roads and trackways, but it sets seed late, so it is vulnerable to grass-cutting in July. Our fanatically early roadside mowing regimes mean that this and other late-seeding plants, such as Common Bistort (p.70), Agrimony (p.142) and Betony (p.143), are not as common as they were.

Plant type Crane's-bill family, Geraniaceae. *Flowers* June–September. *Height* 30–80cm. *Description* Erect, hairy perennial herb. Saucer-shaped flowers are arranged in pairs; petals are 15–18mm across, unnotched and ranging in colour from violet to sky blue. Leaves are deeply palmately lobed and the lobes are pinnately cut with sharp teeth. *Companion species* Common Toadflax (p.74), Meadow Vetchling (right), Red Clover (p.161), Tufted Vetch (p.166) and White Clover (p.167). *Distribution* Native. Common throughout much of Great Britain and Ireland, although very rare or absent in far north-west Scotland and also quite local in parts of south-east England, East Anglia and County Antrim. It is also found as an alien throughout its range. Alien populations have increased since 1962, but native populations have declined because of habitat loss and changes in agricultural practice. It has become restricted to roadsides in many areas, although it is still locally common and a glorious sight in places such as the broad-verged ancient droves of the Cotswolds. *Habitat* Rough grassland on verges, railway banks and stream sides, and in damp hay meadows and lightly grazed pastures, mainly on calcareous soils. Further north, it is less choosy about its soils.

Meadow Vetchling

(Lathyrus pratensis)

Meadow Vetchling is one of the first flowers to give abundant clouds of yellow on roadsides in the early part of the year. After the demure carpets of Primrose (p.103) and Lesser Celandine (p.18) that we enjoy for the first few weeks of spring, this performs on a much bigger scale, and its showiness runs in the family: it is closely related to Broad-leaved everlasting-pea (p.67), as well as garden sweet peas. It flowers from late April and keeps going on lane sides and meadows well into summer. The name vetchling means as it sounds – little vetch – but this species is not at all little, climbing to well over a metre through scrub and hedgerow. The nodules on its roots fix nitrogen from the air and increase the richness of the soil, so, as with Common Vetch (p.75), farmers encourage this slender, scrambling plant to grow in their meadows. It is also rich in protein, particularly in its seeds, making it a valuable food source mixed in grass or hay. Cattle love it.

Plant type Pea family, Fabaceae. *Flowers* April–August. *Height* 30–120cm. *Description* Scrambling perennial herb with leaves divided into two lanceolate leaflets, with tendrils. The leaflets are grey-green, parallel-veined, 1–3cm long and with arrow-shaped stipules. Stems are angled. Flowers are yellow, 15–18mm across, in racemes of five to twelve, on long stalks. Fruit is a pod 20–35mm long, turning black when ripe. *Companion species* Bulbous Buttercup (p.144), Creeping Buttercup (p.149), Common Sorrel (p.147), Meadow Buttercup (p.158) and Tufted Vetch (p.166). *Distribution* Native. Very common throughout the British Isles, but scarce in parts of the Scottish Highlands. *Habitat* Moderately fertile soils on roadside and railway banks, hedges, unimproved pastures and hay meadows.

Melancholy Thistle
(Cirsium heterophyllum)

You will never see this plant in southern Britain. Its range extends as far south as the Derbyshire and Staffordshire moorlands and mid Wales. It forms huge and impressive clumps in Yorkshire and Cumbria and almost anywhere further north. The origin of its common name is that the buds supposedly hang their necks, straightening only as the flowers fully open. The way I see it, however, it is not the buds but the seed heads that hang themselves so distinctively. This is a thistle that is not thistly: it has no prickles on its flowers, leaves or stem. It is closely related to the fashionable *Cirsium rivulare* that many of us grow in our gardens, and it is easy to see why its cultivated relation is so popular: Melancholy Thistle has intense amethyst-purple flowers that last for ages and are loved by pollinator insects. It has declined recently as grass-cutting on roadside verges has been done earlier in the year and hay meadows have been turned into silage fields.

Plant type Daisy family, Asteraceae. *Flowers* July–August. *Height* 45–120cm. *Description* Erect, perennial herb. Basal leaves are green, elliptical-lanceolate, stalked, with soft prickles (not spines). Leaves are 20–40cm long and 4–8cm wide. Upper leaves are unstalked with clasping, cordate bases. All leaves have a white, felted underside. Flower stem is grooved and unbranched. Flower head is solitary, 3–5cm in diameter, with red-purple flowers. *Companion species* Globeflower (p.301), Montbretia (p.98), Sweet Cicely (p.110), Water Avens (p.318) and Wood Crane's-bill (p.121). *Distribution* Frequent to locally common in northern England and Scotland and also found in north Wales. It is absent from southern England and very rare in Ireland. *Habitat* Upland grasslands, damp roadside verges, moist woodland margins, stream banks and hay meadows, often on calcareous or base-rich soils.

Mexican Fleabane
(Erigeron karvinskianus)

The flowers of Mexican Fleabane look like petite and delicate Daisies (p.246), not growing in a lawn but hanging as a flower curtain on a church or village wall. Like Yellow Corydalis (p.121), Mexican Fleabane often forms large colonies, shrouding whole walls in its pretty flowers and leaves. It flowers for ages, often being in bloom by late April and continuing into the autumn. For this reason, many of us have planted it in our gardens to soften stone steps or newly built walls. It spreads by seed, germinating in the smallest crevice, the roots fixing themselves in the nooks and crannies. As its common name suggests, it is native to Mexico, but it has been cultivated in Britain since 1836 and then escaped into the wild. It has increased its distribution in recent years: country villages would look very different now without it. The common name also refers to the burning of related plants (such as Blue Fleabane, *E. acris*) to repel fleas.

Plant type Daisy family, Asteraceae. *Flowers* April–October. *Height* Up to 25cm. *Description* Sprawling, much-branched perennial herb. Leaves are obovate, lobed near the base but unlobed above. Flower heads are white or pale pink and very daisy-like, 15–30mm across. There are usually several flower heads per stem. *Companion species* Ivy-leaved Toadflax (p.93), Maidenhair Spleenwort (p.95), Wall-rue (p.114) and Yellow Corydalis. *Distribution* Introduced. Scattered throughout England and Wales and quite frequent in parts of south-west England. It is very rare in northern England and absent from Scotland. It is rare in Ireland, mostly found in the south east. *Habitat* It is most often naturalised on walls, rock outcrops and cliffs. Stony banks and cracks in pavements are also favoured localities.

Monk's-hood
(Aconitum napellus)

When you whisk past this on the roadside, it looks like a delphinium with deep indigo-blue spires, either on its own or in a small clutch of plants, standing out from all around it. You might assume it is a garden escape, and sometimes it is – Monk's-hood is popular in gardens because of its long flowering season – but not always. The plants that occur in the Welsh Marches and south-west England are considered to be a subspecies, ssp. *napellus*. Monk's-hood is incredibly persistent, living in the shadier patches of lanes and woods for decades or longer in the same place. I remember a clump just outside our neighbouring village in Cambridgeshire when I was a child, which my father said had been there for as long as he could remember. Monk's-hood is extremely poisonous – even very small amounts can have severe effects. It contains aconitine, a neurotoxin that can cause heart failure, and there are reports of people feeling unwell after just smelling the flowers. In parts of Europe, the plant is known as Wolf's Bane, because of its use as a hunter's poison. Nevertheless, it was formerly used as a medicinal herb.

Plant type Buttercup family, Ranunculaceae. *Flowers* May–September. *Height* Up to 1.5m. *Description* Hairless perennial herb. Leaves are palmate and deeply divided to the base. Flowers are arranged in a raceme. Each flower is violet-blue, 3–4cm across, with five petal-like sepals, the rear sepal forming a helmet-shaped hood. *Companion species* Hazel (p.15), Primrose (p.103), Toothwort (p.29) and Wood Sage (p.32). *Distribution* Native. It is considered native only in the Welsh Marches and south-west England. However, it is found as a garden escape throughout the British isles. *Habitat* Damp, open woodland, shady stream banks, roadsides and meadows. It prefers calcareous to mildly acidic ground.

Montbretia
(Crocosmia x crocosmiiflora)

Montbretia's deep, rich bronze-orange makes this a surprising plant to find in the wild, as this colour is rare among British wild flowers. Montbretia is not native. It is a cultivated hybrid that was raised in France in 1880 and introduced to Britain in the same year. It is now quite common, particularly in the west of Britain. I have seen great swathes of it as far apart as the Lizard in Cornwall and Morvern, Argyll. It spreads quite rapidly by vegetative growth, producing chains of knobbly bulbs, as well as short rhizomes that swell to produce new bulbs, so often it appears in a large clump forming a bold strip between a ditch and the road. There are many other, larger-flowered hybrids now available, but this one remains the toughest, thriving in very varied conditions, in sun or part shade on alkaline and acid soils.

Plant type Iris family, Iridaceae. *Flowers* July–September. *Height* 50–60cm. *Description* Erect, patch-forming, hairless perennial herb. It is a horticultural hybrid between two South African species: *C. pottsii* and *C. aurea*. Leaves are sword-shaped and pale green. Spike is two-sided, with orange-red flowers that have uneven, spreading lobes. *Companion species* Bramble (p.66), Fuchsia (p.84), Honeysuckle (p.91) and Melancholy Thistle (p.97). *Distribution* Introduced and quite common throughout Britain and Ireland. It is rare or local on much of the east coast of England and also absent from much of inland Scotland. Since 1962, it has dramatically increased its range eastwards and has consolidated its distribution in the west of Britain and Ireland. Some viable seed is produced, but most populations are thought to have arisen from discarded garden plants and spread by vegetative reproduction. *Habitat* Roadsides, woods, hedge banks, waste ground, sea cliffs and riverbanks.

Mugwort

(Artemisia vulgaris)

Mugwort is not the most exciting plant that you will see on the roadside, but the silver undersides of its leaves and silvery gleam of its flower stems, buds and miniature flowers lift it above the utterly drab. It was thought to have powerful therapeutic uses: the Anglo-Saxons stuffed it into their shoes to prevent travel weariness, and the Victorians put its aromatic leaves into their baths to relieve tiredness. The leaves have also been used as a moth repellant and burned to fumigate sick rooms. Children used to smoke it – it has a slightly tobacco-like taste – and it was sometimes used instead of hops to add bitterness to beer. Its common name is said to derive from the word 'mug', as it has been used to flavour drinks since at least the early Iron Age. Its common relative Wormwood (*A. absinthium*) is the key flavour in the alcoholic drink absinthe.

Plant type Daisy family, Asteraceae. *Flowers* July–September. *Height* 60–120cm. *Description* Erect, downy, tufted, aromatic perennial herb. Leaves are twice pinnate, dark green, hairless on the upper sides, cottony on the undersides, 5–8cm long. They are stalked near the base and stalkless above. Flower heads are small and oval with woolly bracts and red-brown, tubular florets. They are held erect on racemes in a leafy panicle. *Companion species* Bulbous Buttercup (p.144), Common Toadflax (p.74), Creeping Buttercup (p.149) and Meadow Buttercup (p.158). *Distribution* Introduced, probably by the Romans. It is very common throughout much of the British Isles. However, it is more localised in upland regions of Wales and very rare in the Highlands of Scotland. In Ireland, it is also quite localised and more common in the east than in the west. *Habitat* Roadside verges, waysides, waste places, tips and rough ground, usually on relatively fertile soils.

Musk-mallow

(Malva moschata)

This is the Cinderella of the mallows, a more delicate and pretty plant than most of its relations, such as the chunkier Common Mallow (p.73) and Tree-mallow (p.421). It has fine, feathery stem leaves and soft, sugar-almond-pink (and often white) flowers, which tend to be clutched in a group at the top of its main stem. The flowers are softer in colour and texture than those of its relations, but still have marked veining on the petals, drawing pollinator insects into their centres. Bees, in particular, are frequent visitors. Musk-mallow's name originates from the fragrance of its foliage: when the weather is warm, the leaves give off a sweet musky smell. During the day, this is very faint, but it gets more powerful in the evening. It has been grown as a popular garden plant for centuries.

Plant type Mallow family, Malvaceae. *Flowers* July–August. *Height* 30–50cm. *Description* Erect, sparsely hairy perennial herb. Stem leaves are cut much deeper than those of any other British mallow into narrow segments. Basal leaves are kidney-shaped and only shallowly lobed. Flowers are 3–6cm across, solitary in the leaf axils and in a terminal cluster. *Companion species* Agrimony (p.142), Betony (p.143), Meadow Crane's-bill (p.96), Lucerne (p.95), Rough Hawkbit (p.162) and Viper's-bugloss (p.214). *Distribution* Native. Frequent to common in most of Great Britain, but rare in Scotland. In Ireland, it is occasional to locally frequent. Populations in northern Scotland and Ireland are mapped as introduced. *Habitat* Roadsides, hedge banks and grasslands, especially on sand and clay. It also grows on woodland edges, pastures, field borders, riverbanks and grassy wastelands, preferring unshaded or lightly shaded situations. It is tolerant of moderate levels of grazing and mowing, and its seed is long-lasting in the soil.

Narrow-leaved Lungwort
(Pulmonaria longifolia)

You might have seen a form of this plant in people's gardens – the introduced Lungwort (*P. officinalis*), which has been cultivated in Britain since before 1597. Narrow-leaved Lungwort is the rare native species, and its wildness is its virtue. Both are lovely to find, so bright in their variety of flower colours – from deepest blue to magenta and purple in the newly emergent buds – and so early and long in their flowering. That is why we love them in shady corners of our gardens. I have seen the native form growing on a grave in the New Forest, looking like something that had been planted. It had in fact made its own way there and had been in the same spot for decades (churchyards are often excellent places for wild flowers, where plants can escape modern agricultural systems).The characteristic variation in flower colour gives them the alternative common name Soldiers and Sailors, in reference to the different colours of their uniforms.

Plant type Borage family, Boraginaceae. *Flowers* March– May. *Height* Up to 30cm. *Description* Downy, rhizomatous, perennial herb. Leaves are narrow (lanceolate), pointed, long-stalked with pale white spots. Basal leaves persist through the winter. Flowers are blue, pink and purple, the corollas 6mm across, with many glandular hairs. Fruit is an oval, rounded nutlet. The leaves of the alien species are oval-cordate, with more prominent white spots and larger flowers (corollas 10mm across). *Companion species* Bluebell (p.2), Bugle (p.68), Common Dog-violet (p.5), Early Dog-violet (p.8), Lesser Celandine (p.18), Sweet Violet (p.111) and Wood Anemone (p.30). *Distribution* Native. Rare, confined to the New Forest, east Dorset and the Isle of Wight. In those areas it is relatively common. The introduced form was first recorded in the wild in 1793 and is now scattered throughout Britain, more frequently in the south, especially near London. There are also smaller concentrations near Glasgow and Edinburgh. *Habitat* Shady grassland, woodlands and scrub, banks and rough ground.

Navelwort
(Umbilicus rupestris)

Navelwort looks as if it is made of rubber, with fleshy, round leaves and a central dimple in each leaf, reminiscent of a human belly button – hence its name. Those leaves – which shrivel up and disappear as soon as the flower spikes spring into action – also look like thick, old-fashioned coins, earning it the other common name of Pennywort. The roots creep into the nooks and crannies of drystone walls in the sunken lanes and churchyards of the West Country. In the summer, tall, narrow flower spikes erupt, following the line of the wall. Each one has a red stem and much paler flower bobbles, looking like an upright fibre-optic wand with miniature bulb lanterns all the way up it. There is something sub-aquatic about the whole plant, like a sea creature that has rooted in a wall.

Plant type Stonecrop family, Crassulaceae. *Flowers* June–August. *Height* 10–40cm. *Description* Erect perennial herb. Leaves are circular (1–7cm across), fleshy and dark green, with a central 'navel' and rounded teeth, on a long stalk. Stem leaves become smaller going up the stem. Inflorescence is a long, tapered spike of greenish-white, bell-shaped, pendant flowers, each 8–10mm long. The size of the plant depends on its location. It is larger in damper, shadier situations than on drystone walls or exposed cliffs. *Companion species* Hart's-tongue (p.15), Maidenhair Spleenwort (p.95) and Pellitory-of-the-wall (p.102). *Distribution* Native. It is mostly confined to the west of a line from Southampton to the Mersey, being common throughout Wales and south-west England. It is scattered and local to the east of this and absent from much of eastern England. It is also found in Cumbria, the west coast of Scotland and most of Ireland. *Habitat* Walls, rock crevices and stony hedge banks, mainly on acidic substrates. In Cornwall, it has been seen as an epiphyte on the boughs of large trees.

Oak
(Quercus robur and *Q. petraea)*

Oak has long been Britain's favourite tree. The Domesday Book measured an area of woodland according to the number of pigs it could support, which largely depended on the acorn crop from oaks. These hugely important food sources, rich in protein, fat and carbohydrates, support many birds, including woodpeckers, ducks and pigeons. Pedunculate Oak (*Q. robur*) produces more acorns than Sessile Oak (*Q. petraea*). The fruits are dispersed by animals, particularly squirrels and jays, which hoard them for future use. If they forget where they have hidden their buried stash, or die before they can eat them, the acorns grow into trees. Less well known than the acorns, Oak flowers are hanging, fluffy, acid-green catkins which turn a hedge the freshest green.

Plant type Beech family, Fagaceae. *Flowers* April–May. *Height* Up to 30m. *Description* Monoecious tree. Pedunculate Oak has a broader crown and has more spreading branches than Sessile Oak. The key difference is in the leaves and acorns. Pedunculate Oak has almost stalkless leaves and long-stalked acorns, while Sessile Oak has stalked leaves and almost stalkless acorns. Pedunculate Oak also has leaves with rounded basal lobes, whereas the leaves of Sessile Oak taper to the stalk. *Companion species* Crab Apple (p.77), Elder (p.80), Hawthorn (p.89) and Traveller's-joy (p.112). *Distribution* Native. Pedunculate Oak is common throughout the British Isles, except in remote parts of north and west Scotland. It is also local in western Ireland. Sessile Oak has a more westerly distribution and is quite scarce in some parts of eastern England, Scotland and central Ireland. *Habitat* Pedunculate Oak is found on a wide variety of soils, particularly those that are heavy and fertile. Sessile Oak prefers well-drained, shallow, acidic soils. It is often the dominant oak in upland areas.

Oxford Ragwort
(Senecio squalidus)

This is the showiest of ragworts, with shorter, brittle stems, stockier plants and bigger flowers than the other species; it also flowers at least a month earlier. Its name tells an unusual story. An introduction from southern Europe, it was first recorded in 1794 as an escape from the Oxford Botanic Garden (the original plants were said to have been gathered from Mount Etna). It was recorded at Oxford railway station in 1879, by which time the Great Western Railway had opened, linking Oxford and London. Oxford Ragwort made the most of this new corridor of opportunity – the well-drained ballast underneath the railway tracks provided similar conditions to the volcanic rock of its native environment. Its seeds, which have a 'parachute' of hairs, were easily swept along amid the turbulence created by the steam trains, and Oxford Ragwort romped away.

Plant type Daisy family, Asteraceae. *Flowers* May–December. *Height* Up to 30cm. *Description* Erect annual or short-lived perennial herb, often woody at the base. Leaves are more-or-less hairless, deeply divided (one to two times pinnate), with all lobes narrow and pointed. Flower heads are bright yellow, 15–20mm across, with ray florets usually longer than 8mm. These longer-branched, looser inflorescences distinguish it from Common Ragwort (p.242), which has leaves with narrower, more pointed lobes and a less spreading habit. Welsh Groundsel (*S. cambrensis*) looks similar, but has smaller ray florets (4–7mm long). *Companion species* Butterfly-bush (p.237) and Rosebay Willowherb (p.258). *Distribution* Alien, a neophyte. The most common ragwort in British cities, it remains mainly an urban plant, much rarer in the countryside. It is found throughout England and Wales but is more local and scarce in northern England and central Wales, especially in upland regions. In Scotland it is mostly confined to the lowland belt around Edinburgh and Glasgow and is very scattered north of there. In Ireland, it is scattered along the coast with clusters near urban centres. *Habitat* Roadsides, waste places, walls, railways, cinders and gardens, where it is often established on well-drained soils.

Pellitory-of-the-wall
(*Parietaria judaica*)

An individual spike of this is nothing to write home about, but you cannot ignore the huge, dark green and red curtains of it that completely clad the shadier, cooler sides of walls, particularly in south-west Britain. Like other wall plants, it takes root in cracks, apparently existing on almost nothing, and it grows in similarly barren ground on rocks and cliffs as well as in richer soils at the base of hedges. The central stem is crimson-red, matching the translucent, ant-like flowers that form in the leaf axils all the way up it. They nestle against the stem, clumped together, looking more like a growth than flowers. The leaves give away its family – nettle – and despite their smooth edge, they have a veined, indented surface and texture reminiscent of those of Common Nettle (p.241). The common name sounds rather more glamorous than the plant appears: it comes from the species name *Parietaria*, which is derived from the Latin *paries*, meaning 'wall'. It often grows on the walls of abbeys and priories, which may be due to the fact that – like Sweet Cicely (p.110) and Bilberry (p.349) – it was widely planted by medieval herbalists, who used it as a remedy for urinary disorders.

Plant type Nettle family, Urticaceae. *Flowers* June–October. *Height* 30–60cm. *Description* Hairy perennial herb. Stems are cylindrical, red and branched. Leaves are alternate, oval-lanceolate, untoothed, up to 7cm long. Flowers are arranged in clusters, the male and female flowers separate, with the females towards the centre, each with a greenish, red-tinged, four-lobed calyx. *Companion species* Garlic Mustard (p.84), Ivy-leaved Toadflax (p.93) and Prickly Sowthistle (p.256). *Distribution* Frequent to locally common in England and on the Welsh coast; occasional to rare in Scotland, becoming absent in the north. It is frequent in the south of Ireland. *Habitat* Cracks and mortar crevices of brick and stone walls, building rubble, rocks, cliffs and steep-sided hedge banks. It prefers dry, sunny, sheltered spots, and is often found in built-up areas or not far from habitation.

Periwinkle
(*Vinca major/V. minor*)

A child could draw a Periwinkle, its flat, almost square-petalled flowers slightly spiralling around the sunken centre like a Catherine wheel. The petals are purple, paling to white-mauve towards the centre, and, as with Bluebell (p.2), the odd pure-white one can be found. The buds are perfect: tightly twisted like an umbrella, long and thin with a bright mauve tip. There are two species, the Greater and Lesser Periwinkle, both garden escapes. *V. major* has slightly larger flowers and is generally chunkier, with broader, longer-stalked leaves. Lesser Periwinkle (*V. minor*) is more delicate. Both species spread not by seed but by strong rooting runners, and this helps to tell them apart: the Lesser species roots at each leaf node, the Greater only at the runner's tip.

Plant type Periwinkle family, Apocynaceae. *Flowers* March–May. *Height* Lesser has stems up to 1m long, Greater 1.5m long, but both are prostrate. *Description* Evergreen, creeping perennials with opposite, oval, untoothed leaves, which are hairless, elliptical and shiny dark green. Flowers, situated in the leaf axils, are five-petalled (2.5–3cm across for the Lesser, 3–5cm across for the Greater), twisted in bud and slightly twisted when fully open. The calyx teeth of the Lesser are lanceolate and hairless, whereas the Greater has hairy calyx teeth. *Companion species* Common Dog-violet (p.5), Male-fern (p.19), Sweet Violet (p.111) and Wild Strawberry (p.120). *Distribution* Usually considered an introduction. *V. minor* was recorded as being grown in British gardens by 995. It is now widespread as an escape, much more frequent in the south of England and scarce in north-west Scotland. *Habitat* Found in a wide range of habitats, many of which are typical of introduced species, such as roadside banks, verges and waste places, especially close to houses. They are also occasionally found in ancient woodland, where, rather like Bluebell and Wood Anemone (p.30), they may form extensive carpets.

Polypody
(Polypodium vulgare)

This grows like a moustache on drystone walls, or bursts out of the base of fallen trees. It is evergreen, going a bit crispy in winter, with fresh leaves unravelling from the base in spring. The leaves emerge from a long, creeping, scaly rhizome, a bronze, woolly link between each frond. The fronds are simple, just once pinnate. There are three species of Polypody – the common, the Intermediate (*P. interjectum*) and the Southern (*P. cambricum*) – which are closely related and tricky to tell apart, but the common Polypody is most often seen. Like other ferns (such as Hart's-tongue, p.15, and Lady-fern, p.17), Polypodys were among the species that the Victorians developed a fascination for, and they collected natural variants and mutations. Some of the surviving clones, such as *P. cambricum* 'Falcatum O'Kelly', have been passed between enthusiasts for decades, or even centuries.

Plant type Polypody family, Polypodiaceae. *Height* 5–25cm. *Description* Evergreen, rhizomatous fern. Leaves are oblong, once pinnate, up to 25cm long, borne singly on creeping rhizomes. Each leaf usually has twelve to thirty pairs of pinnae, which do not become shorter or inflexed (curved inwards) towards the base. By contrast, the leaves of Southern Polypody are usually triangular, while those of Intermediate Polypody are usually oblong-lanceolate. Both species have leaves that may grow to 40cm long and have the lowest pair of pinnae inflexed towards the base of the stem. *Companion species* Hart's-tongue (p.15). It is an epiphyte on Oak (p.101) and other deciduous trees. *Distribution* Native. Occurs throughout Britain, although more common in the west than in the east. It is quite local in south-east England and scarce or absent in much of the East Midlands, Lincolnshire and south-east Yorkshire, although it is more frequent in Norfolk. In Ireland, it is common in the north and south, but very rare in central Ireland. *Habitat* Sheltered places, such as old and drystone walls, hedge banks, tree stumps and moist rocks. Polypody is confined to acid sites, while Southern Polypody comes from limestone districts.

Primrose
(Primula vulgaris)

One of the great sights at the end of winter is the first crinkly, Savoy cabbage-like leaves of a Primrose pushing through the soil. These are closely followed by the flowers of our *Prima Rosa*, which trumpets the start of the growing year. Primrose can produce flowers in every shade from deep yellow to the palest cream; in our lane in Sussex there are several clumps of a dusty pink one, probably a hybrid with a garden polyanthus. The flowers have a wonderful scent, sweet and violet-like, which draws in pollinators, both bees and butterflies. Their slightly sticky seeds attract ants, which disperse them.

Plant type Primrose family, Primulaceae. *Flowers* March–June. *Height* Up to 15cm. *Description* Perennial with wrinkled leaves that are hairless above, stalkless, obovate to spoon-shaped, gradually tapering to the base. Pale yellow flowers are held upright and always single on woolly, leafless stalks. Corolla is 20–40mm across, five-lobed, and each lobe has a shallow notch. Calyx tube is woolly and five-notched. *Companion species* Cuckooflower (p.297), Greater Stitchwort (p.87) and Wild Strawberry (p.120). *Distribution* Native. Occurs throughout Britain and Ireland and is absent or rare only in a few parts of the Scottish Highlands and the area surrounding the Wash. *Habitat* North-facing banks and hedgerows in sites shaded from hot sun. It needs regular bursts of light to flower and set seed. It is an ancient woodland indicator species and thrives particularly in coppiced woods. It also grows on coastal slopes and shaded montage cliffs, where it can form extensive carpets. In the west it grows in a wider variety of sites because of higher rainfall.

Pyrenean Lily
(Lilium pyrenaicum)

It is an exhilarating moment when you find a clump of Pyrenean Lily beside the road, a rare but possible event, particularly in Cumbria, where it has been naturalised since the mid nineteenth century. This is a native of the Pyrenees, where it is found in mountain meadows and on rocky slopes. The flowers have the typical Turk's-cap lily shape, the petals reflexed back in a curve onto the stem, like a turban. Each individual flower is exquisite and cheerful, a slightly limey yellow with stipples of the darkest purple. When the filaments fully ripen, they add a searing scarlet-orange, which is almost neon in its intensity. The green stigma protrudes from the flower even further, often dusted with the pollen's brilliant pigment. The flowers have a strong, unpleasant, foxy smell.

Plant type Lily family, Liliaceae. *Flowers* Late May–July. *Height* 80–100cm. *Description* Medium to tall perennial herb, often forming clumps. Leaves are linear-lanceolate, alternate, bright green, usually three-veined. Flowers, arranged in a raceme of one to eight, are greenish yellow with purple lines and spots on the perianth segments. Reddish-brown anthers are very prominent. *Companion species* Bulbous Buttercup (p.144), Common Bistort (p.70), Creeping Buttercup (p.149), Meadow Buttercup (p.158), Sweet Cicely (p.110) and Wood Crane's-bill (p.121). *Distribution* Introduced. It has become established in some areas as an escape from cultivation. It is very rare in the east of England and restricted to isolated spots, with loose concentrations in south-west England, south-west Wales, Cumbria, Yorkshire and eastern Scotland. *Habitat* Roadsides, woodlands, wood borders and hedgerows, often occurring in isolated clumps arising from discarded or deliberately planted garden stock. It is tolerant of both acid and alkaline soils.

Raspberry
(Rubus idaeus)

The wild Raspberry might not be as plump as its many cultivated forms, but it tastes intensely delicious. I spent a lot of time as a child (and still do) on the west coast of Scotland, where big stands of Raspberry are a common sight beside the road. You can easily pick a feast in five minutes, because the birds do not seem to relish the berries as we do. They crop like an autumn raspberry, a few ripening at a time over a long season. Raspberries have a definite preference for the north, liking the high rainfall, which is higher in the west: I have rarely seen them in the east of England. If you live in raspberry country, it is well worth introducing a few of these into native hedges in your garden; they are quite easy to root from cuttings. Raspberry leaf infusions have long been used – and still are – to ease the pain of childbirth, and raspberry vinegar is a traditional remedy for colds and fevers.

Plant type Rose family, Rosaceae. *Flowers* June–August. *Height* 1.5m. *Description* Erect, suckering perennial shrub. Stems are rounded and have straight, slender prickles. Leaves are pinnate, with three to seven oval, toothed leaflets, green above, woolly white beneath. Flowers, 9–10mm across, are white with narrow petals and arranged in panicles. *Companion species* Honeysuckle (p.91), Melancholy Thistle (p.97) and Montbretia (p.98). *Distribution* Native. It is most abundant in the cooler, wetter and more acid parts of western and northern Britain, rare only in the far north of Scotland, the west of Ireland and around the Wash. It is absent from Orkney and Shetland. *Habitat* Hedgerows, open woodland, downland scrub and heathland. It also occurs on rough and waste ground as an escape from cultivation. In the uplands, it grows on the drier ledges of basic crags and ravines and below base-rich cliffs.

Russian Comfrey

(Symphytum x *uplandicum)*

This is a hybrid between Common Comfrey (p.71) and Rough Comfrey (*S. asperum*), and with all that hybrid vigour, it is a plant that you will notice even as you drive past in your car – big, clump-forming and hairy. But it is not as rough-and-ready as it might first appear. Take a look at its emerging flowers, as intricate as the carved scrolls at the top of an Ionic column. The purple of the flower can be intense and positively ecclesiastical, lots of red in the colour rather than blue adding to its richness, but its tone is variable and you may see some duller mauve to almost pink forms. This has all the beneficial uses of its less-glamorous cousin Common Comfrey, with double the panache. It backcrosses with Common Comfrey, forming a wide range of intermediate types in pink and purple colours, which appear all over lanes and roadsides in late spring and summer. They are always heaving with honeybees and bumblebees.

Plant type Borage family, Boraginaceae. *Flowers* May–July. *Height* 30–120cm. *Description* Perennial herb with purplish-blue or deep red flowers and very rough, bristly stems, which are narrowly winged. Leaves are hairy, pale green, oval, slightly cordate at the base. *Companion species* Alexanders (p.62), Cow Parsley (p.77), Garlic Mustard (p.84), Red Campion (p.24) and White Campion (p.115). *Distribution* Introduced to Britain in 1870 as a forage plant for animals and widely cultivated in the late nineteenth and early twentieth centuries. It is still on the increase and is now the most common comfrey in the British Isles, apart from in north-west Scotland and Ireland, where it is local or rare. *Habitat* Usually found on rough and waste ground, roadsides, railway banks, hedge banks and woodland margins. Like Common Comfrey, it is also found on the edges of streams and rivers.

Rustyback

(Asplenium ceterach)

Rustyback is one of those plants that, once noticed, is never forgotten. The fronds curl in on themselves in drought, revealing the copper-coloured underside of the leaves. This means that you often see the front and the back of the leaves at the same time. As the leaves age, the copper deepens to brown, but Rustyback is evergreen and remains all year. Also known as Scaly Spleenwort, it appears in tufts on ruins, old walls and churches, where the short, tough roots push themselves right into the crevices. With our great burst of building during the twentieth century, this is one of the few plants that has increased, but its spread has slowed with the move towards treating the walls of interesting old buildings with herbicides. This is done to stop damage by plant roots, but it has made Rustyback less common, as have the reuse and renovation of old buildings and the re-pointing of old mortar.

Plant type Spleenwort family, Aspleniaceae. *Flowers* Spores ripen April–October. *Height* 3–10cm. *Description* Small, tufted evergreen fern. Fronds are dark green, once pinnate, and have a leathery texture on the upper sides. Lobes (pinnae) are broad-based, oval to triangular in shape, blunt and usually untoothed. The underside of the fronds has a dense, felt-like covering of brown scales. These scales often project beyond the margin of the fronds, giving the upper sides a brown edge. Sori are often hidden by the brown scales. *Companion species* Ivy-leaved Toadflax (p.93), Maidenhair Spleenwort (p.95), Wall Lettuce (p.113) and Wall-rue (p.114). *Distribution* Native. Widespread throughout the British Isles and common in Ireland and western Britain. It is rare in much of eastern England and absent from the far north of Scotland. *Habitat* Usually found in sunny places on rocks and old walls, mostly on basic substrates such as limestone or mortar. It also tucks itself into rock crevices in limestone pavements.

Salsify
(*Tragopogon porrifolius*)

I love the flowers of Salsify. I first saw them wild in Greece and I longed to bring seed home with me. Two weeks later, I saw them again, beside the road in Norfolk. It is not native, but has escaped from vegetable gardens, where it has a long history of cultivation. The roots are said to taste of oysters crossed with parsnip – it is one of my mother's favourite vegetables – but in the wild it stands out for the magnificent, smoky purple daisy flowers which shut by noon. After a few days come the huge, dandelion-clock seed heads, which are truly magnificent. These great powder-puff spheres – together with those of Salsify's close relation Goat's-beard (p.153), which are smaller – are the most impressive seed heads of any of our wild flowers. Unlike those of dandelions, they last in a vase if you pick them.

Plant type Daisy family, Asteraceae. *Flowers* Late May–July. *Height* Up to 120cm. *Description* Erect, branching, hairless biennial herb. Leaves are linear and blue-green. Stem is swollen just beneath the flower heads and contains a milky juice. Flower heads are 30–50mm across and have mauve-purple florets and long bracts. Salsify has similar foliage to Goat's-beard's, but that has yellow florets. A hybrid occurs occasionally between the two species. *Companion species* Fennel (p.81), Goat's-rue (p.86) and Pyramidal Orchid (p.210). *Distribution* Introduced. A native of southern Europe. It is found throughout England, but has a south-easterly bias. It is very localised in most places, although quite frequent in the Thames Estuary, and is often found near the sea. It is very rare in Scotland, Wales and Ireland. *Habitat* Road verges, sea walls, rough grassland and cliffs. Once abundant in fallow land reverting from arable at Ranscombe Farm Reserve in Kent, it became increasingly rare as the turf matured.

Shining Crane's-bill
(*Geranium lucidum*)

It is the shininess of the leaves of this geranium that make it stand out from the other common members of its genus. The leaves provide a bright, clean backdrop to the flowers, which are much pinker than those of Meadow Crane's-bill (p.96), but similar to those of Herb-Robert (p.91). They are small, shaped like miniature garden pelargonium leaves, but the overall impact is of brimming health and vigour. The nodes from which the leaf stalks spring are a rich, bloody red. As with all crane's-bills, the seed pods of this one are shaped like the skull and beak of a crane or heron. In the autumn, and when the plants are growing in a dry place – particularly on or at the base of walls – the leaves turn a brilliant red. This is due to the same pigment that occurs in Herb-Robert.

Plant type Geranium family, Geraniaceae. *Flowers* May–August. *Height* 30–40cm. *Description* Fleshy-stemmed, branched, ascending and almost hairless annual herb. Leaves are shiny green (although often tinged with red), deeply five-to-seven-lobed and long-stalked. Each lobe has two to three blunt teeth. Flowers are pink, 8–9mm across, with five un-notched petals. Sepals are green, hairless and keeled, and form a five-angled calyx. The shiny, lobed leaves and almost hairless stems distinguish this species from other geraniums. *Companion species* Hairy Bitter-cress (p.251), Lords-and-Ladies (p.19) and Navelwort (p.100). *Distribution* Native. Very common throughout the British Isles except the far north. Absent from much of the Scottish Highlands and local in the west of Ireland. It can be invasive and has increased significantly in range and abundance recently. *Habitat* Usually on rocky outcrops and scree in uplands and hedge banks, walls and roadsides in lowlands. It prefers calcareous soils, but it is also frequent in artificial environments such as waste ground and railways.

Spiked Star-of-Bethlehem
(Ornithogalum pyrenaicum)

This native – or probably native (see below) – bulb has tall, airy spikes of pale greenish-white starry flowers, like a sparkler. The leaves come first and then wither as the flower spikes emerge, resembling an ear of corn with their tight buds. Known in the area around Bath since at least the sixteenth century, it is also known as Bath Asparagus, and it does look like a spring asparagus stem, and tastes similar to asparagus when cooked. It was commercially collected for a while and sold in Bath markets, and local people still harvest it on a much smaller scale. Collecting the stems does no harm as it reproduces by bulb, not seed, and it is the leaves, not the flower stems, which feed the bulb during the following year.

Plant type Asparagus family, Asparagaceae. *Flowers* April–June. *Height* 50–100cm. *Description* Erect perennial herb, 50–100cm tall. Leaves are linear, grey-green, 30–60cm long, all basal, withering before the flowers open. Inflorescence is a dense, many-flowered raceme of white, six-petalled, star-like flowers. Fruit is a capsule, 8mm long. It is taller and much more densely flowered than its close relative Star-of-Bethlehem (p.369). *Companion species* Bluebell (p.2), Cleavers (p.238), Dog's Mercury (p.8), Herb-Robert (p.91), Ramsons (p.23), Wood-sorrel (p.33) and, less frequently, Solomon's-seal (p.26). *Distribution* Probably native. Some botanists argue that it is more likely to be a legacy of the Roman occupation of the Bath and Avon area. Confined to east Somerset, Wiltshire, Gloucestershire, Berkshire and Bedfordshire. Within these counties it is quite frequent and can be very abundant locally. It is also found rarely as an alien elsewhere in the British Isles. *Habitat* Road verges, rough grassy banks and woods (ash, field maple and elm). It prefers neutral, clay-rich soils that overlie well-drained rocks.

Spanish Bluebell
(Hyacinthoides hispanica)

It cannot compete with the incredible scent and dramatic yet delicate beauty of our native Bluebell (p.2), but the Spanish Bluebell from Portugal and Spain is quite pretty, like a form of hyacinth. There is something rather brutish about it, however. It forms stocky, robust-looking plants in good clumps, usually scattered quite widely from one another, not forming a continuous carpet. It was introduced into British gardens as early as written records exist in the seventeenth century, and was recorded in the wild by 1909. It hits the headlines every spring as a cause of botanical anxiety, because increasingly it is cross-breeding and muddying the pure genetics of our British native form. For this reason, we are encouraged to control vigorous populations in the garden by removing faded heads before they self-seed. Whereas the Spanish Bluebell thrives only in sun and is in no danger of colonising woods, the hybrid (p.3) tolerates shade and is creeping in around the edges of many of our best Bluebell places.

Plant type Asparagus family, Asparagaceae. *Flowers* April–May. *Height* 20–50cm. *Description* Hairless, perennial bulb. Easy to distinguish from the native Bluebell, as its flower stems are thicker and vertical with no apical curve. Flowers are paler blue, with lots of pink and white forms in cultivation, much wider in the bell, with green not yellow stamens, equally spaced all the way around the stem. Perianth segments are flared slightly, but not curled right back, and they have no scent. *Companion species* Red Campion (p.24) and White Campion (p.115). *Distribution* Introduced, now quite common. Naturalised in wasteland and open scrubby areas near towns and gardens, where they have been planted or discarded, and may be increasing slowly. *Habitat* Open, sunny habitats in waste ground, lanes and quarries, but not in woods.

Spindle

(Euonymus europaeus)

A good bush of spindle stands out a mile in an autumn hedgerow, a brilliant pink beacon among the ochre, brown and crimson turning leaves of the Hawthorn (p.89), Elder (p.80), Oak (p.101) and Blackthorn (p.64) among which it often grows. Looked at closely, the seed pods resemble puffy Shakespearean pantaloons, with rich orange seeds hanging within them. The leaves also turn rich deep reds and oranges, starting at the tip and moving towards the stem. Spindle is easily overlooked at other times of the year, with its small, white, four-petalled flowers, although these are a valuable source of nectar for hoverflies, bees and other insects. As its name suggests, Spindle was sometimes used for making the wooden spools on which wool was wound before the invention of the spinning wheel. The wood was ideal for this purpose because it is heavy, smooth and straight. It was also used to make toothpicks, knitting needles and skewers, as it can be cut into a sharp point. Spindle berries are mildly poisonous.

Plant type Spindle family, Celastraceae. *Flowers* May–June. *Height* 2–6m. *Description* Much-branched shrub or small tree. Leaves are green, oval-lanceolate, finely toothed, 3–13cm long and arranged opposite one another. Flowers are arranged in groups of three to ten, which are situated in the leaf axils. Each flower has four greenish-white petals and four stamens. Fruit is a bright pink, four-lobed berry, 10–15mm across, which splits along its seams to expose the orange seeds. *Companion species* Blackthorn, Elder, Hawthorn and Oak. *Distribution* Native. Frequent in southern England, but more local in northern England, Wales and Ireland. It is rare in Scotland, and many populations may be introductions or escapes. *Habitat* A species of hedgerows, open woodland and scrubland on moderately fertile soils. It is most common on alkaline soils, but will grow on acid but free-draining and fertile ground.

Sweet-briar

(Rosa rubiginosa)

Sweet-briar is the eglantine rose of poets and writers. It was one of the favourite plants of Vita Sackville-West, who planted a hedge of it in her garden at Sissinghurst, where it remains. She loved it for the fragrance of its leaves, particularly on muggy evenings after rain. 'You do not need to crush a leaf . . . to provoke the scent,' she wrote: 'it swells out towards you of its own accord, as you walk past, like a great sail filling suddenly with a breeze off those Spice Islands which Columbus hoped to find.' The hips are magnificent, too, big, fat and scarlet. The specific name *rubiginosa* means 'rusty' and refers to the often brownish-red colour of the stems and leaves.

Plant type Rose family, Rosaceae. *Flowers* June–July. *Height* Up to 2m. *Description* Erect, deciduous shrub. Prickles are unequal in size, hooked and mixed with stout bristles. Leaves are pinnate with oval leaflets that are rounded at the base and covered with sticky, apple-scented hairs (glands). Flower stalks (pedicels) are also covered in these glandular hairs. Flowers are bright pink, 2.5–4cm across. Sepals persist on the fruit. Sweet-briar is easy to distinguish from Dog-rose (p.79), which has more strongly hooked prickles and does not have sticky, apple-smelling glands on its leaves. It also has slightly larger and paler flowers than Sweet-briar. *Companion species* Bramble (p.66), Dog-rose, Field-rose (p.82) and Honeysuckle (p.91). *Distribution* Native. Found throughout Great Britain and Ireland, but rare in most areas. It is perhaps most frequent in south-east Scotland and also on some of the chalk downlands of southern England. In Ireland, it is very local throughout but slightly more frequent in the east than in the west. Some populations have been lost because of habitat destruction, but it is increasing as an alien as a consequence of planting on amenity ground and along roadsides. *Habitat* Characteristically found in scrub and hedgerows on chalk and limestone, but also found in quarries, on railway banks and in waste ground.

Sweet Cicely
(Myrrhis odorata)

This is a plant with a strong north/south divide. It flowers throughout parts of Yorkshire, Northumberland and the Borders in May, frothy and white on the roadside, yet it is hardly found in the south. It is like a shorter, stockier version of Cow Parsley (p.77), with delicate, ferny leaves. It has therapeutic uses, as an antiseptic and soother of the stomach; probably because of this, it is common on archaeological sites of medieval monasteries. The fresh spring leaves have a gentle liquorice, Chervil-like taste, and the seed pods are delicious, too, a wild alternative to Liquorice Allsorts. With Hemlock (p.304) being in the same family, you should be careful when identifying umbellifers before you eat them. Sweet Cicely's distinguishing characteristic is its strong aniseed scent and its seeds, which are more strongly ridged than those of other umbellifers.

Plant type Carrot family, Apiaceae. *Flowers* May–June. *Height* Up to 180cm. *Description* Robust, erect perennial herb. Stems are hollow and slightly downy. Leaves are finely divided (two to four times pinnate), fern-like, also downy, often with white blotches at the base, up to 30cm long. *Companion species* Alexanders (p.62) and Green Alkanet (p.88) on medieval monastery sites; Male-fern (p.19), Meadow Crane's-bill (p.96) and Melancholy Thistle (p.97) on northern roadsides. *Distribution* Introduced. A native of the Alps, Pyrenees, Apennines and the Balkan Peninsula, it is now the most common spring-flowering umbellifer in northern and western England and Scotland, although largely absent from the far north west of Scotland. It is quite frequent in Wales and Northern Ireland, but very scattered elsewhere in England. *Habitat* Hedge banks, woodland margins, roadside verges, riverbanks and other grassy places.

Sweet Vernal-grass
(Anthoxanthum odoratum)

This green-bladed grass, with its sedge-like flowers and habit – tufted and stiff, with smooth, unbranched stems and finely pointed, flat leaves – stands out for two reasons. Together with Meadow Foxtail (p.158), it is the earliest common grass to come into flower (hence its name). It is often covered in pollen by the middle of April, and from mid spring until late summer it fills the air with a sweet, grassy fragrance, which is to most of us the smell of summer. This new-mown hay scent, for which it is named, comes from a chemical called coumarin, which is also found in Woodruff (p.32) and White Melilot (p.116). Sweet Vernal-grass is one of the worst grasses for provoking asthma and hay fever. Its Latin genus name is taken from the Greek *anthos* meaning 'flower' and *xanthos* meaning 'yellow', and, by midsummer, it does indeed turn a rich straw-gold.

Plant type Grass family, Poaceae. *Flowers* April–June. *Height* Up to 50cm. *Description* Erect, tufted, short-lived perennial herb. Leaves are sparsely hairy, 1.5–5mm wide, flat and finely pointed. Sheaths have a conspicuous ring of hairs at the junction with the blade. Ligules are blunt, 1–5mm long. Inflorescence is a dense, spike-like panicle, green at first, although golden once over. Each spikelet is 6–10mm long with three flowers, the lower two of which are sterile with awns. *Companion species* Bluebell (p.2), Bush Vetch (p.69), Greater Stitchwort (p.87), Pignut (p.161) and Yorkshire-fog (p.169). *Distribution* Native. Found throughout Britain and Ireland and very common in many areas. It is no longer used in grass-seed mixes. *Habitat* A wide variety of grassland habitats, including road- and lane sides, old pastures and meadows, hill grassland, heaths, the drier parts of mires and sand dunes. It is most frequent on acid soils and avoids drought-prone or waterlogged sites.

Sweet Violet

(Viola odorata)

With its huge and extraordinary, slightly marzipan scent, this is one of our most marvellous native flowers, which comes at least a month earlier than other violets. Have an eagle eye for the purple, or rarer white, form, and always stop to smell them. They are a gift to be prized on an early spring walk. The oil distilled from the petals has been used to make scent and to flavour sweets since the time of Cleopatra, and they are still used commercially in Turkey to make violet sugar. In the past, when it was much more abundant, Sweet Violet flowers were strewn on the floors of churches and cottages to conceal bad smells. As well as their delicious scent, they contain ionine, which dulls our sense of smell. Bees love it and, like several other violets, it is a key food source for five of the fritillary butterflies (see Common Dog-violet, p.5).

Plant type Violet family, Violaceae. *Flowers* Mainly March. *Height* 3–6cm. *Description* Perennial with five-lobed, deep purple (or white, and sometimes other colours) flowers on leafless stems above neat rosettes of shield-shaped hairy leaves, indented at the edge. Sweet Violet is easy to confuse with both dog-violets (pp.5 and 8), but unlike these *V. odorata* is scented and its sepals are blunt. Sweet Violets also flower earlier and usually appear in small clumps, not drifts. They are a darker, more uniform purple. Their leaves are hairy and the leaves and flowers are on separate stems. Reproduction is by seed and rooting stolons. *Companion species* Lesser Celandine (p.18) and Wood Anemone (p.30). *Distribution* Native and widespread across the British Isles, but very rare throughout much of Scotland. *Habitat* An ancient woodland indicator species, it grows in light shade in ancient woodlands and in more open habitats on lightly shaded road verges, railway and hedge banks and scrub, usually on calcareous soils.

Tansy

(Tanacetum vulgare)

The unmistakable flowers of Tansy look as though they have had all their petals removed, leaving only the central bright yellow boss on the flowering stem. It is like a plant that has gone wrong, on which every flower seems to be a mutant. It forms big, bushy clumps with bright green, ferny leaves, which overhang roads and lanes, the stems arching out over the tarmac a little. It was widely grown in medieval gardens as a culinary and medicinal herb, and it is often difficult to distinguish between introduced and native populations. The leaves smell and taste pungent and bitter; they were eaten in the spring to detoxify the body after winter, and were used to treat infestations of worms. They were also used as an alternative to expensive spices, a staple of the kitchen herb garden, with a warm flavour a little similar to that of nutmeg and cinnamon (it was called sweet mace in Derbyshire), often combined with egg. I grow an acid-green-leaved version of this in my garden, *Tanacetum* 'Isla Gold'.

Plant type Daisy family, Asteraceae. *Flowers* July–October. *Height* 30–100cm. *Description* Erect, hairless perennial herb. Leaves are 15–25cm long, twice pinnate, alternately arranged up the stem. Flower heads are yellow and button-like, 7–12mm across, without ray florets and arranged in dense, umbel-like inflorescences. Seeds are hairless and lack a pappus (feather-like parachute). *Companion species* Cow Parsley (p.77), Hogweed (p.156) and Japanese Knotweed (p.252). *Distribution* Native. Common throughout most of Great Britain except in upland regions, such as the Cambrian Mountains, the Pennines and the Scottish Highlands, although it is found on the Outer Hebrides and Shetland. It is scattered throughout Ireland, but not considered native there. *Habitat* Field borders, riverbanks and roadsides.

Three-cornered Garlic
(Allium triquetrum)

First recorded as an escape near Helston, Cornwall, in 1874, this has become the Japanese Knotweed of the south west. Particularly on the Scilly Isles, it carpets the lane sides and corners of fields and spreads very quickly. Passing traffic, and the air turbulence caused by it, is thought to assist seed dispersal, which explains its greater abundance along busy roads. Also known as Triangular-stalked Garlic, it is edible and can be used in the same way as Ramsons (p.23), the flowers scattered in salads and its foliage and flowers used to make an intense but delicious soup. There is some evidence that it is causing damage to common plants such as Bluebell (p.2), as well as rarer plants, on the cliffs of the Lizard. Because of this it is now one of the species listed in Schedule 9 of the Wildlife and Countryside Act, which makes it illegal to introduce the plant into the wild. It is one of the best plants to forage – the more you harvest, the better.

Plant type Onion family, Alliaceae. *Flowers* April–June. *Height* 20–50cm. *Description* Herbaceous perennial with umbels of drooping, long-stalked, white flowers with perianth segments 12–18mm long. Leaves are flat or keeled, 12–20cm by 5–10mm. Stem is strongly three-angled. *Companion species* Fennel (p.81), Garlic Mustard (p.84), Lesser Celandine (p.18) and Navelwort (p.100). *Distribution* Introduced for cultivation from the western Mediterranean, where it grows in damp shady places, often by streams. It had become established by 1849. It is scattered across the British Isles, but more common in the south, especially in Cornwall and along the south coast. It is gradually moving up the country, with numbers increasing rapidly. *Habitat* Usually found in places typical of introduced species, such as roadsides, hedge banks, field margins and waste ground. It grows in sun and shade.

Traveller's-joy
(Clematis vitalba)

Our native clematis has small, white, sea anemone-like flowers in summer, each of the petals thin and needle-like. As with other clematis species, the flowers smell of vanilla: pollinator insects love them. The flowers are followed by crimson-hearted seed heads, which look like creamy spiders packed together in a huddle, every leg fluffing up into a cottony powder puff – that is why it is also known as Old-man's-beard. Its wide, stretching vines swathe many sheltered hedgerows through autumn and into winter, lining paths, roads and railways, particularly on chalk. I sometimes pick them before they blow completely to use in Christmas decorations. If you leave the stem ends in a dilute solution of glycerine for a couple of weeks, or zap them with hairspray, you can hold most of the fluff in place. It was particularly loved by the herbalist John Gerard, who found it 'decking and adorning ways and hedges, where people travel, and thereupon I have named it the travellers' joy'.

Plant type Buttercup family, Ranunculaceae. *Flowers* July–August. *Height* Stems up to 30m long. *Description* Woody climbing plant. Bark is fibrous and peeling. Leaves are opposite and compound with oval, toothed and pointed leaflets. Flowers are 2cm across with hairy, greenish-cream petals, no sepals and many stamens. *Companion species* Black Bryony (p.63), Bramble (p.66), Common Ivy (p.73) and Elder (p.80). *Distribution* Native. Common in southern England and Wales, less frequent to the north and west. It is rare in Scotland and perhaps not native there. It is not thought to be native in Ireland or the Isle of Man, although it is quite common in the south and east of Ireland. *Habitat* Hedgerows, woodland edges, glades and scrubland. It clambers over walls and ruined buildings, railway embankments and sand dunes. It is most frequent on base-rich soils and lime mortar.

Vervain
(Verbena officinalis)

Vervain crops up on trackways, parking places and gravel drives, where you cannot believe that there is anything in the stones on which it could survive. It thrives where little else, apart from deep-rooted docks, can eke out an existence. It can grow quite tall and upright, or much more prostrate, forming big plants that stretch at least a metre across. Its flowers are a pale and pretty pinky mauve. Vervain is the only member of its family found wild in the British Isles, but you may recognise it because it bears a strong resemblance to *V. rigida* and *V. bonariensis*, popular garden plants that provide reliable summer colour. Its narrow trumpet flowers, tall, thin flower spikes and long flowering season are typical of the vervain family, whose Latin generic name, *Verbena*, refers to plants that were used by Druids during sacrifices. Vervain is known to have been grown in Britain since the Neolithic period and was widely cultivated and venerated in medieval gardens for its medicinal qualities: it was used to treat headaches and to help those who could not sleep. Vervain is related to the South American native that we call Lemon Verbena (*Aloysia citrodora*), which is still widely used in a tisane to aid sleep.

Plant type Vervain family, Verbenaceae. *Flowers* June–September. *Height* 30–75cm. *Description* Erect, branched perennial herb. Leaves are deeply pinnately lobed, bristly, 2–7cm long and arranged in opposite pairs. Flowers are small, bluish pink and arranged in slender, elongated terminal spikes. Each flower has five sepals and a two-lipped, five-lobed corolla. *Companion species* Basil Thyme (p.191), Broad-leaved Dock (p.236), Curled Dock (p.245) and Pineappleweed (p.255). *Distribution* Introduced, although some botanists consider it to be native. It is common in southern England and south Wales but becoming rare in northern England. It is absent from Scotland and occasional in Ireland. *Habitat* A plant of open, disturbed ground on free-draining and usually calcareous soils. Typical habitats include roadsides, quarries, grassland, scrub, woodland rides and clearings, walls, sheltered coastal cliffs and stream sides.

Wall Lettuce
(Mycelis muralis)

You will notice Wall Lettuce not for its tiny, lemon-yellow, Dandelion-tassel flowers, but for its shape and the colour of the stems and basal leaves. In the shade, it can be a messy and straggly-looking plant, but in better light, it forms an airy, elegant cloud with rich crimson stems and flower calyces. The stems shoot out vertically from walls and cliffs, their roots tucked into the tiniest crevice, standing straight out from flat rocks or stone surfaces like skeletal flags, with almost no leaves. If you know where to find them, you can harvest the long-stalked, edible basal leaves early in the year – they taste best before the plants flower. If lettuce has ever bolted in your garden, you will recognise this as a relation of cultivated garden lettuce. Like other lettuces, its stems contain a milky fluid called lactucarium, a mild opiate, and it was eaten by the Romans and Egyptians to induce sleep.

Plant type Daisy family, Asteraceae. *Flowers* June–September. *Height* 25–100cm. *Description* Erect, hairless perennial herb. All leaves are quite thin and reddish-tinged. Lower leaves are pinnatifid, lyre-shaped, with triangular lobes and winged stalks. Upper leaves are stalkless, less deeply lobed and have arrow-shaped bases that clasp the stem. Flower heads are small, usually not more than 1cm across, and have five yellow florets. They are arranged in an open panicle with branches joining the main stem at right angles. *Companion species* Maidenhair Spleenwort (p.95), Wall-rue (p.114) and Yellow Corydalis (p.121). *Distribution* Native. Common throughout most of England and Wales, although absent from the far south west and parts of eastern England. It is more local in Scotland and introduced in Ireland. *Habitat* Shaded walls, rock outcrops, hedge banks, woodland, wood margins and scrub, especially on chalk and limestone.

Wall-rue
(Asplenium ruta-muraria)

It is easy to recognise Wall-rue, because it looks more like a herb – a curly-leaved chervil or mustard – or like its namesake, Rue (*Ruta graveolens*), than a fern. The paler green, new growth stands up and out above the darker, older rosette, which clings closest to the wall. Each of the fronds is divided into lobes, which have three or sometimes four lobules to them, their tips just notched into little stubby fingers. Wall-rue used to be as common as muck, but it has declined during the twentieth century, particularly in industrial areas. Together with many lichens, it is sensitive to air pollution, and, as people buy up and restore old buildings, the over-vigorous re-pointing of old lime mortar walls is almost certainly another factor in its decline. As with Rustyback (p.105), the use of herbicide sprays on old church walls and ruins to prevent plant roots causing further damage has also decreased its numbers.

Plant type Spleenwort family, Aspleniaceae. *Height* 3–12cm. *Description* Small tufted fern. Fronds are evergreen, long-stalked and triangular to ovate in outline, twice pinnate, 3–12cm long. Individual segments are leathery, fan-shaped, bluntly toothed, dull green, 2–8mm long. Sori are linear. *Companion species* Pellitory-of-the-wall (p.102) and Wall Lettuce (p.113). *Distribution* Native. Common throughout most of Britain and Ireland, except the north of Scotland, where it is quite local and generally more frequent near the coast. It is also less frequent in parts of the east of England, especially Cambridgeshire, Suffolk and Essex. *Habitat* Occurs naturally on limestone and other basic rocks, where it grows on steep, bare faces and in crevices, as well as in hollowed clints in limestone pavement. It also grows on walls and man-made structures of all types, which are now its most important habitat in lowland areas.

Welsh Poppy
(Meconopsis cambrica)

All poppies are beautiful, but this brilliant yellow one, its petals slightly crumpled like the finest linen, is one of the loveliest. Unlike Common Poppy (p.241), which has scraggy foliage, Welsh Poppy has handsome, bright green hummocks of leaves, as healthy and vibrant as the flowers themselves. Strictly speaking, this is not an official poppy. It used to be in the *Papaver* genus, but its seed-releasing mechanism is different – through slits in the seed pods rather than a 'pepper-pot' head – so it is in the genus *Meconopsis*, named after a Greek word for 'looking like a poppy'. Welsh Poppy has been cultivated as a garden flower for centuries, loved for its tolerance of light shade and its habit of cropping up – self-sown – on the edges of paths and at the base of walls.

Plant type Poppy family, Papaveraceae. *Flowers* June–August. *Height* 30–60cm. *Description* Almost hairless perennial herb. Like all members of the poppy family, it has flowers with four petals and two sepals (but these fall off when the flower opens). Both the flowers and the latex in the stems and leaves are yellow. Leaves are pinnate and the capsule is elliptical, 2.5–3cm long. Yellow Horned-poppy (p.427) also has yellow flowers, but it is easily distinguished by its two-celled, sickle-shaped seed pod, which grows to 30cm long. It also grows in a different habitat – coastal shingle. *Companion species* Alexanders (p.62), Creeping Thistle (p.150), Hogweed (p.156) and Sweet Cicely (p.110). *Distribution* Native. Only scattered populations in Wales, south-west England and Ireland are definitely native, and these are probably in slow decline. It is far more common as an alien species in the British Isles and occurs throughout, with a westerly bias. Even in the regions where the plant is considered native, it is more frequent as an alien and is spreading in this form. *Habitat* Damp, rocky woodlands and shaded cliff ledges. It is also grown in gardens and has become widely naturalised on hedge banks, walls, roadsides and waste ground.

White Bryony
(Bryonia dioica)

I like the pale, creamy-green flowers of White Bryony, which tends to clamber up split chestnut and barbed-wire fences in our part of the world, lacing between the different layers. With its palmate leaves and tightly curled tendrils, you could easily think this was a wild vine, or a wild cucumber, to which it is related. For the later weeks of spring and right through summer, it is covered in flowers, the male flowers bigger and showier than the female. Then come the berries – red, shiny and highly poisonous, like those of its namesake Black Bryony (p.63). White and Black Bryony are not related. They are both dioecious, with separate male and female plants, but they belong to entirely different families. Black Bryony is a member of the yam family, a monocotyledon with tuberous rhizomes, heart-shaped leaves and smaller flowers. White Bryony is the only wild-growing British member of the gourd family, which includes melons, pumpkins, cucumbers and squash.

Plant type White Bryony family, Cucurbitaceae. *Flowers* May–September. *Height* Up to 4m. *Description* Climbing perennial herb with stems that are bristly and angled. Leaves are dull green and palmately lobed with spirally coiled tendrils rising from the leaf-stalk axils. Flowers are pale green. Male flowers are 12–18mm across, slightly larger than female flowers. Fruit is 5–8mm across. *Companion species* Bramble (p.66), Hawthorn (p.89), Oak (p.101) and Rosebay Willowherb (p.258). *Distribution* Native. Common in most of England, although largely absent from the far north and north west, south west and the Weald. It also occurs as a native in eastern Wales. It is a very rare alien in Scotland and Ireland. *Habitat* Well-drained, often base-rich soils in hedgerows, scrub and woodland borders, and on rough and waste ground.

White Campion
(Silene latifolia)

White Campion, along with its relation Red Campion (p.24), is one of the cheeriest plants of any roadside and hedgerow. The Red grows happily in more shade than the White, but they often grow side-by-side on a bank or grass verge. They flower continuously from spring until autumn and make a lovely bunch of flowers, lasting well over a week in water if you sear the stem end in boiling water for twenty seconds. If you see this in abundance it is fine to pick just a few. The puffy crimson calyx behind the petals, which resembles pink-and-red-striped Elizabethan breeches, is particularly noticeable in the White. Both species cross-fertilise, creating many crosses in different tones of pink. These will backcross with their parents to further increase the colour range. Like so many white flowers, White Campion has an evening scent – slightly spicy and clove-like – which keeps it busy with moths and night-pollinating insects.

Plant type Pink family, Caryophyllaceae. *Flowers* May–October. *Height* 30–100cm. *Description* Sticky, hairy, annual to perennial dioecious herb. Leaves are situated opposite one another and are elliptical-lanceolate in shape. The flowers form in the leaf axils, with usually several buds in each. They are 25–30mm across with deeply forked petals. Male flowers have ten stamens; female flowers have five styles. *Companion species* Cow Parsley (p.77), Garlic Mustard (p.84) and Red Campion. *Distribution* Introduced, but has occurred in Britain since at least the Bronze Age (there are fossil records). It is a common plant in most of Britain, although it is less frequent in the south west, most of Wales and western Scotland. *Habitat* Being an annual, White Campion is usually found in disturbed places: roadsides, arable land, hedge banks and waste places. It prefers deep, well-drained soils.

White Dead-nettle
(Lamium album)

Cows grazing a field will leave this until last. They hate its smell, which, as with all dead-nettles, is released as soon as you crush even a small amount of leaf. Cattle might not like it, but it is an incredibly valuable plant for pollinating insects and an important nectar source for bumblebees, particularly foraging queens emerging from hibernation. The flower has evolved to accommodate them. The lower lip acts as their landing platform, from which they feed on the abundant nectar at the bottom of the tube; try sucking on it and you will get a delicious drop of sweet nectar – but you need to get there in the morning to beat the bees. We used to do this as children. The upper hood conceals and protects the stamens, so as the bee probes into the tube of the flower, its upper surface brushes the stamens and becomes covered in pollen, which it then carries off to the style of another flower. As with Red Dead-nettle (p.257), the leaves and young stems are edible – tender and juicy before they flower. Use them raw in salads, or steam them and serve like Greek *horta*, with olive oil and lemon juice. You can also use the leaves and young tops – as you would ordinary nettles – in a soup.

Plant type Dead-nettle family, Lamiaceae. *Flowers* May–December. *Height* 20–60cm. *Description* Erect, hairy perennial herb. Leaves are 3–7cm long and nettle shaped, but do not sting. White flowers are in dense, well-spaced whorls, corollas 2mm long. *Companion species* Common Nettle (p.241), Garlic Mustard (p.84), Green Alkanet (p.88) and Soft-brome (p.165). *Distribution* Introduced by the Romans and now very common throughout Britain, except in north-west Scotland. It is rare throughout most of Ireland, except the east. *Habitat* A characteristic plant of roadsides and hedgerows, as well as secondary woodland.

White Melilot
(Melilotus albus)

This airy plant is often self-sown into cracks and crevices beside the road, its spikes curving out into the danger zone to be decapitated by passing cars. The individual flowers are tiny, but there is such a mass of them that the spikes resemble feathery plumes. Like the yellow form, Tall Melilot (*M. altissimus*), it was introduced as a fodder crop and medicinal plant: herbalists used it to make ointments and poultices to reduce swellings, blisters and bruises. It is a rich source of nectar for pollinating hoverflies and bees. In each flower, the stigma and stamens are held stiffly inside the joined lower petals. The weight of a big insect landing on a flower is enough to press the lower petals downwards, so that the stigma touches the underside of the insect's body and is fertilised by the pollen there. While drying, White Melilot has a lovely scent, like that of new-mown hay. This is derived from the coumarin in its leaves and stalks, the same substance that gives Sweet Vernal-grass (p.110) its delicious smell.

Plant type Pea family, Fabaceae. *Flowers* June–August. *Height* 60–120cm. *Description* Spring-germinating annual with white flowers 4–5mm long. Inflorescence is a many-flowered erect raceme. Leaves are trifoliate, rather like clovers, but leaflets are sharply toothed. Stems are erect and branched. Pod is 3–5mm, hairless and brown when ripe. *Companion species* Cock's-foot (p.145), Creeping Thistle (p.150) and Curled Dock (p.245). *Distribution* Introduced. Found throughout the British Isles. It is most frequent in the London area and home counties, although there are centres of distribution around Merseyside and the West Midlands. It is absent from the uplands of Wales and Scotland, although it is found in lowland parts. *Habitat* Waste or disturbed ground, in railway sidings and by roadsides, often as a relic of cultivation.

Wild Cherry

(Prunus avium)

Wild Cherry's blossom is so transient that it can be gone – depending on the weather – in a matter of days. We have several plants in the hedges around Perch Hill and we love the sweet, deliciously scented flowers, but it takes just one bad rain storm or spring gale and they are lost for another year. In July they will be covered in fruit, half the size of a domestic cherry but just as shiny and red. They can taste either sweet or bitter – it varies from tree to tree – but they have an intense flavour ideal for cherry brandy. Fill the bottom of a jar with cherries, add sugar and brandy, and store for three or four months, shaking it every so often. Sieve out the fruit, taste and add more sugar if you need it. These shrubs and trees also look good in early autumn, the leaves turning a mix of yellows and reds. The timber is valuable for furniture, bowls and boxes, being tough and a reddish brown, which, like mahogany, can be polished to a high shine.

Plant type Rose family, Rosaceae. *Flowers* April–May, often just before or at the same time as the leaves emerge. *Height* Up to 25m if left unclipped. *Description* Deciduous tree. Wild Cherry has a distinctive, peeling bark with horizontal lines. Leaves are oval-elliptical, toothed, hairless above, downy below. White flowers are in umbels of two to six. Red fruit is 1cm across. *Companion species* Bramble (p.66) and Hedge Bindweed (p.90). *Distribution* Native. Occurs throughout the British Isles but is local or rare in north-west Scotland and Ireland. It has also been widely planted, so it is difficult to distinguish between native and alien populations. *Habitat* An ancient woodland indicator species, it occurs in woodland and hedgerows on fertile soils, but it is also widely planted as an ornamental or fruit tree in parks and gardens. It often forms large colonies by spreading with its suckers.

Wild Clary

(Salvia verbenaca)

Many will recognise Wild Clary as a relative of culinary sage and the other salvias that we grow in our gardens. It has the telltale square, branched stems, which are tinged with red, and two-lipped flowers with a hood and a more open, curved bottom lip. The lower lip has three lobes with two distinctive white marks. This species is less showy than most other salvias, as the calyx is almost as long as the flower petals and holds them in a way that seems to stop this plant reaching its full purple-velvet potential. It could be easily confused with Meadow Clary (p.206), but this is a much rarer, showier and more glamorous plant, with less deeply cut leaves and larger flowers. Wild Clary's flowers and leaves, like those of culinary sage, are edible, but it is rare enough in most parts of the country to say that it is better not to harvest it.

Plant type Dead-nettle family, Lamiaceae. *Flowers* May–August. *Height* 30–80cm. *Description* Downy, aromatic perennial herb with a rosette of oval-oblong, cordate, stalked, jagged-toothed leaves at the base, each 4–12cm long. There are few stalkless stem leaves. Inflorescence is a spike of whorled flowers, each with a sticky/downy two-lipped calyx (7mm long) and a two-lipped violet-blue corolla, up to 7mm long with an arched upper lip, often well hidden in the calyx. *Companion species* Alexanders (p.62), Autumn Lady's-tresses (p.190) and Red Valerian (p.407). *Distribution* Native. Locally frequent in the south and east of England, scattered elsewhere in Great Britain and rare in Ireland. In some areas, such as Cornwall and Sussex, its distribution is coastal. *Habitat* Open grassland on sunny banks, sand dunes and roadsides, usually on well-drained, base-rich soils, including sticky calcareous clays that are wet in winter and baked dry in summer. In Suffolk and Sussex, it is often associated with churchyards.

Wild Parsnip
(Pastinaca sativa ssp. *sylvestris)*

If, like me, you like umbellifers, you will love this tall acid-green-to-yellow-flowered plant, which looks like a more robust form of the beautiful garden herb dill. Wild Parsnip is an excellent ornamental addition to a wild-flower meadow or patch. It self-sows, so it is not recommended for immaculate borders, but tucked in among rough grass somewhere it will brighten up its corner and scatter itself from one year to the next. Like many umbellifers, it is adored by soldier beetles – several can be seen at once perching on a single umbel, feeding on the pollen and nectar. The name 'parsnip' is thought to derive from the Latin generic name *Pastinaca*, which may come from *pastus*, the Latin word for 'pasture' – the place where it is often found. Alternatively, its origin may be the Latin *pastinare*, 'to dig', the root being the plant's most valuable part. The roots of Wild Parsnip are quite spindly and mean, and develop a hard inedible core when they get older, but you can use the leaves to give a strong parsnip flavour to soups and chop them finely to add to salads.

Plant type Carrot family, Apiaceae. *Flowers* July–August. *Height* 30–120cm. *Description* Erect, medium to tall, branched, hairy perennial herb. Stems are furrowed, angled and hollow. Leaves are once pinnate with five to eleven oval, lobed and toothed leaflets. Flowers are yellow, in five- to fifteen-rayed umbels, 5–10cm across. Fruit is oval, flattened and winged. There are three subspecies of *P. sativa* found in Britain; the other two are ssp. *urens* (Eastern Parsnip) and ssp. *sativa*, which is the culinary parsnip, usually an escape from cultivation. *Companion species* Chicory (p.70), Common Sorrel (p.147) and Meadow Crane's-bill (p.96). *Distribution* Native. Common in southern, central and eastern England, but very rare in Scotland and Ireland and mainly introduced. It is occasional to locally frequent in Wales. *Habitat* Roadsides, grassland, scrub and wasteland on both neutral and calcareous grassland.

Wild Plum
(Prunus domestica)

This is not one plant, but several, all with similar blossoms but variable fruit. What is considered to be Wild Plum includes at least three subspecies. Ssp. *domestica* produces plums and has sparsely hairy, spineless twigs. Ssp. *insititia* produces damsons and bullaces and has densely hairy, sometimes spiny twigs. Ssp. *italica* is more or less intermediate between the two and produces small greengages. Whichever variety you find, the fruit makes superb jam, chutneys, fruit 'cheese' – a thick jelly to eat with meat or cheese – and excellent ice cream. If you spot a tree in the hedge in spring, it is worth making a note to return later in the year to harvest some fruit. Some botanists consider specimens of ssp. *italica* to

be native in British hedges and woodlands; others believe that the three subspecies are all introduced. Like other fruit trees, it has hard wood that is useful to turners and its bark yields a good yellow dye.

Plant type Rose family, Rosaceae. *Flowers* April–May. *Height* Up to 8m. *Description* Large, deciduous shrub or tree. Leaves are obovate to elliptical, up to 8cm long. Flowers are white and five-petalled. Blossom looks similar to that of Blackthorn (p.64) and Cherry Plum (p.69), but comes a good month later, flowering on the bare branch, like Blackthorn (by contrast, Cherry Plum blossom comes at the same time as the unravelling leaves). *Companion species* Black Bryony (p.63), Elder (p.80) and Hawthorn (p.89). *Distribution* Introduced archaeophyte. It has been grown in Britain since at least 995 and was first recorded in the wild in 1777. It is common throughout most of England and Wales except in remote upland areas. It is more localised in Scotland and mostly confined to the lowlands. In Ireland, it is found throughout, but more frequently in the east than in the west. It is often still planted in Kent and Sussex as a windbreak and pollinator for fruit orchards. *Habitat* Hedgerows, scrubland, wood borders and wasteland.

Wild Strawberry
(Fragaria vesca)

I remember walking along a wooded strip below some basalt cliffs in the west Highlands of Scotland in May: the hillside, above and below, was spattered with Wild Strawberries. They did not flower in deep shade, but wherever there was light coming through the trees, there were carpets of them. The whole place smelt and looked like paradise. Each plant had several bright white, potentilla-like flowers, with the pleated, notched glossy leaves – like the leaves in a woodcut – providing a plate for the strawberry to sit on. The flower stems are strong enough to hold the flowers up and out, but as the fruit fattens, their weight pulls the stem over so that the strawberries hang down and the flowers stand above them. These are fruit to eat as you walk, a mouthful of sweet wood.

Plant type Rose family, Rosaceae. *Flowers* April–June. *Height* 5–30cm. *Description* Perennial herb with long runners and long-stalked, trifoliate, glossy-green, hairy leaves. Each leaflet is 1–6cm long. Flowers are white, five-petalled and 12–18mm across. Fruit is like a miniature garden strawberry, 1–2cm long. Barren Strawberry (p.62) looks similar, but does not produce fruit. It is also easily distinguished by its flower, which has sepals that are longer than the petals. *Companion species* Bluebell (p.2), Germander Speedwell (p.85), Lesser Celandine (p.18), Wood Anemone (p.30) and Wood-sorrel (p.33). *Distribution* Very common throughout the British Isles, although a bit less frequent in northern Scotland. *Habitat* Dry, sometimes stony soils on hedge banks, in woodland and scrub, railway banks and roadsides and on basic rock outcrops and screes in upland areas. It also colonises open ground in quarries and chalk pits, and grows on walls. It reproduces by seed and spreads with long, arching runners, forming distinct patches of strawberries from which you can gorge.

Wild Privet
(Ligustrum vulgare)

You seldom see the flowers or berries of privets when they are grown in hedges, because the shrubs are usually cut each year, removing the flowering wood. Unclipped, however, they are covered in flowers, which resemble delicate, miniature versions of pure-white lilac. Unlike most hedgerow blossoms, the flowers last well, the bushes flowering for most of the summer; they also have a delicious sweet scent, which makes them worth picking – sear the stem end in boiling water for thirty seconds to make them last in water. The shiny, ebony berries that come next also last well, often remaining on the branch until winter. The berries of Wild Privet are poisonous and can be fatal to small children. Wild Privet's dull, leathery, dark green leaves usually drop in late autumn, leaving the berries showing clearly. This is its big difference from the introduced evergreen Garden Privet (*L. ovalifolium*).

Plant type Ash family, Oleaceae. *Flowers* June–July. *Height* 1–3m. *Description* Semi-evergreen shrub. Leaves are elliptical, 3–6cm long and opposite one another. Flowers are white, 4–5mm across, with stamens projecting from the four-lobed corollas. They are arranged in terminal panicles. Fruit is 6–8mm across. *Companion species* Black Bryony (p.63), Hedge Bindweed (p.90), Honeysuckle (p.91) and Large Bindweed (p.94). *Distribution* Native. Found throughout Britain and Ireland and common in many areas, but rare in northern Scotland and mostly absent from the Highlands. *Habitat* Hedgerows, woodland and scrub, preferring well-drained, calcareous or base-rich soils. It is an early invader of calcareous grassland, forming large suckering patches that are difficult to clear due to the lack of single trunks. It also occurs as a garden escape and a relic of cultivation.

Wood Crane's-bill
(Geranium sylvaticum)

This grows in the brighter patches of woods and hedgerows and on many roadsides in the higher areas of northern England – Yorkshire, Cumbria and Northumberland – where it forms wonderful wild gardens. It is also a key feature of the declining upland hay meadows of the Yorkshire Dales. Mixed with plants such as Sweet Cicely (p.110), Lady's-mantle (p.156), Wood Avens (p.31) and the delicate Broad Buckler-fern (p.3), it dominates the show. You can tell it apart from the more southern species Meadow Crane's-bill (p.96) by its slightly smaller, purplish (rather than bluey) flowers, which have a white eye at their centre. Rarely, other colour variants occur, from pure white to pinkish purple, and all make good garden plants. This is an important source of food for pollinating insects. Like all the larger-flowered crane's-bills, it is full of nectar and comes alive with butterflies and bees as soon as the sun comes out.

Plant type Crane's-bill family, Geraniaceae. *Flowers* June–July. *Height* Up to 70cm. *Description* Compact, erect perennial herb. Leaves are five- to nine-lobed (divided approximately four fifths of the distance to the base) and bluntly toothed. Flowers, 10–15mm across, are purplish pink with unnotched petals (occasionally slightly notched). *Companion species* Broad Buckler-fern, Lady's-mantle, Sweet Cicely and Wood Avens. *Distribution* Native. Common in the north of England and Scotland. It is very rare south of the Yorkshire Dales, although there are a few scattered colonies in Wales that are considered to be native. There are also a few populations on the north-east coast of Ireland, which are thought to be native. It has declined at the edges of its range because of the use of fertilisers on its hay-meadow habitat. *Habitat* Damp woodland and hedge banks, as well as pastures, meadows and rock ledges, on base-rich or calcareous soils.

Yellow Corydalis
(Pseudofumaria lutea)

A species native to the foothills of the central and eastern Alps in Italy, Switzerland and Yugoslavia, this has long been cultivated as a cottage-garden plant because it flowers for much of the year. It is now very common in the wild, but it still looks like an Italian spiv. There is hardly a church wall in our part of the world not softened by this pretty-leaved, yellow-flowered wall plant: analysis of walls in south Essex found this species in 18 per cent of all the sites surveyed. It is also very abundant in London, usually growing out of cracks in pavements and walls. Yellow Corydalis is one of the fumitories, which all have delicate, hairless, rather ferny foliage, with tubular, two-lipped flowers. However, its yellow flowers distinguish it from other fumitories found wild in the Britain Isles – they all have white or purple flowers.

Plant type Poppy family, Papaveraceae. *Flowers* May–August, but it can go on flowering until November, particularly in warm urban areas, such as London. *Height* 30cm. *Description* Hairless, stout, much-branched, erect perennial herb. Leaves are pinnate with a terminal leaflet (no tendrils). Yellow flowers are tubular, two-lipped, 12–18mm long, in a raceme of five to ten. *Companion species* Maidenhair Spleenwort (p.95), Mexican Fleabane (p.97) and Red Valerian (p.407). *Distribution* Introduced, probably by the Romans, and first recorded in the wild in 1796. Widespread by the early 1800s, it has increased gradually ever since. It is now commonly found throughout England and Wales, except in upland regions, where it is more local. In Scotland, it is less frequent and more common near the east coast; it remains virtually absent from the Highlands. In Ireland, it is very rare and confined to a handful of scattered populations, mostly in the north. *Habitat* Most frequently found rooted into the crevices of old mortared walls, pavements and other masonry, and on brick rubble and stony waste ground. Once established in an area, it can quickly colonise new sites.

Greater Stitchwort (p.87) and Dandelions (p.246), Hurst Green, East Sussex, 3 May.

Ivy-leaved Toadflax (p.93), Moreton, Dorset, 8 May.

Bluebell (p.2), Greater Stitchwort (p.87) and Red Campion (p.24), Warkleigh, Devon, 14 May.

Dog-rose (p.79), the Burren, County Clare, Ireland, 22 June.

Elder (p.80), the Burren, County Clare, Ireland, 22 June.

Bettenham Lane, Sissinghurst, Kent, 7 September

Common Ivy (p.73) and Traveller's-joy (p.112), Chalford Hill, Gloucestershire, 3 November

Chalford Hill, Gloucestershire, 6 December.

Common Ivy (p.73), Chalford Hill, Gloucestershire, 6 December.

Meadow

In the Middle Ages, and right up to the invention of the tractor, in a culture that relied on animals for energy, nothing was more important to the economy than a hay meadow. Now that central relationship with the grassy and flowery world has disappeared, and this is the habitat that we have lost more than any other – the fields where the grass is longer than on the tight sward of our downs and dales, the meadows that are cut for hay. Almost all have now been sprayed and resown, with more productive grasses to create more hay or with short-term rye-grass leys.

The meadows we have left are very rare, places to revel in. In these unimproved fields, the flowers are often thick on the ground and hugely varied. You can sit down and play the game of how many species you can find in the metre around you. In May and June, the upper storey will be full of Common Sorrel, Ribwort Plantain and the crimson blobby heads of Salad Burnet. There will be lots of buttercups, too: Bulbous, Creeping and the tallest of all, Meadow Buttercup.

A little below them in the next layer down are Rough Hawkbit, Oxeye Daisy and Yellow-rattle. Yellow-rattle is a key plant, parasitic on grasses, depleting their lushness enough to allow wild flowers to thrive. The more Yellow-rattle, the more wild flowers you are likely to see, and with the help of Yellow-rattle, many of the meadow restorations of the past twenty years are slowly creeping back to previous levels of plant diversity.

There is more to find in a slightly lower middle layer. Common Spotted-orchid, Common Bird's-foot-trefoil, Red and White Clover, Yarrow and Pignut. In the grasslands around where we holiday on the west coast of Scotland, Pignut is as common as Cow Parsley in May and June, only much finer and more beautiful, about a quarter of Cow Parsley's scale.

Looking almost at ground level, you will find the most delicate things, which you might not notice as you stride along. These are small but still highly glamorous: Common Milkwort in its intense blue, pink or occasional white, and the cheery white, blue-veined flowers of Common Eyebright, all held together in a cloud of Fairy Flax. The white flowers of Fairy Flax are tiny, just a fleck, but there are so many of them that they can haze the bottom storey entirely.

In a few special sites where the ground is heavy or moist, you may find fields full of Green-winged Orchid, or carpets of the most exquisite of our wild flowers, the chequerboard Fritillary (illustrated opposite). I have a meadow near me at Marden in Kent, where the whole field turns magenta in the middle of May with Green-winged Orchid. The field is immediately to the left of the main train line to London, and from the train window, about two minutes out of Staplehurst station, you can see thousands of orchids, as if someone has laid out a magenta-red carpet stretching from hedge to hedge.

Meadow flowers come and go quite quickly, evolved to drop their seed before the hay is cut and stored away. But if the meadow is left uncut, there may be banks of purple Tufted Vetch, magenta Betony and golden Dyer's Greenweed, pierced by the vertical spires of yellow Agrimony. These continue on through summer and in many fields they will persist on the track sides and steeper banks that have escaped the grass harvest. They go on looking good well into autumn, and give a varied contour to our meadows through the winter until the grass and flowers come again in spring.

You may also see Bluebell (p.2), Bracken (p.351), Bugle (p.68), Burnet-saxifrage (p.192), Chalk Milkwort (p.194), Common Field-speedwell (p.240), Common Marsh-bedstraw (p.295), Common Toadflax (p.74), Cowslip (p.195), Cuckooflower (p.297), Daisy (p.246), Dandelions (p.246), Early Marsh-orchid (p.298), Early-purple Orchid (p.9), Field Scabious (p.198), Germander Speedwell (p.85), Goat Willow (p.86), Grass Vetchling (p.200), Greater Knapweed (p.201), Greater Stitchwort (p.87), Harebell (p.202), Hedge Bedstraw (p.202), Heath Spotted-orchid (p.359), Herb-Robert (p.91), Hoary Plantain (p.203), Lady's Bedstraw (p.205), Meadowsweet (p.314), Meadow Vetchling (p.96), Musk-mallow (p.99), Northern Marsh-orchid (p.315), Primrose (p.103), Quaking-grass (p.211), Ragged-Robin (p.317), Red Bartsia (p.256), Red Valerian (p.407), Salad Burnet (p.213), Sheep's Sorrel (p.366), Shepherd's-purse (p.260), Silverweed (p.418), Small Scabious (p.214), Spring Squill (p.420), Sweet Cicely (p.110), Sweet Vernal-grass (p.110), Tormentil (p.371), Water Avens (p.318), Wild Thyme (p.217), Wood Crane's-bill (p.121) and Wood Sage (p.32).

Adder's-tongue
(Ophioglossum vulgatum)

This is a fern that does not look like a fern. It more resembles a green version of Lords-and-Ladies (p.19) crossed with Common Twayblade (p.148). It makes me think of a snake charmer's cobra unravelling from its green basket, and it is one of those plants that once seen and identified is never forgotten. You might confuse it with Small Adder's-tongue (*O. azoricum*), but this is only 3–8cm tall and normally has two to three fronds together; Adder's-tongue has just one. There is also a very rare third Adder's-tongue, Least Adder's-tongue (*O. lusitanicum*), which is confined to Guernsey and a few square metres in the Isles of Scilly. It is 1–2cm tall.

Plant type Adder's-tongue family, Ophioglossaceae. *Height* Up to 12cm. *Description* Rhizomatous deciduous fern. Fronds are forked into two parts – a vegetative, leaf-like blade and a fertile, tongue-like, long-stalked spike. The vegetative blade is solitary, yellowish green, oval-lanceolate to oblong, blunt with no midrib, fleshy, stalkless, 4–15cm long. The fertile blade (not always present) has a long stalk, 10–15cm long, enclosed at the base by the vegetative blade. The fertile part (the spike) is 2–5cm long with sixteen to forty stalkless green sporangia. *Companion species* Bulbous Buttercup (p.144), Common Spotted-orchid (p.148), Common Twayblade, Cowslip (p.195), Creeping Buttercup (p.149) and Green-winged Orchid (p.154). *Distribution* Native. Locally frequent throughout England and Wales except Devon and Cornwall, where it is quite rare. It is quite rare in Scotland, most frequent on the west coast. Throughout Ireland, it is scattered and rare in most areas. It has declined catastrophically because so many meadows have been agriculturally improved. *Habitat* Meadows/pasture and open woodland on neutral, mildly acidic to base-rich clay/silt soils in damp spots.

Agrimony
(Agrimonia eupatoria)

I was a junior member of the Wild Flower Society (p.496) as a child, and every year I kept a wild flower diary, recording the plants I found. I will always remember Agrimony because it was alphabetically the first plant on the printed list, so I wanted to tick it off quickly. I love it for its verticality, its tall, tapering spires of primrose yellow like those of a verbascum, but without the down, and finer. The ancient unimproved meadows near where I live in the Sussex Weald are thick with this plant, and it looks good from May, when the flower spikes first draw out in tight bud, until late autumn, when the stem has distributed its seeds and collapsed back down. The seed sets late, so Agrimony is vulnerable to grass-cutting in July and changes in traditional meadow management, with grass-cutting for silage done too early. The seed case is incredibly spiny, so it sticks to passing animals to be distributed. If you walk through a meadow full of Agrimony in late summer, these cling fast to your clothes like burs. The individual seed pods are highly distinctive – large and goblet-shaped, green washed with rust, with a grooved, castellated top.

Plant type Rose family, Rosaceae. *Flowers* June–September. *Height* Up to 60cm. *Description* Erect, hairy perennial herb. Leaves are pinnate and toothed, and have smaller leaflets between the main ones, of which the largest are up to 6cm long. Yellow flowers are 5–8mm across, in long spikes. *Companion species* Betony (opposite), Common Spotted-orchid (p.148), Musk-mallow (p.99) and Yellow-rattle (p.168). *Distribution* Native. Frequent or common throughout most of the British Isles, except northern Scotland and some parts of central Wales, where it is rare or absent. *Habitat* Field borders, hedge banks, woodland margins and rides, open grassland, roadsides, railway banks and waste places.

Autumn Hawkbit
(Scorzoneroides autumnalis)

This nectar-rich plant plays an important role in any meadow because it goes on flowering longer than most, providing an important source of food for insects late in the year. It is popular with bees and butterflies, but you will see hoverflies visiting the flowers most frequently. For this reason, it is a popular addition to wild-flower meadow seed mixes, giving colour to the grass right up to the first frosts of autumn. It also tolerates trampling and mowing and can therefore survive in a lawn. As soon as regular mowing stops, Autumn Hawkbit will flower as fast as Dandelions (p.246). It is also competitive in longer, coarser grass and adaptable to many habitats, so it occurs in every part of the British Isles.

Plant type Daisy family, Asteraceae. *Flowers* June–October. *Height* Up to 60cm. *Description* Erect, branched, almost hairless perennial herb. Leaves are deeply pinnately lobed and have forked hairs on the undersides. Flower heads are yellow. The ruff of bracts at the base of the flower head tapers gently to the stalk. Yellow-flowered, dandelion-like members of the daisy family can always be difficult to identify at first. However, this is one of the easiest, as it has a branched flower stem (often two to three times branched), almost hairless stems and leaves that are very deeply lobed. *Companion species* Bulbous Buttercup (p.144), Common Bird's-foot-trefoil (p.145), Common Sorrel (p.147), Creeping Buttercup (p.149), Hedge Bedstraw (p.202), Lady's Bedstraw (p.205) and Meadow Buttercup (p.158). *Distribution* Native. Very common. *Habitat* Most frequent on neutral or calcareous substrates in meadows, pastures, open scrub, heaths, moorland, salt marshes, fixed dunes and roadsides in the lowlands. It also occurs on scree, flushes and lake margins in the uplands.

Betony
(Stachys officinalis)

You can tell by its top and bottom lip and square stem that Betony is one of the dead-nettles, but it is by far the brightest, with intense magenta flowers standing well out from the clutch of calyces at the top of the stem. In other dead-nettles, the petals tend to nestle right in, being held more tightly by the calyces around them, but in Betony the flowers appear bold and proud. In the area around Perch Hill in the Sussex Weald on heavy clay, it thrives and forms large and splendid patches in ancient unimproved fields, often colonising the slightly better-drained edges of trackways, its magenta glow broken by the vertical yellow spires of Agrimony (opposite). Betony flowers for months, coming into bloom with Oxeye Daisy (p.159) and Selfheal (p.163) in early summer, still going strong with Agrimony well into autumn.

Plant type Dead-nettle family, Lamiaceae. *Flowers* June–September. *Height* 10–60cm. *Description* Sparsely hairy, erect perennial herb. Basal leaves are oblong, coarsely toothed, cordate and long-stalked, 3–7cm long. Stem leaves are similar but in pairs and stalkless near the top of the stem. Inflorescence is a short, oblong, whorled spike. Flowers have a calyx 7–9mm long with bristle-pointed teeth and a red-purple corolla, 15mm long. Occasional albinos have gleaming white flowers and Granny Smith-green foliage. *Companion species* Agrimony, Common Spotted-orchid (p.148), Devil's-bit Scabious (p.151), Heath Spotted-orchid (p.359), Rough Hawkbit (p.162) and Yellow-rattle (p.168). *Distribution* Native. Common throughout most of England and Wales except in East Anglia, where it is more locally distributed. It is rare in Scotland, mostly confined to the south; in Ireland, most colonies are in the south west, although there are also a few in central Ireland. *Habitat* Meadows, grassland, heaths, hedge banks, open woods and woodland rides and margins on damp and heavy ground (it is an ancient woodland indicator species). It occurs occasionally on cliff-top grassland in a dwarf form. It favours acid soils, but can also grow on neutral and mildly calcareous substrates.

Bitter-vetch
(Lathyrus linifolius)

Vetches provide some of the earliest splashes of strong colour in our lanes, hedge banks and meadow edges. While the purple Bush Vetch (p.69) seems to be ubiquitous and flower for longest, there are other more interesting and colourful varieties. Bitter-vetch has flowers that are a brilliant magenta when they first emerge, and vivid green leaves edged with crimson. It is showy in spring and can be big and bushy, so one might assume that it is a garden escape. In fact, it is native. Vetches are easy to confuse, but the colours of their flowers do not overlap much. This one could be mistaken for Grass Vetchling (p.200), which has similarly coloured flowers, but the latter has different leaves, like those of a grass. Bitter-vetch's foliage resembles that of linum, or flax – hence its Latin name, *linifolius*.

Plant type Pea family, Fabaceae. *Flowers* April–July. *Height* 15–40cm. *Description* Erect, hairless perennial. Leaves have two to four pairs of narrow, lanceolate, grey-green leaflets, each of which is 1–4cm long, and no tendrils. The lack of tendrils helps distinguish it from Bush Vetch. Flowers are in racemes of two to six; each flower is about 12mm long and crimson, later turning blue or green. *Companion species* Bracken (p.351), Bugle (p.68) and Greater Stitchwort (p.87). *Distribution* Native. Found throughout Britain and Ireland, most common in the north and west. Absent from a large area in central and eastern England (particularly East Anglia); absent or very rare in much of central-eastern Ireland. *Habitat* Moist, infertile, neutral and acidic soils in heathy meadows, lightly grazed pastures, grassy banks, wood banks and old sessile oak coppice cut for charcoal and tanbark in western Britain, as well as lane sides and open woodlands; also on stream banks and rock ledges in the uplands.

Bulbous Buttercup
(Ranunculus bulbosus)

From a distance, it is not easy to tell which buttercup is which – and often there is a mixture, with Meadow Buttercup (p.158) the commonest. One way to distinguish between them is to look at the sepals at the back of the flower. With Bulbous Buttercup, they are reflexed right back on to the stem, bent away from the petals. This species also flowers earlier, and the base of its stems is slightly bulbous. Bulbous Buttercup and the other two field buttercups (Creeping and Meadow, pp.149 and 158) are usually so abundant wherever they appear that you can pick great bunches of them in spring and early summer to bring inside. Sear the stem end in boiling water for thirty seconds to make the petals hold, and arrange in a bucket or large jug with the first of the Common Sorrel (p.147) with which it often grows.

Plant type Buttercup family, Ranunculaceae. *Flowers* March– June. *Height* 10–45cm. *Description* Hairy perennial herb. Leaves are three-lobed. Yellow flowers on grooved stalks have five petals. It can be easily distinguished from Creeping Buttercup and Meadow Buttercup by its reflexed sepals and the absence of runners. Meadow Buttercup also tends to be taller, with more finely divided leaves and ungrooved flower stalks. *Companion species* Common Sorrel, Creeping Buttercup, Fairy Flax (p.152), Meadow Buttercup and Common Milkwort (p.147). *Distribution* Native and very common throughout the British Isles, apart from in Scotland, where it is more localised and absent from many inland areas, especially in the west. *Habitat* This prefers drier grassland than the other meadow buttercups, and it is often found at the top of slopes on well-drained, neutral or calcareous soils in meadows, pastures and dunes. It is absent from highly productive, fertile grassland and from strongly acidic soils.

Cock's-foot
(Dactylis glomerata)

Cock's-foot is a whopper, a coarse-leaved grass, sometimes standing as high as my waist, that easily crowds out more delicate meadow wild flowers, such as milkworts, Fairy Flax (p.152) and Lady's Bedstraw (p.205). It is common and distinctive, with stiff, densely clustered flower spikes, which are big and fat on tall, wiry stems, looking and feeling more like a lump of thick, hairy fabric than a flower of a grass or grain. Its leaves are so sharp-edged that they can cut your fingers if you pick it. The flowers start a grey-green in late spring, gradually fading to pale straw as they get more covered in pollen. Its clusters of flower spikelets have a vague similarity to a chicken's foot – hence its common name. Despite its coarseness, Cock's-foot has been sown for centuries in hay meadows and pastures because it yields lots of quick-growing herbage, which cattle love and thrive on, at least until its leaves have grown very large and coarse.

Plant type Grass family, Poaceae. *Flowers* Late May–September. *Height* Up to 1.4m. *Description* Robust, almost hairless perennial herb. Leaves are stiff, keeled and rough, up to 1cm wide. Ligules are jagged, 2–10mm long. Inflorescence is 2–15cm long, erect and branched, with one or two lower branches diverging from the stem at 45 degrees and several more densely clustered upper branches. All branches have dense bunches of flattened green or purplish spikelets. Each spikelet is 5–7mm long. *Companion species* Agrimony (p.142), Betony (p.143), Pignut (p.161) and Rough Hawkbit (p.162). *Distribution* Native. It occurs throughout the British Isles and is very abundant in most regions except the far north of Scotland. *Habitat* Native. A common component of meadows, downland, roadsides, lawns, wasteland and rough ground on a wide range of fertile, neutral and basic soils.

Common Bird's-foot-trefoil
(Lotus corniculatus)

The yellow flowers and red buds are the giveaway of this plant – it is also known as Eggs and Bacon. It forms extensive carpets in meadows, roadsides and in grasslands above cliffs in places such as the Lizard in Cornwall. One of our commonest meadow wild flowers, it is the larval food plant of the Common Blue, Green Hairstreak and Dingy Skipper butterflies and a popular source of nectar. It is often grown by bee-keepers for this reason, providing a valuable food source for months at a stretch (particularly important in late summer, when pollen and nectar are more scarce). On dry, chalky downs and on the coast, it is often replaced – or growing beside – Horseshoe Vetch (p.204), and it is easy to get muddled between the two. Common Bird's-foot-trefoil has leaves with only five leaflets: a pair at the base of the leaf stem and a triplet further up. Horseshoe Vetch has many leaflets (four to five pairs). The flowers of Common Bird's-foot-trefoil also tend to be bigger. Horseshoe Vetch's branched seed pods are divided into miniature horseshoe shapes along their length, the segments breaking apart bit by bit when they ripen. By contrast, those of Common Bird's-foot-trefoil look like a bony bird's foot and, when ripe, they break apart and ping out all their seeds in one go.

Plant type Pea family, Fabaceae. *Flowers* May–September. *Height* 10–40cm. *Description* Low, creeping, hairless perennial herb. Flowers are deep yellow, often orange-tinged, red in bud, 15mm long, two to eight per head. Leaflets are oval. *Companion species* Dyer's Greenweed (p.152), Pignut (p.161), Red Clover (p.161) and Tufted Vetch (p.166). *Distribution* Native. Common everywhere in the British Isles. It is now often sown in wild-flower mixtures on roadside verges and naturalises further from there. *Habitat* It occupies a broad range of grasslands, including well-drained meadows, chalk and limestone downs, hill pastures and montane rock ledges. It also occurs on coastal cliff tops, shingle and sand dunes. It is absent only from the most acidic and infertile soils.

Common Eyebright
(Euphrasia nemorosa)

This perky little plant dots the grass with bright white, cheery flowers, creating a flower-studded tapestry alongside Common Milkwort (opposite), Fairy Flax (p.152) and Tormentil (p.371) where the soil is poor. If you have a close look at one of the flowers, you will see the deep purple ink lines that draw insects into the centre and the yellow heart where the style and anthers are held. A matching yellow splotch on the bottom lip must be there to attract pollinators and mark out their landing pad. Eyebrights are semi-parasitic herbs on grasses. Like Yellow-rattle (p.168), they weaken the grasses, making room for more wild flowers. Some are also semi-parasitic on legumes, such as clovers. There are twenty-one species (which may hybridise), and unless you are a specialist it is well-nigh impossible to distinguish between them. Common Eyebright is the most widespread.

Plant type Broomrape family, Orobanchaceae. *Flowers* July–August. *Height* 15–20cm. *Description* Short, erect, branched perennial herb. Leaves are oval, sharply toothed, 6–12mm long, arranged in opposite pairs, dark green, sometimes tinged purplish. Flowers are situated in leafy spikes and have white, two-lipped corollas, sometimes tinged with blue or lilac. The lower lip is longer than the upper, 5–8mm long. *Companion species* Autumn Hawkbit (p.143), Common Milkwort, Common Spotted-orchid (p.148), Fairy Flax, Heath Spotted-orchid (p.359), Rough Hawkbit (p.162) and Tormentil. *Distribution* Native. Widespread in Britain and Ireland, but largely confined to chalk and limestone districts and quite local outside those areas. It is most abundant on the chalk of southern England and in Cumbria and south Wales. *Habitat* Short grasslands, heaths, downs and dunes, open scrub, woodland rides and upland moorlands.

Common Knapweed
(Centaurea nigra)

Its showy relation Greater Knapweed (p.201) has bigger, fluffier, more eye-catching flowers, but Common Knapweed is one of the strongest-growing meadow plants we have. It can turn into a bit of a brute in a meadow that is not cut and managed, which is why cutting the hay in mid to late July is good management practice – at least in the southern half of the country – to keep the various species in balance. The wild-flower meadow expert Charles Flower describes how he fenced off an area of grass newly sown with wild-flower mix on his farm in Wiltshire. He cut and managed the fenced area, but left a small strip outside the fence unmanaged. After ten years, instead of the fifteen species of wild flower originally introduced, there were just three in the unmanaged area, including Common Knapweed. However, its high-quality nectar makes it a key food source for butterflies and bumblebees. Its petals are edible and may be used in salads.

Plant type Daisy family, Asteraceae. *Flowers* June–September. *Height* 15–60cm. *Description* Erect, hairy perennial herb. Leaves are usually unlobed, oblong to linear-lanceolate although sometimes pinnatifid. Lower leaves are stalked, upper leaves unstalked. Flower heads are solitary, 2–4cm across, and have red-purple florets. The base of the flower head is spherical and has bracts that have triangular, almost detached brown or black tips. *Companion species* Agrimony (p.142), Autumn Hawkbit (p.143), Betony (p.143), Burnet-saxifrage (p.192), Common Sorrel (p.147), Field Scabious (p.198), Rough Hawkbit (p.162) and Small Scabious (p.214). *Distribution* Native. Common throughout the British Isles. *Habitat* A wide range of grassland habitats, meadows and pastures, sea cliffs, roadsides, railway banks, scrub, woodland edges, field borders and waste ground.

Common Milkwort

(Polygala vulgaris)

The value of Common Milkwort in our landscape lies in the rarity of its blue among other wild flowers. It sings out, despite the flower's minute scale, speckling the greens, yellows, whites and pinks of the meadow tapestry. The colours of individual plants vary, with white, pink and pale blues appearing (it has one of the widest colour variations of any native wild flower), but it is the deep, rich, delphinium blue that creates such a perfect colour balance alongside other species. Common Milkwort is a reliable indicator of a good-quality habitat. Its generic name is derived from the Greek *poly*, meaning 'much', and *gala*, meaning 'milk'. This may derive from the belief that (given as a supplement) it increased nursing mothers' milk and is thought to have had the same effect on cattle grazing milkwort-rich pastures.

Plant type Milkwort family, Polygalaceae. *Flowers* May–September. *Height* Up to 30cm. *Description* Low, branching, spreading, almost hairless perennial herb, with woody-based stems. Leaves are oval to elliptical, all arranged alternately (no basal rosette) and becoming longer further up the stem. Flowers are 5–8mm long and have three very small outer sepals and two larger, lateral, inner sepals, which may be blue, white or pink. The three true petals are joined into a whitish-fringed tube. There are usually between ten and forty flowers per raceme. The fruit is a capsule, with the inner sepals persisting. This is the most common milkwort in the British Isles. *Companion species* Common Knapweed (p.146), Cowslip (p.195), Fairy Flax (p.152), Hoary Plantain (p.203), Salad Burnet (p.213) and Yellow-rattle (p.168). *Distribution* Native. Found throughout the British Isles. In the chalk and limestone districts of England it can be locally very abundant. It is more localised elsewhere and is absent from areas where the soils are unsuitable. *Habitat* Grassland habitats, preferring short, moderately infertile, neutral to basic soils. Typical locations include downland, sand dunes, crags and other hill slopes. It may also be found in acidic grasslands, heaths and fens.

Common Sorrel

(Rumex acetosa)

In combination with Meadow Buttercup (p.158), Common Sorrel makes our fields at Perch Hill glow with colour in May and June. The flowers of the two plants hover at about the same level, just above the grasses. When I look down across the slope of a field, the gold and rust are mixed together. For me, this is the moment when spring turns into summer. The Latin specific name *acetosa* is derived from the Latin word for vinegar, *acetum*, and the leaves do have a distinctly sharp and lemony taste. Both in the garden and in the wild, Sorrel is one of the first green plants to appear in spring, and it is an excellent addition to a leaf salad. If you find plenty of it, it is also excellent for sauces and soups, and you will do the plant no harm by picking its leaves. Remove the midrib and stem, then finely chop or purée the leaves with yoghurt for a cold sauce, or warmed double cream for a hot sauce, to serve with chicken or fish.

Plant type Knotweed family, Polygonaceae. *Flowers* May–June. *Height* 30–80cm. *Description* Variable, erect, short to tall, hairless, dioecious perennial herb. Leaves are arrow-shaped (the basal lobes pointing backwards), up to 10cm long, stalked near the base of the plant but stalkless and clasping the stem above. Stipules are brown. Inflorescence is much branched and has loose whorls of very small, reddish flowers. *Companion species* Bracken (p.351), Creeping Buttercup (p.149), Meadow Buttercup and Pignut (p.161). *Distribution* Native and very common throughout the British Isles. *Habitat* Neutral to slightly acidic soil in meadows, pastures, woodland rides and glades, mountain ledges and shingle beaches. Sorrel is deep-rooted and so able to resist herbicides, and is therefore persistent in sprayed, re-seeded hay meadows.

Common Spotted-orchid
(*Dactylorhiza fuchsii*)

The *Dactylorhiza* group of orchids is a botanical minefield, with several easily confused. The first stage of identification is to look at the leaves. If they are spotted, you are probably looking at Common Spotted-orchid, Early-purple Orchid (p.9) or Heath Spotted-orchid (p.359). Most Marsh-orchids, which look similar in the flower, do not have spots on the leaves. To distinguish between the three spotted species, look at the shape of the spots. If they are large and elongated, the plant is almost certainly Common Spotted-orchid; if they are round, it is Early-purple Orchid, which usually flowers earlier and has darker purple flowers. If the spots are small and randomly scattered on narrower leaves, it is probably Heath Spotted-orchid. Common Spotted- and Heath Spotted-orchids often hybridise, leading to more confusion.

Plant type Orchid family, Orchidaceae. *Flowers* May–July. *Height* Up to 70cm, usually 15–50cm. *Description* Hairless, erect perennial herb with lanceolate leaves, keeled, with longitudinal dark blotches. The spike typically has between twenty and seventy flowers, although up to 150 have been recorded. Flowers are white to pale pink with variable dark reddish markings. The lip is deeply three-lobed; the central lobe is narrower than the two side lobes and is at least as long or longer. Heath Spotted-orchid has a broader, less strongly three-lobed lip. *Companion species* Common Twayblade (p.148), Green-winged Orchid (p.154) and Pignut (p.161). *Distribution* Native. Common throughout Britain and Ireland but local in the far north of Scotland, much of Cornwall and south-west Ireland. This is our most widespread orchid. *Habitat* Neutral or base-rich soils in a wide range of habitats: meadows, deciduous woodland, scrub, roadsides, chalk grassland, marshes, dune slacks, fens and mildly acidic heaths.

Common Twayblade
(*Neottia ovata*)

It might be superficially dull, with green flowers tightly attached to a hairy brown stem, but look more closely at Common Twayblade and you will see that it is full of miniature laughing angels with their hands held above their tiny, bright yellow faces. The whole performance comes shooting up out of a pair of relatively huge, veined, hosta-like leaves. The plant can reproduce vegetatively, so it often grows in dense clusters, a patch of five or ten plants quite close together. It could be confused with Lesser Twayblade (*Neottia cordata*), but that is much smaller with reddish stems and flowers, and it grows in a different habitat (moorland, bogs and pine woodland). Other green-flowered orchids, such as Man Orchid (p.206) and Musk Orchid (p.207), have more plentiful, narrower leaves.

Plant type Orchid family, Orchidaceae. *Height* Up to 60cm. *Description* Erect perennial herb. At the base of the stem (or just above) is a single pair of large, oval-elliptical, strongly ribbed green leaves. There are only a few small, bract-like leaves above this. Flowers are small and yellow-green, arranged in a loose raceme, 7–25cm long. *Companion species* Adder's-tongue (p.142), Common Spotted-orchid (p.148), Goat's-beard (p.153) and Green-winged Orchid (p.154). *Distribution* Native. Found throughout the British Isles and quite common in much of southern England, but rare in the north of Scotland. *Habitat* It occupies a wide variety of habitats, usually woodland and slightly damp or shady grassland on quite a broad range of soils, from calcareous to mildly acidic. It also appears in scrub, sand dunes, dune slacks, limestone pavement and heathlands; in Anglesey and Ireland it also grows in fens. It frequently occurs on railway banks and in disused quarries and sandpits, sometimes in large colonies.

Creeping Cinquefoil
(Potentilla reptans)

This has flowers almost the size of a garden potentilla: big, open, golden-yellow saucers that look like ironed-flat buttercups. You can see each petal edge clearly, with the green calyx showing behind. Just like Wild Strawberry (p.120), to which it is related, it has a prominent yellow dome at the centre of the flower, mounded up with stamens and anthers. Superficially, the leaves and flowers look like a bigger version of another relative, Tormentil (p.371), but *P. reptans* has a creeping habit (hence its name), new stems sprawling out in all directions and rooting at the leaf nodes. As well as growing on grasslands and on track sides in meadows, this is quite common in mown grasslands, garden lawns and roadsides. There it may spread very quickly by its rooting runners and, like Creeping Buttercup (left), it can become an invasive weed.

Plant type Rose family, Rosaceae. *Flowers* June–September. *Height* Sprawls to 30–100cm. *Description* Creeping perennial herb with long trailing shoots. Leaves are palmate, long-stalked, divided into five to seven leaflets, each up to 3cm long, oblong and toothed. Yellow flowers are solitary with five petals (sometimes four or six). The smaller Tormentil is similar and may sometimes be found growing near by. However, it does not have stems that root at the nodes and has flowers with four petals. Trailing Tormentil (*P. anglica*) is even more similar. It has rooting stems, but the leaves are shorter-stalked than those of Creeping Cinquefoil and the flowers usually have only four petals (sometimes five). *Companion species* Germander Speedwell (p.85), Herb-Robert (p.91), Tormentil and Wood Sage (p.32). *Distribution* Native. Common throughout England, Wales and Ireland. In Scotland, it is confined to the lowlands in the south and is rare north of the Clyde and Firth of Forth, where scattered populations are not considered native. *Habitat* Meadows, grassland, hedgerows, banks and roadsides, woodland rides and waste and cultivated ground, generally on neutral to limey soils, but sometimes on mildly acidic soils.

Creeping Buttercup
(Ranunculus repens)

As a gardener or a farmer, you can easily come to hate Creeping Buttercup. It quickly colonises an unweeded corner, producing great numbers of runners from the original mother plant, reaching up to 50cm, each one rapidly rooting to form a colony of further offspring. In a damp meadow grazed by cattle, it rapidly takes over. Cattle and horses do not eat it. Protoanemonin in the sap gives the leaves a bitter taste, and it is probably poisonous. As the grass around it is removed by grazing, the buttercup has room to spread. Its quick-growing numbers make it a huge task to eradicate by hand, and ploughing only chops it up and spreads the runners further. However, this grazing farmer's *bête noire* is a good-looking invader. It may represent the opposite of botanical richness, but it can transform dull, horse-grazed meadows into fields of gold in May and June.

Plant type Buttercup family, Ranunculaceae. *Flowers* May–August. *Height* Up to 60cm (but usually shorter). *Description* Short to medium perennial herb, which produces rooting runners. Leaves are hairy and three-lobed, with the middle lobe having a longer stalk. All the leaves have light spots. Flowers are deep yellow, 20–30mm across, with spreading, not reflexed, sepals. Flower stalks are grooved. *Companion species* Thyme-leaved Speedwell (p.165) and White Clover (p.167). *Distribution* Native and extremely common throughout the British Isles. Like Meadow Buttercup (p.158), it occurs everywhere. *Habitat* It will grow almost anywhere, but is most typical of disturbed habitats on damp or wet nutrient-rich soils, including woodland rides (it is more common in woodland than either Bulbous or Meadow Buttercup), ditch sides, farm gateways, gardens and waste ground. It is also found as an arable weed on cultivated ground and occurs in damp or periodically flooded grasslands, in dune slacks and on lake shores.

Creeping Thistle

(Cirsium arvense)

When we bought the rather neglected farm at Perch Hill, every field was stuffed full of Creeping Thistle. This plant is every farmer's – and gardener's – nightmare. Its small purple flowers form copious amounts of seed, which waft about on late summer and autumn days like a snowstorm. It spreads by seed and from fragments of rhizome broken up by ploughing or other disturbance, and spreads rapidly by its creeping roots. Once it is more than a few inches tall, cattle and sheep eat round it and leave it to grow, allowing it to flower and set seed. If you continue to graze, mow or top it hard, little by little, year on year, it will decrease. Creeping Thistle is normally dioecious, with male and female florets on separate plants, but because it is so common, pollination is frequent. Despite it being a pest to us, a stand of flowering Creeping Thistle is an invaluable source of nectar for many insects, including butterflies.

Plant type Daisy family, Asteraceae. *Flowers* July–September. *Height* Up to 90cm. *Description* Creeping perennial herb. Stems are erect, often branched, furrowed but unwinged. Leaves are oblong-lanceolate, pinnatifid with spines on the wavy, toothed edges. The upper sides of the leaves are hairy, the undersides sometimes cottony. Lower leaves are stalked, while upper leaves clasp the stem. Flower heads are 1.5–2.5cm across, arranged in open clusters with mauve florets. *Companion species* Bulbous Buttercup (p.144), Common Sorrel (p.147), Creeping Buttercup (p.149) and Meadow Buttercup (p.158). *Distribution* Native. Ubiquitous throughout Britain and Ireland, absent only from a few 10km squares in north-west Scotland and western Ireland. *Habitat* Overgrazed pastures, hay meadows and rough grassy places, roadsides, arable fields and other cultivated land, as well as waste ground.

Crested Dog's-tail

(Cynosurus cristatus)

This is a delicate little grass: neat, pert and perfect. The flower spikes are distinctive, like a stiff, narrow bottlebrush crossed with an ear of corn, with the flowers and fluff on just one side of the stem, like the underside of a golden retriever's tail. Each tuft of the brush is separate, coming off the central stem at just less than a right angle; its one-sidedness looks odd, as if each flower spike has been sliced in two, but it gives the grass its elegance. Crested Dog's-tail is an important grass for insects – the larval food plant of the Essex Skipper, Small Skipper and Meadow Brown Butterflies – but it is not a particularly useful fodder grass, because it has rather fine, thin leaves, mostly at the base, so it does not produce much bulk. It is, however, suitable for sheep, which feed away happily on pastures thick with it. Crested Dog's-tail is also easy and quick to establish, so it is frequently used in seed mixtures for new lawns and pastures. Richard Mabey writes in *Flora Britannica* that it was used for making bonnets.

Plant type Grass family, Poaceae. *Flowers* June–August. *Height* 10–75cm. *Description* Tufted, erect, hairless perennial grass. Leaves are glossy green, 1–4mm wide, with straw-coloured sheaths. Ligules are short and truncate. Spike-like inflorescence is dense, stiff and one-sided, 3–5cm long. It has fertile and sterile spikelets. The sterile spikelets have narrow, fan-shaped florets with bristle-like lemmas and glumes, while the fertile spikelets have larger, broader lemmas and glumes. *Companion species* Common Bird's-foot-trefoil (p.145), Red Clover (p.161) and Tufted Vetch (p.166). *Distribution* Native. Common throughout the British Isles. *Habitat* A wide range of swards, especially short or heavily grazed calcareous or neutral grassland, both improved and semi-improved. It avoids waterlogged ground and is often found alongside footpaths.

Deptford Pink
(Dianthus armeria)

The ancestors of many of our cottage garden plants, members of the pink family are irresistible enough in a garden, but they are even more exciting to find in the wild. In the case of the Deptford Pink it is tempting to pick some, but this plant is now very rare, with as few as thirty sites in England (most in the south) and four in Wales. It now covers only 7 per cent of its historic range – we have lost more of this plant than almost any other. The causes of its decline are the same as that of many other wild flowers: conversion of grassland to arable; abandonment of traditional grassland management; overgrazing in some areas, undergrazing in others, resulting in the replacement of grassland with scrub and woodland. The use of herbicides and fertilisers has not helped, either, and many of its original sites have been lost to urban development. It is a classic victim of modernity.

Plant type Pink family, Caryophyllaceae. *Flowers* July–September. *Height* 30–60cm. *Description* Erect biennial herb with dark green leaves. Basal leaves are lanceolate; stem leaves are linear, keeled and pointed. Flowers, 8–13mm across, have five rose-red, fringed petals and are in dense clusters. Sepals are fused into a cylindrical tube. *Companion species* Common Knapweed (p.146), Crested Dog's-tail (opposite), Lady's Bedstraw (p.205) and Red Valerian (p.407). *Distribution* Probably native, although some people wonder if it is a long-standing alien – its largest populations are in Buckfastleigh in Devon, and it may have been a monastic introduction. It is classified as an endangered species. *Habitat* Open, disturbed grassland in pastures, field margins, woodland edges and waysides. Many sites today are along road verges and railway cuttings, particularly in Devon and Cornwall. It prefers dry, slightly limey soils, but has been recorded on acidic peat.

Devil's-bit Scabious
(Succisa pratensis)

I have great affection for this plant because it is all over the sweetest areas of grass on the west coast of Scotland, where I spent a lot of time during my childhood and still go now. There is always plenty of it in the dry sunny spots where you set up camp to have a picnic. It is a much bluer mauve than either Field Scabious (p.198) or Small Scabious (p.214) and, unlike them, it is almost fully spherical, the outside flowers reflexed right back onto the stem. Like other members of the teasel family, it is rich in pollen and nectar – it is the larval food plant of the Marsh Fritillary butterfly and the Narrow-bordered Bee Hawk-moth. Its name apparently stems from its abruptly shortened root: the Devil is said to have bitten it off in a rage at its ability to cure all ailments.

Plant type Teasel family, Dipsacaceae. *Flowers* June–October. *Height* Up to 70cm. *Description* Erect, perennial herb. Leaves are elliptical-lanceolate, undivided, more or less untoothed, sometimes blotched and slightly hairy. Flower heads are 1.5–2.5cm wide, lilac to dark violet-blue, the outer florets no larger than the inner. Both Small Scabious and Field Scabious have pinnate leaves and outer florets larger than inner florets. *Companion species* Bulbous Buttercup (p.144), Common Eyebright (p.146), Common Milkwort (p.147), Creeping Buttercup (p.149), Meadow Buttercup (p.158) and Sheep's Sorrel (p.366). *Distribution* Native and ubiquitous. It occurs throughout the British Isles and is common in localised areas, especially in northern and western Britain. It is scarce only in intensively farmed areas. *Habitat* Extraordinary range of moist to moderately free-draining habitats. It can be very plentiful on both acid heathland and chalk downland, although it favours mildly acidic soils. It occurs in upland meadows, in woodland rides, in mires and in uplands on cliff ledges and in ravines.

Dyer's Greenweed
(Genista tinctoria)

This is a wild flower with real resonance for me, as it was one of the first interesting plants we found when we arrived at Perch Hill seventeen years ago. The farm had been sprayed and reseeded, and most of the fields were not flower-rich. There is a field on the farm that overlies a spring and the topsoil had, one wet winter, slid off its subsoil down the hill. You can hardly walk there now without fear of twisting your ankle, but the field is reverting to the wild, with more flowers creeping in. Dyer's Greenweed is the star of that field, one of the few showy wild flowers specific to acid meadows and longer grasslands. Its common name refers to the yellow dye obtained from the flowering stems, which could be made green by mixing it with the blue dye from woad.

Plant type Pea family, Fabaceae. *Flowers* June–August. *Height* 20–50cm. *Description* Small deciduous shrub. Leaves are oval-lanceolate, pointed, with hairs only on the margins. Inflorescence is a long raceme of yellow five-petalled flowers, each of which may be up to 15mm long. Pods are hairless. Prostrate forms are found in Devon, Cornwall and Pembrokeshire. *Companion species* Agrimony (p.142), Betony (p.143), Oxeye Daisy (p.159) and Rough Hawkbit (p.162). *Distribution* Native. Quite frequent in parts of southern England, south Wales and the Welsh borders. It is more localised elsewhere and is rare in some places, such as Norfolk and north Wales. It is absent from Ireland and only just extends into southern Scotland. It was widely grown as a dye plant, and naturalised relics of cultivation have probably extended its distribution. *Habitat* Rough, lightly or ungrazed grassland on poorly drained soils. It occurs in rough pastures, old meadows, grassy heaths, cliffs, road verges and field edges on heavy soils, usually calcareous to slightly acidic clays.

Fairy Flax
(Linum catharticum)

You may not notice Fairy Flax in the grass of a meadow as you walk. It is so tiny – its white flowers smaller than the nail on my little finger – and its web of stems so delicate that it is easy to miss, but once you have been introduced to it, you will see it everywhere. It is the ubiquitous bottom storey of summer meadows on almost all types of soil, providing a white fuzz just a few centimetres off the ground. It is particularly noticeable where the grass is thin, in the presence of Yellow-rattle (p.168), which is parasitic on grasses and reduces their vigour, giving plants such as Fairy Flax more of a look-in. Fairy Flax is a marker of ancient, flower-rich, unimproved grasslands, so where you see it, you will often find other interesting things. The vernacular name probably originates from its small size; it is a miniature version of the common cultivated flax, which we have grown in this country for centuries.

Plant type Flax family, Linaceae. *Flowers* June–September. *Height* Up to 15cm. *Description* Slender, erect, low to short annual herb. Leaves are narrow, oblong, blunt, opposite. Inflorescence is narrow, lax and forked with white flowers, each of which is 4–6mm across. When in bud, the inflorescence nods. With its delicate, white flowers carried on slender, wire-like stems, this plant looks similar to Squinancywort (*Asperula cynanchica*), with which it often grows in calcareous grassland. However, the flowers of Squinancywort have only four petals, not five. *Companion species* Common Eyebright (p.146), Common Knapweed (p.146), Common Milkwort (p.147) and Yellow-rattle. *Distribution* Native. Common throughout most of Britain, although local in a few areas. *Habitat* Dry, infertile calcareous or limey substrates. It is also found in flushed sites on neutral or mildly acidic soils. It occurs in a wide range of calcareous grasslands, mires and flushes, in short-sedge fen meadows, on outcrops and ledges of basic rock, road cuttings, quarry spoil and lead-mine debris, and very locally on dry heaths.

Fritillary
(Fritillaria meleagris)

This is our most exotic flower, its chequered bells suggestive of the lanterns in a Bedouin's tent. They look like stained glass when the light is coming through them, each pale cell outlined by a darker frame. The combination of the heavy hanging head and thin leaves is elegant, balletic. Fritillaries push out of the ground with their buds held erect, bending over to flower before going erect again to seed. Presumably, being streamlined helps them push through the ground; they bend over when in flower to protect the pollen, becoming erect again to maximize seed dispersal. The reason these are now so rare is that, as bulbs, they can be destroyed by just one ploughing of a site where they may have been for centuries. You can spray a meadow with herbicides when the Fritillary bulbs are not in active growth and you will hardly touch them, but ploughing breaks the bulbs into smithereens.

Plant type Lily family, Liliaceae. *Flowers* April–May. *Height* 20–40cm. *Description* Erect hairless, perennial herb. Distinctive chequered pink or purple (occasionally white) flowers are usually solitary, drooping, 3–5cm across, with six perianth segments forming a parallel-sided cup. Leaves are few, alternate and linear. *Companion species* Cuckooflower (p.297), Dandelions (p.246) and Goat Willow (p.86). *Distribution* Rare, but locally scattered across Britain as far north as the Scottish Borders. There is a debate about whether or not it is native in Britain, with some key botanists stating that its late discovery as a wild plant shows that it is an introduction. Others consider it native to traditionally managed flood-plain meadows in south-central and eastern England. *Habitat* Damp, sometimes winter-flooded, neutral grasslands, usually those managed for hay with aftermath grazing. It is frequently planted in other grassland habitats.

Goat's-beard
(Tragopogon pratensis)

When writing a selective book, with only five hundred flowers included, it is necessary to exclude some plants. For me, the yellow daisies – hawkweeds and their lookalikes – were among the first to go. Many of them are similar, but it was a sad slice to lose, as this is one of the groups that my father specialised in. That is why I had to include a few of the best ones, such as Goat's-beard, named for its extraordinary seed heads, which look like dandelion clocks but are three times the size. It has heavy-headed flowers standing on top of tall, slightly wavery and unadorned stalks. They stay open only until midday, giving the plant another name, Johnny-go-to-bed-at-noon (or sometimes Jack-). Without the flowers it is difficult to spot in long grass. It has thin and scraggly edible roots, which taste slightly of parsnips.

Plant type Daisy family, Asteraceae. *Height* 30–100cm. *Description* Erect annual or short-lived perennial herb. Leaves are grey-green, linear-lanceolate, hairless, keeled lengthwise and sheathing at the base, 10–30cm long. Flowering heads are yellow, solitary, up to 5cm across, with eight or more equal green bracts. *Companion species* Adder's-tongue (p.142), Common Bird's-foot-trefoil (p.145), Common Twayblade (p.148), Green-Winged Orchid (p.154) and Yellow-rattle (p.168). *Distribution* Native. Common throughout most of England except the far south west, where it is local. In Wales, its distribution is largely coastal. In Scotland, it is mostly confined to the east coast and the lowlands. In Ireland, its distribution is scattered and localised. *Habitat* Tall grassland in meadows and pastures, on field margins, sand dunes, roadsides, railway banks and waste ground. It tolerates occasional mowing, but with the decline of traditional hay meadows it has become restricted to more disturbed habitats.

Great Burnet
(Sanguisorba officinalis)

Great Burnet is a tall, upright plant with flowers that look like the crunchy blue, sugar-coated variety of Liquorice Allsorts, except that these are not blue but a deep purple-claret, turning green below. The leaves are more showy than the flowers, bright green and always healthy-looking. They are collected in a series of leaflets arranged around a red-green stem, the edges serrated as if with crimping shears, the tip of each crimp lined with the finest pencil outline of crimson. This plant is often daubed with cuckoo spit, secreted by insects called froghoppers, whose nymphs live in the froth. The word burnet probably comes from the French *brunette* in reference to the red-brown colour of the flowers. The leaves – like those of its cousin Salad Burnet (p.213) – are edible, but rather bitter and too tough, in my view, to be a nice addition to a salad.

Plant type Rose family, Rosaceae. *Flowers* June–September. *Height* Up to 1m. *Description* Hairless perennial herb. Leaves are pinnate with three to seven pairs of oval, toothed leaflets that are green above, greyish beneath. Inflorescence is a dense, oblong flower head, 10–30mm long, with many tiny, dull crimson flowers. Each flower is bisexual, with both stamens and stigmas but no petals. Salad Burnet is much smaller, with round flower heads that are clearly divided into male or bisexual flowers below and female flowers above. *Companion species* Cowslip (p.195), Green-winged Orchid (right), Meadow Foxtail (p.158) and Meadowsweet (p.314). *Distribution* Native. Great Burnet has a peculiar, disjointed distribution. It is common throughout much of central and northern England, but absent from much of the south and east, apart from a few scattered outliers. It is common in south and central Wales, but rare in north Wales. It reaches only the southernmost part of Scotland and is very rare in Ireland. *Habitat* Neutral grassland, occurring on alluvial or peaty soils in damp or dry, unimproved pastures, hay meadows and marshy meadows, on river banks and lake shores and in base-enriched flushes on grassy heaths.

Green-winged Orchid
(Anacamptis morio)

The best time to see Green-winged Orchids is at first light on a clear morning, when every buttercup, every grass blade is glassy with dew, and spider's webs are highlighted and haloed around the orchids. Ten minutes from where I live is Marden Meadow in Kent, one of the best Green-winged Orchid sites in Britain. Sprinkled by the thousand between Common Bird's-foot-trefoil (p.145), Goat's-beard (p.153), Yellow-rattle (p.168) and the buds of Dyer's Greenweed (p.152), the orchid flowers are exotic and otherworldly. The field is turned magenta for most of May and into early June, so vivid that you might notice it as you whistle past on the London train. The stripes on its hood give it the alternative name of Green-veined Orchid.

Plant type Orchid family, Orchidaceae. *Flowers* Late April–June. *Height* 10–30cm. *Description* Glossy green elliptical-lanceolate leaves form a rosette and ascend the stem. Flowers are purplish (also rose-pink and white in large, strong colonies) and arranged in a spike. The lip is pinched, three-lobed and broader than long, with a paler pink, crimson-spotted patch in the centre. Sepals and upper petals form a purple hood with prominent green stripes. It is slightly shorter and more uniform than the other early spring-flowering orchid, Early-purple Orchid (p.9), which flowers first and has black-splotched leaves. *Companion species* Adder's-tongue (p.142), Common Twayblade (p.148), Cowslip (p.195), Early-purple Orchid and Goat's-beard. *Distribution* Native. Occurs throughout England, although it is rare or absent in much of the Midlands and northern England. There are scattered populations along the Welsh coast, in central and eastern Ireland and in south-west Scotland. Once common, it is now very local throughout its range. With increased ploughing and improvement of grassland, it has vanished from half of its historical range and in many counties it is reduced to a handful of sites. *Habitat* Damp to dry, base-rich to mildly acidic soils. It may also grow on sand dunes, heaths, roadsides, chalk and limestone downs, quarries, gravel pits and lawns. It is intolerant of shade and cannot survive in woodland.

Hogweed
(Heracleum sphondylium)

One of our most ubiquitous wild flowers, Hogweed appears in long, uncut grasslands in meadows and beside the road. Its creamy, flat umbellifer flowers are not exceptional in themselves, but because this has been such a huge beast in our countryside for so long, many of us have come to love it. The buds are lacy, washed all over with pink-crimson. The introduced Giant Hogweed (p.85) is twice the size, the tallest herb in Britain and Ireland. Its stems are red-spotted, and if you touch them on a hot sunny day, it can cause severe skin burns and blistering, so people try to eradicate it. The smaller native form (which has plain green stems) has much lower toxin levels and is not harmful to most people. Its flowers are hugely attractive to soldier beetles and on a sunny day there may be several on one flower head.

Plant type Carrot family, Apiaceae. *Flowers* June–September. *Height* Up to 2m. *Description* Biennial with leaves that are once pinnate, grey-green, 15–60cm long, with coarse, toothed leaflets. Umbels are 5–15cm across with many rays, no bracts and bristle-like bracteoles. Flowers are white or pinkish, 5–10mm across, the fruit flattened, oval. Umbellifers can be hard to tell apart. The species that occupies the most similar habitat is Cow Parsley (p.77), but this flowers earlier (April–June) and has oblong seeds and leaves that are two to three times pinnate. *Companion species* Bulbous Buttercup (p.144), Common Sorrel (p.147), Creeping Buttercup (p.149), Meadow Buttercup (p.158) and Red Clover (p.161). *Distribution* Native. Very common throughout the British Isles, becoming local in far north-west Scotland. *Habitat* Dry or moist, neutral to calcareous soils. It occurs in uncut meadows, rough and disturbed grassland, woodland rides, scrub, riverbanks, stabilised dunes, coastal cliffs and waste ground.

Lady's-mantle
(Alchemilla vulgaris agg.*)*

Their fluffy, feather-duster heads in brilliant acid green make Lady's-mantle a popular summer garden plant. Most of us grow the introduced *A. mollis*. This is slightly taller than our native form, but both have almost identical leaves, resembling fresh green lily pads designed to catch the dew or rain. They fold up slightly at night like an upside-down umbrella, catching the dew on their soft hairs, the tiny holes in the leaf surface allowing them gradually to absorb the water if needed. These hairs give them a wonderful texture – soft, downy yet distinctly silken – and you can imagine them making an incredible dress – hence the common name. In Yorkshire and Cumbria, this plant grows commonly beside the road in brilliant miniature wild gardens, mixed with other garden-worthy plants, such as Wood Crane's-bill (p.121), Water Avens (p.318) and Sweet Cicely (p.110). This Lady's-mantle is in fact a collection of microspecies differing only in the smallest characteristics.

Plant type Rose family, Rosaceae. *Flowers* June–September. *Height* 5–45cm. *Description* Spreading or erect herbs with palmately lobed, pleated leaves. Each microspecies may be distinguished by characteristics such as leaf shape, presence and type of hairs. The small, yellow-green flowers which are arranged in clusters (cymes) have four sepals, no petals and four epicalyx lobes, which are shorter than the sepals. The introduced *A. mollis* is bigger and has epicalyx lobes that are as long as the sepals. The much smaller Alpine Lady's-mantle (p.348) is confined to mainly mountainous areas of northern England, Scotland and Ireland. *Companion species* Sweet Cicely, Water Avens and Wood Crane's-bill. *Distribution* Native. Widespread throughout the British Isles, but local. Most of the Lady's-mantle microspecies are more frequent in (or confined to) north-western parts of the British Isles. *Habitat* Grassy banks, rough pasture, hay meadows and mountain flushes. Some microspecies prefer calcareous soils, while others prefer neutral or acidic soils.

Lesser Stitchwort
(Stellaria graminea)

This is the baby brother to Greater Stitchwort (p.87). With its stragglier plants, smaller flowers and almost grass-like leaves, it is generally more delicate and petite-looking than the lush Greater form. In fact, it looks like Common Chickweed (p.239), but with different leaves. Examined closely, its pretty stamens, which are each capped by an amber-coloured anther, stand out as high as the petals around them. Its five petals are fully divided into ten, and you can see the green calyx clearly behind. By contrast, Greater Stitchwort's petals are divided to less than halfway, so the calyx is fully hidden, with the overall effect being more white than green. Lesser Stitchwort tends to grow in rather different places from Greater Stitchwort, preferring old pastures and less disturbed ground. It is quite a common find in the unimproved meadows around us at Perch Hill, but I have also seen it thriving in lush riverside meadows in Hampshire. Its leaves are a much brighter, fresher green than those of both Greater and the similar-looking Marsh Stitchwort (*S. palustris*), and they are always smooth, not jagged-edged.

Plant type Pink family, Caryophyllaceae. *Flowers* May–June. *Height* 15–60cm. *Description* Perennial herb with leaves that are narrow-lanceolate, arranged in pairs, 1.5–4cm long. Unlike the leaves of Greater Stitchwort, they are smooth-edged and untoothed with no stipules. White flowers, 5–18mm across, are in forked cymes and usually have five sepals and five petals (although the latter are sometimes absent), and superior ovaries. *Companion species* Common Spotted-orchid (p.148), Greater Stitchwort and Pignut (p.161). *Distribution* Native. Occurs throughout the British Isles, but it has become less common as meadows have been re-sown and improved. *Habitat* A common plant of rough grassland, permanent pasture, grassy commons, woodland rides and clearings, roadsides and hedge banks on acid soils, which tend to be well drained.

Lesser Trefoil
(Trifolium dubium)

It is easy to get Lesser Trefoil, one of the yellow-bobble brigade, confused with other things. It is similar to Black Medick (p.64), but that is very downy and has pods that are spirally coiled and turn black when ripe, while Lesser Trefoil is almost hairless and has straight (not coiled) pods. The lime-green to yellow flowers have the shape of pompom dahlias, completely encircling the stem. The leaves are lightly veined, with a shallow or sometimes heart-shaped notch at the tips. It can also be muddled with Hop Trefoil (*T. campestre*), but the latter has larger flower heads (10–15mm across). Many Irishmen consider Lesser Trefoil to be the true shamrock, worn to bring good luck and protect against 'evil'. Various other plants also stake a claim to this, including White Clover (p.167), Black Medick and Wood-sorrel (p.33).

Plant type Pea family, Fabaceae. *Flowers* May–September. *Height* 20–50cm. *Description* Low, almost hairless annual. Leaves are trifoliate, with heart-shaped leaflets; the terminal leaflet has a stalk that is longer than the stalk of the other two leaflets. Flower heads are 5–7mm across, with usually less than 25 flowers per head. Flowers are yellow and 3–4mm long, becoming brown with age. *Companion species* Creeping Thistle (p.150), Dandelions (p.246) and Red Bartsia (p.256). *Distribution* Native. Common throughout Britain and Ireland, although local in the north of Scotland, apart from coastal areas. *Habitat* Hay meadows, waysides and waste places, and also frequent in lawns. It is most frequent in dry grasslands, but can be abundant, too, in winter-flooded meadows and damp pastures, and can thrive even in nutrient-enriched situations. It also occurs in open habitats, such as on rock outcrops, quarry spoil and railway ballast, as well as short, open grassland, such as lawns, road verges and along tracks, and occasionally in arable.

Meadow Buttercup

(Ranunculus acris)

As the tallest and most majestic of the three common buttercups, with a tendency to grow in meadows grazed by dairy cows, Meadow Buttercup almost certainly gives this family its name. The leaves and stalks have a bitter taste, which makes them unpalatable to grazing animals, but, unlike Creeping Buttercup (p.149), it is easily controlled by regular mowing. In Wensleydale and other Yorkshire Dales, these buttercups are part of the landscape. In late May, the drystone walls and scattered barns are interspersed with carpets of buttercup gold, each element integral to the traditional hay-meadow system. In the early months of the year, cattle are let out for an early bite on the drier fields. Then, in late spring, they are moved off the hay meadows to other pastures. The grass is cut for hay in July (the buttercups become more palatable when dry), after which the cattle return until it gets too cold and wet. They are moved into the barns, fed on hay, and their muck is spread onto the fields.

Plant type Buttercup family, Ranunculaceae. *Flowers* May–August. *Height* 20–100cm. *Description* Erect, medium to tall, hairy perennial. Stems are branched and leaves are deeply divided into three to seven wedge-shaped lobes, each of which is also deeply toothed. Flowers are bright yellow, 15–25mm across, with spreading (not reflexed) sepals, on ungrooved stalks. *Companion species* Bulbous Buttercup (p.144), Common Sorrel (p.147), Creeping Buttercup and Oxeye Daisy (opposite). *Distribution* Native and very common throughout the British Isles. *Habitat* Characteristic of unimproved hay and water meadow on a wide variety of soils, avoiding only very dry or acid conditions. It also grows on dune grassland, in montane flushes and in tall-herb communities on rock ledges.

Meadow Foxtail

(Alopecurus pratensis)

This grass flowers earlier than most, with flower spikes in a halo of smoky purple or yellow-orange pollen by the middle of April. Each is cylindrical, like a miniature bulrush, and this form, together with the ruddy colour of its anthers, gives the grass its name. Among the common grasses, only Sweet Vernal-grass (p.110) is out by the same time of year. The flower is similar to that of Timothy (p.166), but Meadow Foxtail tends to have a smaller flower head and makes a shorter plant, and it goes over just as Timothy is coming out. Meadow Foxtail also grows in damper grasslands. It is a larval food plant of the Small Skipper and Essex Skipper butterflies.

Plant type Grass family, Poaceae. *Flowers* April–June. *Height* 30–100cm. *Description* Tufted perennial. Leaves are flat with hairless blades, cylindrical sheaths and truncate ligules (1–2.5mm long). Inflorescence is a green- or purple-flushed dense, cylindrical panicle, 2–10cm long and 5–10mm wide. Spikelets are elliptical to oblong, 4–6mm long, one-flowered. Glumes are lanceolate, pointed and fringed with hairs on the keels. Lemma is oval, blunt and keeled with an awn projecting 3–5mm from the back. You can tell Meadow Foxtail apart from Timothy and cat's-tails only by looking closely at the flower's spike. The glumes of Meadow Foxtail are awnless, while the lemmas are awned. Timothy and cat's-tails have awned glumes but awnless lemmas. *Companion species* Cuckooflower (p.297), Meadow Vetchling (p.96) and Tufted Vetch (p.166). *Distribution* Native. Common throughout the British Isles except in north-west Scotland and the far west of Ireland, where it is more localised. *Habitat* A wide range of grasslands, particularly those with moist, fertile soils. It also occurs on roadsides and woodland margins. It avoids waterlogged habitats, and is absent from light and dry soils.

Oxeye Daisy
(Leucanthemum vulgare)

A widely recognised and much-loved wild flower, Oxeye Daisy is easy to grow and quick to self-sow, so it is a popular choice among people creating wild-flower meadows. As one of the first flowers to colonise unsprayed grassland, it is gradually making a return to verges, set-aside land and even lawns. It is so common that it is often called Dog Daisy, and the Latin name is pretty dismissive, too, meaning 'common white flower'. The edible flowers have a distinctive taste and smell, rather like chrysanthemums, which the Japanese use to flavour delicate jellies. You could do the same with Oxeye Daisies, or simply scatter a few petals over a salad or cold soup. They also make a delicious flower tempura.

Plant type Daisy family, Asteraceae. *Flowers* Late May–September. *Height* 20–70cm. *Description* Erect, short to tall, slightly hairy perennial herb. Basal leaves are dark green, oblong to spoon-shaped, toothed, on long stalks, in a rosette. Stem leaves are alternate, stalkless, oblong, deeply toothed and clasping the stem. White flowers are 2.5–6cm across. Flower heads have white ray florets centred round a yellow disc, like that of the common Daisy (p.246) but larger. It has a genetically dwarf variety (5–10cm tall), which occurs in exposed Atlantic locations, such as the west Lizard in Cornwall, and could be confused with a lawn daisy. Oxeye Daisy may also be confused with Shasta Daisy (*L.* x *superbum*), a garden hybrid found as an escape in disturbed ground and wasteland, which has larger flowers (6–10cm). *Companion species* Common Bird's-foot-trefoil (p.145), Meadow Buttercup (opposite) and Red Clover (p.161). *Distribution* Native. Very common throughout the British Isles, becoming local only in the Scottish Highlands. It is regularly sown in wild-flower mixes and naturalises easily from there. *Habitat* It is found in many grassy habitats, especially meadows and pastures that are cut or moderately grazed, preferring well-drained, neutral to base-rich soils. It also occurs on coastal cliffs, stabilised dunes, waste ground and by railways and newly sown roadsides.

Meadow Saxifrage
(Saxifraga granulata)

You may recognise Meadow Saxifrage from rockeries and gardens, where it has always been popular. Its close relative Londonpride is a classic plant for lining cottage garden paths. Meadow Saxifrage's white flowers are made up of five fully rounded petals, which dive at the centre into a deep, green-veined cup from which the golden yellow stamens stand out. Saxifrage means 'stone breaking', and the genus is named because many of its members have a habit of growing in rock crevices on hills and mountains. Not this one – Meadow Saxifrage loves a lusher existence, growing in meadows and lowlands. The bulbils that form at ground level, between the base of the stem and the stalked leaves, are worth a close look. They are the plant's means of reproduction, each one breaking off to form a new young plant.

Plant type Saxifrage family, Saxifragaceae. *Flowers* April–June. *Height* 10–50cm. *Description* Perennial herb. Kidney-shaped basal leaves are strongly jagged-edged, 2–3cm across, bluntly toothed, with scattered hairs and long stalks. Stem leaves are smaller, narrower and shorter-stalked. Flowers are white, 1–2cm across, in loosely branched clusters of two to twelve. Flower stalks are sticky-hairy. *Companion species* Common Bird's-foot-trefoil (p.145), Goat's-beard (p.153) and Oxeye Daisy (right). *Distribution* Native. Found throughout most of Britain but very local or rare in many areas. It is absent as a native from much of south-western England and is scarce in Kent. It is not found in most of the Scottish Highlands or Ireland. It is quite frequent in Norfolk and Suffolk, the Midlands, the Pennines and south-eastern Scotland. *Habitat* Moist but well-drained, often lightly grazed, base-rich and neutral grassland, unimproved pastures and hay meadows, and grassy banks. More rarely, it occurs on shaded riverbanks and in damp woodland. It is locally naturalised near houses and in churchyards.

Pepper-saxifrage
(Silaum silaus)

Pepper-saxifrage is an indicator of the sort of old, agriculturally unimproved, mildly acid or neutral pasture land that is almost a distant memory – more than 97 per cent of this habitat has been lost during the past fifty or so years. I notice this pretty umbellifer most in late summer beside the road and in the few old bits of pasture in the Sussex Weald, and I pick the odd sprig for wild-flower arrangements. In the field and in the vase, it makes an airy, lacy upper storey with taller grasses, such as Soft-brome (p.165) and Cock's-foot (p.145), overlaying carpets of richly coloured plants, such as Red Clover (p.161) and Betony (p.143). Its umbels of golden to yellow-green flowers resemble a smaller form of Fennel (p.81), and its delicate leaves are quite similar, but they are less highly cut and ferny, without the aniseed smell. The common name is misleading: it is not related to any flower in the saxifrage family; nor does it taste of pepper.

Plant type Carrot family, Apiaceae. *Flowers* June–August. *Height* 20–100cm. *Description* Slender, branched, erect perennial herb. Leaves are two to three times pinnate with linear, pointed leaflets, 1–5cm long. Umbels are 2–6cm wide and have five to ten rays without bracts and linear bracteoles. Fruit is oval and shiny brown-purple. Sulphur-yellow flowers are 1.5mm across. *Companion species* Betony, Cock's-foot, Red Clover and Soft-brome. *Distribution* Native. Quite frequent in much of southern, central and eastern England but localised in north-west England and absent from Ireland, much of Wales and far south-west England. There are scattered populations in south-east Scotland. *Habitat* Damp, unimproved neutral grassland, usually on clay soils. Habitats include hay and water meadows, species-rich pastures, roadsides, chalk downs, railway banks and vegetated shingle.

Perennial Rye-grass
(Lolium perenne)

This is an extremely pert and upright grass with vertical green stems and small, flat, bead-like flower heads (spikelets) arranged alternately up the top section of the stem. As well as being a wild native grass, it has been cultivated since at least the seventeenth century for hay and grazing – it is one of our most nutritious native grasses. It now dominates much of the countryside and, particularly when fed with nitrogen, it outdoes weaker-growing grasses, such as Sheep's-fescue (p.213), and more interesting wild flowers. Perennial Rye-grass is added to lawn seed mixtures because its glossy, bright green leaves give the lawn an emerald sheen.

Plant type Grass family, Poaceae. *Flowers* Late May–September. *Height* 25–90cm. *Description* Loosely tufted perennial grass. Leaves are 2–6mm wide with a prominent midrib. Inflorescence is 4–30cm long, with spikelets alternating up the stem in two opposite rows. Spikelets are stalkless, 7–20mm long, flattened, with their narrow sides facing the stem. Lemmas are awnless. Italian Rye-grass (*L. multiflorum*) is similar, but it has lemmas with long awns and broader leaves. *Companion species* Daisy (p.246), Dandelions (p.246), Red Clover (opposite), Soft-brome (p.165), White Clover (p.167) and Yorkshire-fog (p.169). *Distribution* Native. Very common throughout the British Isles, becoming more localised in far north-west Scotland. There are many cultivated strains. *Habitat* Usually a plant of improved grassland, widely sown in amenity grassland and new arable pasture fields (because it is cheap and tolerant of heavy tramping) and hay meadows. It is found widely in other habitats, including downland, rush pasture, inundated grasslands and road verges. It favours fertile, heavy, neutral soils, but it is also found on mildly acidic soils.

Pignut
(Conopodium majus)

Hundreds or thousands of Pignut plants growing together can look marvellous, forming a light white fog about a foot off the ground across a field. There is a traditionally managed hay meadow in our valley at Perch Hill, which has never been sprayed or ploughed, where Pignut creates a carpet interrupted only by the shade of the odd hawthorn tree. This is a classic species of acid grazed pasture, where it often grows under Bracken (p.351); it is a common sight mixed up with buttercups in the Yorkshire Dales. Its common name comes from its tubers. Pigs were trained to rootle them out for human consumption – they taste a bit like hazelnuts. There is not a high return for your labours, but you can forage the odd one to add to a salad or taste on a walk. Follow the main stalk down into the soil and then dig out the root with a sharp stick or garden fork. The bigger the plant, the bigger the pignut.

Plant type Carrot family, Apiaceae. *Flowers* May–June. *Height* 30–50cm. *Description* Erect, almost hairless perennial herb. Small white flowers (1–3mm across) are arranged in an umbel, 3–7cm across, with six to twelve rays. Bracts are absent or few (one or two). Leaves are two to three times pinnate and deeply cut. *Companion species* Bulbous Buttercup (p.144), Common Bird's-foot-trefoil (p.145), Meadow Buttercup (p.158) and, creeping out from the wood, Bluebell (p.2) and Bracken. *Distribution* Native. Common throughout the British Isles. It is absent only from the areas surrounding the Wash. It has declined locally because of the loss or improvement of its grassland habitats. *Habitat* Fairly dry acid pasture, often in areas of high rainfall, or shaded meadows and pastures, hedgerows, roadside verges, copses and woodlands. It grows on a wide range of acidic and base-rich soils.

Red Clover
(Trifolium pratense)

One of our most widespread and common species, Red Clover (which is, in fact, pink or reddish purple) is also an important food plant for many insects. Its flowers are rich in pollen and nectar, essential for honey- and bumblebees – it has in the past been known as 'bee bread'. It flowers long and hard, first blooming early in May and continuing until the later parts of summer and autumn, when there are fewer flowers around for insects to forage. Like all leguminous plants, Red Clover fixes nitrogen from the air via tiny bacteria-rich nodules all over its roots. These turn nitrogen into salts, which plants can then absorb. Zigzag Clover (*T. medium*) is similar to Red Clover, and quite commonly found alongside it. You can tell them apart by Zigzag's narrower, dark green leaflets, which have a very faint white spot (Red Clover's are usually clearly marked with a pale V). The robust Red Clover sown as a fodder crop is not usually the native wild flower but a different, agriculturally selected variety, *T. pratense* var. *sativum*. Both this and the wild form are invaluable food crops for cattle: the phrase 'living in clover' almost certainly originates from the contentment of cows grazing a field thick with this plant.

Plant type Pea family, Fabaceae. *Flowers* May–September. *Height* 10–40cm. *Description* Very variable, hairy perennial herb. Trifoliate leaves have grey-green, oval to elliptical leaflets, often with a characteristic V mark. Stipules are triangular, brown and purple-veined, while the flower heads are globose, 30mm long, often paired and more or less stalkless, with a pair of leaves below. Individual flowers are pink to reddish purple, 12–18mm long. *Companion species* Common Bird's-foot-trefoil (p.145), Red Bartsia (p.256), Tufted Vetch (p.166) and Yellow-rattle (p.168). *Distribution* Native and common throughout the British Isles. *Habitat* It grows in a wide range of grasslands: pastures, meadows, rough grassland, roadside verges and cultivated ground. It is also an important species in sown nectar mixes for honeybees and other pollinating insects.

Ribwort Plantain

(Plantago lanceolata)

The flowers and seed heads of Ribwort Plantain, striking your boot as you stride along through a meadow, make an incredibly satisfying noise. They sound like a little drummer, drumming a tattoo as you walk. The flowers start as dark, bristled torpedoes and gradually transform into dried turd-like cigars, like deer droppings, with a frizz of white stamens haloing the top. The leaves are handsome: bold, upright and strongly ribbed. When there are lots of these colonising an old hay meadow, they are as important as grasses in forming the backdrop to the flowers. It can be mistaken for Greater Plantain (*P. major*), which has longer-stalked, much rounder, oval to elliptical leaves and a longer, yellow-green inflorescence. Hoary Plantain (p.203) is also similar, but it tends to grow more in calcareous grassland and has pretty, pink-haloed flowers and greyish, downy, diamond-shaped leaves.

Plant type Plantain family, Plantaginaceae. *Flowers* May–August. *Height* 10–40cm. *Description* Rosette-forming perennial herb, with flower stems above the leaves. Leaves are all basal, lanceolate, untoothed, either spreading or erect, with three to five strong parallel veins. Flower stalk is deeply furrowed and silky, terminating in an oblong inflorescence of many tiny flowers, each with a green calyx, brownish corolla and long, white protruding stamens. *Companion species* Chalk Milkwort (p.194), Common Eyebright (p.146), Common Milkwort (p.147), Fairy Flax (p.152) and Yellow-rattle (p.168). *Distribution* Native and very common throughout the British Isles. *Habitat* Grassland, on all soils except strongly acid. It occurs in meadows and pastures, in upland grasslands, on rock ledges and crevices, sand dunes and cliffs (including sites subject to sea spray), roadsides and riverbanks, in cultivated and waste ground and on walls.

Rough Hawkbit

(Leontodon hispidus)

Some might say that Rough Hawkbit is a dull, dandelion-like plant with little to commend it, but that would be rather harsh. In the unimproved, heavy Wealden clay meadows surrounding Perch Hill, this is one of the flowers that provide colour for longest, splotching the lower levels of grass all over with tiny daubs of intense gold, like an early twentieth-century painter's idea of what a flower meadow should look like. As with all members of the daisy family, what appear to be petals are in fact individual florets, and these each form their own miniature seed head, all of them collected together into a dandelion-like clock. The seeds are among the easiest to collect, and they germinate easily, so you can introduce this plant successfully into a wild corner of your garden.

Plant type Daisy family, Asteraceae. *Flowers* June–September. *Height* Up to 60cm. *Description* Hairy perennial herb. Leaves are very hairy, lanceolate and wavy toothed, narrowed to the base and all in a basal rosette. Inflorescence stem is leafless, unbranched and equally hairy. Flower heads are 2.5–4cm across with golden yellow florets far longer than the bracts. Hawkbits resemble cat's-ears, such as Spotted Cat's-ear (p.419), because they both have yellow flowers, basal leaf rosettes, leafless inflorescence stems and feathered seeds. Cat's-ears differ in having lots of tiny, narrow, papery, scale-like bracts on the receptacle below the florets, whereas hawkbits do not. *Companion species* Agrimony (p.142), Betony (p.143), Heath Spotted-orchid (p.359) and Yellow-rattle (p.168). *Distribution* Common throughout the British Isles except in Scotland, where it occurs only in the south. It is also extremely rare in much of Cornwall. *Habitat* Dry, neutral or acidic soils, occurring in hay meadows, pastures and other grasslands, on roadside verges, railway banks and rock ledges, and in quarries.

Selfheal
(Prunella vulgaris)

Selfheal makes me think of a merry-go-round in miniature, the whorl of purple flowers like the horses hanging out from the centre as they turn. The whole thing is tiny, the flower spike usually standing less than 15cm tall. Its bright purple, velvet flowers look good and fresh in the grass for at least four months, and wild pollinators love it: bees, hoverflies and butterflies. It looks like a smaller, more trailing form of Bugle (p.68), and the two often grow together, so many people confuse them. Selfheal grows in sunnier spots than Bugle, which tends to thrive on woodland edges in part shade. As its name suggests, Selfheal was once an important therapeutic plant. Its leaves were pulverised and mixed with wood ash to make poultices to dress skin wounds, and a syrup made with the flowers and leaves was thought to cure inflammation of the throat and tonsils. Together with White Clover (p.167), it is one of the first wild flowers to creep into areas of rough grass left unmown in a garden.

Plant type Dead-nettle family, Lamiaceae. *Flowers* June–October. *Height* Up to 20cm. *Description* Sparsely downy, erect perennial herb, which is often short-lived, behaving like an annual. Leaves are oval, untoothed, short-stalked, dull green in colour. It produces creeping runners. Flower stems have a dense, oblong-shaped inflorescence with very hairy bracts. Each flower is a two-lipped corolla, 10–14mm long, which is usually violet but occasionally white or pink. *Companion species* Bugle, Creeping Buttercup (p.149), Pignut (p.161) and Silverweed (p.418). *Distribution* Native. Very common throughout Britain and Ireland. *Habitat* Neutral and calcareous grassland, growing in wood clearings, meadows, pastures, lawns, roadsides and waste ground. It is typically associated with moist, fertile soils.

Sneezewort
(Achillea ptarmica)

At a glance, you might think this was the ubiquitous Yarrow (p.167), which grows on almost every lane and roadside in summer and autumn. It is closely related, but Sneezewort has larger individual flowers, each with a distinctive eye at its centre, a flat grey-and-yellow domed disc typical of the daisy family, around which all the petals are arranged. Its leaves are also different: dark glossy green, linear-lanceolate (rather like a carnation leaf) and strongly saw-edged. Sneezewort has declined significantly during the twentieth century, with losses increasing more recently as a result of land drainage and habitat destruction. You will still see it in old, unimproved meadows and areas of grassland that have not been sprayed, particularly those that are more acidic and peaty, but it is now a rare find. Its name stems from its once-widespread use as a tincture (made from the leaves) to fight coughs and colds.

Plant type Daisy family, Asteraceae. *Flowers* July–August. *Height* 20–60cm. *Description* Tufted perennial herb. Leaves are linear-lanceolate, 1.5–6cm long, hairless but finely and sharply toothed. Flower heads usually have five white ray florets and many greenish-white disc florets and measure 12–18mm across. *Companion species* Betony (p.143), Common Marsh-bedstraw (p.295), Devil's-bit Scabious (p.151), Early Marsh-orchid (p.298), Heath Spotted-orchid (p.359), Northern Marsh-orchid (p.315) and Tormentil (p.371). *Distribution* Native. Found throughout Britain but frequent only in the north and west, quite rare in chalky and intensely farmed areas. *Habitat* A wide range of soils, tending to be damp, including fen and water meadows, rush pasture, marshes, stream sides, wet heath, springs and flushes on hill slopes and occasionally wet woodland.

Soft-brome
(Bromus hordeaceus)

This looks more like a grain than a grass, with prominent whiskers forming a halo enclosing the whole flower spike. That is the origin of its genus name: brome is the English version of the Greek word *bromos*, meaning 'oats'. Each spikelet is beautiful, divided clearly into eight or ten different florets – upright, elliptical dew drops, quite tightly packed and curving off the stem – and the whole flowering spike often shines like a beacon among other grasses, remaining bright green and fresh as the rest begin to turn. It is variable in height, sometimes making only a few inches on very poor ground, or forming a flower spike nearly a metre tall if the soil is good. There are several subspecies in Britain, of which ssp. *ferronii* and ssp. *thominei* are small plants characteristic of dry, coastal habitats, such as dunes and cliff tops.

Plant type Grass family, Poaceae. *Flowers* June–August. *Height* 5–80cm. *Description* Annual grass. Leaves are flat, softly hairy, 2–7mm wide. Ligules are blunt, toothed, 2.5mm long. Inflorescence is an erect panicle, 5–10cm long, with many round, conical, stalked spikelets, 12–25cm long. Spikelets are usually quite soft and hairy, although sometimes hairless. *Companion species* Perennial Rye-grass (p.160), Red Clover (p.161), Spring Squill (p.420), White Clover (p.167) and Yorkshire-fog (p.169). *Distribution* Native. Common throughout England, Wales and southern Scotland but more local in the Highlands, where it is more coastal in its distribution. It is common in the east of Ireland but more localised in the west. *Habitat* Moderately fertile neutral soils, particularly favouring disturbed or open habitats. It occurs in pastures and hay meadows and on coastal cliffs; it is also introduced as an impurity in grass seed to arable fields, track sides and waste ground. It does not form a persistent seed bank and is intolerant of heavy grazing or frequent mowing. It tends to avoid wet or very acidic sites.

form upright flower spikes, with up to thirty flowers on each spike. It also grows in traditional hay meadows, alongside other pretty and delicate plants, such as eyebrights and Sheep's Sorrel (p.366). It is equally at home on high mountains, where it forms much more prostrate, creeping patches, hunkered down against the weather.

Plant type Speedwell family, Veronicaceae. *Flowers* March–October. *Height* 10–15cm. *Description* Creeping perennial herb with stems up to 30cm long, rooting at the nodes. Leaves are simple, elliptical, untoothed, hairless, 1–1.5cm long. Flowers have white or pale blue corollas with dark blue lines, 5–6mm across. They are arranged in erect, terminal, many-flowered racemes with bracts longer than the flower stalks. *Companion species* Common Eyebright (p.146) and Sheep's Sorrel. *Distribution* Native and very common throughout Britain and Ireland, although slightly less frequent in the west of Ireland. *Habitat* It will grow on a wide variety of soils, but prefers slightly acid soil and damp ground, including acid grasslands and moorlands, woodland rides, heaths, flushes, damp rock ledges, cultivated land, lawns, waste ground and damp paths.

Thyme-leaved Speedwell
(Veronica serpyllifolia)

You have to get down on hands and knees to appreciate this plant, but this is worth doing to see its beautiful, ice-blue flowers with strong flares of blue-purple splaying out from a bright green heart. The flowers are paler and subtler than those of its relative Germander Speedwell (p.85), and its leaves are much smaller, too. They do not look like the leaves of a speedwell at all, but are delicate and thin, scattered up the stem like thyme – hence the common name. This is a very variable plant, whose appearance varies according to where you find it. It is often found growing in very compacted soil at the edge of the entrance to a field, or in a bitten-to-the-ground horse paddock, and it can form carpets beneath Creeping Buttercup (p.149). You may see it growing as a weed on the lawn and in the garden, where it tends to

Timothy
(Phleum pratense)

One of our commoner grasses, Timothy looks like a miniature bulrush. Its shape does not change through the summer, but when in full flower it is covered in pollen. Even when browned and going over, it retains the cat's-tail or bulrush shape. It is a fine-leaved grass that cannot compete with more vigorous grasses, such as Cock's-foot (p.145) or Perennial Rye-grass (p.160). When fields containing Timothy are given over to permanent pasture rather than being allowed to grow on to hay every couple of years, it tends to disappear. Historically it has also been sown, chiefly for hay. It is quite hard and coarse while growing, little relished by cows, horses or sheep, but when made into hay just as its seeds are ripening, it is nutritious. It is named after an American farmer called Timothy Hanson, who introduced its seed to the eastern seaboard of America around 1720. Previously an unregarded weed of water meadows and low-lying grasslands, it became an important source of hay for British farmers.

Plant type Grass family, Poaceae. *Flowers* June–August. *Height* Up to 1.5m. *Description* Tufted, hairless perennial herb. Leaves are flat and ligules blunt. Inflorescence is cylindrical and up to 15cm long. Although the inflorescence is dense and spike-like in appearance, it is actually a branched collection of many stemmed flowers, or spikelets, each 2–3mm long. *Companion species* Bulbous Buttercup (p.144), Common Bird's-foot-trefoil (p.145), Common Sorrel (p.147), Creeping Buttercup (p.149), Lesser Stitchwort (p.157) and Meadow Buttercup (p.158). *Distribution* Native. Very common throughout the British Isles, becoming local or rare only in the Scottish Highlands and parts of the northern Pennines, Suffolk and western and southern Ireland. *Habitat* Grasslands of all kinds. It is particularly fond of heavy soil.

Tufted Vetch
(Vicia cracca)

A favourite of mine, this summer wild flower is quietly pretty, creating lovely shapes and mixtures of colours. Farmers love it, too, as it grows quickly and provides plentiful and nutritious fodder. It often grows with plants such as Meadow Buttercup (p.158), Meadow Vetchling (p.96) and bedstraws, its purple pea flowers, ageing to blue, adding bright dashes of colour to the meadow carpet. I love the way that it mounds up like surf on a beach, one great arm of a plant folding itself up and over other things so that you get great heaps of it. The leaves are fine, too, each one made up of many canoe-shaped leaflets, the midrib ending in a curly, clinging spring, which allows the plant to crawl and clamber all over its neighbours without choking them, making beautiful, ready-made arrangements. I often think I would love to cut one of these combinations with the single swipe of a sickle and put it in a vase.

Plant type Pea family, Fabaceae. *Flowers* June–August. *Height* 20–200cm. *Description* Downy, climbing perennial herb. Leaves consist of eight to thirteen pairs of leaflets terminating in a branched tendril. Each leaflet is oval-lanceolate, typically 10–25mm long. Flowers are 8–12mm long and arranged in dense racemes of ten to forty flowers. Seed pods are 10–25cm long, with two to six seeds. Tufted Vetch is easy to recognise because no other native legume has such long, dense racemes of purple flowers. *Companion species* Common Bird's-foot-trefoil (p.145), Hedge Bedstraw (p.202), Lady's Bedstraw (p.205), Meadow Buttercup and Meadow Vetchling. *Distribution* Native. Very common throughout the British Isles, becoming scarce only in the Scottish Highlands. *Habitat* Hedgerows, waysides, wood borders, scrubby grassland and river and canal banks. It also occurs in permanent pastures and hay meadows, arable field edges, marshes and tall-herb fens, but avoids permanently wet sites.

White Clover
(Trifolium repens)

White Clover is one of the wild flowers richest in pollen and nectar, hugely important for insects. Almost all of us have this ubiquitous plant in our lawns, but we rarely leave the mowing long enough for it to flower. If we moved from a weekly to a fortnightly regime, or even better a three-weekly one – at least in parts of our gardens – we would increase significantly the amount of food available to declining honeybee pollinators. Just sit and watch a patch of White Clover for a few minutes and you will see what I mean. As soon as the sun comes out it will be teeming with insect life. White Clover fixes nitrogen from the air, providing natural fertilisation for the soil, and it roots at its leaf nodes, so grows quickly and lushly. The only downside to this is that the grasses are kept so well fed by the clover that they can out-compete interesting plants.

Plant type Pea family, Fabaceae. *Flowers* June–September. *Height* It grows out to 50cm. *Description* Low, creeping and rooting perennial herb. Leaves are more or less hairless, trifoliate and long-stalked. Leaflets are elliptical to oval with a white spot and translucent veins. Flower heads are globular, also on long stalks rising from the leaf axils. Individual flowers are white, sometimes tinged with pink, 7–10mm long. Calyx teeth are about half the length of the tube. *Companion species* Common Bird's-foot-trefoil (p.145), Lesser Trefoil (p.157) and Red Clover (p.161). *Distribution* Native. Very common throughout the British Isles and found almost everywhere. *Habitat* Grasslands on all but the wettest or most acidic soils and waste ground. It is very tolerant of grazing, mowing and trampling and can adapt to a wide range of habitats, although it is often scarce or absent in taller grassland. It is widely sown as a component of short- and medium-term leys, and on roadsides. Many commercial cultivars are available.

Yarrow
(Achillea millefolium)

In summer, when there is so much else in flower, this ubiquitous plant can be easy to ignore. But in the autumn, when many wild flowers have gone over and the lane sides and pastures are draining of colour, Yarrow comes into its own. Its flowery, flat plateaux stand out, providing the odd splotch of grey-white. One of the reasons that Yarrow is so successful is that it can withstand herbicides. It has a very deep root system, which enables it to survive and compete with grass growth. Yarrow also has the ability to send out runners, so it can make new plants from small fragments of its rhizomes. Pink and rich red forms sometimes occur in the wild, and these have been widely used in the breeding of many handsome coloured forms for the garden.

Plant type Daisy family, Asteraceae. *Flowers* June–October. *Height* 8–40cm. *Description* Very variable, patch-forming, downy perennial herb. Leaves are feather-like – lanceolate in outline but divided (two to three times pinnate) into linear segments. Lower leaves are stalked, upper leaves are stalkless. Flower heads are 4–6mm across, white (occasionally pink), arranged in dense, umbel-like corymbs. The whole flower head may, at first glance, superficially resemble that of an umbellifer, but the individual flower heads are distinctly daisy-like. *Companion species* Common Toadflax (p.74), Red Clover (p.161), Tufted Vetch (opposite) and Yorkshire-fog (p.169). *Distribution* Native. It is very common throughout Britain and Ireland. *Habitat* It is found in grassland habitats, ranging from lawns to mountains and heathlands, as well as on coastal sand dunes and stabilised shingle, waysides and waste ground. It tolerates drought and grows in most soils except the most nutrient-poor, permanently waterlogged or strongly acidic.

Yellow-rattle
(Rhinanthus minor)

This is one of our most important meadow wild flowers, because it creates an environment in which other wild flowers will thrive. It is a common denominator among many of our most flower-rich places, occurring in a variety of habitats. You may not at first spot it amid the variety that surrounds it, but it is a key to the other flowers' success. It is a hemiparasite, which fixes its roots onto the root system of any adjacent grass and extracts the water and minerals it needs. This weakens the grass and hence the main competition, allowing more delicate and often more colourful and interesting wild flowers to do well.

Charles Flower, the wild-flower meadow restoration expert, describes this decrease in grass strength and the resulting decline in productivity in his book *Where Have All The Flowers Gone?* He cites a small meadow on his farm in Wiltshire, which used to produce 240 bales of hay. When the Yellow-rattle was fully established within a few years of its introduction, the harvest was reduced to ninety bales, a reduction of more than 60 per cent. It is easy to see why farmers would have considered it a pest, since it robbed them of precious grass to feed their animals in winter. Many were keen to get rid of it as soon as herbicides became available, often without realising the detrimental effect that this would have on the wild flowers in their fields.

In fact, it is easy to get rid of Yellow-rattle without resorting to chemicals. It can be prevented from setting seed – and so being an annual, from perpetuating itself – by allowing cattle to graze the field. They love Yellow-rattle: as soon as they are let in, it is the first thing they eat.

Related to Lousewort (p.308), Yellow-rattle has yellow flowers with a top and bottom lip and two small, deep purple teeth on the upper lip. Once the flowers begin to age, the calyx behind them swells into a silver sphere – the rattle – in which the seeds gradually ripen. In my part of the world, it is known as Yellow Bollocks or Rattle Bollocks, and you can see why. As the rattle dries, it opens, and as it shakes in the wind, the seeds are dispersed.

This wild-flower-lover's friend is versatile and easy to grow, thriving on heavy clay, acid soils or thin limey chalk. It should be sown in late summer or early autumn, when the seed is fresh but the soil is still warm. Stored seed does not germinate as well, which is why buying seed is expensive, but once you have established a few plants of your own, they are prolific and you can reap your own seed. If possible, open up the sward to allow the seed to make contact with bare earth. On a small scale in a garden this could be achieved by sowing onto molehills or any disturbed ground, creating a nucleus from which it can spread, year on year.

On a field scale, the solution is autumn animal grazing, which helps to clear out old grasses. Yellow-rattle seed is a lightweight disc, very thin but wide (4mm), which can easily get caught up in dead vegetation rather than ending up flat on the soil surface, where it can germinate. Grazing animals open up the sward by pulling at it and eating it. Then, by walking about and 'poaching' the ground – making a muddy, pitted surface – they tread in the seed.

Yellow-rattle is fun and easy to sow, by walking up and down the field, broadcasting it from the bag. Old Sussex farmers say that before you sow you need to reduce the sward through grazing to the point where you can see a sixpence at twenty yards – a good measure of just how low it needs to be to guarantee success. Once Yellow-rattle is established, other wild flowers will come.

Recently, Yellow-rattle has been widely used in wild-flower mixes to suppress vigorous grasses and give wild flowers a chance. Some people have worried about this, fearing that Yellow-rattle will become invasive, but with grazing, or an early cut before the seed ripens, its spread is reversible. Common Eyebright (p.146) is another parasitic plant on grasses, but it does not have nearly such an immediate effect.

Plant type Broomrape family, Orobanchaceae. *Flowers* May–August. *Height* Up to 50cm. *Description* Erect, annual, hairless parasitic herb. Leaves are narrow-lanceolate, coarsely toothed and slightly wrinkled on the outer edge, stalkless and arranged in opposite pairs. Flowers are situated in short leafy spikes. Each flower has a flattened calyx that becomes inflated and bladder-like in fruit. Corolla is yellow and two-lipped; the upper lip has two short teeth and the lower lip is three-lobed. *Companion species* Common Eyebright, Common Milkwort (p.147), Common Spotted-orchid (p.148), Quaking-grass (p.211) and Rough Hawkbit (p.162). *Distribution* Native. Found throughout Britain and Ireland and still common in many areas. However, it has declined during the twentieth century, especially in the east of Britain and the south of Ireland. This is probably due to the loss of hay meadows because of agricultural intensification and the resulting ploughing and widespread use of herbicides. *Habitat* Nutrient-poor grasslands, including permanent pastures, hay meadows, the drier parts of fens, on the machair in the Outer Hebrides, flushes in lowland, upland grasslands and montane ledges. Also roadsides and waste ground.

Yorkshire-fog
(Holcus lanatus)

Yorkshire-fog turns fields beige-pink in early summer. The flower spikes are dark to begin with, compact miniature cigars in a gentle smoky crimson, which softens as they open up, each flower head splaying out from the main stem one by one until the whole spike is a beautiful buff-pink. It gradually fades in autumn to the colour of mushroom soup. Lie down on the ground to see it backlit with other grasses, such as Soft-brome (p.165) or Perennial Rye-grass (p.160), whose pert straight lines are a good contrast to the smudge of Yorkshire-fog. Its common name originates from the Old Norse *fogg*, meaning 'long, lax, damp grass', but it is also a good description of the misty effect of the grass when seen at a distance. When young, Yorkshire-fog can provide grazing for animals, particularly on poor soils, but it is not plump and succulent, so cows do not like it. Both leaves and flowers often remain untouched in pastures and meadows when other grasses have been cropped around them.

Plant type Grass family, Poaceae. *Flowers* July–September. *Height* 30–100cm. *Description* Tufted perennial herb. Leaves are grey-green, flat, soft and downy. Ligules are blunt, 1–4mm long. Spikelets are two-flowered, 4–6mm long, white or pink-purple, with oval, hairy glumes arranged in a spreading panicle. *Companion species* Hedge Bedstraw (p.202), Perennial Rye-grass, Red Clover (p.161) and Soft-brome. *Distribution* Native. Ubiquitous and very common throughout the British Isles. *Habitat* Grasslands of all kinds, such as meadows, lawns, woodland rides and clearings, roadsides, waste ground and rough grassland. It is tolerant of a broad range of soils, including clays, loams and sands. It grows in dry to winter-wet, acidic to calcareous soils, and is most vigorous in moist but not waterlogged habitats. It tolerates mowing and heavy grazing, but not trampling.

Green-winged Orchid (p.154), Marden Meadow, near Staplehurst, Kent, 17 May.

Meadow Buttercup (× 1.8) near Oakridge, Gloucestershire, 24 May

Bluebell (p.2), Pignut (p.161) and Ribwort Plantain (p.162), Ardtornish, Morvern, Argyll, 5 June.

Meadow Buttercup (p.158), Common Sorrel (p.147) and Pignut (p.161), Burtersett, North Yorkshire, 13 June.

Common Knapweed (p.146) and Dyer's Greenweed (p.152), near Ashburnham, East Sussex, 30 June.

Common Knapweed (p.146) and Common Sorrel (p.147), near Perch Hill, East Sussex, 30 June.

Perennial Rye-grass (p.160), Soft-brome (p.165) and Yorkshire-fog (p.169), RSPB reserve, Dungeness, Kent, 1 July.

Hedge Bedstraw (p.202) and Tufted Vetch (p.166), Magdalen Hill Down, Hampshire, 5 July.

Red Clover (p.161), Hogweed (p.156) and Meadowsweet (p.314), Northton, South Harris, Outer Hebrides, 23 July.

Chalk Down & Limestone Dale

The flowers on the grasslands of the downs and dales on sweet chalk and limestone are slow to get going in the spring. But once they come, colourful yet delicate, these areas become the floweriest parts of the world in late spring and early summer. The ground is poor and thin, so the strong grasses cannot outdo the slower and weaker-growing wild flowers. That is the secret to this richness – its poverty.

When you drive through chalk or limestone country, the arable fields appear much the same as on a richer clay or loamy soil, full of vigour from the artificial fertilisers applied. It is on the roadsides and in the few unimproved or restored grassy pastures that you really notice the difference. Cowslips spread out as far as you can see, or you may find a chance elaborate tapestry of golden-green Crosswort merging into carpets of Germander Speedwell, Ground-ivy and the slower-to-open flowers of Wild Thyme. I came across a perfect miniature garden of these late last April on the North Downs in Kent. It made me realise that wild flowers often outdo anything you can find combined in a garden.

I remember as a child finding Pasqueflower on Therfield Heath in Hertfordshire in the middle of spring. I have an image in my head of big patches of it, laid out like Liberty bags across the short grass. If you go there now, you will find in truth that it is a light dusting of that vivid purple, but even so, this is a flower vision that will stay with you for life.

It is worth planning to visit one of the extraordinary orchid sites of east Kent. I found seven species of orchid in one chalk down field there last June. As well as miniature forests of Common Twayblade and lots of the deep pink, narrow spires of Chalk Fragrant-orchid, there were the much rarer Monkey Orchid, Man Orchid, Late Spider-orchid and Musk Orchid, with Lady Orchid growing near by on the edge of a wood. Here were flower riches I had never expected to find in the British Isles.

Glowing yellow Lady's Bedstraw flowers away for months in summer, with splashes of white, fluffy Hedge Bedstraw mixed in. Then there are the feather-like, red-pink flowers of Sainfoin. This was my favourite wild flower as a child. I loved its colour and its shape and the fact that you never found one but twenty or a hundred. Through all of these are scattered the pale mauve daubs of Field Scabious and the darker, richer purples from Greater Knapweed and Wild Marjoram, as well as the frolicking, twisting and turning mounds of Tufted Vetch.

In June and July, the bright yellow cartwheel flowers of Common Rock-rose often carpet the sunny south side of a hill on chalk, with Harebell and Chalk Milkwort poking up between them. The landscape takes on the character of a Pointillist painting.

The miniature drumstick heads of Ribwort and Hoary Plantain create the upper storey with the grasses, striking your boots in a rhythm as you walk. But it is in the winter that these take the visual centre stage. The seed heads of plantains, mixed with blobs of Betony and the tall, twisting spires of Agrimony, outlined and twinkling with frost, make the monochrome winter downland almost as beautiful as it is in the full froth of summer.

Autumn Gentian
(Gentianella amarella)

This is by far the most common of the gentian family and, while pretty enough, it is not as much of a show-stopper as the other species. The whole plant is rather stiff and upright, covered with flowers that look like miniature crocus trumpets, stacked in several layers on top of one another. Also known as Felwort, it has flowers that are often a rich purple on the outside, particularly at the petal tip, and paler mauve within. They may also appear in a dull greyish mauve, pale blue, pink or white, but never that intense, characteristic gentian blue. If you peer into one of the flowers, you will see a fuzz of bright white hairs, like spun sugar on the top of a fancy pudding. This is a key difference between this species and the 'true' blue gentians, and one of the things that puts Autumn Gentian into its own genus.

Plant type Gentian family, Gentianaceae. *Flowers* July–August. *Height* 5–30cm. *Description* Erect biennial herb. Usually five to ten (exceptionally up to fourteen) pairs of oval-lanceolate, pointed leaves, each 1–2cm long, emerge from a basal rosette of usually spoon-shaped leaves. Flowers have long, four- to five-lobed, bell-shaped corollas, 14–28mm long. *Companion species* Autumn Lady's-tresses (p.190), Common Centaury (p.194), Horseshoe Vetch (p.204) and Yellow-wort (p.217). *Distribution* Native. Found throughout the British Isles. It is quite frequent in some regions with well-drained basic soils, such as the chalk downs of southern England and limestone districts, such as the Cotswolds, White Peak of Derbyshire and Yorkshire Dales. There has been a decline in some places caused by habitat loss. *Habitat* Well-drained basic soils, typically occurring in grazed chalk and limestone grassland, on calcareous dunes and machair, on spoil tips and in cuttings and quarries.

Autumn Lady's-tresses
(Spiranthes spiralis)

This small, slender plant is a challenge to find, even if you know where it is likely to be. Its irregular flowering season does not help – one year, it will flower in early August, the next year, a month later. It can appear suddenly in large numbers where a mowing or grazing regime is relaxed for a month or two and plants have a chance to flower. It loves short grass, and is sometimes found on garden lawns in chalky parts of the country, such as Hampshire, Sussex and Kent, which are not mown religiously. All Lady's-tresses orchids, including Irish Lady's-tresses (p.306), look as they sound, with an upright flower spike resembling a spiralling plait of hair, particularly when still in bud with the flowers packed in tightly. It is worth getting down to have a close look. Each white flower is slightly sparkling, as if it were diamond-dusted, and has a distinctive scent of coconut.

Plant type Orchid family, Orchidaceae. *Flowers* August–September. *Height* 3–15cm. *Description* Short, erect perennial herb. The stem has scale-like green leaves. Basal leaves die back before the inflorescence has appeared. A new, small rosette of oval-triangular blue-green leaves appears adjacent to the flower spike – the beginnings of the plant that will flower the following year. Flowers have narrow, blunt-lanceolate perianth segments and a green-centred lip with a frilly white edge. *Companion species* Autumn Gentian (left), Autumn Hawkbit (p.143) and Yellow-wort (p.217). *Distribution* Native. Locally frequent in southern England and along the Welsh coast, but becoming increasingly rare further north. It has declined as a result of agricultural intensification and undergrazing. *Habitat* Short, dry, unimproved, well-grazed grasslands on dry calcareous soils, especially on chalk and limestone, and on cliff tops and sand dunes.

Basil Thyme
(Clinopodium acinos)

You might find this when parking on a track beside an arable meadow on chalky ground and nearly put your foot on it as you get out of the car. That is where it tends to grow, in open, sunny spots with excellent drainage. Mildly aromatic, it used to be harvested as a substitute for thyme, but it is now too rare to pick. It has declined hugely during the twentieth century because of increased use of herbicides and, in Ireland, gravel extraction. In many areas, it is no longer found in arable fields, surviving only in less intensively managed habitats. Like many of the dead-nettle family, Basil Thyme is popular with bees and other insects.

Plant type Dead-nettle family, Lamiaceae. *Flowers* May–August. *Height* 15cm. *Description* Creeping or ascending annual or short-lived perennial herb. Leaves are oval-elliptical, more or less hairless, shallowly toothed, up to 1.5cm long. Stems are hairy. Inflorescence is whorls of four to six flowers, each of which has a violet-coloured corolla, 7–10mm long, with white blotches on the lower lip. It is closely related to Common Calamint (*C. ascendens*) and Wild Basil (p.215), but those plants are bigger, with taller, denser flower spikes. *Companion species* Bee Orchid (right), Common Rock-rose (p.195) and Vervain (p.113). *Distribution* Native. A local species mostly confined to the chalk and limestone in southern and eastern England. However, there are scattered or isolated populations throughout England and the north and south of Wales. It is also quite frequent in Norfolk. There is a native population on the east coast of Scotland near Edinburgh. It is rare as an alien in Ireland. *Habitat* Disturbed ground, where it does not have to compete with longer-lived species. It favours disused quarries, roadside banks, track ways, traditionally managed arable fields and steep grassland on thin soils.

Bee Orchid
(Ophrys apifera)

This is a thrilling plant to find, with its pale pink, striped green wings and telltale protuberant lip with bumblebee markings. It is usually short and stocky, but is occasionally found in a giant version, with up to ten flowers on each spike. Plants in the genus *Ophrys* mimic insects and can release pheromones to attract the male of the relevant species, which then spreads pollen from plant to plant. If you find one Bee Orchid, keep looking – there are bound to be more, because, unlike other members of the genus, this species has given up on insects and resorted to self-pollination. Soon after the flowers open, the pollinia are released from the green beak structure above the lip, known as the column, and dangle out until the breeze blows pollen onto the stigma. This ensures that the seed set is plentiful and accounts for Bee Orchid's capacity to colonise new sites quickly.

Plant type Orchid family, Orchidaceae. *Flowers* June–July. *Height* 10–40cm. *Description* Erect perennial herb. Leaves are greyish green, prominently veined and elliptical-oblong, mostly in a basal rosette but also up the stem. The spike normally has two to nine widely spaced flowers. Each flower has three pale pinkish-white oval sepals. The two upper petals are much smaller than the sepals and vary from strap-shaped to triangular and are pink or green. The lip is tongue-shaped, convex, furry and rich brown, with elaborate markings. *Companion species* Common Spotted-orchid (p.148) and Horseshoe Vetch (p.204). *Distribution* Native. Common throughout England, although becoming rare in the north and west. It is largely coastal in Wales and was found recently in Scotland. It is more local in Ireland, most frequent in the limestone districts of central Ireland. *Habitat* Well-drained calcareous grassland, particularly on chalk or limestone.

Burnet-saxifrage
(*Pimpinella saxifraga*)

This is the Pignut (p.161) of chalk meadows, a delicate-flowered and pretty white umbellifer, which forms a lacy bottom storey beneath the flowering heads of grasses. The common name is confusing, because it is neither a burnet nor a saxifrage: burnet comes from the shape of its basal leaves, which look a bit like those of Salad Burnet (p.213), and saxifrage comes from its traditional herbal use to combat kidney and bladder stones (*saxifraga* means 'stone-breaker' in Latin). The flowers are visited by many different insects, and Burnet-saxifrage is the larval food plant of several moth species. The leaves are edible and taste peppery: collect them before the plants flower to add to a salad or mix them into cream cheese or a salsa verde.

Plant type Carrot family, Apiaceae. *Flowers* July–September. *Height* 30–100cm. *Description* Downy, slender, erect perennial herb. Leaves are usually once pinnate; stem leaves are usually twice pinnate and have very narrow leaflets. Stem is rough and round. Flowers are white, very small (2mm across), with short styles. Fruit is oval, 3mm long. The absence of a ruff of bracts and bracteoles helps to distinguish this species from other umbellifers, such as Cow Parsley (p.77) and Wild Carrot (p.424). *Companion species* Common Knapweed (p.146), Rough Hawkbit (p.162), Small Scabious (p.214) and Wild Marjoram (p.216). *Distribution* Native. Common throughout most of the British Isles, although scarce in northern Scotland and the south-west and north of Ireland. *Habitat* Grassy habitats on well-drained soils, favouring those which are calcareous or otherwise base-rich, but also on acidic sands. It occurs on grazed and ungrazed chalk and limestone downs, in rough pasture and other grassland, in woodland edges and open rides and less frequently on roadsides and rough ground.

Burnt Orchid
(*Neotinea ustulata*)

If it were ten times bigger, this plant's flower spikes might look like those of Lady Orchid (p.17), each flower a princess in a fantastic ball gown. But this orchid, named after the burnt appearance of its spikes, is so small that it is difficult to spot. Even though I had been told where it was growing, I once spent forty minutes walking round a small spot of Yorkshire field, eyes fixed on the grass, before I found it in a group of three or four, the only ones of its kind in a magnificently flowery meadow. These tuberous orchids replace their old tubers each year and, quite often, one tuber may produce two or more new tubers, so clumps of two or more plants are not infrequent. Like so many relatively long-lived perennials, however, it takes only one well-seeded flowering stem every few years to perpetuate a colony.

Plant type Orchid family, Orchidaceae. *Flowers* From the middle of May. The less frequent var. *aestivalis* flowers late June–early August. *Height* 8–15cm. *Description* Leaves are elliptical-oblong, pale green, mostly forming a basal rosette. Inflorescence is a small, dense spike of fifteen to fifty flowers, with an overall cylindrical shape. Flowers have a deeply lobed white lip, speckled with purplish red blotches. Sepals and petals form a hood, which is dark purplish red at first, fading later. *Companion species* Chalk Milkwort (p.194), Common Bird's-foot-trefoil (p.145), Common Rock-Rose (p.195), Cowslip (p.195), Hoary Plantain (p.203) and Horseshoe Vetch (p.204). *Distribution* Native. Confined to England, with an isolated population in south Wales. Very scarce, and declining. Its distribution largely reflects chalk and limestone formation. *Habitat* Limestone downland on south- or west-facing slopes. It prefers a short sward and often grows on the terraces created by soil creep on steep slopes.

Carline Thistle

(Carlina vulgaris)

When you first see Carline Thistle, you may think it is a seed head left from the previous year, all colour gone and the head dried and crispy. But this is how the flowers of Carline Thistle open, simple discs in the washed-out colour of old manuscripts, looking like blooms that have been picked, dried and scattered on the grass. The plants usually emerge with just a single flower head, six at most, their short stems preventing the highly branched habit of most other thistles. Carline Thistle is a good indicator of species-rich grassland. As a biennial, it favours short, open turf, which allows its seeds to germinate annually. Without competition from coarse-growing species, it thrives alongside exciting plants such as Autumn Gentian (p.190) and Yellow-wort (p.217). The flowers act like barometers, opening when it is sunny and closing with cloud or rain.

Plant type Daisy family, Asteraceae. *Flowers* July–October. *Height* 10–20cm, occasionally taller. *Description* Low, erect, spiny biennial herb. Leaves are thistle-like: lanceolate, lobed, fringed with weak spines, cottony on the undersides. Flower heads are 3–4cm across when fully open. Inner bracts are spreading, resembling ray florets, linear with an almost metallic straw-yellow colour. The real florets in the centre of the flower head are a darker, brownish yellow. *Companion species* Autumn Gentian, Dwarf Thistle (p.197), Perforate St John's-wort (p.209) and Yellow-wort. *Distribution* Native. Frequent and locally very abundant in much of England and Wales, especially in areas dominated by well-drained calcareous soils. In Scotland, it is mostly confined to the coast. It is common in the centre of Ireland. *Habitat* Well-grazed, dry, infertile meadows; also in more open habitats, including dry rock ledges, screes, quarry floors, coastal cliffs and sand dunes.

Chalk Fragrant-orchid

(Gymnadenia conopsea)

The elegant, bright pink flower spikes of this orchid are strongly and exotically scented, with a perfume like a heady, slightly spicy clove mixed with tuberose, similar to that of philadelphus. It is worth lying down to get your nose near the flower. The scent draws pollinators in, but the spur is very long, so only insects with an equally long proboscis can feed. Various butterflies and day-flying moths are up to the task, but as the scent gets stronger at dusk, night-flying moths are probably the most important pollinators. Like many orchids, this has a symbiotic relationship with a mycorrhizal fungus, which is required for seeds to germinate and develop.

Plant type Orchid family, Orchidaceae. *Flowers* June–July. *Height* 40cm. *Description* Erect, hairless perennial. Leaves are green, unspotted, oblong-lanceolate and keeled. Inflorescence is a dense, many-flowered cylindrical spike of small, rosy-pink flowers. Each flower is 8–12mm across with a long spur (up to 20mm), two wings and a lower three-lobed lip that is broader than it is long, with the upper sepal and two lateral petals forming a helmet. Chalk Fragrant-orchids look quite similar to Pyramidal Orchid (p.210), but the latter has darker, brighter flowers that form a conical spike and is not scented. *Companion species* Common Centaury (p.194), Oxeye Daisy (p.159) and Pyramidal Orchid. *Distribution* Native. Widespread throughout the British Isles, although local in many areas. Where it does occur, it is often abundant. In southern England, its distribution follows the chalk and limestone. It is local or rare in Devon, Cornwall and the Midlands. *Habitat* A characteristic plant of unimproved chalk downland in southern England, it is also found on limestone pavement, less acid heaths and base-rich fens. It grows in artificial habitats, too, including quarries and railway banks.

Chalk Milkwort
(Polygala calcarea)

Milkworts provide one of the first strong patches of colour in the short grass of spring. Although tiny, you cannot miss them as you walk across the downland where they grow. At close quarters they look sub-aquatic, like pieces of blue coral with pale, bluey-white tentacles, fully extended. Each flower has three small green outer sepals and two big bluish inner sepals, which almost conceal the petals, the bottom one of which is fringed and tentacle-like. The chalk-loving variety is usually a bright gentian blue, zingier than blue forms of Common Milkwort (p.147), although paler, whitish-blue flowers also occur. Chalk Milkwort has a shorter flowering season than Common and Heath Milkwort (p.357), which both flower often into September.

Plant type Milkwort family, Polygalaceae. *Flowers* May–June. *Height* 5–10cm. *Description* Low, hairless, perennial herb. Leaves are narrow-lanceolate, without stipules. It has small, irregular flowers with three tiny outer sepals and two large, coloured, lateral, petal-like ones, as well as three very small true petals, which are joined together into a whitish-fringed tube. Its lower leaves, which usually form a basal rosette, are larger than the upper leaves. In Common Milkwort the reverse applies. *Companion species* Burnt Orchid (p.192), Common Bird's-foot-trefoil (p.145), Crosswort (p.196), Horseshoe Vetch (p.204) and Wild Thyme (p.217). *Distribution* Native. Confined to chalk and limestone in southern England, with an outlying population on the limestone of Northamptonshire and Lincolnshire. However, even within this range, it is curiously absent from many areas of apparently suitable unimproved grassland. *Habitat* Much fussier than Common Milkwort, needing tightly grazed chalk and limestone grassland, usually on warm, south-facing slopes.

Common Centaury
(Centaurium erythraea)

One of the sweetly prettiest of our wild flowers, Common Centaury has long-lasting rose-pink petals arranged round a golden heart of anthers. Each stem holds a mass of flowers, with up to fifty or so on one plant. It can be hugely abundant in the right habitats on freely drained chalk or sand. With its broad, rather fleshy leaves, it looks more like a bulb than an annual, but an annual is what it is, a relation of the gentians. There is great variation in its size. You will see it quite tall and slender, with stems up to 40cm, but it can be a quarter of that height and very branched, with a large flower clump at the top of a short stem. That is how it appears in places that are heavily grazed, and in wind-beaten spots, such as the tops of the cliffs on the Lizard in Cornwall, where it looks like an alpine flower in its stature and sugary glamour.

Plant type Gentian family, Gentianaceae. *Flowers* June–October. *Height* 10–40cm. *Description* Hairless, erect annual. Basal leaves are obovate, 5mm across or wider, forming a rosette; stem leaves are oval-elliptical and never parallel-sided. Pink flowers are 10–12mm across. *Companion species* Autumn Gentian (p.190), Common Bird's-foot-trefoil (p.145), Common Spotted-orchid (p.148), Pyramidal Orchid (p.210) and Yellow-wort (p.217). *Distribution* Native. Common throughout England and Wales, except in upland areas. It is mostly restricted to coastal and lowland areas in Scotland and occurs throughout Ireland. *Habitat* Like most annuals, it favours disturbed ground. It occupies a broad variety of habitats and is capable of growing on both acid and alkaline soils. It is most abundant on chalk downland, but also occurs in clay meadows, woodland rides and tracks, coppice clearings, heathland and arable field edges.

Common Rock-rose
(Helianthemum nummularium)

I have fond memories of finding Common Rock-rose with my father in Devon when I was a child. My sister was at school there, and we used to plan spring and early summer botanising trips around visits to see her. As a result of discovering it in the wild, my parents grew many different rock-rose varieties in their garden – on chalk in Cambridgeshire – lining a path on both sides, scalloping the edge with reds and oranges as well as the native white and yellow species. Every June, the open sunny flowers overlapped, the intense splotches of brilliant colour, one on top of another, looking like a van Gogh painting. I have loved rock-roses ever since. *Helianthemum* alludes to the bright flowers – derived from the Greek *helios*, meaning 'sun', and *anthemon*, meaning 'flower' – and may also refer to the fact that the flowers open only in sunlight.

Plant type Rock-rose family, Cistaceae. *Flowers* June–September. *Height* 5–30cm. *Description* Prostrate, many-branched shrub. Bright yellow flowers are 2–2.5cm across and located in one- to twelve-flowered lax inflorescences. Leaves are 0.5–2cm long, oblong, green, mostly hairless above, woolly below. Stem is woody. *Companion species* Chalk Milkwort (opposite), Crosswort (p.196), Germander Speedwell (p.85), Hedge Bedstraw (p.202) and Lady's Bedstraw (p.205). *Distribution* Native. In England, the distribution of Common Rock-rose is largely confined to the chalk and limestone, but it extends to mildly acid pastures and heaths on well-drained soils in eastern Scotland and base-rich soils over basalt in north-east England and eastern Scotland. It is very rare in Ireland, known in only one locality in Donegal. It has declined since 1950, mostly as a result of conversion of chalk grassland to arable and reversion to scrub. However, where it does occur, it is often very frequent. *Habitat* A plant of short grassland on chalk and limestone in the south, growing in dry, acid, fescue/bent grassland in the northern part of its range. It is also found occasionally on the edge of scrubland, on cliffs, rocks and scree and on roadside banks.

Cowslip
(Primula veris)

Cowslips are a good indication that the soil is sweet and that other wild flowers will be thriving near by. With widespread sowing and planting of Cowslips on roadsides and motorways, it is difficult to tell what is wild and what is introduced, but a drift of Cowslips lifts the spirits, however it got there. The Cowslip is the larval food plant of the Duke of Burgundy butterfly, arguably second to the High Brown Fritillary as the most endangered butterfly in Britain and Ireland. The female selects only the most lush, greenest plants that grow in half shade beside encroaching scrub or tussock. The more Cowslips we have for her, the better.

Plant type Primrose family, Primulaceae. *Flowers* April–May. *Height* 10–30cm. *Description* This perennial herb is similar to Oxlip (p.21), with flowers in umbels at the top of each stem. Cowslips have more wrinkled leaves, gradually tapered leaf stalks and egg-yolk-yellow flowers (8–10mm across) with orange streaks at their heart. Oxlips have pale primrose-yellow flowers, which are larger and less tubular. When Primrose (p.103) and Cowslip hybridise, False Oxlip (p.81) is the result. *Companion species* Germander Speedwell (p.85), Green-winged Orchid (p.154) and Salad Burnet (p.213). *Distribution* Native. Frequent to very locally abundant in England, although absent or rare in some areas, such as the Weald. In Scotland, it is largely confined to the east. Until recently, numbers of wild Cowslips had fallen drastically, but with more carefully controlled mowing of grass verges in rich areas, they are beginning to recolonise. *Habitat* They thrive in almost any kind of grass so long as it is left short at the end of the year. They love chalk, but you will also see them on seasonally flooded soils, in scrub or woodland rides and edges, calcareous cliffs and on road verges.

Crosswort
(*Cruciata laevipes*)

If you live on clay, you are not likely to know this plant. I thought it was rare until I started to visit chalk downlands and realised that from late April until June it is – on almost any chalk down – literally everywhere. On the North Downs in Kent, it fills the air with the scent of honey and forms carpets of acid green, its colour broken only by the purple leaves of Ground-ivy (p.14) and splashes of brilliant-blue Germander Speedwell (p.85). It is a hive of insect activity, with hoverflies and bees of all kinds feeding on its ample quantities of pollen and nectar. You can tell this is a bedstraw from the tiny, starry flowers grouped in puffs of colour around a square stem, and the whorls of small leaves with gaps of clear stem in between. Bedstraws all have a long flowering season.

Plant type Bedstraw family, Rubiaceae. *Flowers* April–June. *Height* 30–60cm. *Description* This perennial plant is easy to identify because its oval-elliptical leaves, their margins rolled back, are arranged together in whorls of four in the form of a cross (hence its common name). Stems are square, softly hairy, creeping at the base and erect where flowering, with pretty clouds of small green-yellow flowers in clusters at the base above the leaf whorls. After the flower come hairless dark purple nutlets, 1.5mm across, which ripen to black. *Companion species* Germander Speedwell, Ground-ivy, Hoary Plantain (p.203), Lady's Bedstraw (p.205) and Ribwort Plantain (p.162). *Distribution* Native. Common throughout England but absent from parts of the West Country and west Wales. In Scotland it is native only in the south east. It is also scarce in parts of East Anglia and the Midlands. *Habitat* Usually found on well-drained neutral or calcareous soils, typically occurring in ungrazed grassland, open scrub, hedge banks, woodland rides and edges and on waysides.

Dark-red Helleborine
(*Epipactis atrorubens*)

Dark-red Helleborine is the femme fatale of wild flowers: sultry, proud and exotically beautiful, but maybe not entirely friendly. The only fresh thing about it is the green of its leaves. Otherwise, it is all darkness and seduction. It is highly localised and rare (but not extremely so), and confined to hard limestone areas. I remember finding it as a child with my father in the Burren, Ireland, and I found it coming into flower there again last summer. One particular sunny hillside was scattered with at least a hundred plants, a few in groups but most in splendid isolation, each gracing its own particular patch of limestone pavement like a queen on her throne.

Plant type Orchid family, Orchidaceae. *Flowers* June–July. *Height* 15–60cm. *Description* Robust perennial herb. Stems are reddish with a dense covering of white hairs. Five to ten leaves are oval-elliptical, pointed, keeled and arranged in two opposite rows. Flowers are arranged in a dense, one-sided raceme of eight to forty flowers. Each flower has three sepals and three petals, all oval-triangular and deep red-purple in colour, with a distinctive yellow anther cap. The lower petal forms a lip. *Companion species* Bloody Crane's-bill (p.393), Common Valerian (p.74), Maidenhair Fern (p.404), Mountain Avens (p.361), Red Valerian (p.407) and Rustyback (p.105). *Distribution* Native. Very rare, confined to the north Wales coastline, Peak District, Yorkshire Dales, Morecambe Bay, southern Lake District, North Pennines and County Durham. It is also found in northern Scotland. In Ireland, it is confined to the Burren. *Habitat* Strongly associated with limestone, where it occupies a variety of habitats, usually in open, sunny conditions but sometimes in the moderate shade of ash woodland on limestone pavements.

Dropwort
(Filipendula vulgaris)

With its Hawthorn-blossom-like flowers on top of long, thin stems, and buds like little cream bubbles washed with red, Dropwort looks a lot like Meadowsweet (p.314), the fluffy-flowered plant that occurs very commonly all over damp meadows and marshes. Dropwort is a rarer, fussier plant, which grows in much drier habitats only on base-rich, alkaline soils. It is often cultivated in its double-flowered form. Meadowsweet and Dropwort are close relations, both incredibly pretty with a sweet, soft, honey-like scent, flowering for ages. The generic name *Filipendula* is derived from two Latin words – *filum*, meaning 'thread', and *pendulus*, 'hanging' – and refers to the underground tubers that hang from narrow, thread-like roots.

Plant type Rose family, Rosaceae. *Flowers* June–August. *Height* 10–50cm. *Description* Erect, tufted perennial herb. Leaves are pinnate with eight to twenty-five pairs of narrow, oblong, toothed leaflets that are shiny green on both sides. Cream flowers are 10–20mm across, slightly tinged with red on the outside, with usually six petals, arranged in dense, flat-headed clusters. *Companion species* Betony (p.143), Common Centaury (p.194), Common Restharrow (p.396) and Lady's Bedstraw (p.205). *Distribution* Native. It occurs throughout England, although it is local and rare in many areas. It is most frequent in south-central England. It is also found in Wales, although it is rare as a native. In Scotland, there are a handful of colonies in the south, while in Ireland it is confined to the Burren. It has declined in southern England because of the conversion of chalk downland to arable and lack of grazing. *Habitat* Calcareous grassland, mostly on chalk and limestone downland. However, it is also found on heathland and coastal grassland (such as the Lizard) on other basic rocks.

Dwarf Thistle
(Cirsium acaule)

The flowers held on the shortest of stems, this looks like a plant that has been hammered by grazing, as if every time it has tried to grow it has been bitten off and stunted (hence its other common name of Stemless Thistle). That is not what has happened. This is how the plant grows, with the brilliant purple thistle flower opening almost at ground level. Its punch of colour is surrounded by a halo of sharply prickly, deep green leaves with shiny upper sides, a perfect contrast to the flowers – they would make a lovely buttonhole. Dwarf Thistle is also known as 'picnic thistle', as it often grows in areas of grassland that look ideal for a picnic, although you would not want to sit on one of these. Like many thistles, it provides a rich nectar source for insects, including bumblebees and late summer butterflies, such as Chalkhill Blue, Adonis Blue and Silver-spotted Skipper.

Plant type Daisy family, Asteraceae. *Flowers* June–September. *Height* 5–10cm. *Description* Low, rosette-forming perennial herb. Leaves are deeply pinnatifid, wavy-edged and spine-tipped, hairless above but hairy underneath, 10–15cm long. Flower heads are bright red-purple, stalkless (rarely stalked to 10cm), usually solitary but sometimes in groups of two to four. *Companion species* Carline Thistle (p.193), Common Centaury (p.194), Hedge Bedstraw (p.202) and Lady's Bedstraw (p.205). *Distribution* Native. Common in much of southern England, but rare in Devon and Cornwall and largely absent from the Weald of Kent and Sussex. It becomes increasingly scarce north of a line from the Seven Estuary to the Humber Estuary and does not extend any further north than the North York Moors. It is absent from most of Wales, mostly confined to south Wales near the English border, although there is an isolated colony in Pembrokeshire. *Habitat* Short swards on base-rich soils, particularly on chalk and limestone. The northerly and westerly limits appear to be determined by summer warmth, and in areas such as the Yorkshire Wolds and Derbyshire it is almost wholly confined to south-west-facing slopes.

Early Spider-orchid
(*Ophrys sphegodes*)

The name of this exotic-looking orchid comes from the fat, velvety lip (labellum) of its flower. It is furry on the outside, but has a smooth, hairless, reflective patch in the centre (the speculum) – the two parts together suggest a fat spider. But it is bees, not spiders, which flock to this plant. The male solitary bee *Andrena nigroaenea* attempts to mate with it, collecting pollen on its head, which it then deposits on other flowers. This is less successful than it sounds: self-pollination is thought to be the main process by which the flowers set seed. One of the best places to see it is Samphire Hoe on the Kent coast, which is where this photograph was taken. In some areas these exotic orchids are so thick that, tiptoeing along, you feel as if you are in a Mediterranean country, your every step potentially crushing another flower.

Plant type Orchid family, Orchidaceae. *Flowers* April–June. *Height* 5–15cm; at coastal locations it may reach 45cm. *Description* Flower has green oval-oblong sepals, green, sometimes brown strap-shaped petals and a brown furry lip with an X or H-shaped blue-grey speculum. Grey-green leaves are elliptical-oblong, forming a rosette and ascending the stem. Easy to distinguish from other insect-mimicking orchids. Both Late Spider-orchid (p.205) and Bee Orchid (p.191) have white or purplish-pink sepals, while Fly Orchid (p.10) has a narrower lip and grows in woodland or scrubland. *Companion species* Cowslip (p.195) and Crosswort (p.196). *Distribution* It has been lost from nearly three quarters of its historical range and is extinct in many English counties. Most of the losses occurred in the nineteenth century, mainly because of the ploughing of chalk/limestone grassland. The remaining populations are between Durlston and St Aldhelm's Head on the Isle of Purbeck, Dorset;

between Beachy Head and Castle Hill on the South Downs in East Sussex; and the North Downs in east Kent. There are isolated recent records from Gloucestershire, Wiltshire, Northamptonshire and Suffolk. *Habitat* Usually on closely grazed chalk or limestone grassland, often near the coast. Favours disturbed areas, perhaps because they have plenty of bare ground for the germination of seed.

Field Scabious
(*Knautia arvensis*)

Descendants of this pretty wild flower have become some of our favourite cottage garden plants, and rightly so. It flowers for months, right through the summer, and has high-quality nectar for butterflies and bees. Many insects home in on it above other chalk meadow flowers, and finches and linnets also love its seed. It is the largest scabious in the British Isles, with bumper-sized flowers in the palest, softest mauve, fading to a rose pink-mauve at its heart. The anthers look like tiny, pink, gravity-free bugs floating about in the lilac atmosphere of the flower below. There may be as many as fifty flowers on one plant, with buds forming continually through the summer. For all these reasons it has become a popular addition to wild-flower seed mixes, but it germinates well only on chalky soil.

Plant type Teasel family, Dipsacaceae. *Flowers* July–September. *Height* Up to 1m. *Description* Roughly hairy perennial herb with basal leaves that are usually unlobed but toothed, and stem leaves that are deeply pinnatifid with an elliptical end leaflet. Flower heads are variable in colour, usually a soft pale mauve and sometimes lilac, 2–4cm across. *Companion species* Common Knapweed (p.146), Devil's-bit Scabious (p.151), Greater Knapweed (p.201), Hedge Bedstraw (p.202), Hogweed (p.156), Lady's Bedstraw (p.205) and Small Scabious (p.214). *Distribution* Native. Common throughout most of the British Isles, although absent from north-west Scotland and local or rare in the Weald, mid Wales and parts of west Ireland. *Habitat* Calcareous and neutral grassland on well-drained soils in rough pasture, open hedgerows and wood borders, and as a colonist on roadside verges, railway banks and grassy waste ground. It is also a locally common weed of cultivation, especially field borders on chalk. It is associated with longer, less heavily grazed swards than Small Scabious, and it is not as frequent on rabbit- or sheep-grazed pasture as either Small Scabious or Devil's-bit Scabious. Despite this, it is much more widespread than Small Scabious.

Frog Orchid
(Coeloglossum viride)

This orchid is now so rare that I have seen miniature plants in nature reserves covered with cages to protect them from being squashed. It was once quite common in southern England, but it is now largely confined to slopes of chalk and limestone downland that have escaped ploughing or improvement. It is not rare everywhere: I have seen Frog Orchids on machair in the Outer Hebrides in huge colonies of a hundred or more. The individual flowers look just like a frog in full hop, its legs extended as it shoots from place to place. The colour of the flower spike and individual flowers varies from bright acid green to a dusky, smoky red-carmine.

Plant type Orchid family, Orchidaceae. *Flowers* June–August. *Height* 4–15cm, exceptionally up to 25cm. *Description* Short, erect perennial herb. Leaves are dark green and oval, mostly in a basal rosette, with one or two narrower leaves up the stem. The spike has five to twenty-five flowers, occasionally up to fifty. Flowers are green to brownish purple with the sepals and upper petals forming a hood and the lower petal elongated into a tongue-shaped lip with two small terminal lobes. *Companion species* Burnet Rose (p.68), Lesser Butterfly-orchid (p.359) and Kidney Vetch (p.403). *Distribution* Native. Widely distributed throughout the British Isles, but very local, rare or absent in places. It is common in parts of upland Scotland and northern England. It is also found locally on the downlands of central southern England. In East Anglia, it is reduced to a few populations. *Habitat* Various grassland habitats on calcareous or neutral soils. It prefers more damp north-facing slopes to drier south-facing slopes. In the north and west it is found on limestone pavements, rock ledges, roadside verges, upland flushes and mountain pastures, scree and coastal dunes.

Grass Vetchling
(Lathyrus nissolia)

An incredible needle of brilliant carmine pink sparkling in the long, ungrazed grass like a jewel, this has to be one of my favourite flowers. Each flower is tiny and a whole plant has only twenty or so, but the effect is like a Dürer etching: it makes you home in on a three-inch square and notice every blade of grass and flower within it. Its leaves look just like grass, so you only notice it during the months when it is in flower. The actual flower stems are so fine that they disappear in the grass and the flowers look as if they are floating in mid air. These are followed by flat, pea-like seed pods, 3–6cm long, which also look as though they are levitating.

Plant type Pea family, Fabaceae. *Flowers* May–July. *Height* Up to 90cm. *Description* Autumn-germinating annual, with leaves similar to those of grasses – hairless, long and thin with no leaflets. Flowers are magenta-crimson, 8–18mm long, solitary or in twos. Pods are 2–3cm long, brown, hairless and straight, becoming pale brown when ripe. *Companion species* Chalkland grasses and grassland vetches, such as Common Vetch (p.75), Meadow Vetchling (p.96) and Tufted Vetch (p.166). *Distribution* Native and locally common, but confined to southern England and south Wales. It is most frequent in south-eastern England and in the Thames Estuary area – at Plantlife's Ranscombe Farm Reserve, for instance – and occurs in countless thousands in 'new' grasslands on thin soils on land that has been reverted from arable. Scattered populations in northern England, west Wales and Scotland are not considered to be native. *Habitat* Open, often disturbed (but ungrazed in summer) habitats on chalk and heavy calcareous soils. It is also found on grassy banks, verges, railway banks, woodland rides and coastal grassland and shingle.

Greater Knapweed
(*Centaurea scabiosa*)

Big and showy, like a cross between a cornflower and a thistle, it is no wonder that this plant is so popular in wild-flower mixes. It is a valuable nectar source for insects and a favourite flower of butterflies. It also has therapeutic properties: Nicholas Culpeper wrote that Greater Knapweed 'is good for those who are bruised by any fall, blows, or otherwise, by drinking a decoction of the herb roots in wine, and applying the same outwardly to the place'. Its Latin species name is derived from the Latin *scabere*, 'to scratch', probably because it was believed to cure skin problems, such as sores, rashes and itchiness. It is also host to the handsome parasitic Knapweed Broomrape (*Orobanche elatior*), a feature of road verges and fields across Salisbury Plain.

Plant type Daisy family, Asteraceae. *Flowers* June–August. *Height* 30–80cm. *Description* Erect, downy perennial herb. Leaves are deeply pinnatifid, 10–25cm long, stalked near the base, stalkless further up the stem, which is grooved and branched. Flower heads are solitary, 3–6cm across, with bright purple-red florets (sometimes white), the outer of which are enlarged. *Companion species* Bush Vetch (p.69), Field Scabious (p.198), Hedge Bedstraw (p.202), Hogweed (p.156), Lady's Bedstraw (p.205), Red Clover (p.161), Small Scabious (p.214) and White Clover (p.167). *Distribution* Native. Frequent to locally very common throughout England and Wales, although absent from some areas without suitable soils, such as mid Wales and the Weald. It is rare in Scotland, although locally frequent where it does occur. It is also locally frequent in central Ireland. *Habitat* Dry, usually calcareous soils. It is found in grassland, scrub and woodland edges, on cliffs, roadsides, railway banks, quarries and waste ground.

Hairy Violet
(*Viola hirta*)

Named for its hairy leaves, this has flowers like those of Sweet Violet (p.111), although they are sometimes a little bluer. The key difference is that they have no scent. The leaves emerge curled up like little cigars, opening as they grow, but remain narrower than those of the sweet form. I love all violets because they come so early in the year; if these flowered in June, we might notice them less. Violets are always tricky to tell apart, but they do have distinct characteristics. Like Sweet Violet, this has flowers and leaves arising directly from the rootstock on separate stems. There are no stems on which leaves and flowers are mixed, as in Common Dog-violet (p.5) and Early Dog-violet (p.8).

Plant type Violet family, Violaceae. *Flowers* March–May. *Height* 2–20cm. *Description* Low, hairy perennial herb. Leaves are ovate, deeply cordate, long-stalked and covered in spreading hairs. Flowers have five blunt green sepals and five violet-blue to deep purple flowers. Like Sweet Violet, Hairy Violet has flowers with blunt sepals (those of both dog-violets are pointed). *Companion species* Spurge-laurel (p.27) and Stinking Hellebore (p.27). *Distribution* Native. Distribution reflects its preference for calcareous soils, so it is locally common in much of central and southern England except in areas dominated by acidic rocks, such as the Weald. It is more local in northern England. In Wales, it is almost entirely confined to (or near) the north and south coasts. In Scotland, it is found only in the south, while in Ireland there are three isolated concentrations. *Habitat* Open habitats on calcareous soils, such as short grassland or open scrub on downland, rocky slopes, limestone pavement, woodland borders and rides, and sometimes base-flushed but more acidic riverside substrates. It also occurs on roadsides and railway banks.

Harebell

(Campanula rotundifolia)

There is almost nothing as pretty or as delicate as Harebell (or Bluebell, as the Scottish call it). Its petals are a June sky blue and, when it first opens, it hangs its head demurely, like a Pasqueflower (p.209), but with a finer, more delicate texture, slightly translucent when backlit. The round basal leaves often wither away by the time the plant is in flower, which adds to its airy, floaty appearance. The seeds are tiny and wind-dispersed. When the flowers begin to go over, their heads lift and the stem becomes more upright. Then small pores develop in the base of the seed capsule, allowing the seeds to be shaken out as the plant sways in the breeze.

Plant type Bellflower family, Campanulaceae. *Flowers* July–September. *Height* 15–40cm. *Description* Short, erect, hairless perennial herb. Stems creep, then ascend. Basal leaves are long-stalked, round, cordate-based; stem leaves are linear and stalkless. Flowers are bell-shaped, pendant, pale blue, 12–20mm long, in lax panicles. Clustered Bellflower (*C. glomerata*) is quite similar, but has oval leaves and erect, not drooping, flowers in a dense cluster. Nettle-leaved Bellflower (p.21) and Spreading Bellflower (*C. patula*) are taller herbs of woodlands. *Companion species* Hoary Plantain (p.203), Lady's Bedstraw (p.205), Red Clover (p.161), Ribwort Plantain (p.162), Selfheal (p.163) and White Clover (p.167). *Distribution* Native. Occurs throughout Britain, although it is very rare in much of south-western England (for which there is no explanation) and in the area surrounding the Wash. In Ireland, it is mostly restricted to the north and west, especially near the coast. This once-common plant has declined severely in many areas as a result of the loss of fine grassland habitats. *Habitat* Dry, open, infertile habitats and fine grasslands on undisturbed ground. It is a characteristic plant of old downland, hillsides, heaths, fixed dunes, machair, rock ledges, roadsides and railway banks. It tolerates a wide range of soil pH, being found on both mildly acidic and calcareous substrates, and heavy metal-tolerant strains are known. It cannot tolerate damp soil conditions.

Hedge Bedstraw

(Galium album)

With its tiny white flowers on long and elegant stems, this is the puffy-cloud relation of yellow Lady's Bedstraw (p.205). They often grow together in an airy mass punctuated by other chalk downland and lane-side plants, such as scabious or knapweed, or the pretty, purple Tufted Vetch (p.166). Hedge Bedstraw is the more robust and stronger-growing of the two, and fares better in a wider range of habitats – hence its other name of Common Bedstraw. It is quite a tough and bristly plant, so it is unlikely that it was, as Lady's Bedstraw was, used to stuff mattresses, probably giving the family its common name. You can use Hedge Bedstraw flowers in an infusion, which tastes gently sweet and is said by herbalists to help fight cancer and anaemia and detoxify the liver, kidneys and pancreas.

Plant type Bedstraw family, Rubiaceae. *Flowers* June–September. *Height* Up to 1m. *Description* Scrambling perennial herb. Stems are four-angled; leaves, in whorls of six to eight, are one-veined, lanceolate, edged with forward-pointing prickles, 8–25mm long. Inflorescence is a loose panicle of many small white flowers, each with a four-lobed corolla, 3–4mm across. *Companion species* Common Knapweed (p.146), Field Scabious (p.198), Lady's Bedstraw, Small Scabious (p.214) and Tufted Vetch. *Distribution* Native. Very common throughout southern England. Widespread but less frequent in northern England and Wales, becoming rare in Scotland. Scarce in Ireland and not considered to be native there. It may be increasing on roadsides because of its use in seed mixtures. *Habitat* Hedgerows, hedge banks and rough and permanent grassland on calcareous soils. It also occurs on railway banks, roadsides, woodland edges, scrub and waste ground.

Henbane
(Hyoscyamus niger)

My grandmother had some beautiful 1930s playing cards, whose cream surface was veined with purple-black, as if they had sucked up ink. As I child I loved this snakeskin quality, and the flowers of Henbane remind me of it. Their sultry look and nasty smell make it pretty clear that Henbane is a seriously poisonous plant. It is a member of the nightshade family and all its parts are toxic, containing the same active ingredients as Deadly Nightshade (p.6). The symptoms of poisoning include delirium, convulsions and disturbed vision, and if enough is ingested, it can cause coma and death. The infamous herbal doctor-cum-murderer Dr Crippen was said to have used a poison made from Henbane to murder his wife in 1910 before he dismembered her body.

Plant type Nightshade family, Solanaceae. *Flowers* June–August. *Height* 30–80cm. *Description* Annual or biennial herb. Leaves are sticky-hairy, oval-oblong, greyish green, alternate, 6–20cm long, often toothed and clasping the stem. Flowers are solitary, in the leaf axils; they have funnel-shaped, five-lobed corollas that are a dull yellow with purplish veins and centre. Fruit is a large capsule, 1–2cm long. *Companion species* Common Ragwort (p.242) and Hound's-tongue (p.204). *Distribution* Thought to be introduced (although some botanists consider it native), with continuous archaeological records from the Bronze Age onwards. It is scarce, found mostly in southern and eastern England. In Scotland, Ireland, Wales, northern and south-west England, it is rare and largely confined to the coast. *Habitat* Dry and calcareous soils, particularly chalk and coastal sands. It prefers disturbed sites, such as rabbit warrens, waste ground, farmyards and building sites. As with many other species that favour disturbed ground, its seed can remain dormant for years before germinating.

Hoary Plantain
(Plantago media)

I used to think of plantain as the root vegetable of the wild-flower world: robust, efficient, architectural, but not beautiful. When I saw Hoary Plantain in full flower, I realised that I was wrong. It has slightly ripply, plate-shaped leaves, lightly indented by their longitudinal veins, and a series of green flower spikes, haloed in pink-lilac stamens, a puff of smoke among the grass. This is the only plantain to be insect-pollinated, which explains its strong scent. The pale, young leaves of any plantain are edible, both raw and cooked. This and Greater Plantain (*P. major*) have a distinctive mushroomy, slightly bitter flavour. You can harvest the whole rosette from beneath with a sharp knife.

Plant type Plantain family, Plantaginaceae. *Flowers* May–August. *Height* 20cm. *Description* Perennial herb with five to nine veined, downy, elliptical grey-green leaves with short stalks forming a flat basal rosette. Inflorescence is an oblong spike, 2–6cm long, bearing many scented flowers with white corollas and pinkish stamens. The much commoner Greater Plantain has long-stalked, almost hairless leaves and dull greenish-white flower stalks. *Companion species* Chalk Milkwort (p.194), Common Bird's-foot-trefoil (p.145), Common Milkwort (p.147), Fairy Flax (p.152) and Yellow-rattle (p.168). *Distribution* Native. Occurs throughout most of England but quite scarce in the far south west and rare in Wales. Confined to southern Scotland; isolated colonies in the north are considered to be alien. Not native to Ireland, although there are several introduced colonies. *Habitat* Chalk and limestone soils, but it also occurs on heavy clay. Its main habitats are downland grassland and tracks, calcareous pasture and mown grassland (such as churchyards). It is less frequent in hay meadows and on fixed dunes, and is sometimes found in water meadows that receive calcareous water.

Horseshoe Vetch
(*Hippocrepis comosa*)

To the untrained eye, the yellow vetches can look bewilderingly similar. But a few telltale signs make them easy to tell apart. The two most alike in terms of season, flower and habit are Horseshoe Vetch and Common Bird's-foot-trefoil (p.145), which often grow side by side. But Common Bird's-foot-trefoil has only a pair of leaflets on the main stem where each leaf parts from it, with a triplet of leaflets as the main body of the leaf, and it tends to have bigger flowers. By contrast, Horseshoe Vetch has ten to twenty leaflets to every leaf, and its clustered seed pods are divided into horseshoe shapes all the way along, the segments breaking apart when they are ripe. It is the larval food plant of two of the quintessential butterfly species of southern English calcareous grassland: Chalkhill Blue and Adonis Blue.

Plant type Pea family, Fabaceae. *Flowers* April–July. *Height* 5–20cm. *Description* Spreading hairless perennial herb with a woody stem at the base. Leaves are pinnate with four to five pairs of leaflets and a terminal leaflet (no tendril), 5–8cm long. Inflorescence is a long-stalked whorl of five to twelve yellow flowers, each 8–10mm long. *Companion species* Common Bird's-foot-trefoil, Crosswort (p.196) and Germander Speedwell (p.85). *Distribution* Native. Its distribution follows the chalk and limestone. Thus it is found on the North and South Downs, the Chilterns, Salisbury Plain, Cranborne Chase, the Isle of Wight, the Cotswolds, the Mendips, the Lincolnshire Wolds, the limestone of Yorkshire and Cumbria and the limestone of south Wales, with an isolated colony on Great Orme's Head, Llandudno. Within these areas it can be locally abundant. *Habitat* Sunny pastures on chalk and limestone and rock ledges on limestone cliffs. It is one of the best indicators of unimproved calcareous grassland.

Hound's-tongue
(*Cynoglossum officinale*)

You can tell that Hound's-tongue is a cynoglossum, like the spring-flowering, forget-me-not-like flowers that some of us grow in our gardens. Their flower spikes have the characteristic scorpion-tail curl at their stem end, although the flowers are not blue but a deep, clotted-blood red. Both the common and generic names refer to its long, soft leaves, which resemble a hound's tongue. The whole plant has a strong and quite nasty smell, said to be like that of dog's pee or a nest of mice. On chalk and limestone, it used to be very common, but it has declined noticeably during the twentieth century. This is largely due to habitat loss, but herbicide spraying has also had a drastic effect.

Plant type Borage family, Boraginaceae. *Flowers* June–August. *Height* 30–60cm. *Description* Erect, downy biennial. Basal leaves are elliptical, stalked and silky, 10–25cm long; upper leaves are lanceolate and stalkless. Inflorescence is a forked cyme of flowers, each with funnel-shaped, five-lobed, purplish-red corollas up to 1cm across. Flowers have short stalks, no more than 5mm long. Fruit is a flattened nutlet, 5–6mm across, covered with hooked bristles. *Companion species* Common Knapweed (p.146), Common Ragwort (p.242), Perforate St John's-wort (p.209), Weld (p.264), Wild Mignonette (p.216) and Viper's-bugloss (p.214). *Distribution* Native. It is locally frequent in most of southern and eastern England and coastal parts of Wales, but rare in northern England and Scotland. In some regions, such as the chalk and limestone districts of southern England, it can be quite common. In Ireland, it is mostly confined to the east coast. *Habitat* Disturbed ground on dry, usually base-rich soils. Typical habitats include woodland edges and clearings, hedgerows, open grassland, downland, field edges and shingle.

Lady's Bedstraw
(Galium verum)

This is one of my favourite wild plants. Individually, it has tiny, delicate flowers, but lots of them together make the ground look as though it is puffing with yellow, sulphurous smoke. It smells delicious, too – like hay mixed with honey – and the scent remains even when it is dried. That is why it was harvested for stuffing pillows and mattresses, particularly on beds used by women who were about to give birth (hence its name). Because of its high acid content, it was also used as a rennet substitute to colour and flavour cheese – mixed with nettles, it was a key ingredient of Double Gloucester. It is surprising to think, when you see it growing happily and strongly on chalk, that this is one of the weakest wild flowers, easily crowded out by more robust plants. It is often most abundant on very poor chalk soil or other very thin, limey soils, where hungry bruisers have less of a chance.

Plant type Bedstraw family, Rubiaceae. *Flowers* July–August. *Height* Up to 60cm long. *Description* Perennial herb with sprawling, then erect, four-angled stems. Leaves are linear, shiny and in whorls of eight to twelve. Flowers are golden yellow, very small (corollas 2–3mm across) and in leafy panicles. Fruit is 1.5mm long, smooth, becoming black when ripe. Its yellow flowers distinguish it from other members of the bedstraw family, although a hybrid, which also has pale yellow flowers, occurs with Hedge Bedstraw (p.202). *Companion species* Common Knapweed (p.146), Greater Knapweed (p.201), Tufted Vetch (p.166) and Wild Mignonette (p.216). *Distribution* Native. Common throughout Britain and Ireland, although becoming more restricted to the coast in the westernmost extremities of Britain and in Ireland. There have been local declines due to grassland improvement and it is now absent from inland parts of Devon and parts of north-west Scotland. *Habitat* Well-drained, relatively infertile neutral or calcareous soils. Habitats include hay meadows, pastures, chalk and limestone downland, rock outcrops, quarries, coastal cliff tops, dune grasslands and machair, roadsides and railway banks.

Late Spider-orchid
(Ophrys fuciflora)

Insect-imitating *Ophrys* orchids are numerous in the Mediterranean, but we have only four here: Fly Orchid (p.10), Early Spider-orchid (p.198), Bee Orchid (p.191) and Late Spider-orchid. Of these, Late Spider-orchid is the rarest because the bee that pollinates it lives on the Continent and is not found in Britain, so seed-set is very rare. The flowers are long-lived, however, and the plants also reproduce vegetatively, forming strong clumps over decades. Many of these were lost during the twentieth century, as a result of the destruction of chalk grassland. The species was also severely hit by the myxomatosis outbreak in the 1950s, when the consequent death of grazing rabbits caused areas of grassland to succumb to scrub and woodland. This exotic and beautiful species has been reduced to about five hundred plants in the British Isles, and the flowering population is considerably smaller.

Plant type Orchid family, Orchidaceae. *Flowers* Late May– June. *Height* Up to 40cm, although usually less than 20cm. *Description* Erect perennial herb. Leaves are oblong-elliptical, grey-green and with prominent veins. The spike has between one and fourteen flowers. Each flower has three sepals, usually pink, sometimes white or darker pink, often with a green vein. The two small upper petals are usually triangular and pink. The lower petal or 'lip' is dark brown, similar to that of Bee Orchid but larger. The feature that distinguishes it from Bee Orchid is that the yellow, terminal appendage of the lip sticks forward. *Companion species* Columbine (p.4), Common Centaury (p.194), Common Twayblade (p.148), Man Orchid (p.206) and Musk Orchid (p.207). *Distribution* Native. Confined to a dozen or so populations on the North Downs between Wye and Folkestone. *Habitat* Well-drained calcareous chalky soil in species-rich, closely grazed grassland.

Man Orchid
(Orchis anthropophora)

You need to get down on hands and knees to appreciate the distinctive flowers of this small orchid. The overall colour is usually a clear Chartreuse green. Its shape is that of a long-bodied man, with long arms almost down to the floor and often, but not always, a small appendage between the legs. He is wearing a big biker's helmet or large turban, the edges of which are often outlined with the deepest crimson. Individual flower spikes vary, and in some the legs and arms are also crimson. The French call this either Hanged Man or Naked Man Orchid.

Plant type Orchid family, Orchidaceae. *Flowers* May–June. *Height* 10–40cm (can be up to 65cm). *Description* Perennial herb. Grey-green leaves are oblong-lanceolate, in a basal rosette and up the stem, 6–10cm long, often with a few transverse wrinkles. Inflorescence is a dense spike of up to fifty flowers. Each flower is yellowish green, nearly always tinged with red, with three sepals and three petals. The two upper petals and all the sepals form a close helmet, while the lower petal forms a four-lobed lip. *Companion species* Lady Orchid (p.17). *Distribution* Native. It has been lost from about half its historical sites, and it declined significantly during the twentieth century, destroyed by ploughing, scrub encroachment, spray drift and inappropriate roadside cutting regimes. It is now confined to southern and eastern England. The North Downs of Kent and Surrey are the stronghold for the species, where it is locally common. Elsewhere it is very rare. *Habitat* Well-drained calcareous grassland. It is often found in old chalk pits and limestone quarries, and on roadside verges. It can put up with some shade and is often found at the edge of scrub. Continuous heavy grazing is detrimental, and will eventually wipe it out.

Meadow Clary
(Salvia pratensis)

A beautiful, intense purple-blue flower, the colour of a bishop's cassock, this is now very rare in the British Isles. It is still quite common on the Continent, but with the widespread destruction of meadows and traditionally managed grasslands, it now occurs in only twenty-one native locations (most of the decline took place before 1950). The ancestor of many of our garden salvias, its status as a native plant is sometimes questioned because it was known in Elizabethan gardens before it was recorded in the wild. More recently, it has become a popular plant of wild-flower seed mixes, so you will see it by the roadside more commonly. It is a criminal offence to collect it from the wild.

Plant type Dead-nettle family, Lamiaceae. *Flowers* June–July. *Height* 30–100cm. *Description* Erect downy perennial. Leaves are oval to oblong with a heart-shaped (cordate) base, bluntly toothed, slightly wrinkled, 7–15cm long, in a rosette at the base and up the stem. Flowers are violet-blue (occasionally pink or white) with two-lipped corollas; the upper lip forms a hood that encloses the stamens. Stamens are articulated, with an arching upper filament topped by the anther and a short, flap-like lower appendage in the lip. When a bee lands on the lip it depresses this flap, causing the upper part of the stamen to arc down so that the anther dusts the bee with pollen. *Companion species* Black Medick (p.64), Common Bird's-foot-trefoil (p.145), Red Clover (p.161) and White Clover (p.167). *Distribution* Generally considered to be native. Almost confined to southern England, where it is very rare. It is most frequent in the Oxfordshire Cotswolds. As a casual alien, it has a wider distribution. *Habitat* Unimproved grassland, lane sides, road verges and disturbed ground on well-drained soils overlying chalk and limestone.

Monkey Orchid
(*Orchis simia*)

This is exceptionally rare, with only three sites in the British Isles. Each bright flower, a mixture of white to very pale pink and bright magenta, looks like a monkey, with a big head, very long, thin, stringy arms and legs, a speckled chest and a long tail. The tips of the arms and legs are often curved upwards and forwards. The flowers, which have a faint vanilla scent, are all very close together, the monkeys often looking as if they have been thrown into a random heap. The other telltale sign of this orchid – unique among British varieties – is that it opens (and so goes over) from the top down. Most flower spikes develop the opposite way round, the flowers at the top of the spike opening last.

Plant type Orchid family, Orchidaceae. *Flowers* Mid May–early June. *Height* 15–30cm, occasionally to 45cm. *Description* Erect hairless perennial. The lip of the flower is deeply lobed, white, flushed purplish pink at the edges and heavily speckled purplish pink in the centre. Upper petals and sepals form a helmet. Thick green stem is washed brown-purple at the tip and grey-green leaves are oval-oblong. *Companion species* Chalk Milkwort (p.194), Common Bird's-foot-trefoil (p.145), Common Milkwort (p.147), Common Twayblade (p.148), Early-purple Orchid (p.9) and Wild Thyme (p.217). *Distribution* Native. One of our rarest wildflowers. By the 1920s, it had severely declined, an effect of the ploughing of chalk grassland and collection of specimens. Only one substantial colony was left, at Hartslock Nature Reserve in Oxfordshire, where it persists today. It was rediscovered in east Kent in the 1950s and seed was taken to Park Gate Down Nature Reserve in Kent, which now supports a healthy population. *Habitat* Chalk grassland, usually on south-facing slopes. It dislikes heavy grazing, so it is associated with scrub cover.

Musk Orchid
(*Herminium monorchis*)

The only species of the genus *Herminium* found in Britain, this is a very tricky orchid to find. Even if you know vaguely where it is, you can spend ages locating it – the tiny flower spikes are a grass-like yellow-green, so it is well camouflaged and easily mistaken for a sprig of the richer yellow Lady's Bedstraw (p.205), with which it often grows. Once you have spotted it, you are likely to find a few, as it reproduces vegetatively and can appear in large stands of dozens of plants. The flowers are pollinated by a broad variety of insects, including flies, gnats, beetles and parasitic wasps, but, despite its name, it has no apparent scent. It is probably the most boring-looking orchid in the country and, being so difficult to find, it is one for devotees.

Plant type Orchid family, Orchidaceae. *Flowers* June–July. *Height* Up to 30cm, usually 2–15cm. *Description* Erect perennial herb. Leaves are keeled, bright green, oblong to oval-lanceolate, all in a basal rosette that overwinters. Inflorescence is a densely flowered spike of usually twenty to thirty small, bell-shaped flowers, sometimes up to seventy. *Companion species* Common Centaury (p.194), Common Twayblade (p.148), Lady's Bedstraw and Yellow-wort (p.217). *Distribution* Native. Confined to chalk and limestone in southern England. It is rare or local wherever it occurs and colonies are often very small. It has declined significantly during the twentieth century with the ploughing and improvement of downland pastures. The best site is Noar Hill in Hampshire, where four- or five-figure counts are usually made. *Habitat* Calcareous grassland on chalk or limestone. It prefers a short, open, herb-rich sward and is unable to compete with rank grasses. It is often found on narrow terraces on steep downland slopes.

Pasqueflower

(Pulsatilla vulgaris)

Also known as pulsatillas, these are the *Vogue* models of the wild-flower kingdom, when each flower is backlit, trapped in a halo of light. They never form the solid, clumped spectacle that Oxlips and Fritillaries do. Instead they scatter themselves sparsely over thin, chalky pastures, lying there like beautiful girls left in the ballroom at the end of the dance, their dusky purple dresses folded around them. Have a really close look at them. The golden yellow anthers at the flower's centre are a perfect contrast to the velvet-textured purple petals. A gentle fuzz of very fine hairs covers the calyx and leaves. The feathery, anemone-like seed pods are also exquisite. These are worth travelling miles to see.

Plant type Buttercup family, Ranunculaceae. *Flowers* April–May. *Height* 4–12cm. *Description* Perennial herb with greyish, feathery leaves that are twice pinnate and hairy. Solitary bell-shaped purple flowers, 5–8cm across, have a tuft of yellow stamens and are held erect at first, drooping later. Fruits develop long, silky plumes. *Companion species* Burnt Orchid (p.192), Chalk Milkwort (p.194), Common Juniper (p.354), Common Rock-rose (p.195), Cowslip (p.195) and Horseshoe Vetch (p.204). *Distribution* Native. Rare. A species of chalk downland and the great limestone belt that runs from Bristol to Lincolnshire, including the Cotswolds, one of its remaining strongholds. Oddly absent from chalk areas where one might expect it to be, such as the North and South Downs and Salisbury Plain. Reduced to about twenty colonies, of which only a few can be regarded as large and expanding – some sites number fewer than ten plants each. Pasqueflower is archetypal of species that have suffered from the fragmentation of formerly expansive unimproved grasslands, systematically dying out from isolated sites as they became temporarily overgrown. *Habitat* Characteristically a plant of grazed downland, mainly in places with high summer temperatures, high sunshine and low rainfall, but this does not always apply. On Therfield Heath near Royston, Hertfordshire, it grows in a rabbit- and sheep-proof enclosure and is now largely absent from the heavily nibbled grazed downs beyond.

Perforate St John's-wort

(Hypericum perforatum)

This is one of the strongest-growing meadow flowers, particularly on chalk or limestone, where it can form large, extensive colonies, taking over swathes of ground. It looks like Common Ragwort (p.242) from a distance, and in some countries it is listed as a noxious weed. It has lots of small, sharp-yellow flowers, with distinct tufts of anthers radiating from their hearts. The petals have characteristic black dots all the way round their edges. Perforate St John's-wort is used in the treatment of depression and is commercially grown in some countries for that reason. You can take it in many forms, as pills, tea bags or tinctures, but in large doses it can be poisonous, causing skin irritation and restlessness. You can tell this species from its relatives by holding a leaf up to the light. The leaf surface is covered with pale spots, making it appear perforated – hence the species name. In fact, the dots are glands, filled with fragrant oils and other chemical compounds.

Plant type St John's-wort family, Hypericaceae. *Flowers* June–September. *Height* 30–90cm. *Description* Erect perennial herb. Stems are round with opposite ridges. Leaves are elliptical to oblong, blunt, hairless and quite small (1–2cm long). Flowers are golden yellow, 2cm across, with pointed sepals and black dots around the edges of the petals. St John's-worts can be difficult to tell apart at first, but they are easy to distinguish once you know the key characteristics. Stems can be round or square, hairy or hairless, with raised ridges or without; leaves may be hairy or hairless, with or without translucent dots; flowers have either black dots on the petals or no dots. *Companion species* Broad-leaved Dock (p.236), Creeping Thistle (p.150), Curled Dock (p.245) and Viper's-bugloss (p.214). *Distribution* Native. Very common throughout the British Isles, except the far north of Scotland and west of Ireland. It extended its range into Scotland along the railways during the twentieth century. *Habitat* Meadows, hedge banks, open woods, roadsides and along railways. It often grows in dry, calcareous habitats, particularly in areas of heavy rabbit browsing.

Purple Milk-vetch
(Astragalus danicus)

When you are lucky enough to come across clumps of what looks like a purple-flowered Red Clover (p.161), you have found Purple Milk-vetch. This now-rare plant thrives on impoverished soils – the thinnest Breckland sand or most free-draining chalk or limestone – probably because it stands a better chance of survival in poor ground that bigger, quicker-growing plants cannot tolerate. Because of agricultural improvement and lack of grazing, Purple Milk-vetch has declined over many decades, particularly on the chalk in southern England and limestone in northern England. It is now considered endangered. There is hope, however: work in the Breckland, East Anglia, funded by Plantlife and managed by the Forestry Commission, has brought back a fantastic population, probably from buried seed, on land cleared of pines and de-stumped.

Plant type Pea family, Fabaceae. *Flowers* May–June. *Height* 5–35cm. *Description* Low perennial herb. Leaves are hairy, pinnate, 3–7cm long, with leaflets 5–12mm long. Stipules are fused at the base. Flowers are bluish purple, up to 18mm long. Fruit is a pod, 7–10mm long, with white hairs. *Companion species* Black Medick (p.64), Selfheal (p.163) and White Melilot (p.116). *Distribution* Native. Very local. Its distribution is scattered and difficult to explain. It is not in places that it should be. It occurs on the eastern coast of Scotland and northern England (north of Flamborough Head) and there are a few populations in the Isle of Man, inland Scotland and the Western Isles, as well as on the west coast of Ireland. It also occurs on the chalk of England (although it is mysteriously absent from much of the North and South Downs). *Habitat* Short, unimproved turf on species-rich, well-drained calcareous soils, predominantly on chalk and limestone, but also on sand dunes and machair.

Pyramidal Orchid
(Anacamptis pyramidalis)

The least weird of British orchids, this is generously pretty with dense, distinctively shaped flower spikes in brilliant pink. Once common in old meadows on chalk, it is now something of a rarity. I came across a sad sight last summer: a swathe of twenty or so Pyramidal Orchids beside a road on the South Downs. There had been at least double that number the day before, but a roadside flail had sliced through more than half the group, beheading them before their seed was ripe. Despite this sort of treatment, Pyramidal Orchid has fared better than other orchid species because its seeds have a longer viability. It is scented, with a foxy, musky smell, which draws in different butterflies and moths.

Plant type Orchid family, Orchidaceae. *Flowers* June–August. *Height* 20–40cm, occasionally up to 75cm. *Description* Erect, hairless perennial herb. Leaves are green, unspotted, keeled and lanceolate, arranged spirally in a rosette and up the stem. The spike is dense, dome-shaped or conical and 2–5cm long. Between thirty and one hundred flowers are closely packed together. Each flower is deeply three-lobed with a long spur, the upper sepal and two petals forming a helmet. *Companion species* Black Medick (p.64), Common Bird's-foot-trefoil (p.145), Oxeye Daisy (p.159), Red Clover (p.161) and White Clover (p.167). *Distribution* Native. Quite common on chalk and limestone in southern England. Confined to the coast towards the north and west of England and Wales, it is rare in Scotland and frequent to locally common in Ireland. *Habitat* Well-drained calcareous soils. It is found in shortly grazed downland, dune slacks and on cliff tops, and in the longer grass of semi-stable dunes, scrub, roadside verges and churchyards. It also grows in the grikes of limestone pavement, on disturbed ground and, in the Hebrides, on machair.

Quaking-grass
(Briza media)

Like a series of raindrops hanging from a stem, this is one of our most delicate and elegant grasses. It is a soft hay-green when it flowers in early summer, turning more dun as it ages. The flower stems are like the finest hairs, almost invisible, so the flower spikelets appear to dance and quake even in a light breeze, which gives this grass its common name. Quaking-grass appears where the ground is thin and poor, forming a light smoky covering over chalk and limestone grasslands. It is not a vigorous species and has comparatively little foliage, so it is not used as fodder or sown in improved pastures. It is often a marker of interesting, species-rich, unimproved meadows. Its larger relative Greater Quaking-grass (*B. maxima*) is often seen in gardens, picked for flower arrangements. I grow them both at Perch Hill.

Plant type Grass family, Poaceae. *Flowers* June–August. *Height* 10–40cm. *Description* Erect perennial with creeping roots. Leaves are flat, lanceolate and pointed, up to 4mm wide at the base. Ligules are short and truncate (1mm long). Inflorescence is a loose, branched panicle, 5–8cm long, with many long-stalked, pendulous spikelets. Each spikelet is oval-shaped, flushed with purple and 4–5mm in width and length. *Companion species* Bee Orchid (p.191), Carline Thistle (p.193), Chalk Fragrant-orchid (p.193) and Pyramidal Orchid (p.210). *Distribution* Native. Common throughout much of Great Britain but rare in the far south-west of England and in north-west Scotland. It is more localised in parts of the Cambrian mountains, the Weald of Kent and Sussex and the Wash. It is common in central Ireland but quite scarce in both the south-west and north. *Habitat* Most frequently found in unimproved, species-rich, well-grazed grassland on infertile, calcareous soils, favouring well-drained slopes.

Sainfoin
(Onobrychis viciifolia)

With its showy, feather-like flower spikes in a bright, rich pink, Sainfoin is one of my long-standing favourites. The individual flowers are like those of a pea (and this is a legume), but every spike has up to one hundred flowers, stacked in layers, one on top of another. Its showiness and colour give it the other common names of Cock's Head and Cock's Comb: in full flower, it was thought to look like the head of a cockerel. There are two colour forms: the richer-coloured native form and a paler-flowered seventeenth-century introduction (it was grown widely as a fodder plant until the nineteenth century, and the name Sainfoin originates from French – *sain* meaning 'wholesome' and *foin* meaning 'hay'). The native is more prostrate in its habit. Sainfoin has distinctive seed pods, which are large and round, downy and toothed, like a series of spiny footballs, each one holding a seed. The pod does not split open, but attaches itself to an animal for wide dispersal.

Plant type Pea family, Fabaceae. *Flowers* June–August. *Height* 20–40cm. *Description* Erect or (sometimes) prostrate perennial herb. Leaves are pinnate, with six to twelve pairs of leaflets. Flower spikes are on long stalks, with rich pink (sometimes salmony), red-veined flowers, each 10–12mm long. Pods are 6–8mm long. *Companion species* Common Bird's-foot-trefoil (p.145), Horseshoe Vetch (p.204), Red Clover (p.161), White Clover (p.167) and Wild Mignonette (p.216). *Distribution* Native or alien. The chalk grassland (prostrate) form may be native, but the more frequent erect form is considered to be imported from central Europe. It is locally frequent in southern England, occasional to rare in northern England, and absent from Ireland. In Wales and Scotland it is very rare and found only as an alien. The non-native form is increasing because of its use in wild-flower seed mixes and its presence as a contaminant of grass seed. *Habitat* Unimproved chalk grassland. The more robust alien variants are found on grassy banks and roadsides, and by tracks on chalk, less often on other calcareous soils. They can be abundant on newly sown roadsides.

Salad Burnet
(*Sanguisorba minor*)

Like plantains, burnets provide a detailed foliage backdrop to more glamorous grassland flowers, their embroidered textures breaking up the repetitive shapes of grass leaves in wild-flower-rich fields. In the case of Salad Burnet, the leaves are dark green on top and silvery below with deep crimson stems, the individual lobe of each leaf so elegantly serrated it looks as though it has been cut with crimping scissors. The flowers hover above like round red marbles with splotches of green. Its common name comes from the fact that the fresh spring leaves are edible and said to taste of cucumber, although they have always seemed rather bitter to me.

Plant type Rose family, Rosaceae. *Flowers* May–September. *Height* 15–40cm. *Description* Hairless, erect, branching, evergreen perennial herb. Basal leaves are pinnate with three to twelve pairs of rounded, toothed leaflets that smell of cucumbers when crushed. Inflorescence is a globular head (the 'marble') of tiny flowers: the lower flowers are yellow-green, male or bisexual with long stamens, the upper ones reddish and female with two feather-like purple stigmas. It could be confused with Great Burnet (p.154), but this is larger (up to 1m in height), with not round but more elongated flower heads, and it grows on heavier soils. *Companion species* Common Bird's-foot-trefoil (p.145), Common Spotted-orchid (p.148), Green-winged Orchid (p.154), Horseshoe Vetch (p.204) and Wild Thyme (p.217). *Distribution* Frequent to locally abundant in England and Wales, although absent from much of central Wales and north Devon. It is very rare in Scotland, being confined as a native to the south. In Ireland it is local, mostly found in central Ireland. *Habitat* Dry, infertile grassland on chalk and limestone, but also occurring on boulder clay. It is often abundant on downland, but also grows in rock crevices, scree, quarries and on roadside banks.

Sheep's-fescue
(*Festuca ovina*)

As its name suggests, this pinky-purplish-flowered grass is a valuable pasture grass for sheep, because it forms densely tufted clumps that make good grazing. It is a common species of pastures, particularly on poor, well-drained soils of chalk and limestone, where it often grows alongside Quaking-grass (p.211). Like that species, Sheep's-fescue is often an indicator of herb-rich, unimproved grassland. This one, however, is more widespread than Quaking-grass, as it also grows on heaths, moors and mountain pastures, a fact in part due to its variability – a number of difficult-to-separate subspecies are known. On higher ground, it provides good grazing where lusher vegetation struggles to flourish, so it is a key grass for upland and heathland farmers. It is also one of the larval food plants of the

Meadow Brown, Small Heath and Gatekeeper butterflies and the primary larval food plant of the Silver-spotted Skipper butterfly – now a rarity of chalk downland in southern England.

Plant type Grass family, Poaceae. *Flowers* Late May–July. *Height* 5–60cm. *Description* Variable, densely tufted perennial grass without rhizomes. Leaves are blue-green, bristle-like, 3–15cm long and 0.5mm wide. Leaf sheaths are split halfway to the base. Inflorescence is erect with oblong spikelets, 5–6mm long, with three to nine violet-tinged florets. Lemmas are pointed and have awns at their tips. There are several species of fescue that are similar to Sheep's-fescue, and even experienced botanists have difficulty recognising some species. Confusion is most likely with Red Fescue (*F. rubra*), which also has bristle-like leaves but is often taller (up to 100cm) and has creeping rhizomes. *Companion species* Common Centaury (p.194), Quaking-grass and Yellow-wort (p.217). *Distribution* Native. Common throughout Great Britain. It is more local in Ireland. *Habitat* It is drought-tolerant and therefore often abundant on poor, well-drained soils. Although it is associated with chalk and limestone grassland, it is found as high as 1200m in the Scottish Highlands. In fact, it is often the dominant grass species in upland regions, occurring on heaths and moors, mountain slopes, rock ledges and sea cliffs.

Small Scabious
(Scabiosa columbaria)

It is easy to see why this plant is known as the pincushion flower, with lots of densely packed miniature flowers making up what appears to be a single flower head. It has smaller, more globular flower heads than the fatter-bloomed Field Scabious (p.198), with the outer petals a little reflexed back towards the stem, and generally it makes smaller plants. It is also less robust and will not persist in rank, ungrazed grass. It has long, deep tap roots, so it can survive in a drought and on thin, infertile, dry chalk, where there is less competition from more vigorous plants. Like most members of the teasel family, this has energy-rich nectar and is loved by bees, butterflies and moths. Culpeper recommends using the juice of the plant to clear pimples and freckles from the face and to treat dandruff or itching of the scalp.

Plant type Teasel family, Dipsacaceae. *Flowers* July–September. *Height* 15–70cm. *Description* Short to medium, slender, erect perennial herb. Basal leaves are long-stalked, obovate and pinnatifid with a large terminal leaflet, forming a rosette. Upper leaves are stalkless with linear lobes. Flower head is 2–3cm across, made up of many densely packed five-lobed corollas in blue-violet (sometimes pale lilac). *Companion species* Devil's-bit Scabious (p.151), Field Scabious, Lady's Bedstraw (p.205) and Sainfoin (p.211). *Distribution* Native. Frequent to locally common in England and Wales, very rare in Scotland and absent from Ireland. Its distribution follows chalk and limestone. Thus it is quite local or scarce in areas of south-west England, mid Wales and the West Midlands, where limestone soils are infrequent. *Habitat* Dry, infertile soils. Habitats include calcareous pastures on downs, hill slopes and banks, and it is occasionally found on cliffs and rock outcrops and in disused chalk and limestone quarries.

Viper's-bugloss
(Echium vulgare)

Like the wild delphinium of the Mediterranean, Viper's-bugloss gives us huge swathes of intense, brilliant blue. Standing tall and upright, it is the perfect backdrop to almost any other wild flower. It was made famous by Derek Jarman's garden at Dungeness in Kent, and more of us should grow it in our gardens, because it is dripping with nectar. You will often see it covered with four or five burnet moths at once, as well as countless bees and butterflies. Like lungworts, it has red buds, opening to purple and fading to the characteristic bright blue. Particularly when it is still in bud, each group of flowers on the central stem looks like a coiled snake (hence the name), or a millipede arching out from the centre where the flowers first open. It looks spectacular, but it is unpopular with some farmers as one plant can generate a swathe the following year.

Plant type Borage family, Boraginaceae. *Flowers* June–September. *Height* Up to 80cm. *Description* Erect, bristly, multi- or solitary-stemmed biennial herb. Basal leaves are strap-shaped with a prominent central vein but no apparent side veins, while stem leaves are shorter and stalkless. Blue flowers, arranged in cymes, are 15– 20mm long and funnel-shaped with protruding red stamens and unequal lobes. *Companion species* Creeping Thistle (p.150), Hemlock (p.304), Perforate St John's-wort (p.209) and Weld (p.264). *Distribution* Native. Widespread throughout England (most common in the south and east) and Wales, and found as a native in southern Scotland and eastern Ireland. *Habitat* Grassy and disturbed habitats on well-drained soils. It is found in bare places on chalk and limestone downs, on heaths, in quarries and chalk pits, in cultivated and waste land, along railways and roadsides and by the coast on cliffs, sand dunes and shingle.

Wild Basil
(Clinopodium vulgare)

Wild Basil is one of those pink tubular flowers of which there are so many to confuse with one another in summer. At a glance, it could be Hedge Woundwort (p.90) or Wild Marjoram (p.216), but it looks most like Common Calamint (*Clinopodium ascendens*), to which it is related. Wild Basil is generally more delicate-looking than the others, if rather untidy in its overall ensemble. It thrives only with little competition on thin, chalky, infertile soils. Its common name is misleading, because it does not taste or look anything like the culinary herb basil. The name 'basil' comes from the Greek word *basilkon*, meaning 'kingly', and is a reference to the plant's pungency and value in medicine. It is edible, with a mild aromatic taste somewhere between mint and Wild Marjoram, but it is not nearly as strong as either. Its flowers are good added to a salad. Like other members of the dead-nettle family, this is attractive to bees and butterflies and a valuable source of late summer pollen.

Plant type Dead-nettle family, Lamiaceae. *Flowers* July–September. *Height* 10–40cm. *Description* Erect, hairy perennial herb. Stems are unbranched or slightly branched. Leaves are oval, stalked, blunt and rounded at the base, 2–5cm long, resembling those of Wild Marjoram. Flowers are situated in dense whorls in the leaf axils and have bright rose-purple, two-lipped corollas, 15–20mm long. *Companion species* Carline Thistle (p.193), Lady's Bedstraw (p.205) and Wild Marjoram. *Distribution* Native. Common in the south and east, becoming occasional to the north. Absent from the far north-west of Scotland and very rare as an introduction in Ireland. *Habitat* Hedges, woodland margins, coarse scrubby grassland, coastal cliffs and sand dunes, typically on dry calcareous soils. It is also found on waste ground.

Wild Liquorice
(Astragalus glycyphyllos)

This sprawling, prostrate plant has stems that bend each time they branch, giving it a distinctive zigzagging style as it sprawls out over the ground. It has pale pompom flower heads, each made up of fifteen to twenty miniature pea-shaped flowers. Particularly when not in flower, it can be confused with other vetches, but it lacks the usual tendrils at its leaf tips and instead has a leaflet. It is not the same as the liquorice used to make sweets. The true liquorice, *Glycyrrhiza glabra*, is native to south-east Europe and west Asia and is no longer found in the British Isles. It was once grown here, especially around Pontefract, West Yorkshire, where it was used in liquorice confectionary: its roots were pulped and its juice condensed. The two plants' similar names are derived from the Greek *glycyphyllos*, meaning 'sweet leaf', and the edible roots and stems of both do have a sweet, aniseedy flavour.

Plant type Pea family, Fabaceae. *Flowers* July–August. *Height* Sprawls to 60–100cm. *Description* Hairless, flat-growing perennial herb. Leaves are pinnate, 10–20cm long, with elliptical leaflets, each 15–40cm long, and arrow-shaped stipules at the base. Inflorescence is a raceme of cream flowers, 2–5cm long. Each flower has the typical flower structure of members of the pea family and is 10–15mm long, later ripening to produce banana-shaped pods, 20–25mm long. *Companion species* Oxeye Daisy (p.159), Small Scabious (opposite) and Wild Basil (p.215). *Distribution* Native. Found throughout much of Britain as far north as Inverness. In Wales it is confined to just a handful of colonies, and it is absent from Devon, Cornwall and Ireland. *Habitat* Cliffs, wood borders, chalk pits and scrubby grassland on railway banks and road verges. It grows mainly on calcareous soils and thrives on warm, sheltered banks and hollows without too much grazing.

Wild Marjoram
(Origanum vulgare)

Walking through chalky fields of Marjoram is one of the wild-flower highs of summer. The pretty, airy, pale mauve flowers contrast with the deeper red-purple buds, creating a bi-colour haze. The whole place is filled with oregano scent, and insects buzz around manically as soon as the sun comes out – there are few such long-flowering plants so rich in nectar. The leaves and flowers taste as delicious as they smell, but they are not palatable to grazing animals, so the flowers usually survive well into autumn. Garden forms include a gold-leaved cultivar and a white-flowered variety. They all do best on chalk and will not grow and flower as well on heavy soils, but they do fine in a sunny area of my garden on Wealden clay, with extra grit added to the planting holes.

Plant type Dead-nettle family, Lamiaceae. *Flowers* July–August. *Height* 30–60cm. *Description* Erect, tufted, stiff perennial herb. Leaves are oval, pointed, untoothed (or slightly toothed) and stalked, 1.5–4.5cm long, arranged in opposite pairs. Flowers are in dense, rounded panicles and have rosy pink, two-lipped corollas, 6–8mm long, with protruding stamens. White-flowered plants are quite common. Wild Marjoram's distinctive scent makes it easy to identify. Wild Basil (p.215) grows in the same habitats, but its flowers are a darker rosy purple, weakly scented and arranged in whorls in the leaf axils. *Companion species* Crosswort (p.196), Hedge Bedstraw (p.202), Lady's Bedstraw (p.205), Pyramidal Orchid (p.210), Wild Basil and Wild Mignonette (right). *Distribution* Native. Common to very locally abundant in the south of England, becoming more local in the north of England, Wales and Scotland. It is very rare or absent in north-west Scotland and frequent in central Ireland. *Habitat* Dry, infertile, calcareous soils in grassland, hedge banks and scrub, as well as grassy, chalky places in woodland rides. It is a colonist of bare or sparsely vegetated disturbed ground, including quarries and road verges, and in some places, it has spread rapidly into former set-aside land. It is occasionally naturalised from gardens, and is intolerant of heavy grazing.

Wild Mignonette
(Reseda lutea)

The yellow-green vertical flower spikes of Wild Mignonette are always easy to spot from a distance, standing proud above the grasses and flowering plants that surround it. Like its larger cousin Weld (p.264), it has a bold, architectural presence amid a mass of chalk-loving wild flowers, cutting through the horizontal froth of plants such as Hedge Bedstraw (p.202), Lady's Bedstraw (p.205) and Tufted Vetch (p.166). It is also a plant of chalk field margins and arable crops, where its distinctive shape is easy to spot scattered among wheat or barley, mixed with Common Poppy (p.241) in those incredibly rare unsprayed arable fields. Its common name derives from the French *mignon*, which means 'dainty'.

Plant type Mignonette family, Resedaceae. *Flowers* June–August. *Height* Up to 70cm. *Description* Hairless, branched, bushy biennial or perennial herb. Stems are erect or sprawling, ribbed and branched. Leaves are once or twice pinnately cut, arranged in a rosette and up the stem. Flowers are arranged in conical racemes. Each flower is yellowish green, with six sepals, six petals and twelve to twenty stamens. Fruit is a warty, oblong capsule, 7–12mm long. *Companion species* Common Poppy, Perforate St John's-wort (p.209), Weld, Wild Marjoram (left) and Viper's-bugloss (p.214). *Distribution* Native or alien. Common throughout most of England, although local in the south west and largely absent from upland areas. It is absent from much of mid Wales, although quite common in north and south Wales. In Scotland, it is largely restricted to lowland areas in the south. *Habitat* Well-drained soils in open habitats. It occurs on waste ground and roadside verges, marginal grassland, disused railway land, quarries, arable land, disturbed chalk and limestone grassland around rabbit warrens, and fixed sand dunes.

Wild Thyme
(*Thymus polytrichus*)

Whether you are walking across chalk downs, clay pastures or Highland hills, you will see and smell wild thyme from May until early autumn. If the sun is out, the whole plant will be moving with feasting bees and butterflies. Wild Thyme is at its most impressive when it colonises mole- and anthills, carpeting them all over like brilliant purple pouffes scattered randomly across a sunny hillside. Unlike the thyme that we use in the kitchen, this species is practically tasteless. You can, however, use it like lavender to scent linen and clothes, as its dried flowers retain their scent for years.

Plant type Dead-nettle family, Lamiaceae. *Flowers* May–August. *Height* 10cm. *Description* Low, creeping, carpet-forming perennial herb. Leaves are 4–8mm long, oval-elliptical, only faintly scented. Flowers are rose-purple in crowded, dense clusters, with a strong scent. Flower stems are four-angled, hairy on two opposite faces but hairless on the other two. Three species of thyme are found in the British Isles. Breckland Thyme (*T. serpyllum*), found only in the Breckland, East Anglia, has flower stems that are hairy all round. Large Thyme (*T. pulegioides*) is more erect, growing to 20cm in height. Its flower stems are hairy only on the angles and it has a stronger scent. *Companion species* Crosswort (p.196), Thyme Broomrape (p.421) and Tormentil (p.371). *Distribution* Native. Found throughout the British Isles, but uncommon in regions dominated by acid substrates. Most frequent in Wales, south-central England, Cumbria, the north Pennines and Scotland. In Ireland it is largely restricted to the coast, and it is rare in the English Midlands, East Anglia and central Ireland. *Habitat* Free-draining, calcareous or base-rich substrates, including chalk, limestone, sands and gravels. It occurs in short grassland on heaths, downland, sea cliffs and sand dunes, and on rock outcrops and hummocks in calcareous mires. It is also frequent in upland grassland and on montane cliffs, rocks and ledges.

Yellow-wort
(*Blackstonia perfoliata*)

Yellow-wort is a graceful plant, particularly in its taller forms, with egg-yolk yellow, star-like flowers that contrast beautifully with silvery leaves. It is closely related to the earlier-flowering Common Centaury (p.194) and, apart from the flower colour, the two plants look quite similar. The specific name *perfoliata* is Latin for 'through the leaves' and refers to the stem, which appears to pierce the waxy leaves. The six- to eight-petalled flowers are typical of the gentian family, fused into a tube at the base, splitting near the petal tip. They flare out fully only in the morning, closing up tightly in the early afternoon.

Plant type Gentian family, Gentianaceae. *Flowers* June–October. *Height* 15–40cm. *Description* Erect, hairless, waxy annual herb. Basal leaves are obovate and form a rosette; stem leaves are oval, triangular and in pairs that are fused around the stem. Yellow flowers are arranged in loose, branched cymes and have six- to eight-lobed corollas, 8–15mm across. *Companion species* Autumn Gentian (p.190), Carline Thistle (p.193), Chalk Fragrant-orchid (p.193), Dwarf Thistle (p.197) and Pyramidal Orchid (p.210). *Distribution* Native. Common in England, more local in Wales, very rare in Scotland, locally common in Ireland. It is absent or rare in many parts of north-west England, mid Wales, Norfolk and inland Cornwall and Devon (where it is confined to the coast). Scottish colonies are not thought to be native – native distribution is not considered to extend beyond north-west Yorkshire and Northumberland. *Habitat* Open, dry (but frequently winter-wet), often stony, shallow basic soils. Its main habitats are calcareous grasslands and fixed sand dunes, but it can be an abundant colonist of disturbed ground, including quarries, railway cuttings, road verges and path sides.

Early Spider-orchid (p.198), Samphire Hoe, Kent, 4 May.

Crosswort (p.196) and Germander Speedwell (p.85), Dean, Bishop's Waltham, Hampshire, 12 May.

Leyburn Old Glebe Field, near Wensley, North Yorkshire, 12 June.

Common Bird's-foot-trefoil (p.145), Red Clover (p.161), Salad Burnet (p.213) and Yellow-rattle (p.168), Leyburn Old Glebe Field, near Wensley, North Yorkshire, 12 June.

Greater Knapweed (p.201), Field Scabious (p.198), Hedge Bedstraw (p.202) and Lady's Bedstraw (p.205).
Magdalen Hill Down, Hampshire, 5 July.

Field Scabious (p.198) and Kidney Vetch (p.403), Magdalen Hill Down, Hampshire, 5 July.

Harebell (p.202), Lady's Bedstraw (p.205), Marram (p.405) and Selfheal (p.163), Luskentyre, South Harris, Outer Hebrides, 22 July.

Seed heads and anthills, Strawberry Banks Nature Reserve, near Chalford, Gloucestershire, 20 November

Arable & Wasteland

Summer is the colourful high point for arable and wasteland 'weeds'. The year starts quite dull, with flowers such as Hairy Bitter-cress and Red Dead-nettle beginning the wild-flower show as early as February. The ever-flowering Shepherd's-purse, which gardeners think of as a bane, can be delicate and beautiful, especially when backlit by the low light of early spring.

This is the habitat of annuals, which thrive in disturbed ground, their seeds – many of which can survive for decades, even centuries, in the soil – turned over and exposed to light that will spark their germination. With ploughing or digging, earthworks or tipping, perennials are cleared, leaving a gap that annuals can exploit. Their seeds drift in to empty ground and can form a massive army, but they need time to grow and reach their flowering size. That is why glamour comes a little later in an arable field or in the corner of a patch of wasteland.

In May, once the days lengthen and the sun offers more warmth, prettier, showier annuals begin to bloom. I love the rich, dark flowers of Common Fumitory and its elegant grey-green leaves, forming a smoke-like ground cover. Common Field-speedwell may not be as large-flowered and intense in colour as the Germander species, but when the sun is on it, it forms a lovely trickle of blue across bare ground. The cheery, acid-green cartwheels of Sun Spurge provide splotches of intense colour, together with the floriferous, intense-coloured Scarlet Pimpernel, which can take over the whole margin of a field, and equally abundant swathes of Field Forget-me-not and, if you are lucky, Field Pansy.

Last year, on a walk through a barley field, I came across a corner where you could not see the soil for Field Pansy. The crop had for some reason failed in this patch – maybe because of grazing rabbits – and with no competition or shade from the barley, the pansy had gone haywire. With the widespread use of herbicides, you do not see Field Pansy, or any of these arable weeds, as often as you used to, but where they escape the spray, they can appear not by the ten, but by the thousand.

One of the great sights of the summer countryside in fields without herbicides is a cornfield full of poppies on an early June day. If there are poppies, there are probably many other interesting things: the elegant, twisting spires of Wild Mignonette, so loved by pollinator insects, the ground-carpeting, starry flowers of Field Madder and, in a very few sites, the great pink saucers of Corncockle. It is worth a trip to Plantlife's Ranscombe Farm Reserve in Kent at the end of June for a glimpse of these.

In the Outer Hebrides, spraying has never been widespread. The small arable fields are as flower-rich as they always have been, wild flowers filling the landscape as far as the eye can see. On the west side of the islands, near the shore where the white sand is mixed with centuries of added seaweed, the flowers in these machair fields often outdo the crop they have been sown with. Everyday plants, including Sun Spurge, Common Fumitory, Tufted Vetch and Perennial Sowthistle, are joined by what have become rarities: Corn Marigold and Cornflower.

Broad-leaved Dock
(Rumex obtusifolius)

The chunkiest of the common docks, with big, coarse leaves, Broad-leaved Dock is often a pest in the garden, particularly on the lawn. Its deep tap root is tricky to get rid of. If you pull it up, but leave a small section behind, it just regrows. It is a prolific seed producer, too. One plant can produce up to 60,000 seeds a year, and each seed may survive for up to fifty years. Together with Spear Thistle (p.261), Creeping Thistle (p.150), Curled Dock (p.245) and Common Ragwort (p.242), it is one of five species listed under the Weeds Act 1959, which obliges landowners to prevent it from spreading to agricultural land. Having said this, in an area of rough grassland, wasteland or beside the road its rust-red flower heads and seed pods can look marvellous. I pick and arrange them in a large jug with one of the meadow buttercups – they make a good combination and, by cutting them, I help to prevent a few plants at least from romping away.

Plant type Knotweed family, Polygonaceae. *Flowers* June–October. *Height* Up to 120cm. *Description* Stout, robust perennial herb. Lower leaves are up to 25cm long, oval-oblong with cordate bases, slightly wavy-edged. Upper leaves are narrower. Inflorescence is branched, green to rust-red, leafy below; tepals are 5–6mm long, triangular and deeply toothed, with a wart on at least one of them. It is most easily confused with Curled Dock, and hybrids between the two are common. *Companion species* Bulbous Buttercup (p.144), Creeping Buttercup (p.149), Creeping Thistle, Curled Dock, Meadow Buttercup (p.158) and Spear Thistle. *Distribution* Native. Common throughout the British Isles. *Habitat* Disturbed or trampled ground on most types of soils, except acid peat. It is a coloniser of field margins, hedge banks, roadsides, stream- and riverbanks, ditches and neglected cultivated ground.

Bugloss
(Anchusa arvensis)

The plants of Bugloss are as untidy as they come, the leaves so hairy that they are bristly, the stems covered with dense stubble. The common name originates from two Greek words meaning 'ox tongue', because its leaves are supposed to look or feel like one. These leaves are often windburnt, black around the edges, so one might wonder what there is to recommend this plant. The answer is its flowers, which are a beautiful, deep, June-sky blue, pretty en masse, particularly from a distance, when a clump makes a blue smudge on the edge of a field or in a vegetable patch. That is the sort of place it likes: disturbed, rich soil in full sun. Bugloss has edible flowers, which look pretty scattered over a salad.

Plant type Borage family, Boraginaceae. *Flowers* June–September. *Height* 15–40cm. *Description* Erect, bristly annual herb. Leaves are lanceolate-oblong, wavy edged, toothed, stalked near the base but clasping the stem above, up to 15cm long. Inflorescence is often forked, with leafy bracts. Blue, five-lobed flowers are no more than 5–6mm across with narrow calyx teeth. The corolla tube has a distinct curve, and the mouth of the tube is closed by five white, hairy scales. It has a four-seeded fruit. *Companion species* Creeping Thistle (p.150), Pineappleweed (p.255) and Silverweed (p.418). *Distribution* Introduced, probably as a contaminant of arable seed. Common in much of central and eastern England, especially East Anglia, Lincolnshire and the Severn Valley. It is very rare or absent in many upland regions. It is quite frequent along some stretches of the east coast of Ireland, but very rare inland. Bugloss has declined with agricultural intensification. *Habitat* A weed of arable fields and waste ground, it prefers well-drained calcareous or sandy soils, but it also occurs near the sea on sandy heaths and in disturbed dunes.

Butterfly-bush
(Buddleja davidii)

Good old Butterfly-bush is one of our loveliest wasteland plants, with tall, candelabra-like flowers in a range of purples and mauves. It smells delicious – sweet and honey-like – and comes alive with butterflies and bees as soon as the sun comes out. It was introduced in the 1890s from China, where it grows wild on rocky scree slopes on the Tibetan-Chinese border. It was first recorded in the wild in Britain in 1922. Like Oxford Ragwort (p.101), it has been helped by the railways, which act as a series of corridors along which its seeds can disperse – the railway ballast provides a habitat similar to that of its wild Tibetan homeland. As a favourite nectar source of many butterflies, it was encouraged by conservation organisations, but there is a growing awareness that its invasiveness may do more harm than good – it can damage butterfly habitats because it shades out caterpillar food plants. It is becoming a problem plant on some nature reserves in southern England.

Plant type Figwort family, Scrophulariaceae. *Flowers* June–September. *Height* Up to 5m. *Description* Shrub. Oval to lanceolate leaves are toothed, with fine white hairs on the undersides, arranged opposite one another. Flowers are mauve-purple and arranged in a dense, conical panicle. Each flower has four petals fused into a tube and four stamens. *Companion species* Broad-leaved Dock (p.236), Curled Dock (p.245), Red Valerian (p.407) and Wild Teasel (p.265). *Distribution* Recent introduction. Common throughout much of England and Wales, apart from the most remote regions. It is less frequent in Scotland and mostly confined to the lowlands around Edinburgh and Glasgow and near the coast. It is scattered throughout Ireland and more frequent in the east than in the west. It increased rapidly in the second half of the twentieth century and has continued to increase since. *Habitat* Well established on waste ground, by railways, in quarries, on roadsides and generally in urban habitats, where it often grows on walls and neglected buildings. It prefers dry, disturbed sites, where large populations can develop from its wind-dispersed seed.

Caper Spurge
(Euphorbia lathyris)

There is something reptilian and insect-like about Caper Spurge: it looks like a cross between an iguana and a stick insect. The whole plant is gawky and angular, its 'flowers' diamond-shaped and its bluish-green leaves neatly rigid and tiered regularly, almost at right angles, up the stem. Caper Spurge emerges from the ground as one single stem, but it does not branch, forking only at the top to hold the flowers. The fruits are big and round, nestled in the calyx, and look remarkably like those of the true caper (*Capparis spinosa*). Like all euphorbias, however, this is poisonous. Its milky latex sap causes a rash in many people and it would be dangerous to eat. For this reason, it is sometimes grown as a mole deterrent. It has an amazing capacity for springing back from long-buried seed.

Plant type Spurge family, Euphorbiaceae. *Flowers* May–July. *Height* Up to 1.2m. *Description* Tall, erect, hairless biennial. Leaves are waxy, grey-green, strap-shaped, blunt, 4–20cm long, arranged in four vertical rows. Inflorescence is a two- to six-rayed umbel with triangular-lanceolate bracts at the base. Each flower has crescent-shaped glands and a pair of upper bracts, broader than the bracts at the base of the umbel, with a cordate base. Fruit is 8–20mm long. The other common wild spurge, Wood Spurge (p.33), is distinguished from Caper Spurge by its downy, reddish stem. *Companion species* Bitter-vetch (p.144), Dandelions (p.246), Greater Stitchwort (p.87), Red Campion (p.24) and White Campion (p.115). *Distribution* Introduced: an archaeophyte. Found throughout the British Isles but common only in southern England and the Welsh Borders. It is very rare in Scotland and Ireland. In most areas it is a casual or naturalised alien originating from bird-sown seed or as an escape from cultivation. However, in some woods it is more persistent and some botanists have suggested that it may be native. *Habitat* Disturbed habitats or places with plenty of bare ground, including roadsides, abandoned gardens, old quarries and rubbish tips; it also occurs in open woodland.

Cleavers
(Galium aparine)

Cleavers can be the bane of your life as a gardener, germinating by the thousand with its hairy, sticky leaves and sticky green miniature-football seed heads (hence its other common name of Sticky Willy), which climb up and strangle precious garden plants. It does have redeeming qualities, though. For a start, it is edible – surprisingly good as a wilted green and traditionally fed to geese and chickens, giving it yet another common name: Goose Grass. It also has therapeutic uses. The Jodrell Laboratory at the Royal Botanic Gardens, Kew, in Surrey, has been collecting records of herbal remedies from visitors, and Cleavers keeps appearing. Older visitors report that its leaves can be made into a paste or poultice and applied to the skin after bad cuts or burns; this has now been tested and Cleavers found to increase the production of scab-forming Fibrinogen. Clinical trials have proved that a paste of Cleavers is one of the few effective remedies for intractable leg ulcers, which are notoriously difficult to treat.

Plant type Bedstraw family, Rubiaceae. *Flowers* June–August. *Height* Up to 200cm. *Description* Scrambling, sprawling or ascending annual herb. Stems are rough, four-angled and covered in bristly, backward-pointing prickles. Leaves are elliptical-lanceolate, one-veined, edged with backward-pointing prickles, arranged in whorls of six to nine up the stem. White flowers are four-petalled, 2mm across and arranged in axillary clusters of two to five. *Companion species* Broad-leaved Dock (p.236), Common Chickweed (p.239), Common Nettle (p.241), Curled Dock (p.245) and Lesser Burdock (p.253). *Distribution* Native. Very common throughout Britain and Ireland, except the Scottish Highlands. *Habitat* Cultivated land, hedges, riverbanks, waysides, soil heaps and waste places.

Colt's-foot
(Tussilago farfara)

One of the first things to emerge early in spring, Colt's-foot can form huge, expansive carpets on newly disturbed ground. When Samphire Hoe on the Kent coast was created with spoil from the Channel Tunnel, and the site was sown with seed from the Downs, two of the first colonisers were Colt's-foot and the very rare Early Spider-orchid (p.198). The flowers come first: bright, wide, golden-yellow daisies with scaly crimson stems. Only once these are dying back do the leaves appear: large flat fans, dark green on their upper surface and brilliant white-silver below. Its Latin genus name comes from *Tussis ago*, meaning 'to drive out a cough'. It was a remedy for coughs and respiratory diseases, and a tincture of its leaves is still added to some cough sweets.

Plant type Daisy family, Asteraceae. *Flowers* March–April, even February in an early year. *Height* Up to 30cm. *Description* Low to medium, creeping perennial herb. Leaves are broad, rounded-triangular, cordate-based, downy on the upper side, felted on the underside, 10–20cm across and long-stalked. Flower head is solitary, yellow, 15–35mm across, on a stout, erect, leafless, scaly stem up to 15cm tall. *Companion species* Creeping Buttercup (p.149), Creeping Thistle (p.150) and Shepherd's-purse (p.260). *Distribution* Native. Common throughout the British Isles, becoming local in far north Scotland. The seeds are like Dandelions' parachutes (p.246), needing only the slightest of draughts to keep them airborne – hence their widespread distribution and rapid colonising of bare ground. *Habitat* Often a pioneer in a range of moist or dry, often disturbed habitats, including sand dunes and shingle, cliff slopes, landslides, spoil heaps, seepage areas, rough grassland, crumbling riverbanks, waste places and roadside verges. It can also be a troublesome arable weed.

Common Chickweed
(Stellaria media)

When this is leafy and lush with new growth in the spring, it makes brilliant emerald-green cushions wherever it grows. At this stage, before many of the flowers have appeared and the leaves toughened, it makes good eating: succulent and slightly sweet, reminiscent of cornsalad or a sweet lettuce – an excellent addition to a spring salad bowl, as sometimes served by smart restaurants, which have baskets of Chickweed delivered to them by commercial foragers. It used to be fed to chickens – hence its common name. Look for the single line of hairs on the stem, which directs dew downwards towards a pair of leaves, where it is absorbed and reserved for use in times of drought. Once its small white stars (stellarias) begin to bloom, it merges into the clan of other small, white-flowered plants, such as stitchworts and mouse-ears. However, stitchworts have long and thin leaves, while mouse-ears are hairier.

Plant type Pink family, Caryophyllaceae. *Flowers* Year round. *Height* 5–30cm. *Description* Low-sprawling, straggly annual. Stems are round with a single line of hairs running down them. Leaves are bright green, oval and soft, pointed with long stalks (although the uppermost have no stalks). White flowers, 8–10mm across, have five deeply divided petals. *Companion species* Common Field-speedwell (p.240), Common Fumitory (p.240) and Fat-hen (p.247). *Distribution* Native and very common all over the British Isles. *Habitat* Found in a wide range of disturbed habitats, especially in nutrient-enhanced conditions, this conspicuous garden weed is also a serious weed of agricultural crops. It increases with fertiliser treatment and is resistant to a number of common selective herbicides. It also inhabits manure heaps, sewage works, walls and recently established plantations, and is a characteristic plant of coastal strands and seabird rocks.

Common Evening-primrose
(Oenothera biennis)

This species looks similar to Large-flowered Evening-primrose (*O. glazioviana*), and despite the latter's slightly larger flowers, it is tricky to tell the difference between the two. They grow in the same sorts of places and cross-breed like mad. On a late summer evening, you cannot drive in town or country without being almost certain to see Common Evening-primrose. It is often in a big, bold drift on the central reservation or in scrappy corners beside the road, its large, primrose-yellow, open saucers in groups of five or six at the top of every stem. Most of the flowers do not open until the evening, when they are pollinated by night-flying moths. Some Evening-Primrose hybrids are quite fragrant and have been used to create garden plants. The plant is also cultivated on an agricultural scale for its oil, which is said to relieve the symptoms of premenstrual syndrome, lower cholesterol and blood pressure and possibly slow the progression of rheumatoid arthritis and multiple sclerosis.

Plant type Willowherb family, Onagraceae. *Flowers* June–August. *Height* 1–2m. *Description* Tall herb with alternate leaves. Flowers are arranged in leafy spikes, each with four yellow petals and strongly reflexed sepals. This species has smaller petals (15–30mm long) than other Evening-primroses, with green sepals and a style the same length as the filaments. Stems are green at the top without red bulbous-based hairs. *Companion species* Cleavers (p.238), Common Toadflax (p.74) and Fennel (p.81). *Distribution* Introduced. Common throughout much of England and Wales, although largely absent from some remote upland regions and rare north of a line from the Humber Estuary to Morecambe Bay. It is found in Scotland and Ireland, but only rarely and often near the coast. *Habitat* Light, disturbed soils, particularly on sand. Typical habitats include waste ground, railway sidings, roadsides, riverbanks, quarries, sand pits and agricultural ground. It also occurs in coastal situations, such as sand dunes and seashores.

Common Field-speedwell
(Veronica persica)

This is not as showy as Germander Speedwell (p.85), with single flowers on each stem rather than a clutch, but it is the commonest of the speedwell family and can be seen wherever there is disturbed or bare ground. The Common form has a big white splotch at the centre of the flower, filling the whole of the bottom petal and bleeding out into the other three, whereas the flower of Germander Speedwell is pure blue with a thin white ring at its heart. I have it in my vegetable patch – it loves to be out in the open, in full sun and with plenty of water – and I am always trying to weed it out before it sets seed. It is pretty and cheerful, but it needs removing. Like Field Forget-me-not (p.248), its seeds remain viable in the soil for years and continue to germinate throughout the year and from year to year, so it can quickly colonise a new patch.

Plant type Speedwell family, Veronicaceae. *Flowers* Year round. *Height* 10–30cm. *Description* Branched, spreading, hairy annual with bright green, short-stalked leaves, 1–3cm long, which are oval-triangular and toothed and arranged alternately along the slim, gangly stems. Bright blue flowers are 8–12mm across with four petals, solitary, on long stalks rising from the leaf axils. The lower lip of the flowers is white. *Companion species* Common Chickweed (p.239), Common Fumitory (p.240) and Fat-hen (p.247). *Distribution* Introduced (probably native to the mountains of the Caucasus and northern Iran – hence its other common name of Persian Speedwell) and first recorded in the wild in 1826. Since then it has spread rapidly and it is now very common throughout the British Isles, rare or absent only from parts of western Scotland and western Ireland. *Habitat* Typically found on arable field edges, but also in other cultivated areas and waste ground on a wide range of fertile soils. This speedwell is a sure sign of human activity.

Common Fumitory
(Fumaria officinalis)

Since I was a child I've loved Fumitory, its strange, deep crimson, candle-like flowers standing out rich and dark against the delicate silver-green leaves. It reminded me of a long, thin sea anemone or coral, with its tentacles spreading out down the stem. As elegant as its garden cousins dicentras, or bleeding hearts, it flowers from the middle of spring right through the summer, filling the edges and corners of fields and wasteland areas wherever the ground is disturbed. The name Fumitory is derived from the medieval Latin *fumus terrae*, meaning 'smoke of the earth', and the way the plant spreads its delicate bluish-green, highly cut foliage over the surface of the soil is reminiscent of dispersing smoke. If you pull a fumitory from the ground, its roots give off an acrid, gaseous smell, like the fumes of nitric acid.

Plant type Poppy family, Papaveraceae. *Flowers* May–October. *Height* 20–50cm. *Description* Delicate, scrambling or erect, hairless annual. Leaves are two to three times pinnate and have flat, lanceolate, grey-green leaflets. Flowers are tubular and two-lipped and have two tiny sepals, two inner petals and two larger outer petals, 6–9mm long, pink-purple with a reddish-black apex. There are up to twenty flowers on each spike and often more than five spikes on a single plant. Fruit is a green, globe-shaped nutlet containing one seed. *Companion species* Common Chickweed (p.239), Prickly Sowthistle (p.256), Red Clover (p.161), Red Dead-nettle (p.257), Shepherd's-purse (p.260) and White Clover (p.167). *Distribution* May have been introduced by the Romans, but very common throughout most of Britain, becoming local only in some upland areas. In Ireland it is mostly restricted to the east. *Habitat* Arable fields, allotments, gardens and other disturbed land; most commonly found on calcareous soils. Most germination takes place in the spring but, as with many of these cornfield and garden weeds, the seed – dormant in the ground – remains viable for years.

Common Nettle
(Urtica dioica)

Common Nettle is hardly beautiful, but it has other things going for it. It is edible, best picked when the leaves are in their first flush of youth, and makes a delicious spring soup. Nettles are a key food plant for some of our loveliest butterflies – the Peacock, Small Tortoiseshell, Comma and Red Admiral – and they make an excellent nitrogen-rich fertiliser for the garden. If you harvest the leaves in May, chop them into a dustbin, fill it with water and leave them to stew for a couple of weeks, you can pour off the smelly liquid and use it to feed leafy greens and lettuce. Nettles are also a reliable marker of nitrogen- and phosphate-rich soils, often associated with man, and they can persist for exceptionally long periods of time. According to Richard Mabey, they clearly show the sites of Romano-British villages on Salisbury Plain, which are still dense with nettles 1,600 years after Roman occupation ended.

Plant type Nettle family, Urticaceae. *Flowers* June–August. *Height* Up to 1.5m. *Description* Dioecious, erect perennial herb with far-creeping rhizomes. Flowers are arranged in drooping, catkin-like inflorescences. Leaves are oval, cordate and pointed, arranged in opposite pairs. Both leaves and stem are covered with stinging hairs that release irritant histamine-containing juice when broken. Strong winds can damage and blacken the leaf edges. *Companion species* Cleavers (p.238), Cock's-foot (p.145), Creeping Thistle (p.150), Curled Dock (p.245) and Spear Thistle (p.261). *Distribution* Native. Very common throughout the British Isles. It appears to have increased since the 1950s, perhaps with the increased use of artificial fertilisers. *Habitat* Woods, scrub, unmanaged grasslands, fens, riverbanks, hedgerows, roadsides, manure heaps, cultivated and waste ground.

Common Poppy
(Papaver rhoeas)

A field full of poppies is the stuff of Monet posters and the 1970s Cadbury's Flake advert. It is the redness of the red that give them such mass appeal, such a strong ladybird contrast to the black at the centre of each flower. They look so ethereal, and indeed the petals may be shed after a single day, but a plant can produce up to a hundred flowers in a summer and it is more durable than it looks. Poppies thrive in disturbed ground, with the seed lying dormant for decades until it is activated by soil disturbance. That is what happened on the battlefields of the First World War: the churning up of the soil stimulated a mass poppy germination, creating carpets of flowers. Today, we see this effect – all too rarely – when farmers fail to spray a young crop of wheat or barley or miss a strip down a field. Poppies then germinate like mad. Common Poppy and its close relations, Rough Poppy (p.258), Long-headed Poppy (*P. dubium*) and Prickly Poppy (*P. argemone*), were almost certainly introduced, mixed up with the seedcorn of the first Neolithic settlers.

Plant type Poppy family, Papaveraceae. *Flowers* June–August. *Height* 20–60cm. *Description* Bristly, erect annual herb with pinnate leaves and flowers 7–10cm across. Capsule is globular and hairless. It is the most common member of the poppy family. *Companion species* Long-headed Poppy, Opium Poppy (p.254), Prickly Poppy, Weld (p.264) and Wild Mignonette (p.216). *Distribution* Introduced. Common throughout England and Wales except in upland regions. In Scotland and Ireland, it is more frequent in the south and east. It is sensitive to herbicide, but can be abundant in unsprayed strips in fields. *Habitat* Disturbed soil in arable fields, field margins, waste ground and other disturbed and open habitats. It is most frequent on light and calcareous soils.

Common Ragwort

(Senecio jacobaea)

You should pull this out by the roots whenever you see it, but do not drop it. You must remove what you have pulled. The leaves are poisonous and can cause irreversible cirrhosis in the livers of animals. Horses and cattle do not usually eat it when it is growing – you can see that in a heavily grazed field, in which everything but Ragwort has been eaten to the ground. But they will eat it when it is dead or dried, even though the toxin remains active. Contained in hay, Common Ragwort is responsible for half the cases of livestock poisoning seen in Britain each year. It spreads by seed and, like many wasteland plants, it is a huge seed producer and exceptionally invasive. Ragworts are the larval food plant of the beautiful Cinnabar moth, whose bold yellow-and-black-striped caterpillars can be seen feeding on the leaves.

Plant type Daisy family, Asteraceae. *Flowers* June–October. *Height* Up to 1m. *Description* Erect branched biennial or perennial. Stems are furrowed, more or less hairless. Basal leaves are pinnatifid, irregularly lobed, resembling those of cabbage or kale. Stem leaves are more deeply divided with short, bluntly toothed terminal lobes. Flower heads are yellow, 15–25mm across, arranged in dense, umbel-like corymbs. *Companion species* Bulbous Buttercup (p.144), Curled Dock (p.245), Creeping Buttercup (p.149), Creeping Thistle (p.150), Meadow Buttercup (p.158), Scentless Mayweed (p.259) and Spear Thistle (p.261). *Distribution* Native. Common everywhere, absent only from a few 10km squares in the Scottish Highlands. Despite being listed under the Weeds Act 1959, which obliges landowners to prevent it from spreading to agricultural land, it remains one of our most common wild flowers. *Habitat* Grassland, especially neglected, rabbit-infested or overgrazed pastures. It also grows on sand dunes, in open woods and woodland rides, and on scrub, waste ground, road verges and waysides, rocks, screes and walls.

Corncockle

(Agrostemma githago)

This is the most glorious of our cornfield weeds. How could you better the bright pink, open saucers, with their insect-runway markings drawing bees and butterflies into the white throat of the flower? Corncockle is a native of the Mediterranean and was introduced as a grain contaminant; it has been present in Britain almost certainly since the Iron Age. It was common until the twentieth century, but has declined dramatically during the past hundred years. Farmers thought of it as a pest. Its seeds are roughly the same size as those of wheat or barley, and ripen at much the same time, so they would get muddled up and lower the quality of flour. Early seed cleaning failed to separate the seeds, so when a new crop was sown, the Corncockle was planted back into the field. With the advent of better seed cleaning in the 1920s, Corncockle disappeared virtually overnight. Its fate was sealed with the appearance of selective herbicides in the 1950s. It is now almost extinct in Britain.

Plant type Pink family, Caryophyllaceae. *Flowers* June–August. *Height* 30–100cm. *Description* Tall, erect, hairy annual herb with lanceolate leaves. Flowers are reddish purple (occasionally white), 2–5cm across. Calyx tube is ribbed and very hairy. Sepals are narrow, leaf-like and much longer than the broader-notched petals. Some forms have sepals that are the same length as the petals, but these are introduced cultivars. *Companion species* Common Poppy (p.241), Scentless Mayweed (p.259), Shepherd's-purse (p.260) and Sun Spurge (p.262). *Distribution* Introduced. Formerly considered an agricultural pest, it is now extremely rare in its traditional cornfield habitat, with only a few populations considered 'natural'. The Ranscombe Farm population on the Plantlife reserve is perhaps the most famous, but even this may be a southern European subspecies impostor. It is more often found as a component of sown wild-flower meadows, and such populations are found throughout Britain, more frequently in southern and eastern England. *Habitat* An annual weed of cereal and other arable crops, tolerant of various soil types.

Cornflower

(Centaurea cyanus)

With their Catherine wheels of brilliant blue, Cornflowers are some of our prettiest wild flowers. They used to be so common, turning fields blue with their flowers, that they had a colour named after them. A juice was extracted from the flowers and mixed with alum to make a watercolour. Richard Mabey quotes Edward Salisbury describing a cornfield near Oxford in 1926, the year in which the Prince of Wales visited. It 'looked as though it had been sown for the occasion, since it was red, white and blue with Poppies, Scentless Mayweed and *Centaurea cyanus*'. We still get mayweed and poppies like this, but the idea of wild Cornflowers in such abundance is magnificent. The plant is now very rare, with all the usual factors to blame: improved seed-cleaning techniques, herbicides and fertilisers, the destruction of arable field margins and the sowing of more chunky, competitive crop varieties. The combination has all but wiped out wild Cornflowers, although there has been a slight resurgence in the past twenty years.

Plant type Daisy family, Asteraceae. *Flowers* June–August. *Height* 20–90cm. *Description* Erect annual herb. Lower leaves are stalked, pinnately divided and 10–20cm long. Upper leaves are linear-lanceolate and stalkless. Flower heads are bright blue, 1.5–3cm across, on long stalks. Bracts have jagged, toothed edges. *Companion species* Common Poppy (p.241), Corn Marigold (right) and Field Madder (p.249). *Distribution* Introduced: it has been here since the Iron Age. It is found throughout Britain and most frequent in central and southern England. Almost all recent records are of garden escapes and sown plants on roadsides and waste ground. It is extremely rare in arable fields,where it was once so common that it was regarded as a pest. *Habitat* It prefers light and sandy soils.

Corn Marigold

(Chrysanthemum segetum)

The good old Corn Marigold is a brilliantly cheery plant, resembling miniature yellow sunflowers en masse among the corn. Its flowers and leaves are edible – the Japanese use them more than we do – and good scattered in a salad or wilted as a vibrant green. Introduced as a contaminant of grain, Corn Marigold was once considered a serious arable weed and has long been persecuted. Henry II issued an ordinance against the plant in the twelfth century – the earliest known example of such an act in Britain. It was also included on John Fitzherbert's blacklist of plants in *The Book of Husbandry* (1523). It is now decreasing in all parts of the country thanks to increased liming of arable fields and widespread use of herbicides. I have seen occasional non-sprayed arable fields in places such as Benbecula in the Outer Hebrides, where Corn Marigold is so thick that it appears to outnumber the crops – no wonder it was so hated by farmers.

Plant type Daisy family, Asteraceae. *Flowers* June–October. *Height* 20–50cm. *Description* Erect, hairless, spring-germinating annual herb. Leaves are alternate, grey-green, fleshy and deeply toothed. Flower heads are golden yellow, daisy-like and solitary, usually 3.5–6.5cm across. *Companion species* Bugloss (p.236), Common Poppy (p.241), Shepherd's-purse (p.260), Sun Spurge (p.262) and Tufted Vetch (p.166). *Distribution* Introduced. Found throughout Britain. Its distribution is patchy: it is common in some regions, such as East Anglia and the Midlands, but rare in others, including Kent and Sussex. In Scotland, it is largely confined to the lowlands and the east coast, but is abundant in the small cornfields of the Outer Hebrides. In Ireland, it is most frequent in the east and rare in the west. *Habitat* Light, sandy or loamy soils that are deficient in calcium and rich in nitrogen, as found in arable fields.

Corn Mint
(*Mentha arvensis*)

The mauve-purple puffs in the leaf axils of this pretty plant are made up of lots of miniature flowers, merging into fluffy spheres around the central stem. Like all dead-nettles, Corn Mint is loved by insects, endlessly visited by bees and hoverflies when the sun is shining. The leaves may not have such a good flavour as native Peppermint (*M.* x *piperita*), but they still make good mint tea. It is ornamental, too, one of the parents of the widely grown garden variety Ginger Mint, which has similarly vibrant leaves. Corn Mint gets its name from its usual habitat, around the edges of arable fields, and it is the commonest British mint that grows away from water. It will also thrive in damp ground, where it may grow with the similar-looking Water Mint (p.321). The two can hybridise, making identification tricky, but the pure species has stamens that project outside the flower, whereas in hybrids the stamens tend to be contained within.

Plant type Dead-nettle family, Lamiaceae. *Flowers* June–October. *Height* 10–30cm. *Description* Variable, downy, prostrate or erect perennial herb. Leaves are elliptical, rounded, shallowly toothed, blunt-tipped and stalked, 2–6cm long. Flowers are mauve (occasionally white), 3–4mm long, in dense whorls in the leaf axils. Calyx is bell-shaped and very hairy with short triangular teeth. *Companion species* Common Fumitory (p.240), Red Clover (p.161), Tufted Vetch (p.166), Water Mint and White Clover (p.167). *Distribution* Native. Found throughout Britain, but more abundant in the south (where it is common). It is locally common in the lowland regions of Scotland, but rare in the far north-west. In Ireland, it is more local than in England and absent from much of central-eastern Ireland. *Habitat* Arable fields, woodland rides (particularly in damp areas), marshy pastures and waste places.

Curled Dock
(*Rumex crispus*)

Like its relation Broad-leaved Dock (p.236), Curled Dock can be a pest when it appears where you do not want it – you should get in quick and uproot it if you see it in your vegetable garden or lawn. It is listed under the Weeds Act 1959, controlling its spread to agricultural land, because it contains high levels of oxalic acid, which is mildly toxic and may cause illness in livestock if eaten in large amounts. Even so, there is an architectural elegance to this plant, with its narrow, crinkle-edged leaves and stately, Golden Delicious-green flower spikes, which deepen to red. It is a little more refined, less brutish than its broad-leaved relation, with which it often grows side by side. A distinctive ecotype, ssp. *littoreus*, thrives on shingle beaches all around the coast.

Plant type Knotweed family, Polygonaceae. *Flowers* June–October. *Height* Up to 120cm. *Description* Stout perennial herb. Leaves are oblong-lanceolate, rounded to the base and undulate at the edges. Inflorescence is branched and open. Inner tepals are 4–5mm long, not toothed, and usually have warts on all three sides (sometimes only on one side). The presence/number of warts on the inner tepals is one of the most reliable methods of distinguishing between different dock species. *Companion species* Broad-leaved Dock, Common Sorrel (p.147), Creeping Thistle (p.150), Hogweed (p.156) and Spear Thistle (p.261). *Distribution* Common throughout the British Isles, although slightly less frequent than Broad-leaved Dock in most areas. It is absent from the most remote parts of the Scottish Highlands. *Habitat* Waste ground, roadsides, disturbed pastures and arable land; also a range of coastal habitats including drift lines, shingle beaches, sand dunes, tidal river banks and the uppermost parts of salt marshes. Ssp. *littoreus* also grows on shingle coasts.

Daisy
(Bellis perennis)

We need to become less fanatical about the mowing of lawns, park grasslands, grassy lane sides and village greens, so that we can allow the good old Daisy to flower more often. Like White Clover (p.167), Daisy is an invaluable source of food for important pollinating insects, such as hoverflies and honey- and bumblebees, and we could increase their food provision many times by moving from a weekly to a fortnightly or three-weekly mowing regime. Daisies close in dull, cloudy weather, when there are few pollinating insects flying, but they become a hive of activity as soon as the sun is bright. They are edible: the flowers do not taste of much, but the rosette is good added to a salad or steamed and eaten as a slightly succulent wilted green.

Plant type Daisy family, Asteraceae. *Flowers* April–October. *Height* 3–12cm. *Description* Low, rosette-forming, winter-green perennial herb. Leaves form a basal rosette and are obovate, blunt-tipped and blunt-toothed, 2–4cm long. Flower heads are 16–25mm across, with many spreading white ray florets, yellow disc florets and many green, oblong bracts. Flower head stems are hairy, leafless and 3–12cm tall. The dwarf variety of Oxeye Daisy (p.159) looks rather like it, but that grows in a few very exposed sites and has narrower, deeply toothed leaves. *Companion species* Red Clover (p.161), Ribwort Plantain (p.162) and White Clover. *Distribution* Native. Very common throughout the British Isles. It is one of the most widespread wild flowers. *Habitat* Short grasslands and meadows on almost all soils, often in areas that are heavily grazed or trampled. It does best in sites that are relatively wet for at least part of the year. It is familiar as a weed of lawns, verges and pastures, but also grows in more natural habitats, including stream banks, lake margins and dune slacks.

Dandelions
(*Taraxacum* agg.)

Why include Dandelions in a book about wild flowers, when everybody knows what they look like? It is to remind us to eat the baby leaves, ideally before the plants come into flower in the middle of spring. Picked young from your lawn, or any area of grass, these leaves have a good flavour. They are a little bitter, like those of Chicory (p.70). The French pick them for the classic *salade du pissenlit au lard*, fried bacon scraps and croutons served on a bed of dandelion leaves. Once the plants come up to flower, the leaves toughen and become more bitter. This is not a single species but an aggregate of several hundred microspecies, all quite similar in appearance. The seed heads have that fantastic chimney-sweep brush appearance. They are one of the few weeds that can overtake grass.

Plant type Daisy family, Asteraceae. *Flowers* March–October. *Height* 5–30cm. *Description* Low perennial herbs with a tap root and basal rosette of sparsely hairy, lanceolate, lobed and toothed leaves. Flower heads are yellow, 2–6cm across, solitary, on leafless, unbranched, hollow stems that contain a milky latex. Each flower head contains up to 200 individual florets. There are often several flower stems per plant. *Companion species* Daisy (p.246) and Ribwort Plantain (p.162) in lawns; Greater Stitchwort (p.87), Green Alkanet (p.88) and Red Dead-nettle (p.257) in lane sides. *Distribution* Native. Very common throughout the British Isles, occurring almost everywhere. *Habitat* Ubiquitous in a wide range of habitats, although best known as weeds of lawns, allotments and waste ground. They love disturbed sites. Some microspecies are associated with natural or semi-natural habitats, including sand dunes, chalk grassland, fens, flushes and cliffs.

Dark Mullein
(Verbascum nigrum)

Dark Mullein is one of the best-looking plants that you will find in wastelands and scrappy corners, particularly if you live on chalk. It has tall, narrow flower spikes studded with small, bright yellow, saucer-like flowers. Look closely to see the furry, velvety purple stamens, each topped by brandy-snap-brown anthers, a lovely contrast to the bright petal behind. This is a biennial, which germinates when ground is disturbed. It may appear suddenly in great quantities by a new road or building site, then disappear again. The common name mullein is derived from the Old French *moleine*, which comes from the Latin *mollis*, meaning 'soft', and refers to the mullein's felted leaves, although the darker leaves of Dark Mullein are not as soft and delicious to look at as those of Great Mullein (p.250). Dark Mullein is the food plant of the nationally scarce and declining Striped Lychnis moth.

Plant type Figwort family, Scrophulariaceae. *Flowers* June–September. *Height* 50–120cm. *Description* Biennial herb. It forms a rosette of leaves in the first year and dies after a display of flowers in the second year. It is smaller and less robust than Great Mullein, to which it is similar in appearance, although it has an angled stem and leaves that are dark green above and only thinly downy (not woolly). It sometimes has white flowers. *Companion species* Curled Dock (p.245), Hedge Bedstraw (p.202), Lady's Bedstraw (p.205), Oxeye Daisy (p.159) and Wild Marjoram (p.216). *Distribution* Native. Occasional in England and Wales, locally common in the south and east (but rare in Kent and East Sussex). It is rare in Ireland and Scotland. Garden escapes have blurred the distinction between native and alien populations. *Habitat* Dry hedge banks, wasteland, roadsides and grassland on calcareous or sandy soils. It is also found on walls and cultivated ground.

Fat-hen
(Chenopodium album)

Fat-hen's fleshy, grey-green, meal-covered leaves might look boring, but they taste delicious. Pick them at their lushest, before the flower spikes begin to stretch out from the centre of the plant, to get the best equivalent of wild spinach: earthy-tasting (but not muddy) and slightly sweet. You can chop them up and eat them raw in salads or wilt them briefly in olive oil or butter and eat them just like spinach – they are good mixed with nettle tops. Long-prized for its edible leaves, Fat-hen had the Old English name of *melde*. I was brought up near Melbourne, just outside Cambridge, whose name stems from Meldeburna, meaning 'stream on whose banks melde grew'. Fat-hen is also known to have been one of the last meals of Tollund Man, a 2,000-year-old corpse found preserved in a peat bog in Jutland, Denmark. There used to be many more species, which are now rare or have died out as market gardens, manure piles and middens have become a thing of the past.

Plant type Goosefoot family, Amaranthaceae. *Flowers* June–October. *Height* 30–100cm. *Description* An aggregate of eight similar and difficult-to-identify species. Overall, it is a very variable, erect, annual herb. Stem is often tinged reddish. Leaves are grey-green, lanceolate to diamond-shaped, and usually covered in a whitish mealy substance. They may be lobed or bluntly toothed. Inflorescence is erect and dense, with many small, greyish, five-tepalled flowers, 2mm across. *Companion species* Lesser Burdock (p.253), Scentless Mayweed (p.259) and Shepherd's-purse (p.260). *Distribution* Native. Common throughout most of Britain and Ireland, especially southern England. It is more local in western Ireland and in upland areas. It is rare in north-west Scotland. *Habitat* Disturbed, nutrient-rich sites, such as waste ground, cultivated fields, gardens, rubbish sites and soil heaps.

Field Bindweed
(Convolvulus arvensis)

The stripy pink-and-white flowers of Field Bindweed are as cheery as a stick of Brighton rock, but farmers feel anything but cheery when they find patches of this in their fields. Like Hedge Bindweed (p.90), it has spaghetti-like roots, every bit of which can make a new plant if broken off and left in the ground. The roots go deeper than those of Hedge Bindweed, so it is even more difficult to eradicate, except with the use of herbicides. Left growing, the stems become quick-forming mats across arable fields and gardens, climbing up and over plants in their way. The generic name of the whole family is derived from this behaviour – the Latin *convolvo* means 'to intertwine'. The roots also gradually exhaust the soil of nutrients, making Field Bindweed a pernicious weed in the field and garden, especially on neutral or calcareous soils.

Plant type Bindweed family, Convolvulaceae. *Flowers* June–September. *Height* Up to 2m. *Description* Hairy/hairless creeping and/or climbing perennial herb. Leaves are oblong, arrow-shaped, stalked, 2–5cm long with hairless stems. Flowers are solitary, trumpet-shaped, white or pink with white stripes, up to 3cm across, weakly almond-scented. They are very sensitive to the weather and will close in rain and at night, opening in sunny weather. Fruit is a round capsule. Hedge Bindweed is larger, with leaves up to 15cm long and white (occasionally pink) flowers. Sea Bindweed (p.410) is a creeping perennial easily recognised by its kidney-shaped leaves; its flowers are twice the size of Field Bindweed's. *Companion species* Common Fumitory (p.240), Common Poppy (p.241), Shepherd's-purse (p.260) and Sun Spurge (p.262). *Distribution* Native. Very common throughout most of England and Wales, becoming rare in upland areas, such as the Cambrian Mountains and the Pennines. It is common in the Edinburgh/Glasgow area of Scotland, but rare elsewhere. In Ireland, it is frequent to local and more common near the east coast. *Habitat* Waste or cultivated ground, waysides and railway banks, open scrub and rough or short grassland, including disturbed chalk downland.

Field Forget-me-not
(Myosotis arvensis)

We moved into Perch Hill eighteen years ago, on 1 May. The woods were full of bluebells, and the whole garden was pale blue with carpets of this little plant, also known as Common Forget-me-not. At first we liked it, and the following year I planted tulips to go with its colour, but then I spent three years weeding it out, trying not to allow future generations to flower. I have not let it near the place since. It produces a huge amount of seed, and one plant will be a hundred the following year – the more you turn over your soil with seed already in, the more it germinates. Field Forget-me-not flowers are pretty en masse, but there are bigger, showier garden hybrid forms based on the Water Forget-me-not (p.320), with every part of the plant at least twice the size of this arable and garden weed. It was Coleridge who popularised the name Forget-me-not in his poem 'The Keepsake', written in 1802. He in turn got it from a German folk tale – see p.320 for the original story.

Plant type Borage family, Boraginaceae. *Flowers* April–September. *Height* 15–40cm. *Description* Downy annual or biennial herb with blue flowers. Similar to Wood Forget-me-not but less showy, with smaller flowers (3–5mm across), and a corolla tube shorter than the calyx. Leaves are spotted red with red margins. *Companion species* Cleavers (p.238), Field Pansy (p.249) and Shepherd's-purse (p.260). *Distribution* Introduced, probably by the Romans, and widespread across the British Isles, although less frequent in north-west Scotland and western Ireland. *Habitat* Open, disturbed ground, especially cultivated fields. It may also grow on woodland edges, open grassland, hedges, scrub, roadsides, walls and quarries.

Field Madder

(Sherardia arvensis)

Unlike so many arable annual flowers, such as Common Poppy (p.241), Corncockle (p.242) and Cornflower (p.244), which were introduced as contaminants of arable seed, Field Madder is a true native. It is an understorey plant that is very common in disturbed ground and, rather like Fairy Flax (p.152) in a summer meadow, can occur in such numbers that the plants almost link up to form an airy carpet two or three inches above the ground. You may not notice it to begin with, but once you get your eye in, you will see plenty of it. It is one of the bedstraws, which is obvious at a glance: it has the square stems and miniature star-shaped flowers, collected in the leaf axils, that are typical of the bedstraw family. A red dye can be extracted from the roots, but it is not as intense as the colour obtained from Wild Madder (p.426), so Field Madder has never been grown specifically for that purpose.

Plant type Bedstraw family, Rubiaceae. *Flowers* June–July. *Height* 5–40cm. *Description* Prostrate, bristly, annual herb. Leaves are lanceolate, unstalked, pointed and in whorls of six. Flowers are white to pink, violet or pale purple, 3mm across, arranged in terminal clusters and surrounded by a ruff of bracts. Fruit is globose, 4mm long. *Companion species* Bugloss (p.236), Common Poppy and Wild-oat (p.264). *Distribution* Native. Like many cornfield weeds, it is common where arable is common – in the south and east of Great Britain (i.e. most of England) – becoming rare and local towards the north and west, and rare in Scotland. It follows the same pattern in Ireland, and is common in areas where arable is common. Its abundance is now much reduced because of agricultural intensification. *Habitat* Principally a plant of cultivated places and recently disturbed soil, occurring in open, drought-prone grasslands, sheltered cliffs, sand dunes, arable fields, waste ground, waysides and verges.

Field Pansy

(Viola arvensis)

Field Pansy is intriguing to find because it's so obviously the wild ancestor of plants that many of us grow in our gardens. Its cheerful flowers are outward-facing and slightly upturned, primrose-yellow on their periphery, their golden hearts slashed seven times with purple-black lines. This is a prolific self-seeder – if you get one, you get a hundred, or probably more like a thousand. It could be confused with the rare Mountain Pansy (p.362), which also has yellow flowers, but these are of a brighter colour than those of Field Pansy and much larger; they also grow in totally different habitats. You are more likely to see Wild Pansy (p.265) in the same sorts of places as Field Pansy, but that has purple wings and a yellow chin. Like all pansies, the flowers are edible.

Plant type Violet family, Violaceae. *Flowers* April–July. *Height* 15–20cm. *Description* Short, hairy annual herb. Oblong leaves are broadest above the middle and bluntly toothed. Stipules are pinnate but with a large, leaf-like terminal lobe. Pale yellow or cream flowers, 8–20mm from top to bottom, have green sepals protruding from behind their petals. *Companion species* This often grows in carpets on the edges of arable fields on its own, but you will also see it with a scattering of other annual weeds, such as Common Chickweed (p.239), Common Fumitory (p.240) and Shepherd's-purse (p.260). *Distribution* Introduced, probably by the Romans, and common throughout Britain apart from upland areas. It is very local in north-west Scotland. In Ireland it is mostly confined to the east and is very rare or absent in the west. *Habitat* Usually found on light, well-drained soils in cultivated fields, in old gravel and sandpits and on waste ground where soil is disturbed. It still occurs in many intensively farmed arable fields.

Fool's Parsley
(Aethusa cynapium)

The leaves and flowers of this pretty little umbellifer look a bit like a fine form of flat-leaved parsley. It can sometimes crop up in disturbed ground in a vegetable patch, so the two can be confused. However, Fool's Parsley is poisonous, and you will be able to tell the difference as soon as you crush the leaves. They give off a nasty acrid smell that is distinct from the bright scent of parsley. They are also a much darker green and more finely divided than garden parsleys. The leaves contain a toxic compound called cynopine, and the symptoms of poisoning are heat in the mouth and throat. The generic name *Aethusa* comes from this symptom, derived from the Greek word *aithos*, meaning 'fire'. Fool's Parsley also looks quite similar to Cow Parsley (p.77), but it is hairless, flowers later and has different seeds. Those of Cow Parsley are narrow and oblong, whereas the fruit of Fool's Parsley are oval, deeply ridged and hairless.

Plant type Carrot family, Apiaceae. *Flowers* July–August. *Height* Up to 50cm. *Description* Branched annual or biennial herb. Leaves are triangular in outline and finely divided (two to three times pinnate). Flowers are small, white and arranged in terminal umbels that have no bracts at the base but have three to four narrow, conspicuous, drooping bracteoles on the partial umbels. Fruit is 3–4mm long. *Companion species* Common Poppy (p.241), Red Dead-nettle (p.257) and Scarlet Pimpernel (p.259). *Distribution* Native. It is found throughout England, Wales and southern Scotland, becoming more local to the north and west. It also occurs throughout much of Ireland, most frequently in the south east, but it is not considered to be native there. *Habitat* Wasteland, arable ground, gardens, hedgerows and other disturbed soils. The seeds can remain dormant in the ground for at least ten years.

Great Mullein
(Verbascum thapsus)

The commonest of the mulleins, this is an impressive spire of a plant, a straight, unbranched velvety column of flower and stem standing to the height of a human, its basal leaves like huge felted trays. The velvetiness of its leaves may deter herbivores, and the hairs also disrupt the flow of air across the leaf, reducing evaporation, so Great Mullein can put up with baking heat. It has such an architectural presence that you cannot miss even a solitary specimen, but, as a huge producer of seed, it is often found en masse in groves or forests, which flower through the summer. The plant itself is poisonous, but the dried flowers and crushed leaves are used to make cough medicines. A yellow dye may be extracted from the flowers.

Plant type Figwort family, Scrophulariaceae. *Flowers* June–August. *Height* Up to 2m. *Description* Stout, white, woolly, mostly unbranched biennial. Leaves are oval-elliptical, up to 45cm long, alternate, with winged stalks. Inflorescence is a dense terminal spike with bright yellow, five-lobed flowers, 1.5–3cm across, the lowest lobe marginally larger than the others. The key difference from other verbascums is that the anthers are less than 2mm long and the two lower filaments (stamens) are hairless. *Companion species* Common Figwort (p.72), Common Poppy (p.241), Weld (p.264) and Wild Mignonette (p.216). *Distribution* Native. Common throughout the British Isles except in north-west Scotland and some upland parts of England and Wales. *Habitat* Open scrub and hedge banks, waysides, railway banks and sidings, waste ground and quarries. It prefers well-drained soils, and is a frequent garden escape, establishing itself well on rubbish tips.

Ground-elder
(Aegopodium podagraria)

There are few gardeners who have not had Ground-elder – and hated it – as a coloniser of a corner of their patch. It is one of those perennial 'weeds' that spreads by a spaghetti network of very deep underground roots, which are almost impossible to excavate. If you leave only a small section in the ground, it has the potential to create a new plant, making Ground-elder difficult to eradicate. Once it has a small hold in your garden, it will creep out at several metres a year. The white airy flowers are pretty and typical of umbellifers, but the leaves are very different from those of most other umbellifers, such as Cow Parsley (p.77) or Wild Angelica (p.324), looking more like those of the unrelated Elder (p.80) – hence its name. It is thought that Ground-elder was introduced by the Romans for its herbal and medicinal virtues (they believed that it cured gout). It is also edible, the leaves slightly lemony and aromatic, good eaten as a wilted green.

Plant type Carrot family, Apiaceae. *Flowers* Late May–July. *Height* 40–100cm. *Description* Erect, vigorous, hairless, carpet-forming perennial. Leaves are once or twice trifoliate, with oval-elliptical leaflets, each 2–7cm long. White (occasionally pink) flowers are 2–3mm across, in many-rayed umbels (2–6cm across) with no bracts or bracteoles. *Companion species* Cleavers (p.238), Common Nettle (p.241), Creeping Thistle (p.150), Ground-ivy (p.14), Hedge Bindweed (p.90) and Spear Thistle (p.261). *Distribution* Introduced. Found throughout the British Isles and very common in most areas. *Habitat* Wide variety of disturbed habitats, especially hedgerows, road verges, churchyards, neglected gardens and waste ground. It typically occurs near habitation or in the vicinity of abandoned settlements, such as in woodlands.

Hairy Bitter-cress
(Cardamine hirsuta)

This appears to be quite an unexceptional little plant, with white, cress-like flowers above a basal rosette of indented leaves. The reason to get to know it is that its leaves taste delicious: sweeter than Watercress (p.320), with a mild peppery flavour. They make a punchy, strong addition to a winter or early spring salad. In my garden, this plant is one of the earliest to germinate, appearing in almost any open or disturbed ground, right in under hedges as well as out in the sun. I can start picking it with Dandelion leaves (p.246) before the winter ends, adding in Common Chickweed (p.239) at the beginning of spring for an excellent foraged harvest. But it comes with a word of warning in the garden. It grows astonishingly quickly, has explosive seed pods and rapidly takes over in spite of its small size. It is often introduced as a weed in containerised plants and gets a hold from there.

Plant type Cabbage family, Brassicaceae. *Flowers* March–September. *Height* 20–30cm. *Description* Slender annual herb with white flowers, 3–4mm across. Leaves are pinnate and mostly form a basal rosette. Basal leaves have many pairs of small, round, angled leaflets, which are hairy on their upper surface. The upper leaf leaflets are much narrower. Stems are wavy or straight, branching mostly from the base. Easy to confuse with Wavy Bitter-cress (*C. flexuosa*), but that species is perennial and often slightly larger. It also has flowers with six stamens, whereas Hairy Bitter-cress has flowers with only four. *Companion species* Cleavers (p.238), Green Alkanet (p.88) and Germander Speedwell (p.85). *Distribution* Native and common throughout the British Isles, although more local in north-west Scotland and western Ireland. *Habitat* Cultivated and disturbed ground. Also found by streams and in woods, and frequently on rocks and scree, especially limestone.

Hairy Tare
(Vicia hirsuta)

Popping up in ungrazed or unmown grass, studding it with pretty speckles of colour, Hairy Tare has lots of tiny pale mauve flowers. Tares are fine in grass and meadows, but have long had a reputation for being an irritating infester of crops. They scramble through arable fields, clinging on to the sown plant by their tendrils and strangling anything they use as their climbing frame. Indeed, they feature in a parable told by Jesus of a man who sowed seed in his field, but whose 'enemy came and sowed tares among the wheat . . . When the blade was sprung up and brought forth fruit, then appeared the tares also' (Matthew 13: 24–30). Hairy Tare, as its name suggests, has seed pods coated in fine hairs.

Plant type Pea family, Fabaceae. *Flowers* May–August. *Height* 30–80cm. *Description* Slender, short, trailing or scrambling annual herb. Leaves are pinnate, divided into four to ten pairs of linear-oblong leaflets. Inflorescence is a one-sided raceme with one to ten lilac-white flowers, 4–5 mm long, with equal calyx teeth all longer than the calyx tube. Pod is 10mm long, downy, usually with two seeds. There are two similar species. Smooth Tare (*V. tetrasperma*) has unequal calyx teeth and its pod is hairless and four-seeded. Slender Tare (*V. parviflora*) is local, rare and declining. It has larger flowers. *Companion species* Fat-hen (p.247) and Shepherds-purse (p.260). *Distribution* Native. Common in England, Wales and lowland Scotland. It is very local or absent in upland areas. In Ireland it is most frequent on or near the east coast, becoming local or rare inland. Smooth Tare has a more south-easterly distribution than Hairy Tare, although it still reaches southern Scotland. *Habitat* Set-aside fields, the edges of arable fields, rubbish tips, waste ground, road and railway banks, scrubby grassland, hedgerows, sheltered sea cliffs and stable shingle beaches.

Japanese Knotweed
(Fallopia japonica)

This huge perennial weed has exceptionally deep roots and extraordinary vigour. It can push its way up through solid concrete and tarmac and resists the repeated use of systemic herbicides. It is able to grow from root fragments as small as a little finger. That partly explains its rapid spread: when it became too vigorous in gardens, it was often thrown over the garden hedge onto rubbish tips, railway banks and riversides, where it could root and grow unrestricted. Japanese Knotweed was introduced in the early nineteenth century as an ornamental plant for water gardens. It was not recorded in the wild until 1886, but by 1920 it was well established. It is now the most pernicious weed in Britain, and it is illegal to plant it deliberately in the wild. A government study in 2003 estimated that the cost of eradication would be £1.56 billion. Its young, tender stems are edible and taste of rhubarb (one of its common names is Sally Rhubarb), and are good in pies and jam.

Plant type Knotweed family, Polygonaceae. *Flowers* August–October. *Height* Up to 2m. *Description* Tall, erect, thicket-forming hairless perennial. Stems are reddish and zigzagging and the plant spreads by rhizomes to form dense clumps. Leaves are hairless, oval-triangular, pointed, 6–12cm long, with truncate leaf bases. White flowers are arranged in branched, short-stemmed inflorescences. Fruit is brown, glossy and three-angled. *Companion species* None. It crowds out everything else. *Distribution* Introduced. It is found throughout most of Britain and Ireland and is very common in many areas. It is absent only from the most remote upland regions. It is also quite scarce in central Ireland, but it is spreading. *Habitat* Waste ground, roadsides, canal, river and railway banks and, in Scotland, along the shores of sea lochs.

Lesser Burdock

(Arctium minus)

There is something brutish but magnificent about Lesser Burdock, one single plant rocketing out of the ground and quickly forming a mountain of leaves. It is a sign of abandoned arable fields, and appears in the Bible as that, a weed of laziness and decline. Referring to the presence of Lesser Burdock in a farmer's field is an insult, although it romped away all over the country in the era of set-aside fields. It is a biennial, whose spiny flower buds and seed pods come in the second year. It looks like a green-stemmed rhubarb, with leaves a similar shape and size, but Lesser Burdock has tufty, purple, thistle-like flowers and Velcro-like seed pods. Our dogs always get covered in these from head to toe during walks in autumn or winter. Its spines are curved at the tip for better sticking, making this one of the best-adapted plants for efficient and widely spaced seed dispersal. Its roots can be eaten, roasted or fried like needle parsnips.

Plant type Daisy family, Asteraceae. *Flowers* July–September. *Height* 60–130cm. *Description* Medium to tall, downy, branched biennial herb. Stems are woolly and furrowed, often reddish. Leaves are oval, up to 50cm long, longer than they are wide, with cordate bases, and many spiny bracts, each with spreading, hooked tips. *Companion species* Bulbous Buttercup (p.144), Creeping Buttercup (p.149), Curled Dock (p.245), Meadow Buttercup (p.158), Spear Thistle (p.261) and Wild Teasel (p.265). *Distribution* Native. Common in England and Wales, although more local in Scotland, especially in the Highlands. In Ireland, it is generally more common in the east than in the west. *Habitat* Anywhere, apart from the most acidic soils. It occurs on waste ground, roadsides, railway banks, rough pastures, sand dunes, woodlands, scrub and hedgerows.

Night-flowering Catchfly

(Silene noctiflora)

Night-flowering Catchfly looks rather feeble during the day – like a person with consumption. All the stuffing goes out of it and the flowers close up. At night, however, it opens its flowers and exudes its perfume to attract the night-flying moths that pollinate it. The stem is covered in sticky hairs, which ensure that pollen adheres to the insects attempting to reach the nectar. Some insects become permanently stuck to the stem, but catchflys are not carnivorous (unlike sundews), so they do not eat them. Although the flowers are bisexual, the anthers produce pollen before the stigma is able to receive it, thus preventing self-pollination. The seeds can remain viable for many years. Night-flowering Catchfly has undergone a dramatic decline since the 1950s, due to increased use of fertilisers and herbicides and the shift from spring-sown to autumn-sown crops. It is a late seed dropper, so autumn ploughing wrecks its chances of setting seed.

Plant type Pink family, Caryophyllaceae. *Flowers* July–August. *Height* 15–60cm. *Description* Erect, hairless, spring-germinating annual herb. Leaves are oval-lanceolate, usually stalked near the base, narrower and unstalked above. Flowers remain inrolled during the day but expand at night. Once expanded, they are 17–19mm across with five deeply notched petals that are pink on the upper sides and creamy yellow on the undersides, arranged in few-flowered clusters. *Companion species* Common Poppy (p.241), Rough Poppy (p.258) and Wild Mignonette (p.216). *Distribution* Introduced, probably by the Romans. Mostly confined to south-central and eastern England, where it is common in some areas, particularly Norfolk. *Habitat* Usually cultivated land but sometimes open waste ground. It prefers dry, sandy and calcareous soils.

Opium Poppy
(Papaver somniferum)

Delicate and beautiful, the newly opened flowers of Opium Poppy are like handfuls of crumpled silk. They come in a lovely array of colours, from strong pinks and reds to washed-out mauve. There are also double forms, escaped into the wild from gardens, which range from blacks through to reds and pinks to white. This is the famous poppy from which opium, and hence morphine, codeine and heroin, are derived. When the unripe seed pod is scratched, it oozes a milky latex, which contains poisonous alkaloids and can be collected and dried. I have seen fields of it near Stonehenge in Wiltshire, grown to supply the pharmaceutical industry. Named after the Roman god of sleep, Somnus – a reference to its narcotic properties – it has been cultivated throughout Asia and Europe since at least 2000BC; it was grown in Switzerland during the Stone Age, probably for food. The ripe, dry seeds can be baked into bread and cakes and are often sprinkled on top of bagels and pastries. They contain an oil that can be extracted and used for cooking and soap making.

Plant type Poppy Family, Papaveraceae. *Flowers* June–August. *Height* Up to 80cm. *Description* Medium to tall, stout, almost hairless perennial herb. Leaves are oblong, unlobed, wavy, coarsely toothed and waxy green. Flowers are white, pale lilac or pink, often with a large, dark blotch at the base of each petal, with yellow anthers, 8–18cm across. *Companion species* Fat-hen (p.247), Pineappleweed (opposite) and Scentless Mayweed (p.259). *Distribution* Introduced, probably by the Romans. It is common in England and lowland parts of Wales, either as a garden escape or a relic of cultivation. In Scotland, it is local, more frequent near the coast and absent from the Highlands. In Ireland, it is more frequent in the north east. *Habitat* Roadsides, waste ground and rubbish tips, and occasionally in arable fields as a relic of cultivation.

Perennial Sowthistle
(Sonchus arvensis)

It is hard to believe that any sowthistle could be beautiful, but, when seen en masse, the Perennial species truly is. It has large, flat flower heads, like Dandelions' (p.246) but twice as wide, made up of many individual yellow tassel flowers. The calyx below the flower head is a dusky blackish green and, when caught in the light, the tiny hairs all over it make it look dusted with glitter. Each complete flower spike is made up of several well-spaced flowers on long, thin stems, the plants standing tall and airy, well above the barley or wheat with which they grow. Farmers are not keen on them as they contaminate the crop, and the widespread use of herbicides has made them a much rarer sight in the past fifty years. Perennial Sowthistle, like the rest of this family, is edible, and its leaves – fleshier and less bitter than those of Dandelions – and flowers have been used in salads for centuries.

Plant type Daisy family, Asteraceae. *Flowers* July–October. *Height* 60–150cm. *Description* Tall, erect perennial herb with creeping stolons. Stem is furrowed and hollow. Leaves are pinnatifid and edged with fine spines. Stem leaves have rounded bases that clasp the stem. Flower heads are a rich golden yellow, 40–50mm across, in loosely branched inflorescences. *Companion species* Bugloss (p.236), Common Poppy (p.241), Corn Marigold (p.244) and Prickly Sowthistle (p.256). *Distribution* Native. Common throughout England and Wales, becoming largely restricted to coastal or lowland areas in Scotland. It occurs throughout Ireland. *Habitat* It is frequent in arable fields (hence its other common name of Corn Sowthistle) and on waste ground, as well as roadside verges, ditch and river banks, sea walls and the upper parts of beaches and salt marshes, particularly along strand lines. It prefers disturbed, nutrient-rich, mildly acid to basic soils.

Pineappleweed
(Matricaria discoidea)

You may smell Pineappleweed before you see it. Each plant is erect and bush-like, but it forms a carpet made up of many small plants, and as you walk on it and crush the leaves, they release a strong smell of pineapple. The flowers also look like miniature pineapples, each one a prominent yellow-green boss with no petals encircling it. Native to north-east Asia, Pineappleweed was introduced to the Royal Botanic Gardens at Kew in Surrey from Oregon, USA, in the eighteenth century. It is now one of our fastest-spreading plants, its seeds probably picked up in mud by walking boots, car tyres and farm vehicles and spread from field to field. The dried flower heads can be used to make an infusion, which tastes like chamomile tea and may be given to treat indigestion and insomnia.

Plant type Daisy family, Asteraceae. *Flowers* Late May–November. *Height* 5–30cm. *Description* Low, branched annual herb. Leaves are bright green and very finely divided into narrow, thread-like segments. Flower heads are conical, 5–8mm across, with greenish-yellow disc florets but no ray florets. Its leaves are similar to those of Scentless Mayweed (p.259), but the absence of white ray florets and the distinctive smell make Pineappleweed easy to distinguish. *Companion species* Red Bartsia (p.256) and Silverweed (p.418). *Distribution* Introduced. First cultivated in Britain in 1781 and recorded as an escape from Kew Gardens in 1871. It is now found almost everywhere in the British Isles, except parts of the Scottish Highlands and the far west of Ireland. *Habitat* Wherever ground has been disturbed. Typical habitats include driveways and the edges of pavements. It usually thrives on fertile ground in lowland areas and occurs in arable crops.

Prickly Sowthistle

(Sonchus asper)

Rose Gray of the River Café taught me the value of Prickly Sowthistle. I had always disliked this boring, yellow-flowered thistle with spiny leaves, which grows all over disturbed ground. Then I learned that the leaves are a good addition to a spring salad. The taste and texture are best before they start to flower in late spring, so before you put this invasive garden weed on the compost heap, harvest the leaves through March and April. In northern Italy, the leaves form part of the classic wild leaf salad *insalata di campo*. When the basal rosettes are young and the prickles not yet formed, they have a good, slightly crunchy texture and a mild, Chicory-like bitterness. The common name refers to the supposed popularity of this plant with sows, which were said by William Coles (a seventeenth-century botanist) instinctively to eat it after giving birth, to help increase their milk yield.

Plant type Daisy family, Asteraceae. *Flowers* June–October. *Height* Up to 120cm. *Description* Variable, erect, robust, hairless annual. Leaves are shiny green, pinnately lobed or unlobed, very spiny with basal lobes (auricles) that clasp the stem. Flower heads are golden yellow, 1.5–2.5cm across, arranged in lax clusters. Seeds are smooth between the ribs. *Companion species* Garlic Mustard (p.84), Herb-Robert (p.91) and Pellitory-of-the-wall (p.102). *Distribution* Native. The most common sowthistle, it is found throughout the British Isles, absent only from the most remote parts of the Scottish Highlands. *Habitat* Cultivated and waste ground and waysides on fertile, mildly acid or calcareous soils. It occurs on rough grassland, scrub, roadside verges, quarries, rock outcrops, railway lines, arable fields, manure heaps, gardens and waste places. It prefers dry, sandy soils and is intolerant of grazing, but it can be an invasive weed of bare ground.

Red Bartsia

(Odontites vernus)

This scraggy-looking plant pops up on arable field edges and may be dotted right through a field unless it has been sprayed with herbicide. It can appear as an occasional plant or in huge carpeting colonies, often around gateways and field entrances, turning the earth a dusky purple-pink. You will also see it on salt marshes and above the high-tide mark of beaches and rocky seashores. It is closely related to eyebrights (including Common Eyebright, p.146) and, like them, it is a hemiparasite on the roots of grasses, taking water and minerals from them. Grasses will be weakened by Red Bartsia, allowing more wild flowers to flourish. Red Bartsia is an important pollen source for bees, particularly favoured by carder bees. Its generic name comes from *odons*, the Greek word for 'tooth', because its flower spike was believed to look like a line of teeth and, made into a paste, was widely considered to cure toothache.

Plant type Broomrape family, Orobanchaceae. *Flowers* June–August. *Height* Up to 50cm. *Description* Variable, short, erect, slender, downy annual. Stem is often branched, slightly square. Leaves are oblong to lanceolate, toothed, unstalked, 1–3cm long. Inflorescence is a leafy, branched raceme. Calyx is green, bell-shaped and four-lobed. Flowers are red to pink, up to 9mm long, two-lipped; the lower lip is three-lobed. Anthers protrude slightly from the flower. *Companion species* Common Eyebright, Pineappleweed (p.255) and Silverweed (p.418). *Distribution* Native. Common throughout most of the British Isles apart from upland regions, such as the Scottish Highlands, the Pennines and Snowdonia, where it is scarce or absent. *Habitat* Short, often trampled grasslands, tracks, waste places, the edges of arable fields, gravelly and rocky seashores and salt marshes. It can tolerate a wide range of soils.

Red Dead-nettle
(Lamium purpureum)

This flowers for much of the year, often starting in February and continuing into the following winter. That is its main attribute – it is an important early food source for bees – together with the pretty red-purple wash that spreads over the top few whorls of leaves on some plants. The common name comes from the fact that it looks like a nettle, but does not sting. Like the nettle, it is edible, both raw and stir-fried – exactly the sort of plant that would be collected as *horta*, or wild greens, throughout the Mediterranean countries when vegetables were scarce. You should harvest the leaves when its flowers are out and its leaves still fresh but of maximum size, in late spring and early summer.

Plant type Dead-nettle family, Lamiaceae. *Flowers* February–October. *Height* 10–30cm. *Description* Erect, downy annual that varies in appearance depending upon its habitat. In open situations, it is short and spreading; in shadier places, it is taller and more upright. Flowers are pink-purple in a dense inflorescence. Corolla is 10–15mm, longer than the calyx. Leaves and bracts are heart-shaped to oval, toothed, purplish in colour, 1–5cm long. Stem is much branched. On first appearance, this looks like Henbit Dead-nettle (*L. amplexicaule*), but that has stalkless upper leaves that clasp the stem. It can also be confused with Cut-leaved Dead-nettle (*L. hybridum*), with which it often grows. However, the latter is generally more slender and less downy, and has leaves that are more deeply cut. It also has conspicuous rings of hairs towards the base of the inside of the corolla. *Companion species* Common Chickweed (p.239) and Marsh Woundwort (p.313). *Distribution* Almost certainly not native, but ubiquitous in most of the British Isles apart from north-west Scotland, where it is more local. *Habitat* This coloniser of fertile and disturbed ground thrives in gardens, hedgerows and hedge banks, and on roadside verges, along railways, around rocky outcrops and in rough grassland.

Redshank
(Persicaria maculosa)

Redshank resembles a miniature bottlebrush, with pale pink, open flowers that have deeper pink buds among them. It makes scraggy plants, tall, thin and highly branched, each stem ending with a dense cluster of flowers. This is one of the most common persicarias, the prominent black splotch central on its lower leaves, making it easy to identify. Its spindly nature means that you will often see it collapsed over, beaten down by the wind or rain and trailing along the ground. As with many cornfield annuals, it appears not in ones and twos but in tens or hundreds, almost always collected in the most trampled parts of fields, on the edges of tracks or around gateways. This is a plant you'll often find in your garden. Its leaves and new shoots are edible and can be eaten as a green vegetable or added to a salad, although the mild flavour is bland, so it is best mixed with other things.

Plant type Knotweed family, Polygonaceae. *Flowers* June–October. *Height* Up to 70cm. *Description* Short to medium, erect or sprawling, branched, hairless annual herb. Stems are red, swollen above the leaf bases. Leaves are lanceolate, tapered to the base, green, often with black blotches and 5–10cm long. Flowers are pink and small in dense, stout, oblong clusters. *Companion species* Common Field-speedwell (p.240), Pineappleweed (p.255) and Silverweed (p.418). *Distribution* Native. Common throughout Britain and Ireland except in the Highlands of Scotland and a few parts of western Ireland. *Habitat* Open ground on a wide range of soils, particularly those that are rich in nutrients. It can be a pestilential weed of cultivated land and in gardens, but it is also found by ponds, lakes, streams and ditches, in waste places, on roadsides and railways. It is most abundant on heavy, non-calcareous soils.

Rosebay Willowherb
(Chamerion angustifolium)

By far the most spectacular of the willowherb family, this has magnificent, feather-like flower plumes made up of fifty or more individual flower heads. It is almost always a bright magenta, with the occasional white albino form. The white is very popular for growing in gardens as it puts up with tricky conditions. It is beautiful, but horribly invasive. After the flowers come vast amounts of feathery seed, which blow around like flotsam and jetsam. It is also called Fireweed because of its frequency on fire sites, and this is often where it crops up in woods, when someone has been coppicing and has lit a fire to burn the spoil twigs and small branches. During the Second World War, Rosebay Willowherb was one of the first plants to brighten London's bomb sites, appearing in great sheets between the ruined buildings.

Plant type Willowherb family, Onagraceae. *Flowers* July–September. *Height* Up to 120cm. *Description* Erect perennial herb. Leaves are alternate, lanceolate and spirally arranged up the stem. Flowers are rose-purple, 2–3cm across, with the upper petals broader than the two lower petals, borne in spikes. *Companion species* Agrimony (p.142), Common Nettle (p.241) and Common Toadflax (p.74). *Distribution* Native. Widespread and very common throughout most of the British Isles, except some parts of western Ireland and northern Scotland, where it is local. Rosebay Willowherb was a rare species of uplands in the early nineteenth century, but by the middle of the twentieth century it had extended its range and is now (possibly from a foreign source) one of the most successful colonisers of waste places. *Habitat* Moderately fertile soils, forming dense stands on disturbed, often burnt ground, on heaths, in woodland rides and clearings, on sand dunes and along track sides, roadsides and railways.

Rough Poppy
(Papaver hybridum)

Rough Poppy looks like the weedy relation of Common Poppy (p.241), its flowers not as rich a red (there is more blue in them) and generally smaller and scraggier, but from a distance it is tricky to tell them apart. Only when you see the seed pod can you tell that Rough Poppy is a different species. Its head is much rounder and fatter, with very pronounced, curved spines over its whole surface. It is also much more strongly ribbed longitudinally, splitting the seed head into definite segments. Rough Poppy is more specific about where it lives, largely confined to chalk. Like all cornfield weeds, it has declined substantially with the increased use of herbicides. It is now becoming quite rare and is significantly more unusual to find than Common Poppy.

Plant type Poppy family, Papaveraceae. *Flowers* June–August. *Height* Up to 50cm. *Description* Short to medium, hairy annual herb. Leaves are pinnately lobed. Flowers are 2–5cm across (much smaller than those of Common Poppy) and the petals do not overlap. It has four crimson petals with a dark blotch at the base. Fruit is a rounded capsule covered with stiff, yellowish bristles. *Companion species* Common Poppy, Field Madder (p.249) and Scentless Mayweed (p.259). *Distribution* Introduced. Mostly confined to southern and eastern England, although there are outlying populations to the north and west, for example in south-west England, Pembrokeshire, southern Scotland and the east coast of Ireland. Even in its heartlands in the Chilterns, the North and South Downs and Salisbury Plain, it is now only locally common. *Habitat* More confined to well-drained calcareous soils than other poppies. It is usually found as a weed of cereals and sugar beet, although it may be found in other disturbed habitats.

Scarlet Pimpernel
(Anagallis arvensis)

Scarlet Pimpernel looks as though it has just been picked off the pages of a medieval manuscript, its trailing sprigs curving round the letters on the vellum, its flowers bright and cheery. It looks so perfect that it is hard to believe that it is real, particularly where it appears in the weedy corners of arable fields, a smart aristocrat among the louts of Prickly Sowthistle (p.256) and emerging docks – its name is derived from the Old French word *pimper*, meaning 'trim' or 'smart'. When it is in full flower, the long, slender flower stalks are upright and perky; when in fruit they droop and run along the ground. There are not many British wild flowers of this colour, a clear, brilliant scarlet. As regular as clockwork on sunny days, its flowers open at 8am and shut at 3pm (and remain closed during wet or cloudy weather) – hence local names such as Change-of-the-weather in Norfolk and Shepherd's Sundial in Somerset.

Plant type Primrose family, Primulaceae. *Flowers* May–October. *Height* Up to 20cm. *Description* Low, prostrate or ascending, hairless annual herb, which spreads to 30cm long. Stems are four-angled, with opposite pairs of oval, pointed, stalkless leaves, which have black gland dots on the undersides. Flowers are scarlet (although sometimes blue or flesh-coloured, called var. *carnea*), solitary, 10–15mm across, arranged on slender stalks in the leaf axils. Calyx teeth are narrow, pointed and nearly as long as the corolla, like a pronounced star behind each flower. *Companion species* Common Fumitory (p.240) and Shepherd's-purse (p.260). *Distribution* Native. Common throughout most of England and Wales, although rare or absent in upland regions. In Scotland it is largely coastal, while in Ireland it is more frequent in the south east, becoming more local and coastal in the north east. *Habitat* Open habitats, as an arable or garden weed; also grows around rabbit warrens and in rocky and bare sites, including coastal cliffs (we photographed it on the Lizard in Cornwall), chalk downland, heaths and sand dunes. It has a preference for lighter, well-drained soils.

Scentless Mayweed
(Tripleurospermum inodorum)

You will see this bright white daisy plant with its yellow flower centres everywhere in summer. Each flower is small, but they appear in great sprays, often forming the understorey in arable field margins that have escaped herbicide sprays. They also carpet waste ground and new road cuttings and embankments on motorway verges. Scentless Mayweed is common because it is not fussy, growing on both heavy and well-drained soils in acidic and chalky places. The reason it is called Scentless is that its similar-looking relation Scented Mayweed (*Matricaria chamomilla*) has an aromatic scent to its leaves, although Mayweed is a confusing name for both plants, because they do not flower in May, but usually in July. The common name is in fact derived from the word 'maiden', as the plant was used in the past for treating gynaecological pain.

Plant type Daisy family, Asteraceae. *Flowers* July–September. *Height* 10–50cm. *Description* Annual or perennial herb. Leaves are alternate, hairless and very finely divided into thread-like segments (two to three times pinnate). Flower heads are 2–4.5cm across with white ray florets and yellow disc florets arranged in loose inflorescences. *Companion species* Common Poppy (p.241), Corn Marigold (p.244), Fat-hen (p.247) and Pineappleweed (p.255). *Distribution* Introduced, but there are archaeological records of Scentless Mayweed in the British Isles dating from the Bronze Age. It is common throughout England and Wales but less frequent in Scotland, apart from in the south and east. In Ireland, it is more frequent in the east and rare in the west. *Habitat* Arable fields, farm tracks and gateways and waste ground on a wide range of disturbed, fertile soils. It is also found on roadsides, railway ballast and spoil heaps.

Shepherd's-purse
(Capsella bursa-pastoris)

You will see this extremely common plant in all disturbed ground – bare earth in a vegetable patch, allotment, arable field or building site. Its flowers are tiny and white, its leaves in a basal rosette, a bit like a less spiky dandelion. One tends not to give it a second glance. But once it is going over, Shepherd's-purse gains an airy elegance. Each seed pod is a heart-shaped purse, like those in which shepherds carried their food, held singly on a little stem away from the centre of the plant, giving it a light and delicate silhouette. The stems and purses are green, washed with smoky purple. We found this corner of a cornfield stuffed full of Shepherd's-purses; backlit by the evening light, they looked lacey and beautiful. The raw leaves have a mild peppery flavour and crisp texture – a good addition to a leaf salad. They are also used in Asian cooking, and in China there are cultivated varieties. In Shanghai, they are stir-fried with bamboo shoots and included in a kind of meat dumpling. In Korea, the leaves are par-boiled and served with soy sauce.

Plant type Cabbage family, Brassicaceae. *Flowers* Year round. *Height* 5–40cm. *Description* Annual or biennial herb. At the base of its erect stem is a rosette of pinnately lobed (although sometimes undivided) leaves. Stem leaves have arrow-shaped auricles. White flowers are arranged in a raceme and are 2.5mm across. Fruit are triangular with an indent, held erect on long stalks 6–9mm long. *Companion species* Common Fumitory (p.240), Scarlet Pimpernel (p.259) and Sun Spurge (p.262). *Distribution* Introduced. It has probably been with us since Roman times and is now extremely common everywhere, apart from the far north-west of Scotland. *Habitat* Abundant on waste ground and in gardens and frequent in cultivated fields, particularly among broad-leaved crops.

Small Toadflax
(Chaenorhinum minus)

I am fond of this little plant, as I remember being drawn to its cheery flowers as a child – they look like the flowers of a snapdragon, but in miniature. It is in fact closely related to Snapdragon (*Antirrhinum majus*), although that species is native to the Mediterranean and not found wild in the British Isles. Small Toadflax used to grow commonly on cultivated farmland, but it is a classic example of a once-abundant plant that has declined significantly in recent years. Agricultural intensification and widespread use of herbicides have hit it hard, particularly in Ireland. It is now more likely to be found by railways and railway yards and in vegetable patches. I know a vegetable garden at Cuckmere Haven in Sussex where this is one of the commonest 'weeds', much prettier to have around than the usual Cleavers (p.238) and Hairy Bitter-cress (p.251).

Plant type Speedwell family, Veronicaceae. *Flowers* June–October. *Height* 8–25cm. *Description* Low, slender annual. Stems are erect and branched. Leaves are linear to lanceolate, blunt, toothed and alternate. Flowers have pale purple, two-lipped corollas, 6–8mm long. There is a yellow patch on the lower lip. Each flower is situated on a long stalk rising from the leaf axils. Most other toadflaxes have broader leaves. *Companion species* Common Fumitory (p.240), Dandelions (p.246), Shepherd's-purse (left) and Sun Spurge (p.262). *Distribution* Introduced, probably by the Romans. It is common throughout most of Britain, becoming less so towards the north and west. It is very rare in the north of Scotland. It is local in Ireland, mainly found in the east. *Habitat* Open habitats on well-drained, often calcareous soils, including cultivated fields, forestry tracks, rough waste ground, old walls, quarries and along railways.

Soapwort
(Saponaria officinalis)

The mild but delicious, slightly clove-like smell of this late summer-flowering plant is much stronger at night. Soapwort is pollinated by moths, in particular the Hummingbird Hawk-moth. Its generic name is derived from the Latin word for 'soap', and it was indeed used as a detergent because it contains saponins, compounds that lubricate and absorb dirt particles. Simply rubbing a leaf will produce a slight, slippery froth. When boiled in water, Soapwort produces a lathery liquid, which was used for washing wool and woollen cloth. We would be wise to grow a few of these night-scented, nectar-rich flowers in our gardens, to help revive moth populations.

Plant type Pink family, Caryophyllaceae. *Flowers* July–September. *Height* 30–90cm. *Description* Erect, hairless perennial herb. Leaves are ovate to elliptical and up to 5cm long. Inflorescence is a forked cyme of pink flowers, each 2.5cm across, with unnotched petals, ten stamens and a five-lobed calyx tube. It is easily distinguished from pink-flowered campions (its near relations), by its unnotched and untoothed petals and its hairless stems and leaves. *Companion species* Butterfly-bush (p.237), Common Nettle (p.241) and Wild Teasel (p.265). *Distribution* Introduced, probably by the Romans. It is quite common throughout much of England and Wales, although it is rare in the most remote upland regions. It is more localised in Ireland and rare in Scotland. It is well naturalised in damp woods and along streams in south-west England and north Wales, where it is sometimes considered native as it is often found far from human habitation. *Habitat* Grassy places on hedge banks, quarries, roadsides, railway banks, tips and waste ground, where it is often a garden escape.

Spear Thistle
(Cirsium vulgare)

I love this impressive plant. The calyx below the flower is like the sort of headdress that Elizabeth Taylor would have worn, or the mace of a Norman knight. The spikelets are geometrically arranged around a slightly less than spherical, silvery grey blob, out of which the radiant magenta topknot of the flower emerges, as brilliant as a Sikh's turban. Its leaves are horrible and vicious, mean little things with ugly long spikes, but I sometimes cut off the flower bubbles and float them in a dish on the table. Like Creeping Thistle (p.150), it is unpopular with gardeners, farmers and even some conservationists, and is often treated with herbicides. It is an invasive species in Australia and is listed as an injurious weed in the UK, probably still increasing in man-made habitats.

Plant type Daisy family, Asteraceae. *Flowers* July–September. *Height* 30–150cm. *Description* Biennial herb. Stem is cottony with interrupted spiny wings. Leaves are lanceolate and pinnately lobed with spiny margins and prickly hairs on the upper surface. Basal leaves are 15–30cm long and short-stalked. Stem leaves are smaller and stalkless and have long terminal lobes – the 'spears'. Flower heads are purple, 20–50mm long by 25–40mm across, in a panicle or flat-topped loose cluster, or sometimes solitary. Bracts are yellow-spined, long and arched. *Companion species* Cleavers (p.238), Common Nettle (p.241), Common Ragwort (p.242) and Scentless Mayweed (p.259). *Distribution* Native. One of the commonest thistles throughout Britain and Ireland. *Habitat* More or less ubiquitous, especially on fertile, base-rich or calcareous soils. It is found in a wide variety of habitats, such as overgrazed pastures and rough grassland, sea cliffs, dunes, drift lines and well-drained, fertile, disturbed habitats, including arable fields, spoil heaps, waste ground and burnt areas in woodland.

Springbeauty
(Claytonia perfoliata)

This unusual-looking plant cannot be mistaken for anything else, its white flowers emerging from the slightly fleshy, shield-shaped leaves like miniature teacups on a green tray. Its succulent appearance hints at its seaside origins. I grow it as a winter salad leaf – it is also known as Miner's Lettuce or Winter Purslane – and it is one of the hardiest annuals I have come across, which will only germinate as temperatures cool in the autumn. It is reliably cut-and-come-again, with leaves shooting back within a week, even when it is cold and wet. It has a gentle flavour, a little like that of spinach, but its texture is more succulent. In the spring, it prefers to grow in a little shade.

Plant type Blinks family, Montiaceae. *Flowers* May–July. *Height* 20–30cm. *Description* Hairless, lax annual. Basal leaves are long-stalked, but stem leaves are fleshy and joined in a pair, forming a ring around the stem. Flowers are white, very small and dainty, 5–8mm across, with four or five flowers in a clutch, fully encircled as if on a saucer by a round to oval leaf. *Companion species* Common Chickweed (p.239), Fat-hen (p.247), Shepherd's-purse (p.260) and Sun Spurge (p.262). *Distribution* Introduced in the mid eighteenth century from the Pacific coast of North America, where it is native from Alaska to Mexico, as well as Cuba. First recorded in the wild in 1849, and now established throughout the British Isles except in south-west England, Wales and Ireland. There is a lot of it around London and in East Anglia. *Habitat* This is a seaside plant, especially on light sandy soils that warm up early in the year. However, it occurs inland, too, on arable ground and wasteland, along roadsides and in churchyards, on light, sandy open grassland. It is absent from wet and ill-drained soils and from limestone.

Sun Spurge
(Euphorbia helioscopia)

Like hats for Ladies Day at Ascot, these often single-stemmed flowers are a complicated affair, their saucer-like bases topped by several compact ornamental roses, all in searing acid green. As with most spurges, the male and female flowers are separate. What looks like the 'flower' consists of a single female ovary on a stalk surrounded by a cluster of tiny male flowers. If you take care to keep its sap out of your eyes, Sun Spurge makes a marvellous cut flower with a faint honey scent (plunge its stems into boiling water for twenty seconds to seal in the poisonous sap and make them last up to a week in water). The species name *helioscopia* is from the Greek for 'looking at the sun', and that is exactly what they do, their flat flowers following the light through the day as it moves across a field. It looks particularly good growing with crimson-flowered Common Fumitory (p.240).

Plant type Spurge family, Euphorbiaceae. *Flowers* May–October. *Height* 10–30cm. *Description* Short to medium, virtually hairless, erect, annual herb. Leaves are obovate, blunt, tapering to the base (broadest above the middle), finely toothed near the tip. Flowers are green, in a five-rayed umbel, with five large obovate bracts at the base. Glands are oval and green; seeds are brown. Sun Spurge has segmented seed heads that explode with a loud bang to release the seeds. *Companion species* Common Fumitory, Red Dead-nettle (p.257) and Shepherd's-purse (p.260). *Distribution* Introduced, but has been with us probably since the Romans. It is common throughout much of Britain and Ireland, although absent from much of the Scottish Highlands and becoming local in the west of Ireland. This is one of the commonest euphorbias in northern Europe. *Habitat* Occurs on cultivated and disturbed ground in gardens, wasteland and arable fields, particularly with root and leaf crops. It thrives on dry, well-drained, neutral or base-rich soils in sun-warmed situations.

Weld
(Reseda luteola)

The tall, slightly wavering green spires of Weld transform depressing wastelands, lay-bys and railway sidings into wild gardens. Like sunflowers, Weld is heliotropic – the flowers follow the sun. Why more of us do not grow it in our patches, I do not know, but I am planting more of it in mine, in combination with Viper's-bugloss (p.214), with which it often grows in the wild. On the coast near Dungeness in Kent, several trackways and scrappy bits of land have this duo growing in great swathes – nothing I could conjure in my head could be better. Its other common name is Dyer's Rocket, and it has been used since Neolithic times to make a yellow dye. It was grown for this reason in east Kent, Essex and Yorkshire, one of the ancient trio of medieval dyers' plants, with Woad for blue and Wild Madder (p.426) for red.

Plant type Mignonette family, Resedaceae. *Flowers* June–August. *Height* 50–150cm. *Description* Erect perennial or biennial herb. Leaves are lanceolate, undivided and wavy edged. Flowers are greenish yellow with four petals and four sepals, arranged in long, narrow racemes. Fruit is globular. *Companion species* Colt's-foot (p.238), Common Poppy (p.241) and Viper's-bugloss. *Distribution* It may or may not be native. Some botanists think that it is native on chalk and sandy soils in southern and eastern England, but its distribution may have been extended by cultivation. It is common throughout most of England, becoming local in upland regions and parts of Devon and Cornwall. In Wales, it is more local and largely restricted to the coast. It is found only in southern Scotland and a few coastal locations further north, and in Ireland, it is more frequent in the east. *Habitat* Dry disturbed ground on neutral or base-rich soils on roadsides, waste ground, brickyards, gravel pits and urban demolition sites.

Wild-oat
(Avena fatua)

I remember as a child going to stay with a farmer friend of my parents in Somerset. We spent a day, ten or fifteen of us, walking in a line through fields of oats, pulling out Wild-oats as we went. It was important to weed them out while they were still green: Wild-oat tends to seed before the cultivated crop, so it had to be removed before it was ripe and dropping. This grass is a rampant self-seeder – hence the euphemism 'sowing wild oats'. Whenever I see Wild-oat, I think of that farm, but I love the look of it in an arable field: tall, airy, skeletal and elegant, usually standing at twice the height of the crop all around it. It is one of the ancestors of cultivated oats, but it has a smaller grain.

Plant type Grass family, Poaceae. *Flowers* June–September. *Height* Up to 150cm. *Description* Tall, erect, annual grass. Leaves are flat, 3–15 mm wide, with hairy basal sheaths. Inflorescence is 10–40cm long, with whorls of wide-spreading branches that have pendulous spikelets. Each spikelet is 18–25 mm long, two- to three-flowered; when in fruit, the flowers start to separate from one another. Oat grasses are distinguished by their long awns, which develop a kink about halfway along as the fruit matures. This is a dispersal device, which starts to rotate once wetted. *Companion species* Creeping Thistle (p.150) and Fat-hen (p.247). *Distribution* Introduced, probably by the Romans. It is common throughout most of England and Wales except in upland districts, where it is more localised. It is confined to the lowlands and coast in Scotland and is absent from the far north-west. It is local in Ireland, more frequent in the east than in the west. *Habitat* Arable land, especially in cereals. It is also found on roadsides and waste ground and is resistant to some herbicides.

Wild Pansy
(Viola tricolor)

It is always a thrill to find the wild origins of a much-grown ornamental garden plant. My father described large drifts of Wild Pansy when he was botanising in Dorset and Devon in the 1930s. At that time, both Wild Pansy and Field Pansy (p.249) were very common on disturbed ground on the lane sides and fields. I saw it there in abundance with him when I was a child. The huge increase in our use of fertilisers and herbicides has caused this and other arable flowers to decline massively, and it is now quite rare. In the wild, it germinates early in the year and flowers all summer long, but in gardens you can sow it in September for flowers right through winter. Also known as Heartsease, its flowers are edible.

Plant type Violet family, Violaceae. *Flowers* April–July. *Height* 20–30cm. *Description* Annual or short-lived perennial. Leaves are oval at the base; upper leaves are narrower (usually lanceolate), all bluntly toothed. Flowers are a mixture of blue-violet, yellow and white, 1.5–2.5cm long. They may be sometimes entirely yellow (ssp. *curtisii*, which is perennial) or blue-violet. Yellow forms may be confused with the more common Field Pansy, but Wild Pansy has petals longer than the sepals. The cultivated garden pansy, *V.* x *wittrockiana* (more common in urban areas), is distinguished from Wild Pansy by its larger flowers (35mm long) and overlapping petals. *Companion species* Common Fumitory (p.240) and Field Pansy. *Distribution* Native. Found throughout the British Isles and frequent in many areas, but quite scarce in the West Country, Scottish Highlands and inland Ireland. It has also become scarce in much of south-east England. *Habitat* Dry and disturbed areas with little competition. It is found on dunes and other sandy areas, on acidic grassland on heaths and hills, and in cultivated ground, gardens and waste places.

Wild Teasel
(Dipsacus fullonum)

Wild Teasel looks good at almost all stages, its fresh flower heads like spiny goose eggs with a belt of mauve anthers around their middles. As the band moves up the flower head, so the clutch of feeding insects moves with it. Then, as it goes over and the seeds form, it becomes the feeding ground for finches – particularly goldfinches –which feast on its plump and abundant seed. Its common name originates from the use in the textile industry of the flower of a cultivated variety, Fuller's Teasel (*D. sativus*). This has hooked spines on the end of the bracts, which were used to 'tease' out wool fibres prior to spinning – a practice known as carding. On Gloucestershire farms, you would sometimes find fields called teasel grounds, where they were grown for the local fullers.

Plant type Teasel family, Dipsacaceae. *Flowers* July–August. *Height* Up to 2m. *Description* Tall, stout biennial herb. Leaves are oblong-elliptical at the base, covered in swollen prickles. Stem leaves are lanceolate, opposite, fused to form a cup at the base, with prickles on the underside of the midribs. Flower heads are 3–8cm long and egg-shaped, with several linear bracts (5–9cm long) below the base and shorter bracts among the florets. These are longer than the lilac corollas, which are 5–7mm long. *Companion species* Broad-leaved Dock (p.236), Common Ragwort (p.242), Curled Dock (p.245) and Lesser Burdock (p.253). *Distribution* Native. It is common throughout most of England but becoming more local in the north. In Scotland, it is mostly confined to the south and east. In Wales, it is common in lowlands but rare (or absent) from the Cambrian mountains. In Ireland, it is very local to rare. *Habitat* Heavy, neutral clay soils in rough grassland, wood margins, thickets and hedgerows, and on roadsides and waste ground on a wide range of soil types.

Common Fumitory (p.240), Red Dead-nettle (p.257) and Common Chickweed (p.239), Moreton, Dorset, 8 May.

Common Poppy (p.241), Ranscombe Farm Reserve, Kent, 9 June.

Ground-elder (p.251), near Ashburnham, East Sussex, 30 June.

Common Poppy (p.241), Perforate St John's-wort (p.209) and Viper's-bugloss (p.214), Ranscombe Farm Reserve, Kent, 30 June.

Viper's-bugloss (p.214) and Weld (p.264), near Dungeness, Kent, 1 July.

Bugloss (p.236), Common Poppy (p.241) and Sun Spurge (p.262), Balranald, North Uist, Outer Hebrides, 24 July.

Corn Marigold (p.244), Benbecula, Outer Hebrides, 25 July.

Common Ragwort (p.242) and Spear Thistle (p.261), Polochar, South Uist, Outer Hebrides, 26 July.

Soapwort (p.261), Stroud Valley, Gloucestershire, 16 August.

Rosebay Willowherb (p.258), Sapperton, Gloucestershire, 7 December.

Water & Wetlands

I love a chalk stream, the clear water filling its banks to the point of absolute
fullness, with large tussocky islands of River Water-crowfoot and the odd
trout wavering slightly, its head facing upstream. Around the stream edge,
there will be Brooklime, Watercress and Common Comfrey from early in the
year, and the very poisonous Hemlock Water-dropwort. That will flower from
early summer, its white clouds like a more robust form of Cow Parsley, with
the big, yellow Monkeyflower clucking cheerily around its ankles. My
husband, Adam, recently rediscovered fly-fishing, and I like the excuse it gives
me to spend days pottering around, botanising in places such as these.

Streams, rivers and ponds on heavy clay or peat are very different places,
with a less clear and shiny beauty. In March and April, in quite dark, damp
patches of a wood, you will come across Marsh-marigold, lighting up the
whole place like a beacon. Where we live, we have a shallow, swamp-like pond,
which we discovered only last year. Just more than wellington-boot deep, it is
ten metres across and full to the brim with these big, rubbery, boisterous
plants – the spring equivalent of our native Yellow Water-lily.

Carpets of Golden-saxifrage shimmer on the banks or in hollows where
the ground is damp on heavy soils. It has acid-green bracts around more
golden flowers, the whole plant looking angular and jointed, like the wheels
of a Meccano set. There is Cuckooflower here, too, light drifts of soft pink,
just dots, but lots of them. In a damp, cool spring, there is a grassy triangle
between roads near my home which is carpeted with Cuckooflower, mainly
in pale pink but with the odd seam of white through the middle. Some years,
this looks magnificent, but in other dry springs, it hardly appears.

The buttercup-like Lesser Spearwort grows almost anywhere with
its roots properly in even slightly running water. In a bog or marsh, this
spearwort can mark out clearly the exact course of a flowing stream,
the solid carpet of yellow curving like a snake between the green-brown
rushes and sedges, marking the stagnant bog all around it.

It is worth keeping your eyes peeled for more localised plants: the
elegant, pink, allium-like Flowering-rush, which forms clumps on the edges
of shallow ditches, streams and ponds, and the waxy, creamy White Water-lily.
This can fill small Scottish lochs or lochans from bank to bank in the summer.
Another flower that I have always loved is Marsh Cinquefoil, with its jagged,
elegant calyx and its incredible colour, a deep mahogany crimson. It reminds
me of the garden plant astrantia, resembling a rich-coloured Tudor ruff. In
North Uist on the Outer Hebrides last year, we came across a huge, shallow
boggy pond that was edged with this, maybe a thousand plants circling the
deeper water like the rings around a dark, watery planet.

There are several wonderfully showy rarities to be found in the better
preserved areas of wetland. On the edges of clean, un-nitrogenated water,
look out for the tropical orchid-like flowers of Bogbean and, in the water, the
standing stems of Water-violet. It is worth a late spring trip to the north of
England to find the primrose-yellow Globeflower. This fills whole sections of
damp and marshy fields in Yorkshire, merging with the deep pink Bird's-eye
Primrose. Finding those two together – en masse – has been one of my life's
wild-flower high points.

Amphibious Bistort
(Persicaria amphibia)

Amphibious Bistort looks like hundreds of miniature pink bottlebrushes poking out of the shallows of a lake or pond. Its wide, flat, strap-shaped leaves form an almost solid canopy over the water's surface, with vertical flower spikes breaking through. The first section of the flower spike is a narrow pinkish stem, which is topped by the sugary pink cigar. Seen from a distance, it looks as if someone has poured strawberry mousse onto the water. Amphibious Bistort is usually found in the shallows, but it may grow in water up to 3m deep and is capable of spreading rapidly to cover a small pond. It generally grows floating in water, but you will occasionally see it erect in an arable field on dry ground. Terrestrial plants are much less floriferous than their aquatic equivalents. It has been widely introduced outside its native range; in some places in North America it is considered to be a noxious weed.

Plant type Knotweed family, Polygonaceae. *Flowers* July–September. *Height* 30–70cm above water's surface. *Description* Short to medium, hairy, hairless or bristly, branched perennial herb. Leaves are oval to oblong-lanceolate with rounded bases, up to 15cm long, hairless when floating, hairy when on land, sometimes black-blotched. Inflorescence is 2–4cm long, densely flowered. Each flower is pink or greenish white, 2–3mm long, with five protruding stamens and two stigmas. On dry land, Amphibious Bistort can be distinguished from Common Bistort (p.70) and Redshank (p.257) by its hairy leaves. *Companion species* Bulrush (p.293), Common Water-crowfoot (p.297) and Mare's-tail (p.308). *Distribution* Native. Found throughout Britain, although largely absent from upland regions. It is quite local in far south-west England. In Ireland, it is found throughout, but is generally more frequent in the east than in the west. *Habitat* Lakes, ponds, canals, slow-flowing rivers and ditches. It is also a terrestrial plant found in damp places on watersides, in marshes, wet meadows and dune slacks, and as a weed of cultivated land. It is usually found in non-calcareous waters.

Arrowhead
(Sagittaria sagittifolia)

The leaves of this plant look so much like arrowheads that if you asked people to guess its name, most would get it right. These large (5–20cm), arrow-shaped leaves, bright green and healthy-looking, are in fact just one of three types of leaves that Arrowhead may have. Strap-like leaves are also usually submerged beneath the water, and oval leaves float on the water's surface. The flower spikes have widely spaced whorls of white flowers on vertical stems. They open only from late afternoon to early evening. As with other waterside plants, the top leaves are a useful perch for emergent dragonflies. The larvae climb out of the water onto an Arrowhead leaf platform. If they do not get eaten by a bird, they hatch out of their larval cases and unfurl their wings, using the flat leaf surface as their first launch pad. The closely related Duck-potato (*S. latifolia*) is cultivated in China and Japan for its starch-rich tubers, which are sliced up and stir-fried. We have never had a tradition of this with our native form, which is now too scarce to harvest.

Plant type Water-plantain family, Alismataceae. *Flowers* July–August. *Height* Up to 1m. *Description* Erect, hairless, monoecious submerged or emergent aquatic perennial herb. Inflorescence is an erect, whorled raceme with female flowers located at the base and male flowers above. Female flowers are globular. Male flowers have white petals with a purple spot at the base. *Companion species* Water-plantain (p.322) and Yellow Water-lily (p.324). *Distribution* Native. Locally frequent throughout much of England, especially central England, but rare in the north and south west. It is found in Scotland only as an occasional introduction, and is confined in Wales to the south and English border region. It is local in Ireland. *Habitat* Still or slow-moving, shallow calcareous or eutrophic water.

Bird's-eye Primrose

(Primula farinosa)

Tiny and delicate they might be, but Bird's-eye Primroses are deeply glamorous and exciting to find. They grow only in the north of England, flowering for the last month of spring and into early summer. When southerners such as me are lucky enough to find them, it makes us want to do a jig. Their flowers are arranged in a little clutch at the top of the stem, with the emerging buds, stems and leaves all dusted in a silvery, flour-like powder (the species name *farinosa* comes from the Latin for flour or fine meal: *farina*). Like other wild members of the Primrose family – Cowslip (p.195), Primrose (p.103) and Oxlip (p.21) – they are loved by pollinator insects. During the half hour that we spent photographing them, there were only a few minutes when a bee or hoverfly was not perched on one of their landing platforms, feeding.

Plant type Primrose family, Primulaceae. *Flowers* May–June. *Height* Up to 15cm. *Description* Small perennial herb with a basal rosette of leaves that produces a long-stalked umbel of rosy-pink flowers, each of which is 1cm across with a yellow 'eye' centre. Leaves are spoon-shaped to elliptical. *Companion species* Common Butterwort (p.294), Early Marsh-orchid (p.298) and Grass-of-Parnassus (p.302). *Distribution* Native. Rare and nationally scarce, confined to northern England – Lancashire, Yorkshire (particularly the Craven district of North Yorkshire), County Durham (especially Upper Teesdale) and Cumbria. *Habitat* Typically found along stream sides and in wet, usually spring-fed, calcareous flushes, where lime-rich water runs or seeps through peat, mostly on upland Carboniferous limestone (on north- rather than south-facing slopes). They also seem to like areas where slippage has opened up the turf; they occur on upland farms where hoofed grazing livestock have pitted the soil.

Blue Water-speedwell

(Veronica anagallis-aquatica)

Where its relation Brooklime (p.292) is a stocky, rugby-player type of water-speedwell, Blue Water-speedwell is a willowy long-distance runner, carrying very little weight. It grows out from the shallows of beautiful chalk streams in the West Country and wafts like airy curtains of soft pale blue and green over the water. There is a similar Pink Water-speedwell (*V. catenata*), with pale pink flowers instead of blue. The leaves, raw or cooked, are edible and rich in Vitamin C. They are delicious in salads with lemon dressing, but the same precautions should be taken as when collecting other freshwater plants, such as Watercress (p.320), because of the risk of liver fluke. If there are sheep, cattle or rabbits grazing with access to the water, and the water is not fast-flowing, it is safest to eat this cooked.

Plant type Speedwell family, Veronicaceae. *Flowers* June–August. *Height* Up to 30cm. *Description* Robust perennial herb with fleshy, creeping and ascending stems. Leaves are oval-lanceolate, pointed, with bases clasping the stems. Inflorescence is a many-flowered raceme located in the leaf axils, each flower pale blue, 5–6mm across. It grows as a vegetative plant submerged in shallow water or as a flowering emergent, or as a terrestrial plant in marshy habitats and marshy ground at the water's edge. *Companion species* Hemlock Water-dropwort (p.304), Lesser Water-parsnip (p.307) and Watercress. *Distribution* Native. It is found throughout Britain, most common in a broad band stretching from Dorset to East Anglia and Lincolnshire. Elsewhere, it is more local, although there are concentrations on the east Scottish coast. It is frequent in central Ireland. *Habitat* Margins or shallow waters of pools, ponds, drainage ditches and streams in still or slow-moving water, marshy meadows and wet mud.

Bogbean
(Menyanthes trifoliata)

The flower spikes of Bogbean erupt out of shallow water, each petal stuck all over with what looks like fraying nylon string. In silhouette, the flower could be an impressive cake topped with spun-sugar icing. They look exotic and tropical, more like something you would expect to see in an Indonesian rainforest than in a bog in Britain. The sixteenth-century herbalist John Gerard sung its praises: 'Towards the top of the stalks standeth a bush of feather-like flowers of a white colour, dasht over slightly with a wash of light carnation.' Its seed pods are round and shiny green, fat and full like a series of gobstoppers on the stem. In contrast to the flowers' fineness, the leaves are chunky, like a rubbery lily pad divided into three (hence the species name *trifoliata*). They look like broad beans, which is the reason for this plant's common name.

Plant type Bogbean family, Menyanthaceae. *Flowers* May–June. *Height* 10–30cm. *Description* Perennial herb with creeping stems that bear long-stalked, grey-green, trifoliate leaves with oval, untoothed leaflets, 3–7cm long. Flower stem is a raceme, erect and leafless, with white flowers, which are five-lobed, creating a star-shaped corolla that is fringed with white hairs. *Companion species* Amphibious Bistort (p.288), Marsh Cinquefoil (p.309), Water Forget-me-not (p.320) and Yellow Iris (p.324). *Distribution* Native. Occurs throughout the British Isles. Common in many areas, including the north and west, but less frequent in parts of the Midlands and eastern England. Bogbean has decreased as a result of the drainage of wetlands in both historic and recent times, and it is now rare in many English counties, such as Kent. It is now more frequent in some areas as a planted ornamental rather than as a native plant. *Habitat* Shallow edges of lakes, pools or slow-flowing rivers, or in swamps, flushes or dune slacks. It tolerates a wide range of water chemistry, and prefers sun to shade.

out jolly quickly if the habitat becomes too coarse and rank. But when conditions improve again, for example in the divots of a cattle footprint, it can freely regenerate from buried seed, soon forming a glorious new flowering patch and producing lots of seeds with which to recharge the seed bank.

Plant type Primrose family, Primulaceae. *Flowers* June–August. *Height* Up to 15cm. *Description* Hairless, creeping, mat-forming perennial herb. Leaves are oval, short-stalked, 5–10cm long, in pairs. Flowers are five-petalled, solitary, up to 14mm across, located in the leaf axils. *Companion species* Heath Spotted-orchid (p.359), Lesser Spearwort (p.307) and Marsh Pennywort (p.312). *Distribution* Native. It is found throughout the British Isles, but is very rare or local in many areas. It is common in Wales, the west coast of Scotland, Cumbria and south-west England. It is almost entirely absent from the Scottish Highlands and Southern Uplands. In Ireland, it occurs throughout, with a westerly bias. *Habitat* Damp ground, often where there has been some disturbance of the soil or where there is little competition.

Bog Pimpernel
(Anagallis tenella)

This pretty, delicate flower is a good indicator of short, species-rich, damp, peaty turf, which is often well grazed and full of miniature beauties. It is soft pink from a distance, but in close-up each flower is white with pink veins. Like its relative Scarlet Pimpernel (p.259), it has flowers that open fully only in the sunshine and close in cloudy weather. It forms precise, lily-pad-like splotches, which are often big. This is because it produces stems that lace themselves over the damp turf, rooting at the nodes as they go along. One stem can be up to 20cm long, but once rooted, a node will produce new stems that spread out further in all directions. This fast-creeping plant excels at recolonising lost ground. It requires short turf or damp, open peat or sand, so it dies

Broad-leaved Pondweed

(Potamogeton natans)

There are many pondweeds, and it is easy to get bogged down in which one is which, but this is the most common species in many regions. It occurs all over the British Isles, from shallow water in lochans in the Outer Hebrides to ditches in East Anglia and a village pond in Cornwall. The large, flat, strap-shaped leaves are green with a distinctive coppery hue, and you can see that bronze haze over the water from quite a distance. Its abundance in many places is due to the fact that it will grow almost anywhere. Give it some water and it will romp away, no matter if the water is nutrient-poor, nutrient-rich, acid or alkaline. It prefers moderate depths of 1–2m, but it may be found in depths of more than 5m, as well as shallow swamps. This highly successful plant is invaluable to lots of pond life, oxygenating the water, giving shelter to small fish and providing an ideal surface for emergent dragonfly and damselfly larvae.

Plant type Pondweed family, Potamogetonaceae. *Flowers* Late May–September. *Height* 3–8cm above water surface. *Description* Perennial herb. Leathery, dark green, oval-elliptical, floating leaves are 5–10cm long with translucent longitudinal veins. There are no submerged leaves, although there are submerged grass-like leaf stalks known as phyllodes. Stipules are large, 4–17cm long. Inflorescence is a dense, cylindrical spike. Pondweeds can be extremely difficult to identify. Their appearance can vary greatly depending on the speed and depth of the water. The most reliable characteristic with which to identify Broad-leaved Pondweed is the presence of a buff-coloured, flexible joint a little way below the top of the leaf stalk. *Companion species* Bogbean (p.291), Water Lobelia (p.321) and Water-violet (p.322). *Distribution* Native. Found throughout Britain and Ireland and common in most areas. *Habitat* A floating aquatic in still or slowly moving water. More rarely it is found with submerged leaves in faster-moving streams and rivers.

Brooklime

(Veronica beccabunga)

The fleshy texture of its stems and leaves makes Brooklime look more like a salt-marsh or coastal plant than one of rivers, ponds and streams, but its flowers show immediately that it is a member of the speedwell family. It is as if Germander Speedwell (p.85), one of our most beautiful wild flowers, has been stuck onto a fat-thighed scurvygrass plant, the delicate blue flowers in groups on thin stems arising from the leaf axils, the main stem chunky with even chunkier leaves. Brooklime is not related to scurvygrasses, but it is edible (its leaves are unpleasantly bitter) and effective – it used to be eaten with Watercress (p.320) and oranges to protect against scurvy. It grows on the water line of a riverbank, and you will see it in damp hollows that dry out in the summer. It can make big, lush clumps, partly floating on water in a stream's shallows, or smaller, almost prostrate, creeping patches in muddy hollows. Like many plants of wetlands, it has hollow stems. This allows for oxygen and other gases to be easily transferred from the aerial parts of the plant to the roots.

Plant type Speedwell family, Veronicaceae. *Flowers* May–September. *Height* 20–60cm. *Description* Hairless perennial herb. Stems creep and root along the ground. Blue flowers have corollas, 7–8mm wide, located in many flowered racemes arising from the leaf axils. Leaves, 3–6cm long, are oval, blunt, shallow-toothed and short-stalked, in opposite pairs. *Companion species* Celery-leaved Buttercup (p.294) and Watercress. *Distribution* Widespread and common throughout Britain and Ireland, except the Scottish Highlands, where it is largely absent. *Habitat* Shallow water, by rivers, streams and ponds, and in ditches, marshy hollows in pastures, flushes, wet woodland rides and rutted tracks.

Bulrush
(Typha latifolia)

When I worked as a florist in London, Bulrushes were incredibly fashionable. The window dressers of the more chic shops liked the boldness of these brown cigars on their bright green stems – the slimline Lesser Bulrush (*T. angustifolia*), was the most popular of all. But the Bulrushes had a trick to play. When they are ripe and ready to distribute their seed, they go off like Champagne bottles, the seeds frothing out from the top in great powdery puffs. If you pick them, it is wise not to store them inside for long. Until the 1970s, this plant was known to botanists as Reedmace, and the true Bulrush is actually another species. The reason for the name change is that illustrations of the story of Moses in the Bulrushes were given away at Sunday schools during the 1970s, showing a baby in its basket among what is clearly *T. latifolia*. Children were therefore taught that the tall, brown sausages on sticks were called Bulrushes, and the name has stuck.

Plant type Bulrush family, Typhaceae. Flowers June–July. *Height* 1.5–2.5m. *Description* Hairless, aquatic or semi-aquatic, rhizomatous herbaceous perennial. Leaves are 16–18mm across. Inflorescence has no gap between male and female flowers. The female part of the spike is 3–4cm wide, brown and sausage-shaped. The male part, which is fluffy and yellow with a bract at its base, rises from the top of the female part. *Companion species* Flowering-rush (p.299), Water-plantain (p.322) and Yellow Iris (p.324). *Distribution* Native. Common throughout most of Britain and Ireland, becoming scarce in upland regions and towards the north and west. *Habitat* An emergent in shallow water or on exposed mud at the edges of lakes, ponds, canals, ditches, streams and rivers. It spreads by wind-dispersed seeds, often colonising newly excavated ponds and ditches, subsequently spreading by vegetative growth.

Butterbur
(Petasites hybridus)

This forms large, carpeting colonies in damp roadsides and ditches all round the country. The flower stems erupt first, each one a spike with a hundred or so pale pink, tassled flower heads. These then develop into seed pods that resemble pipe cleaners, on their own short stems. With so many flowers on every spike and such large colonies, Butterbur is an excellent early source of pollen and nectar for hive bees – it is often planted deliberately for this reason. Once the flower spikes are fully up, the leaves follow, impressively lush for this early in the year. They are on a lily-pad scale and look good when it is not too hot; on a warm, sunny May day, the whole thing flops like a half-deflated balloon. The large, pliable leaves give the plant its common name: they were picked and used to wrap blocks of butter before fridges arrived on the scene. The Latin genus name, *Petasites*, also refers to the leaf size, derived from the Greek *petasos*, meaning 'a broad-brimmed felt hat'.

Plant type Daisy family, Asteraceae. *Flowers* March–May, sometimes as early as February. *Height* 10–40cm. *Description* Dioecious, patch-forming perennial herb. Leaves are long-stalked, heart-shaped, cordate, pointed and toothed, up to 10cm wide at first but becoming larger (up to 90cm) in summer. Inflorescence has many pink, brush-like flower heads. Male flower heads are 7–12mm long; females 3–6mm. It spreads mostly vegetatively from rhizome fragments, which explains why it often occurs in large, single-sex colonies. *Companion species* None: it tends to take over wherever it grows. *Distribution* Native. Locally frequent throughout much of the British Isles but absent from the Scottish Highlands and rare in the far south east of England and mid Wales. Frequent throughout much of Ireland, although rare in some areas, such as the far south west. Colonies in these areas are thought to be introduced. *Habitat* Moist, fertile, often alluvial soils by watercourses, in wet meadows, marshes, flood plains and copses, and on roadsides, often in or on the sides of ditches.

Celery-leaved Buttercup
(Ranunculus sceleratus)

This is exactly what its name suggests: a plant with leaves and stalks like those of celery, with small buttercup flowers. The yellow petals are quickly dwarfed by the expanding green seed boss at the centre of each flower. These miniature green lychees make it look like Pineappleweed (p.255), but on a bigger, taller plant. When a pond dries in the summer and the mud at its edge appears half-dried and cracked, that is where you will find Celery-leaved Buttercup. The seeds are long-lived and the plant may reappear after many years' absence, particularly if the ground is disturbed by cattle as they stodge about at the edge of a cow drink. It is highly poisonous – as bad as Lesser Spearwort (p.307) – and if eaten by cattle it will dry up their milk if it does not kill them. If handled by us, it causes skin blisters.

Plant type Buttercup family, Ranunculaceae. *Flowers* May–September. *Height* Up to 60cm. *Description* Erect annual herb with basal leaves that are deeply three-lobed, shiny green and hairless. Stem leaves are even more divided, on short stalks. Yellow flowers are 5–10mm across with reflexed sepals. Fruit consists of many achenes in an elongated, bright green head. Goldilocks Buttercup (p.11) is the most similar species but generally it grows in a woody habitat and has kidney-shaped basal leaves. *Companion species* Brooklime (p.292) and Water Mint (p.321). *Distribution* Native. Common throughout most of England but becoming more restricted to the coast in the south west and north, as well as in Wales and Scotland. Rare in the north of Scotland. In Ireland, it is most abundant in the east, becoming local and rare in the west. *Habitat* Shallow water or wet, disturbed, nutrient-rich mud, especially at the edges of ponds, ditches, streams or rivers poached by livestock. It is salt-tolerant and frequent on grazed estuarine marshes.

Common Butterwort
(Pinguicula vulgaris)

This is an insectivorous plant, much like a sundew (see Round-leaved Sundew, p.365). Each leaf is curled at the edges and, when an insect lands, the sticky surface of the leaf holds it fast. The victim's struggle to free itself activates a curling mechanism on the leaf margin. The leaf then secretes digestive enzymes to break down the still-living body, and absorbs the nutrients through its surface. When it gradually opens again, the undigested bits are blown or washed away. Its flowers vaguely resemble a violet in a kind of old-lady mauve – hence its other common name of Bog Violet.

Plant type Bladderwort family, Lentibulariaceae. *Flowers* May–July. *Height* 5–15cm. *Description* Rosette-forming, insectivorous perennial herb. Leaves are yellow-green, oval-oblong, pointed, 2–8cm long, in a basal rosette. Inflorescence has a solitary flower, each with a two-lipped, bluntly lobed calyx and a violet corolla, 10–15mm long, up to 12mm wide, with a white throat, and spur, 4–7mm long. There are two other British species. Large-flowered Butterwort (*P. grandiflora*) from south-west Ireland has larger flowers, with the white patch on the throat streaked with purple. Pale Butterwort (p.362) is smaller, with pale, lilac-pink flowers that bloom later. *Companion species* Golden-saxifrage (p.302), Grass-of-Parnassus (p.302), Round-leaved Sundew (p.365) and Water Avens (p.318). *Distribution* Native. Common throughout Scotland and Wales and in much of England, north of the Humber Estuary. In the rest of England it is scarce, but occurs in Norfolk, some of the southern English heathlands and the Lizard in Cornwall. It declined significantly in lowland England during the nineteenth century and this has continued since. *Habitat* Damp ground and rocks in upland regions, although it occurs more widely in bogs and flushes.

Common Fleabane
(*Pulicaria dysenterica*)

As yellow daisies go, this is showy. It is similar in flower structure to our common Daisy (p.246), the petals narrow and needle-like, the central boss raised, but it has broader flowers and its stems are three times taller. The centre is a rich saffron yellow-orange, the petals a dandelion yellow. Common Fleabane is one of the last things to give colour to ditches and damp roadsides, forming big clumps in late summer, which continue into autumn. The leaves have a strong smell, like camphor crossed with chrysanthemum, and there is a long tradition of using them in houses to keep flies and fleas at bay. They were hung in dried bunches above doors or burnt on the fire, giving the family its common name. Fleabanes are closely related to the plant from which the insecticide pyrethrum is extracted (a tanacetum native to the Balkan Peninsula). Common Fleabane was also used on the Continent for the treatment of dysentery – hence its Latin species name.

Plant type Daisy family, Asteraceae. *Flowers* August–September. *Height* 20–60 cm. *Description* Erect, clump-forming, hairy, branched perennial herb. Leaves are downy, oblong, 3–8cm long, arranged alternately up the stem. Lower leaves narrow into a stalk. Upper leaves are heart-shaped at the base and clasp the stem. Flower heads are 1.5–3cm across, with golden yellow florets. Ray florets are twice as long as disc florets. Bracts are narrow and pointed. *Companion species* Gypsywort (p.303), Indian Balsam (p.305) and Water Mint (p.321). *Distribution* Native. Common in most of Great Britain south of a line from Morecambe Bay to the Humber Estuary, except in upland areas. North of this line it becomes increasingly scarce. In Ireland, it is more localised, although it is quite common on the south and east coastlines. *Habitat* Dampish roadsides, ditches and meadows, riverbanks and marshes on a wide range of soil types.

Common Marsh-bedstraw
(*Galium palustre*)

Bedstraws have a lot to recommend them. They fill the grass with fluffy colour, looking from a distance like puffs of smoke scattered across the plants growing alongside them. They flower for ages, and they also have a soft, honey-like fragrance. Common Marsh-bedstraw is a delicate but wide-spreading species, which can grow up to a metre, particularly if supported by rushes and grasses. It thrives in much damper conditions than any of its common relations, and that is how it can be distinguished from the white-flowered and similar-looking Heath Bedstraw (p.356). It is also noticeably slenderer and more dainty than the very common Hedge Bedstraw (p.202) and much more sprawling and airy than the compact, ground-hugging Heath Bedstraw. There are two similar but rarer species of damp places: Slender Marsh-bedstraw (*G. constrictum*) is now confined to short turf in and around seasonal pools in the New Forest, and Fen Bedstraw (*G. uliginosum*) occurs in fens and fen grasslands.

Plant type Bedstraw family, Rubiaceae. *Flowers* June–August. *Height* Up to 1m. *Description* Slender perennial herb with creeping, ascending or scrambling stems. Like all bedstraws, it has four-angled stems, but they are quite variable – they may be smooth or rough. Leaves are linear-lanceolate to elliptical, blunt, up to 3.5cm long, with backward-pointing prickles on the leaf edges. They are arranged in whorls of four to six. Flowers are white, 3–4.5mm across, in a pyramid with widely spreading panicles. *Companion species* Marsh Pennywort (p.312) and Marsh Valerian (p.313). *Distribution* Native. Occurs throughout Britain and Ireland and is common in most areas. *Habitat* Seasonal or permanently wetland habitats, including wet meadows, marshes, fens, ditches, ponds and lakesides. It prefers non-calcareous substrates.

Common Meadow-rue
(Thalictrum flavum)

The contrast between the pale creamy flowers and grey-green leaves is what makes Common Meadow-rue such a pretty plant. The undersides of the leaves are slightly silvery, adding to the elegance that has encouraged many of us to grow a European relative, *Thalictrum flavum* ssp. *glaucum*, in damp spots in our gardens. The flowers of both look like powder puffs, with huge numbers of primrose-yellow stamens producing tons of pollen, so that in my garden you sometimes get pale yellow patches on the path beneath a flower spike. The flowers do not have scent, but this pollen abundance is enough to draw in hoards of pollinator insects to seek out the nectar at the base of each flower. The foliage is thought to be toxic to cattle: Common Meadow-rue is a member of the buttercup family, most of which are poisonous. The leaves resemble the garden herb rue – hence its common name.

Plant type Buttercup family, Ranunculaceae. *Flowers* July–August. *Height* 50–100cm. *Description* Erect perennial herb. Leaves are two to three times pinnate with wedge-shaped leaflets, 1–2cm long, which are longer than they are broad. Flowers are small and arranged in dense panicles. Each flower has four sepals and many yellow stamens. Fruit is 1.5–2.5mm long and six-ribbed. Lesser Meadow-rue (p.403) is slenderer, and has a more branched and spreading habit, and broader leaflets. *Companion species* Marsh Cinquefoil (p.309), Marsh-marigold (p.311) and Meadowsweet (p.314). *Distribution* Native. It is quite frequent in much of central and eastern England, but rare in the south-east and south-west corners. It is also rare in Wales and occasional in Ireland. A few scattered colonies in Scotland are not considered to be native. *Habitat* Fens, ditches and stream sides, and tall vegetation in wet meadows. It is found where the substrate or water is base-rich.

Common Sedge
(Carex nigra)

Sedges are often confused with grasses, but they are a different group of plants. They have stems that are solid and unjointed, usually triangular in cross-section and with three rows of leaves (grasses have only two rows). One of the largest groups of flowering plants in Britain, with about 75 species, they are most easily identified by their fruit, which, rather than their flowers, is what distinguishes them from one another. I used to think of sedges as little brown blobs, with the exception of a few eye-catchers that were either pretty or odd. But then I found one or two that epitomised the description of brown blob – and came to like them. Common Sedge has blue-green leaves, which provide a strong contrast to the black-fruiting female flower spikes. In its own small way, it is interesting and fun, like an alien geek that needs to change its hairdresser.

Plant type Sedge family, Cyperaceae. *Flowers* May–July, fruiting in June–August. *Height* Up to 70cm, and can form large tussocks, but very variable and can be as short as 7cm on grazed land. *Description* Tufted, rhizomatous perennial herb. Leaves are 1–3mm wide and glaucous. Ligules are rounded, 1–3mm long. Inflorescence has one to four female spikes and one to two male spikes. Fruits are 2.5–3.5mm long, faintly ribbed. Bracts are leaf-like, the lowest as long as the inflorescence. Fruit are hairless and slightly flattened. Other distinguishing features are its creeping rather than clump- or tussock-forming habit, and the two feathery styles on top of the ovary. *Companion species* Grass-of-Parnassus (p.302), Lesser Spearwort (p.307) and Lousewort (p.308). *Distribution* Native. Found throughout Britain and Ireland and common in most areas. *Habitat* Wide range of wet habitats – fens, fen meadows, bogs, stream sides and flushes, wet grassland and dune slacks – except those that are extremely basic or acidic.

Common Water-crowfoot

(Ranunculus aquatilis)

Shallow village ponds have become rarer during the past fifty years, but that is where you will see this white buttercup. Most of the plant exists under water, the leaves floating on the surface and the flowers standing proud, an inch or two above. One of the main distinguishing features between water-crowfoots is their leaves: some have so-called laminar leaves, which float like miniature water-lily pads; others have capillary leaves, which are submerged and composed of many divided linear segments. This species characteristically has a mixture of both. The capillary leaves are adapted to maximise photosynthesis and are important for the oxygenation of the pond's water – that is why this species is found at aquatic nurseries: it helps to keep wildlife ponds clear and healthy. Plants growing in fast-flowing water tend to have fewer or no laminar leaves, whereas those in sitting water – like this one – have plenty. But the main characteristic of Common Water-crowfoot is that it is hugely variable according to where it grows, forming short or very long stems with mainly laminar or mainly capillary leaves.

Plant type Buttercup family, Ranunculaceae. *Flowers* May–June. *Height* 2.5–10cm. *Description* Flowers are 1–2cm across, white with yellow centres, their petals not overlapping. Laminar leaves are divided into three lobes, each lobe further divided, with blunt teeth at the edge. Fruit stalks curve downwards into the water, with globe-shaped, large fruiting heads. It is rather similar to Pond Water-crowfoot (*R. peltatus*), but the Common species has round nectaries at the base of the petals rather than pear-shaped ones. *Companion species* Amphibious Bistort (p.288) and Fringed Water-lily (p.300). *Distribution* Native. Occurs throughout the British Isles, although less frequent in the north and scarce in some parts of southern England, such as Sussex and Cornwall. *Habitat* Shallow waters in marshes, ponds and ditches, and at the edge of slow-flowing streams and sheltered lakes. It occurs chiefly in water that is eutrophic and at least mildly base-rich, and is favoured by a degree of disturbance.

Cuckooflower

(Cardamine pratensis)

Wherever there is a damp patch in a lane or field, or on the edge of a ditch beside the road, there will be a pale-pink puff of Cuckooflower. The flowers vary from pink to pure white, not in a random scattering but in definite bands of colour. Locally, double-flowered forms of the plant are also common, adding to its prettiness. Its stems come in a variety of colours, too, from a smoky, slate-like purple to bright, sharp green. On heavy soil, you sometimes get whole fields of this, broken only by the odd Dandelion (p.246). Its common name of Cuckooflower is shared with several other plants, such as Wood Anemone (p.30) and Red Campion (p.24), whose flowers also open as the first cuckoo sings. Other common names include Lady's Smock and Milkmaids. This is an important wild flower for insects. It is a key larval food plant of both the Orange-tip and Green-veined White butterflies, and its flowers are visited by long-tongued hoverflies and bee flies. The young leaves are edible for us, too, tasting a little spicier than those of its cousin Hairy Bitter-cress (p.251).

Plant type Cabbage family, Brassicaceae. *Flowers* March–June. *Height* Up to 60cm. *Description* Lower leaves have large, round leaflets, the terminal leaflet being kidney-shaped and much the largest. Upper stem leaves have narrower leaflets. Pale lilac or pink flowers, 12–18mm across, are usually veined with darker violet. *Companion species* Dandelions, Garlic Mustard (p.84) and Lords-and-Ladies (p.19). *Distribution* Native. Very common throughout the British Isles, occurring wherever there is moisture, from the edges of bogs in the Outer Hebrides to damp patches on the banks of streams in southern England. *Habitat* Hedgerows, roadsides, stream sides, woods, wet meadows, fens and flushes on moderately fertile, seasonally waterlogged soils. It is also found occasionally in gardens.

Dame's-violet
(Hesperis matronalis)

Like many people, I grow this in my garden for its clouds of mildly scented flowers and the fact that it grows quite happily in light shade. Also known as Sweet Rocket, it has the added bonus of appearing at a downtime during the middle of May, when spring bulbs are mostly over but roses and perennials are yet to begin. When self-sown in the wild, it grows as a mixture of the mauve and white forms, the white having the stronger perfume. It does not need damp soil to grow, but it does best either with moisture or dappled shade. It is not a native plant, but a garden escape, a wild species from southern Europe and western Asia cultivated here since at least 1375. It is called Dame's-violet because it has always been picked and brought into the house. Double forms have been grown in gardens for centuries, but changing fashion, debilitation by virus and difficulties of propagation have reduced these to a rarity. Like all members of the cabbage family, its flowers are edible, and I sometimes freeze petals or whole flowers picked from my garden in ice cubes or ice bowls.

Plant type Cabbage family, Brassicaceae. *Flowers* May–July. *Height* 80–90cm. *Description* Biennial or perennial herb. Lanceolate leaves are pointed, stalked, hairy and toothed; stems are often branched, hairy and leafy. Fragrant violet or white flowers are 18–20mm across, arranged in a long-stalked raceme. Seed pods look like an upright clutch of fine French beans. *Companion species* Lesser Burdock (p.253), Foxglove (p.10) and Ribwort Plantain (p.162). *Distribution* Probably introduced by the Romans, it is relatively common throughout the British Isles, much more so in the north, although less frequent in upland regions of Scotland. *Habitat* Shaded, moist habitats, such as hedgerows, wood borders, riverbanks, roadsides and waste ground, usually near habitation.

Early Marsh-orchid
(Dactylorhiza incarnata)

The colour of Early Marsh-orchid can vary hugely, from a pale, fleshy pink to something even darker than an Early-purple Orchid (in the case of *D. i.* ssp. *pulchella*). This variability is typical of the *Dactylorhiza* – spotted- or marsh-orchids – which are difficult to identify because they are closely related and hybridise like mad. Early Marsh-orchid has five subspecies, of which the most common is ssp. *incarnata* (pictured here), with usually pale pink flowers loosely gathered at the head of its rather chunky stem. Ssp. *ochroleuca* is creamy white, and ssp. *cruenta* has spotted leaves and pinkish-mauve flowers. The squat ssp. *coccinea* grows on the damp dune slacks up Britain's west coast. It has spectacular brick-red flowers without a hint of blue.

Plant type Orchid family, Orchidaceae. *Flowers* Mid May to late June. *Height* Up to 60cm. *Description* Erect, hairless perennial herb. Lanceolate leaves are keeled, up to 3.5cm wide, unspotted, and held at 45 degrees to the stem, typically with a narrowly hooded tip. *Companion species* Bog Pimpernel (p.291), Common Butterwort (p.294), Marsh Thistle (p.312) and Water Avens (p.318). *Distribution* Native. The most widespread of the Marsh-orchids, occurring throughout the British Isles, but it is always local. It is rare in parts of central England and Kent, and has disappeared from almost half of its sites in Britain and a third in Ireland as a result of drainage and habitat loss. *Habitat* Ssp. *incarnata* is found on calcareous to neutral soils in damp to wet grassland. It is especially characteristic of unimproved wet meadows on flood plains, but is also found in spring-fed flushes, dune slacks and chalk quarries (where compaction leads to seasonal waterlogging). Other subspecies prefer slightly different habitats: ssp. *pulchella* is found in valley bogs and acid marshes on heathland.

Fine-leaved Water-dropwort
(Oenanthe aquatica)

This is the less common relation of the ubiquitous Hemlock Water-dropwort (p.304) and, like that species, it grows in running water ditches and slow-running streams. Its roots sit in the water or in a tussock on the bank, half in and half out of the water. It has leaves that are paler green than those of Hemlock Water-dropwort, finely cut and elegant, not unlike those of Cow Parsley (p.77). It is also poisonous, but less dangerous than the Hemlock form. The symptoms of poisoning include giddiness, vertigo, failure of circulation and, if you have eaten lots, coma. Water-dropworts share their common name with the unrelated grassland plant Dropwort (p.197). The name describes their tubers, which are attached to the roots by narrow, thread-like stalks.

Plant type Carrot family, Apiaceae. *Flowers* June–September. *Height* 30–100cm. *Description* Bushy aquatic tuberous annual or biennial herb. Stem is hollow and very swollen near the base (3–4cm thick), with many fine ridges and transverse joints. Leaves are three times pinnate, with leaflets that are hair-like when submerged but lanceolate and finely toothed when above water. Umbels are short-stalked, situated in the leaf axils, with four to ten rays, few or no bracts, and bristle-like bracteoles. Flowers are white, 2mm across. Fruit is oval, 3.5–4.5mm long. *Companion species* Hemlock Water-dropwort, Water-plantain (p.322) and Water-violet (p.322). *Distribution* Native. In England and Wales the distribution is patchy – it is most frequent (locally common) to the east of a line from Selsey Bill in West Sussex to Flamborough Head in east Yorkshire, but it is also locally frequent in the West Midlands, Welsh Borders and Somerset Levels. Outside these areas it is scattered and rare. It is locally frequent in central Ireland. *Habitat* Still or slow-moving water, usually occurring on deep, silty, often eutrophic substrates in shallow ponds and ditches, often where water fluctuates in depth. It also grows in open vegetation by sheltered lakes, reservoirs, canals, streams and rivers, and in marshes and seasonally flooded depressions that dry out in summer.

Flowering-rush
(Butomus umbellatus)

I have great affection for this plant, because a good clump of it grew near to where I was brought up, just outside Cambridge. There was a slow-running stream – really more of a ditch – filled with Flowering-rush, and we made a pilgrimage to see it every year. It seemed such a brilliantly surprising plant – such boring, iris-like leaves, matching those of the Yellow Iris (p.324) all around it, but then came the most delicious, sugar-almond pink, open buttercup flowers, each with a clutch of deep pink carpels at its heart, every flower head like an upside-down umbrella standing at least a foot taller than everything else. It reminded me of a huge and impressive garden allium more than a plant of a village ditch, and I loved it. Flowering-rush used to be so common in parts of the river Thames that Geoffrey Grigson nicknamed it Pride-of-the-Thames. It is now much rarer there as a result of dredging. It has been introduced as an ornamental plant in gardens and is now considered an invasive alien species in the Great Lakes region of the United States.

Plant type Flowering-rush family, Butomaceae. *Flowers* July–September. *Height* Up to 150cm. *Description* Tall, hairless erect perennial. Leaves are linear, pointed and twisted, as long or a little shorter than the flowering stems. Flowering stems are round, terminating in an umbel of many unequally long-stalked flowers. Sepals and petals are both rosy pink, although the sepals are smaller than the petals. There are six to nine stamens. *Companion species* Amphibious Bistort (p.288), Water-plantain (p.322) and Yellow Iris. *Distribution* Native. It is found throughout Britain and Ireland, although it is native only in England and Wales. It is frequent to locally common in England, especially in the Midlands, but is rare in Wales and absent from far south-west England and north-west England (except as an alien). Its two natural strongholds are probably the Norfolk Broads and the Somerset Levels. *Habitat* Calcareous, often nutrient-rich water at the edges of rivers, lakes, canals and swamps.

Fool's-watercress
(Apium nodiflorum)

As its name implies, you can easily confuse this with Watercress (p.320). They both grow in similar spots, quite often growing together in the shallows of fairly fast-running streams or around chalk springs, and the leaves are similar. In fact, Watercress is an unrelated member of the cabbage family. The way to tell them apart is to look at the leaf stalks where they join the main stem. Fool's-watercress has sheathing, inflated bases to the leaf stalks, characteristic of the umbellifer (or carrot) family. These are absent in Watercress. The leaves of Fool's-watercress are generally paler green with lightly serrated edges and pointed tips, in contrast to the smooth edges and rounded tips of Watercress leaves. Fool's-watercress also starts to flower a couple of months later, from midsummer onwards, and although it is edible, it tastes bland. People in the West Country – where it is common – traditionally picked it for cooking with meat in pasties and pies. When in leaf it can be easily confused with Lesser Water-parsnip (p.307), but that has reddish-purple stems. Lesser Water-parsnip is poisonous, so be absolutely sure that you know which of these similar-looking plants you are picking before you eat any.

Plant type Carrot family, Apiaceae. *Flowers* July–August. *Height* Up to 80cm. *Description* Prostrate to ascending perennial herb. Umbels have three to twelve rays and are short-stalked or unstalked with very small, white flowers. Leaves are once pinnate with four to six pairs of oval, shallow-toothed, bright green leaflets. Stems are finely grooved and root at the lower nodes. Fruits are 1.5–2.5mm, longer than wide, with thick ridges. *Companion species* Hemlock Water-dropwort (p.304), Lesser Water-parsnip and Watercress. *Distribution* Native and common in England, Wales and Ireland, but rare in Scotland, except in some parts of the Western Isles. *Habitat* Shallow water in streams, ditches, swamps and marshes, and on seasonally exposed mud at the edges of ponds, lakes, rivers and canals, sometimes scrambling into nearby vegetation. It is characteristic of nutrient-enriched sites.

Fringed Water-lily
(Nymphoides peltata)

Although this looks as if it would be at home in the rivers and ponds of the Orient, it grows quite commonly in village and field ponds and in slowly moving rivers and canals. From a distance, it looks like a brilliant Yellow Water-lily (p.324), and if you were whizzing past, you would assume that was what it was. However, the two plants are not related. Fringed Water-lily has smaller flowers, which it holds up, perky and proud, a little above the water's surface. Looked at closely, the petal edges are finely frizzed, as if they have been cut with crimping shears – it looks more like its relative Bogbean (p.291), with its bizarre frilly flowers, than a water-lily. The leaves are lily-pad-shaped, but they are small with a deep crimson underside. Fringed Water-lily has been planted as an ornamental in village and garden ponds and can become invasive. All parts of the plant are edible, but it is no longer widespread enough to harvest.

Plant type Bogbean family, Menyanthaceae. *Flowers* June–September. *Height* Flowers stand up to 10cm above the water. *Description* Aquatic rhizomatous perennial herb with round- to kidney-shaped, deeply cordate, floating leaves, very much like those of true water-lilies. Flowers, which arise from the leaf axils, are yellow, with a five-lobed corolla, 3cm across, fringed with small, fine hairs. *Companion species* Flowering-rush (p.299), Water-plantain (p.322) and Yellow Iris (p.324). *Distribution* Native. It occurs throughout England and is quite common in many waterways, wetlands and rivers, although it is becoming less frequent in the north and very rare in Scotland and Ireland. It is considered by some botanists to be native only in a small part of its range – in some East Anglian fens and in the Thames Valley. It has been widely introduced by deliberate plantings or from discarded surplus stock. *Habitat* Water 0.5–2m deep in lakes, ponds, slow-flowing rivers, canals and large fenland ditches. As a native, it is a plant mainly of calcareous and nutrient-rich water.

Frogbit
(Hydrocharis morsus-ranae)

Frogbit looks like a three-petalled trillium floating on the water, its distinctive flowers scattered across shiny miniature lily-pad leaves. Close to, the petals have a delicate texture, like those of a poppy, cut out of crumpled silk. The flowers can also be tinged with pink, so they look iridescent, like mother-of-pearl. They have an ingenious system to avoid being frozen and killed by winter weather. In late summer and early autumn, they produce special winter buds, which sink to the bottom of the water and remain dormant in the mud. When spring arrives, the buds develop into small plants that rise to the surface and start growing again. Any seeds produced also sink into the pond or lake, rising to the surface the following spring. Its common name comes from the belief in ancient Greece that Frogbit was devoured by frogs, and it does, indeed, provide good cover for tadpoles, newts and dragonfly larvae.

Plant type Frogbit family, Hydrocharitaceae. *Flowers* July–August. *Height* Spreads to 50–100cm. *Description* Free-floating dioecious herb with long runners that are not rooted in the mud. Leaves are round and kidney-shaped, up to 3cm across, stalked with papery stipules. The undersides of the leaves are often reddish brown. Flowers are unisexual and have three green sepals and three crumpled white petals, with a yellow spot at the base of each petal. There are usually two to three male flowers together, but females are always solitary. Male flowers have nine to twelve stamens. *Companion species* Fringed Water-lily (left), Lesser Pond-sedge (p.306) and Water-violet (p.322). *Distribution* Native. Scattered throughout England, Wales and Ireland. It is absent from Scotland, except as a rare introduction. *Habitat* Sheltered parts of lakes, ponds, canals and ditches. It prefers shallow, calcareous water and tends to be an indicator of good, clean water.

Globeflower
(Trollius europaeus)

Globeflower inspires one of those moments when you think, 'Heavens alive, look at the riches of this country!' I have seen them in North Yorkshire in big drifts, like a field of buttercups but with flowers five times the size. They are incredibly showy, with a sophisticated poise that could not be more different to the milkmaid simplicity of buttercups. Each flower makes a neat globe, which opens only just enough – in warm weather – to let small insect pollinators in. A possible reason for this roundness and tightness is that the species is really a rock-ledge and mountain flower at heart, which has colonised upland hay meadows as we have created them – the cold and wet of the mountains would be a jolly good reason to close up and protect its anthers and stigmas. The illustrator Anne Pratt described a lovely scene in the nineteenth century: 'Globe flowers are gathered in Westmorland, with great festivity, by youth of both sexes in the beginning of June … it is usual to see them return from the woods of an evening laden with these blossoms.' Massive drainage and the turning over of meadow to arable farming has made these much rarer.

Plant type Buttercup family, Ranunculaceae. *Flowers* May–August. *Height* 40–70cm. *Description* Palmate, deeply toothed leaves, which look similar to those of Meadow Crane's-bill (p.96), and bright yellow flowers with five to fifteen petal-like sepals that form a neat globe enclosing small, strap-shaped, nectar-secreting petals. Flowers are 2.5–5cm across and often twice as wide as they are tall. *Companion species* Early Marsh-orchid (p.298), Meadowsweet (p.314) and Water Avens (p.318). On drier ground: Melancholy Thistle (p.97) and Wood Crane's-bill (p.121). On cliffs: Roseroot (p.365). *Distribution* Native. Rare, confined to northern England, Wales, Scotland and the north west of Ireland. *Habitat* Found in cool, damp habitats, such as hay meadows, stream and riverbanks, lake margins, open woodland and rock ledges. Basic soils are preferred, and it is associated with limestone. Although sensitive to grazing, it may persist as a small, non-flowering plant in uplands.

Golden-saxifrage
(Chrysosplenium oppositifolium/C. alternifolium)

I am a lover of acid green, and the way that it brightens everything around it and is beautiful with every colour. That is why I have always been fond of this miniature euphorbia-like plant, plastered to the edges of watery hollows, spring flushes and bog waterfalls and running along as brilliant ribbons on the edges of dark streams. Richard Mabey tells us that in the Vosges mountains in France, the leaves are eaten under the name of *Cresson des roches*, but in the British Isles the plant is not common enough to pick in any quantity. There are two species, *C. oppositifolium* and *C. alternifolium*. The stalked leaves are in opposite pairs on the first, and alternate down the stem of the second. *C. oppositifolium* prefers acid soils, whereas *C. alternifolium* prefers more base-rich soils and is found in grikes and sinkholes in limestone, but they also grow together. *C. alternifolium* does not form such spreading large mats, but grows as taller, chunkier plants.

Plant type Saxifrage family, Saxifragaceae. *Flowers* April–May, sometimes as early as March. *Height* 5–15cm. *Description* A low, sprawling mass of leafy shoots that root at intervals, the leaves rounded and bluntly toothed, with stalks no longer than the leaf blades. Flowers are yellow-green. Most saxifrages have five sepals, five petals and ten stamens, but these have four sepals, no petals and eight stamens. The alternate-leaved variety has kidney-shaped leaves, which have wide, squarish teeth at their edge and longer stalks and flower stems. *Companion species* Bugle (p.68), Lesser Celandine (p.18) and Yellow Archangel (p.35). *Distribution* Native. Common in south-west and western Britain. Local elsewhere and scarce in the east, particularly East Anglia. Absent from Shetland. *Habitat* Damp, mossy areas by springs, streams in woods and around and under mountain rocks, especially on acid soils.

Grass-of-Parnassus
(Parnassia palustris)

I am not the only one to count Grass-of-Parnassus among my favourite plants. It was voted the favourite flower of both Cumbria and Sutherland in Plantlife's County Flowers campaign. Like a serene and beautiful buttercup in pure white, the flowers translucent with a network of veins, it would inspire the most perfect wedding dress: the skirt substantial yet ethereal, the bodice a light, smoky pink with golden-yellow embroidery – I will do my damnedest to persuade one of my daughters to walk down the aisle in it. Grass-of-Parnassus is common in damp places with high rainfall, and I used to find lots of it during childhood holidays on the west coast of Scotland. The name Grass-of-Parnassus was given after it was found on Mount Parnassus in Greece.

Plant type Grass-of-Parnassus family, Parnassiaceae. *Flowers* July–October. *Height* 10–30cm. *Description* Erect, hairless perennial herb. Leaves are oval-cordate and long-stalked. There is one stalkless, cordate leaf on the stem. Flowers are solitary, 15–30mm across, with five white, green-veined petals, five fertile stamens, five fan-shaped, gland-tipped, sterile stamens and four stigmas. *Companion species* Autumn Hawkbit (p.143), Bog Pimpernel (p.291), Meadowsweet (p.314), Red Clover (p.161), Rough Hawkbit (p.162) and Yellow Iris (p.324). *Distribution* Native. Frequent in much of Scotland and northern England. In Wales, it is confined to the far north. It is quite common in central Ireland, but absent from the south west. It was formerly found in much of central lowland England, but is now very rare, although quite frequent in Norfolk. Modern drainage, eutrophication and neglect of its fenland habitat has consigned it to near extinction. *Habitat* Streamside flushes, mires, dune slacks, wet pastures, moorland and machair. It prefers base-rich soils.

Great Willowherb
(Epilobium hirsutum)

There are two willowherbs that you cannot fail to notice in the wild: Rosebay Willowherb (p.258), with its tall, feather-like flower plumes, and Great Willowherb. This has larger individual flowers than the Rosebay form, but there are fewer of them, and they are more spaced out, so it lacks the oomph of its relation. The magenta flowers have a prominent, four-pointed star stigma at the centre and, as with all willowherbs, its flowers are stuck out at the end of a long, thin pod. They smell like cooked fruit, which gives this plant its common name of Codlins-and-cream. Great Willowherb spreads rapidly by underground stems, so it rarely occurs in ones and twos, more like fifties and hundreds. This enables it to form large clumps to the exclusion of other plants. The fat grey and black caterpillars of the Elephant Hawk-moth feed on the leaves and may be seen during the day on the lower leaves and stem.

Plant type Willowherb family, Onagraceae. *Flowers* July–August. *Height* 80–150cm. *Description* Tall, hairy perennial herb. Stems are round and very hairy. Leaves are lanceolate, stalkless, 6–12cm long and arranged in opposite pairs that clasp the stem. Flowers are deep purple-pink, 15–23mm across, with a four-lobed stigma. *Companion species* It tends to grow in isolation. *Distribution* Native. Very common throughout most of England, Wales and Ireland, but in Scotland it is almost entirely restricted to the Lowlands and the east coast. It is rare or absent from the west of Scotland, Orkney, Shetland and the Western Isles. *Habitat* Beside rivers, streams, lakes, ponds and ditches, as well as in fens and marshes. It is often an indicator of rather neglected and abandoned damp lands. It occurs less commonly in drier situations, such as woodland edges, rides and hedgerows. However, it is intolerant of shade. It is usually found on calcareous or base-rich soils.

Gypsywort
(Lycopus europaeus)

The leaves of Gypsywort are elegant and jagged, like those of nettles, but soft-looking and non-threatening, arranged very neatly up the stem. They are the reason that you will notice this plant, rather than its small and insignificant dead-nettle flowers, which huddle in spherical pompoms, tight to the stem. It is called Gypsywort because the leaves produce a black dye that was once used by gypsies to darken their skin. They apparently did this to masquerade as fortune-tellers and magicians from Egypt and Africa, as dark skin was thought to give them greater credibility. It was also used to dye cloth: the herbalist John Gerard considered that cloth dyed with Gypsywort would keep its dark colour for ever. Most dead-nettles used to be harvested for eating as a wilted green, but not this one. It has very little flavour and is stringy.

Plant type Dead-nettle family, Lamiaceae. *Flowers* June–September. *Height* 30–100cm. *Description* Variable, erect, slightly hairy perennial herb. Stem is square. Flowers are arranged in well-spaced, dense whorls situated in the leaf axils. Leaves are jagged-edged, elliptical-lanceolate, pinnately lobed, 5–10cm long and short-stalked. Each flower has a bell-shaped calyx and a four-lobed, white corolla, 3mm across, the lower lip spotted with purple, with two protruding stamens. *Companion species* Common Fleabane (p.295), Great Willowherb (p.303), Indian Balsam (p.305) and Water Mint (p.321). *Distribution* Native. Frequent throughout much of England and Wales but rare in the north and scarce in upland areas. In Scotland, it is frequent near the west coast but rare elsewhere. It is found throughout Ireland but is quite local in many areas. *Habitat* Wet habitats, usually on mineral or peaty soils, including the banks and margins of lakes, rivers, ditches and streams, as well as fens and dune slacks, and damp woodland clearings.

Hemlock
(Conium maculatum)

Hemlock looks innocent, like Cow Parsley (p.77), but taller. Like Deadly Nightshade (p.6), it is an exciting plant to find because it is incredibly poisonous. All parts of it are highly toxic, containing a neurotoxin called coniine, which paralyses the respiratory nerves, causing death by suffocation. The seeds contain particularly high concentrations. It is said to be poisonous to cows while, improbably, not affecting horses, sheep and goats. Plants growing in full sunshine are the most virulently poisonous. Socrates was one of its famous victims, sentenced to death by a cup of Hemlock juice. Fortunately, cases of Hemlock poisoning are rare, because it smells horrible. You only have to sniff a crushed leaf and its sourness would put you off eating any part of it. The Latin genus name derives from the Greek *konos*, meaning 'spinning top', in reference to the vertigo you experience as the first stage of poisoning.

Plant type Carrot family, Apiaceae. *Flowers* June–July. *Height* Up to 2m. *Description* Erect perennial or biennial herb. Fern-like leaves are 30cm long, white umbels 2–5cm across. Fruit is distinctive, being globular with wavy ridges. It looks like a larger version of Cow Parsley, which is edible, so the differences are important to note. Hemlock is taller and hairless and has a purple-spotted stem. Cow Parsley has a plain green stem. *Companion species* Cleavers (p.238), Common Nettle (p.241) and Viper's-bugloss (p.214). *Distribution* Introduced, probably by the Romans. Common throughout the British Isles, except in north-west Scotland. It is absent from much of inland Scotland and parts of mid Wales and the Pennines; local in much of Ireland, but more frequent in the south. *Habitat* Damp places, such as ditches and riverbanks. Drier habitats include rough grassland, waste ground, rubbish tips and roadsides. It is a colonist of disturbed areas.

Hemlock Water-dropwort
(Oenanthe crocata)

There is hardly a hundred-yard stretch in the chalk streams of the West Country that does not have a good colony of this tussock-forming plant. Around me in Kent and Sussex, it packs freshwater ditches, its leaves creating a ribbon of brilliant green at the water's edge. It looks so tempting and edible, and it smells sweet and wine-like. But Hemlock Water-dropwort is highly poisonous and probably responsible for more human deaths that any other British plant. There have been several recent deaths, particularly among tourists, who mistake it for Wild Celery (*Apium graveolens*) and eat it raw, boiled or in soup. All parts of the plant are toxic, especially the tubers, and more than half of cases of human poisoning are fatal. If you find an umbellifer with finely divided leaves near or in the water, do not pick it. Even if it is not this one, it is likely to be a water-dropwort, and all British species are poisonous.

Plant type Carrot family, Apiaceae. *Flowers* June–July. *Height* Up to 150cm. *Description* Robust, erect, hairless perennial herb. Stems are hollow, cylindrical and grooved. Leaves are triangular, three to four times pinnate, the leaflets being wedge-shaped, toothed and tapered to the stalk. Umbels are stalked, 5–10cm across, with many linear bracts and bracteoles. Flowers are 2mm across, with unequal petals. Fruit is cylindrical, 4–6mm long. *Companion species* Monkeyflower (p.315), River Water-crowfoot (p.317) and Watercress (p.320). *Distribution* Native. Very common in southern England and western Britain. In East Anglia, the East Midlands, much of east Yorkshire and inland Scotland, it is rare or absent. In Ireland, it is common in the north east and south west, but rare in the centre. *Habitat* Ditches, banks of streams, rivers, canals, lakes and ponds, roadside culverts, marshes and wet woodland, the tops of beaches and on flushed sea cliffs.

Hemp-agrimony
(Eupatorium cannabinum)

The name Hemp-agrimony is incredibly misleading, as this plant is not related to hemp or Agrimony (p.142). The leaves are a bit like those of cannabis (hemp) and it was once mistakenly classed with Agrimony, but it could not look more different. It is a towering giant of a plant, standing to almost human height in good ground, with every stem topped by large, dirty-pink, powder-puff flowers, which stay on the plant for months. When the flowers first open, they are a cleaner colour, but this muddies and browns over time. The overall effect by the end of summer is grimy. Its dark crimson stems are the most handsome part of the plant, and this colour has been picked up in several garden forms, which have deep purple flowers. Hemp-agrimony is very attractive to butterflies and other insects, and the garden hybrids make excellent nectar-rich additions to borders.

Plant type Daisy family, Asteraceae. *Flowers* July–September. *Height* Up to 150cm. *Description* Tall, downy, clump-forming perennial herb. Basal leaves are stalkless, trifoliate or five-lobed, with elliptical-lanceolate, toothed leaflets, 5–10cm long. Each flower head has five to six reddish-pink tubular florets and eight to ten purple-tipped bracts, arranged in dense, branching, rounded panicles up to 15cm across. Seeds are black with white pappus hairs. *Companion species* Great Willowherb (p.303), Indian Balsam (right) and Meadowsweet (p.314). *Distribution* Native. Common in much of southern England and Wales, but becoming less frequent to the north. In Scotland, it is confined to near the coast and is absent from the far north. In Ireland, it is found throughout but is rather localised in most areas. *Habitat* It prefers dampish or wet ground, and is often found along the margins of streams, rivers, lakes, ponds and ditches and in marshes, fens, damp woods and heaths, mires and meadows. It is found less frequently in drier habitats, although it does sometimes crop up on waste ground and chalk grassland.

Indian Balsam
(Impatiens glandulifera)

Indian (or Himalayan) Balsam engenders different reactions. Some people are fond of it and like to see it along riverbanks and on the edges of village ponds. Others hate it with a passion. That is because it was introduced as a garden plant from the Himalayas and has now become very invasive. The tallest non-climbing annual in Britain (it can grow up to 3m in a year), it was first recorded in the wild in 1855 in Middlesex and its increase was slow until the middle of the twentieth century. Since then, it has escaped onto riverbanks and found its ideal habitat, spreading rapidly along river courses and achieving a rampaging spread. The plants can project their seeds explosively, up to a distance of four metres – if you stand by a clump in the early autumn, you will see them do it. The seeds often drop into the river, travelling wherever it goes. It is particularly invasive on rivers that tend to flood, as flooding creates the bare open ground on which it can quickly get a foothold.

Plant type Balsam family, Balsaminaceae. *Flowers* July–October. *Height* Up to 3m. *Description* Tall, hairless, reddish-stemmed annual. Leaves are lanceolate-elliptical, sharply toothed and arranged in whorls of three. Flowers are purplish pink, five-petalled, 25–40mm long, arranged in racemes of five or more. They are irregular in shape, with broad lips, narrower hoods and short, curved spurs, and have a sweet, somewhat sickly scent. Fruit is a club-shaped capsule. *Companion species* Tends to form a monocultural swathe. *Distribution* Introduced. Widespread throughout the British Isles and common in most areas, although it remains rare in northern Scotland and central Ireland. *Habitat* Along riverbanks and other waterways. It is also found in damp woodlands, mires and flushes.

Irish Lady's-tresses
(Spiranthes romanzoffiana)

There is something shell-like about Irish Lady's-tresses, as if a stack of miniature molluscs were arranged, one on top of the other, up the pale green stem. The Irish species is not as plaited as Autumn Lady's-tresses (p.190). Its species name is after Nicholas Romanzof, a Russian minister of state, because it was first discovered in 1828 in Alaska, then a Russian territory. The flowering time varies according to the weather and moisture levels in the soil, so it can be tricky to find. I remember spending hours, even days, with my father, looking for this in a peaty bog at Drimnin on the Morvern peninsula on Scotland's west coast, where he had found it years before. We found it in some years and not in others. Now, it has disappeared.

Plant type Orchid family, Orchidaceae. *Flowers* July–August. *Height* 12–35cm. *Description* Stout, erect perennial herb. Leaves are lanceolate-linear, mostly in a basal rosette and held erect. There are usually a few sheathing, bract-like stem leaves. Inflorescence is a compact spike of three rows of small, creamy-white, tubular flowers, each 8–11mm long, spiralling round the stem. *Companion species* Grass-of-Parnassus (p.302) and Heath Spotted-orchid (p.359). *Distribution* Native. Very local and scattered in the north and west of Ireland. It occurs locally in western Scotland. There is one population on the edge of Dartmoor in south Devon. *Habitat* Nutrient-poor, permanently damp grassland, sometimes where it is flushed with ground water but more usually close to a river or loch shore. It prefers mildly acidic to neutral grassland but may sometimes grow on more alkaline substrates. In the Hebrides, it is often found in the marginal land between lime-rich machair and inland acidic moorland. It is also sometimes found among sphagnum moss on disused peat workings.

Lesser Pond-sedge
(Carex acutiformis)

The rich, velvet, brown-black flower spikes of this sedge make it stand out from the crowd, like pointed paintbrushes on the edge of a pond, river or stream. They look like bittern heads, alert and upward, half hidden by a mixture of the new green and older, more silvery leaves around them. Each has white anthers on a dark background. Spend some time with Lesser Pond-sedge and it becomes a beautiful thing, its leaves ribbed and upright, just curving over at the tip and distinctly silver. It grows best by water, lush among the highly cut leaves of Hemlock Water-dropwort (p.304) or handsome architectural foliage of Wild Angelica (p.324), with its roots almost in the water. You will also see tussocks of it around the base of willow trees, both curving in over the water. Sometimes the bank erodes enough to cause a huge tussock to fall into the water, to root somewhere further downstream.

Plant type Sedge family, Cyperaceae. *Flowers* July–September. *Height* 60–160cm. *Description* Tufted herb with sharply three-angled stems. Leaves are glaucous, keeled or pleated, drooping at the tips, up to 160cm long and 10mm wide. Sheaths are streaked with red and ligules pointed, 5–15mm long. Inflorescence has two to three male spikes (each 1–4cm long) above and three to four female spikes (2–5cm long) below. Male and female spikes are short-stalked. Female glumes are narrow, pointed and brown with a pale midrib. Fruit is oval with a short beak. *Companion species* Common Comfrey (p.71), Common Nettle (p.241), Hemlock Water-dropwort and Wild Angelica. *Distribution* Native. Quite common throughout most of England, although rare in the far south west. In Scotland, it is mostly restricted to the lowlands. In Wales, it is absent from the most remote, upland regions. In Ireland it is mostly found in the east, where it is local. *Habitat* Damp meadows and swamps; also on the edges of ponds, rivers and streams, often occurring in extensive stands. It is notably shade tolerant.

Lesser Spearwort
(Ranunculus flammula)

A buttercup-like plant, which occurs in many places, this always grows in the damp, in ditches or wet hollows, not out in the middle of a meadow. It is common and can form huge colonies if the conditions are right: I came across a snake of it curling over a bog in South Harris, Outer Hebrides, a defined, colonising carpet, 200 metres across, in shallow, slow-running, peaty water that was a little deeper than the bog around it. From a distance, its flower carpets are reminiscent of meadow buttercups, although their simple, undivided leaves are very different. If grazing is too heavy, it may become invasive on acid bogs. This is poisonous and animals will not eat it, so it is able to spread unchecked. It has a bigger relation, Greater Spearwort (*R. lingua*), which is taller (50–120 cm) and has stem leaves that are narrower, more linear and up to 25cm long. Greater Spearwort also has brighter and larger flowers.

Plant type Buttercup family, Ranunculaceae. *Flowers* May–September. *Height* Up to 50cm. *Description* Hairless, erect or creeping perennial herb. Stem is hollow, sometimes rooting at the nodes. Basal leaves are spear-shaped; stem leaves are lanceolate. Flowers are yellow, 8–20mm across, on furrowed stalks. *Companion species* Bog Pimpernel (p.291), Common Sedge (p.296) and Monkeyflower (p.315). *Distribution* Native. Found throughout Britain and very common in some areas, especially in the north and west. It is absent from a few small, intensively managed agricultural areas of England. *Habitat* Wet habitats, particularly those with seasonal water level fluctuations. It is found in springs and flushes, around ponds, on lake shores and stream sides, in dune slacks, marshes, water meadows, flood pastures, bogs and in ditches and track ruts. It usually grows in shallow water over neutral or acidic soil.

Lesser Water-parsnip
(Berula erecta)

The waterside umbellifers are enough to give anyone a headache, trying to work out which is which. From a distance, all of them look quite similar – Hemlock Water-dropwort (p.304), Fine-leaved Water-dropwort (p.299) and this. They all have elegant, finely cut leaves and large white umbellifer flower heads, which come out at about the same time. Looked at more closely, Lesser Water-parsnip has much less finely divided leaves than the water-dropworts. In fact, the most similar common waterside plant is another umbellifer, Fool's-watercress (p.300), but that has less cut, more shallow, bluntly toothed leaves and flower umbels that are more or less stalkless and located only in the leaf axils (not terminal, as in Lesser Water-parsnip). Some records say that Lesser Water-parsnip is poisonous, but less intensely so than water-dropworts. Others say that you can eat the roots. Cattle eat large amounts of water-parsnip with no ill effects.

Plant type Carrot family, Apiaceae. *Flowers* July–August. *Height* 30–100cm. *Description* Erect perennial herb with runners. Leaves are dull, bluish green and once pinnate, with deeply toothed, oval leaflets, 2–5cm long, in seven to ten pairs. Umbels are 3–6cm wide, on short stalks in the leaf axils and terminal. Fruit is almost spherical, 2mm wide. Greater Water-parsnip (*Sium latifolium*) is a much larger plant (up to 2m tall) and rare in most areas, except East Anglia. *Companion species* Fine-leaved Water-dropwort, Fool's-watercress, and Hemlock Water-dropwort. *Distribution* Native. Occurs throughout England and is quite frequent in most areas, apart from the south west and north, where it is rare. It is rare in Scotland and the Cambrian mountains of Wales. In Ireland, it is locally frequent, especially in central Ireland, becoming scarcer to the north and south. *Habitat* A submerged aquatic in rivers and streams, and an emergent species at the edges of lakes, ponds, rivers, ditches and canals. It is also found in marshes and on seasonally flooded wet ground, and usually roots into fine silt or mud.

Lousewort
(*Pedicularis sylvatica*)

This funny-looking plant appears like a large two-lipped flower emerging straight out of the ground without a stem. It is as if someone has scattered flowers all over the turf as they have walked along, a handful clumped together here and another there. If you look a little closer you will see that there is a very short stem with some quite elegant, heavily indented leaves in green, washed carmine and purple. Louseworts are semi-parasitic, usually on the roots of grasses, from which they extract the water and mineral salts they need. It has been thought that Lousewort may be involved in the transmission of liver fluke (parasitic worms that rot the livers of sheep), but this is probably an old wives' tale, most likely originating from the fact that both Lousewort and liver fluke occur in the same sort of wet, sheepy places. The plant is poisonous to animals if eaten in any quantity, so farmers are keen to eradicate it from grazed land.

Plant type Broomrape family, Orobanchaceae. *Flowers* April–July. *Height* 10–20cm. *Description* Low perennial or biennial herb with many stems that are usually hairless. Flowers are pink or red, 15–25mm long. Leaves are lanceolate, 2–3cm long and twice pinnately lobed. *Companion species* Common Sedge (p.296), Dandelions (p.246) and mosses. *Distribution* Native. Widespread across the British Isles, although rare or absent from much of central and eastern England. There has been a widespread decline in southern and eastern England since 1950, due to the loss of heathland and unimproved grassland. *Habitat* It appears in similar places to Marsh Lousewort (p.311), but also in drier places, usually on acidic soils. Habitats range from damp grassy heaths, moorlands and upland flushed grasslands to the drier parts of bogs and marshes.

Mare's-tail
(*Hippuris vulgaris*)

Mare's-tail looks prehistoric, like something that you can imagine being trampled on by dinosaurs. When you catch it at the right flowering moment, you will see that it has a bright pink central stem with whorls of vibrant green leaves arranged like spinning tops all the way up it, one clearly separated from the next. The circumference of the spinning tops decreases as they reach the tip of the spike, and they become more densely packed. In between each whorl are what look like purple eggs – the petal-less flowers – almost touching around the stem. You will see these spikes densely packed on the edge of the water in a shallow pond or marsh. Mare's-tail is said to absorb methane, thus improving the air quality in its immediate surroundings. However, in some parts it is regarded as a troublesome weed, because it can clog up ditches and ponds.

Plant type Mare's-tail family, Hippuridaceae. *Flowers* June–July. *Height* 25–75cm. *Description* Aquatic, unbranched perennial herb that occurs in two growth forms. Plants with long, flaccid, trailing stems grow as submerged aquatics and are sometimes abundant in clear calcareous water. More rigid, stiffly erect shoots grow as emergents at the edges of lakes and ponds, in swamps or in upland flushes. These may be very robust when growing on deep, eutrophic mud. *Companion species* Bogbean (p.291), Marsh Cinquefoil (p.309) and Water Forget-me-not (p.320). *Distribution* Native. It is found throughout most of Britain, apart from Devon and Cornwall, the Cambrian mountains and parts of the Scottish Highlands. In most areas, it is quite local, but it is common in the Norfolk Broads and in the area surrounding the Wash. *Habitat* It prefers nutrient-rich water and is most frequent in lowland, calcium-rich waters of slow-moving rivers and lakesides.

Marsh Cinquefoil
(Comarum palustre)

With its crimson-mahogany petals and spiky, jagged flower shape, this is one of the most striking wild flowers. Once the flowers are over, the seed head swells to look like a blackberry, surrounded by the pointed calyx. It has bold, architectural leaves, bigger and showier than those of other potentillas, dark grey-green on the upper side and silvery below. It also goes by the name Bog Strawberry. I found an entire field of it in South Uist in the Outer Hebrides, looking like an intricately embroidered Middle Eastern carpet, a perfect mix of colour and shape, along with the odd clump of Water Mint (p.321) and Wild Angelica (p.324). It can, rarely, form huge colonies like this because it spreads by creeping underground stems.

Plant type Rose family, Rosaceae. *Flowers* May–July. *Height* Up to 45cm. *Description* Short to medium, slightly hairy perennial herb. Lower leaves are pinnate, divided into five to seven leaflets, each of which is oblong, toothed and 3–6cm long. Upper leaves are palmate or trifoliate. Inflorescence is a loose cyme of maroon flowers, each 2–3cm across. The five sepals are longer and wider than the five linear petals. *Companion species* Grass-of-Parnassus (p.302), Lousewort (p.308), Marsh Lousewort (p.311) and Ragged-Robin (p.317). *Distribution* Native. Occasional to locally abundant throughout Britain, but much more common in northern (upland) England, Scotland, Wales and Ireland. It is absent from much of the English Midlands and southern and eastern England. It has declined as a result of drainage, agricultural improvement and lack of grazing. *Habitat* Permanently flooded swamps and mires and wet meadows where the summer water table lies just below the soil surface. It grows on a wide range of soils. Habitats include the edges of lakes, natural hollows, bog pools, peat cuttings and floating rafts of vegetation.

Marsh Helleborine
(Epipactis palustris)

One of our most beautiful native plants, this stands out from the other damp grassland species like a refined, exotic bird among a flock of sparrows. Its flower spikes are tall, slim and elegant, each main stem a smoky brown-crimson colour that extends onto the short flowering stems. Every individual flower – there may be fifteen or twenty on a spike – looks like a tropical orchid, its articulated lip and top pair of wings pure white, its three outer wings the same smoky brown-crimson, with a prominent bright green stem leaf. It is hard to believe that this is a British native. Marsh Helleborine is a reliable indicator of good, species-rich fen, fen grassland and dune-slack habitat. If you see it, you are likely to see many exciting things, so have a good hunt around.

Plant type Orchid family, Orchidaceae. *Flowers* Late June–early August. *Height* 15–50cm. *Description* Erect perennial herb. Leaves are elliptical to lanceolate, folded, with prominent, pleated veins, up to 15cm long, in two ranks up the stem. Inflorescence is a loose, one-sided raceme. Individual flowers have oval-lanceolate sepals, washed purple with a white border. Inner petals are smaller and blunter, usually paler, with delicate pinkish-purple veins. Lip is modified into a purple-veined, cup-like structure known as the hypochile, with a projecting, frilly, white tip, known as the epichile. *Companion species* Bog Pimpernel (p.291), Common Spotted-orchid (p.148), Early Marsh-orchid (p.298), Grass-of-Parnassus (p.302), Northern Marsh-orchid (p.315) and Yellow-rattle (p.168). *Distribution* Native. Scattered throughout the British Isles, although never common, and very rare in many areas. It is probably most easily seen along the coast – in clay slips and dune slacks. *Habitat* Wet marshy habitats, most frequently dune slacks, marshes and damp meadows.

Marsh Lousewort
(Pedicularis palustris)

The less peculiar, almost pretty species of this semi-parasitic group of plants, Marsh Lousewort stands tall and straight in bogs and marshy heaths. Each plant has a green central stem, ageing to deep crimson, with neat, evenly spaced, straight-flowering stems off to the side – it resembles a stalky Christmas tree that no one has yet got round to decorating properly. The flowers have a swollen calyx, the upper and lower lips looking much like a pink form of the spring and summer meadow plant Yellow-rattle (p.168), although Marsh Lousewort has prettier, highly cut, ferny leaves. It is related to Yellow-rattle: they are both in the broomrape brigade. This is always a cheerful plant to find because it is often an indicator of good-quality, species-rich wetland and suggests that many other interesting plants are around, too. It is as poisonous as it looks, so do not pick it.

Plant type Broomrape family, Orobanchaceae. *Flowers* May–September. *Height* Up to 60cm. *Description* Almost hairless annual to biennial with a single erect, branched stem. Pink-purple flowers are 2cm long, arranged in a loose, leafy spike. The upper lip of the flower is four-toothed. By contrast, Lousewort (p.308) is a perennial, lower in stature, with many spreading stems from the base; the upper lip is two-toothed. *Companion species* Bogbean (p.291), Marsh Cinquefoil (p.309), Ragged-Robin (p.317), and Water Avens (p.318). *Distribution* Native. Formerly recorded throughout the British Isles, the distribution of Marsh Lousewort has declined and is now confined largely to the north and west. However, it is still found in parts of East Anglia, Surrey, Hampshire and Dorset. It is extinct in much of eastern England, but remains common in much of Scotland, north-west England, Wales and Ireland. *Habitat* Found in a wide range of base-rich to acidic, moist habitats, including wet heaths, valley bogs, wet meadows, ditches, fens and hillside flushes. Its sites are usually more enriched than those preferred by Lousewort, but they do also appear together.

Marsh-marigold
(Caltha palustris)

One of my great flower moments of recent years was finding this relatively common plant in a dark, dank corner of a wood five minutes' walk away from where we live. It was in such abundance that it lit up a hidden shallow marshy pond. We had never noticed it before, but there it was, carpets of it, flowering away happily for a good three-month stretch. There were three really beautiful things about it: the black, glimmering water of the woodland bog it was coming out of; the unbelievable lushness of the green leaves; and the yellow, yellow, yellow of the crowding of flowers. It was one of those rare combinations of total purity and total richness. It flowers early, just as spring begins, and when the flowers

are finally over, its jester-hat seed pods look good, too. The whole performance feels rather un-English – big, tropical and high-energy, befitting of its other common name: Kingcup.

Plant type Buttercup family, Ranunculaceae. *Flowers* March–July. *Height* 30–60cm. *Description* Hairless, perennial herb. Leaves are dark green and shiny, the lower ones long-stalked, cordate/kidney-shaped, up to 10cm across. Upper leaves are stalkless and clasp the hollow stems. Large yellow flowers, 15–50mm across, have five petal-like sepals (no true petals) surrounding a mound of abundant anthers. *Companion species* Alder (p.348) and Pendulous Sedge (p.316), with Broad Buckler-fern (p.3), Hart's-tongue (p.15) and Male-fern (p.19) on the drier stumps and tussocks nearby. *Distribution* Native. Widespread and common across the British Isles. It used to be much more common before the drainage of much of our landscape. *Habitat* Occurs in a range of wet habitats, usually in partial shade, such as the edges of rivers, streams, canals, lakes, ponds and ditches and in winter wet meadows and pastures. It may slightly prefer neutral to base-rich, rather than acidic, soils, but in the pond near us, the soil is acid and it looks as happy as Larry.

Marsh Pennywort
(Hydrocotyle vulgaris)

It is difficult to get a sense of the scale of Marsh Pennywort from a photograph, but it is tiny, each leaf about the size of a two-pence coin and hidden right down in the grass. You could be walking across a spongy, peaty field thick with it and notice it only when lots of leaves join up to form a prominent patch with a different texture to everything else. The leaves are slightly succulent and juicy, a contrast to those of the vertical-growing grasses and flowering plants around them. The flowers are minuscule, like tiny collections of miniature sedum heads in dull pink. They are so small that it was often thought that this plant did not produce flowers at all, but if you poke around, you will usually find them. Marsh Pennywort is shaped like its namesake Pennywort, also known as Navelwort (p.100), but that has leaves that are twice the size and flowers that are many times larger.

Plant type Pennywort family, Hydrocotylaceae. *Flowers* June–August. *Height* 2–6cm. *Description* Slender, hairless, prostrate, creeping perennial herb. Leaves are circular, shallow-lobed, 1–5cm wide, on stalks attached to the leaf centres. Flowers (sometimes not present) are pinkish green, no more than 1mm across and in whorls of two to five, on stalks. It is not to be confused with an introduced (North American) relative, Floating Pennywort (*Hydrocotyle ranunculoides*), a pest of canals, ditches and pools. *Companion species* Bogbean (p.291), Bog Pimpernel (p.291), Cuckooflower (p.297), Grass-of-Parnassus (p.302), Lesser Spearwort (p.307) and Marsh-marigold (p.311). *Distribution* Native. Found throughout the British Isles, but rare or uncommon in areas such as the Scottish Highlands, Southern Uplands and central England. *Habitat* Bogs, marshes, fens and dune slacks. In oceanic areas, it grows in drier habitats, such as turfed wall tops.

Marsh Thistle
(Cirsium palustre)

Marsh Thistle is like the Creeping Thistle (p.150) of damp ground, appearing in large numbers threaded through the grass on the edges of streams and rivers. It is more handsome than Creeping Thistle, with tufted flowers in the deepest, regal purple. The stems are surrounded by thorns on all sides and the leaves jagged with pointed needles. That is why it is left upstanding in a grazed damp meadow, the spikes as unpleasant to the mouths of cattle and sheep as they are to us as we brush through them. The flowers start as purple spiny ovals with deep purple florets poking out of the top, looking rather like shaving brushes. Occasionally, there are white ones, too. Like most thistles, Marsh Thistle is extremely attractive to bees, butterflies and other insects. It is the larval food plant of the Painted Lady butterfly, and the seeds are popular with many birds, including goldfinches and linnets.

Plant type Daisy family, Asteraceae. *Flowers* June–September. *Height* Up to 150cm, occasionally twice this size. *Description* Erect biennial plume thistle. Stem leaves are shiny dark green, often purple-flushed, deeply pinnatifid and spiny-edged. Basal leaves are lanceolate and less deeply lobed. Stem is hairy and spiny-winged. Flower heads have reddish-purple florets and measure 1.5–2cm long by 1–1.5cm wide, arranged in crowded clusters. Bracts are purplish, erect and shortly pointed. Spear thistle (p.261) is similar, but that has much longer arched, spiny bracts and looser, fewer-flowered inflorescences with larger flower heads. *Companion species* Common Bird's-foot-trefoil (p.145), Common Marsh-bedstraw (p.295), Marsh Valerian (opposite) and Yellow Iris (p.324). *Distribution* Native. Ubiquitous. *Habitat* Anywhere damp: mires, fens, marshes, damp grassland, rush pastures, wet woodland, montane springs and flushes and tall-herb vegetation on mountain ledges.

Marsh Valerian

(Valeriana dioica)

This is a smaller, stockier version of Common Valerian (p.74), with the same pale pink flowers and straight, strong stems, but the whole plant is about half the size. It is easy to tell the difference by where it is growing, too, because this species appears in places that are properly boggy and wet. The odd plant of Marsh Valerian grows here and there in higher, slightly drier patches of grasses and sedges, but all around those it is hard to avoid getting your feet wet. Common Valerian would not put up with that level of moisture at its roots. Marsh Valerian also flowers a little earlier and is dioecious (hence its name), with male and female flowers on separate plants. The male flowers are bigger, 5mm across and slightly lighter pink than the female flowers, which are 2mm across. It is rich in nectar and an important food source for many insects.

Plant type Valerian family, Valerianaceae. *Flowers* May–June. *Height* 15–30cm. *Description* Erect, hairless perennial herb. Basal leaves are oval-lanceolate, undivided, blunt and spoon-shaped, 2–3cm and long-stalked (Common Valerian has highly divided, pinnate basal leaves). Stem leaves are pinnatifid and almost stalkless. Flowers are pale pink and arranged in terminal heads. It has creeping, rooting stems at the base of the flowering stems. *Companion species* Marsh Cinquefoil (p.309), Marsh Lousewort (p.311), Marsh-marigold (p.311) and Ragged-Robin (p.317). *Distribution* Native. Found throughout Britain as far north as southern Scotland. It is quite common in parts of northern England, Norfolk and East Anglia but is rare in the far South East and also in Devon and Cornwall. It is absent from northern Scotland and Ireland. *Habitat* Marsh Valerian is principally a species of mires, flushes and water meadows, as well as willow and alder fen carr. It prefers calcareous soils.

Marsh Woundwort

(Stachys palustris)

The vertical spires of Marsh Woundwort look their best when backlit by low evening light, the outline of the flower spikes softened by the downy stems and leaves. They have the typical square stems and tubular flowers of the dead-nettle family. The bright pink flowers have darker purple-magenta tiger-skin markings on a white base in the throat, making them the prettiest and most impressive of the woundworts. Marsh Woundwort is reputed to be the most effective 'wound herb' of the woundworts and was often used by the sixteenth-century herbalist John Gerard. He was convinced of its therapeutic properties after a farm labourer in Kent cut his leg with a scythe while harvesting. Gerard was in the area and offered to help. The man declined, saying he could heal the wound himself with the help of a nearby Marsh Woundwort plant. The man applied a poultice made from the leaves each day to his wound, and it healed within a week.

Plant type Dead-nettle family, Lamiaceae. *Flowers* July–September. *Height* 30–100cm. *Description* Erect, bristly perennial herb. Leaves are lanceolate or oblong, 5–12cm long, very short-stalked near the base, stalkless above. Flowers are pink-purple with a white pattern on the lower lip. *Companion species* Cock's-foot (p.145), Common Sorrel (p.147), Purple-loosestrife (p.316) and Yorkshire-fog (p.169). *Distribution* Native. Common throughout the British Isles apart from the Scottish Highlands and north-east England, where it is quite rare. *Habitat* Damp places. It grows by streams, rivers, ditches and ponds, in fens, marshes and swamps, on rough ground and occasionally flooded cultivated fields. It is typically found on intermittently flooded and poorly drained soils. It also occasionally grows on arable land.

Meadow Saffron
(Colchicum autumnale)

This is the nearest we get to a native crocus, its beautiful pink trumpets poking out of closely grazed grass. It is our answer to alpine flowers, but Meadow Saffron appears in late summer, not spring, and thrives in damp ground rather than freely drained sites. The common name refers to its resemblance to the Saffron Crocus (*Crocus sativus*), from which the spice is harvested, although that belongs to the iris family. You can tell that this is a colchicum rather than a crocus because the flowers are bald in the ground with no leaves. The leaves come first, but die down before the flowers appear. All parts of the plant are poisonous and contain the toxin colchicine. This is also harmful to livestock, so it used to be dug out by farmers. It now occurs mostly in clearings and rides within woods, where it poses no threat to grazing animals.

Plant type Meadow Saffron family, Colchicaceae. *Flowers* August–October. *Height* Up to 20cm. *Description* Hairless perennial herb. Leaves are oblong-lanceolate, 1.5–4cm across and glossy green. Flowers arise directly from the ground after the leaves have withered. What appears to be a white flower stalk is actually the perianth tube. Flowers have six rosy-pink perianth segments, 3–4.5cm long, with six stamens and three styles. Fruit is an oval capsule, 3–5cm long. *Companion species* Common Spotted-orchid (p.148), Great Burnet (p.154) and Meadow Buttercup (p.158). *Distribution* Native. Found mostly in an area between Dorset, Shropshire and Oxfordshire, where it may be locally abundant. It occurs as far north as Cumbria and is also known in south-west Ireland. There are records throughout Britain of casuals or naturalised populations originating from garden escapes. Many outlying populations have been lost to agricultural improvement. *Habitat* Meadows and riverbanks. It is also found in some churchyards.

Meadowsweet
(Filipendula ulmaria)

The scent of Meadowsweet is soft and slightly almondy, like marzipan. I can immediately conjure it up in my head, together with the associated hum and buzz of insects. The cream bubble buds and fully emerged flowers look good against the carmine-crimson stems and bold, heavily veined leaves, and its frothy texture is a contrast to the dagger-shaped, green foliage of Yellow Iris (p.324). It is a lovely flower to pick and put in a small bunch beside your bed – give the bunch a shake upside-down to dislodge aging flowers, then sear the stem ends in boiling water for twenty seconds. In the Middle Ages, an infusion of Meadowsweet was used to ease pain, calm fevers and induce sweating. We now know why: its sap contains chemicals in the same group as salicylic acid, the natural painkilling ingredient in Goat Willow (p.86) and the origin of aspirin.

Plant type Rose family, Rosaceae. *Flowers* June–September. *Height* Up to 120cm. *Description* Erect perennial herb. Leaves are pinnate at the base, 30–60cm long, with two to five pairs of large leaflets. Each of the large leaflets is dark green above, pale green and woolly underneath, oval, pointed and sharply toothed, up to 8cm long. Alternating between them are pairs of smaller leaflets, 1–4mm across. Flowers are 4–10mm across with five petals and five sepals, arranged in umbel-like inflorescences. Fruit is composed of several twisted carpels. *Companion species* Hemp-agrimony (p.305), Red Clover (p.161), Tufted Vetch (p.166) and Yellow Iris. *Distribution* Native. Common throughout the British Isles. *Habitat* Damp or wet habitats on moderately fertile, neutral or calcareous substrates: wet woodland, damp meadows, swamps and tall-herb fens, damp roadsides, ditches and railway banks, and montane tall-herb communities.

Monkeyflower
(Mimulus guttatus)

With its wide cheeks and smiling open mouth, Monkeyflower is named for its resemblance to a grinning face, a bit like that of a monkey. It was introduced into water gardens from the damp and foggy islands off the Alaskan coast in the early nineteenth century and was recorded in the wild soon afterwards. Its first sighting was near Abergavenny in Monmouthshire and it has spread far and wide from there. Just as Oxford Ragwort (p.101) and Butterfly-bush (p.237) spread quickly via the developing railway network during the Industrial Revolution, so Monkeyflower was dispersed throughout Britain by the construction of canals in the nineteenth century: its seed floated on the water and, once germinated, spread vigorously on creeping roots. The Latin species name, *guttatus*, means 'spotted' and refers to the prominent bright red spots on the lower lip of the flower. The lip provides a landing platform for pollinator insects, and the spots guide them towards the centre of the flower.

Plant type Monkeyflower family, Phrymaceae. *Flowers* July–September. *Height* 20–45cm. *Description* Erect, perennial herb with creeping stolons. Leaves are oval, toothed, 2–7cm long, opposite one another and clasping the stem. Flowers consist of a green, tubular, five-lobed calyx and a yellow, two-lipped corolla, 3–4cm wide. The lower lip is much longer and three-lobed, with two swellings on the palate that close the throat. *Companion species* Lesser Spearwort (p.307) and Yellow Iris (p.324). *Distribution* Introduced. It is found throughout Britain, more common in northern England, Wales and southern and eastern Scotland. It is rare or local in much of the East Midlands, East Anglia (apart from Norfolk) and Kent. In Ireland, it is common in the north and scattered elsewhere. *Habitat* Wet places by streams, rivers and ponds, in damp meadows, marshy ground and open woodland. It spreads both by seed and vegetatively, rooting from the nodes in wet mud or gravel.

Northern Marsh-orchid
(Dactylorhiza purpurella)

One of our brightest orchids, this has magenta flowers heading towards the blue of those cheap Malaysian orchids you can buy from the supermarket. As with all *Dactylorhiza*, the colour is variable. The flower spikes are tall and densely packed, making this a hugely impressive orchid that should stop you in your tracks. If you are lucky, you may see it by the hundred or even the thousand. This is because it sets seed prolifically and reproduces vegetatively, creating tight clusters of plants.

Plant type Orchid family, Orchidaceae. *Flowers* June–July. *Height* 20–25cm. *Description* Erect perennial herb. Lanceolate leaves are unspotted, 10–20cm long, in two opposite ranks up the stem. Flowers are pale pink to rosy purple, speckled with darker markings, arranged in a dense, conical spike. It has darker flowers and is chunkier, taller and more robust than both Common Spotted-orchid (p.148) and Heath Spotted-orchid (p.359), which you might see in similar if less damp habitats. Southern Marsh-orchid (*D. praetermissa*) looks very similar, but it is taller and flowers earlier in the summer. *Companion species* Meadow Buttercup (p.158), Meadowsweet (opposite) and Ragged-Robin (p.317). *Distribution* Native. Confined to the north and west of a line from the Severn Estuary to the Humber Estuary. Throughout much of this area it is the most common Marsh-orchid –Southern Marsh-orchid replaces it south and east of this line. In Ireland, it is most frequent in the north and is absent from much of central Ireland. *Habitat* Usually in damp, calcareous to neutral grassland, such as dune slacks, damp meadows, wet heathland, fens and marshes and chalk pits. It may also turn up on road verges, brownfield land and even on dry chalk downland, and among arable weeds on previously set-aside land.

Pendulous Sedge
(Carex pendula)

This is often the plant right on the water's edge. The first thing you notice are the long, sharp, elegant spear points of the leaves, each with three or four ribs running the length of it. Sprouting up from among the clump is a slightly taller flower stem, from which a series of flowers hangs. Each flower is a long, pendulous dongle, which begins its life as a simple bendy cylinder, a little fuzzy with white hairs, but ripens into a rich tobacco-brown and slightly swollen flower head, surrounded by a halo of pale golden anthers. It self-sows freely in shade and wet, and, given the chance, will form chunky tussocks in a garden. On my heavy clay, I often dig it out as it creeps out from the wood and romps away in the shade in a well-fed flower bed.

Plant type Sedge family, Cyperaceae. *Flowers* April–May, fruiting June–July. *Height* Forms tussocks up to 70cm across and 180cm tall. *Description* Leaves are keeled but flat and usually 20–100cm long and 15–20mm wide. Inflorescence consists of one to two male spikelets, up to 10cm long, at the tip of the stem and three to four female spikelets, up to 16cm long, spread out further down the stem and drooping (pendulous) when in fruit. Fruit is ovoid to ellipsoid, glaucous-green and three-sided. *Companion species* Cuckooflower (p.297), Golden-saxifrage (p.302) and Lesser Celandine (p.18). *Distribution* Native. Widespread across Britain and Ireland as far north as Inverness. Most frequent in the south, where it is very common. However, it is often grown in gardens and is a frequent escape, so the limits of its native range are obscure. *Habitat* Damp, base-rich, heavy (often clay) soils in shaded habitats. It is found in deciduous woodland (especially ancient woods on clay soils), by ditches, ponds and streams, in hedgerows and on track sides.

Purple-loosestrife
(Lythrum salicaria)

One of our most dazzlingly coloured wild flowers, Purple-loosestrife is like a smaller-scale Rosebay Willowherb (p.258), with plumy spikes of flowers in brilliant magenta. It flowers right through summer and its reliable drama has led many of us to grow it in damp spots in our gardens. The seed pods remain handsome and architectural long after the flowers have gone. Its specific name, *salicaria*, is derived from the generic name for willows, *Salix*. This is because of similarities in their leaves, which in Purple-loosestrife are increasingly narrow and willow-like towards the top of the stem. Pollination is carried out by various long-tongued insects: Brimstone and Comma butterflies seem to like it most. Purple-loosestrife juice is rich in tannins and was once extracted for tanning leather, as an alternative to oak bark. It can create large patches in disturbed wet ground and is considered an invasive species in North America and New Zealand.

Plant type Purple-loosestrife family, Lythraceae. *Flowers* June–August. *Height* Up to 120cm. *Description* Tall, erect, downy perennial herb. Leaves are oval-lanceolate, pointed, untoothed, sessile, 4–7cm long, in opposite pairs or whorls of three at the base, alternate above. Flowers are red-purple, six-petalled, 10–15mm across, located in whorls in the bract axils, forming a dense spike, 10–30cm long. *Companion species* Bramble (p.66), Hogweed (p.156), Lesser Pond-sedge (p.306), Meadowsweet (p.314) and Wild Angelica (p.324). *Distribution* Native. Found throughout Britain and Ireland, except in upland areas, such as the Scottish Highlands and the Pennines. *Habitat* Margins of slow-flowing rivers, canals, lakes, flooded gravel pits, tall-herb fens and willow carr. It thrives in permanently wet or periodically inundated fertile soils and tends to avoid acidic conditions.

Ragged-Robin
(Lychnis flos-cuculi)

Good old Ragged-Robin is many people's favourite, its bright pink flowers looking a bit dishevelled, like a skinny dandy after an all-night party. So many flowers are exercises in perfection and pertness, but Ragged-Robin is cooler than that: a Red Campion that has been through a shredder and now resembles the fluffy sides of a car wash. In the Scottish Highlands and the Outer Hebrides, where it can be scattered widely across damp meadows and around the drier edges of bogs, its fresh flowers are a cheering sight, standing up tall and forming a soft, washy haze amid the dun and khaki of the background. There is also a dwarf form, which grows in some exposed coastal grasslands, hunkered down against the wind and sea spray. This is easy to grow from seed and will quite quickly naturalise, so it has become a popular garden plant for spreading through damp areas beside a pond or in wet wood or shrubbery edges with poorly drained soils. The name *flos-cuculi* means 'cuckoo flower' and, like Cuckooflower (p.297), this flowers when the cuckoos arrive in spring.

Plant type Pink family, Caryophyllaceae. *Flowers* May–August. *Height* Up to 75cm. *Description* Erect, hairy perennial herb. Basal leaves are oblong to spoon-shaped; stem leaves are narrow, lanceolate and rough, but hairless. Flowers have – like Red Campion (p.24) – a swollen, green-striped crimson calyx with deep pink-red petals that are each deeply divided into four very narrow lobes. *Companion species* Grass-of-Parnassus (p.302), Lesser Spearwort (p.307), Marsh Cinquefoil (p.309) and Marsh Lousewort (p.311). *Distribution* Native. Frequent throughout Britain and Ireland, absent only from parts of the Scottish Highlands and intensely agricultural areas. *Habitat* Damp habitats in sun or shade: wet grassland, rush pasture, fen meadow, ditches, tall-herb fen and damp woodland margins.

River Water-crowfoot
(Ranunculus fluitans)

This is the white buttercup flower floating beside Ophelia in John Everett Millais's Pre-Raphaelite painting, a green cushion of its leaves on either side of her body. Each flower has a blazingly golden heart and petals that are faintly veined in grey, the flowers prodding up an inch or two above the water's surface. This species is the long, trailing one that floats in many larger streams and rivers of moderate flow. It is tricky to tell it apart from Stream Water-crowfoot (*R. penicillatus* ssp. *pseudofluitans*), but that occurs more in shallow, riffling chalk streams, such as the Test and the Itchen, where it can carpet the river from bank to bank. Both form an important shelter for trout in the early part of the year. River keepers cut it in mid June to limit the amount of vegetation, which can get in the way of fishermen. They wait to do this until after the hatching of the mayfly, which colonises Water-crowfoot in spring.

Plant type Buttercup family, Ranunculaceae. *Flowers* May–August. *Height* Stems up to 6m long on the water. *Description* Ten species of these sub-aquatic perennials are found in the British Isles, and are difficult to tell apart because of the variation that exists within species, which frequently hybridise. River Water-crowfoot is most easily recognised by its large flowers, which are 2–3cm across with overlapping petals, and the absence of laminar leaves (broad, floating leaves on the surface of the water). It has only feathery, tassel-like leaves, which are streamlined to reduce resistance to the water's movement. Fruit heads have stout stalks, and often project above the water. *Companion species* Blue Water-speedwell (p.289), Watercress (p.320) and Water Forget-me-not (p.320). *Distribution* Native. Occurs throughout the British Isles, although it is scarce throughout much of its range. It is most frequent in the Midlands and Welsh Borders. In Ireland, it is confined to the far north east. *Habitat* Rapidly flowing rivers with a stable substrate. It is usually found in base-rich, chalky water.

Summer Snowflake
(Leucojum aestivum ssp. *aestivum)*

Despite its name, this flowers not in summer but in April and May. The flower is reminiscent of a Snowdrop (p.26), but the whole plant is five times the size, with several elegant flowers hanging from the stem. The flowers have a sweet, gentle scent and look like ballerinas' tutus from *Swan Lake*, each layer of fabric tipped with a splotch of acid green. Many of us grow this in our gardens, where it is popular for brightening up a dingy, dark corner. It forms large clumps and can gradually take over; it has hence escaped into the wild from bulbs that have been discarded. There are now few places where this grows genuinely wild, but they will always be moist with fertile soil, often temporarily flooded, allowing the buoyant black seeds to wash away to new places. There is also Spring Snowflake (*Leucojum vernum*), which is smaller and flowers from January to April, and is sometimes considered native in two sites in Somerset and Dorset.

Plant type Onion family, Alliaceae. *Flowers* April–May. *Height* 30–60cm. *Description* Bulbous herb with three to seven flowers in a loose umbel and an undivided spathe. Perianth segments are 14–18mm long, all alike and equal, obovate and white with a green spot near the tip. The native plant has two sharp stem edges with minute teeth. The introduced garden plant, *L. a.* ssp. *pulchellum*, is a little smaller with glossy mid-green leaves. All snowflakes are similar to Snowdrop, but this flowers earlier, is smaller (15–25cm tall) and has solitary flowers with three perianth segments that are longer than the others. *Companion species* Lesser Celandine (p.18), Primrose (p.103), violets and Wood Anemone (p.30). *Distribution* Native, very local and restricted, but much introduced; there is a question over whether or not it is native at all. *Habitat* Swamps, wet meadows, winter-flooded alder and willow scrub by fresh and tidal rivers. It also occurs as a garden escape near habitation and on rubbish tips.

Water Avens
(Geum rivale)

I love mahogany-crimson flowers, and this is one such. With Water Avens, however, it is not the petals that are crimson but the calyx, which encloses petals of a soft apricot, dusted and lightly veined with purple-crimson, each flower green and gold at its heart. When it is backlit, the apricot petals glow. The buds are like small pointed lanterns, which open into full-blown bell-shaped lamps. Water Avens are like little, late-spring fritillaries, but rather less demonstrative – not boom-boom flowers but the sort you have a private relationship with. The stem matches the calyx in colour, darkest on its sunny side. After the flowers come the light, fluffy balls of the seed heads, each a green globe within a downy halo. In damp ditches and water meadows this plant will grow tall, but I have seen a pygmy version in the wind-blasted landscape of Upper Teesdale, standing just 6cm high. Water Avens hybridises with Wood Avens (p.31) where the two grow close together. The resulting hybrids are fertile and can backcross with both parents, causing a wide variety of appearance in their offspring.

Plant type Rose family, Rosaceae. *Flowers* May–September. *Height* Up to 60cm. *Description* Short, stout, erect perennial herb. Basal leaves usually have three to six pairs of rounded, deeply lobed leaflets; the terminal leaflet is usually unlobed and rounded, while the stem leaves are usually trifoliate. Nodding bell flowers have orange-pink petals, 10–15mm long; sepals and epicalyx are crimson-purple. It has feathery seed heads. *Companion species* Lady's-mantle (p.156), Mare's-tail (p.308), Sweet Cicely (p.110) and Wood Avens. *Distribution* Native. Common in Scotland and northern England, frequent to locally common elsewhere, although rare in south-west England and absent from the south-east corner of England. *Habitat* Mildly acidic to calcareous soils, preferring shaded conditions. It is most common in wet meadows, marshes, fens, open, damp woodlands or glades, and hedge banks, stream sides, mountain pastures and wet rock ledges.

Watercress
(Rorippa nasturtium-aquaticum)

The best Watercress grows in the brilliantly clear chalk streams of Hampshire, Wiltshire and Dorset, forming substantial carpets where the stream is shallow. It is one of our most harvested wild plants, rich in Vitamin C and delicious in a salad or cooked in soup, and the only native British wild flower species that has passed into widespread commercial cultivation. Surprisingly, the older stems are the ones to pick. The young ones may be more tender, but they have little flavour. If you pick it from the wild, beware of the danger of liver fluke, a flatworm that can destroy the livers of cattle and sheep and can also be fatal for humans. You should avoid gathering it from stream banks and areas of slow-flowing water near grazing animals, where the fluke is likely to breed. It is probably safest to cook wild-foraged Watercress rather than eating it raw, as cooking kills the parasite.

Plant type Cabbage family, Brassicaceae. *Flowers* May–October. *Height* Up to 60cm. *Description* Hairless, creeping perennial herb with dark green, pinnate leaves that have oval leaflets. White flowers are 4–6mm across with petals as long as the sepals. Fruit is a pod, 13–18mm long, with two rows of seeds visible inside. The closely related Narrow-fruited Watercress (*R. microphyllum*) has leaves that usually turn purplish in autumn and larger fruits. The unrelated Fool's-watercress (p.300) has the sheathing, inflated leaf stalks characteristic of umbellifers. *Companion species* Blue Water-speedwell (p.289), Hemlock Water-dropwort (p.304) and River Water-crowfoot (p.317). *Distribution* Native. Found throughout Britain and Ireland, although mostly absent from the Scottish Highlands and local in the Cambrian Mountains. *Habitat* In and beside clear, shallow rivers and streams, as well as ditches, ponds, canals and marshes, in both calcareous and acidic areas.

Water Forget-me-not
(Myosotis scorpioides)

This is a luscious forget-me-not, with lots of large flowers for its family, sky blue with yellow centres, packed together. It is obviously related to the scraggy Field Forget-me-not (p.248), but it is in a different class, its flowers up to three times the size. The species name *scorpioides* means 'resembling a scorpion's tail', and it describes the way in which the bud tips unfurl as they come into bloom. All forget-me-nots have this, but the curl is most prominent in this species. Water Forget-me-not usually grows on the edge – not in the water – and functions as a dry resting place for newly emerged insects, such as caddis flies, dragonflies and alderflies. It also provides a source of pollen and nectar for bees. According to legend, it is the Water Forget-me-not that gives the family its common name, adopted from a story in German folklore about a knight who fell into the river as he picked the flowers for his lady. Before he drowned, the knight threw them towards her, crying '*Vergiss mein nicht!*'

Plant type Borage family, Boraginaceae. *Flowers* May–September. *Height* 15–30cm. *Description* Ascending or erect, rhizomatous perennial herb. Stems have spreading hairs below, creeping above. Leaves are oblong, up to 7cm long, three to five times as long as wide. Flowers are up to 8mm across. Forget-me-nots are all quite similar in appearance. The most reliable way to identify Water Forget-me-not is by its broad-based calyx teeth, which form equilateral triangles. Other forget-me-nots have narrow-based calyx teeth in the shape of isosceles triangles. *Companion species* Common Figwort (p.72), Marsh Thistle (p.312), Water Mint (opposite), Welted Thistle (p.323) and docks. *Distribution* Native. Common throughout most of Britain and Ireland. Scarce only in the far south west of England and the Scottish Highlands. *Habitat* Found in damp or wet habitats, usually in fertile, calcareous or mildly acidic soils. It is usually terrestrial, occurring by lakes, ponds, rivers and streams and in marshes and fens, but may sometimes be aquatic, forming submerged patches or floating rafts.

Water Lobelia
(Lobelia dortmanna)

Many of us will recognise the flowers of this plant from the trays of bedding that we see in every garden centre in May. Water Lobelia has a typical lobelia flower, with the narrow tube opening out to five separated petals, three large lower ones and two narrow upper ones. The difference here is that the flowers are a pale mauve-white, often bleaching to pure white as they mature. These flowers hover on narrow stems nearly a foot above the water. The neat linear leaves below the water's surface are in relatively tight clumps, trailing in the shallow water just above the muddy bottom of the ponds and shallow ditches where this tends to grow. The genus was named after Mathias de L'Obel, a French botanist who died in London in 1616 and who made the first records of many British plants.

Plant type Bellflower family, Campanulaceae. *Flowers* July–August. *Height* Up to 60cm from root to flower. *Description* Hairless, erect, aquatic perennial herb with rooting runners. Leaves are linear, fleshy, arched back, 2–4cm long, in a submerged basal rosette. Flowers are pale lilac, nodding, 12–20mm across, in a lax inflorescence of three to ten. Inflorescence stem is leafless, apart from a few scales. *Companion species* Broad-leaved Pondweed (p.292) and White Water-lily (p.323). *Distribution* Native. Confined to northern and western Britain, where it is frequent in localised areas, such as the Lake District, north and west Scotland, Snowdonia and the Cambrian mountains. In Ireland, there are three concentrations in the west. *Habitat* Sheltered shallow water at the margins of mountain tarns and lakes. It grows in acid or peaty water with a stony or gravelly bottom. It is slow-growing, with little ability to withstand shade or competition, and is therefore confined to shallow water.

Water Mint
(Mentha aquatica)

One of the best smells of a summer walk is when you crush a plant of Water Mint under your feet as you tramp across a bog or through a shallow river or stream. The air fills instantly with a sharp green, minty scent. Water Mint goes on growing and flowering deep into autumn. It often grows in huge clumps, as it spreads clonally by extensive rhizomes. It can also root easily from detached rhizome fragments, which are often dispersed by water, so repeated clumps often appear on the edges of a shallow river, ditch or stream. Water Mint does not have the same intensity of flavour as Spear Mint or Apple-mint, and so is less useful for cooking, but it has been used for perfume and flavourings since Roman times.

Plant type Dead-nettle family, Lamiaceae. *Flowers* July–October. *Height* 15–60cm. *Description* Downy, erect, perennial herb. Inflorescence is terminal, often with more whorls below. Corolla is mauve, with stamens projecting from the flower. Leaves are opposite, oval and hairy, with blunt teeth. It is easily distinguished from Corn Mint (p.245) because its main flower is in a rounded, terminal head, with a few subsidiary flowers in the leaf axils. Corn Mint flowers are all tucked into the leaf axils. The two sometimes hybridise. *Companion species* Common Fleabane (p.295), Corn Mint, Gypsywort (p.303), Lesser Pond-sedge (p.306) and Yellow Iris (p.324). *Distribution* Native. Widespread in Britain and Ireland, absent only from higher ground in Scotland. It is the most common of all the mint species. *Habitat* Permanently wet habitats adjacent to open water, often partially or wholly submerged: by ditches, ponds and rivers, in marshes, wet pastures, dune slacks and fens, and in wet woods. It is found on mildly acid to calcareous mineral or peaty soils.

Water-plantain
(Alisma plantago-aquatica)

Water-plantain reminds me of flowering Wild Asparagus (p.423), its tall spikes highly branched, airy and graceful, with small flowers at the end of every stem. Unlike Wild Asparagus, which grows on rocks, sand and shingle, this tends to grow in the shallows of standing water in ponds or in shallow, slow-running streams. The flowers open at the beginning of the afternoon and close during the early evening. Its chief claim to fame, according to Richard Mabey, is that John Ruskin believed that the particular curve of its leaf ribs (together with the southern edge of the Matterhorn, the lip of a nautilus shell and the side of a bay leaf) represented the model of 'divine proportion', one of those shapes on which 'God stamped those characters of beauty which he has made it man's nature to love'. The shape inspired his theory of Gothic architecture. Water-plantain's common name is probably derived from the resemblance of its leaves to those of plantains, although it is not related to those more common plants at all.

Plant type Water-plantain family, Alismataceae. *Flowers* June–August. *Height* 20–100cm. *Description* Aquatic, erect, hairless perennial herb. Leaves are oval, 8–20cm long, on long stalks. Inflorescence is composed of several tiers of whorled branches, which branch again in whorls. Flowers are up to 1cm across, with three blunt green sepals and three rounded pink petals. There are three stamens. *Companion species* Bulrush (p.293), Celery-leaved Buttercup (p.294) and Flowering-rush (p.299). *Distribution* Native. It occurs throughout Britain and is common except in upland regions. It is almost absent from the north of Scotland, apart from a few scattered colonies on the east coast. *Habitat* Exposed mud at the shallow end of still or slow-flowing waters, or in marshes and swamps.

Water-violet
(Hottonia palustris)

This looks like a cross between a candelabra primula and a Cuckooflower (p.297), with delicate, pale mauve-pink flowers, arranged in tiers up the stem, erupting straight out of the water to a good thirty centimetres. The delicate flower varies in colour from off-white to purple, with many different tones in between, each with a yellow eye subdivided by a pink, five-armed star. Like many aquatic plants, it has feathery, fern-like leaves, which in this case are deeply divided as far as the central vein, like the teeth of a double comb. They remain below the water, but look delicate submerged, giving Water-violet the other common names of Featherfoil and Millefolium. Like Common Water-crowfoot (p.297), with the oxygen its leaves produce by photosynthesis it helps to keep the water oxygenated and maintain it as a fresh and clean environment for aquatic animals and plants. This makes it an invaluable plant for domestic and public ponds, as it also looks pretty early in the year, with its ornamental flowers and leaves. Its bushy leaves also provide protection for fish and fry. After the plant flowers, the fruit stalks bend downwards, and the capsules, each containing many small seeds, ripen in the water. *Palustris* is Latin for 'marshy', and many plants in this habitat share the species name.

Plant type Primrose family, Primulaceae. *Flowers* May–June. *Height* 20–40cm. *Description* Aquatic, hairless perennial with submerged or floating pinnate leaves. Inflorescence is erect and leafless, with whorls of three to eight long-stalked, lilac-pink flowers with a yellow eye, 20–25mm across. *Companion species* Amphibious Bistort (p.288), Flowering-rush (p.299) and Frogbit (p.301). *Distribution* Native. Thinly scattered throughout England – and declining – with localised hotspots including the Somerset Levels and East Anglian fens. *Habitat* Still, shallow, base-rich, clear and not eutrophicated water in ponds, ditches, oxbows and backwaters. It can withstand shade and temporary exposure. It is often an indicator of good water quality and typically occurs in the species-rich habitats beloved of aquatic botanists.

Welted Thistle
(Carduus crispus)

This handsome wild thistle stands tall and proud, often overlooking a stream or river like a sentry. Individual plants can be huge, creating clumps almost a metre across, and they often appear singly, marking this species out from many other common thistles, which appear in great clutches. It is one the prickliest plants that you will ever see, every stem, leaf and flower base covered in a haze of lethal prickles, large and small. That is what gives it its common name, as the stems are welted or winged with spines. The reddish-purple flowers, looked at closely, are beautiful, the petals pinky mauve, the stamens a deeper purple, and the contrast between the two as dazzling as a party dress. One flower head is in fact a collection of many small individual flowers, so this, like all thistles, holds an abundance of nectar, which makes it popular with many insects. Welted Thistle is especially loved by butterflies, including the Painted Lady.

Plant type Daisy family, Asteraceae. *Flowers* June–August. *Height* 30–120cm. *Description* Erect, branched biennial. Stems have spiny wings, which stop a little short of the flowering heads. Leaves are dull green and pinnatifid and have spiny-lobed edges and cottony undersides. Flower heads are about 3cm long by 2cm wide and have two-lipped, reddish-purple florets. They are arranged in dense clusters of three to five. Welted Thistle looks most similar to Marsh Thistle (p.312), but that has wings all the way up the stem and more deeply cut leaves. *Companion species* Broad-leaved Dock (p.236) and Water Forget-me-not (p.320). *Distribution* Native. Quite common throughout most of England, although more local in north-west England and rare in Cornwall and Devon. It is also quite local in Wales. In Scotland, it is mostly confined to the lowlands in the south east. In Ireland, it is very local and confined to the east. *Habitat* It favours dampish spots, such as meadows, marshes, ditches, hedge bottoms, roadsides, railway banks, waste places and woodland clearings, rides and margins. It prefers clay, nutrient-rich soils.

White Water-lily
(Nymphaea alba)

This seems almost too huge, too showy and too exotic to be a native. You have to travel to remote lochans on the west coast of Scotland, several hundred feet up, where few people ever go, to know that this is a true British wild flower. It is an incredible thing, with fifteen or twenty pure-white petals in an open cup around a brilliant golden-yellow heart of huge anthers. The flowers open only between midday and late afternoon, closing as light levels fall. They float among their large, shiny green lily-pad leaves, anchored on the pond or lochan floor many feet below. The leaves' lower surfaces often have toothpaste-like squirts of clear jelly, which are water snail eggs. The fleshy stems are edible and were once considered a delicacy; they are still eaten in some parts of the Continent.

Plant type Water-lily family, Nymphaeaceae. *Flowers* June–August. *Height* Stems may grow from a depth of 1.8m. *Description* Aquatic rhizomatous perennial. Leaves are circular, deeply cleft to the stalk, green above, reddish on the undersides; they float on the surface of the water and have veins that join up laterally to form a network. Flowers are white, 10–20cm across, with four sepals that are green on the outside, white on the inside, and twenty to twenty-five petals. Fruit is globe-shaped. *Companion species* Broad-leaved Pondweed (p.292) and Water Lobelia (p.321). *Distribution* Native. It occurs throughout Britain but is local in northern England, Wales and east Scotland. It is most common in the West Midlands, west Scotland and south-east England. In Ireland, its distribution is patchy, although it is generally more common in the west and absent from the south east. *Habitat* Still or slow-moving, nutrient-rich waters with a muddy bottom. It can be found in waters of all sizes, from ponds and drainage dykes to lakes and canals, in depths of up to 3m. It tolerates a wide range of water chemistry, but lacks submerged leaves and is therefore vulnerable to disturbance by boats.

Wild Angelica
(Angelica sylvestris)

The elegant, architectural, bright green leaves of Wild Angelica often provide the first bold foliage on a stream or riverbank from early spring. In summer, it produces creamy-white, often pink-tinged umbellifer flower heads, which last for months. The seed heads are impressive, too, breakfast-plate-sized heads of green beads, each one held out separately on a short stem. Wild Angelica makes such a striking impression that we have gathered lots of garden forms. Wild Angelica is edible. Sections of the stem traditionally have been candied for decorating cakes; the seeds can also be used to flavour cakes, and the leaves added in small amounts (as they have an intense celery/lovage/aniseed flavour) to salads. Wild Angelica has therapeutic properties and was considered to be a universal remedy – hence its 'angelic' name.

Plant type Carrot family, Apiaceae. *Flowers* June–September. *Height* Up to 2m. *Description* Tall, robust, hairless perennial. Stems are purplish, hollow, downy near the base. Leaves are triangular in outline, two to three times pinnate, 30–60cm long. Leaflets are ovate, sharply toothed, 2–8cm long. Leaf stalks are channelled on the upper side, with inflated sheathing bases. Flowers are white, 2mm across, in many-rayed umbels, 3–15cm across, both terminal and in the leaf axils. Fruit is oval, 5mm long with broad wings on the edges. Hogweed (p.156) looks similar but is roughly hairy. *Companion species* Bulbous Buttercup (p.144), Common Sorrel (p.147), Creeping Buttercup (p.149), Hogweed, Lesser Spearwort (p.307) and Meadow Buttercup (p.158). *Distribution* Native. Common everywhere. *Habitat* Mildly acid to calcareous soils in damp woods and carr, damp neutral grassland, marshes, mires, swamps and tall-herb fens, sea cliffs, ungrazed montane grassland and mountain ledges.

Yellow Iris
(Iris pseudacorus)

The vertical swords of Yellow (or Flag) Iris stand in armies across damp fields and shallow ditches almost everywhere. They are a sharp, brilliant-green presence in a late spring meadow, their masculine vigour bringing an astringent element to any pond edge. They look so exciting, but when the flowers come out towards the end of May, they are a bit of a disappointment and, looked at close to, quickly become rather scraggy after opening. *Iris* is Greek for 'rainbow' and refers to this genus's huge and colourful range of flowers – what a shame that nature did not make the ordinary English iris a more elegant hue. Like all irises, Yellow Iris's flower parts come in groups of three. There are three large outer petals with dark veins at their heart, three sepals and three styles. There is no other plant you could confuse this with. The other common wild iris, Stinking Iris (p.28), is much smaller with grey-purple flowers, and is usually found in woodlands and hedge banks. Yellow Iris has dull brown seeds while Stinking Iris's are a brilliant scarlet-orange.

Plant type Iris family, Iridaceae. *Flowers* May–July. *Height* Up to 150cm. *Description* Rhizomatous perennial herb. Leaves are sword-shaped, equalling the inflorescence in height, 15–25mm wide. Inflorescence is branched, with two to three per spathe. Flowers are 8–10cm across, the falls oval-oblong with purple veins and the standards spoon-shaped, 2cm long. Styles are two-lobed. *Companion species* Lesser Spearwort (p.307), Purple-loosestrife (p.316) and Water Mint (p.321). *Distribution* Native. Common throughout Britain and Ireland, apart from upland regions. *Habitat* Wet meadows, wet woods, fens, the margins of lakes, ponds and watercourses, wet dune slacks and, in the north and west of Britain, coastal streams, shingle, upper salt marshes and raised beaches.

Yellow Loosestrife
(Lysimachia vulgaris)

Yellow Loosestrife looks like a golden campanula, with generous, open-saucer flowers that look straight out at you from the vertical stem. The flower colour is a bright contrast to the acid-green leaf, making this a popular plant for pond edges and damp patches in gardens. It lasts well in water, too, if you sear the stem ends in boiling water after picking it. Yellow Loosestrife spreads vegetatively by long, thin rhizomes, so if you find it you usually find lots of it, in big, bold patches. Its common name probably originates from the ancient Greeks' belief that a bunch of this tied to the neck of a horse or ox would repel flies and lessen the animal's strife, making it more docile. It is unrelated to its namesake Purple-loosestrife (p.316), which was thought to have the same effect. Nicholas Culpeper, the seventeenth-century herbalist, advised burning bunches of Yellow Loosestrife at home to drive away gnats and flies. The flowers have no scent and produce no nectar.

Plant type Primrose family, Primulaceae. *Flowers* July–August. *Height* 60–150cm. *Description* Erect, downy perennial. Leaves are oval-lanceolate, pointed, stalkless, black-dotted and 5–12cm long, arranged either opposite one another or in whorls of three to four. It has loose panicles of yellow flowers with corollas 15mm across. *Companion species* Monkeyflower (p.315), Montbretia (p.98) and Purple-loosestrife. *Distribution* Native. Frequent to locally common throughout most of Britain and Ireland, although rare or absent in Scotland and south-east Ireland. *Habitat* Riverbanks, marshes, fens, ponds, alder carr and ditches. It is tolerant of some shade and may form large colonies on permanently wet ground, usually on organic soils. It is sometimes found on mineral soils.

Yellow Water-lily
(Nuphar lutea)

Compared to the elegant and ghostly White Water-lily (p.323), this is rather lumpen, its bright yellow goblet flowers made up of a single row of petals around a prominent central boss made up of many smaller petals. The leaves are huge, reaching 40cm by 30cm, the largest of any British native. When they overlap in a village or field pond, it looks as though you could walk across the water. The flowers smell slightly of alcohol, and this, combined with their shape, has earned them the common name of Brandy Balls or Brandy Bottles. The alcoholic scent attracts small flies, which pollinate the flowers. After pollination, the flowers break off and air bladders in the 'bottles' allow them to stay afloat, so that they can be transported by birds or carried along on the current to distribute the seeds. Eventually these air pockets collapse and the seeds sink to the floor and germinate in the mud. It is more shade-tolerant than White Water-lily, making it a popular garden-pond plant.

Plant type Water-lily family, Nymphaeaceae. *Flowers* June–August. *Height* Up to 5m. *Description* Aquatic, rhizomatous perennial. Leaves are oval, cordate, deeply cleft to the stalk, leathery, on long elastic stems, floating on the surface of the water. Each of the leaves has twenty-three or more veins that divide into twos to form a parallel 'tuning fork' pattern. *Companion species* It forms quite dense colonies on its own. *Distribution* Native. It is found throughout Britain, although it is absent from north-east Scotland and rare in south-west England. In Ireland, it is common, except in the south east. *Habitat* Mildly acidic or basic water in lakes and slow-flowing rivers and large ditches. Its submerged leaves allow it to persist in disturbed sites where the floating leaves are broken off. It is less likely to thrive in polluted water than White Water-lily.

Marsh-marigold (p.311), Sissinghurst, Kent, 3 May.

River Water-crowfoot (p. 317), near Puddletown, Dorset, 8 May.

Common Water-crowfoot (p.297), Beaulieu, Hampshire, 12 May.

Globeflower (p.301), Ashberry Nature Reserve, near Rievaulx, North Yorkshire, 11 June.

Dame's-violet (p.298), Thirsk, North Yorkshire, 12 June.

Water Forget-me-not (p.320), river Ure, near Leyburn Old Glebe Field, near Wensley, Yorkshire, 12 June.

Marsh Helleborine (p.309), Sandwich Bay, Kent, 6 July.

Lesser Spearwort (p. 307), Rodel, South Harris, Outer Hebrides, 23 July.

Amphibious Bistort (p.288) and Common Cottongrass (p.352), Balranald, North Uist, Outer Hebrides, 24 July.

Bulrush (p.293), Toadsmoor Valley, Eastcombe, Gloucestershire, 6 December.

Heath, Moor & Mountain

Heaths are the huge, sandy, sterile tracts of country often used for common land. They fill large parts of Dorset and Surrey and include the unique Breckland in East Anglia. The Breck was near where I lived as a child, and we often headed off there at weekends to botanise. The countryside bored me, pine trees and thin flowers on sand, but once I looked closely, this place was full of riches. Great chunks of this heath have been forested in an attempt to make it productive, and its floweriness has been much reduced, but in the odd place, you will still find the pretty spring flowers of Star-of-Bethlehem or the summer Spanish Catchfly, mixed up with a splash of rusty-red Sheep's Sorrel and the brilliant yellow flowers of Sickle Medick.

The heaths become moors at higher altitude. There, poor drainage fills them with stagnant water and makes them very acid. These bogs can be dreary places with a repetitive flora: mile upon mile of deergrass and rush, lit by the bunny tails of Common and Hare's-tail Cottongrass and the odd miniature spear of Bog Asphodel or bush of Bog-myrtle. Moors often contain beautiful, dark little pools containing White Water-lily, with Grass-of-Parnassus on the banks. Heath Spotted-orchids and Harebells grow on drier, slightly better-drained patches, and on the sites of old buildings there may be Silverweed and sometimes Common Nettle feeding off the phosphates left by animal life.

Of these three related habitats, it is the higher hills and mountains that are most likely to provide the richest collection of wild flowers. Most of our mountains are under ice and snow until at least the middle of spring, so flowers start late at these high altitudes. Even in summer, the environment can be severe, so the plants tend to be tiny, keeping close to the ground to stay out of the wind.

Apart from altitude, acidity is the governing factor. On poorly drained mountains made of impervious rock, the flowers are often similar to those found on peaty moorland. It is only on the freer-draining limestone mountains that the real treasures appear.

You will find wonderful high lawns with Spring Gentian, Mountain Pansy and Mountain Everlasting in limestone places such as Upper Teesdale. In the hills and mountains of the west, you will come across occasional limey patches or strata filled with miniature mountain gatherings of similarly interesting alpines.

As a girl I spent some of the summer holidays with my father botanising on the west coast of Scotland. He had emphysema, so could no longer walk up hills of any decent size, but he sent me up in his place, with detailed maps of where he knew I was likely to discover exciting things. I remember finding thrilling combinations: the gem-like, ruby flowers of Moss Campion were just going over as Mossy and Starry Saxifrage came into flower, together with the chunky, truncheon-like plants of Roseroot and the delicate Alpine Lady's-mantle.

Since rediscovering my love of wild flowers, I have been back up the same hills, Beinn na h-Uamha and Beinn Iadain, and they look exactly as I remember them: slaty purple scree among black, wet cliffs, with these flowers perched in every flattish crevice between. You can sit there surrounded by carpets of wild flowers and, facing west on a clear day, see out to the Cuillin hills of Skye and Rum and to the Outer Hebrides beyond. This pair of Morvern hills are not Monroes – they are scarcely more than 2,000 feet – but sitting up there you feel as if you are in the most incredible place in the universe.

Alder
(*Alnus glutinosa*)

I love the craggy, beaten-up shape of Alder, which often lines a mountain or moorland stream. It flowers long before it leafs, its crimson branches a rich dome of colour through winter and spring. The ripe catkins look like a family of yellow caterpillars, with miniature leg-like nodules in a purple to conker-red brown. When they are tightly closed, that is the only colour you will see, but as they elongate, they turn to primrose. The catkins are the male flower heads, very different to the female flowers, which, when ripe, are like tiny, dark brown pine cones in clutches of three to eight. The seeds are loved by finches, including goldfinches, siskins and redpolls. In autumn, the leaves darken, wither and drop; they do not change colour dramatically.

Plant type Birch family, Betulaceae. *Flowers* February–March. *Height* Up to 20m. *Description* Deciduous monoecious tree. Bark is dark grey and fissured. Twigs are hairless. Leaves do not appear until April. They are dark green, shiny, round, tapered to the stalk, 3–9cm across, with paler, downy undersides. Male and female flowers grow on the same tree. Male catkins are 2–6cm long. Female flowers are green, egg-shaped, 1cm long, with three to eight per stalk. When ripe, they resemble small pine cones and enlarge to about 28mm long. *Companion species* Broad Buckler-fern (p.3), Hemlock Water-dropwort (p.304), Lady Fern (p.17) and Meadowsweet (p.314). *Distribution* Native. Found throughout the British Isles and scarce only in the far north of Scotland and the Outer Hebrides. Alder is less common than it was, because swathes of the damp habitats in which it thrives have been drained for agriculture. *Habitat* It prefers slightly acidic soils and is found along watercourses, such as the banks of rivers, streams, lakes and canals, as well as in bogs, highland hills and mountains, fens, carr and floodplains.

Alpine Lady's-mantle
(*Alchemilla alpina*)

This stands out a mile in its mountain terrain, its brightness a contrast to most of the vegetation, rocks and scree around it. Alpine Lady's-mantle often grows right beside a narrow deer or sheep path, its bright, fluffy, acid-green flower heads and delicate leaves looking like something you might expect to find in a rock garden. The silvery-backed leaves look almost metallic. You can tell immediately that it is in the same family as the larger, lusher lowland meadow and roadside plant Lady's-mantle (an aggregate of thirteen species, p.156), or the garden form *A. mollis*, but each part of Alpine Lady's-mantle is a fraction of the size of those related plants. It needs to grow hunkered down tight to the ground, sheltered against the harshness of the weather. The generic name *Alchemilla* refers to the popularity of some members of the genus with medieval alchemists – it means 'little alchemist'. The common English name Lady's-mantle is a reference to the Virgin Mary, to whom the plant was traditionally dedicated.

Plant type Rose family, Rosaceae. *Flowers* June–August. *Height* 15cm. *Description* Low perennial herb. Leaves are palmate, divided at least halfway to the base into five to seven narrow, toothed lobes with silky, silvery undersides. Flowers are very small, yellow-green, with four sepals but no petals, arranged in many-flowered dense terminal clusters. *Companion species* Heath Milkwort (p.357), Moss Campion (p.360), Mossy Saxifrage (p.360) and Roseroot (p.365). *Distribution* Native. Found throughout the Scottish Highlands and in the mountains of the Lake District. There are a few scattered colonies in the mountainous parts of south-west Ireland. *Habitat* Montane grassland and grass heath, scree, cliffs, rocky streamsides, rock crevices and ledges. It is found in well-drained habitats, in areas of snow lie, and sometimes on mountain slopes subject to severe wind scour. Soils range from acidic to strongly calcareous. It is frequently washed down to lower levels on river gravel, so it can sometimes be seen on lower ground on stream- and riverbanks.

Bell Heather
(Erica cinerea)

Whenever you are looking at postcards at a tourist spot in Scotland, it is the Loch Ness monster, a group of Highland cattle and a mass of Bell Heather across a moorland that you will most often see depicted. In late summer, it turns whole hillsides an incredible magenta-purple, with splotches of the paler mauve-flowered Heather (p.357) sporadically mixed in. Bell Heather is a handy plant to recognise, as it tends to grow on the driest tussocks, so you can use patches of it to navigate a dry route across what might be boggy ground. For this, you must be able to tell it from the similar Cross-leaved Heath (p.354), which prefers much damper ground. Bell Heather is renowned for being easy to grow in gardens, and there are various colour forms that flower at different times of the year. As with all heathers, its flowers are loved by bees and butterflies.

Plant type Heather family, Ericaceae. *Flowers* July–September. *Height* Up to 60cm. *Description* Hairless shrub. Leaves, arranged in whorls of three, are dark green, linear, with revolute (inrolled) margins. Flowers are arranged in elongated racemes – groups extending a little down the stem – and each has a reddish-purple, oval corolla, 5–6mm long, and dark green, hairless sepals. Cross-leaved Heath has whorls of four leaves and its flowers are arranged in umbel-like clusters right at the tip of the stem. *Companion species* Heather, Heath Milkwort (p.357), Oak (p.101), Sheep's Sorrel (p.366) and Slender St John's-wort (p.367). *Distribution* Native. Common in northern and western parts of Britain but much more local in the south and east, and absent from large parts of central England. In Ireland, it is common on both the northern and southern tips but much less frequent in central Ireland. *Habitat* Well-drained, thin, acidic soils, often in the midst of generally damp areas. Typical habitats include dry heaths and open Scots pine and oak woodlands. It is also found on limestone and chalk heaths where the calcareous soils have become leached, resulting in an uppermost layer of acidic soil.

Bilberry
(Vaccinium myrtillus)

Bilberries, also called Blaeberries, are rich in Vitamin C and Vitamin D and have long been known to be excellent for gastrointestinal infections and inflammations. Excavations of the drains of medieval monastic hospitals (such as the one at Paisley Abbey in Scotland) have found traces of these berries in huge quantities. The Bilberry's close American relative, the Blueberry, is now also known to have similarly good health benefits, and clinical trials have suggested that regular consumption of these blue-black berries helps reduce the risk of a plethora of diseases, including cancer and cardiovascular disease. It is a very common shrub in acid, heathy parts of the country, where special curved picking combs-cum-baskets have been devised for the July and August harvest – the berries are often hidden under the leaves.

Plant type Heather family, Ericaceae. *Flowers* April–June. Fruits ripen July–August. *Height* 20–60cm. *Description* Low, hairless, deciduous shrub with four-angled twigs. Leaves are bright green, oval, flat and finely toothed, 1–3cm long, arranged alternately. Flowers are small, with greenish-pink, globular corollas, 4–6mm long, solitary or located in pairs in the leaf axils. Calyx is unlobed. Pollinated flowers ripen to an edible black berry. *Companion species* Bell Heather (left), Bracken (p.351), Hard-fern (p.14) and Heather (p.357). *Distribution* Native. Very common in Scotland, northern and western England, Wales and much of Ireland. It is very rare in most of central and eastern England and absent in many areas. *Habitat* Acidic heaths, moors and uplands and, in Scotland, woodlands. It avoids calcareous soils. It also grows in open woodlands in Devon, Cornwall and elsewhere, particularly former sessile oak coppice woodlands.

Bog Asphodel
(Narthecium ossifragum)

Bog Asphodel is one of the easiest plants to identify in acidic bogs, heaths and moors. Its star-shaped, yellow-tinged, amber flowers are often the only obvious bright colour amid the browns and greens. When walking across heaths and moors, it is a good idea to avoid areas where Bog Asphodel grows. It likes truly wet soil, and is often a good marker of where you will sink into wet peat up to your ankles. The whole plant, including the fruit, turns tawny orange after flowering and keeps its colour through autumn. Its Latin specific name *ossifragum* means 'bone-breaking' – it used to be thought that eating it gave sheep brittle bones, but this is now known to be caused by the absence of mineral salts in the soil where it usually grows. It is slightly toxic, yet very heavily grazed.

Plant type Bog Asphodel family, Nartheciaceae. *Flowers* June–August. *Height* 10–40cm. *Description* Creeping perennial herb with erect flower stems and horizontal rhizomes running along the soil surface. It has fans of flat, two-ranked leaves, 5–20cm long, mostly basal. Inflorescence is an erect raceme with yellow flowers, each of which has six lanceolate perianth segments and six to eight orange-red anthers. *Companion species* Bog-myrtle (right), Common Cottongrass (p.352), Hare's-tail Cottongrass (p.356) and Round-leaved Sundew (p.365). *Distribution* Native. Common in much of northern and western Britain, but rare in the south and east, except in the Hampshire, Dorset and Surrey heaths. It is absent from much of central England and East Anglia. In Ireland, it is common in most places except parts of the south and east. *Habitat* Wet, moderately basic to strongly acidic mineral soils and peats, in a wide range of raised, valley and blanket mire communities, and in wet heaths and flushes. It is intolerant of shade. It is a classic plant of acidic sphagnum bogs and flushes.

Bog-myrtle
(Myrica gale)

Bog-myrtle is strongly aromatic, with an incense-like, eucalyptus smell. The scent comes from a resinous substance exuded by hundreds of tiny yellow glands all over the plant. Its other common name is Sweet Gale. Where we holiday on the west coast of Scotland, Bog-myrtle is very common. When the midges are bad, it is traditionally used as an insect repellent, and it was thought to be effective against fleas. Highlanders used to make what they hoped were flea-proof beds from it. If you are cooking on a barbecue outside and you have bushes near by, you can throw bunches of Bog-myrtle on the fire to keep the bugs at bay; you will sometimes see fishermen wearing sprigs of it in their buttonholes for the same reason. That delicious smell translates into a similar taste: before the use of hops, Bog-myrtle was used to flavour beer.

Plant type Bog-myrtle family, Myricaceae. *Flowers* April–June. *Height* Up to 1.5m. *Description* Erect, deciduous, usually dioecious shrub. Twigs are reddish brown and buds are oval and blunt. Leaves are narrow, grey-green, 2–6cm long, widest above the middle, tapered to the base, serrated at the tip, hairless above, downy below. Flowers are produced in short catkins that appear before the leaves. Fruit is a narrow, winged nut. *Companion species* Common Cottongrass (p.352), Common Sedge (p.296), Hare's-tail Cottongrass (p.356), Lousewort (p.308) and Round-leaved Sundew (p.365). *Distribution* Native. It occurs throughout Britain and Ireland, but is frequent only in Scotland, northern and western Ireland and in localised parts of England and Wales. It is absent from much of central and eastern England. *Habitat* It forms dense thickets in upland bogs, moorland and lowland wet heaths and flushes. It prefers organic base-poor soils with moving groundwater. It is often found in sphagnum bogs.

Bog-rosemary
(Andromeda polifolia)

Despite being in the heather family, this is well named, because it looks like a tussocky rosemary. The upper sides of its leaves are a similar grey-green, with the undersides silver to chalky white and slightly rolled around the edges. In terms of habitat, however, it could not be less like rosemary, which thrives with brilliant drainage. This plant needs the opposite, appearing like a series of mini-hillocks in the midst of a bog, often with water all around it. The flowers are Bell Heather-like, in pale pink to rosy white. Its leaves can be steeped in boiling water for an aromatic tea, but it is now too rare for picking. It has become less widespread because of bog drainage and is now a localised rarity.

Plant type Heather family, Ericaceae. *Flowers* May–August. *Height* Up to 35cm. *Description* Low, hairless dwarf shrub. Stems are branched a little. Leaves are elliptical-lanceolate, pointed, 1.5–3.5cm long, arranged alternately. Flowers are rosy pink, globular (urn-shaped), with five small teeth at the tip. Bog-rosemary is distinguished from most other native heathers by its rounder, more globular flowers, which are arranged in a loose, long-stalked cluster. *Companion species* Bog Asphodel (opposite) and Round-leaved Sundew (p.365). *Distribution* Native. Confined to northern England, southern Scotland, Wales and Ireland. It is most abundant in central Ireland, Dumfries and Galloway, Cumbria, Northumberland and the Cambrian mountains of mid Wales. The raised bogs where it tends to live are the ones targeted by the peat industry for the horticultural trade. The original extent of lowland raised bog has declined by 94 per cent, and Bog-rosemary with it. *Habitat* Moist to wet acidic peaty ground. It is most abundant in lowland raised bogs, with scattered occurences on upland peats.

Bracken
(Pteridium aquilinum)

Bracken is one of the most widely distributed species on earth. In the British Isles, as a result of increased grazing and burning of hillside vegetation, it is on the increase; on many hills it has become an invasive weed, and stock farmers hate it for taking over and sterilising good grazing land. When it grows in a wood, by contrast, the shade keeps it under control and transforms it into something elegant and restrained. In the autumn, some fronds stay green into November, others turn Highland-cattle red. Add to that the extraordinary smell of burnt caramel creams when you walk through it, and you can see why some people love it. The plant is edible, and the young fronds are quite widely eaten in parts of China, Japan and Korea. However, it contains a toxin called ptaquiloside (PTQ), which is thought to be carcinogenic. Bracken is not usually consumed in Britain, although it has been suggested that in Bracken-rich areas, PTQ may leach into the water supply, increasing the risk of gastric and oesophageal cancer.

Plant type Bracken family, Dennstaedtiaceae. *Height* 1–2.5m. *Description* Fronds are deciduous, usually inclined to one side, with a tough texture and two to three times pinnate. The smallest divisions are linear-lanceolate, deeply toothed, with inrolled margins and a dense covering of hairs on the undersides. They are borne at intervals on a creeping rhizome. *Companion species* Bracken releases chemicals that inhibit other plants, so it often carpets hillsides with little else growing beside it. However, it can provide shade to woodland plants, such as Bluebell (p.2). *Distribution* Native. Found throughout the British Isles. Extremely abundant in rough grassland and moorland in the west of Britain. *Habitat* Moorland, hill pasture and other habitats on acidic soils. It is most vigorous when growing in deep loam, sands or alluvium and is rare on base-rich soils.

Broom
(Cytisus scoparius)

Many people recognise Broom, a brilliant yellow-flowered shrub that grows on heathland, railway sidings and scrubby ground. It almost never grows on chalk or limestone. It prefers sandy, acidic soils and is, like Bracken (p.351), a good indicator of soil type. Looked at closely, the flowers are pea-shaped, similar in structure to those of Common Bird's-foot-trefoil (p.145) and Horseshoe Vetch (p.204), but three times the size. The flowers have a delicious smell of vanilla, which wafts around on warm days. Its common name originates from its use for sweeping – its long, whippy, thornless stems are ideal for making a broom, and dry well without becoming rapidly brittle. The twigs were also used in thatching and basket making. A prostrate subspecies (ssp. *maritimus*) can be seen on western sea cliffs, bent over against the wind. The parasitic plants known as broomrapes are so called because one of them – Greater Broomrape (*Orobanche rapum-genistae*), which used to be common but is now quite rare – is a parasite on Broom. The flowers of Broom are edible and make a decorative addition to a spring salad. The flower buds, just before they turn yellow, can also be picked and pickled like capers.

Plant type Pea family, Fabaceae. *Flowers* April–June. *Height* Up to 2m. *Description* Erect, spineless shrub. Stems are five-angled and grooved. Leaves are stalked, each with one to three leaflets. Flowers are golden yellow and 20mm long, arranged on stalks up to 10mm long. It is most likely to be confused with Gorse (p.355), but that has long spines and no leaves, except on very young plants. *Companion species* Butterfly-bush (p.237), Gorse and Heather (p.357). *Distribution* Native. Common throughout most of Britain, although local in some parts of central and eastern England.

It is absent (as a native) from the Outer Hebrides. It is common in the northern and southern extremities of Ireland, but scarce in much of central Ireland. *Habitat* Heaths, open woodland, railway banks, stony riversides and, particularly, roadside banks and verges, where it may often be planted.

Common Cottongrass
(Eriophorum angustifolium)

Cottongrasses are one of the few groups of plants that thrive in the harshest environments, making the most of the opportunity to romp away with little competition. The cotton-wool ball is not the flower but the seed head. The strands begin as short hairs surrounding the ovary, which, after pollination, elongate as the fruit begins to ripen. They are usually in boggier, wetter ground, so if you come across them when out for a walk, they are a pretty reliable marker of the areas best to avoid. Despite their common name of Cottongrass, they are not grasses but sedges. There are four native species in the British Isles, with this one being the most widespread.

Plant type Sedge family, Cyperaceae. *Flowers* May–June. *Height* 20–60cm. *Description* Rhizomatous, erect perennial. Stems are round on the upper side, three-angled below. Leaves are dark green, shiny, channelled, 3–6mm wide, tapering to three-angled. They become wine-red in the summer, a characteristic of this particular species. Stems bear umbels of three to seven drooping spikelets. Perianths are formed of many white, cotton-like bristles, 2–4cm long. Slender Cottongrass (*E. gracile*) is very rare and much smaller, with a three-angled stem throughout, as well as rough, bristly spikelet stalks (which are smooth and hairless in Common Cottongrass). Broad-leaved Cottongrass (*E. latifolium*) also has three-angled stems throughout, as well as flat, yellow-green leaves and rough, bristly spikelet stalks. *Companion species* Bog Asphodel (p.350) and Bog-myrtle (p.350). *Distribution* Native. Found throughout Britain and Ireland, but much more frequent in the north and west of Britain than in the south and east. In much of the Midlands, Suffolk, Essex and Kent, it is rare or absent, although where it does grow it is often abundant. In central and eastern England the species has declined drastically. *Habitat* Open, wet, peaty ground, both calcareous and acidic. It sometimes colonises peat cuttings and often grows in standing water. Its habitats range from upland blanket bogs and hillside flushes to wet heaths and marshy meadows in the lowlands.

Common Juniper
(Juniperus communis)

The tiny juniper tree often clings to the crevices of a windswept cliff face, looking gnarled and ancient. Its yellow flowers are hardly noticeable, forming small green cones. In their second year, these turn dark blue to black, plump and handsome, with a smokiness to their skin, like miniature sloes. These are known as juniper berries, but strictly speaking they are not berries at all. When dry, they add their sharp, clean flavour to marinades for meat – delicious with venison – and give the characteristic flavour to gin. They used to be harvested from wild trees in the British Isles, but are now imported from Eastern Europe and Tuscany, where they grow wild in great abundance. Juniper, together with yew and Scots pine, is one of only three native conifers found in Britain and Ireland.

Plant type Juniper family, Cupressaceae. *Flowers* May– June; fruits September–October. *Height* Usually up to 1m, but can be up to 6m. *Description* Dioecious, evergreen, coniferous tree or shrub. Leaves are narrow, stiff, sharply pointed, 5–15mm long, arranged in threes, with an apple-like scent. Its appearance is very variable. It can be low and prostrate at one extreme, conical or columnar at the other. *Companion species* Bracken (p.351), Primrose (p.103), Wild Strawberry (p.120) and Wild Thyme (p.217). *Distribution* Native. It occurs throughout the British Isles but is frequent only in the uplands of Scotland, northern England, Snowdonia and northern and western Ireland. It has declined severely, and populations on the chalk downs of southern England are a particular concern. *Habitat* In the north, it prefers cold, rainy sites on acid soils. In the south, it is a species of hot, dry, calcium-rich soils and haunts the parched downlands of chalk country. It also occurs very rarely in heathland in southern Britain, in places such as the Lizard, the New Forest and Burnham Beeches in the Chilterns.

Cross-leaved Heath
(Erica tetralix)

This delicate and pretty plant has drooping clusters of pale pink, waxy flowers, which are almost white at the base. This is the heather that grows in damp patches and bogs all over the British Isles, giving it the other common name of Bog Heath. The edges of the leaves are turned down, inrolled, which traps still air and reduces moisture evaporation. You might not think that was necessary in the damp places where this grows, but with the brutal winds that hammer it for long periods, it needs this adaptation to thrive. The leaves are covered in resinous sticky glands, which also help to make it more robust in severe weather. It shares this characteristic with Bell Heather (p.349), which grows in similar areas and can be easily confused with it.

Plant type Heather family, Ericaceae. *Flowers* July–September. *Height* Up to 60cm. *Description* Erect, evergreen dwarf shrub. Leaves are hairy, narrow, grey-green, 2–4mm long, arranged in whorls of four. The margins of the leaves are revolute (inrolled). Flowers have rose-pink corollas, 5–9mm long, and shorter, hairy green sepals, and are arranged in dense, umbel-like clusters. Sprawling branches root as they spread outwards. Bell Heather has darker, richer purple flowers extending further down the stem and leaves arranged in whorls of three, not four. *Companion species* Bell Heather, Bog Asphodel (p.350), Bog-myrtle (p.350), Heather (p.357) and Round-leaved Sundew (p.365). *Distribution* Native. Common in Scotland, Wales and much of northern England. It is far less common in southern England, although it is locally frequent in parts of south-west England, the New Forest and the heaths of the Weald and Thames basin. *Habitat* Mires and wet heaths, especially on nutrient-poor soils.

Gorse
(Ulex europaeus)

Just thinking of Gorse, I can immediately conjure up that sweet, coconut smell that hangs around it, pouring out of the flowers when the sun is out. It is a tough, resilient plant that grows in many windswept places on heaths and moorlands and around the coast. Its spikes are as sharp as a lance, and Gorse often protects immature trees, such as Oak (p.101), Alder (p.348) and ash, from grazing while they are vulnerably small. Given their scent, it is not surprising to learn that the flowers are edible and slightly sweet-tasting. Gorse almost never stops flowering, as the saying goes: 'Kissing is out of fashion when Gorse is out of flower.' It is also the key habitat for the rare and iconic Dartford warbler.

Plant type Pea family, Fabaceae. *Flowers* Year round, but most prolifically in April. *Height* Up to 2m. *Description* Spiny, evergreen shrub with trifoliate leaves when young. Yellow flowers are 10–17mm long. Spines are deeply furrowed, 1.5–2.5cm long. Dwarf Gorse *(U. minor)* is much smaller and often prostrate, although it can be up to 1m tall. Western Gorse *(U. gallii)* is similar to Gorse, but it is usually slightly smaller and has faintly furrowed spines. *Companion species* Alder, Bracken (p.351), Common Sorrel (p.147), Oak and Sheep's Sorrel (p.366). *Distribution* Native. Common throughout the British Isles, although considered alien on the Isle of Man and Outer Hebrides. Gorse has increased hugely in many areas because of the decrease in grazing on lowland grassland, cliff tops and heath. It has also colonised road verges and motorway cuttings. It is encouraged by heath fires, which open the seed pods, remove competition and create bare ground for seedling establishment. *Habitat* Often a good indicator of land that is 'wild' or neglected, it is especially frequent on common lands in the lowlands and upland regions in the west. It is often abundant near the coast and on many of our chalk and limestone downs, although it has a preference for acidic grassland and scrub.

Fir Clubmoss
(Huperzia selago)

This looks like a plant from the bottom of the sea, like a loofah – or clutch of them – in miniature. It stands out on the rocky tops of decent-sized hills and mountains, a sign that you are reaching the zone where you are going to find many other plants worth climbing for, such as Globeflower (p.301), Mossy Saxifrage (p.360), Starry Saxifrage (p.371) and Moss Campion (p.360). Clubmosses are peculiar plants. They look a bit like mosses, but they have a vascular structure (internal water-bearing vessels or veins), whereas mosses do not. They are closely related to ferns, and are one of the oldest groups of plants – their evolutionary history can be traced back at least 400 million years. Fossils found in coal deposits suggest that some species grew up to forty metres tall with trunks nearly two metres wide. The spores of some clubmosses are harvested to make an explosive powder, which was historically used in photography and to make fireworks. It is still used as a lubricating dust on latex products, such as surgical gloves and condoms.

Plant type Clubmoss family, Lycopodiaceae. *Height* Up to 25cm. *Description* Erect perennial herb. Stem is often forked and densely covered in dark green, spirally arranged leaves. Each leaf is minutely toothed and sometimes has small, bud-like plantlets in the leaf axils. The sporangia (spore-producing structures) are yellow and also situated in some of the leaf axils. *Companion species* Globeflower, Mossy Saxifrage, Moss Campion and Starry Saxifrage. *Distribution* Native. It occurs in upland areas, especially Scotland, Wales, Cumbria, the North Pennines and some parts of Ireland, and also rarely on heaths in lowland England, such as the Lizard, Dartmoor and the Blackdown Hills. *Habitat* Upland blanket bogs, heathland and acidic grassland, on nutrient-poor peaty or sandy soils.

Hare's-tail Cottongrass

(Eriophorum vaginatum)

This is easy to distinguish from the other three British plants in its genus (p.352) by its solitary flowers, or spikelets followed by solitary 'cotton-wool' balls. These single balls of fluff look like the tail of a hare, giving this plant its common name. All the other species have multiple flowers and then multiple plumes on each stem. Both Common Cottongrass and Broad-leaved Cottongrass have leaves that are 2–8mm wide, whereas Hare's-tail has more slender leaves. This one also forms distinct tussocks rather than a generalised mat – hence its other common name of Tussock Cottongrass – making it a nightmare to walk through. It creates ankle-twisting terrain and, like the other cottongrasses, it is always a sign of waterlogged acidy bleakness. Skirt around it when you are on a hill walk.

Plant type Sedge family, Cyperaceae. *Flowers* April–May. *Height* 30–50cm. *Description* Tussock-forming perennial herb. Stems are bright green, smooth, rounded near the base, three-angled above. Leaves are long, bristle-like and three-angled, up to 1mm wide at the base. Upper stem leaves have very short blades, or none, but have inflated yellowish sheaths. Flower (spikelet) is solitary and terminal, with a tuft of white perianth bristles, 2cm long, when in fruit. *Companion species* Often dominant or co-dominant with Heather (p.357) where both survive or even increase after burning. *Distribution* Native. This species is more confined to upland districts than Common Cottongrass and thus is less frequent in the south and east of the British Isles and absent from many areas, especially central England. It is common in the north and west of Britain, particularly Scotland, Wales, the Pennines, the Lake District and the North York Moors. There are isolated concentrations on Exmoor, Dartmoor, the New Forest and Wealden Heaths, but it is very scattered elsewhere. It occurs throughout Ireland, but is slightly more common in the North and West. *Habitat* A species of acidic blanket and raised bogs in the uplands, and wet heaths in the lowlands, where it often occurs in great abundance.

Heath Bedstraw

(Galium saxatile)

This is the smallest and most delicate of the common bedstraws, with flower stems skimming just above the grass or moss surface where it grows. It often forms quite extensive mats stretching up to two metres across, spreading itself horizontally rather than vertically, unlike its relations Hedge Bedstraw (p.202), Lady's Bedstraw (p.205) and Cleavers (p.238), which tend to clamber up and over neighbouring plants. You can also tell this species apart by its habitat. It is the only bedstraw of upland places, growing on heaths and leached poor acid soils in areas with high rainfall. There it is often one of the commonest plants, easy to spot in open patches in conifer plantations, where – in the absence of grazing – it forms great billowing mounds of white flowers. The specific name *saxatile* means 'growing on or among rocks' – *saxum* is Latin for 'rock' – and that is where you are likely to find this plant.

Plant type Bedstraw family, Rubiaceae. *Flowers* June–August. *Height* 10–20cm. *Description* Low, mat-forming perennial herb with ascending flower shoots. Leaves are lanceolate, 7–10mm long and arranged in whorls of six to eight on hairless, four-angled stems. Each leaf is one-veined, broadest above the middle, with a pointed tip and forward-pointing prickles along the edges. Flowers are 3mm across, white, four-lobed and arranged in loose cylindrical panicles. Fruit is 1.5–2mm long, hairless and covered in pointed warts. *Companion species* Heath Milkwort (opposite), Sheep's Sorrel (p.366) and Tormentil (p.371). *Distribution* Native. Found throughout Britain and Ireland and common in many areas, especially Scotland, Wales and north-west England. In southern and eastern England, it is much more localised, but is often very abundant where it does occur. It has declined locally in lowland areas as a result of habitat destruction. *Habitat* Infertile acidic soils in heaths, grasslands, open woodlands and sometimes on disturbed or derelict soils.

Heather
(Calluna vulgaris)

Heather, in its white form, is supposed to bring us luck, so many of us recognise it as the flower traditionally sold by gypsies to put in our buttonholes. In its usual pale pink form, more commonly known as Ling in England, it can cover whole hillsides and moors. It is hugely important in upland areas. The young shoots are the principal food source for red grouse, so it is a key plant on many Highland shooting estates. A great range of birds love the seeds, and its honey-scented flowers are a valuable source of nectar for bees and many insects. The English common name Ling is derived from the Anglo-Saxon *lig*, meaning 'fire', and the dead growth makes excellent kindling. Its Latin genus name, *Calluna*, is derived from the Greek for 'to brush', as Heather was also used to make brooms, brushes, baskets and ropes. The lilac flowers produce an orange dye, which was used to colour tweed; they are also used to flavour beer.

Plant type Heather family, Ericaceae. *Flowers* July–September. *Height* Up to 60cm. *Description* Much-branched, dwarf, evergreen shrub. Leaves are small, stalkless, 1–3mm long, triangular and arranged along the stem in four vertical rows. Flowers are small, 2–4mm long, pink (sometimes white) and arranged in dense spikes, 3–15cm long. Each flower has a four-petalled corolla, four-lobed calyx and eight stamens. *Companion species* Bell Heather (p.349), Sheep's Sorrel (p.366) and Slender St John's-wort (p.367). *Distribution* Native. Very common in most of Ireland and northern and western Britain. It is less frequent in southern and eastern England, although it can be abundant in areas dominated by acidic soils. *Habitat* Heathland and moorland. It is also found in open woodlands, especially under oak, birch and pine. It tolerates both dry and damp soils and often grows in wet peat bogs.

Heath Milkwort
(Polygala serpyllifolia)

Milkworts remind me of the flowers you might see in a delicate tapestry, or studding the grass in paintings such as Botticelli's *Primavera*, an exquisite presence despite their minute scale. That is even more the case with this species, surrounded as it often is by dull browns and greens. Walking through rushes and deergrass, you may come upon its scatterings of deep, dark purple to blue on the south-facing slopes of higher, better-drained ground, with splashes of more intense colour from plants such as Alpine Lady's-mantle (p.348), Heath Spotted-orchid (p.359), Purple Saxifrage (p.363), Wild Thyme (p.217) and Yellow-rattle (p.168), creating a perfect rock garden but in the wild. Heath Milkwort replaces Common Milkwort (p.147) on acid soils, and you can pretty much assume that any milkwort growing in heathland or acid grassland is this species. To be sure, however, look at the leaves. The lower leaves of Heath Milkwort are arranged opposite one another towards the base of each stem, whereas those of Common Milkwort are alternate. The flowers of the Heath species are usually slightly smaller, too, and of a deeper but less bright colour than those of the Common form.

Plant type Milkwort family, Polygalaceae. *Flowers* May–September. *Height* Up to 25cm. *Description* Low, scrambling, hairless perennial herb. Leaves are narrow, lanceolate and arranged in opposite pairs, especially near the base, becoming alternate above. Flowers are most commonly purple-blue, but can also be pink or white, formed of three very small outer sepals and two larger inner sepals, with the petals joined into a white tube. Flowers are usually 4.5–6mm long and arranged in racemes of up to ten. *Companion species* Heath Bedstraw (opposite), Lousewort (p.308), Sheep's Sorrel (p.366) and Tormentil (p.371). *Distribution* Native. Occurs throughout the British Isles and is common in many areas, especially in Wales, northern England and Scotland. It can be very abundant. It is local or rare in much of eastern England, particularly in East Anglia and the East Midlands. *Habitat* A characteristic plant of acidic grassland, moorland and heathland.

Heath Spotted-orchid
(Dactylorhiza maculata)

This is a blackcurrant ripple ice cream doing a cancan, a dancing head of a flower in which the white predominates over the purple flecks. It has narrow leaves, which cling tightly to the flower stem, except for the lowest pair, which are broader, spotted and splayed out to either side. Above them stands quite a chunky, densely packed spike of frilly flowers. Often, if you find one, you will find a hundred – they tend to hang around in big swathes. It is often confused with Common Spotted-orchid (p.148), or hybrids between the two, but Common Spotted grows in lower, dryer, less acidic grassland, is usually bigger and has different flower shapes. The lip of the Heath Spotted-orchid is only shallowly three-lobed, and the middle lobe is shorter and more pointed than the rounded side lobes. The reverse is the case for Common Spotted-orchid: its lip is deeply three-lobed and the central lobe is at least as long or longer than the others.

Plant type Orchid family, Orchidaceae. *Flowers* Mid May–July, but in the north it can flower well into August. *Height* Up to 50cm, usually 10–25cm. *Description* Hairless, erect perennial herb. Leaves are lanceolate, keeled, with circular dark blotches. The spike typically has between five and twenty flowers, although sometimes up to fifty. Flowers are white to pale pink with variable dark reddish-purple markings. *Companion species* Bog Pimpernel (p.291), Cross-leaved Heath (p.354), Heather (p.357), Heath Milkwort (p.357) and Round-leaved Sundew (p.365). *Distribution* Native. Found throughout Britain and Ireland but much more common in the north and west (where it is more common than Common Spotted-orchid) than in the south and east. In much of the East Midlands it is a rare flower. *Habitat* Well-drained or wet acidic soils in a wide variety of habitats, including grasslands, moors, heaths, flushes and bogs. It also occurs in pockets of peat on limestone and, more rarely, in open woodland.

Lesser Butterfly-orchid
(Platanthera bifolia)

This is one of my favourite native orchids. I love its subtle colour range of white, lime green and dark green – the colours of a white garden in a single plant. The flowers are highly scented, especially at dusk, presumably to attract moths. Like Greater Butterfly-orchid (p.13), its flowers are loosely and airily arranged around the main stem, but each one is more delicate. You can tell it apart from its larger relative, with which it sometimes grows, by looking into the flowers. In Greater Butterfly-orchid, the pollinia are well separated at the base but converge at the tip, but in this species the pollinia are held parallel all the way down.

Plant type Orchid family, Orchidaceae. *Flowers* June–July. *Height* Up to 45cm. *Description* Erect perennial herb with usually two (but sometimes three) oval, flaccid, shiny green basal leaves and one to five narrower stem leaves. The spike is cylindrical with five to twenty-five creamy- to greenish-white flowers. Each flower has a strap-shaped lip (6–12mm long) and two lateral sepals that spread outwards. The two other petals and upper sepal form a loose hood over the pollinia. A long, curved spur protrudes from the back of the flower. *Companion species* Burnet Rose (p.68) and Kidney Vetch (p.403). *Distribution* Native. Widespread throughout Britain and Ireland, particularly in the north and west, but not common. It is absent from much of central and eastern England and its remaining populations in the south are often small and isolated. It is listed as Vulnerable, but it can be locally abundant, as at Plantlife's Cae Blaen-dyffryn reserve in Carmarthenshire. *Habitat* Moorland in the north and west of Britain, often in quite damp ground, such as on the margins of bogs. On grass heath, it may occur under thin Bracken (p.351). In the south of England, it is found in deciduous woodland and scrub on calcareous soils.

Moss Campion

(Silene acaulis)

I remember Moss Campion from occasional mountain walks as a child, climbing up Beinn na h-Uamha and Beinn Iadain on the west coast of Scotland. It is a plant rarely found below 600 metres, so it was always thrilling to find it on the most out-of-reach rock crevices and ledges. You can walk straight past it in midsummer. By then, its flowers are over, so you will just see bright green domes of miniature leaves mounded up into hummocks like clumps of moss – hence its name. From mid spring to early summer, its brilliant magenta, gem-like flowers scatter thickly over the green cushions. Each five-petalled flower is held on the shortest of stems, which gives this campion its specific Latin name, *acaulis*, meaning 'stemless'. The flowers are pollinated by butterflies, and their brightness attracts insects across long distances. The cushion-forming habit of Moss Campion is an adaption to the alpine environment in which it lives. The dome shape prevents exposure and desiccation in a harsh alpine climate, and the leaves are small and narrow for the same reason. Cushion-forming plants also grow very slowly, so little of the plant is exposed at once. Moss Campion grows at a rate of 0.06cm per year, meaning that individual plants are often impressively old.

Plant type Pink family, Caryophyllaceae. *Flowers* May– August. *Height* Up to 10cm. *Description* Low, tufted, cushion-forming perennial herb. Leaves are linear, fringed with hairs and arranged in tight rosettes. Flowers are rose-pink, 9–12mm across, solitary and short-stalked, with five petals and five sepals. *Companion species* Fir Clubmoss (p.355), Mossy Saxifrage (right), Roseroot (p.365) and Starry Saxifrage (p.371). *Distribution* Native. It is confined to the uplands of northern Scotland, Snowdonia, Cumbria and north-west Ireland. It is locally abundant in northern Scotland, but rare in its other stations. *Habitat* Typically upland cliff ledges, crevices and screes on base-rich substrates. However, it is also sometimes found growing on boulder fields on mountain plateaux, and even in stabilised sand dunes at sea level in northern and western Scotland.

Mossy Saxifrage

(Saxifraga hypnoides)

It is always exciting to come across a patch of Mossy Saxifrage nestled down in the crevices between rocks. This choice of habitat gives the genus its name, from the Latin word *saxifrage*, which means 'stone breaking'. Like an all-in-one miniature rock garden, it offers different points of interest at different stages of development, from blood-red buds to newly emergent, fleshy green rosettes, then tall, red stalks capped with pure white flowers. The appearance of Mossy Saxifrage varies hugely according to where it grows. In very moist sites, it can be long and trailing, whereas in drier or more exposed areas it will form a wide, creeping mat.

Plant type Saxifrage family, Saxifragaceae. *Flowers* May–July. *Height* Up to 20cm. *Description* Mat-forming perennial herb with ascending flowering rosettes and trailing non-flowering leafy shoots. Rosettes are mostly formed of linear, three-lobed leaves, up to 1cm long. Sterile shoot leaves are more or less undivided. Flowers are white, 10–15mm across, with five petals and nodding, often pink-tipped buds. *Companion species* Alpine Lady's-mantle (p.348), Rustyback (p.105) and Spring Sandwort (p.369). *Distribution* Native. Frequent in the upland regions of Britain and Ireland, particularly in Scotland. In England, its native distribution is restricted to Derbyshire and the Lake District, with an outlying population in the Mendips. It occurs throughout the Welsh uplands. In Ireland, it is mostly found in the west and north. *Habitat* Upland habitats, on moist rocks, screes and cliffs, and by mountain streams. It may be found as high as 1,215m, but mostly occurs between 200m and 700m. Occasionally it occurs on sand dunes in lowlands, often in partial shade. It is also cultivated, and sometimes escapes.

Mountain Avens
(Dryas octopetala)

A deliciously pretty plant, made all the more so by the contrast with the rocky, brutal places where it tends to grow. It is usually a plant of high altitudes, but it grows abundantly down to sea level at the Burren in County Clare, Ireland. In that rocky, moon-like landscape, mountain plants grow side by side with lowland beauties, such as Bee Orchid (p.191) and Chalk Fragrant Orchid (p.193) – that is one of the miracles of this extraordinarily plant-rich place. This plant can be confused with white-flowered saxifrages, but these have only five petals, whereas Mountain Avens has eight. In fact, it sometimes has double that number – as many as seventeen have been recorded. The seed heads are almost as showy as the flowers, looking like the ragged flight feathers of a slightly bedraggled duck. These look best when backlit, giving the hillsides and promontories where they grow a soft, white halo. Its leaves resemble miniature oak leaves – hence its Latin genus name, *Dryas*, after dryad, the nymphs of the oak tree.

Plant type Rose family, Rosaceae. *Flowers* May–July. *Height* Up to 8cm. *Description* Low, creeping shrub with leaves that are dark green above, white-woolly below, oblong and toothed. Large white flowers, 2.5–4cm across, have eight petals and a cluster of many golden stamens in the centre. As with many mountain species, flowers are held on short stems. Green sepals are oblong with golden hairs. *Companion species* Dark-red Helleborine (p.196), Fragrant Orchid and Rustyback (p.105). *Distribution* Native. Confined to northern England and north Wales, where it is very rare, and the Scottish Highlands and the north and west of Ireland, where it is locally frequent. *Habitat* Uplands. Typically found on basic ledges and rock crevices on mountains, but also in upland calcareous grassland, and on coastal shell sand and limestone pavement.

Mountain Everlasting
(Antennaria dioica)

When fully out, with its halo of pink on white-silver, this strange-looking plant looks more like a marine coral than a flower. There is no sign of a petal, just tussocky, silver-white brushes on top of short, silvery-green stems. Mountain Everlasting is the only member of its genus found wild in the British Isles, and given its preference for heathland, upland grassland and mountain ledges, you could not confuse it with anything else. It gets the 'Everlasting' part of its name from the fact that plants famously appear in the same spot for decades, and because it dries brilliantly, losing no colour – when it was more prolific, its flowers were gathered in summer and dried as a winter decoration. As its specific Latin name, *dioica*, suggests, it is dioecious, with male and female flowers on separate plants.

Plant type Daisy family, Asteraceae. *Flowers* May–July. *Height* 5–20cm. *Description* Short, erect, stoloniferous perennial herb. Basal leaves are blunt, spoon-shaped, green above and whitish and woolly beneath. Stem leaves are narrower and pointed. Flower heads are dense, terminal umbels with tubular pink florets. Female flower heads are up to 12mm across and have narrow, pointed, erect, pink-tipped bracts. Male flower heads are smaller, up to 6mm across, with blunt, spreading, white-tipped bracts. *Companion species* Moss Campion (p.360), Mountain Pansy (p.362), Spring Gentian (p.368) and Water Avens (p.318). *Distribution* Native. Mostly confined to the west and north of Britain. It is common in the Scottish mountains and parts of Cumbria, the Pennines and Snowdonia. It is rare elsewhere. In Ireland, it occurs throughout, but is quite rare in most areas, apart from the mid-west, where it is common. Mountain Everlasting declined substantially in the first half of the twentieth century, especially in lowland England. *Habitat* Thin, basic to mildly acidic soils. Lowland habitats include chalk and limestone grassland, heathland, coastal cliff tops, sand dunes and machair. Upland habitats include rock ledges, crags, stream sides, screes, well-drained acidic grasslands, healthy pastures and dwarf-shrub heaths.

Mountain Pansy

(Viola lutea)

One of the best wild-flower experiences I have had was in Upper Teesdale in May. Walking through drenching rain around the head of the Cow Green reservoir, I saw the odd clump of pansy on the ground. But once I reached the sugar limestone proper, I could hardly put my foot down without squashing one of these exquisite flowers. The contrast between the harshness of the place and the sweetness of the flowers – in such huge numbers – was a breathtakingly uplifting sight. The ground undulated gently with domes of moss and lichen, and in each of the miniature valleys between them would be a family of pansies. Mountain Pansy is undoubtedly the most beautiful of our wild pansies, with flowers 20–35mm from top to bottom. Attempts to grow it in gardens have always failed. Today's garden pansies are usually derived from a cross between Wild Pansy (p.265) and Mountain Pansy, with a bit of foreign pansy added in.

Plant type Violet family, Violaceae. *Flowers* May–August. *Height* Up to 20cm. *Description* Low, creeping perennial herb with erect flowering stems. Leaves are oval- to broad-lanceolate. The terminal segment of the stipules is not longer than the other segments. Flowers are usually yellow, although often tinged with blue or purple. Many of the Scottish colonies are var. *amoena*, which is entirely purple save for some yellow streaking around the 'eye'. *Companion species* Alpine Lady's-mantle (p.348), Mountain Everlasting (p.361), Spring Gentian (p.368), Spring Sandwort (p.369) and Water Avens (p.318). *Distribution* Native. Confined to upland districts in north and west Britain. It is quite common in the Cambrian Mountains, the Pennines, the Lake District, the Southern Uplands and the Highlands of Scotland (although it is rare north of the Great Glen). There are a few localities in the west and east of Ireland. *Habitat* Shortly grazed grassland on hill slopes and rock ledges. It is often found on metalliferous soils and mildly acidic, leached soils that overlie calcareous rocks. In the west of Ireland it is also found on sand dunes.

Pale Butterwort

(Pinguicula lusitanica)

Rather like Marsh Pennywort (p.312), this is a minute plant that you will not notice unless you are looking for it. But once you have found one, you will go on to see plenty. Like its bigger relation Common Butterwort (p.294), it is a carnivorous plant that digests insects. Its leaves are very sticky. When a fly lands on a leaf, it is held fast. The leaf secretes digestive enzymes and absorbs nutrients and mineral salts from the fly – particularly nitrates and phosphates – through pores in its surface. Being carnivorous gives Pale Butterwort a competitive advantage over other plants in the acidic peat bogs – a low-nutrient habitat – where it tends to grow.

Plant type Bladderwort family, Lentibulariaceae. *Flowers* June–October. *Height* 10–12cm. *Description* Rosette-forming, insectivorous perennial herb. Leaves are olive green with purple veins, oblong, blunt, 1–2cm long. Flowers have corollas 5–8mm across, pale lilac-pink with a yellow throat and a blunt, downward-pointing spur, 2–4mm long. *Companion species* Lesser Spearwort (p.307) and Round-leaved Sundew (p.365). *Distribution* Native. Mostly confined to the west of the British Isles. In England, it is confined to the south between Cornwall and Surrey. In Wales, it is found only in Pembrokeshire. It is common on the west coast of Scotland and also on the Isle of Man. It is scattered throughout Ireland and quite common in some regions, particularly in the west. *Habitat* Sphagnum bogs, wetland and heaths. It grows on damp, bare peat and at the bases of grass, rush or sedge tussocks beside moorland rills, drainage ditches on former bogs, acidic flushes and wet heaths, often in places trampled by livestock or deer.

Petty Whin
(Genista anglica)

Glanced at in passing, this could be the more widespread *Genista*, Dyer's Greenweed (p.152). They are both low-lying shrubs with pea- or broom-like flowers in bright, golden yellow, forming bright splotches of colour in a ground-hugging carpet. Petty Whin flowers earlier and has many spines up its stem (Dyer's Greenweed has spineless stems) and much smaller leaves. It also grows on more open heathlands. Gorses, which look a little similar, also have spines, but these are always branched and the leaves on mature plants are spiny, not flat like those of Petty Whin. If you find this on a sunny day, stop and watch what happens when a bee lands on a flower. As the insect lands on the lip, the flower appears to explode as the join between the keel petals is broken and the coiled-spring-like stamens are released, shooting a cloud of pollen onto the bee.

Plant type Pea family, Fabaceae. *Flowers* May–June. *Height* 30–70cm. *Description* Low, straggling, spiny shrub with oval, hairless, waxy green leaves, 2–8mm long. Flowers are rich yellow, 7–10mm long, arranged in short, terminal racemes. Like all members of the pea family, its flowers have five petals: an erect standard at the top, two wing petals at the sides and two lower petals forming a keel beneath. Seed pods are hairless, swollen and pointed. *Companion species* Heath Spotted-orchid (p.359) and Lousewort (p.308). *Distribution* Native. Found throughout Britain but absent from Ireland. It is common in much of Wales and eastern Scotland and also more locally common in parts of Devon, the New Forest and the Wealden Heaths. It has become much rarer during the past fifty years, particularly in central England and southern Scotland, as a result of the loss of heathlands due to drainage, agricultural improvement and the cessation of grazing. *Habitat* Heaths and moors. It is found in the lowlands on relatively humid grass heaths and around the drier fringes of bogs. In upland areas, it occurs in heathy, damp, unimproved pastures.

Purple Saxifrage
(Saxifraga oppositifolia)

Alpine plants are always exciting to find, so small and yet so showy – you can see why people get obsessed with them. Purple Saxifrage is a perfect example, the earliest flowering of its genus (indeed, of all British mountain plants), with fantastic magenta-purple flowers. These flowers are huge in relation to the rest of the ground-hugging plant, and join up to form a solid carpet. They could compete with any modern bedding plant in their drama, if not their scale, yet this is a wild flower that grows in the harshest environments. Fossil remains of Purple Saxifrage have been found in Cambridgeshire, which probably date from the last ice age or soon after. At that time, temperatures would have been far lower and vegetation in southern Britain similar to that found in Scotland today.

Plant type Saxifrage family, Saxifragaceae. *Flowers* March–May. *Height* 15cm. *Description* Densely tufted, cushion-forming alpine perennial. Tiny oval leaves, 2–6mm long with bristly margins, are arranged opposite one another in four overlapping rows. They have a series of tiny pits near the leaf tips, which secrete lime and appear as a series of tiny white dots. Flowers are rosy purple, 10–20mm across, five-petalled, solitary and almost stalkless. *Companion species* Alpine Lady's-mantle (p.348), Globeflower (p.301) and Mossy Saxifrage (p.360). *Distribution* Native. Quite common in the Scottish Highlands but very local in upland regions in the rest of the British Isles. Although populations are very localised, it can be often quite abundant. *Habitat* A classic mountain plant growing on open, moist but well-drained, base-rich rocks and stony ground, mainly on cliff faces, ledges, stony flushes and scree slopes. It may grow near sea level in far north-western Scotland, but usually at between 300 and 1,000m, exceptionally 1,200m.

Roseroot

(Sedum rosea)

So many of us grow one relation or another of Roseroot in our gardens that we can recognise straight away which family this belongs to. It has thick, fleshy leaves, which are silvery and cactus-like, often edged in pinky red. The soft greenish-yellow flowers are domed on chunky stems held clear above the leaves, flushed smoky pink in bud and as they go over. Roseroot gets its common name because its root smells of Damask roses when cut, and it was widely grown in cottage gardens to make rose-scented water and to supplement perfume in potpourri. Roseroot, like St John's-worts (pp.209 and 367), has been used in European herbal medicine for more than three thousand years to treat depression and alleviate the effects of stress and fatigue. It is thought to moderate levels of dopamine and serotonin.

Plant type Stonecrop family, Crassulaceae. *Flowers* May–August. *Height* Up to 30cm. *Description* Low, tufted, hairless, succulent, dioecious perennial. Leaves are greyish-green (sometimes purple-tinged), flat, oval, toothed, arranged alternately and increasing in size up the stem. Flowers are a dull yellow, four-petalled (although occasionally petals are absent), 5–8mm across and arranged in dense, umbel-like clusters. It is difficult to muddle this with anything else, except possibly other members of the stonecrop family with yellow flowers and succulent, glaucous leaves – Rock Stonecrop (*S. forsterianum*) and Reflexed Stonecrop (*S. rupestre*) – but these have narrower, linear leaves and five-petalled flowers. *Companion species* Alpine Lady's-mantle (p.348), Bilberry (p.349) and Globeflower (p.301). *Distribution* Native. Confined to the north and west of Britain and Ireland. It is quite common in the Highlands of Scotland, but its distribution elsewhere is scattered, with localised concentrations in the Cumbrian mountains, the Pennines, Snowdonia, the Brecon Beacons and along the west coast of Ireland. It is also found very rarely as an escape from gardens in lowland Britain. *Habitat* A plant of mountain ledges and rock crevices, usually, but not always, on calcareous substrates. It will grow at altitudes up to 1,100m, but may also be found near the coast.

Round-leaved Sundew

(Drosera rotundifolia)

The glistening droplets secreted by the glandular hairs on the leaves of Round-leaved Sundew attract midges, which mistake them for water in which they can lay their eggs. The droplets are in fact very sticky, so the midges become trapped. The round leaves on their long stems quickly contract and the brilliant scarlet hairs become prison bars. Other hairs on the leaf margins respond by curling around the midge and secreting enzymes that digest the insect into a form that can be absorbed by the Sundew. After a few days,

the leaf opens again, with only the midge's skeleton remaining. These indigestible bits then get washed or blown away. Sundews do not rely solely upon insect protein for food, but it provides an essential supplement, giving them a competitive advantage over other plants. Up to two thousand insects (mainly midges) may be caught by one Round-leaved Sundew plant in a single summer.

Plant type Sundew family, Droseraceae. *Flowers* June–August. *Height* 10–15cm. *Description* Insectivorous, rosette-forming perennial herb. Leaves are almost circular, long-stalked and covered in sticky, red-tipped glandular hairs. Inflorescence is leafless, with small, white, six-petalled flowers. Flowers sometimes never open and are self-pollinated. *Companion species* Bog Asphodel (p.350), Common Butterwort (p.294), Heath Spotted-orchid (p.359), Lesser Spearwort (p.307) and Pale Butterwort (p.362). *Distribution* Native. Very common in most of Scotland, Wales and Ireland. In England, it is common in Cumbria and the Pennines, and also locally on the North York Moors, Dorset heaths, the New Forest and Surrey heaths. However, it is very rare elsewhere and virtually absent from much of central and eastern England, although it is often plentiful where it does occur. *Habitat* A classic plant of damp, acidic sphagnum bogs, bare, damp peat and flushes in both lowland heath and upland moor. It can be an abundant colonist of ditch sides cut through wet, peaty ground.

Sheep's Sorrel

(Rumex acetosella)

I love to see Common Sorrel (p.147) rippling in the wind
with buttercups on a late spring day, but Sheep's Sorrel is
even nicer. It grows in different places to Common Sorrel,
not so much in open meadows but on stonier soil on the
coast and at higher altitudes. It is shorter and stockier than
Common Sorrel, with densely red stems, yet, like a lichen
scattering itself into stony nooks and crannies, it washes the
area where it is growing with a delicate shimmer of bronze-
red. I have seen it in the North York Moors swathing drystone
walls with its rusty glow, and in patches on the shingle beach
near Dungeness in Kent, creating a translucent haze. Like
Common Sorrel, its leaves contain oxalic acid, which give
them a lemony taste: sorrel is traditionally used to replace
lemon in northern and central European cooking. They
make a delicious addition to a foraged spring salad and are
also good in soups and sauces – best used raw to keep the
colour bright. Wild sorrels have a more intense flavour than
cultivated varieties, so you can use fewer leaves.

Plant type Knotweed family, Polygonaceae. *Flowers* May–
August. *Height* Up to 30cm. *Description* Low, slender, hairless,
dioecious perennial herb. Leaves are shaped like a barbed
spearhead, with basal lobes, like miniature wings, pointing
outwards or forwards. They are up to 4cm long and stalked.
A silvery sheath surrounds the stem and the base of the leaf
stalk. Flowers are greenish to reddish, arranged in a loose,
branched inflorescence. *Companion species* Heath Bedstraw
(p.356) and Sheep's-bit (p.417). *Distribution* Native. Very
common throughout the British Isles. *Habitat* Dry heaths,
non-calcareous sand dunes, shingle beaches and other short,
open grasslands on acidic, impoverished, sandy or stony soils.
It is sometimes found on outcrops of acidic rocks.

Sickle Medick

(Medicago sativa ssp. *falcata)*

Sickle Medick is almost specific to the unique habitat of
the Breckland in East Anglia: open grasslands, heaths and
fallows on very freely drained sandy soil. The Breckland has
an unusual and specific flora, many of which are miniature.
That is not true of Sickle Medick. It forms prominent
patches of sharp, sulphurous yellow beside the road; you
cannot miss it as you drive along. Sickle Medick hybridises
with its close relative Lucerne (p.95) to form the exotic,
beautiful and rare Sand Lucerne (*M. s.* ssp. *varia*). This has
incredible-coloured flowers, sometimes like those of one
of its parents, more rarely a mixture of the yellow and
purple of both of its parents on one flower spike, and even,
occasionally, an extraordinary petrol green.

Plant type Pea family, Fabaceae. *Flowers* June–July. *Height*
30–60cm. *Description* Prostrate or erect perennial herb. Leaves
are divided into leaflets, each of which is narrow, linear and
up to 15mm long. Flowers are yellow, 6–9mm long and
arranged in short racemes, 10–25mm long. Seed pod is sickle-
shaped. This plant is quite similar to Black Medick (p.64)
but it is larger, with narrower leaflets and sickle-shaped pods
that remain green (they do not ripen to black). *Companion
species* Common Toadflax (p.74), Hare's-foot Clover (p.402)
and Lucerne. *Distribution* Native. Scattered sparsely
throughout Great Britain but considered native only to East
Anglia, where it is locally frequent in the Breckland. Within
its native range, it has declined due to habitat loss. *Habitat*
Grassy heaths and coastal grassland, usually on calcareous
soils and sands. It is also found on roadsides, tracks and sea
walls. It does not respond well to heavy grazing by livestock
or rabbits, or to mowing.

Slender St John's-wort
(Hypericum pulchrum)

Many of the St John's-wort family are robust, tall and on the chunky side. They are not, in my view, our most attractive wild flowers, but Slender St John's-wort is a notable exception. This delicate little plant forms light carpets through short grazed grass on old pastures, meadows and coastal heaths. Its bright yellow flowers and matching stamens with orange anthers at their tips identify it immediately as a St John's-wort, but the orange-red-stained, pointed buds, slender stem and finer leaves befit the species name of *pulchrum*, meaning 'beautiful'. Slender St John's-wort grows in exciting places, from the Lizard in Cornwall to the alpine tops of hills and mountains on the west coast of Scotland, and it is often an indicator of species-rich habitats where you will find other interesting things.

Plant type St John's-wort family, Hypericaceae. *Flowers* June–August. *Height* 20–40cm. *Description* Slender, hairless, erect perennial herb. Stems are round, smooth and reddish. Leaves are oval-oblong, blunt with cordate bases that clasp the stem, arranged in opposite pairs and covered with tiny translucent dots. Flowers are 15mm across, with five petals that are reddish on the underside, orange-yellow with red dots on the upper side. Sepals and petals are edged with black glands. *Companion species* Heath Milkwort (p.357), Roseroot (p.365), Tormentil (p.371) and Wild Thyme (p.217). *Distribution* Native. It is found throughout the British Isles and is quite common in most areas, apart from some parts of central and eastern England, where it is local and scarce. *Habitat* Heaths and open woods on non-calcareous, fairly dry, sandy, peaty or leached soils. A dwarf form with prostrate to procumbent stems (var. *procumbens*) occurs in exposed habitats in north and west Scotland and on islands off the coast of west Ireland.

Snowdon Lily
(Gagea serotina)

This is a plant more to dream about than actually to see: its large white flowers, exquisitely beautiful, dusted and veined with the palest purple around a clear yellow centre. It is exceptionally rare, surviving only in five sites in Snowdonia, in precarious and tricky-to-reach rocky outcrops and ledges. It hangs on in these crevices out of the reach of sheep, and if sheep cannot get there, we probably cannot either. There is anxiety that climate change may cause the Snowdon Lily to be lost from Snowdonia: if temperatures increase, more vigorous species are likely to colonise the places where it grows, and it will quickly be outcompeted.

Plant type Lily family, Liliaceae. *Flowers* May–June. *Height* 5–15cm. *Description* Erect, hairless perennial bulb. There are usually two linear, thread-like basal leaves and two to four much shorter stem leaves. Flowers are solitary, bell-shaped, 15–20mm across, with six pointed, white, purple-veined tepals. There are no similar species found in the same habitat other than some white-flowered saxifrages, which have five petals and non-linear leaves. *Companion species* Roseroot (p.365), Sheep's-fescue (p.213) and Spring Sandwort (p.369). *Distribution* Native. Confined to a handful of sites in Snowdonia. Snowdon Lily has only ever been recorded in this area and is thought to be a late glacial relic. It suffered from collecting following its discovery in the seventeenth century and, more recently, overgrazing by sheep has damaged populations. Although very rare in Britain, Snowdon Lily is one of the most widespread members of the lily family, found as far afield as the Himalayas and the east coast of the United States. The nearest colonies to those in Snowdonia are in the Alps. *Habitat* Damp mountain ledges and rock crevices on north- and north-east-facing cliffs. Shady situations are often favoured, as are those sheltered by overhanging rock. Some plants grow in tiny fissures on almost sheer vertical cliffs. Most of the plants grow in small pockets of very thin, weakly acid, humus-rich soils.

Spanish Catchfly
(*Silene otites*)

This delicate heathland plant, which grows in small numbers in parts of the Breckland heath of East Anglia, has tall, narrow flower spikes with lots of flowers, each one held away from the centre of the plant by thread-like stems. The flowers are tiny, in a halo of anthers, with an overall effect of fine filigree lace in a light Jersey cream. Spanish Catchfly is pollinated by night-flying moths, and its exotic, incense-like scent is strongest just after sunset to attract these insects. A weaker scent is also emitted throughout the day, and other insects, such as bees, beetles and flies have been recorded visiting the flowers in daylight. Despite its name, it is in fact a British native. It was once the sole food plant of the confusingly named Viper's-bugloss moth, which is now extinct in Britain.

Plant type Pink family, Caryophyllaceae. *Flowers* June–August. *Height* 20–90cm. *Description* Erect, usually dioecious perennial herb. Basal leaves form a rosette and are dark green, narrow, stalked and spoon-shaped. Stem leaves are linear-lanceolate and stalkless. Stems are sticky and hairy. Flowers are 3–4mm across, with greenish-yellow petals and a bell-shaped corolla. They are arranged in whorled inflorescences. *Companion species* Common Bird's-foot-trefoil (p.145), Hare's-foot Clover (p.402), Purple Milk-vetch (p.210) and Sheep's Sorrel (p.366). *Distribution* Native. Confined as a native to the Breckland in Norfolk and Suffolk, where it continues to decline through loss of habitat, fragmentation and isolation of its sites, and the lack of open disturbed ground within the sites where it still grows. It is a very rare casual elsewhere. *Habitat* Shallow, well-drained, calcareous soils. Typical habitats in the Breckland include roadside banks and grass heaths. It prefers open swards with some ground disturbance to assist germination and recruitment of new plants.

Spring Gentian
(*Gentiana verna*)

Gentians have a colour named after them as their hue is so intense. Only Green Alkanet (p.88) comes near it (and it is not native), and the fact that Spring Gentian lives in such high and austere places makes it even more miraculous. I have seen this with Mountain Pansy (p.362) in Upper Teesdale, a truly sumptuous pairing that is worth travelling a long way to see. The plant itself has never seemed particularly beautiful to me – it is too much like a cigarette holder with a flower stuffed in the end – but its deep blue, which pales as the flower ages, is the reason why it is always such a thrill to find it. It is easy to identify, because the only other plant that looks like it is the closely related Alpine Gentian (*G. nivalis*), an incredibly rare annual growing only in the Scottish Highlands. As the English writer A. C. Benson wrote, Spring Gentian is 'the pure radiance of untroubled heaven'.

Plant type Gentian family, Gentianaceae. *Flowers* April–June. *Height* 2–6cm. *Description* Hairless perennial herb with oval-elliptical leaves, 5–15cm long, mostly in a dense basal rosette. Stem leaves are smaller. Flower is a bright blue corolla tube with oval, spreading lobes, 1.5–2cm across. *Companion species* Bird's-eye Primrose (p.289), Common Bird's-foot-trefoil (p.145), Mountain Everlasting (p.361) and Spring Sandwort (opposite). *Distribution* Native. Confined to Upper Teesdale in northern England and the west of Ireland around Galway Bay. Changes in grazing practices during the past century, with greater sheep numbers and the resulting overgrazing, have caused a catastrophic decline. *Habitat* Calcareous grassland, usually on Carboniferous limestone or associated soils. In Upper Teesdale, it grows on the metamorphosed sugar limestone between 350m and 730m; in the Burren, on limestone pavement and fixed dunes at sea level.

Spring Sandwort
(Minuartia verna)

A couple of years ago I walked up Beinn na h-Uamha, on the west coast of Scotland, to be shown the exceptionally rare Arctic Sandwort. Rare and important it might have been, but I was disappointed to find that it was a rather boring, scrappy little plant, which looked like a tiny form of Chickweed with spidery leaves. It did not steal the show, which is something that could not be said about Spring Sandwort when I saw it in Upper Teesdale nestled next to Alpine Lady's-mantle (p.348) and Spring Gentian (opposite). This also has insignificant leaves, but its pretty, clear white, upright bell flowers are whoppers, quite out of scale on such a tiny, ground-hugging plant. Sandworts are a tricky group of plants to identify as they look similar to mouse-ears and stitchworts. They are all small, with white flowers, but Spring Sandwort has un-notched petals.

Plant type Pink family, Caryophyllaceae. *Flowers* May–September. *Height* 3–15cm. *Description* Low, cushion-forming perennial herb. Leaves are dark green, linear, three-veined, 6–15mm long. Flowers, 8–12mm wide, have white, oval, un-notched petals, slightly longer than the sepals. *Companion species* Alpine Lady's-mantle, Mountain Everlasting (p.361) and Spring Gentian. *Distribution* Native. Confined to north and west Britain, where it is very local. The strongholds of this species are the Yorkshire Dales, the North Pennines and the Peak District. There are also concentrations in the Lake District, north Wales, the Burren in west Ireland, the coast of Northern Ireland and the Highlands of eastern Scotland. There are isolated populations in southern Scotland, the Isle of Man, south Wales, the Mendips and the Lizard in Cornwall. *Habitat* Usually found on calcareous rocks and scree and in sparse, rocky grassland. It has a preference for the spoil heaps of old lead mines. It prefers open sites with reduced competition, but it may suffer from drought in very exposed conditions.

Star-of-Bethlehem
(Ornithogalum umbellatum)

In the Breckland in East Anglia, Star-of-Bethlehem has found a perfect niche and grows in fantastic and spectacular carpets, worth a spring journey to see. You need to be there in the morning: also known as Betty-go-to-bed-at-noon, Shamefaced Maiden and Eleven o'clock Lady, Star-of-Bethlehem shuts up its flowers by the middle of the day, even earlier in overcast weather. It grows in clumps, like hyacinths with much more open flower spikes, resembling a showier, shorter-stemmed, larger-flowered version of Ramsons (p.23), the starry, white flowers gathered at the top of the stem. The closely related Spiked Star-of-Bethlehem (p.107) is native to parts of the West Country and used to be sold in markets as a substitute for asparagus.

Plant type Asparagus family, Asparagaceae. *Flowers* April–June. *Height* 10–30cm. *Description* Short, hairless perennial bulb. It has six to nine leaves, which are linear, channelled, 15–30cm long, with a conspicuous white stripe down the midrib. Flowers are white, 30–40mm across, with six perianth segments, each of which has a distinct green stripe on the back. The flowers are held erect, arranged in a short, loose, pyramidal raceme, with the lower flowers on much longer pedicels than those above. Fruit is an obovate, six-angled capsule, 2–3cm long. It is easily distinguished from Spiked Star-of-Bethlehem by its lower stature, shorter and narrower leaves, fewer-flowered inflorescence and larger flowers. *Companion species* In the Breckland, it tends to grow with other alien species, such as Springbeauty (p.262). *Distribution* Introduced, although some botanists consider it to be native in the Breckland. It was cultivated in Britain by 1548, but not recorded in the wild until 1650 (1772 in the Breckland). It is widely scattered throughout the British Isles and is quite common in parts of central and southern England and East Anglia. *Habitat* A plant of waysides, hedgerows, woodlands, wasteland and rough ground. In East Anglia, it is abundant on sandy soils.

Starry Saxifrage

(Saxifraga stellaris)

Gardeners will recognise Starry Saxifrage. It looks like a smaller version of Londonpride, which often lines paths and flower beds in cottage gardens. But this species is rare, occurring only in damp nooks and crannies at high altitudes. The slightly succulent-looking leaves are hardly noticeable without the flower spikes, but once in flower, the plant is beautiful. It has five-petalled, starry flowers in a clutch of four or five at the top of each tall, narrow, reddish stem, their smoky-pink anthers forming a halo above the characteristic pair of yellow splotches at the base of each petal. Its tough, penetrating roots exploit the natural cracks and crevices in the rock and anchor it so firmly that it has gained the reputation, as other saxifrages have, of being able to carve out its own foothold by cracking the stone (*saxifraga* means 'stone breaker').

Plant type Saxifrage family, Saxifragaceae. *Flowers* June–August. *Height* 5–20cm. *Description* Low, densely tufted perennial herb. Leaves are oval, toothed, 0.5–3cm long, almost stalkless and all in a basal rosette. Inflorescence is a lax, branched cluster of small white, five-petalled flowers, each 10–15mm across. Each petal is quite narrow and has two yellow spots at the base, which are unique to this species among our native saxifrages and make it straightforward to identify when in flower. *Companion species* Fir Clubmoss (p.355), Moss Campion (p.360), Mossy Saxifrage (p.360) and Roseroot (p.365). *Distribution* Native. Confined to upland regions in the north and west of the British Isles. It is found in Snowdonia, the Lake District, the North Pennines, Southern Uplands, Highlands and Hebrides. In Ireland, there are concentrations in County Galway and County Kerry, but it is very thinly scattered elsewhere, mostly near the coast. *Habitat* This classic mountain plant prefers damp places, particularly rocky stream edges, rills, flushes, rock ledges and stony ground, usually on acidic substrates.

Tormentil

(Potentilla erecta)

Tormentil spangles the upland turf, never really seen as a separate flower but rather as the wallpaper that you happen to be walking on. This is the lawn daisy of the upland wild, a good companion to the purple of Heath Milkwort (p.357). These two often grow together, the Milkwort equally spread among Tormentil's yellow stars. Tormentil is a rich source of nectar for mountain and heathland bees and butterflies. It is often jumbled up with Wild Thyme (p.217), the two drawing in pollinator insects from far and wide. Tormentil and Creeping Cinquefoil (p.149) are the commonest plants in their genus and, on first impression, they may be confused. They are easy to tell apart, however, because Creeping Cinquefoil has rooting stems and much larger

flowers – on the scale of buttercups – with five (occasionally six), not four, petals. They also grow in different places: Tormentil avoids the heavy fertile clay and calcareous grassland favoured by the slightly later-flowering Creeping Cinquefoil.

Plant type Rose family, Rosaceae. *Flowers* May–September. *Height* Up to 10cm. *Description* Creeping and ascending, patch-forming perennial herb. Stems are branched, not rooting. Leaves are deep green, silky on the undersides and stalkless, divided into digitate leaflets, each of which is deeply toothed. Yellow flowers, 7–11mm across, have four petals and sit on long stalks in lax clusters arising from the leaf axils. Trailing Tormentil (*P. anglica*) is similar to Tormentil, but it has rooting stems. *Companion species* Bog Asphodel (p.350), Bog Pimpernel (p.291), Common Eyebright (p.146), Heath Milkwort and Heath Spotted-orchid (p.359). *Distribution* Native and very common throughout the British Isles; absent only from parts of East Anglia, such as the area surrounding the Wash. *Habitat* A characteristic and common plant of acidic habitats, such as heath and acid grassland, it is also found in a wide variety of habitats on more or less acidic soils, including lowland, upland and montane grassland, hay and fen meadows, moorland and heathland, blanket and raised mires, open woodland, wood borders and hedge banks.

Roseroot (p.365), Beinn Iadain, Morvern, Argyll, 4 June.

Moss Campion (p.360), Beinn Iadain, Morvern, Argyll, 4 June.

Mossy Saxifrage (p.360), Beinn Iadain, Morvern, Argyll. 4 June.

Mountain Pansy (p.362), Upper Teesdale, County Durham, 13 June.

Hare's-tail Cottongrass (p.356), Upper Teesdale, County Durham, 13 June.

Mountain Avens (p.361), Kinvarra, the Burren, County Clare, Ireland, 21 June.

Bell Heather (p.349), Luskentyre, South Harris, Outer Hebrides, 22 July.

Bog-myrtle (p.350) and Heather (p.357), Loch Skiport, South Uist, Outer Hebrides, 25 July.

Bracken (p.351), Sapperton, Gloucestershire, 7 December.

Coast

The expectable, average Britishness changes at the coast. The effect of salt and wind on whatever is growing means that it is like seeing the British flora transplanted to a slightly different planet – everything shifts. That is one of the reasons why, when you go to the coast, you feel that it is not like home.

Many of the plants are compact and carpeting, hunkered in close to the ground to prevent a wind battering. The leaves often look tough and have a waxy sheen; many, particularly on salt marshes, which are flooded every day, are fleshy and succulent. Salty conditions are toxic to most plants. High concentrations of salt reduce their ability to absorb water. This causes imbalances within the plant and disrupts photosynthesis and respiration. The fleshiness of salt-marsh plants is an adaptation to cope with this, enabling them to store more water in their leaves and stems. That is the only way a plant can survive.

Spring is delayed on the coast. You can come out of the woods and lanes and feel that the winter has scarcely gone. But when spring does arrive, there is a host of treasures. In April, if you go to Samphire Hoe, created by the spoil from the Channel Tunnel on the Kent coast, you will find Early Spider-orchids by the thousand, which have spread from the chalk downlands above. These are the first and one of the most astonishing sights anywhere along our coast.

The Lizard, a hard and rocky peninsula sticking south into the English Channel from the body of Cornwall, full of protected nooks and crannies, is a kind of wild-flower heaven in May. Wide fields of Thrift and Kidney Vetch paint the grasslands above the coves; then on steps going down towards the sea there are colonies of Thyme Broomrape, Lesser Meadow-rue and the extremely rare and protected Chives and Wild Asparagus, growing in such lushness that it is almost a miniature vegetable garden.

In high summer, the shingle promontory of Dungeness in Kent could not be more different. Some of the same plants are here, but it is jewelled with a whole suite of varied forms and colours. Here, you will find the searing red-pink Sea Pea, which billows out above the shingle like a sequinned cloth. Sea-kale is dolloped all over in three-foot-wide cushions, and the smoky purple-blue Viper's-bugloss, wavery yellow spires of Weld, and Red Valerian all contribute to a shimmery summer haze of abundance.

It is also in midsummer that salt-marsh plants are at their peak. On the muddy coast at places such as Stiffkey in Norfolk, there are fields of Common Sea-lavender, the purple carpet a bright contrast to the silveriness of Sea Wormwood. Acres of paler mauve Sea Aster on Harris and South and North Uist in the Outer Hebrides flower gently into the autumn.

Then the coast becomes a bleak place again, with any seed pods or plant skeletons whisked away in an autumn storm. In the winter, you will see the odd hummock of leathery-leaved Sea-holly or Wild Cabbage, as well as durable plants such as Marram, able to stand more severe conditions than most, but the looseness and abundance is scoured away, until next spring.

You may also see Betony (p.143), Bladder Campion (p.66), Bluebell (p.2), Broad-leaved Dock (p.236), Bugle (p.68), Burnet Rose (p.68), Bush Vetch (p.69), Common Bird's-foot-trefoil (p.145), Common Centaury (p.194), Common Chickweed (p.239), Common Evening-primrose (p.239), Common Eyebright (p.146), Common Knapweed (p.146), Common Ragwort (p.242), Common Toadflax (p.74), Common Valerian (p.74), Creeping Thistle (p.150), Curled Dock (p.245), Danish Scurvygrass (p.78), Dark-red Helleborine (p.196), Dyer's Greenweed (p.152), Field Scabious (p.198), Foxglove (p.10), Goat's-beard (p.153), Gorse (p.355), Heath Bedstraw (p.356), Heather (p.357), Hemlock (p.304), Hemlock Water-dropwort (p.304), Hogweed (p.156), Horseshoe Vetch (p.204), Lady's Bedstraw (p.205), Lesser Burdock (p.253), Maidenhair Spleenwort (p.95), Marsh Thistle (p.312), Marsh Valerian (p.313), Oxeye Daisy (p.159), Pineappleweed (p.255), Polypody (p.103), Pyramidal Orchid (p.210), Red Bartsia (p.256), Red Campion (p.24), Red Clover (p.161), Ribwort Plantain (p.162), Rosebay Willowherb (p.258), Rustyback (p.105), Salad Burnet (p.213), Selfheal (p.163), Sheep's-fescue (p.213), Sheep's Sorrel (p.366), Spear Thistle (p.261), Tormentil (p.371), Tufted Vetch (p.166), Viper's-bugloss (p.214), Wall Lettuce (p.113), White Clover (p.167), Wild Clary (p.117), Wild Thyme (p.217), Wood Sage (p.32), Yarrow (p.167), Yellow-rattle (p.168) and Yorkshire-fog (p.169).

Annual Sea-blite
(Suaeda maritima)

This plant of salt marshes and coastal mudflats grows amid carpets of Common Glasswort (p.395). It is fleshy and succulent – as you would expect of a salt-marsh plant – its leaves flatter than those of Glasswort, soft, thin and half-rounded. It stands a little taller than Common Glasswort, looking even more like a grey-green miniature pine tree. It has red staining over some of its lower leaves and at the point where the leaves meet the central stem, and this colouring increases in the autumn. The common name *blite* is an Old English word derived from the Latin for spinach or orache, and it refers to the fact that this plant is good to eat. As with Common Glasswort (which most of us call samphire), you can blanch or fry it and serve it with fish. Young stems are best, harvested in late spring and early summer before it flowers. It is also excellent added to spaghetti vongole.

Plant type Goosefoot family, Amaranthaceae. *Flowers* July–October. *Height* Up to 40cm. *Description* Short to medium, erect, branched annual. Leaves and stems are blue-green, flushed with red and purple. Leaves are alternate, fleshy, half-cylindrical, linear and pointed, 10–50mm long. Flowers are very small (1–2mm across) and green, in clusters of one to three in the axils of the upper leaves. Each flower has five stamens and two stigmas. *Companion species* Common Glasswort, Grass-leaved Orache (p.401), Sea-purslane (p.415) and Sea Wormwood (p.417). *Distribution* Native. Common on the coastline of the British Isles, apart from northern Scotland, where it is local. It is also absent between the Humber Estuary and Redcar in North Yorkshire. *Habitat* Sandy and muddy salt marshes, where it is often a primary colonist growing below the high-water mark. It also grows on the muddy banks of drainage creeks and in saline dune slacks.

Biting Stonecrop
(Sedum acre)

In bud, Biting Stonecrop looks like a mass of acid-green and yellow caterpillars, all crammed together, reaching towards the light. Its stems are segmented and very fleshy, and they accumulate to form large mats, creeping out and over stones, rising and falling over the contours of the land. When the flowers open, they merge into a solid mass of small yellow stars, each with five clearly separated, pointy petals. Biting Stonecrop thrives in infertile soils just inland of beaches and sand dunes, but it also grows on cliffs, walls and rocky hillsides inland as well as on the coast. The leaves are edible and have a peppery taste. It is now often planted on rooftops, as green roofs become ever more fashionable. Traditionally said to hold off fire and lightning, it is ideal for a parched roof habitat because of its tolerance of low-nutrient, very thin soils and baking heat.

Plant type Stonecrop family, Crassulaceae. *Flowers* June–July. *Height* 2–10cm. *Description* Mat-forming perennial herb. Leaves are fleshy, egg-shaped and broadest near the base, yellow-green, 3–6mm long. Flower spikes are branched and do not form dense heads. Yellow, star-shaped flowers are 10–12mm across. Reflexed Stonecrop (*S. rupestre*) also has yellow flowers and often also grows on and in walls, but it is a taller plant with flowers arranged in a dense, umbel-like head. *Companion species* Common Chickweed (p.239), Common Stork's-bill (p.398), English Stonecrop (p.401) and Red Valerian (p.407). *Distribution* Native. Widespread and common throughout most of the British Isles, although in many areas it is more frequent on the coast. In Scotland, it is predominantly coastal; it is absent from the Highlands and very local in the Southern Uplands. In Ireland, it is quite local and more frequent on the coast than in inland parts. It is also absent from parts of mid Wales. *Habitat* Dry, undisturbed and open habitats on thin or skeletal acidic or basic soils. Typical habitats include shingle, sand dunes, cliffs and steeply sloping, south-facing rocks. It is also frequent on walls, roofs, gravel tracks, pavements and road verges.

Bittersweet

(Solanum dulcamara)

The poisonous Bittersweet, also known as Woody Nightshade, has flowers and fruit similar to those of a miniature plum tomato, with straggly, sprawling plants more like a potato (it is closely related to both these edible plants). The flowers have an exotic Ottoman richness about them, like stuffed plush-velvet pantaloons. There is a prostrate form (var. *marinum)*, which grows on shingle beaches, such as Dungeness in Kent. Away from the sea, in woods and hedgerows, it can make a much taller plant, climbing by threading its soft stems in and out of other plants. As its common name suggests, its fruit and leaves taste bitter at first, then sweet. But it is better not to taste them: the berries particularly, but also flowers, leaves and roots, all contain the poison solanine, which some members of the nightshade family, such as Deadly Nightshade (p.6) and Henbane (p.203), have in potentially fatal quantities. Bittersweet is less poisonous, but it can still cause severe stomach problems, vomiting and breathing difficulties.

Plant type Nightshade family, Solanaceae. *Flowers* May–September. *Height* Up to 2m. *Description* Downy, scrambling, woody-stemmed perennial. Alternate leaves are oval, pointed, up to 8cm long, with two spreading lobes (leaflets) at the base. Flowers have five sepals and a purple, five-lobed corolla. Each corolla lobe is pointed and reflexed behind the flower. A prominent cone of yellow stamens, up to 8mm long, projects from the flower. Fruit is a red, oval berry up to 1cm long. *Companion species* Sea-kale (p.412), Sea Pea (p.413), Sheep's Sorrel (p.366) and Yellow Horned-poppy (p.427). *Distribution* Native. Very common in most of England and Wales, except remote regions. It is more local in Scotland, common in the lowlands but almost absent in the Highlands. It is found throughout Ireland, where it is more common in the east. *Habitat* Woodlands, thickets, hedgerows, ditches and, as var. *marinum*, on shingle beaches. It often grows in moist habitats and is common in swamps and tall-herb fens, and beside rivers and lakes, where it can grow in shallow water.

Bloody Crane's-bill

(Geranium sanguineum)

You can see a clump of Bloody Crane's-bill at a good hundred yards, its flowers an intense and zingy magenta. It often grows in savage places, with its roots in what appears to be neat rock. In the limestone pavements of the Burren in Ireland, it sometimes survives on the thinnest layer of organic matter. Such places start with a thin coating of a nutrient-rich algae called nostoc, which forms the base of a slow organic build-up, and Bloody Crane's-bill is often one of the first plants to eke out a living here. It also appears in lusher crevices on the serpentine of the Lizard in Cornwall, and these plants can be big and bushy. The name 'Bloody' comes not from its flowers but from the colour of the stalks, or perhaps the colour that the leaves turn in autumn. As with all wild crane's-bills, its flowers are attractive to bees.

Plant type Crane's-bill family, Geraniaceae. *Flowers* July–August. *Height* Up to 40cm. *Description* Bushy perennial herb. Leaves are 2–6cm across, long-stalked, deeply divided five to seven times, with white hairs on the undersides. Flowers are solitary, 25–35mm across, with unnotched crimson petals. A softer, veined, pale pink form, var. *striatum*, which grows wild on Walney Island off the Cumbrian coast, is widespread in gardens. *Companion species* Burnet Rose (p.68), Lady's Bedstraw (p.205), Sheep's-fescue (p.213), Tufted Vetch (p.166) and Wood Sage (p.32). *Distribution* Native. Scattered and locally frequent throughout Great Britain, but in the south it mainly occurs as an alien, except in a few parts of the south west. In Ireland, it is found mainly in the Burren. *Habitat* Base-rich grasslands and scrub, open rocky woodlands, coastal cliffs and stabilised sand dunes on rocks such as serpentine and dolerite. It occurs mainly on the coast but also inland on limestone pavements and cliff ledges.

Buck's-horn Plantain

(Plantago coronopus)

This handsome, perky little plant crops up all over our coasts, in rocky ledges and in the nooks and crannies and tops of cliffs. Like all plantains, it is happy to be trampled on, so you will often find it right by a path. The leaves clearly distinguish it from Sea Plantain (p.415). They are shaped like a stag's antlers (hence its common name), or perhaps a bird's foot – *coronopus* is Greek for 'crow's foot'. Historically, Buck's-horn Plantain was a local plant inland, typically in thin, dry, sandy or gravelly grassland. Like scurvygrasses, however, it is now increasing inland, especially in the south east and in Cornwall, cropping up quite commonly beside salt-treated roads. All plantains are edible, and this one has tasty leaves with a mild, spinach-like flavour and crunchy texture. Where they appear, they are usually very common, so it is fine to pick a few individual leaves to add to a salad.

Plant type Plantain family, Plantaginaceae. *Flowers* May–July. *Height* 20cm. *Description* Rosette-forming, downy biennial herb. Leaves are finely divided, 2–6cm long, with narrow-linear segments. Flowers are very small and arranged in a dense, oblong and long-stalked spike. They have brown corollas with protruding yellow stamens. Sometimes the leaves are undivided, like those of Sea Plantain. You can tell them apart by counting the number of veins on each leaf: Buck's-horn Plantain has one to three. *Companion species* Common Bird's-foot-trefoil (p.145), Common Chickweed (p.239), Kidney Vetch (p.403), Sea Plantain, Thrift (p.420) and White Clover (p.167). *Distribution* Native. Occurs along the coastline of the British Isles. *Habitat* Dry, open, often heavily trampled habitats on acidic to basic stony or sandy soils and rock crevices. It occurs in open grassland and on heaths, sand dunes, shingle, sea cliffs, sea walls and waste ground.

Chives

(Allium schoenoprasum)

Wild Chives are very rare, but on the Lizard in Cornwall, you can find them in their thousands. Pink globes, purple ones and others almost white: it is worth a special trip to see them. There are breaks in the precipice where the cliff has collapsed, and you can climb down over the boulder-strewn slopes. Close to Kynance Cove there is one of these collapses, on what feels like the outermost promontory. When you peer over the cliff, the grassland looks lusher than that around it. It is swathed in a lava-like river of pink and purple pompoms, cascading almost into the sea. These cliff tops are a carpet of Thrift (p.420) and Kidney Vetch (p.403) in May, and when I first found Chives here, I assumed that they were Thrift, until I saw the leaves. Like those of Thrift, they are crinkled and twisted, long and thin, but unlike Thrift, they are round in cross section.

Plant type Onion Family, Alliaceae. *Flowers* June–July. *Height* 15–40cm. *Description* Short, tufted perennial herb. Stems are cylindrical. Leaves are cylindrical, hollow and erect, all growing from the base. Inflorescence is a dense umbel of pink-purple flowers without bulbils. Each petal has a dark vein down the centre. Stamens protrude only slightly. There is a short, thin, papery spathe of two bracts at the base of the inflorescence. *Companion species* Common Bird's-foot-trefoil (p.145), Kidney Vetch, Sheep's-bit (p.417), Thrift, Wild Asparagus (p.423) and Wild Carrot (p.424). *Distribution* Native. There are scattered native colonies in Cornwall, south Wales, the Wye Valley, northern England and western Ireland. It is always rare. It also occurs an occasional garden escape. *Habitat* Usually on thin soils over limestone, serpentine and basic igneous rocks; it sometimes grows in rank grass on deeper soils, and in crevices of riverside bedrock. As an alien, it grows on roadsides and rubbish tips.

Common Cord-grass
(Spartina anglica)

Common Cord-grass is the equivalent of Marram (p.405) on the salt marsh and tidal mudflats surrounding the river estuaries of the southern coast. Like Marram, which is important for the development and strength of sand dunes, Common Cord-grass has a dense root system that helps bind together the mud where it grows and stops chunks of the estuaries being washed away. It is a key part of our coastal defences and has been widely planted specifically for this purpose – together with the similar hybrid between Small Cord-grass (*S. maritima*) and Smooth Cord-grass (*S. alterniflora*), introduced from America – and now forms extensive stands in many estuaries. There is a fear that both these species have been spreading too rapidly in recent years, colonising too much space and causing the loss of natural intertidal mudflat habitats. In some places, the cord-grasses are outcompeting native plants and beginning to damage fragile ecosystems. This may affect populations of overwintering birds.

Plant type Grass family, Poaceae. *Flowers* July–November. *Height* Up to 130cm. *Description* Tufted, patch-forming, rhizomatous perennial grass. Leaves are quite broad (6–15mm wide), thick, stiff and spreading near the top of the stem. Ligule is a fringe of silky hairs, 2–3mm long. Inflorescence has several erect, non-spreading racemes with one-flowered yellow spikelets. Each spikelet is 14–21mm long and 2.5–3mm wide, with prominent yellow anthers. *Companion species* Annual Sea-blite (p.392), Common Glasswort (right), Common Sea-lavender (p.397) and Sea Aster (p.409). *Distribution* Native. It is locally common on the coastlines of England, Wales and Ireland. In Scotland, it is confined to the south, where it is quite scarce. *Habitat* Coastal and estuarine salt marshes.

Common Glasswort
(Salicornia europaea)

Picking Common Glasswort, or samphire, from the mudflats of the creeks and salt marshes of Norfolk is one of the most rewarding foraging activities there is. Take off your shoes and roll up your trousers, because the mud where this plant grows is deep and sticky and you will quickly become coated in it. It is illegal to uproot the plant, except with the landowner's permission, and it is more responsible – and time-saving, because it needs less cleaning – to cut the tender tops with scissors. The best time of year to pick it is early summer, traditionally after the longest day of the year. Eat it raw or blanch in boiling water for a couple of minutes. Glassworts get their common name from their role in glass-making. Their stems have a high concentration of mineral salts, and they were baked in large pyres to produce mineral-rich ash.

Plant type Goosefoot family, Amaranthaceae. *Flowers* August–September. *Height* 20cm. *Description* Low, hairless, succulent annual. Stems are erect, jointed, translucent, blue or green but often flushed red or pink during flowering. Leaves are scale-like and fused to the stem. Flowers are very small and arranged in clusters of three in the leaf scales. *Companion species* Annual Sea-blite (p.392), Common Cord-grass (left), Common Sea-lavender (p.397) and Sea-purslane (p.415). *Distribution* Native. It is found all along the coast of the British Isles, quite common where its preferred habitat (salt marsh) survives. It is less frequent on hard rock and cliff and shingle coastlines; more frequent in England than in Scotland, Wales and Ireland. *Habitat* Coastal habitats, especially salt marsh, but also creeks, brackish grassland, muddy shingle and sand. It is an effective coloniser of bare mudflats and may form 'lawns' as thick as grass in the early stages. As the mud stabilises, it may become less abundant as perennial species compete.

Common Orache
(*Atriplex patula*)

This is probably the most common orache, which grows in all sorts of disturbed places, including near the sea. It often forms big patches at the top of a beach, with its relative Spear-leaved Orache (p.419) and other driftline plants, such as Sea Mayweed (p.412). Common Orache has a high Vitamin C content and is a mild laxative. The closely related garden species – which is often grown in a red variety (*A. hortensis* 'Rubra') – makes a useful vegetable and self-sows readily (in a tidy garden it can become a weed). The seeds are known to remain viable for up to thirty years. You can use the wild form in the same way, and because it is so abundant, it is a good plant to forage. Oraches are easy to confuse with one another. The key distinguishing characteristic of Common Orache is its gradually tapering, diamond-shaped lower leaves.

Plant type Goosefoot family, Amaranthaceae. *Flowers* July–October. *Height* Up to 100cm. *Description* Very variable, sprawling or erect perennial annual. Stem is often branched and reddish. Leaves are diamond-shaped and taper gradually to the stalk, with sharp, forward-pointing lobes at the base. Upper leaves are linear-oblong. Like other oraches, it has flowers that are small, dull, inconspicuous and arranged in slender leafy spikes. Fruit are enclosed in a pair of leaf-like structures (called bracteoles), which are fused to halfway. *Companion species* Pineappleweed (p.255), Sea Mayweed, Silverweed (p.418) and Spear-leaved Orache. *Distribution* Native. It is common throughout much of Britain and Ireland, although becoming increasingly scarce in north and west Scotland and the west of Ireland. *Habitat* Cultivated ground near the coast, as well as roadsides, manure heaps and waste ground in urban environments. It is also found on fertile soils in semi-natural habitats, such as pond margins.

Common Restharrow
(*Ononis repens*)

The flowers of Common Restharrow look like little pink peacocks with deep pink wings above white faces with pink-flashed beaks. It forms dense carpets, studding the grass with dots of colour. The flowers are right down at ground level, linked together by long straggly stems, which allow this plant to reach more than a metre from a single root. The stems are sticky and put down deep roots, which give the plant its common name: the roots are so strong and fibrous that they could stop a horse-drawn harrow, tangling the blades in their roots, making this plant the bane of the pre-tractor ploughman's life. There is also a larger, shrubbier species called Spiny Restharrow (*O. spinosa*), in which every stem is studded with sharp spines. Both are excellent for planting in newly created perennial wild-flower meadows, because they flower for many months through the summer and autumn and are easy to grow. The spiny species is typically found on heavier soils than Common Restharrow: it grows well where I have introduced it to my wild-flower meadow on heavy clay in Sussex.

Plant type Pea family, Fabaceae. *Flowers* June–September. *Height* Single stems grow 30–60cm long and up to 30cm tall. *Description* Creeping or ascending perennial herb. Stems sometimes have soft, weak spines. Leaflets are trifoliate and bluntly toothed, 10–20mm long, very sticky-hairy with a sweat-like odour. Flowers are 10–15mm long, on short stalks in lax, leafy racemes. Spiny Restharrow has narrower leaflets and deeper purple flowers. *Companion species* Common Bird's-foot-trefoil (p.145), Red Valerian (p.407), Sea-holly (p.411) and Wild Thyme (p.217). *Distribution* Native. Common throughout most of England and Wales, except in areas with strongly acid soils. In Scotland, it is more localised and more confined to the coast. In Ireland, it is commoner in the east. *Habitat* Widespread in grasslands on base-rich, well-drained, light soils, and on calcareous boulder clays. On the coast, it occurs on sand dunes and shingle, and inland it is frequently a colonist of sandy or gravelly road verges.

Common Scurvygrass
(*Cochlearia officinalis*)

I got to know this plant as a child, walking across salt marshes and tussocky peaty inlets beside the sound of Mull, my father getting me to taste the leaves. They are fleshy and succulent, with a mild mustardy flavour, and stuffed full of Vitamin C. That is what gives this family its common name. Before the ready availability of citrus fruit, sailors starved of this key vitamin often fell ill from scurvy. Captains of ships, including Captain Cook, encouraged their crews to pick and preserve scurvygrass and to eat it daily on board to keep them healthy. It used to be confined to the coast, but it has now become common inland – Common Scurvygrass in particular is often seen in full flower in Cornish and Devon lanes. Seeds are blown in or carried from the coast and, as we spread more and more salt on our roads, the resulting salinity allows it to thrive.

Plant type Cabbage family, Brassicaceae. *Flowers* April–August. *Height* 5–50cm. *Description* This is not one but an aggregate (group) of plants, which are all similar biennial or perennial hairless herbs. They have long-stalked, heart-shaped leaves in a basal rosette, triangular, stalkless stem leaves and white flowers 8–10mm across. Danish Scurvygrass (p.78) is much smaller, with ivy-shaped basal leaves and stalked stem leaves. English Scurvygrass (p.399) is more confined to the coast. *Companion species* Curled Dock (p.245), Rock Samphire (p.408), Sea Plantain (p.415) and Silverweed (p.418). *Distribution* Native. It exhibits a strong north-westerly distribution, and occurs along most of the British and Irish coastline. In Devon and Cornwall, Pembrokeshire, the Pennines and parts of Scotland, it also grows beside inland roads. *Habitat* Moist coastal areas, montane habitats in the north and hedge banks in the south west.

Common Sea-lavender
(*Limonium vulgare*)

Like walking into a wood and smelling a mass of bluebells for the first time, finding a salt marsh covered in sea-lavender is one of those exhilarating flower moments that we all need to pack in to our lives. To come across sheets of Common Sea-lavender jumbled up with the upright stems of Sea Wormwood (p.417), the purple, skeletal flowers silhouetted against a bright silver backdrop, is to see nature's gardening at its best. It is all the more beautiful because it is surprising to find so much prettiness in such a harsh, salty, windswept place, where colour is usually reduced. Despite their name, sea-lavenders are not related to lavenders, which are in the dead-nettle family. As with lavenders, though, the flowers are rich in nectar and much visited by bees, butterflies and other insects.

Plant type Thrift family, Plumbaginaceae. *Flowers* July–August. *Height* Up to 40cm. *Description* Erect perennial herb. Leaves are elliptical-lanceolate, 4–12cm long, with pinnate veins. Inflorescence is branching, flat-topped (sometimes rounded) and leafless, with clusters of flowers. Each flower has a pale lilac, sharply five-toothed, ribbed calyx and a corolla, 8mm across, with five pale purplish-blue petals. Anthers are yellow. Two types of sea-lavender are widespread in the British Isles, with this shorter, stockier species more common. Lax-flowered Sea-lavender (*L. humile*) is similar and sometimes hybridises with Common Sea-lavender, which makes identification difficult. *Companion species* Common Cord-grass (p.395), Sea-purslane (p.415) and Sea Wormwood. *Distribution* Native. Quite frequent on much of the coastline of England and Wales, where it may be locally common. It is most abundant between the Humber Estuary and north Kent, in the Solent and adjacent harbours, the Severn Estuary and Morecambe Bay. It is very rare in Scotland (found only in the south) and absent from Ireland. It was formerly found on the Isle of Man, but has not been seen there recently. *Habitat* Ungrazed or lightly grazed muddy salt marshes. Occasionally it also grows among nearby rocks and on the stonework of sea walls.

Common Stork's-bill

(Erodium cicutarium)

The name Stork's-bill refers to the fruit, or seed pod, of this plant. Looking just as it sounds, it is up to 4cm long and much more prominent than those of crane's-bills, to which it is related. The seeds have a complex and intricate method of dispersal. Each beak has five seeds at the base. When the fruit ripens, the beak splits into five segments, each with a seed attached. Each segment then twists into a corkscrew, which flutters to the ground. Absorbing some of the humidity from there, it then changes shape further and spears the soil surface to bury the seed. This is easier on disturbed and very light sandy ground, which explains the plant's mainly coastal or arable field distribution. Backward-pointing hairs ensure that the seed does not re-emerge from the soil; when the conditions are right, it is able to germinate. Common Stork's-bill is one of the larval food plants of the Brown Argus butterfly.

Plant type Geranium family, Geraniaceae. *Flowers* May–July. *Height* Up to 30cm. *Description* Spreading annual herb. Leaves are hairy (sometimes sticky), pinnate, with deeply divided leaflets (almost to the mid-rib). Flowers are rose-purple (although sometimes paler), 7–18mm across, with five petals, often with black spots, arranged in loose umbels of three to seven flowers. Fruit is 5–6.5mm long with a large, rimmed pit at the apex. Sea Stork's-bill (*E. maritimum*) looks similar, but it has undivided leaves and petals that are either not present or fall off soon after opening. *Companion species* Sea Campion (p.411), Sea-holly (p.411), Sheep's Sorrel (p.366) and Thrift (p.420). *Distribution* Native. Found throughout the British Isles, although in the north and west it exhibits a more coastal distribution. It is quite common throughout most of lowland England, but more local in Wales. It is most frequent near the coast. *Habitat* Well-drained sandy and rocky places, sand dunes, and grasslands and heaths above the coast. It is also found on roadsides, stone walls and railway ballast and, occasionally, in woods.

Dodder

(Cuscuta epithymum)

Dodder does not look like a plant. It looks as though someone got carried away unravelling red and yellow nylon fishing line all over the grass. It starts small and then, like a triffid, it takes off, rising up and over huge gorse bushes and anything else in its path, enclosing everything in its net as it goes. The common name may originate from the Frisian *dodd*, meaning 'bunch', or from the Dutch *dot*, meaning 'tangled thread'. It is parasitic on a variety of small shrubs and herbs, most frequently upon Heather (p.357), Gorse (p.355) and Wild Thyme (p.217) – the specific name *epithymum* is Greek for 'upon thyme'. When the seed germinates on soil it quickly grows a shoot that starts to twine around the nearest plant. The shoots grow suckers that penetrate the host, extracting nutrients and anchoring the plant. The root of the Dodder then withers away. Dodder declined greatly in the nineteenth century and early twentieth century, because of the ploughing of lowland heathland and chalk downland, and it is listed as vulnerable. Lack of land management has allowed Heather to crowd it out, but it does well where Heather is open and relatively short, allowing it to germinate and invade.

Plant type Bindweed family, Convolvulaceae. *Flowers* July–September. *Height* As tall as the plant over which it climbs. *Description* Parasitic climbing annual herb without chlorophyll. Stems are red and thread-like. Leaves are reduced to very small scales. Flowers are arranged in dense clusters, 6–10mm across. Each flower has a pink, five-lobed, bell-shaped corolla, 3–4mm across. *Companion species* Gorse, Heather and Wild Thyme. *Distribution* Native. Locally frequent in southern England but very rare north of a line from the Thames Estuary to the Severn Estuary. There are a few scattered colonies in Wales and Ireland. It is most frequent on the heathlands of the New Forest, Dorset, Dartmoor and the Weald. *Habitat* Wherever the host plants grow: coast grasslands, fixed sand dunes and shingle, as well as heathland and downland.

Dune Pansy
(Viola tricolor ssp. *curtisii)*

It is fantastic to find Dune Pansy because it feels so out of place. You could be walking across the arid, harsh environment of a sand dune or in the sandy, dry, well-drained soil just inland of one, and you may find huge carpets of Dune Pansy among much coarser-growing plants, such as Marram (p.405) and Sea Mayweed (p.412). You would have to be hard-hearted not to fall for its sweet, cheerful, outward-looking flowers. Dune Pansy is recognised as a subspecies of Wild Pansy (p.265), but it is perennial, whereas Wild Pansy is always an annual. It looks similar, although Dune Pansy usually (not always) has yellow flowers, and Wild Pansy's are purple and yellow. It is mainly scattered along the coasts of western and northern Britain. I have seen extensive swathes of it in the Outer Hebrides, and it is also found on the dry sandy heaths of the Breckland in East Anglia, one of the few places where inland dunes exist in the UK.

Plant type Violet family, Violaceae. *Flowers* April–September. *Height* 8–10cm. *Description* Low, tufted, hairless perennial. Stipules are large, pinnate, with the end lobe much broader than the other lobes. Flowers are 1.5–2.5cm across from top to bottom. Petals are longer than the sepals. The sand dune habitat is perhaps the best indication of this species. Field Pansy (p.249) has smaller, creamy-yellow flowers (0.8–2cm long), and is usually found in cultivated ground. *Companion species* Marram, Sea Mayweed and Spear-leaved Orache (p.419). *Distribution* Native. It is found rather locally throughout the British Isles. It is never common, and is rare in many areas. There has been some decline in the distribution. Colonies have been lost as a result of agricultural improvement of coastal grassland. *Habitat* Coastal dunes and grassland, although it is occasionally found on heathland inland.

English Scurvygrass
(Cochlearia anglica)

This is the seaside equivalent of the arable weed Shepherd's-purse (p.260). It too is in the cabbage family and it appears – like Shepherd's-purse – in large numbers, not on disturbed ground but on the salt-drenched rocky or peaty water's edge. The rocks around it will be covered in lichens and seaweeds, but Scurvygrass will not often get its roots properly wet. It will be in a band above the normal high-tide mark, so it gets only the occasional dousing at spring tides and when there is a decent storm. The leaves have the classic thick, succulent texture of seaside plants, which would otherwise dehydrate in the high-salt environment. Like all scurvygrasses, it is very high in Vitamin C, and used to form a key part of sailors' diets before the ready availability of long-storing citrus fruit. Ships' crews could pick it and store it in brine or vinegar to retain its valuable vitamin content. It is good to eat, with a mild Horseradish flavour, excellent in salads or chopped up and added to a punchy sauce, such as Béarnaise. The Latin genus name *Cochlearia*, meaning 'bowl of a spoon', comes from the shape of the leaves, which, together with the stem, resemble a teaspoon.

Plant type Cabbage family, Brassicaceae. *Flowers* April–July. *Height* 30cm. *Description* Low biennial or perennial herb with ascending flowering stems. Basal leaves are wedge-shaped, slightly toothed (or untoothed), tapering to the stalk. Upper leaves clasp the stem. White flowers are four-petalled, 9–14mm across, arranged in racemes. Fruit is elliptical and 8–15mm across. *Companion species* Sea Aster (p.409), Sea Sandwort (p.416) and Thrift (p.420). *Distribution* Native. English Scurvygrass is more localised than Common Scurvygrass (p.397) and Danish Scurvygrass (p.78), found mainly on the English and Welsh coastlines. It is quite rare in Scotland and absent from the north of Scotland. *Habitat* Salt marshes on soft, silty substrates and in former areas of mud (and sea walls) near the high-water mark of estuaries and tidal rivers.

English Stonecrop
(Sedum anglicum)

This rubbery plant starts life in the spring as a patch of compact, vivid green, grub-like stems plastering shingle banks at the top of a beach or boulders on top of a mountain. It hunkers right in to the exposed places where it lives, keeping its head down and deriving shelter from the slightly taller foliage and flowers all around it. There are large carpets of it at the shingle beach at Dungeness in Kent, and I have also seen it in rocks and crevices at the tops of hills and Scottish mountains. It seems to be able to thrive, however exposed its situation, gradually forming wide-reaching carpets, never extending its flower heads more than a few centimetres high. It is bright green in the spring, slowly changing to pink and white as the flowers open in early summer: neat, five-petalled, starry white flowers on red-pink stems. English Stonecrop, like Biting Stonecrop (p.392), has a low nutrient demand and will take baking heat, so it is another excellent plant for green roofs.

Plant type Stonecrop family, Crassulaceae. _Flowers_ June–September. _Height_ 2–5cm. _Description_ Mat-forming, evergreen perennial herb. Leaves are egg-shaped, fleshy and bluish green, arranged alternately up the stem. Flowers are white, pink-tinged and 12mm across. Biting Stonecrop is easily distinguished from English Stonecrop by its yellow flowers. _Companion species_ Biting Stonecrop, Polypody (p.103) and Red Valerian (p.407). _Distribution_ Native. One of the commonest stonecrops. It is usually confined to the coast, being very common on the west coasts of the British Isles, but only locally frequent on the south and east coasts. It is occasionally scattered inland, and some of these are likely escapes from cultivation. _Habitat_ Base-poor substrates on rocks, dunes and shingle, but sometimes also dry grassland. It may be found on old walls, rocky hedge banks, quarries and mine spoil.

Grass-leaved Orache
(Atriplex littoralis)

You may wonder why I have included three fleshy-leaved, green-flowered oraches: Common Orache (p.396), Spear-leaved Orache (p.419) and this one. It is because they are all good to eat and often grow in such abundance that, if you are an enthusiastic forager like me, it is worth knowing how to recognise them. Grass-leaved Orache grows above the high-water mark at the top of salt marshes. It has narrower leaves than its relations, so you need to gather more to make it worthwhile, but because it grows in the same places as Common Glasswort (p.395) and Annual Sea-blite (p.392), both delicious and plentiful wild foods, you could easily include a few leaves of this in your foraging basket. Picked in spring, its leaves are tender when raw or can be eaten as a wilted green with a spinach-like taste.

Plant type Goosefoot family, Amaranthaceae. _Flowers_ July–October. _Height_ 50–100cm. _Description_ Medium or tall, erect, branched annual herb. Leaves are alternate, linear-lanceolate, often toothed, unstalked on the upper part of the stem. Flowers are arranged in a long spike that is leafy at the base. Fruit is enclosed in two triangular, toothed bracteoles. _Companion species_ Common Sea-lavender (p.397), Sea-purslane (p.415), Sea Wormwood (p.417) and Thrift (p.420). _Distribution_ Native. Almost confined as a native to the coast. It is locally frequent on much of the British coastline, except in south-west England and north-west Scotland, where it is very rare. In Ireland, it is mostly confined to the east coast, with a few isolated colonies on the west coast. It is also found as an alien further inland, particularly in eastern England, where it is quite abundant. _Habitat_ Open, usually sandy or silty places near the sea, often forming dense stands along salt-marsh drift lines, estuarine banks and sea walls, and on waste ground around docks. It also grows inland as a colonist by salt-treated roads.

Greater Sea-spurrey
(Spergularia media)

As you walk through the damp, salty mudflats and marshes around our coast, you will see that the ground is studded with Greater Sea-spurrey, like daisies in a lawn – its Latin genus name is derived from *spargere*, meaning 'to scatter'. Although its common name implies something large, this is a small, delicate plant, which stands out from the green and greyish sward of the salt marsh with its bright, white to pink, chickweed-like flowers – five-pointed stars about the size of a five-pence coin. Whatever the colour of the flowers, they have white centres and ten prominent stamens. The calyx behind the petals is bright green and also pointed, the same size as the petals, clearly visible between each one. The flowers open only in the morning and early afternoon; they are usually closed by four o'clock.

Plant type Pink family, Caryophyllaceae. *Flowers* June–September. *Height* Up to 30cm. *Description* Hairless, creeping or ascending perennial herb. Leaves are narrow, fleshy and pointed. Flowers are 8–12mm across and vary in colour from deep purple to delicate lilac or white. Roundish black seeds have a whitish papery ring encircling the seed, looking a bit like a tiny flying saucer, 7–10mm long. Lesser Sea-spurrey (*S. marina*) lives in the same sorts of salt-marsh or cliff-ledge habitats. It has even smaller (6–8mm across) flowers that are deep pink, with up to seven stamens. *Companion species* Common Sea-lavender (p.397), Sea Aster (p.409), Sea Wormwood (p.417) and Thrift (p.420). *Distribution* Native. Common on most of the coastline of the British Isles. It has also been recorded in a few inland localities, usually by salt-treated roads. *Habitat* Salt marshes, muddy beaches, banks and low cliffs, tidally inundated dune slacks and the margins of saline ditches in coastal grazing marshes.

Hare's-foot Clover
(Trifolium arvense)

The furry flower heads of Hare's-foot Clover look so much like miniature hare's or rabbit's paws that whenever you see it, you will know exactly what it is. If you look at one of the downy balls more closely, you will see that it is made up of many pale pink flowers collected together on one flower head, with a halo of soft grey down surrounding them. The common name clover is thought to derive from the Latin *clava*, meaning 'club', because the trifoliate leaves resemble the three-lobed club of Hercules. Like other legumes, Hare's-foot Clover has nodules in its roots that fix nitrogen from the atmosphere. This provides a real advantage on the low-fertility, free-draining coastal soils where it tends to grow.

Plant type Pea family, Fabaceae. *Flowers* June–September. *Height* 5–20cm. *Description* Greyish-green, erect, branching annual herb. Leaves are trifoliate with narrow, oblong leaflets, 10–15mm long. At the base of each leaf is a narrow, bristle-tipped stipule. Flowers are creamy white or pink and arranged in soft, hairy, cylindrical heads up to 25mm long, which are located on long stalks (up to 20mm) in the leaf axils. The pinkish tinge is caused by the reddish pointed teeth of the sepals, which are masked by a covering of long white hairs. *Companion species* Dune Pansy (p.399) and Viper's-bugloss (p.214). *Distribution* Quite frequent in parts of eastern and southern England, but more local in the north and largely absent from north-west Scotland. In Ireland, it is found locally on the east coast but is very rare on the west coast. It has declined since the 1950s because of agricultural improvement, habitat loss and cessation of grazing. *Habitat* Rocky or sandy places. Sand dunes and sea cliffs are a favourite habitat, but it is also found inland on acidic heathland, railway ballast, waste ground, set-aside fields and other disturbed grasslands.

Kidney Vetch
(Anthyllis vulneraria)

Like Bluebell woods in May (pp.46–7), the lemony-coloured flowers of Kidney Vetch jumbled up with the pale pink of Thrift (p.420) create one of the top wild-flower sights of the year. They grow together on coastal paths in May, forming vast interlacing tapestries of colour on the tops of cliffs. Kidney Vetch is also a great coloniser of bare ground where the soil is right. Swathes of it appear in cut chalk escarpments for new roads, and it appeared en masse at Samphire Hoe in Kent. Its flowers are generally a good nectar source, although only powerful insects, such as bumblebees, can force open the large, stiff petals to extract it. It is also the sole larval food plant of the smallest British butterfly, the Small Blue.

Plant type Pea family, Fabaceae. *Flowers* May–September. *Height* Up to 30cm. *Description* Prostrate or erect perennial herb. Yellow flowers, located in dense rounded heads (2–4cm wide) of many flowers, have distinctive inflated woolly calyx tubes. Pinnate leaves are 3–6cm long, silky white on the underside, green above. Leaflets are linear-oblong, with the terminal leaflet being much the largest. *Companion species* Common Bird's-foot-trefoil (p.145), Field Scabious (p.198), Red Valerian (p.407), Sheep's-bit (p.417) and Thrift. *Distribution* Native. Widespread throughout the British Isles. It exhibits a coastal distribution in much of its range, especially in the west. Its inland distribution reflects the distribution of the chalk and limestone, although it sporadically occurs on other soils. It is increasing as an alien on roadsides from sown seed mixes. *Habitat* Rock outcrops and open turf on south-facing slopes. On the coast it is found on sea cliffs, shingle and sand dunes. It is usually found on free-draining, neutral-calcareous soils, where it also occurs on grassland that is regularly disturbed but not heavily grazed.

Lesser Meadow-rue
(Thalictrum minus)

This airy, elegant plant has smoky purple stems tipped by small flowers, each one not much more than a clutch of hanging, lemon-yellow stamens. The flowers are unusual, because they do not have petals enclosing the stigma and stamens. This is because Lesser Meadow-rue is usually wind-pollinated and it does not need showy petals to attract insects. On exposed sites, such as the Lizard in Cornwall, it often grows in groups in a sheltered nook, tucked in from the cliff edge, the mass of lacy stems and puffs of yellow resembling the finest hand-painted Chinese wallpaper. In such a situation it is beautifully restrained, but in damp conditions it can grow to more than a metre and can become invasive on rich soil. It is long-lived: one plant in the Avon Gorge has persisted for more than a hundred years.

Plant type Buttercup family, Ranunculaceae. *Flowers* June–August. *Height* 50–120cm. *Description* Branched spreading perennial. Leaves are highly divided (3–4 times pinnate) with small leaflets that are as broad as long. Flowers have four narrow, whitish sepals and many drooping yellow stamens. They are arranged in diffuse, spreading panicles. *Companion species* Chives (p.394), Sea Plantain (p.415), Sheep's-bit (p.417) and Sheep's Sorrel (p.366). *Distribution* Native. It is mostly found in the north and west of the British Isles, and also on the north side of the Chilterns and in Breckland, East Anglia. There are a few isolated colonies on the south-west coast of England. In Ireland, it is very local, with widely scattered colonies, mainly near the coast. It also occurs widely as an alien. *Habitat* Calcareous or other base-rich habitats where competition is low, including fixed dunes, scrubby banks, rocky lake and river edges, limestone and serpentine cliffs, limestone grassland and pavement and montane rock ledges.

Lizard Orchid
(Himantoglossum hircinum)

It is thrilling to find Lizard Orchid, because it looks so extraordinary, like a plant that has arrived from Mars. Standing up to mid thigh, it has tongue-like, lizard-shaped flowers, which protrude right out from the flower spike, falling as the plant goes over. Some of the tongues are as long as my little finger. The flowers smell of goat and are an odd colour, a mix of browns and greens, with an untidy, straggly appearance. The largest population is at Sandwich Bay in Kent, where there were 5,000 flowering spikes in 2000. The Devil's Dyke near Newmarket in Suffolk usually has between 200 and 250 flowering plants.

Plant type Orchid family, Orchidaceae. *Flowers* June–July. *Height* Up to 100cm. *Description* Erect perennial herb. Grey-green leaves are oblong to elliptical, 10–20cm long, forming a rosette and also up the stem. Inflorescence is a dense spike with fifteen to eighty flowers. The sepals and upper petals form a green hood, flushed with purple, and the lower petal forms a three-lobed lip, the lower lobe of which is long, ribbon-like and twisted, white with purple spots at the base, dull purple-brown at the tip. *Companion species* Marram (p.405), Wild Clary (p.117) and Wild Onion (p.427). *Distribution* Native and vulnerable. The range and distribution have varied greatly during the twentieth century, possibly reflecting changes in the climate, with the orchid favouring warmer periods. It has also been suggested that an increase after the First World War may have been due to the return from France of soldiers, who carried the adhesive seeds on their boots. *Habitat* Sand dunes and lightly or ungrazed calcareous grassland. It has a tendency to crop up in unlikely locations. At least six of the nineteen populations recorded in 2000 were on golf courses, possibly spread by golfers' shoes.

Maidenhair Fern
(Adiantum capillus-veneris)

I found Maidenhair Fern forty years ago with my father, in the Burren on the west coast of Ireland, and I discovered it there again this year. One of the most delicate of all our native ferns, it is now extremely rare. The Victorians collected it fanatically, driving it to near extinction. It is still holding on in the nooks and crannies of rocks on coastal and mountain cliffs in a few sites around the British Isles. Its beauty is in its fineness, an almost thread-like (or Maiden-hair) stem linking all the different parts so that the whole appears wavering and mobile. It emerges in late winter and is at its brightest and freshest in spring, although it can be evergreen in very sheltered sites.

Plant type Ribbon Fern family, Pteridaceae. *Height* Up to 30cm. *Description* Perennial fern with a stout, scaly rhizome. Drooping fronds are oval in outline, once to twice pinnate, with black, wiry stalks. Individual leaflets (pinnules) are fan-shaped, lobed and situated on hair-like stalks. Sori are located beneath reflexed lobes on fertile pinnules. *Companion species* Dark-red Helleborine (p.196), Maidenhair Spleenwort (p.95) and Rustyback (p.105). *Distribution* Native. Scattered throughout England, Wales, Ireland and the Isle of Man, although rare in most areas. There is a southerly bias to its distribution in England. However, most of these colonies are in inland regions and are considered to be garden escapes. Native colonies are confined to the coast in south-west England, south Wales, Morecambe Bay, the Isle of Man and the west coast of Ireland. *Habitat* Crevices of damp sea cliffs on calcareous rocks; also in the grikes of limestone pavement. It favours an oceanic climate.

Marram
(Ammophila arenaria)

Marram's beauty is in its greyness; it is as if it has been washed out by its seaside life. Imagine it bright green: it would not have nearly the same peaceful, poetic presence – the difference is like that between fresh-cut timber and driftwood. This coarse grass, which can cut your fingers or bare legs as you push through it, covers sand dunes over huge swathes of our coast, forming big tussocks with straw-coloured foxtail flower spikes. Its root system is a convoluted mat of fibres, which anchors the plant in the sand. The leaves are springy enough to resist strong winds and are covered in glossy cuticles that protect them from abrasive wind-blown sand. The leaf edges curl inwards to help prevent water loss. These qualities make Marram the ideal sand binder, and it is widely encouraged and planted for stabilising mobile sand dunes and strengthening coastal defences. It used to be cut and dried for weaving fishing nets and ropes because, unlike the hollow, cylindrical stems of straw and reed, its flat leaves are very flexible. On Anglesey, it was used for thatching, but it is so important for stabilising dunes that it cannot now be harvested.

Plant type Grass family, Poaceae. *Flowers* July–August. *Height* Up to 120cm. *Description* Tufted, rhizomatous perennial grass. Leaves are grey-green, prominently ribbed, tough, sharply pointed and tightly inrolled, opening only in moist conditions. Ligules are very long (1–3cm) and pointed. Inflorescence is a stout, grey-green, cigar-shaped panicle, 7–20cm long. Spikelets are one-flowered, compressed and 12–16mm long. *Companion species* Common Orache (p.396), Sea Mayweed (p.412) and Spear-leaved Orache (p.419). *Distribution* Native. It grows all along the coastline of Britain and Ireland, although it is more localised on the south coast of England. *Habitat* It is the dominant species of coastal sand dunes.

Marsh-mallow
(Althaea officinalis)

The silk-velvet texture of Marsh-mallow's grey-green leaves makes me want to wrap myself up in them. The fruit has the same feel, with the pale pink flowers providing a beautiful contrast. This mallow forms good-sized clumps, standing to waist height. It inhabits damper places than other members of its family, but it does occur inland. The roots contain high quantities of starch, oils and sugars, and their pulp was used for making marsh-mallow sweets. They were dug up from the marshes on the banks of the Thames, where it no longer occurs – digging up so many of them is probably the reason it has become rare. Marsh-mallow is the sole larval food plant of the Marsh-mallow moth, a very rare species confined to tiny preserved patches on Romney Marsh in Kent and East Sussex, one of the strongholds of the plant.

Plant type Mallow family, Malvaceae. *Flowers* August–September. *Height* Up to 120cm. *Description* Erect, downy, velvety perennial. Leaves are oval, slightly lobed and velvety, 3–8cm across near the base. Flowers are in clusters of one to three in the leaf axils, on stalks shorter than those of the leaves. Each flower is 2.5–4cm across, with pale pink petals, velvety sepals and an epicalyx of six to nine triangular lobes. *Companion species* Common Glasswort (p.395), Goat's-beard (p.153) and Sea-purslane (p.415). *Distribution* Native. Scattered throughout low-lying, coastal areas of southern and eastern England and south Wales. It can be quite frequent where it does occur, but has declined with coastal development and the drainage of coastal wetlands. *Habitat* It is found in a variety of coastal habitats, but favours brackish marshes and the banks of brackish ditches. Marsh-mallow is often found on the upper reaches of salt marshes, in the transitional area between seawater and freshwater habitats.

Oysterplant
(Mertensia maritima)

I first came across Oysterplant in a restaurant in Amsterdam, which was serving oysters with the leaves of this plant in a salad. I could not believe how alike the flavours were. If it were not for their different textures, had I shut my eyes and tasted a small part of a leaf I would have thought I was eating an oyster. You can grow this in a garden, but it grows much better in the wild, forming huge colonies at the tops of shingle and sandy beaches. I have seen carpets of it on the western side of Mull. Its leaves are elegantly silver, with flowering stems that hang with vivid blue bell flowers. Most members of the borage family are bristly or hairy, but Oysterplant is the exception. It has hairless, waxy, succulent leaves, typical of coastal plants. These enable it to grow on saline, very dry shingle beaches and avoid dehydration.

Plant type Borage family, Boraginaceae. *Flowers* June–August. *Height* 30–60cm. *Description* Hairless, prostrate, mat-forming, slightly succulent biennial or perennial herb. Leaves are blue-green, oval, fleshy and stalked near the base. Flowers are stalked and have bell-shaped corollas, 6mm wide, which are pink at first, later turning pale blue. Flowers are arranged in terminal, branching inflorescences. *Companion species* Sea Rocket (p.416) and Sea Sandwort (p.416). *Distribution* Native. Confined to the coastlines of western and northern Britain and Ireland. It is rare in both England and north Wales. It is more frequent on the Scottish coast, but still rather local. In Ireland, it is also very localised but appears to be increasing. Declines have been attributed to recreational pressure, removal of shingle, grazing and storms. *Habitat* Usually gravel and shingle beaches, although sometimes on sand. It also colonises areas of rock and earth that are tipped along the coast. The seeds can survive for long periods in seawater.

Pale Flax
(Linum bienne)

The flowers of Pale Flax are ethereal and beautiful. They look as if the petals would blow away on a gust of wind, and they do not last more than a few hours, perched at the tip of a thin stem with narrow leaves only on the bottom section. While the flowers are short-lived and transient, the plants themselves are robust, growing happily on dry grasslands on the windy south coast and in similarly exposed places in south-east Ireland. Unlike many wild flowers growing in coastal grasslands, Pale Flax is on the increase. The lilac-blue flowers are paler than those of the annual cultivated Flax (*L. usitatissimum*), which is planted in summer arable fields to make linen and to produce the linseed oil used in paints and varnishes. Now widespread as a casual escape from cultivation, it has larger flowers than Pale Flax, but is mostly confined to cultivated ground, waste ground and roadsides.

Plant type Flax family, Linaceae. *Flowers* May–September. *Height* 30–50cm. *Description* Erect, hairless, multi-stemmed biennial or perennial herb. Leaves are narrow, pointed and three-veined, 1–2.5cm long, alternately arranged. Flowers have pale, lilac-blue petals that are 8–12mm long, and pointed sepals. Stigmas are club-shaped. Fruit is a round capsule, 4–6mm across. *Companion species* Lady's Bedstraw (p.205), Sheep's-bit (p.417), Sheep's Sorrel (p.366) and Wild Thyme (p.217). *Distribution* Native. Confined to England, Wales, the Isle of Man and Ireland. It is most frequent in south-west England and along the coast of Wales; more localised in south-east England. In Ireland, it is quite frequent along the south-east coast but very rare elsewhere. *Habitat* Dry, well-drained, permanent pasture on calcareous or neutral soils, usually near the sea. It also occurs on path and field margins, roadsides, railway banks and old quarries.

Parsley Water-dropwort
(Oenanthe lachenalii)

Parsley Water-dropwort is well presented, as if it has been done up smartly for a party. It has one of the finest flower heads of all the umbellifers, with each clearly separated branch of the flower and each individual flower within each branch looking as though it has been cut from the most delicate pure white lace. Its flowers look bright and clean and stand out strongly against the narrow, grey-green foliage, as well as the other greens and browns that often surround it. It is usually found in brackish water near the coast, but not always. I have seen it growing in East Anglian inland fens as well as in marshes near the coast. The generic name *Oenanthe* may originate from the Greek words for 'wine' and 'flower', because of the plant's vine-like smell. That might make it seem rather tempting, but like all water-dropworts, Parsley Water-dropwort is poisonous.

Plant type Carrot family, Apiaceae. *Flowers* June–September. *Height* Up to 1m. *Description* Erect, branched, hairless perennial herb. Basal leaves are twice pinnate with narrow, bluntly elliptical-obovate, lobed leaflets. Stem leaves are narrower and untoothed. Flowers are white (with a tinge of pink), on slender rays, in open umbels with oval bracts. It is less toxic than Hemlock Water-dropwort (p.304). *Companion species* Marsh Thistle (p.312), Marsh Valerian (p.313) and Wild Leek (p.426). *Distribution* Native. It has a mostly coastal distribution in Britain and Ireland, where it is not uncommon. It is absent from the north and east coasts of Scotland, and rare on the east coast of northern England. *Habitat* In coastal areas, it occurs in the uppermost parts of salt marshes, in rough grassland in drained estuarine marshes and by brackish dykes and the lower reaches of tidal rivers. Inland, it is found in base-enriched habitats: marshes, fen meadows and tall-herb fen.

Red Valerian
(Centranthus ruber)

This grows in swathes on the coast, from the shingle beaches of Dungeness in Kent to the limestone pavements of the Burren in Ireland. Curtains of it also appear in crumbly village and old church walls and steps. It looks as though one plant has started off a Red Valerian waterfall, scattering seed into every cranny below. The roots then bury into crevices in the rock, giving the plant a firm anchorage. Red Valerian comes in three colour forms, which often grow closely together: deep red, pink-magenta and pure white. It is not native – it was introduced to Britain from the Mediterranean before 1600 – but it has been here for so long and is so well established that it feels like one of ours. Nectar-rich, with a long flowering season, it is a valuable plant for butterflies and bumblebees. Its long, thin flowers are accessible to these long-tongued insects, but not to wasps and hoverflies. The fruits have a fluffy pappus, which aids wind dispersal.

Plant type Valerian family, Valerianaceae. *Flowers* June–August. *Height* 30–80cm. *Description* Erect perennial herb. Leaves are grey-green, oval-lanceolate, untoothed, 5–10cm long. Inflorescence is a terminal panicle of deep pink, scarlet or white flowers, each with a corolla 5mm across and 8–10mm long, with a pointed spur a further 3–4mm long and a solitary protruding stamen. White variants may be confused with Common Valerian (p.74), but that species has divided (pinnate) leaves and unspurred flowers with three protruding stamens. *Companion species* Sea-kale (p.412), Sheep's-fescue (p.213) and Sheep's Sorrel (p.366). *Distribution* Introduced. It was grown in Britain before 1597 but not recorded in the wild until 1763. Red Valerian is very common in the south of Britain but becomes rare further north and is mostly absent from northern and western Scotland, apart from a few coastal colonies. In Ireland, it is quite common in the south and east, but rare in much of the north and west. *Habitat* Thoroughly naturalised on sea cliffs, limestone rocky outcrops and pavements, rocky waste ground, quarries, railway banks, old walls and buildings and in other well-drained, disturbed and open habitats.

Rock Samphire
(Crithmum maritimum)

The succulent stems and leathery leaves of Rock Samphire are an adaptation to the highly saline habitat in which it grows – on almost every stretch of cliff and rocky seashore on the British coast. This is not related to what most of us call samphire: Common Glasswort (p.395), the fleshy, edible plant that covers coastal mudflats, which you can buy from fishmongers in early summer. Rock Samphire is an evergreen sea-cliff plant with a herby, slightly lemony flavour, which was hugely popular as a brined and pickled vegetable in the sixteenth and seventeenth centuries. It is at its most tender and delicious before it flowers, so it is best picked in May or early June. Add the tender young leaves to salads or pickle them in a dill-rich mix, to make a delicious accompaniment to cold meats, pork or duck rillettes, or a plate of bread and cheese. Valuable for its high Vitamin C content, it used to be widely harvested all around our coast, but it is now only rarely foraged.

Plant type Carrot family, Apiaceae. *Flowers* June–August. *Height* Up to 30cm. *Description* Spreading perennial herb. Leaves are triangular in outline and deeply divided once or twice into narrow, fleshy, rounded segments. Flowers are yellow-green, 2mm across, arranged into many-rayed umbels, 3–6mm wide, with narrow bracts and bracteoles. *Companion species* It usually grows on its own in a rocky crevice. *Distribution* Native. It occurs on the western and southern coastlines of Britain. On the west coast, it reaches no further north than Ayrshire and Islay, while on the East Anglian coast it does not reach further north than Suffolk. It is found along the Irish coast, less frequently in the north. *Habitat* Spray-drenched rock crevices and ledges on sea cliffs, coastal rocks and stabilised shingle; also in maritime grassland and artificial habitats, such as harbour walls and stone sea defences. It appears indifferent to soil reaction, being found on many rock types, from chalk and limestone to granite.

Scot's Lovage
(Ligusticum scoticum)

The wild coastal form of the garden herb lovage has similar-tasting leaves and seeds, like intense, smoky celery. When you bruise or crush a leaf, it fills the air with a strong smell of parsley crossed with celery. It grows on the rocky coasts of Scotland and Northern Ireland, where its young and tender stems and leaves have long been harvested to be chopped and added to meats or prepared as a salad. The natives of the Shetland Islands have a traditional affection for it and used to eat it raw, as well as boiled, giving it the Gaelic name *siunas*. It is too rare now for picking, tending to survive in impossible-to-reach crevices on sheer cliffs. The seeds of Scot's Lovage drop into the water from these precarious sites and float off, retaining some viability after a year in seawater, hopefully washing up somewhere suitable to germinate.

Plant type Carrot family, Apiaceae. *Flowers* July. *Height* 20–90cm. *Description* Stocky, hairless perennial herb. Stems are stiff, ribbed and often purplish. Leaves are once or twice trifoliate, dark shiny green and leathery, with toothed leaflets, each 3–5 cm long. Leaf stalks have inflated, sheathing stems. Inflorescence is a dense umbel (4–6cm across) of small, greenish-white flowers, each of which is 2mm across, with linear bracts and bracteoles. You could confuse this with Alexanders (p.62), but that has acid-green flowers and is very rare on most of the Scottish coast, where Scots Lovage is found. *Companion species* It tends to grow on its own in rocky crevices. *Distribution* Native. It is quite frequent and locally common on the coasts of Scotland and Northern Ireland, but absent from England and Wales. *Habitat* Coastal rock crevices and free-draining skeletal soils by the sea. Habitats include cliffs, rocky shores and platforms, spray-drenched shingle, stabilised sand dunes and stone sea-defence walls.

Sea Arrowgrass
(Triglochin maritima)

The vertical spires of Sea Arrowgrass, rich green dusted with amber, moving to green-yellow, are an interesting contrast to the fluffy pink-and-mauve abundance of Thrift (p.420), Sea Aster (right) and Common Sea-lavender (p.397) on the salt marshes and peaty sea loch edges where it grows. The spikes look like a Bog Asphodel (p.350) that is still in bud, or one of those baby corn-on-the-cobs stretched to three or four times its natural length. The spire is not perfectly vertical, but bends and wavers slightly as it climbs. Rising above the vegetation and flowers around it, it is often visible from thirty metres away. Sea Arrowgrass is wind-pollinated, so there is no need for brilliant colours to draw pollinators in. Each spike is made up of small, nondescript rows of flowers, which, rather like the yellow-green flowers of Wild Mignonette (p.216) or Weld (p.264), have a discreet but definite presence.

Plant type Arrowgrass family, Juncaginaceae. *Flowers* July–September. *Height* Up to 50cm. *Description* Short to medium, erect, hairless, rhizomatous perennial herb. Leaves are linear, fleshy and half-cylindrical but not furrowed or aromatic. Inflorescence is a dense raceme of many fleshy, green, short-stalked flowers. Fruit is egg-shaped, 3–4mm long. It can be confused with Sea Plantain (p.415), although that has a more compact flower spike. *Companion species* Common Sea-lavender, Sea Aster, Sea Plantain and Thrift. *Distribution* Native. It is found along the British and Irish coasts. There are also a few inland sites. *Habitat* Saline habitats. It is typical of coastal and estuarine salt marshes and closely grazed brackish grassland, where it is usually found in closely grazed turf. It is also found along the banks of brackish drainage dykes and in grassy places along rocky shores. Very rarely, it grows on salt-treated roads.

Sea Aster
(Aster tripolium)

Looked at individually, Sea Aster is a bit dishevelled and weather-beaten, the petals ramshackledly arranged around a typical aster yellow heart. But a mass of it can be a great sight from afar, stretching as far as the eye can see in a drifty, distant haze. I remember coming across it in North Uist in the Outer Hebrides on a beautiful day. The carpet of Sea Aster mauve was continual from where we stood for a few hundred yards until it met a slither of pure white sand and then turquoise sea. It felt as if we had landed in paradise. As with many coastal plants – and particularly those of the salt marsh – its leaves are very fleshy in adaptation to their saline habitat. The leaf thickness makes it tougher, better to withstand the salt spray and severe winds that are common on the coast, and the extra leaf bulk enables it to retain fresh water in its leaves.

Plant type Daisy family, Asteraceae. *Flowers* July–October. *Height* 15–100cm. *Description* Hairless annual or short-lived perennial. Leaves are fleshy, linear-lanceolate, untoothed, 7–12cm long. Stem is reddish, erect and often branched at the base. Flower heads are 8–20mm across with spreading mauve ray florets and yellow disc florets, and are borne in large, usually flat-topped panicles. Garden escape Michaelmas-daisies look quite similar, but do not have fleshy leaves. *Companion species* Common Cord grass (p.395), Common Scurvygrass (p.397), Sea Arrowgrass (left), Sea Milkwort (p.413) and Sea Plantain (p.415). *Distribution* Native. It is locally common along most of the coastline of the British Isles, becoming scarce only in the far north of Scotland. *Habitat* Low elevations in ungrazed or lightly grazed salt marshes, especially along creek sides, and also on muddy sea banks, tidal riverbanks and in brackish ditches. In western Britain and Ireland it also grows among rocks and on exposed sea cliffs. It occurs very locally in inland salt marshes and recently it has been recorded beside salt-treated roads.

Sea Beet

(Beta vulgaris ssp. *maritima)*

The leathery, upright leaves and densely packed green flower spikes of Sea Beet appear all over the cliffs and seashore; it is able to withstand sea spray because of its waxy leaf texture. It is particularly noticeable in spring, where there are few other plants on the same scale around it. By summer, it has merged into the general coastal lushness, but it is remarkable for looking strong and healthy even after a spring storm. This is the progenitor of an important group of cultivated plants, including sugar beet, beetroot and perpetual spinach. It has itself been grown for at least two hundred years for its long, fleshy roots and highly nutritious leaves. You can certainly forage for it because it is so abundant, the leaves best when big and lush in spring, before they toughen up as the plants flower. They are best de-stemmed and eaten raw in a salad with other strong-tasting leaves – and particularly good mixed with Watercress (p.320) and purslane and topped with a strong blue cheese. Sea Beet also makes a robust-tasting soup and is lovely as a creamed green to eat with meat or fish.

Plant type Goosefoot family, Amaranthaceae. *Flowers* July–September. *Height* Up to 1m. *Description* Sprawling, hairless perennial herb. Leaves are glossy, dark green, narrow, oblong, untoothed with a cordate base. Stem is fleshy with red stripes. Flowers are green and have five sepals. *Companion species* Common Orache (p.396), Red Valerian (p.407) and Thrift (p.420). *Distribution* Native. Confined to the coast. It is common in England and Wales, but less so in Scotland. In Ireland, it is common on most of the east and south coastlines, but less so on the north-west coastline. *Habitat* Coastal rocks and cliffs, salt-marsh drift lines, sea walls and sand and shingle beaches, favouring nutrient-enriched sites, such as seabird cliffs and coastal paths popular with dog walkers.

Sea Bindweed

(Calystegia soldanella)

Wouldn't it be lovely to eat out of a bowl that looked like this, a soft and subtly coloured version of Brighton rock? The porcelain-like pink and white trumpet flowers identify Sea Bindweed immediately: there is nothing else that remotely resembles it growing on the coast. Its relation Field Bindweed (p.248) is often stripy, too, but its stripes are paler, and it does not have the small and very characteristic kidney-shaped leaves of the sea species. Unlike other bindweeds, Sea Bindweed does not wind around other plants. Instead, it trails over the upper parts of beaches, its stems often partially buried beneath the shingle or sand. Up it pops again to form another stripy colony, typically just above the highest seaweed line. The young shoots are edible and used to be cooked or pickled as a samphire substitute, but it is now probably not frequent enough to forage.

Plant type Bindweed family, Convolvulaceae. *Flowers* June–August. *Height* Sprawls to 60cm. *Description* Creeping, hairless perennial herb with far-creeping rhizomes. Leaves are fleshy and kidney-shaped, 1–4cm across. Flowers have trumpet-shaped corollas, 2.5–4cm across, pink with white stripes. They have five stamens and bracts that are shorter than the five sepals. *Companion species* Common Orache (p.396), Sea Beet (left), Sea-holly (opposite), Sea Rocket (p.416) and Spear-leaved Orache (p.419). *Distribution* Native. It is found along much of the coast of Britain and Ireland – I have seen it on beaches from the Outer Hebrides to Kent – although it is never particularly common. It is quite scarce on the coasts of north-east England and eastern Scotland. It is also very localised on the coasts of southern England and western Ireland. *Habitat* Coastal sand dunes and above the strand line on shingle and sandy beaches.

Sea Campion

(Silene uniflora)

Walk by the sea on a blustery spring morning and Sea Campion will be one of the few plants whose flowers are already on show. The nearest bit of coast to where I live is the shingle beach at Dungeness in Kent, and there Sea Campion mixes with the odd clump of Wallflower (p.422), providing the first sign of new spring life. There are huge and architectural mounds of Sea-kale (p.412) and clumps of Red Valerian (p.407), but neither show any sign of bud or flower until spring is nearly over. I love the three colours of Sea Campion – the dark bluey green of the leaves, the smoky purple of the calyx and the undiluted white of the petals. The common name Campion is said to derive from the Latin *campus*, meaning 'plain' or 'sport's field'. The flowers were used in the floral crowns with which the winners of Roman public games were decorated. This is also where 'champion' comes from.

Plant type Pink family, Caryophyllaceae. *Flowers* May–August. *Height* Up to 25cm. *Description* Prostrate, usually hairless perennial herb with erect flowering shoots. Leaves are elliptical to lanceolate, fleshy, waxy and bluish grey. White flowers, 20–25mm across, have notched petals and a cylindrical-oblong calyx tube, 17–20mm long. *Companion species* Biting Stonecrop (p.392), English Stonecrop (p.401), Red Valerian, Sea-kale and Wallflower. *Distribution* Native. Found along the coastline of the British Isles and common in many places, especially along the west coast. It is absent from some stretches of the east coast. It is also found inland in some upland parts of the British Isles, although such colonies are quite localised. *Habitat* Sea cliffs, ledges, rocky ground, shingle beaches and sea walls. It is able to tolerate high levels of nutrient enrichment, enabling it to thrive in seabird colonies. It is also found on inland shingle deposits, such as stream- and riversides.

Sea-holly

(Eryngium maritimum)

Sea-holly is in a class of its own, with its angular, jagged grace and effortless glamour. The silver-frosted, holly-like leaves emerge in mid spring and look good until late autumn – the frosting is in fact a waxy cuticle, which covers the leaf surface, preventing water loss and protecting the leaves against the harsh seaside wind and sun. The flower heads have an egg-like centre, encircled with what looks like a Tudor ruff. They start blue-silver, drying to a more washed-out, driftwood colour, elegant to the very last. Not surprisingly, many of us have introduced this to the drier patches of our gardens and it does well on freely drained soil. Until the twentieth century, it was a common sight on sandy beaches round the coast, but for a variety of reasons – some people digging them up to take home; others ripping them out from popular tourist beaches because of their prickles – it is now quite rare and considered endangered. It has been crossed with other European natives to form some excellent garden plants.

Plant type Carrot family, Apiaceae. *Flowers* July–September. *Height* 30–60cm. *Description* Branched, spiny, hairless perennial. Leaves are waxy, grey-green and 5–12cm long, with thick, spiny margins. Basal leaves are palmate and stalked; stem leaves are stalkless. Like true thistles, the flower head is a collection of many tiny flowers, the whole spike a dense, oval umbel, 25–40mm long. Each individual flower is clear blue and has spine-like, three-lobed bracts. *Companion species* Common Stork's-bill (p.398), Marram (p.405), Wild Onion (p.427) and Yellow Horned-poppy (p.427). *Distribution* Native. Locally frequent along most of the coasts of Britain and Ireland, although very rare in north-east England and absent from eastern and northern Scotland. *Habitat* Usually sand dunes, although occasional on shingle.

Sea-kale
(Crambe maritima)

If I drive to the coast from where I live and walk along the shingle beach at Dungeness, one of the first plants I see in spring is Sea-kale. Its newly emerged leaves decorate the beach in well-spaced dollops, like sub-aquatic growths of coral on the seabed. Every leaf is a glamorous mix of grey and purple, with a puckered shape, as if someone has threaded around its edge and pulled the string to gather it. When light-deprived, the leaves are a great delicacy: tender and cabbagey. My mother used to grow it in her garden, the crowns earthed up and blanched under forcing pots, like rhubarb. The white, honey-scented flowers, beloved of pollinator insects, taste delicious, too. Sea-kale has declined in many parts of its range, probably as a result of increased sea-defence works. Collecting it would be frowned upon, particularly as many of its localities are protected for wildlife. This has led to a gradual increase in some areas.

Plant type Cabbage family, Brassicaceae. *Flowers* May–June. *Height* 40–60cm. *Description* Large, stout, clump-forming perennial herb. Basal leaves are large, quite fleshy, waxy and strongly glaucous, pinnately lobed with undulate, wavy margins, up to 100cm long. Upper leaves are smaller and narrower. Flowers, 10–15mm across, are arranged in dense, broad, flat-topped panicles. Fruit is spherical and pea-shaped – it floats in the sea and remains viable in salt water, which allows it to colonise new shingle. *Companion species* Bittersweet (p.393), Red Valerian (p.407), Sea Campion (p.411), Sea Pea (opposite) and Yellow Horned-poppy (p.427). *Distribution* Native. It is found along the coast of the British Isles, commonest on the south and east coasts between Dorset and Suffolk. It is rather rare and local in Devon and Cornwall. It is also quite common on the coasts of north Wales, Cumbria and Dumfries and Galloway. It is absent from the coast of northern Scotland. *Habitat* Shingle and boulder beaches, occasionally on dunes (where they overlay shingle) and cliffs. It is often found where there is a rich accumulation of seaweed humus.

Sea Mayweed
(Tripleurospermum maritimum)

It is very easy to walk past this and think that it is just another white daisy. But Sea Mayweed is a pretty plant, which is worth a second look for its simple, single flowers with broad, showy white petals around a golden heart. The leaves are elegant, too, highly cut and almost ferny. They are slightly succulent – like those of many coastal plants – so they can retain moisture and tolerate harsh, drying seaside conditions. Sea Mayweed can become massive, a metre-high globe, growing on highly nitrogenated guano-drenched cliffs and the grasslands above and below. It cannot tolerate grazing, so where sheep can get at it, it does not survive. This looks very much like Scented Mayweed (*Matricaria chamomilla*), although neither its leaves nor its flowers are scented. Scentless Mayweed (p.259) is also similar, but it does not have fleshy leaves.

Plant type Daisy family, Asteraceae. *Flowers* July–September. *Height* 60cm. *Description* Low to medium biennial or occasionally annual herb. Stems are spreading or prostrate, and hairless. Leaves are alternate, twice to three times pinnately lobed, with short, fleshy segments. Flower heads are 15–50mm across, long-stalked and solitary, with white, spreading ray florets and yellow disc florets. Fruit has two elongated black spots (oil glands) on one side. Scentless Mayweed has fruit with circular oil glands. *Companion species* Common Orache (p.396), Marram (p.405), Sea Rocket (p.416) and Spear-leaved Orache (p.419). *Distribution* Native. Common on most of the coast of Britain and Ireland. It is scarce in a few localised stretches, such as the coast between Dungeness in Kent and Selsey Bill in West Sussex. *Habitat* It is found in a wide range of coastal habitats, including open sand, shingle, cliffs, walls and waste ground. It often grows on the drift line, and is also found rarely inland on road verges.

Sea-milkwort
(Glaux maritima)

Sea-milkwort's small, bright pink flowers are like beacons in the reduced-colour surroundings of the salt marshes, shingle, sandy beaches and cliffs where it grows. The generic name *Glaux* is of Greek origin and means 'bluish green', a reference to the tone of its leaves. This unusual-looking plant looks as if it is covered with the lightest sheen of smoky silver. It is the only British native in this genus. The sepals act as petals, with five pink lobes and no true petals to the flowers. The flowers are unstalked, each tucked in to the base of a leaf. As you would expect, Sea-milkwort has succulent leaves, which form large carpeting colonies that can be seen from quite a distance, even when not in flower. The plants creep along the ground, their stems rooting as they spread, making dense monocultural patches. Its common name is probably due to its slight resemblance to the dark blue-purple Common Milkwort (p.147). It is small like a milkwort – usually about 10cm high – but it spreads out to many times that diameter.

Plant type Primrose family, Primulaceae. *Flowers* June–August. *Height* 10–30cm. *Description* Creeping and ascending perennial herb. Leaves are quite fleshy, strap-shaped and blunt, 4–12mm long, arranged opposite one another. Flowers are solitary, 5mm across, with a pink, five-lobed calyx located in the leaf axils. Sea Sandwort (p.416) has similar foliage but greenish-white flowers. *Companion species* Common Scurvygrass (p.397), Sea Arrowgrass (p.409), Sea Aster (p.409) and Sea Sandwort. *Distribution* Native. Common along the coast of the British Isles. It occurs at a very few inland localities. *Habitat* It typically forms dense colonies on moist, saline soils. Habitats include salt marshes, strand lines, damp shingle, wet sand, brackish dune slacks, aerobic mud and spray-drenched rock crevices.

Sea Pea
(Lathyrus japonicus)

The Sea Pea is one of our showiest wild plants. Its spectacular-coloured flowers are always a joy to find, billowing out all over the shingle banks at Dungeness in Kent. The seeds are quite large, like a smaller version of the garden pea, and Richard Mabey writes in *Flora Britannica* of a story that 'during a seventeenth-century famine on the Suffolk coast, villagers kept themselves alive by eating these peas'. They are dispersed by the sea and can remain floating and viable for up to five years: the little offshoot colonies that we have in the north of England and Ireland are due to seed floating in from our own coast or possibly that of America. This durability also accounts for its extensive native range, along much of the coast of Europe, North and South America and even the Pacific coast of Asia. The flowers are pollinated by long-tongued bumblebees, attracted by the brilliant colour and abundant nectar and pollen.

Plant type Pea family, Fabaceae. *Flowers* May–August. *Height* Sprawls up to 100cm long. *Description* Prostrate, almost hairless perennial herb. Leaves are pinnately divided into two to five pairs of grey-green leaflets, terminating with a fleshy tendril (occasionally this is absent). Each tendril is elliptical and rather blunt, 2–4cm long. Flowers are pink-purple (fading to blue), 14–20mm long and arranged in racemes of five to fifteen. Pod is hairless, 3–5cm long and quite similar to that of a garden pea. *Companion species* Red Valerian (p.407), Sea-kale (p.412), Sheep's Sorrel (p.366) and Yellow Horned-poppy (p.427). *Distribution* Native. Scattered along the coast from Great Yarmouth to Rye in south-east England. It is very rare on the coast away from there, but it is found in Dorset and on the Isle of Wight. There are colonies in Northumberland, Angus and Aberdeenshire. It is also scattered, very rarely, along the southern and western coasts of Ireland. *Habitat* Coastal shingle, where it forms conspicuous patches, and, less frequently, fixed sand dunes and dune-covered shingle ridges.

Sea Plantain
(Plantago maritima)

This is a compact, coastal form of the plantain family, which looks similar to Buck's-horn Plantain (p.394), but has straight-tipped, miniature strap-shaped leaves without the antler-like fork at the ends. It might have a couple of teeth on the sides of each leaf, but not the regular horns of the Buck's-horn Plantain. Sea Plantain comes into flower later, too. The flowers are dull, like tiny yellow-green to brown bulrushes. It is one of the few plants that can survive in a salt marsh, where twice a day much of the vegetation is inundated with seawater. It is smaller and lower growing on saturated mud, taller in less salty situations. Like other seaside plants, such as Danish Scurvygrass (p.78), which carpets central reservations with its white flowers in spring, Sea Plantain has spread recently along salt-treated roads, particularly in Scotland.

Plant type Plantain family, Plantaginaceae. *Flowers* June–August. *Height* 5–20cm. *Description* Woody based, almost hairless perennial herb. Leaves are narrow, linear and fleshy, held erect. Inflorescence spike is 2–6cm tall, on a long, erect, unbranched, unfurrowed stalk. Stamens are pale yellow. The leaves are much narrower than those of Ribwort Plantain (p.162) and the inflorescence is more elongated. Buck's-horn Plantain differs in its flat rosette of downy and more divided (pinnatifid) leaves. However, occasionally Buck's-horn Plantain has undivided leaves, in which case it may be separated from Sea Plantain by having leaves with only one to three veins (Sea Plantain has three to five veins on each leaf). *Companion species* Buck's-horn Plantain, Sea Aster (p.409), Sea-milkwort (p.413) and Sea Sandwort (p.416). *Distribution* Native. It is quite common on most coastlines and is also found in some inland areas, particularly in western and northern Scotland, Snowdonia and the north Pennines. *Habitat* A typical plant of salt marshes, it is also found in short, brackish grassland and the crevices of sea cliffs. In mountainous regions, it is often found beside streams.

Sea-purslane
(Atriplex portulacoides)

The blue-green leaves of Sea-purslane form mud-carpeting colonies in the mudflats, creeks and estuaries of the East Anglian coast. Its leaves, stems and bobbly, amber-grey flowers have a slightly mealy texture, as if they have been dipped in bronze-coloured flour and dusted off gently. The dull, dense flower spikes make it immediately recognisable as a member of the edible goosefoot family, and you can eat the leaves raw or quickly cooked (they turn a brilliant green). They are best picked off the main stem, so harvest the stem tips with scissors and pick off the leaves. Sea-purslane has a particular liking for the edges of small patches of salt water, and in the salt marshes and estuaries of Suffolk and Norfolk, every creek and inlet drainage channel is bordered with a light grey band of this plant. Sea-purslane seed is an important part of the winter diet of the twite and corn bunting.

Plant type Goosefoot family, Amaranthaceae. *Flowers* July–September. *Height* Up to 80cm. *Description* Low shrub. Leaves are stalked, elliptical, untoothed and arranged opposite one another. Flowers are very small, greyish and stalkless, with five sepals, arranged in dense spikes. Fruit is enclosed by a pair of triangular bracteoles that are broadest at the three-lobed tip. *Companion species* Common Sea-lavender (p.397), Grass-leaved Orache (p.401), Sea Arrowgrass (p.409) and Sea Wormwood (p.417). *Distribution* Native. It is common on the south and east coasts of England between the Humber Estuary and Cornwall. It is also quite common on the south coast of Wales and between Anglesey and Cumbria. It is found on the coastlines of Northumberland, the Isle of Man and Dumfries and Galloway, but is absent from the rest of Scotland. It is quite frequent on the east coast of Ireland, but rare in the west. *Habitat* It forms a conspicuous zone along the upper levels of coastal and estuarine marshes and it also fringes the tops of the banks of salt-marsh creeks and pools. In west Britain and Ireland, it also occurs locally on coastal rocks and cliffs.

Sea Rocket
(Cakile maritime)

With its pink, white or lavender flowers and bright green, lush leaves, Sea Rocket is one of the prettiest coastal plants. It reminds me strongly of a more delicate, single-flowered version of a garden stock. This tends to form a narrow but distinct line along the top of a beach, getting its nourishment from the extra organic matter that collects at the storm-tide line. It is often surrounded by driftwood, seaweed and even litter. Like many coastal species, it has succulent leaves and stems that have evolved to retain water, so it can survive in the free-draining sand. Sea Rocket is a pioneer species, able to grow where few other plants can survive. It produces a long taproot that anchors it in the sand. This also stabilises the sand, which often accumulates around the base of the plant and forms into miniature dunes, which may or may not gradually build into something much larger. Bees, flies, beetles and butterflies pollinate the flowers, and the seeds are distributed by the tide. This is not the rocket that is widely cultivated – Sea Rocket has a very bitter taste, although the leaves are rich in Vitamin C. It has only ever been eaten as a famine food.

Plant type Cabbage family, Brassicaceae. *Flowers* June–August. *Height* Up to 50cm. *Description* Prostrate to erect, hairless, succulent annual. Leaves are linear to oblong, shiny, simply or pinnately divided. Flowers are 6–12mm across and held in racemes. Fruit is fleshy stalked, 10–25mm long. *Companion species* Common Orache (p.396), Sea Mayweed (p.412) and Spear-leaved Orache (p.419). *Distribution* Native. Frequent along much of the coastline of Britain and Ireland. It is localised in a few areas, such as the Severn Estuary, south-west Ireland and north-west Scotland. *Habitat* Sandy seashores and coastal dunes, often most abundant along the winter storm-tide line, where there is a plentiful supply of nutrients.

Sea Sandwort
(Honckenya peploides)

This spreads out in bright green carpets over shingle beaches all round our coast. It stands out for its colour, with many leaves around it being grey. As with many coastal species, the fleshiness of its succulent and glossy leaves means that the plant can put up with the thrashing of the weather and the high-salt environment. The small flowers are hardly noticeable, pale green-white and tucked between the leaves. Sea Sandwort is known as Sea Purslane in North America because the leaves are edible. They are tender and sweet in the spring, good in a salad and an excellent replacement for peas in a vegetable soup. Sea Sandwort is one of the earliest colonisers of sand dunes and shingle, making it important as one of the main defenders of Britain's shores. It has a strong network of roots, which anchor it in the sand or shingle, enabling the plant to act as a miniature windbreak. Slowly, more and more sand accumulates around it to form the beginning of a dune. If the wind changes direction and the plant gets buried, it sends up new shoots, which also root. It continues to grow in severe and barren circumstances, quickly forming large, tangled mats that help to rebuild and protect the coastline.

Plant type Pink family, Caryophyllaceae. *Flowers* May–August. *Height* 15–20cm. *Description* Succulent, creeping perennial herb. Leaves are oval, pointed, hairless, fleshy and stalkless, 6–18mm long. Flowers have five blunt, unnotched petals, which are about the same length as the sepals, and ten stamens. *Companion species* Common Stork's-bill (p.398), Sea Campion (p.411), Sea-holly (p.411) and Sea-kale (p.412). *Distribution* Native. Locally common on much of the coast of Britain and Ireland. It is scarce only on a few stretches of coastline in eastern and southern England. *Habitat* It may be abundant on shingle beaches and as a pioneer colonist of foreshore dunes.

Sea Wormwood
(*Artemisia maritima*)

The clean and fresh silver stems and leaves of Sea Wormwood provide an invaluable lift in the colour palette of the salt marshes where it grows. The plants are at their brightest before flowering, dulling a little when the boring yellow, bobbly flowers appear. Sea Wormwood is related to Mugwort (p.99), the silver-leaved plant that appears along the roadside in summer, but its leaves are a much brighter silver and all the better for it. As a backdrop to the purples and mauves of Common Sea-lavender (p.397) or Sea Aster (p.409) when they flower in summer, it creates a plant combination to rival any that you will find in a carefully planned garden. Sea Wormwood has a distinctive smell that it shares with garden artemisias, a strong, bitter scent that is sharp and refreshing.

Plant type Daisy family, Asteraceae. *Flowers* August–September. *Height* 20–50cm. *Description* Erect or spreading, strongly aromatic perennial herb. Leaves are 2–5cm long, woolly on both sides, stalked at the base, stalkless above, twice pinnate with blunt, linear segments and no more than 1mm wide. Flower heads are 1–2mm across, drooping with yellow or reddish florets, and arranged in panicles. *Companion species* Common Sea-lavender, Grass-leaved Orache (p.401), Sea Arrowgrass (p.409) and Sea Aster. *Distribution* Native. Quite frequent on much of the coastline of Great Britain, especially from the Humber Estuary to the Isle of Wight. It is absent from the coasts of north and west Scotland and much of south-west England. In Ireland, it is found on both the east and west coasts, but is rare. *Habitat* Sea Wormwood favours the upper levels of salt and brackish marshes. It may also be found in the brackish dykes of drained, estuarine marshes, as well as sea cliffs, shingle, walls and waste ground close to the sea. The banks of tidal rivers are another favoured habitat.

Sheep's-bit
(*Jasione montana*)

It is the true sky-blueness of Sheep's-bit that is remarkable, a beautiful resonant colour that pings out at you as you walk along a cliff top. There is no other plant with colour quite like it. In habit, it is a stocky, floriferous plant, hunkered in against the rocks where it grows and ideally suited to its exposed coastal habitat. It looks like a scabious, each flower head a mass of fifty or more little flowers collected together in a pincushion, although it is unrelated to the scabious clan, being in the bellflower family. As with scabious, the florets are rich with a huge harvest of nectar. This makes them highly alluring to bees, wasps and butterflies. When the leaves or stem of Sheep's-bit are bruised, they emit a strong and rather nasty smell. Despite this, sheep love to graze it, inspiring its common name.

Plant type Bellflower family, Campanulaceae. *Flowers* May–August. *Height* 5–30cm. *Description* Erect or sprawling biennial herb. Basal leaves, which form a rosette, are strap-shaped, wavy edged, slightly toothed and short-stalked, up to 5cm long. Stem leaves are shorter and stalkless. Flowers are pale blue, very small (5mm across) in dense rounded heads, 10–30mm across. It is superficially similar to scabiouses, but there are differences in flower structure and colour and leaf shape: for example, the leaves of Sheep's-bit are alternate and undivided, while scabiouses have opposite leaves that are often very divided. *Companion species* Common Bird's-foot-trefoil (p.145), Kidney Vetch (p.403), Sheep's-fescue (p.213), Sheep's Sorrel (p.366) and Wild Carrot (p.424). *Distribution* Native. Sheep's-bit has a predominantly westerly distribution. It is most frequent in south-west England, Wales, Cumbria and the south-west coast of Scotland. In the east of the British Isles, it is rare and mostly confined to the coast and the Wealden Heaths. In Ireland, its distribution is predominantly coastal and most frequent in the south. *Habitat* Acidic, shallow, well-drained soils. It occurs on sea cliffs, maritime grasslands and heaths and stabilised sand dunes and, inland, on heathland, stone walls, hedge banks and railway cuttings.

Silverweed
(*Potentilla anserina*)

I was brought up surrounded by this plant. Its paint-pot yellow flowers, bright and cheery in the most trampled-on places around gates and trackways, are like those of a yellow Wild Strawberry (p.120), but a good three times the size, just skimming above the leaves. Like the strawberry, Silverweed spreads by runners, which are much more quick-growing in the case of Silverweed. Its leaves are elegant, chiselled and silvery (especially on the undersides), which gives the plant its common name, and in shape they look like miniature palm trees. The roots are edible, and it was even cultivated in some upland areas of Britain, providing an important crop from prehistoric times until the introduction of the potato in the sixteenth century. This was desperation food, as the roots are thread thin, but you can eat them raw, boiled or baked, and they were also dried and ground into flour for bread or gruel. They are high in magnesium and phosphorus, and are said to taste like parsnip or turnip. Known as *brisgean* in Gaelic, it was an important food in the Hebrides, crucial in times of famine, growing in poor soil where little else thrived.

Plant type Rose family, Rosaceae. *Flowers* May–August. *Height* 10–15cm. *Description* Short, hairy, creeping perennial herb. Leaves are pinnate and often silvery in colour, forming rosettes. There are fifteen to thirty-five oblong, sharply toothed leaflets. Yellow, five-petalled flowers, 15–20mm across, are solitary on long stalks in the leaf axils. *Companion species* Common Chickweed (p.239), Pineappleweed (p.255) and Red Bartsia (p.256). *Distribution* Native. Common throughout Britain and Ireland apart from the Scottish Highlands. *Habitat* A sign of disturbed ground, it thrives in places that have seasonal inundation with fresh or brackish water, such as upper salt marsh, shorelines, dunes, rough ground and roadsides.

Slender Thistle
(*Carduus tenuiflorus*)

This is a thistle by Giacometti, strung out and interesting for its bony, spiny presence. Its pink to pale mauve flowers are smaller than those of most thistles and it stands out for being unbranched, with the flowers arranged around just one central stem. It often grows right by the sea, which gives it the other common name of Seaside Thistle. Slender Thistle has spiny wings running up the stem, so you could confuse it with Marsh Thistle (p.312), but that can get a lot taller and has a much darker flower and stem. Another similar species is Plymouth Thistle (*C. pycnocephalus*), a long-standing introduction to the Devonian limestone cliffs at Plymouth, where it persists. Slender Thistle is considered a noxious weed in many places outside its native range, such as North America and Australia.

Plant type Daisy family, Asteraceae. *Flowers* June–August. *Height* 15–100cm. *Description* Medium annual or biennial herb. Stems have broad (up to 5mm), spiny wings. Leaves are lanceolate and lobed with spiny margins, covered in a white cotton substance. Flower heads are 6–10mm across, with oval-lanceolate bracts that are tipped with outward-curving spines. Spear Thistle (p.261) also has winged stems, but has narrower leaves with much longer spines and a larger ruff of bracts. Creeping Thistle (p.150) is also similar, but has unwinged stems. *Companion species* Bittersweet (p.393), Hemlock (p.304), Sheep's Sorrel (p.366) and Viper's-bugloss (p.214). *Distribution* Native. Frequent to locally common on much of the British coastline. It is very rare on the coasts of northern and western Scotland and on the east coast of England between Norfolk and the Scottish border. It is rare inland, and most of these occurrences are considered to be aliens. In Ireland, it is occasional to locally frequent in the east, very rare in the west. *Habitat* Dry, coastal grasslands, seabird colonies, sea walls, upper edges of beaches, sandy waste ground and roadsides. It occurs on well-drained soils, often, but not always, as an alien.

Spear-leaved Orache
(Atriplex prostrata)

Spear-leaved Orache is the biggest and fleshiest of this edible family of coastal plants, and so the most useful to harvest – you can pick a basket quickly and you will not be doing the environment any harm. It is a common plant, which tends to grow in great abundance. Similar to Fat-hen (p.247), it is a spinach-like wild green, which is good served as a base for fish or pork, stuffed with rice and herbs. Like Danish Scurvygrass (p.78) and Sea Plantain (p.415), this is becoming increasingly common inland along main roads that are salted heavily in winter. It is also common on tips, and you may see lush crops of it on and at the base of field muck heaps, as well as in non-herbicide-sprayed cultivated land.

Plant type Goosefoot family, Amaranthaceae. *Flowers* July–October. *Height* 70cm. *Description* Spreading, prostrate or erect annual herb. Leaves are arrow-shaped (hence its other common name, Hastate Orache), alternate and 3–6cm long, with basal leaves at right angles to the stalk. Flowers are unisexual (male and female have separate flowers) and arranged in dense panicles. Fruit has bracteoles that are fused at the base, but not above. Common Orache (p.396) has diamond-shaped leaves that gradually taper to the stalk, while Grass-leaved Orache (p.401) has lanceolate leaves. *Companion species* Common Orache, Sea Mayweed (p.412) and Sea Rocket (p.416). *Distribution* Native. It is common throughout most of England and Wales, except in upland areas. It is more localised in Scotland and Ireland and exhibits a strongly maritime distribution. *Habitat* Beaches, salt marshes and other open, often wet, saline habitats near the sea. It also occurs inland in disturbed areas on moist, fertile, neutral soils, such as the trampled margins of ditches and ponds, cultivated land, tips and waste ground.

Spotted Cat's-ear
(Hypochaeris maculata)

The leaves of Spotted Cat's-ear look and feel like leopard's ears, with a soft, furry texture and random splotches of dark colour. They remind me of those lettuces and chicories with crimson patches that I have seen in Italian markets and fashionable restaurants. The common name is a reference to the shape of the bracts beneath the flower heads, which are said to look like the ears of a domestic cat. Spotted Cat's-ear is one of the most handsome of this dandelion-like genus, but sadly it is also one of the rarest, occuring in rocky, isolated colonies in Cornwall, Cumbria, north Wales and the Channel Islands, and on chalk downland at the northernmost end of the Chilterns into East Anglia. It has been lost from half of its sites since the nineteenth century as a result of habitat loss, principally caused by ploughing and general improvement of natural grassland, as well as undergrazing. It is now confined to twelve localities.

Plant type Daisy family, Asteraceae. *Flowers* June–August. *Height* Up to 60cm. *Description* Rosette-forming, hairy perennial herb. Leaves are green with dark purple blotches, glossy, wavy-toothed, bristly hairy and 7–15cm long, all in a basal rosette. Flower heads are lemon yellow, 3–5cm across, with bristly, usually unbranched stems. Spotted Cat's-ear is easily distinguished from other dandelion-like flowers by its purple-blotched leaves. *Companion species* Common Restharrow (p.396), Thyme Broomrape (p.421), Tormentil (p.371) and Wild Thyme (p.217). *Distribution* Native. Very rare and still declining. *Habitat* Free-draining, usually base-rich substrates. It occurs on chalk and limestone downland, on coastal cliffs over limestone and serpentine, and on wind-blown calcareous sand on the north Cornwall coast. In Jersey, it grows on exposed granite cliffs.

Spring Squill
(Scilla verna)

This flowers so prettily, so early, in such wind-bashed and blasted conditions, that it is a stalwart. It is worth a trek to the coast of the Lizard in Cornwall to see the tapestry of Spring Squill mixed with Sea Campion (p.411) and Thrift (right) and the odd clump of taller Bluebell (p.2). The leaves come up first, dark green and narrower than those of Bluebell, often with a pronounced curl in their shape – once you know them, you will recognise them straight away. The flowers – on short stems to keep them hunkered down – remind me of Spanish Bluebells (p.107): they are the same pale blue with a darker central stripe to each petal, but held facing up, not hanging from the stem. Some stems look top heavy, with a posse of eight or ten flowers on each; others are more modest, with just four or five. They have a faint, sweet scent.

Plant type Asparagus family, Asparagaceae. *Flowers* April–June. *Height* 5–15cm. *Description* Low, hairless perennial bulb. Leaves are narrow, linear and curly, appearing before the flowers in winter/early spring. Flowers are pale violet-blue, 10–16mm across, with six spreading (not joined) petals (correctly, they are tepals) arranged in a dense raceme of two to twelve flowers. Each flower has a purplish bract, longer than the flower stalk. *Companion species* Bluebell, Sea Campion, Thrift. *Distribution* Native. Confined to the west coast of Britain, with a few outlying colonies on the north and east coast of Scotland (frequent in Orkney and Shetland) and Northumberland. It is also found on the north-east coast of Ireland. Although it is very localised, it is often abundant. *Habitat* Short turf and maritime heath on exposed cliff tops and rocky slopes near the sea, sometimes within the zone regularly affected by seawater spray. In areas with a pronounced oceanic climate, it can occur inland on heathland.

Thrift
(Armeria maritima)

Thrift, or Sea Pink, is one of our commonest and prettiest coastal flowers. It is evergreen, and its new, bright green leaves – which resemble short, tough chives – appear through the spring. In May, its hummocks become covered with little pink flowers, each one a fat-headed hatpin stuck into a pincushion. There are some islands in the Hebrides that look pink from five miles out to sea because of the Thrift that covers them; there are also incredible drifts of it on the Lizard in Cornwall. There, collections of plants join up to form trampolines, their springy roots and leaves giving the turf a wonderful bounce underfoot. Thrift looks good even when it is brown and dried, matching the lichens and seaweeds on the rocks around it. Its long roots reach down to levels where the water supply is constant, so it can survive severe weather, infertile soils and high concentrations of salt. The family name, Plumbaginaceae, originated because it was thought that all the plants in this family could cure lead poisoning.

Plant type Thrift family, Plumbaginaceae. *Flowers* April–October. *Height* 5–30cm. *Description* Carpet-forming perennial herb. Leaves are narrow, linear and more or less hairless, with a single vein, 2–10cm long. Inflorescences are dense, terminal, rounded heads (1.5–2.5cm across) of pink or white flowers, on thin stems. *Companion species* Common Bird's-foot-trefoil (p.145), Dyer's Greenweed (p.152), Kidney Vetch (p.403) and Sheep's-bit (p.417). *Distribution* Native. Common on most coastlines throughout the British Isles, especially in the west. It occurs inland in a few upland regions. It also occurs as an occasional garden escape, mostly in southern England. *Habitat* Found in almost every kind of seashore location, from sea cliffs to stone walls, stabilised shingle beaches and salt marshes. Inland, it grows on montane rock ledges, stony flushes and windswept moss heaths, around old lead workings and other metalliferous mine wastes, and on riverside shingle. It also occurs beside salt-treated roads.

Thyme Broomrape
(Orobanche alba)

It is always rather thrilling to find a broomrape. Like oysters and toadstools, these plants are strange, ugly and alluring, like a species that you would find on the moon. The name of the family comes from Greater Broomrape (*O. rapum-genistae*), a parasite of broom that used to be very common but sadly is now much decreased. The second part of the name, 'rape', refers to the way that the swollen base of the stem resembles the tuber of a turnip (*Brassica rapa*). This species is parasitic on Wild Thyme (p.217), and you will always find it in close proximity to a good colony of Wild Thyme on dry cliffs and grasslands in plant-rich places, such as the Lizard in Cornwall. It opens purplish red, gradually browning to brick red as it ages.

Plant type Broomrape family, Orobanchaceae. *Flowers* June–August. *Height* Up to 25cm. *Description* Short, stout, erect annual or perennial herb. Stems are dark purplish red-brown, covered in glandular hairs. Leaves are reduced to lanceolate scales, as are bracts. Flowers are also purplish red, with a two-lipped, five-lobed corolla, 15–25mm long. Broomrapes are all parasitic herbs that can be quite similar in appearance, which could make identification tricky. However, they usually have a specific plant that they will parasitise on, which makes them easier to distinguish. *Companion species* Common Bird's-foot-trefoil (p.145), Dyer's Greenweed (p.152), Tormentil (p.371) and Wild Thyme. *Distribution* Native. This is a very local species. Its stronghold is the west coast of Scotland, but it also occurs to in Wensleydale in north Yorkshire, the coast of Ireland (mostly on the west coast, but there is one site on the south coast) and the south coast of Cornwall. The size of colonies can fluctuate greatly from year to year. *Habitat* Mainly a feature of dry cliff communities, although it does occur on limestone in the Yorkshire Dales.

Tree-mallow
(Malva arborea)

When I first saw this tall, shrubby mallow in the wild, I assumed it was a garden escape. There was a trend for mallows in the 1980s and 1990s, the most common being Garden Tree-mallow (*M.* x *clementii*). True Tree-mallow is not an escape at all but a native – although many sites have arisen from garden cast-outs. It has large magenta flowers, rich in pollen and nectar, which deepen to a rich purple-crimson towards the centre. Seabirds are thought to spread the seeds, which may float long distances – they have an impermeable outer case and can remain viable for years. Tree-mallow is increasing rapidly on the coasts of some Scottish islands and sea cliffs where puffins breed, raising concerns that it may threaten puffin habitats. The increased nutrients and disturbance from the birds encourages the spread of the plant, which swamps the open, bare ground that puffins need for burrowing and nesting.

Plant type Mallow family, Malvaceae. *Flowers* July–September. *Height* Up to 3m. *Description* Erect, shrub-like biennial herb. Leaves are rounded with five to seven lobes. Flowers are 3–5cm across and arranged in terminal racemes, at least two per leaf axil. *Companion species* Sea Beet (p.410), Sea Mayweed (p.412) and Thrift (opposite). *Distribution* Native in western Britain but not eastern Britain. It is mostly confined to the coastlines of Wales and southern England. On the east coast, it is mostly confined to the south of Norfolk; on the west coast, it is frequent south of Morecambe Bay but very rare further north. It occurs on the Isle of Man and the Irish coast. It also occurs inland as a rare alien. *Habitat* Shallow, guano-enriched soils, most frequently among vegetation in seabird roosts and on ground enriched by garden water. Plants are killed by severe frost, which is why it is rarely native inland.

Tutsan
(Hypericum androsaemum)

Right through summer Tutsan provides a succession of bright yellow flowers, small shallow saucers with a fuzz of yellow stamens, like a sea anemone. After the flowers come the berries, which start green, change to a glossy, cherry red and finally turn black in little bunches above the regularly arranged oval leaves. Many people grow this robust plant in the shady spots of their gardens, particularly in the rainier, northern parts of the British Isles. The whole thing turns a rich range of colours – green, ochre, red and crimson – in the autumn, which adds a daub of colour to a dark and dingy corner. At that stage, its leaves have a faint, warm, rather delicious smell, like resin mixed with fruit. This traditionally led to the leaves being used as bookmarks, even until quite recently, particularly in Bibles.

Plant type St John's-wort family, Hypericaceae. *Flowers* June–August. *Height* 40–100cm. *Description* Low deciduous shrub with red stems and oval, stalkless leaves, 5–10cm long. Flowers, usually just one or two together, have yellow petals less than 15mm long and green sepals that are equal to or longer than the petals. Stamens are very prominent – as long as the sepals. Fruit is a small red berry, 5–8mm across, later turning black. *Companion species* Wall Lettuce (p.113), Wild Madder (p.426) and Wood Sage (p.32). *Distribution* Native. Considered to be native in the south and west of Britain, as well as Ireland. It also occurs widely but less frequently in the east of the British Isles and throughout its native range as an alien. *Habitat* Cliffs, woodlands and hedge banks, avoiding acid soils. In the south west, it is a characteristic plant of the high banks of Devon and Cornish hedges, while in northern England and the Burren in Ireland it grows in the grikes of limestone pavement. It occurs outside its native range in much drier, semi-natural and artificial habitats, presumably bird-sown.

Wallflower
(Erysimum cheiri)

We have been growing this native of Greece and the Aegean Islands in our gardens since the Middle Ages. It was often planted in the walls of castles and manor houses, so that the scent would waft through the windows into the rooms. Its perfume is one of the supreme plant scents – sweet but not cloying, heady but not overwhelming – which will fill the air on a warm spring day. First recorded in the wild in 1548, it is widely naturalised throughout central, western and southern Europe. It grows wild in cracks and holes in old walls and, famously, is scattered all over the tops of the White Cliffs of Dover. It has spread along the coast from there, dotted along the shingle beach at Dungeness, where it does not look as if it has been growing wild for 500 years. Rather, it looks as though it has just strolled out of a neighbouring garden.

Plant type Cabbage family, Brassicaceae. *Flowers* April–June. *Height* 20–60cm. *Description* Perennial herb with oblong-lanceolate leaves, 5–10cm long, and forked hairs on leaves and upper stems. Flowers are bright orange-yellow to dark crimson (most cabbages have yellow, white or pink flowers), 2.5cm across. They have four petals, with sepals half the length of the petals, arranged in a stalked raceme. Fruit is a narrow, flattened, hairy pod, 2.5–7cm long. *Companion species* Polypody (p.103) and Red Valerian (p.407). *Distribution* Introduced, probably by the Romans. It is found throughout Britain but is more frequent in the south, becoming rare/absent in the north. Its distribution is largely coastal, but it is found inland, particularly in the London region, the Midlands and in Dorset and Somerset. In Scotland, it is mostly restricted to the east coast. In Ireland, its distribution is scattered and it is very rare in most regions. *Habitat* Widely naturalised on old walls, cliffs and rocks, particularly on calcareous substrates, where it is often persistent. It tolerates poor, thin, dry soils, but a warm site is essential.

White Rock-rose
(Helianthemum apenninum)

The south-facing slopes of Brean Down in Somerset and Torbay in Devon are turned white with an abundance of this rock-rose in spring. These are the only two places in the British Isles where you will see it. It is very common in Mediterranean grasslands, and the reason why it is restricted to these two coastal areas of Britain is the subject of much botanical discussion. One theory is that it is a relic of the flora that would have colonised Britain before the arrival of deciduous trees in the period after the last ice age. Gradually, large trees, such as oak, lime and ash, took over much of the grassland habitat, pushing sun-loving, delicate plants out to coasts, gorges, cliffs and river gaps, where thin soils prevented large trees from taking hold. This theory is now thought to be simplistic, as there were almost certainly large areas of grassland in the great forests kept open by giant browsing herds, so the distribution of White Rock-rose may just be down to chance.

Plant type Rock-rose family, Cistaceae. *Flowers* April–July. *Height* Creeps horizontally up to 50cm. *Description* Prostrate, downy shrub. Leaves are narrow, elliptical-oblong, greyish green, downy on the upper sides, with inrolled margins. Flowers are white, 10–15mm across, with five petals and five sepals. It cannot be confused with Common Rock-rose (p.195), because that has yellow flowers. Perhaps the most similar flower is Wild Strawberry (p.120), but that is easily distinguished by its foliage. White Rock-rose has thin, thyme-like leaves up the stem, while Wild Strawberry has broad, bright green leaves divided into three flat leaflets. *Companion species* Common Bird's-foot-trefoil (p.145), Horseshoe Vetch (p.204) and Wild Thyme (p.217). *Distribution* Native. Confined to coastal grassland near Weston-super-Mare in Somerset and Torquay in Devon. There has been a decline in abundance at some of its sites because of lack of grazing, which causes the grassland to become rank and leads to shrub encroachment. *Habitat* Dry, rocky, coastal, south-facing limestone grassland and cliff edges.

Wild Asparagus
(Asparagus prostratus)

True Wild Asparagus is so rare that it is on the endangered plant list. It is quite unlike the erect, tall-growing Garden Asparagus (*A. officinalis*) that grows as an escape on golf courses and sand dunes along our coast. Wild Asparagus is prostrate and, at first glance, looks more like Common Juniper (p.354). I have seen it on the Lizard in Cornwall, with some plants grazed right down, poking out horizontally from the rocks like miniature fir trees, others more luxurious, running along the boulders like delicate, ferny fabric. This often grows cheek by jowl with Lesser Meadow-rue (p.403), the highly cut leaves of both plants lacing and patterning the green and red serpentine rock behind them. You should never pick Wild Asparagus: it needs to become more abundant, not less. Garden Asparagus is much more widely distributed and quite frequent in much of southern and eastern England.

Plant type Asparagus family, Asparagaceae. *Flowers* June–September. *Height* Up to 30cm. *Description* Prostrate, hairless, dioecious perennial with creeping rhizomes. Stems are procumbent to slightly erect. Leaves are reduced to small scales with clusters of four to fifteen cladodes (flattened stems that look like leaves) in their axils, which are 2–16mm long, glaucous and rigid. Flowers are unisexual, 4.5–6.5mm long, with greenish to pale yellow, bell-shaped, six-lobed perianths, located in the axils of the scale leaves. Fruit is a red berry. *Companion species* Lesser Meadow-rue, Sheep's-fescue (p.213), Wild Carrot (p.424) and Yorkshire-fog (p.169). *Distribution* Native. Confined to Cornwall, Dorset, south Wales and south-east Ireland. There has been a slight decline recently both in distribution and abundance. Many remaining populations are small and have only one sex remaining. *Habitat* Sea cliffs and sand dunes. On cliffs, it prefers free-draining, rocky soils and is often found growing through a dense mat of Red Fescue (*Festuca rubra*). On sand dunes, it prefers the edges of paths.

Wild Cabbage

(Brassica oleracea var. *oleracea)*

The new spring leaves of Wild Cabbage are smoky grey, stalked and veined in bleeding violet-purple, just as showy as the ornamental cabbages sold at garden centres. The leaves dull a bit as they start to flower in May, their tall, airy stems of yellow flowers lasting through summer. This is a noble beast, a plant reminiscent of an ancient dinosaur, with all the freedom and vigour of a pre-tamed life. It is the origin of all the brassicas we grow in our vegetable gardens. It was probably first cultivated in the Mediterranean by the Greeks and Romans, and our seed-grown modern varieties will revert gradually to something similar after several self-sown generations on the edges of compost heaps.

Plant type Cabbage family, Brassicaceae. *Flowers* May–August. *Height* Up to 60cm. *Description* Robust, hairless perennial herb. Leaves are fleshy, undulate, waxy, grey-green and pinnately lobed near the base. Upper leaves clasp the stem. Inflorescence is a loose-flowered raceme (2–3cm across) of large, lemon-yellow flowers. Like all cabbages, its flowers have four petals, arranged in a cross, and four sepals. There are many other yellow-flowered brassicas, but most have tight clusters of flowers. *Companion species* Early Spider-orchid (p.198), Red Valerian (p.407), Rock Samphire (p.408) and Wallflower (p.422). *Distribution* Native. Confined as a native to a handful of very localised sites, mostly along the south coast from Kent to Cornwall, but also along the coasts of south Wales, north Wales and North Yorkshire. There are a few localities in Scotland where it is considered native. It is often abundant where found – some coastal colonies can number several thousand plants. Some botanists doubt that Wild Cabbage is native, but the colonies on the White Cliffs of Dover are regarded as having the strongest claim, having been recorded there for more than four hundred years. *Habitat* Native only on coastal cliffs, usually chalk and limestone, where it is found on exposed rocks and cliff-top grassland and at the base of cliffs. Inland colonies are usually garden escapes.

Wild Carrot

(Daucus carota ssp. *carota)*

I love the white, lacy umbels of Wild Carrot. The crimson to pale pink buds are almost as good, then the seed pods – little green, bead-like seeds on a Catherine wheel of narrow stems. These invert as they dry into a concave bird's nest. If you look closely at a flower head, you will usually see one deep blood-red flower right at the heart. This gives rise to the common name for Wild Carrot of Queen Anne's Lace. Queen Anne was said to have been sowing lace when she pricked her finger and a drop of blood stained the middle of the flower. Wild Carrot is the ancestor of the cultivated carrot, and the leaves and roots smell of carrots, although the roots are too thin to be used as a vegetable.

Plant type Carrot family, Apiaceae. *Flowers* June–August. *Height* Up to 100cm. *Description* Erect, branched perennial herb. Stem is solid and ridged. Leaves are finely divided (three times pinnate). Umbels are many rayed, 3–7cm wide, with many divided bracts forming a 'ruff' beneath. Each flower is 2–3mm across. Fruit is oval, 2.5–4mm long, with four ridges of long spines on the corners. It looks similar to Hogweed (p.156) and Wild Angelica (p.324), but Hogweed has creamier flowers and Wild Angelica has more domed flowers, and the leaves are very different. *Companion species* Buck's-horn Plantain (p.394), Salad Burnet (p.213) and Sea Plantain (p.415). *Distribution* Native. Occurs throughout the British Isles, but is mostly confined to the coast in northern England, Wales and Scotland. It is rare on the east coast of Scotland. In Ireland, it is common, except in some inland parts of Northern Ireland. *Habitat* Dunes and cliff tops near the coast. It grows best on fairly infertile, well-drained, often calcareous, soils. It also occurs on disturbed or open turf on chalk downs, rough pastures on roadsides, waysides and railway banks, quarries, chalk and gravel pits, and waste ground.

Wild Leek

(Allium ampeloprasum)

Wild Leeks are an impressive sight, their towering grey-green stems standing to shoulder height, their flower buds like turned finials. When you find them, it looks as if someone has created an allotment in the middle of nowhere and filled it only with leeks. These are the ancestors of the garden leek and have been growing in the wild since Roman times. They are very rare, growing only on rocky and waste places on the coasts of Cornwall, Somerset, Glamorgan, Pembroke and Guernsey, but you cannot miss them where they grow. Once the buds split open, the large flower globes look much like decorative garden alliums. Each head consists of a ball of bulbils, every one capable of growing where it falls. Around these open small pink flowers, which are thick with nectar, making Wild Leek a Mecca to pollinating insects. It reproduces largely vegetatively by bulbils, rather than by seed.

Plant type Onion family, Alliaceae. *Flowers* July–August. *Height* 60–200cm. *Description* Robust perennial herb. Stems are round. Leaves are grey-green, linear, flat but keeled, rough-edged and up to 60cm long. Flowers are off white to pale purple and bell-shaped, in a dense, many-flowered, globular umbel, 7–10cm across. All parts have a strong onion scent. *Companion species* Hemlock Water-dropwort (p.304), Perennial Rye-grass (p.160) and Red Campion (p.24). *Distribution* Introduced, probably by the Romans. It is mostly confined to the far south west of England and the Channel Islands, where it is locally common. There are a few scattered colonies on the coast of Ireland and the Welsh and southern English coasts. *Habitat* Among rank vegetation in sandy and rocky places near the sea, especially in old fields and hedge banks, on sheltered cliff slopes, by paths and tracks and in drainage ditches and other disturbed places.

Wild Madder

(Rubia peregrina)

This spiky, scrambling plant pokes out between rocks on the coast and in limestone pavements. You can tell it is a member of the bedstraw family by its star-like flowers and square stems, but the flowers are bigger and the plants much larger and more robust than other native members. It is also an evergreen, whereas most bedstraws die down in winter. The flowers are all five-petalled, with each petal ending in a little topknot, and they are a pale, straw yellow rather than the golden yellow of Lady's Bedstraw (p.205). The buds and calyces at the top of each flower stem are a distinctive smoky, pinkish brown, giving a unique colour combination to this plant, which is famous as a source of pink dye (although the principle source of the dye, Madder, is a different species, *R. tinctorum*, introduced from Asia). Wild Madder is one of the few plants that has increased in its distribution as a result of the relaxation of grazing on cliff-top grassland.

Plant type Bedstraw family, Rubiaceae. *Flowers* June–August. *Height* Up to 150cm, but scrambling rather than upright. *Description* Evergreen, woody perennial. Stems are four-angled, sharply prickly edged and wide-spreading. Leaves are elliptical-lanceolate, shiny dark green and leathery, prickly-edged, 2–6cm long, and arranged in whorls of four to six. Flowers have yellow-green, five-lobed corollas, 5mm across. Fruit is a black berry, 4–6mm across. *Companion species* Tutsan (p.422), Wall Lettuce (p.113) and Wood Sage (p.32). *Distribution* Native. Largely confined to south-west England, Wales and the southern half of Ireland, with a few outlying populations on the coasts of Kent and Sussex. It is found inland in some areas, such as Somerset. *Habitat* Cliffs, scrubby grassland or rocky slopes. It may also grow on walls, hedge banks and, occasionally, on calcareous soils inland.

Wild Onion
(*Allium vineale*)

Wild Onion looks so much like one of the smaller garden alliums that you might assume it is a garden escape. But this is a true British native. Two other varieties are sometimes recognised: var. *compactum*, which has bulbils only, and var. *capsuliferum*, which has flowers only. Each bulbil can develop into a new plant. Wild Onion was once considered a harmful weed of cereal crops in southern England – it can resist many selective weedkillers – but it is now a rarer find. The leaves may be used as a garlic or onion substitute; they are best in the spring, as by summer they are rather stringy. The bulbs have a strong garlicky smell and flavour, but are quite small. You can also eat the bulbils, which have a similar taste. The juice of the plant has been used as a moth repellant, and may be rubbed onto exposed parts of the skin to deter biting insects.

Plant type Onion family, Alliaceae. *Flowers* June–July. *Height* Up to 80cm tall. *Description* Variable perennial herb. Two to four leaves are half cylindrical, grooved and hollow, 20–60cm long. Inflorescence usually has both bulbils and flowers, and a papery bract (spathe) at the base, which does not exceed the flowers. Bulbils are oval and greenish purple. Flowers have pink or white perianth segments, 5mm long, and stalks 1–2cm long. *Companion species* Red Valerian (p.407). *Distribution* Native. It occurs throughout much of Britain and Ireland, most frequently in southern England, becoming increasingly restricted to the coast in northern England and Scotland. Wild Onion is locally frequent in the southern half of Ireland, but absent from the northern half, except as a rare garden escape. *Habitat* It prefers dry, calcareous or neutral grasslands and is often found on coastal sand dunes as well as cliff edges, roadsides, hedgerows and cultivated ground.

Yellow Horned-poppy
(*Glaucium flavum*)

To look at the flowers of Yellow-horned Poppy, you would not think that the petals stood a chance in the exposed and windy places where this plant grows. Surprisingly, however, one flower can last several days. Like many seaside plants, it has silver leaves – a beautiful contrast to the zingy lemon-yellow of the flowers – that are crenellated like the battlements of a Scottish castle. This has never been a common plant and it is always exciting to find it. It has been lost from some sites because of coastal defence work and trampling on tourist beaches. Yellow-horned Poppy can germinate from very old seed, as Richard Mabey recounts in *Flora Britannica*. Twenty-five plants were found in a newly dug drainage ditch half a mile from the sea near Greenhithe in Kent. The site corresponded to the position of the old coastline before the drainage of coastal marshes, so the plants must have germinated from seed aged between 300 and 700 years.

Plant type Poppy family, Papaveraceae. *Flowers* June–August. *Height* 20–90cm. *Description* Tall, branched herb. Leaves are waxy, hairy and pinnately lobed near the base. Stem leaves are less deeply divided. Flowers are yellow, 6–9cm across, and produce a long, sickle-shaped capsule up to 30cm long. It produces a yellow latex from the cut stems and leaves. *Companion species* Bittersweet (p.393), Red Valerian (p.407), Sea-kale (p.412) and Sea Pea (p.413). *Distribution* Native. It is confined to the coast, most frequent in the south east. On the east coast, it is found as far north as Fife; on the west, as far north as Argyll. In Ireland, it is mostly confined to the east. *Habitat* Well-drained habitats near the coast with a preference for basic, rather than acidic soils: shingle banks, stony beaches and, more rarely, among loose rock, on eroding cliffs and on the bare tops of chalk cliffs.

Sea-kale (p.412); Dungeness, Kent, 7 June.

Thrift (p.420), Kynance Cove, the Lizard, Cornwall, 18 June.

Chives (p.394) and Common Bird's-foot-trefoil (p.145), Kynance Cove, the Lizard, Cornwall, 18 June.

Hemlock Water-dropwort (p.304) and Wild Leek (p.426), Kynance Cove, the Lizard, Cornwall, 19 June.

Bloody Crane's-bill (p.393), the Burren, County Clare, Ireland, 21 June.

Red Valerian (p.407), the Burren, County Clare, Ireland, 22 June.

Common Sea-lavender (p.397), Stiffkey, Norfolk, 13 July.

Common Sea-lavender (p.397) and Sea Wormwood (p.417), Stiffkey, Norfolk, 13 July.

Sea Rocket (p.416), Northton, South Harris, Outer Hebrides, 23 July.

Sea Aster (p.409), Balranald, North Uist, Outer Hebrides, 24 July.

Glossary of Family Names

Adoxaceae (Moschatel family)
Small rhizomatous perennials with divided leaves and usually five small flowers borne in a dense, cube-shaped head. Flowers have five united petals (four in terminal flower), five (or four) stamens, each divided into two half-stamens. Fruit is a dry drupe.

Alismataceae (Water-plantain family)
Hairless aquatic herbs characterised by untoothed, parallel-veined, ovate or arrow-shaped (sagittate) leaves and flowers arranged in umbels, each with three petals, three sepals and a superior ovary. Seeds are arranged in dense heads quite similar to those of buttercups. They are not closely related to plantains.

Alliaceae (Onion family)
Herbaceous perennials with rhizomes, bulbs or corms and all leaves basal. Flowers are single or in an umbel, often with papery bracts at the base, with six perianth segments (which may all be similar, or the inner three joined into a cup), six stamens and an ovary with three cells but one style. Fruit is a capsule splitting into three.

Amaranthaceae (Goosefoot family)
Often weedy, annual or perennial herbs or shrubs with usually alternate, slightly fleshy leaves and small greenish flowers in dense clusters in the leaf axils. Flowers have a green or papery perianth of up to five partly joined segments, one to five stamens and three styles. Fruit is a single-seeded capsule or achene.

Apiaceae (Carrot family)
Annual or perennial herbs easily recognised by the umbrella-like inflorescences (umbels) and the often inflated, sheathing bases to the leaf stalks. Leaves are alternate, often pinnate and without stipules. Flowers are typically small and have five petals, five sepals (although many genera have

none), five stamens and two stigmas. Several species have a ruff of bracts at the base of the primary umbel, and bracteoles at the base of the secondary umbel. Fruit is dry, often ribbed, and divides into two parts.

Apocynaceae (Periwinkle family)
Creeping, somewhat woody-based evergreen perennials with simple, oval, opposite leaves, showy flowers with five sepals, fused at the base, and five somewhat oblique petals spreading from a slender corolla tube.

Aquifoliaceae (Holly family)
Evergreen shrubs or trees with simple, alternate, often spiny leaves, usually dioecious, with small clusters of white, four-parted flowers in the leaf axils. Fruit is a berry-like drupe with four seeds.

Araceae (Lords-and-Ladies family)
Rhizomatous or tuberous perennial herbs characterised by a distinctive spiked inflorescence of tiny flowers known as the spadix (male and female flowers sometimes on separate parts), which is enclosed in a large leaf-like bract, the spathe. Most species are tropical.

Araliaceae (Ivy family)
Evergreen or deciduous shrubs, herbaceous perennials or climbing evergreen shrubs with alternate, often palmately lobed or divided leaves and umbels of small flowers with five minute sepals, five petals and five stamens. Fruit is a black berry containing up to five seeds.

Asparagaceae (Asparagus family)
Diverse family including rhizomatous and bulbous perennials, evergreen shrubs and tree-like perennials with simple, often narrow, rarely spiny-edged leaves usually in a basal rosette. Flowers may be solitary, in racemes or panicles, often showy, with six generally similar perianth segments, six stamens

and a three-celled ovary developing into a capsule or a berry with one or more seeds.

Aspleniaceae (Spleenwort family)
Mostly small, tufted evergreen ferns with undivided, forked, or one to three times pinnate fronds and oblong or elongated sori that are situated along the side veins of the frond undersides.

Asteraceae (Daisy family)
Large family of annuals, perennials and shrubs with simple or palmately or pinnately lobed leaves and many small florets borne on a receptacle, forming dense flower heads that resemble a single flower sitting within a ruff of sepal-like involucral bracts. Each floret has five stamens that are joined to form a tube, often with the style projecting from the tip. There are two types of floret: disc florets, which have a funnel-shaped, five-lobed corolla; and ray florets, which have a long, petal-like flap extending from one side of the corolla; individual florets may be hermaphrodite or unisexual. Some species have flower heads composed solely of ray florets (such as Dandelions), while others have flower heads composed solely of disc florets (such as Pineappleweed). Many species have a combination of both, the typical daisy flower head, with a central area of disc florets surrounded by a ring or rings of ray florets. The calyx, known as the pappus, may be absent, reduced to cup of tiny scales, or represented by a plume of silky hairs, which assists wind dispersal of the achenes.

Balsaminaceae (Balsam family)
Annual or perennial herbs with succulent stems bearing simple, alternate, opposite or whorled leaves and one or more flowers in terminal cymes or in leaf axils. Flowers are two-lipped, with three petal-like sepals, one with a nectar-secreting spur, and five,

partly united petals. The five stamens are joined round the ovary. The fruit is a capsule that opens explosively throwing the seeds some distance.

Betulaceae (Birch family)
Deciduous trees or shrubs with toothed, undivided, alternate leaves. Flowers are tiny, borne in catkins, male and female on the same tree. Male catkins are drooping, with many small, scale-like bracts, each with up to three flowers; female catkins are upright or nodding, with two or three flowers to each small bract. Fruit is a tiny nut, usually with a rounded, membranous wing.

Blechnaceae (Hard-fern family)
Tufted evergreen ferns with once-pinnate fronds produced at the end of scaly rhizomes. The fertile (spore-producing) fronds bear elongated sori either side of the midrib of each pinna and usually differ in appearance from the sterile (non-spore-producing) fronds.

Boraginaceae (Borage family)
Annual or perennial herbs, mostly coarsely hairy or bristly, although a few are hairless. All have alternate, undivided leaves without stipules, and flowers arranged in curved or forked cymes, with a five-toothed calyx, a five-lobed corolla, five stamens and a fruit of four nutlets.

Brassicaceae (Cabbage family)
Annual or perennial herbs with alternate, simple or pinnately lobed leaves without stipules. Flowers have four petals arranged in a cross, four sepals, two stigmas, six stamens (occasionally fewer). Ovary is superior, two-celled and ripens to form a capsule that opens from the bottom upwards by two valves, to release the seeds. Many species are annual weeds of disturbed ground.

Butomaceae (Flowering-rush family)
Hairless aquatic herbs with long, narrowly strap-shaped leaves and flowers arranged in a terminal umbel on a stem longer than the leaves. Each flower has three sepals and three petals, nine stamens and a tight cluster of six carpels.

Campanulaceae (Bellflower family)
Annual or perennial herbs, usually with white sap and unlobed alternate leaves. Flowers are regular and bell-shaped or irregular and two-lipped, solitary or in racemes, spikes or tight clusters, with five partly joined petals, five stamens and an inferior ovary producing a capsule or berry with many small seeds.

Cannabaceae (Hop family)
Annual or perennial, mostly dioecious herbs, sometimes vigorous twining climbers, with alternate or opposite palmately divided leaves. Small greenish flowers, the males in loose clusters or panicles, the females in dense clusters, sometimes forming cone-like fruiting clusters (hops).

Caprifoliaceae (Honeysuckle family)
Herbs, shrubs or woody climbers with opposite leaves, no stipules and flowers arranged in heads or umbels. Flowers may be regular or irregular, with five petals, fused at the base, five sepals, five stamens and inferior ovaries that ripen into fleshy fruit (or rarely into capsules). Showy sterile outer flowers are sometimes present.

Caryophyllaceae (Pink family)
Large family of herbs with untoothed and unlobed leaves that are usually arranged in opposite pairs and do not have stipules. Flowers are typically arranged in cymes and have five sepals and five petals (although sometimes four of each). Many species have notched petals. The number of stamens is usually twice the number of sepals and there are two, three or five styles. Ovary is superior and fruit is a one-celled capsule.

Celastraceae (Spindle family)
Evergreen or deciduous shrubs, small trees or climbers with opposite or alternate leaves. Small, mostly greenish flowers are borne in cymes in the leaf axils, and have four or five sepals, petals and stamens. Fruit is a somewhat fleshy, sometimes lobed capsule splitting to reveal brightly coloured seeds (the colour is from a fleshy coating known as an aril).

Cistaceae (Rock-rose family)
Low-growing, downy shrubs or herbs with simple elliptical leaves arranged in opposite pairs and flowers with five strongly veined sepals (three large, two very small), five petals and many stamens that move away from the ovary when touched.

Colchicaceae (Meadow Saffron family)
Perennial herbs growing from corms, with narrow, strap-shaped leaves appearing in the spring, and crocus-like flowers opening in autumn after the leaves have died down. Flowers have six similar tepals united below to form a long tube, six stamens and a superior three-celled ovary developing into a capsule with many seeds.

Convolvulaceae (Bindweed family)
Annual or perennial herbs, usually climbing, with alternate, undivided leaves; occasionally parasitic and lacking green pigment. Flowers are mostly showy, funnel-shaped and solitary in leaf axils, or tiny in dense clusters.

Cornaceae (Dogwood family)
Small perennial herbs or large deciduous shrubs with simple, opposite leaves and no stipules. Small flowers are borne in umbels at the ends of branches, with four sepals, petals and stamens and a two-celled ovary developing into a fleshy drupe containing one or two seeds.

Crassulaceae (Stonecrop family)
Succulent annual or perennial herbs with alternate or spirally arranged, often very fleshy leaves and flowers mostly in terminal cymes, each with four or five sepals, petals and carpels; there are four, five, eight or ten stamens.

Cucurbitaceae (White Bryony family)
Annuals or perennials with scrambling or climbing stems, often with tendrils, and alternate, usually palmately lobed leaves without stipules. Flowers have five sepals, five petals, three or five stamens and two to three stigmas. Many familiar vegetables are members of this family, including pumpkins, cucumbers, marrows and watermelons.

Cupressaceae (Juniper family)
Monoecious or dioecious, evergreen trees or shrubs that may be distinguished from other conifers by their opposite or whorled leaves. This family includes cypresses and junipers, such as Common Juniper.

Cyperaceae (Sedge family)
Rhizomatous herbaceous perennials with often three-angled stems and grass-like, alternate leaves whose base sheaths the stem. Flowers are tiny, grouped into spikelets, male and female flowers often in separate spikelets on a stem. Fruit is a nutlet.

Dennstaedtiaceae (Bracken family)
Large and vigorous perennial ferns with deciduous fronds borne singly along extensive rhizomes. The fronds are two to three times pinnate and do not have scales at the base. The only native species is bracken.

Dioscoreaceae (Black Bryony family)
Twining herbaceous perennials growing from a tuber, with undivided, alternate leaves. Dioecious, with flowers either solitary or in racemes in the leaf axils, with six sepal-like perianth segments, six stamens and a three-celled ovary with a single style. Fruit is a berry.

Dipsacaceae (Teasel family)
Erect herbs quite similar to members of the daisy family. Flowers are small with inferior ovaries and are arranged in dense heads on a common receptacle with a ruff of bracts beneath each head. However, members of the teasel family also have an epicalyx and narrow, sometimes bristle-like sepals, as well as a tubular, four- to five-lobed corolla. There are two to four stamens and a simple or two-lobed stigma.

Droseraceae (Sundew family)
Small, rosette-forming, herbaceous perennials with reddish leaves covered with sticky hairs to trap and digest small insects. Flowers are in simple cymes, white, regular, with five to eight sepals, petals and stamens, and two to six styles. Flowers often don't open,

being self-pollinated to produce a small, many-seeded capsule.

Dryopteridaceae (Buckler-fern family)
Perennial ferns with fronds that are once to twice pinnate and borne in crowns or in tufts along a creeping rhizome. Sori are located on the side veins on the undersides of some of the pinnules.

Ericaceae (Heather family)
Diverse family of evergreen or deciduous dwarf shrubs, trees and small perennials, with undivided leaves arranged alternately or sometimes opposite on the stems. Flowers have three to five sepals and petals that may be separate or joined. There are as many stamens as petals, or twice the number. The ovary has up to nine cells and a single style. Fruit may be a capsule, berry or drupe. Many are lime-haters.

Euphorbiaceae (Spurge family)
Only two genera in this large family are native to Britain: *Euphorbia* and *Mercurialis*. They may be annual or perennial herbs. Leaves are usually simple and alternate; flowers are often small and complex; the fruit is a three-celled capsule. Stems contain an acrid sap that is watery in *Mercurialis* and a milky latex in *Euphorbia*. Species belonging to *Mercurialis* have dioecious flowers and two-celled ovaries and fruits, while species belonging to *Euphorbia* have monoecious flowers and three-celled ovaries and fruits.

Fabaceae (Pea family)
Annual or perennial herbs, shrubs or trees easily recognised by their distinctive, five-petalled, 'pea-shaped' flowers. The uppermost petal forms an erect 'standard', the two lateral petals form 'wings', and the two lowermost petals form a boat-shaped 'keel'. Each flower has five sepals usually joined into a tubular or bell-shaped calyx, ten stamens of which all or nine are fused into a tube, one style and a superior ovary. Leaves are usually trifoliate or pinnate. Fruit is a pod that splits into two valves to release the seeds.

Fagaceae (Beech family)
Deciduous or evergreen, monoecious trees with simple or deeply lobed alternate leaves with stipules. Flowers are small, the males in nodding catkins or clusters, the females in groups of up to three. Ovary has three or six cells and up to nine styles. Fruit is a nut more or less surrounded by an involucre of woody scales.

Gentianaceae (Gentian family)
Hairless annual or perennial herbs with opposite, untoothed, unstalked leaves, no stipules and forked cyme inflorescences. Flowers have superior ovaries, a four- to five-lobed calyx and a four- to five-lobed corolla.

Geraniaceae (Crane's-bill family)
Annual or perennial herbs with alternate, palmate or pinnate leaves with stipules. Flowers are often quite attractive and have five petals, five sepals, five or ten stamens, five stigmas and a five-celled, superior ovary with a distinctive long beak.

Grossulariaceae (Gooseberry family)
Small deciduous shrubs with alternate, palmately lobed leaves without stipules. Flowers are solitary or in racemes and have five sepals, five petals, two styles joined at the base, an inferior ovary and a berry fruit. Many species are cultivated.

Hippuridaceae (Mare's-tail family)
Aquatic rhizomatous perennial herbs with undivided, thread-like leaves in whorls, and tiny flowers borne singly in the leaf axils. Flowers may be male, female or bisexual and consist of little more than an ovary with a thread-like style and one stamen. Fruit is a small nut with one seed.

Hydrocharitaceae (Frogbit family)
Hairless, aquatic, floating or rooted perennials with submerged or floating (occasionally emergent) leaves. Flowers are usually dioecious, arising from the leaf axils, with three petals, three sepals and inferior ovaries.

Hydrocotylaceae (Pennywort family)
Small herbaceous perennials with prostrate, rooting stems bearing rounded, alternate leaves with stipules. Flowers are small, in umbels, with five minute sepals, five petals, five stamens and a two-celled ovary. Fruit separates into two dry parts when ripe.

Hypericaceae (St John's-wort family)
Distinctive perennial herbs or shrubs characterised by opposite, stalkless, untoothed, simple leaves without stipules and yellow flowers with five sepals, five petals, many stamens, usually joined into three or five bundles, superior ovaries and dry or berry-like fruit capsules. Some have translucent glands on the leaves and many also have coloured glands on the petals and/or sepals.

Iridaceae (Iris family)
Plants with narrow, parallel-veined leaves, inferior ovaries, perianth segments joined into a tube at the base and three stamens. Members of the *Iris* genus have a distinctive flower structure, with three outer tepals (falls) and three erect inner tepals (standards). There are also three, petal-like styles with branched tips (crests). Fruit is a capsule.

Juncaginaceae (Arrowgrass family)
Rhizomatous perennial herbs with narrow, mostly basal leaves forming a rosette, and almost leafless stems bearing a raceme of inconspicuous flowers, each with six tepals, six stamens and a six-celled ovary maturing into a fruit of three or six sections, each containing one seed.

Lamiaceae (Dead-nettle family)
Distinctive family of annuals, perennials and dwarf shrubs easily recognised by their square stems, opposite leaves (without stipules) and often aromatic leaves. Calyx is usually five-toothed and two-lipped; corolla is usually four- or five-lobed and two-lipped. There are usually four stamens (occasionally two) and a four-lobed superior ovary. Fruit is a cluster of four nutlets.

Lentibulariaceae (Bladderwort family)
Insectivorous plants, either rootless aquatics with finely divided leaves incorporating bladder-like traps, or rosette-forming terrestrial perennials with simple, slimy leaves. Upright stems bear single flowers or short racemes, the flowers two-lipped, with spurred corollas and two stamens; fruit is a capsule.

Liliaceae (Lily family)
Bulbous herbs with stems bearing simple, alternate or whorled leaves and one or more flowers in racemes or clusters. Flowers have six tepals and a three-celled ovary developing into a capsule.

Linaceae (Flax family)
Erect, hairless annuals or perennials with narrow, stalkless leaves without stipules and flowers arranged in loosely forked cymes. Each flower has five sepals, five petals, five stamens and superior, five-celled ovaries forming a capsular fruit.

Lycopodiaceae (Clubmoss family)
Perennial, evergreen, spore-producing plants with small, simple leaves arranged in four ranks or spirally around the stem. Sporangia are borne in leaf axils, and are sometimes cone-like in appearance. Despite their name and superficial resemblance, they are not mosses as they have a vascular structure. In fact, they are more closely related to ferns. Fossils dating from the Carboniferous period suggest that clubmosses were once far more common and grew to heights more than thirty metres.

Lythraceae (Purple-loosestrife family)
Annual or perennial herbs with simple, mostly opposite or whorled leaves lacking stipules. Flowers are borne in the upper leaf axils, singly or clustered, and have usually six sepals united into a tube with six petals at the top, six or twelve stamens and a two-celled ovary forming a capsule opening by two valves.

Malvaceae (Mallow family)
Hairy annuals, perennials, shrubs or trees with alternate, simple or palmately lobed, stalked leaves with stipules. Flowers are with or without an epicalyx, solitary or in racemes or panicles, often in the leaf axils, usually between one and six together. Flowers have five sepals, five petals and many stamens joined into a tube and a superior ovary.

Melanthiaceae (Herb-Paris family)
Perennial herbs growing from a short rhizome, the one native genus having usually four elliptic leaves in a whorl at the top of the stem. Flower is solitary, terminal, with two whorls of usually four narrow, spreading tepals, twice as many stamens, and a four-celled ovary developing into a black berry that splits when ripe.

Menyanthaceae (Bogbean family)
More or less aquatic perennial herbs spreading by stolons, with alternate, simple or three-parted leaves sheathing at the base of the leaf stalk. Flowers are in clusters in the leaf axils or in short racemes, with five sepals, five partly united, fringed petals, five stamens and a one-celled ovary developing into a capsule.

Montiaceae (Blinks family)
Annual or perennial herbs with simple, slightly succulent, alternate, opposite or basal leaves and flowers with two sepals, five petals, usually five stamens and a capsule fruit. Only Blinks (*Montia fontana*) is native to the British Isles, although several species are naturalised here.

Myricaceae (Bog-myrtle family)
Small, deciduous dioecious shrubs, often spreading by suckers, with aromatic, undivided, alternate leaves and small flowers lacking a perianth, borne in erect catkins; male flowers have four stamens, female flowers a one-celled ovary. Fruit is a small nut.

Nartheciaceae (Bog Asphodel family)
Rhizomatous perennial herbs with erect, linear, mostly basal leaves and a stem bearing a short raceme of small flowers with six similar tepals that persist after flowering, six stamens with hairy filaments, and a capsular fruit.

Nymphaeaceae (Water-lily family)
Aquatic perennial rhizomatous herbs with alternate, undivided leaves that typically float on the water surface and solitary, long-stalked flowers that are held on or above the water surface. Each flower may have four to six sepals and nine to thirty-three petals arranged in a spiral. Fruit is a spongy capsule with eight or more cells, which breaks up to release the seeds.

Oleaceae (Ash family)
Deciduous or evergreen trees and shrubs with opposite, simple or pinnate leaves. Flowers have either four sepals or none, and the same number of petals. Petals, when present, are mostly united into a four-lobed tube. Ovary is superior. Fruit is a capsule, winged achene or a berry.

Onagraceae (Willowherb family)
Annual, biennial or perennial herbs with opposite or alternate undivided leaves. Flowers are solitary or in terminal racemes, with two or four sepals, two or four petals, two, four or eight stamens and an inferior ovary. Fruit is a capsule or berry with many seeds, or a few-seeded nut.

Ophioglossaceae (Adder's-tongue family)
Distinctive ferns with forked fronds, one part being a simple or pinnately divided vegetative leaf, the other a fertile spike.

Orchidaceae (Orchid family)
Perennial herbs with bilaterally symmetrical flowers in racemes or spikes. Each flower has three sepals, three petals and an inferior ovary. Sepals are usually alike, but the lowermost petal is usually different from the others and forms a lip (labellum). Male and female parts of the flower are fused into a single structure known as the column. Fruit is a capsule containing many dust-like seeds. This is one of the largest families of flowering plants, with about 18,500 species, the vast majority of which are found in the tropics. Most are epiphytes (living in trees), although all British species are geophytes (living in the ground).

Orobanchaceae (Broomrape family)
Perennial or annual herbs, fully or partially parasitic on roots of other plants. Total parasites lack chlorophyll and have scale-like white or pale brown leaves on erect stems. Semi-parasitic species are mostly annuals with alternate or opposite green leaves. Flowers are borne in spikes or racemes on erect stems, with a four-lobed calyx and tubular, two-lipped corollas. Fruit is a capsule.

Oxalidaceae (Wood-sorrel family)
Perennial herbs with distinctive trifoliate leaves and five-petalled flowers.

Papaveraceae (Poppy family)
Annual or perennial herbs with two sepals and four petals. Many also have a white, yellow or orange latex in the stem and leaf canals.

Parnassiaceae (Grass-of-Parnassus family)
Perennial herbs with simple, mostly basal leaves, an erect stem bearing a single leaf, and a solitary terminal flower with five sepals, five white petals, five stamens alternating with five conspicuous, much-divided staminodes (sterile stamens). Ovary has four united carpels, appearing one-celled, and four styles. Fruit is a capsule.

Phrymaceae (Monkeyflower family)
Perennial herbs spreading by leafy stolons, growing in wet places, with simple, toothed, opposite leaves, no stipules, and two-lipped flowers in terminal racemes. Flowers are yellow or reddish, with a tubular, five-lobed calyx and corolla with a two-lobed upper lip and three-lobed lower lip, four stamens and a two-celled ovary. Fruit is a two-celled capsule with many small seeds.

Plantaginaceae (Plantain family)
Annuals or perennials with leaves in a basal rosette and dense spikes of tiny, usually green flowers on long, leafless stalks. Each flower has four sepals, four petals and four stamens.

Plumbaginaceae (Thrift family)
Perennial herbs, mostly growing in coastal areas, with undivided, basal leaves and flowers in branched cymes or dense heads. Papery calyx has five lobes; corolla has five pink or blue petals joined at the base, and five stamens; ovary is one-celled with five styles. Fruit is a capsule with one seed.

Poaceae (Grass family)
The largest family of flowering plants in Britain and Ireland, with about 200 native and naturalised species. Annual or perennial herbs with long, narrow, alternate leaves, hollow, cylindrical stems, and flowers arranged in terminal inflorescences. As grasses are wind-pollinated, they lack a perianth – they have no need for one as they do not need to attract any pollinators. Instead, the stamens and/or stigmas are enclosed in a pair of scales – an upper palea, and a lower lemma. These florets are clustered into spikelets, which have another pair of scales at the base, known as glumes. The number of florets in a spikelet is often important for identification, as is the structure of the inflorescence: for example, broad, open panicle or narrow spike. The length and shape of the ligule (the small flap at the junction between the leaf sheath and blade) and the presence or absence of bristles (awns) at the tips of the lemmas and glumes are also useful characteristics for identification.

Polygalaceae (Milkwort family)
Slender, hairless, perennial herbs with narrow-lanceolate leaves without stipules and strongly irregular flowers. There are three small, outer sepals, two large inner sepals and three petals that are joined in a whitish tube. Eight stamens are also joined in a tube with the petals. Ovary is superior and fruit is a compressed capsule.

Polygonaceae (Knotweed family)
Large family of herbs, shrubs and climbers, usually with rather small pink, white, brown or green flowers and alternate, undivided and untoothed leaves. A distinctive characteristic of the family is the tubular, papery stipule at the base of each leaf stalk. Each flower has three to six tepals arranged in two whorls, a superior ovary, two to three stigmas and six to nine stipules. Fruit is an achene.

Potamogetonaceae (Pondweed family)
More or less aquatic annuals and perennials, with undivided, alternate or opposite, floating or submerged leaves, the stalks often sheathing the stem. Flowers are in short spikes or solitary, with four tepals and stamens and usually four carpels producing a fruit of four one-seeded achenes or drupes.

Primulaceae (Primrose family)
Variable family of annual or perennial herbs with simple or pinnate leaves without stipules. Flowers are bisexual with usually five petals joined into a corolla tube at the base and an equal number of sepals and stamens. Ovary is superior (except in Brookweed, *Samolus valerandi*) and fruit is a one-celled capsule with many seeds.

Pteridaceae (Ribbon Fern family)
Tufted perennial (rarely annual) ferns with short rhizomes, fronds that are one to two times pinnate, and linear or rounded sori covered by the rolled-under frond margins or naked. Fertile and sterile fronds are similar in some species, distinct in others.

Ranunculaceae (Buttercup family)
Annual or perennial herbs or woody climbers, with alternate, simple, palmately lobed or divided or pinnate leaves without stipules. Flowers have superior ovaries with many stamens, usually five or more sepals and five or more petals (*Clematis* has only four sepals), and numerous separate carpels. Fruit is usually a cluster of achenes or follicles, sometimes with a persistent, long, feathery style. The distinction between sepals and petals is often unclear and both are often referred to as perianth segments. Most members of the family are more or less poisonous.

Resedaceae (Mignonette family)
Annual or perennial herbs with simple or pinnate, alternate leaves and racemes of irregular flowers with four to six sepals, four to six petals, seven or more stamens and a one-celled ovary. Fruit is a capsule open at the apex even when unripe.

Rosaceae (Rose family)
A large family of trees, shrubs and annual or perennial herbs, the alternate, simple or compound leaves with stipules. Flowers usually have five sepals and five petals, although some species have only four of each. The numbers of stamens is usually two, three or four times the number of sepals. An epicalyx that resembles a second ring of sepals is sometimes present. Fruit is one or several achenes, follicles, simple or compound drupes, or fleshy 'false fruits' such as apples and roses, in which the achenes are embedded in the fleshy receptacle. This economically important family includes many well-known, fruit-producing plants as well as popular ornamental species.

Rubiaceae (Bedstraw family)
Distinctive herbs with four-angled stems and leaves arranged in whorls of four to twelve. Small flowers, which are arranged in axillary or terminal inflorescences, and have four- to five-lobed corollas and sepals that are either very small or absent. Ovary is inferior and there are four to five stamens. Fruit is comprised of either two fused nutlets or a berry.

Salicaceae (Willow family)
Deciduous trees and shrubs with male and female flowers on separate plants (dioecious). Leaves are alternate, simple and have stipules. Flowers are borne in catkins, each with a bract but no perianth; male flowers have one to many stamens, females a one-celled ovary with one forked style. Fruit is a one-celled capsule, which opens to release silky-plumed seeds.

Santalaceae (Bastard-toadflax family)
The native species can be semi-parasitic perennial herbs with simple, alternate leaves, or evergreen shrubs with opposite leaves. The former have terminal cymes of small bisexual flowers with five tepals and stamens, the fruit a nut. The shrubs are dioecious, with flowers in clusters of three to five, the males with four tepals each bearing an anther, the females with smaller tepals and a one-celled ovary; fruit is a usually one-seeded berry.

Saxifragaceae (Saxifrage family)
Annual or perennial herbs with simple or divided, alternate (rarely opposite) or all basal leaves. Flowers have four or five sepals and petals, three to ten stamens and a flat or cup-shaped receptacle with two more or less joined carpels. Golden-saxifrages have four sepals, no petals and eight stamens. Many species are cushion-forming alpines.

Scrophulariaceae (Figwort family)
Annual, biennial or perennial herbs, or deciduous or evergreen shrubs with simple alternate or opposite leaves, no stipules and flowers solitary or in racemes or panicles. Flowers have a four- to five-lobed calyx and corolla, the latter somewhat irregular in native species, and four or five stamens. Ovary is two-celled. Fruit is a capsule with many small seeds.

Solanaceae (Nightshade family)
Annual or perennial herbs or shrubs with usually alternate leaves, no stipules and flowers solitary or in cymes or racemes, with five sepals, five-lobed corollas and five stamens, often projecting in a column. Fruit is a berry or capsule. Many plants are very poisonous, although the tubers and fruit of some species are important foods (such as potatoes, peppers and tomatoes).

Thymelaeaceae (Mezereon family)
Deciduous or evergreen shrubs with simple, alternate leaves and flowers in small clusters in the upper leaf axils. Flowers have four coloured, petal-like sepals, no petals and eight stamens; fruit is a drupe with one seed. All species and all parts are poisonous.

Typhaceae (Bulrush family)
Rhizomatous perennial herbs usually growing in or by water, with long, linear alternate leaves and flowers in a terminal spike, panicle or short raceme. Often monoecious, with male and female flowers in separate parts of the inflorescence. Flowers are reduced to a few scales or bristles with up to eight stamens in the males, one or two joined carpels in the females. Fruit is a small capsule or dry drupe.

Ulmaceae (Elm family)
Tall deciduous trees with rough bark and alternate, unlobed, toothed, rough, asymmetrical leaves (the base of the leaf blade extends further down one side than the other). Flowers appear before the leaves and are very small and arranged in globular heads. Each has a four- to five-lobed perianth and four to five red stamens. Fruit is a distinctive achene surrounded by an oval, notched wing.

Urticaceae (Nettle family)
Annual or perennial herbs with simple, opposite or alternate leaves, with or without stipules, and separate male and female flowers on the same plant or on separate plants. Each very small flower has a green, four-lobed perianth, males with four or five stamens, females with a silvery, much-branched style. Fruit is a small achene. Members of the genus *Urtica* have stinging hairs throughout.

Valerianaceae (Valerian family)
Annual or perennial herbs with opposite, undivided or pinnate leaves, no stipules and small flowers arranged in umbel-like cymes. Each flower has a small, rim-like calyx (which develops long feathery hairs in *Centranthus*), a funnel-shaped, five-lobed corolla, sometimes with a long spur, and an inferior ovary; fruit is a small nut.

Verbenaceae (Vervain family)
Annual or perennial herbs with square-sectioned stems bearing simple or pinnately lobed, opposite leaves. Flowers in terminal spikes, sometimes forming a corymb, with a five-toothed calyx, slightly two-lipped, tubular corolla and four stamens. Ovary is four-celled, developing into a cluster of four nutlets.

Veronicaceae (Speedwell family)
Annual or perennial herbs and small shrubs with alternate or opposite leaves, rarely all basal, and flowers solitary in the leaf axils or in terminal or lateral racemes. Calyx is four- or five-lobed; corolla is more or less deeply four- or five-lobed, sometimes two-lipped and spurred. Usually two or four stamens are attached to the corolla tube. Ovary is two-celled with one style. Fruit is a two-celled capsule with many small seeds.

Violaceae (Violet family)
Perennial or annual herbs with alternate, stalked leaves that have pairs of stipules at the leaf bases. Flowers are solitary and irregular, with five sepals and five petals, the lowermost of which has a backward-pointing spur. Fruit is a three-valved capsule.

Woodsiaceae (Lady-fern family)
A rather diverse family of ferns with short or long, scaly rhizomes, and fronds usually in tufts, although sometimes singly along the rhizome. Fronds are one to four times pinnate; sori may be rounded, oblong or hook-shaped and may be naked or covered when young by a similar-shaped membrane, the indusium.

Glossary of Species Names

Note that the endings of many species names may vary, depending on the gender of the generic name.

Acanthodes Spiny
Acinos Small aromatic plant
Acre Sharp
Aculeatus Prickly
Aestivum Of summer
Affinis Related to
Alba White
Alpina Alpine
Amarella Somewhat bitter
Aquaticum/aquatica Growing in water
Aquilinum Eagle-like
Amphibium Amphibious
Angustifolia With narrow leaves
Apifera Bee-bearing
Argentea Silvery
Arvensis In fields
Auriculata With auricles
Autumnalis Of autumn
Bifolia With two leaves
Bolbosus Bulbous
Calcarea Growing on chalk
Caerulea Dark blue
Canadensis Of Canada
Canina Pertaining to dogs
Chrysantha With golden flowers
Ciliata Fringed with hairs
Cinerea Grey
Communis Common
Comosa Tufted
Compacta Compact
Coronopus Crow's foot
Densiflora With dense flowers
Dentata Toothed
Dilatata Expanded
Dioica Dioecious
Dulcis Sweet
Effusum Spreading
Elata Tall
Elegans Elegant
Eupatoria After King Eupator
Farinosa Mealy
Flavescens Yellow
Flexuosa Tortuous
Formosa Beautiful
Fruticosus Shrubby
Fulva Tawny
Germanica Of Germany
Gigantea Very large
Glandulosa Glandular
Glutinosa Sticky

Gracilis Graceful
Grandiflorus With large flowers
Helix Twining
Hirsuta Hairy
Hirtum Hairy
Humilis Low growing
Incarnata Pink
Japonica Of Japan
Laevigatum Smooth
Lanceolata Spear-shaped
Lasiocarpa With woolly fruits
Latifolia With broad leaves
Linifolius With narrow leaves
Lucens Shiny
Lupulina Hop-like
Lutea Yellow
Macrantha With large flowers
Maculata Spotted
Maritima Growing near the sea
Matronalis Of matrons
Minima Small
Minor Small
Montanum Of mountains
Multiflora Multi-flowered
Nana Dwarf
Natans Floating
Nervosa With veins
Nidus-avis Bird's nest
Nobilis Noble
Non-scripta Not written
Norvegica Of Norway
Nudicaulis With bare stems
Nudiflorus With bare flowers
Nutans Nodding
Obtusifolius With blunt leaves
Odoratum Scented
Officinalis/officinale Of the shop
Oleracea Like a vegetable
Olustratum Black vegetable or pot herb
Orientalis Eastern
Ossifragrum Bone-breaking
Pallida Pale
Palustris Of marshes
Paniculata With flowers in panicles
Parviflora With small leaves
Pendula Pendulous
Petraea Growing on rocks
Praecox Early
Pratensis/pratense Of meadows
Pulchellum Pretty

Purpurea Purple
Racemosa With flowers arranged in racemes
Repens/reptans Creeping
Rotundifolia With round leaves
Rugosa Wrinkled
Sagittifolia With arrow-shaped leaves
Sanguineum Bloody
Saxifraga Stone-breaking
Sceleratus Poisonous
Schoenoprasum With rush-like leaves
Scoparius Like a broom
Splendens Splendid
Spinosus/spinosa Spiny
Spinosissima Very spiny
Spiralis Spiral
Stolonifera With stolons
Sterilis Sterile
Striata Striped
Sylvatica/sylvaticum Of woods
Sylvestris Of woods
Tenella Dainty
Tenuiflorum With slender flowers
Tomentosus Hairy
Trifoliata With three leaves
Uniflora With one flower
Ustulata Scorched
Myrtillus Small myrtle
Verna/vernus Of spring
Verticillatum With whorled leaves or flowers
Viridifolia With green flowers
Vulgaris/vulgatum Common

Glossary of Botanical Terms

Terms denoted with an asterisk * are illustrated on pp.462–3.

Achene Small, dry, single-seeded fruit.

Annual Plant that completes its life cycle, from germination to seed production, in one year.

Auricle* Small, 'ear-like' lobe at the base of a leaf.

Awn* Bristle-like projection at the tip or back of a lemma or glume.

Axil Angle between the stem and a flower, leaf or branch. A flower is axillary if it is located in the axil.

Basal leaves* Lowest group of leaves on the stem of a plant.

Basal rosette* Ring of leaves at the base of a plant (sometimes termed 'rosette').

Biennial Plant that completes its life cycle, from germination to seed production, in two years and does not flower in the first.

Bifid Split or cleft into two (usually a petal).

Bract 1. Leaf-like structure that is located where the flower stalk joins the stem.* 2. In umbellifers, whorl of small leaves at the base of the main umbel.

Bracteole 1. Small, leaf-like structure located on a flower stalk. 2. In umbellifers, whorl of small leaves at the base of a secondary umbel.

Bulbil Small bulb located in the axil of a leaf or flower.

Calcareous soil Alkaline soil that is rich in calcium carbonate. Often soil that overlies limestone and chalk geology.

Calyx* Collective term for the sepals of a flower, which usually form a whorl.

Calyx teeth Lobes of a calyx tube.

Calyx tube Tube formed by sepals when they are fused at the base.

Capsule A succulent or spongey fruit, usually one-seeded and with a stony coat.

Carpel Part of the female organ of a flower. The female organ (gynoecium) is divided into carpels, each of which has a style at its tip. In some plants, such as tulips and poppies, carpels are fused, whereas in others, such as buttercups, they are separate.

Cladode Leaf-like structure that is actually a flattened stem.

Cordate Leaf with two rounded basal lobes.

Corolla* Collective term for the petals of a flower, which usually form a whorl.

Corolla tube Tube formed by petals when they are fused at the base.

Corymb* Inflorescence in which the flower stalks are progressively shorter, so that all the flowers are at the same level.

Cyme* Inflorescence in which the terminal flower is the first to open, followed by flowers that are located in the bract axils further down the inflorescence stalk.

Cucullate Leaf with a hooded tip.

Dichotomous key Key used to identify a plant by selecting from pairs of diagnostic features.

Digitate leaf* Palmate leaf with very narrow, finger-like leaflets.

Dioecious Species with male and female organs on separate plants.

Drupe Dry, many-seeded dehiscent fruit formed from one carpel.

Epicalyx* Calyx-like whorl of bract-like leaflets beneath the true calyx.

Epichile In helleborine orchids, the heart-shaped outer portion of the lip of the flowers.

Eutrophic Water that has a high primary productivity due to excessive amounts of nutrients. Eutrophication is the addition of large amounts of nutrients to a water body, usually with adverse effects on its biodiversity.

Falls In irises, drooping outer perianth segments.

Floret Individual flower in a compound flower head.

Frond Leaf of a fern, comprising frond blade and stalk.

Glaucous Green colour tinged with blue-grey.

Globose Describes a flower that is spherical in shape (also Globular).

Glume 1. In grasses, the pair of scales at the base of a spikelet.* 2. In sedges, the single scale.

Hastate leaf* Spearhead-shaped leaf, with basal lobes spreading outwards.

Hemiparasite Plant that has green leaves (i.e. it produces chlorophyll) but also gains some of its nutrients from the roots of other plants.

Herb Plant that dies back to ground level each winter.

Hypochile In helleborine orchids, the cup-shaped inner portion of the lip of the flowers.

Indented leaves Strongly toothed leaves.

Inferior ovary Ovary below the calyx of a flower.

Inflorescence stalk* Stalk on which a group of flowers is situated.

Involucre Whorl or ruff of bracts at the base of a flower head (usually in daisies).

Involucral bract Bract that forms part of a calyx-like whorl (involucre) at the base of a flower head.

Keel In peas, the two lower, partly joined petals that form a shape similar to that of the keel of a boat.

Keeled Leaf that is folded lengthwise and has a keel-like ridge down the lower surface.

Labellum Lip of an orchid.

Lanceolate leaf* Long, narrow leaf that is widest near the base and tapers gradually to the tip.

Leaflet Separate leaf segment of a compound leaf.

Lemma* Lower of the two scales that enclose the florets of a grass (the upper scale is known as the palea).

Ligule 1. Small flap usually found at the junction of the leaf blade and the leaf sheath. 2. The ray of a daisy flower.

Midrib Central vein of a leaf, which is often raised and thicker than the others.

Monocotyledon One of the two sub-divisions of flowering plants. Monocotyledons are usually parallel-veined and have only one leaf to the seedling.

Monoecious Having separate male and female flowers on the same plant.

Mycorrhiza Fungal cells that live within or immediately around the roots of vascular plants.

Nectary Structure within a flower that secretes nectar to attract insects.

Nutlet Small, dry, one-seeded fruit enclosed by a woody shell.

Obovate leaf* Leaf that is broadest above the middle and tapers suddenly to a blunt tip but more gradually to its base.

Ovate leaf* Egg-shaped leaf, which is broadest near the base and about twice as long as broad.

Palate In figworts, a two-lobed swelling on the lower lip of the flowers.

Palmate leaf* Compound leaf with more than three leaflets, which all radiate from the top of the leaf stalk.

Palmately lobed leaf* Lobed leaf with all the main veins radiating from the top of the leaf stalk.

Panicle Branched inflorescence.

Pappus Tuft of hairs attached to the fruits of plants in the daisy and valerian families.

Pedicel Flower stalk.

Perianth* Collective term for the sepals and petals when they are indistinguishable from each other or there is only one whorl of segments.

Perennial Plant that has a lifespan of more than two years and may flower on more than one occasion.

Petiole Leaf stalk.

Phyllode Flattened leaf stalk.

Pinna (plural: pinnae)* Primary division of a fern frond, or any pinnate leaf.

Pinnate leaf* Compound leaf with leaflets arranged in opposite pairs along the leaf stalk.

Pinnatifid leaf* Leaf that is pinnately lobed but not cut to its midrib, such as an oak leaf.

Pinnule* Secondary division of a fern frond, or pinnate leaf.

Raceme Unbranched inflorescence in which the individual flowers are stalked.

Reflexed sepals Sepals that are sharply curved back.

Rhizome Creeping underground stem.

Red List International Union for Conservation of Nature (IUCN) list of threatened species.

Rugose Leaves that are rough and wrinkled.

Saprophyte Organism that does not produce chlorophyll but gains its nutrients from dead or decaying organic matter.

Sepal Part of the outer whorl of floral leaves that surrounds petals.

Sheath Lower part of a leaf, which encloses the stem.

Sorus (plural: sori)* Spore-producing organ of a fern, usually located on the underside of the frond.

Spadix Fleshy, densely flowered inflorescence typical of arums, such as Lords-and-Ladies.

Spathe Large bract that wraps around inflorescence, most notable in arums and some members of the lily family.

Speculum Elaborate, often shiny pattern on the lip of orchids in the *Ophrys* genus.

Spikelet 1. In grasses, usually stalked cluster of florets with a pair of glumes at the base.* 2. In sedges, stalked cluster of florets situated in the axil of a bract.

Sporangium (plural: sporangia)* In ferns, a spore capsule, usually grouped with other sporangia into a sorus.

Spur Tubular, nectar-secreting projection at the back of a flower.

Stamen* Male reproductive organ of a flower, consisting of anther and filament.

Standard 1. In peas, erect upper petal. 2. In irises, one of the erect, inner segments in the perianth of a flower.

Stigma The receptive tip of a carpel in the gynoecium of a flower.

Stipe* Stalk of a fern.

Stipule* Leaf-like or scale-like structure at the base of a leaf stalk.

Stolon Creeping stem, rooting at the nodes and sometimes producing a new plant at its tip.

Style* Part of the female organ of a flower, usually an elongated column with a stigma at its tip.

Superior ovary Ovary situated above the calyx, petals and stamens of a flower.

Tepal Individual segment of a perianth (alternative word for perianth segment).

Terminal At the end of a stem.

Terminal lobe Lobe at the tip of a leaf.

Umbel* Flat-topped inflorescence with multiple branches that rise from the same point at the top of the main stem. These branches may divide in a similar manner again (compound umbel).

Unisexual Flower that has only male or female reproductive organs.

Vegetative reproduction Production of a new plant without the use of seeds or spores. It may occur by several means, including division, production of tubers and suckering from roots or by stolons.

Whorled leaves* Three or more leaves arising from a stem at the same point.

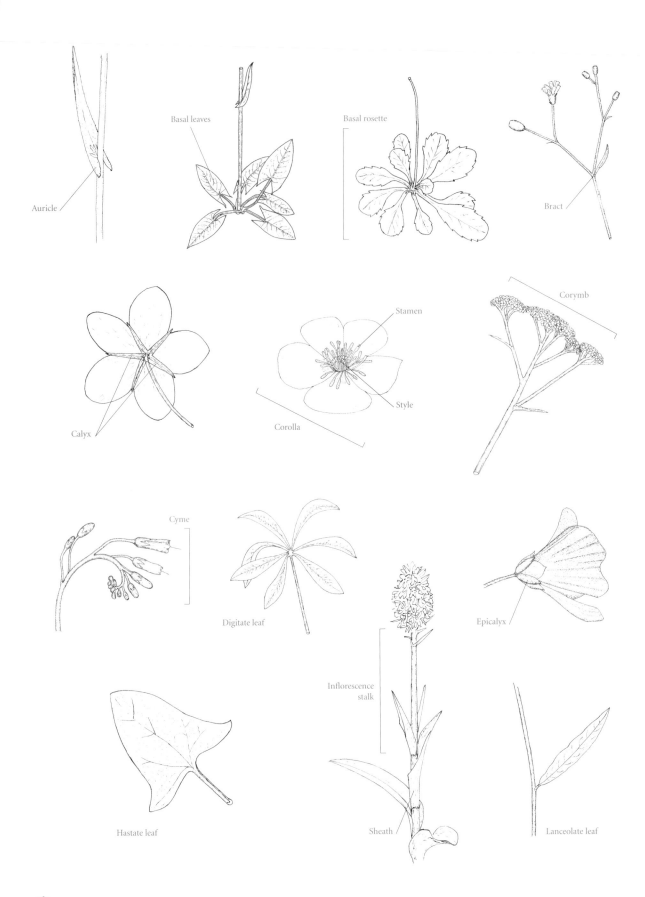

Auricle

Basal leaves

Basal rosette

Bract

Calyx

Stamen

Style

Corolla

Corymb

Cyme

Digitate leaf

Epicalyx

Inflorescence stalk

Hastate leaf

Sheath

Lanceolate leaf

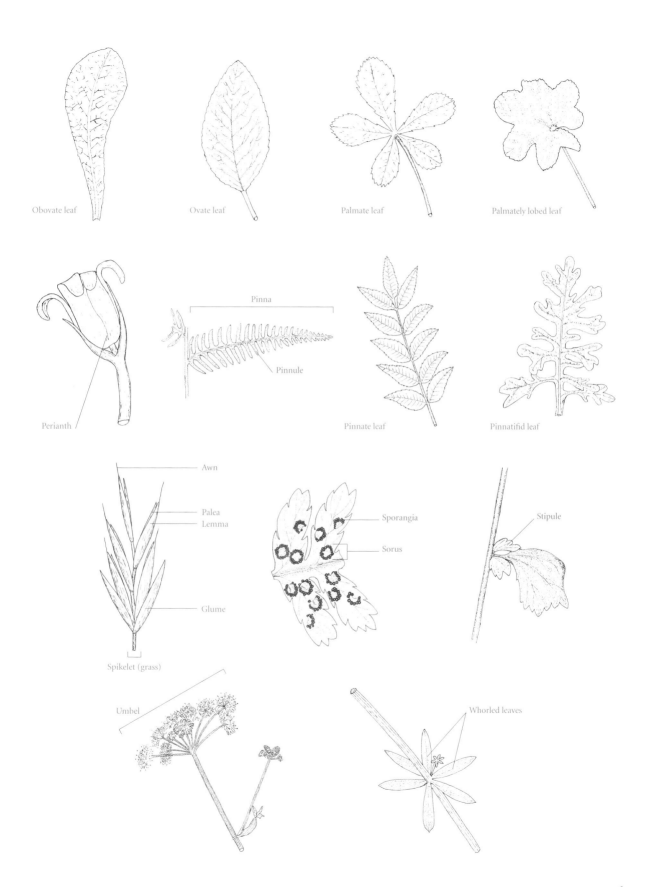

Obovate leaf

Ovate leaf

Palmate leaf

Palmately lobed leaf

Perianth

Pinna

Pinnule

Pinnate leaf

Pinnatifid leaf

Awn

Palea

Lemma

Glume

Spikelet (grass)

Sporangia

Sorus

Stipule

Umbel

Whorled leaves

Index by Petal Colour

White & Cream

Yarrow
Achillea millefolium
p.167

Sneezewort
Achillea ptarmica
p.163

Ground-elder
Aegopodium podagraria
p.251

Fool's Parsley
Aethusa cynapium
p.250

Water-plantain
Alisma plantago-aquatica
p.322

Garlic Mustard
Alliaria petiolata
p.84

Three-cornered Garlic
Allium triquetrum
p.112

Ramsons
Allium ursinum
p.23

Wood Anemone
Anemone nemorosa
p.30

Wild Angelica
Angelica sylvestris
p.324

Mountain Everlasting
Antennaria dioica
p.361

Cow Parsley
Anthriscus sylvestris
p.77

Fool's-watercress
Apium nodiflorum
p.300

Daisy
Bellis perennis
p.246

White Bryony
Bryonia dioica
p.115

Hedge Bindweed
Calystegia sepium
p.90

Large Bindweed
Calystegia silvatica
p.94

Shepherd's-purse
Capsella bursa-pastoris
p.260

Hairy Bitter-cress
Cardamine hirsuta
p.251

White Helleborine
Cephalanthera damasonium
p.29

Enchanter's-nightshade
Circaea lutetiana
p.9

Springbeauty
Claytonia perfoliata
p.262

Traveller's-joy
Clematis vitalba
p.112

English Scurvygrass
Cochlearia anglica
p.399

Mountain Avens
Dryas octopetala
p.361

Snowdon Lily
Gagea serotina
p.367

Danish Scurvygrass
Cochlearia danica
p.78

Marsh Helleborine
Epipactis palustris
p.309

Snowdrop
Galanthus nivalis
p.26

Common Scurvygrass
Cochlearia officinalis
p.397

Mexican Fleabane
Erigeron karvinskianus
p.97

Hedge Bedstraw
Galium album
p.202

Hemlock
Conium maculatum
p.304

Common Eyebright
Euphrasia nemorosa
p.146

Cleavers
Galium aparine
p.238

Pignut
Conopodium majus
p.161

Japanese Knotweed
Fallopia japonica
p.252

Woodruff
Galium odoratum
p.32

Lily-of-the-valley
Convallaria majalis
p.18

Meadowsweet
Filipendula ulmaria
p.314

Common Marsh-
bedstraw
Galium palustre
p.295

Hawthorn
Crataegus monogyna
p.89

Dropwort
Filipendula vulgaris
p.197

Heath Bedstraw
Galium saxatile
p.356

Wild Carrot
Daucus carota ssp.*carota*
p.424

Wild Strawberry
Fragaria vesca
p.120

White Rock-rose
Helianthemum
apenninum
p.423

Giant Hogweed
Heracleum mantegazzianum
p.85

Wild Privet
Ligustrum vulgare
p.120

Sweet Cicely
Myrrhis odorata
p.110

Hogweed
Heracleum sphondylium
p.156

Fairy Flax
Linum catharticum
p.152

White Water-lily
Nymphaea alba
p.323

Dame's-violet
Hesperis matronalis
p.298

Honeysuckle
Lonicera periclymenum
p.91

Fine-leaved Water-dropwort
Oenanthe aquatica
p.299

Frogbit
Hydrocharis morsus-ranae
p.301

Gypsywort
Lycopus europaeus
p.303

Hemlock Water-dropwort
Oenanthe crocata
p.304

Henbane
Hyoscyamus niger
p.203

Crab Apple
Malus sylvestris
p.77

Parsley Water-dropwort
Oenanthe lachenalii
p.407

White Dead-nettle
Lamium album
p.116

White Melilot
Melilotus albus
p.116

Spiked Star-of-Bethlehem
Ornithogalum pyrenaicum
p.107

Oxeye Daisy
Leucanthemum vulgare
p.159

Bogbean
Menyanthes trifoliata
p.291

Star-of-Bethlehem
Ornithogalum umbellatum
p.369

Summer Snowflake
Leucojum aestivum ssp. *aestivum*
p.318

Spring Sandwort
Minuartia verna
p.369

Wood-sorrel
Oxalis acetosella
p.33

Grass-of-Parnassus
Parnassia palustris
p.302

Wild Plum
Prunus domestica
p.119

Wild Madder
Rubia peregrina
p.426

Burnet-saxifrage
Pimpinella saxifraga
p.192

Bird Cherry
Prunus padus
p.63

Arrowhead
Sagittaria sagittifolia
p.288

Ribwort Plantain
Plantago lanceolata
p.162

Blackthorn
Prunus spinosa
p.64

Elder
Sambucus nigra
p.80

Lesser Butterfly-orchid
Platanthera bifolia
p.359

Common Water-
crowfoot
Ranunculus aquatilis
p.297

Meadow Saxifrage
Saxifraga granulata
p.159

Greater Butterfly-orchid
Platanthera chlorantha
p.13

River Water-crowfoot
Ranunculus fluitans
p.317

Mossy Saxifrage
Saxifraga hypnoides
p.360

Barren Strawberry
Potentilla sterilis
p.62

Watercress
*Rorippa nasturtium-
aquaticum*
p.320

Starry Saxifrage
Saxifraga stellaris
p.371

Wild Cherry
Prunus avium
p.117

Field-rose
Rosa arvensis
p.82

English Stonecrop
Sedum anglicum
p.401

Cherry Plum
Prunus cerasifera
p.69

Burnet Rose
Rosa pimpinellifolia
p.68

Field Madder
Sherardia arvensis
p.249

White Campion
Silene latifolia
p.115

Greater Stitchwort
Stellaria holostea
p.87

Guelder-rose
Viburnum opulus
p.88

Night-flowering Catchfly
Silene noctiflora
p.253

Common Chickweed
Stellaria media
p.239

Field Pansy
Viola arvensis
p.249

Sea Campion
Silene uniflora
p.411

Common Comfrey
Symphytum officinale
p.71

Sweet Violet (white form)
Viola odorata
p.111

Bladder Campion
Silene vulgaris
p.66

Hare's-foot Clover
Trifolium arvense
p.402

Greater Sea-spurrey
Spergularia media
p.402

White Clover
Trifolium repens
p.167

Irish Lady's-tresses
Spiranthes romanzoffiana
p.306

Scentless Mayweed
Tripleurospermum inodorum
p.259

Autumn Lady's-tresses
Spiranthes spiralis
p.190

Sea Mayweed
Tripleurospermum maritimum
p.412

Lesser Stitchwort
Stellaria graminea
p.157

Marsh Valerian
Valeriana dioica
p.313

Moschatel
Adoxa moschatellina
p.20

Sea Beet
Beta vulgaris ssp.
maritima
p.410

Spurge-laurel
Daphne laureola
p.27

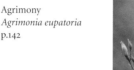
Agrimony
Agrimonia eupatoria
p.142

Yellow-wort
Blackstonia perfoliata
p.217

Winter Aconite
Eranthis hyemalis
p.30

Alpine Lady's-mantle
Alchemilla alpina
p.348

Marsh-marigold
Caltha palustris
p.311

Wood Spurge
Euphorbia amygdaloides
p.33

Lady's-mantle
Alchemilla vulgaris agg.
p.156

Greater Celandine
Chelidonium majus
p.87

Cypress Spurge
Euphorbia cyparissias
p.78

Kidney Vetch
Anthyllis vulneraria
p.403

Corn Marigold
Chrysanthemum segetum
p.244

Sun Spurge
Euphorbia helioscopia
p.262

Wild Liquorice
Astragalus glycyphyllos
p.215

Golden-saxifrage
*Chrysosplenium
oppositifolium/
C. alternifolium*
p.302

Caper Spurge
Euphorbia lathyris
p.237

Common Orache
Atriplex patula
p.396

Crosswort
Cruciata laevipes
P.196

Fennel
Foeniculum vulgare
p.81

Spear-leaved Orache
Atriplex prostrata
p.419

Broom
Cytisus scoparius
p.352

Lady's Bedstraw
Galium verum
p.205

Petty Whin
Genista anglica
p.363

 Horseshoe Vetch
Hippocrepis comosa
p.204

 Meadow Vetchling
Lathyrus pratensis
p.96

 Dyer's Greenweed
Genista tinctoria
p.152

 Sea Sandwort
Honckenya peploides
p.416

 Rough Hawkbit
Leontodon hispidus
p.162

 Wood Avens
Geum urbanum
p.31

 Tutsan
Hypericum androsaemum
p.422

 Scot's Lovage
Ligusticum scoticum
p.408

 Yellow Horned-poppy
Glaucium flavum
p.427

 Perforate St John's-wort
Hypericum perforatum
p.209

 Pyrenean Lily
Lilium pyrenaicum
p.104

 Common Rock-rose
*Helianthemum
nummularium*
p.195

 Slender St John's-wort
Hypericum pulchrum
p.367

 Common Toadflax
Linaria vulgaris
p.74

 Stinking Hellebore
Helleborus foetidus
p.27

 Spotted Cat's-ear
Hypochaeris maculate
p.419

 Common Gromwell
Lithospermum officinale
p.72

 Green Hellebore
Helleborus viridis
p.13

 Yellow Iris
Iris pseudacorus
p.324

 Common Bird's-foot-
trefoil
Lotus corniculatus
p.145

 Musk Orchid
Herminium monorchis
p.207

 Yellow Archangel
Lamiastrum galeobdolon
ssp. *montanum*
p.35

 Yellow Pimpernel
Lysimachia nemorum
p.35

Yellow Loosestrife
Lysimachia vulgaris
p.325

Wall Lettuce
Mycelis muralis
p.113

Pellitory-of-the-wall
Parietaria judaica
p.102

Pineappleweed
Matricaria discoidea
p.255

Daffodil
Narcissus pseudonarcissus
p.6

Herb-Paris
Paris quadrifolia
p.16

Welsh Poppy
Meconopsis cambrica
p.114

Bog Asphodel
Narthecium ossifragum
p.350

Wild Parsnip
Pastinaca sativa ssp.
sylvestris
p.119

Black Medick
Medicago lupulina
p.64

Common Twayblade
Neottia ovata
p.148

Silverweed
Potentilla anserina
p.418

Sickle Medick
Medicago sativa ssp.
falcata
p.366

Yellow Water-lily
Nuphar lutea
p.325

Tormentil
Potentilla erecta
p.371

Common Cow-wheat
Melampyrum pratense
p.5

Fringed Water-lily
Nymphoides peltata
p.300

Creeping Cinquefoil
Potentilla reptans
p.149

Dog's Mercury
Mercurialis perennis
p.8

Common Evening-
primrose
Oenothera biennis
p.239

Oxlip
Primula elatior
p.21

Monkeyflower
Mimulus guttatus
p.315

Man Orchid
Orchis anthropophora
p.206

False Oxlip
Primula x *polyantha*
p.81

Cowslip
Primula veris
p.195

Lesser Spearwort
Ranunculus flammula
p.307

Biting Stonecrop
Sedum acre
p.392

Primrose
Primula vulgaris
p.103

Creeping Buttercup
Ranunculus repens
p.149

Roseroot
Sedum rosea
p.365

Yellow Corydalis
Pseudofumaria lutea
p.121

Celery-leaved Buttercup
Ranunculus sceleratus
p.294

Common Ragwort
Senecio jacobaea
p.242

Common Fleabane
Pulicaria dysenterica
p.295

Wild Mignonette
Reseda lutea
p.216

Oxford Ragwort
Senecio squalidus
p.101

Meadow Buttercup
Ranunculus acris
p.158

Weld
Reseda luteola
p.264

Pepper-saxifrage
Silaum silaus
p.160

Goldilocks Buttercup
Ranunculus auricomus
p.11

Yellow-rattle
Rhinanthus minor
p.168

Spanish Catchfly
Silene otites
p.368

Bulbous Buttercup
Ranunculus bulbosus
p.144

Red Currant
Ribes rubrum
p.24

Alexanders
Smyrnium olusatrum
p.62

Lesser Celandine
Ranunculus ficaria
p.18

Autumn Hawkbit
*Scorzoneroides
autumnalis*
p.143

Perennial Sowthistle
Sonchus arvensis
p.255

Prickly Sowthistle
Sonchus asper
p.256

Lesser Meadow-rue
Thalictrum minus
p.403

Gorse
Ulex europaeus
p.355

Tansy
Tanacetum vulgare
p.111

Lesser Trefoil
Trifolium dubium
p.157

Common Nettle
Urtica dioica
p.241

Dandelions
Taraxacum agg.
p.246

Sea Arrowgrass
Triglochin maritima
p.409

Dark Mullein
Verbascum nigrum
p.247

Wood Sage
Teucrium scorodonia
p.32

Globeflower
Trollius europaeus
p.301

Great Mullein
Verbascum thapsus
p.250

Common Meadow-rue
Thalictrum flavum
p.296

Colt's-foot
Tussilago farfara
p.238

Dune Pansy
Viola tricolor ssp. *curtisii*
p.399

Scarlet Pimpernel
Anagallis arvensis
p.259

Fuchsia
Fuchsia magellanica var.
macrostema
p.84

Opium Poppy
Papaver somniferum
p.254

Carline Thistle
Carlina vulgaris
p.193

Water Avens
Geum rivale
p.318

Fox-and-cubs
Pilosella aurantiaca
p.82

Red Valerian
Centranthus ruber
p.407

Lizard Orchid
*Himantoglossum
hircinum*
p.404

Common Sorrel
Rumex acetosa
p.147

Frog Orchid
Coeloglossum viride
p.200

Bird's-nest Orchid
Neottia nidus-avis
p.2

Sheep's Sorrel
Rumex acetosella
p.366

Marsh Cinquefoil
Comarum palustre
p.309

Late Spider-orchid
Ophrys fuciflora
p.205

Salad Burnet
Sanguisorba minor
p.213

Montbretia
Crocosmia x
crocosmiiflora
p.98

Fly Orchid
Ophrys insectifera
p.10

Great Burnet
Sanguisorba officinalis
p.154

Hound's-tongue
Cynoglossum officinale
p.204

Early Spider-orchid
Ophrys sphegodes
p.198

Common Figwort
Scrophularia nodosa
p.72

Wallflower
Erysimum cheiri
p.422

Common Poppy
Papaver rhoeas
p.241

Navelwort
Umbilicus rupestris
p.100

Corncockle
Agrostemma githago
p.242

Bog-rosemary
Andromeda polifolia
p.351

Flowering-rush
Butomus umbellatus
p.299

Bugle
Ajuga reptans
p.68

Columbine
Aquilegia vulgaris
p.4

Sea Rocket
Cakile maritime
p.416

Chives
Allium schoenoprasum
p.394

Lesser Burdock
Arctium minus
p.253

Heather
Calluna vulgaris
p.357

Wild Onion
Allium vineale
p.427

Thrift
Armeria maritima
p.420

Sea Bindweed
Calystegia soldanella
p.410

Marsh-mallow
Althaea officinalis
p.405

Sea Aster
Aster tripolium
p.409

Nettle-leaved Bellflower
Campanula trachelium
p.21

Green-winged Orchid
Anacamptis morio
p.154

Purple Milk-vetch
Astragalus danicus
p.210

Cuckooflower
Cardamine pratensis
p.297

Pyramidal Orchid
Anacamptis pyramidalis
p.210

Deadly Nightshade
Atropa belladonna
p.6

Welted Thistle
Carduus crispus
p.323

Bog Pimpernel
Anagallis tenella
p.291

Butterfly-bush
Buddleja davidii
p.237

Slender Thistle
Carduus tenuiflorus
p.418

Common Knapweed
Centaurea nigra
p.146

Marsh Thistle
Cirsium palustre
p.312

Early Marsh-orchid
Dactylorhiza incarnata
p.298

Greater Knapweed
Centaurea scabiosa
p.201

Spear Thistle
Cirsium vulgare
p.261

Heath Spotted-orchid
Dactylorhiza maculata
p.359

Common Centaury
Centaurium erythraea
p.194

Basil Thyme
Clinopodium acinos
p.191

Northern Marsh-orchid
Dactylorhiza purpurella
p.315

Small Toadflax
Chaenorhinum minus
p.260

Wild Basil
Clinopodium vulgare
p.215

Deptford Pink
Dianthus armeria
p.151

Rosebay Willowherb
Chamerion angustifolium
p.258

Meadow Saffron
Colchicum autumnale
p.314

Foxglove
Digitalis purpurea
p.10

Dwarf Thistle
Cirsium acaule
p.197

Field Bindweed
Convolvulus arvensis
p.248

Great Willowherb
Epilobium hirsutum
p.303

Creeping Thistle
Cirsium arvense
p.150

Ivy-leaved Toadflax
Cymbalaria muralis
p.93

Broad-leaved Willowherb
Epilobium montanum
p.67

Melancholy Thistle
Cirsium heterophyllum
p.97

Common Spotted-orchid
Dactylorhiza fuchsii
p.148

Dark-red Helleborine
Epipactis atrorubens
p.196

Broad-leaved Helleborine
Epipactis helleborine
p.4

Autumn Gentian
Gentianella amarella
p.190

Chalk Fragrant-orchid
Gymnadenia conopsea
p.193

Bell Heather
Erica cinerea
p.349

Shining Crane's-bill
Geranium lucidum
p.106

Water-violet
Hottonia palustris
p.322

Cross-leaved Heath
Erica tetralix
p.354

Meadow Crane's-bill
Geranium pratense
p.96

Marsh Pennywort
Hydrocotyle vulgaris
p.312

Common Stork's-bill
Erodium cicutarium
p.398

Herb-Robert
Geranium robertianum
p.91

Indian Balsam
Impatiens glandulifera
p.305

Hemp-agrimony
Eupatorium cannabinum
p.305

Bloody Crane's-bill
Geranium sanguineum
p.393

Stinking Iris
Iris foetidissima
p.28

Fritillary
Fritillaria meleagris
p.153

Wood Crane's-bill
Geranium sylvaticum
p.121

Field Scabious
Knautia arvensis
p.198

Common Fumitory
Fumaria officinalis
p.240

Sea-milkwort
Glaux maritima
p.413

Red Dead-nettle
Lamium purpureum
p.257

Goat's-rue
Galega officinalis
p.86

Ground-ivy
Glechoma hederacea
p.14

Purple Toothwort
Lathraea clandestina
p.23

Toothwort
Lathraea squamaria
p.29

Purple-loosestrife
Lythrum salicaria
p.316

Burnt Orchid
Neotinea ustulata
p.192

Sea Pea
Lathyrus japonicus
p.413

Tree-mallow
Malva arborea
p.421

Red Bartsia
Odontites vernus
p.256

Broad-leaved Everlasting-pea
Lathyrus latifolius
p.67

Musk-mallow
Malva moschata
p.99

Sainfoin
Onobrychis viciifolia
p.211

Bitter-vetch
Lathyrus linifolius
p.144

Common Mallow
Malva sylvestris
p.73

Common Restharrow
Ononis repens
p.396

Grass Vetchling
Lathyrus nissolia
p.200

Lucerne
Medicago sativa ssp.
sativa
p.95

Cotton Thistle
Onopordum acanthium
p.75

Common Sea-lavender
Limonium vulgare
p.397

Water Mint
Mentha aquatica
p.321

Bee Orchid
Ophrys apifera
p.191

Water Lobelia
Lobelia dortmanna
p.321

Corn Mint
Mentha arvensis
p.245

Early-purple Orchid
Orchis mascula
p.9

Ragged-Robin
Lychnis flos-cuculi
p.317

Oysterplant
Mertensia maritima
p.406

Lady Orchid
Orchis purpurea
p.17

Monkey Orchid
Orchis simia
p.207

Pale Butterwort
Pinguicula lusitanica
p.362

Harsh Downy-rose
Rosa tomentosa
p.89

Wild Marjoram
Origanum vulgare
p.216

Common Butterwort
Pinguicula vulgaris
p.294

Meadow Clary
Salvia pratensis
p.206

Thyme Broomrape
Orobanche alba
p.421

Hoary Plantain
Plantago media
p.203

Wild Clary
Salvia verbenaca
p.117

Marsh Lousewort
Pedicularis palustris
p.311

Bird's-eye Primrose
Primula farinosa
p.289

Sanicle
Sanicula europaea
p.25

Lousewort
Pedicularis sylvatica
p.308

Selfheal
Prunella vulgaris
p.163

Soapwort
Saponaria officinalis
p.261

Amphibious Bistort
Persicaria amphibia
p.288

Pasqueflower
Pulsatilla vulgaris
p.209

Purple Saxifrage
Saxifraga oppositifolia
p.363

Common Bistort
Persicaria bistorta
p.70

Dog-rose
Rosa canina
p.79

Small Scabious
Scabiosa columbaria
p.214

Redshank
Persicaria maculosa
p.257

Japanese Rose
Rosa rugosa
p.94

Spring Squill
Scilla verna
p.420

Moss Campion
Silene acaulis
p.360

Wild Thyme
Thymus polytrichus
p.217

Common Vetch
Vicia sativa
p.75

Red Campion
Silene dioica
p.24

Salsify
Tragopogon porrifolius
p.106

Bush Vetch
Vicia sepium
p.69

Bittersweet
Solanum dulcamara
p.393

Red Clover
Trifolium pratense
p.161

Periwinkle
Vinca major/V. minor
p.102

Betony
Stachys officinalis
p.143

Common Valerian
Valeriana officinalis
p.74

Hairy Violet
Viola hirta
p.201

Marsh Woundwort
Stachys palustris
p.313

Common Cornsalad
Valerianella locusta
p.71

Mountain Pansy
Viola lutea
p.362

Hedge Woundwort
Stachys sylvatica
p.90

Vervain
Verbena officinalis
p.113

Early Dog-violet
Viola reichenbachiana
p.8

Devil's-bit Scabious
Succisa pratensis
p.151

Tufted Vetch
Vicia cracca
p.166

Common Dog-violet
Viola riviniana
p.5

Russian Comfrey
Symphytum x
uplandicum
p.105

Hairy Tare
Vicia hirsuta
p.252

Wild Pansy
Viola tricolor
p.265

Blue

 Monk's-hood
Aconitum napellus
p.98

 Bluebell (Native-Spanish Hybrid)
Hyacinthoides x *massartiana*
p.3

 Heath Milkwort
Polygala serpyllifolia
p.357

 Bugloss
Anchusa arvensis
p.236

 Bluebell
Hyacinthoides non-scripta
p.2

 Common Milkwort
Polygala vulgaris
p.147

 Harebell
Campanula rotundifolia
p.202

 Sheep's-bit
Jasione montana
p.417

 Narrow-leaved Lungwort
Pulmonaria longifolia
p.100

 Cornflower
Centaurea cyanus
p.244

 Pale Flax
Linum bienne
p.406

 Blue Water-speedwell
Veronica anagallis-aquatica
p.289

 Chicory
Cichorium intybus
p.70

 Field Forget-me-not
Myosotis arvensis
p.248

 Brooklime
Veronica beccabunga
p.292

 Viper's-bugloss
Echium vulgare
p.214

 Water Forget-me-not
Myosotis scorpioides
p.320

 Germander Speedwell
Veronica chamaedrys
p.85

Spring Gentian
Gentiana verna
p.368

 Green Alkanet
Pentaglottis sempervirens
p.88

 Common Field-speedwell
Veronica persica
p.240

Spanish Bluebell
Hyacinthoides hispanica
p.107

 Chalk Milkwort
Polygala calcarea
p.194

 Thyme-leaved Speedwell
Veronica serpyllifolia
p.165

Index by Common Name

Holly 16
Honeysuckle 91
Hop 92
Hop Trefoil 157
Hornbeam 92
Horseradish 93
Horseshoe Vetch 204
Hound's-tongue 204

I

Indian Balsam 305
irises
    Stinking Iris 28
    Yellow (Flag) Iris 324
Irish Lady's-tresses 306
Ivy, Common 73
Ivy-leaved Toadflax 93

J

Jack-by-the-Hedge see Garlic Mustard
Jack-go-to-bed-at-noon see Goat's-beard
Japanese Knotweed 252
Japanese Rose 94
Johnny-go-to-bed-at-noon see Goat's-beard
Juniper, Common 354

K

Kidney Vetch 403
Kingcup see Marsh-marigold 311
knapweeds
    Common Knapweed 146
    Greater Knapweed 201

L

Lady-fern 17
Lady Orchid 17
Lady's Bedstraw 205
Lady's-mantle 156
    Alpine Lady's-mantle 348
Lady's Smock see Cuckooflower
Lamb's Lettuce see Cornsalad
Leek, Wild 426
Lent Lily see Daffodil
Lesser Burdock 253
Lesser Butterfly-orchid 359
Lesser Celandine 18
Lesser Meadow-rue 403
Lesser Periwinkle 102
Lesser Pond-sedge 306
Lesser Spearwort 307
Lesser Stitchwort 157
Lesser Trefoil 157
Lesser Water-parsnip 307
lilies
    Pyrenean Lily 104
    Snowdon Lily 367
Lily-of-the-valley 18
Ling see Heather
Liquorice, Wild 215
Lizard Orchid 404
Lords-and-Ladies 19
Lousewort 308
    Marsh Lousewort 311
Lucerne 95
    Sand Lucerne 366
Lungwort, Narrow-leaved 100

M

madders
    Field Madder 249
    Wild Madder 426
Maidenhair Fern 404
Maidenhair Spleenwort 95
Male-fern 19
mallows
    Common Mallow 73
    Marsh-mallow 405
    Musk-mallow 99
    Tree-mallow 421
Man Orchid 206
Mare's-tail 308
Marjoram, Wild 216
Marram 405
Marsh-bedstraw, Common 295
Marsh Cinquefoil 309
Marsh Helleborine 309
Marsh Lousewort 311
Marsh-mallow 405
Marsh-marigold 311
Marsh-orchid, Early 298
Marsh Pennywort 312
Marsh Thistle 312
Marsh Valerian 313
Marsh Woundwort 313
May-tree see Hawthorn
mayweeds
    Scented Mayweed 259, 412
    Scentless Mayweed 259
    Sea Mayweed 412
Meadow Buttercup 158
Meadow Clary 206
Meadow Crane's-bill 96
Meadow Foxtail 158
meadow-rues
    Common Meadow-rue 296
    Lesser Meadow-rue 403
Meadow Saffron 314
Meadow Saxifrage 159
Meadowsweet 314
Meadow Vetchling 96
medicks
    Black Medick 64
    Sickle Medick 366
    Spotted Medick 64
Melancholy Thistle 97
melilots
    Tall Melilot 116
    White Melilot 116
Mexican Fleabane 97
Mignonette, Wild 216
Milkmaids see Cuckooflower
Milk-vetch, Purple 210
milkworts
    Chalk Milkwort 194
    Common Milkwort 147
    Heath Milkwort 357
    Sea-milkwort 413
Millefolium see Water-violet
Miner's Lettuce see Springbeauty
Mistletoe 20
Monkeyflower 315
Monkey Orchid 207
Monk's-hood 98
Montbretia 98

Moschatel 20
Moss Campion 360
Mossy Saxifrage 360
Mountain Avens 361
Mountain Everlasting 361
Mountain Pansy 362
Mugwort 99
mulleins
    Dark Mullein 247
    Great Mullein 250
Musk-mallow 99
Musk Orchid 207

N

Navelwort 100
Nettle, Common 241
Nettle-leaved Bellflower 21
Night-flowering Catchfly 253
Northern Marsh-orchid 315

O

Oak 101
Onion, Wild 427
Opium Poppy 254
oraches
    Common Orache 396
    Grass-leaved Orache 401
    Hastate Orache see Spear-leaved Orache
    Spear-leaved Orache 419
orchids
    Autumn Lady-tresses 190
    Bee Orchid 191
    Bird's-nest Orchid 2
    Burnt Orchid 192
    Chalk Fragrant-orchid 193
    Common Spotted-orchid 148
    Early Marsh-orchid 298
    Early-purple Orchid 9
    Early Spider-orchid 198
    Fly Orchid 10
    Frog Orchid 200
    Greater Butterfly-orchid 13
    Green-veined Orchid see Green-winged
        Orchid
    Green-winged Orchid 154
    Heath Spotted-orchid 359
    Irish Lady's-tresses 306
    Lady Orchid 17
    Late Spider-orchid 205
    Lesser Butterfly-orchid 359
    Lizard Orchid 404
    Man Orchid 206
    Monkey Orchid 207
    Musk Orchid 207
    Northern Marsh-orchid 315
    Pyramidal Orchid 210
    see also helleborines
Oxeye Daisy 159
Oxford Ragwort 101
Oxlip 21
    False Oxlip 81
Oysterplant 406

P

Pale Butterwort 362
Pale Flax 406
Palm Tree see Goat Willow

Index by Latin Name

Index by Family Name

Botanical Associations

Botanical Society of the British Isles
Principal society dedicated to the study of the British and Irish flora. It publishes the *New Journal of Botany* (formerly *Watsonia*) and a thrice-yearly newsletter. It also organises field meetings and conferences (www.bsbi.org.uk).

Butterfly Conservation
Charity for the conservation of butterflies, moths and the environment (www.butterfly-conservation.org).

Flora Locale
Charity that aims to promote good practice in the use and sourcing of wild flowers in habitat creation and restoration projects in Britain and Ireland (www.floralocale.org).

The Grasslands Trust
Charity focused on the protection and restoration of grassland habitats for the benefit of wildlife and people (www.grasslands-trust.org).

The National Trust
Organisation dedicated to preserving the cultural and environmental treasures in Britain, which protects over 350 historic houses, gardens and ancient monuments (www.nationaltrust.org.uk).

Plantlife
Charity focused on the conservation of wild flowers and other plants. It carries out practical conservation work, manages nature reserves, influences policy and legislation and runs events (www.plantlife.org.uk).

The Wild Flower Society
Society for amateur botanists and wild-flower lovers, which promotes the knowledge and conservation of British flora and organises field meetings (www.thewildflowersociety.com).

The Wildlife Trusts
The 47 individual Wildlife Trusts collectively manage more than 2,000 nature reserves, many of which are excellent botanical sites (www.wildlifetrusts.org).

The Woodland Trust
Conservation charity in Britain concerned with the protection and sympathetic management of native woodland heritage (www.woodlandtrust.org.uk).

Courses for the identification of wild flowers

Field Studies Council
Wild flower and other plant identification courses based at centres around the UK (www.field-studies-council.org).

Institute of Ecology and Environmental Management
The professional body that supports ecologists and environmental managers runs training workshops in topics including basic botany and plant identification (www.ieem.net).

Workers' Educational Association
The association's adult education courses around the country include several focusing on plants and wild flowers (www.wea.org.uk).

Botanic gardens and local environmental studies or education centres also run wild-flower identification courses for the general public.

Select Bibliography

Back, Phillippa, *The Illustrated Herbal* (Hamlyn, 1987).

Baker, Margaret, *Discovering the Folklore of Plants* (Shire, 1996).

Blamey, Marjorie, and Grey-Wilson, Christopher, *The Illustrated Flora of Britain and Northern Europe* (Hodder & Stoughton, 1989).

Clapham, A. R., Tutin, T. G., and Moore, D. M., *Flora of the British Isles* (Third Edition, Cambridge, 1987).

Clarke, William, *First Records of British Flowering Plants* (West, Newman & Co, 1900).

Cooper, Marion, and Johnson, Anthony, *Poisonous Plants and Fungi: An Illustrated Guide* (HMSO, 1988).

Culpeper, Nicholas, *Culpeper's Complete Herbal* (Standard, 2007).

Edwards, Mike, and Jenner, Martin, *Field Guide to the Bumblebees of Great Britain and Ireland* (Ocelli, 2005).

Flower, Charles, *Where Have All the Flowers Gone?* (Papadakis, 2008).

Foley, Michael, and Clarke, Sidney, *Orchids of the British Isles* (Griffin Press, 2005).

Garrard, Ian, and Streeter, David, *The Wild Flowers of the British Isles* (Macmillan, 1983).

Harrap, Anne, and Harrap, Simon, *Orchids of Britain and Ireland: a field and site guide* (A&C Black, 2005).

Irving, Miles, *The Forager Handbook* (Ebury, 2009).

Keble Martin, William, *Concise British Flora in Colour* (Michael Joseph, 1975).

Mabey, Richard, *Flora Britannica* (Sinclair-Stevenson, 1996).

Mabey, Richard, *Food for Free* (Collins, 2007).

Phillips, Roger, *Grasses, Ferns, Mosses and Lichens of Great Britain and Ireland* (Ward Lock 1980).

Phillips, Roger, *Wild Flowers of Britain* (Pan Books, 1977).

Poland, John, *The Vegetative Key to the British Flora* (Botanical Society of the British Isles, 2009).

Pratt, Anne, *The Flowering Plants, Grasses, Sedges and Ferns of Great Britain* (Frederick Warne, 1855–1873).

Pratt, Anne, *Wild Flowers of the Year* (Religious Tract Society, 1913).

Preston, D. A., et al, *New Atlas of the British and Irish Flora* (Oxford University Press, 2002).

Reader's Digest Association, *Field Guide to the Wild Flowers of Britain* (Reader's Digest Association, 1982).

Rose, Francis, *Grasses, Sedges, Rushes and Ferns of the British Isles and North-western Europe* (Viking, 1989).

Rose, Francis, *The Wild Flower Key* (Frederick Warne, 2006).

Spencer-Jones, Rae, and Cuttle, Sarah, *Wild Flowers of Britain and Ireland* (Kyle Cathie, 2005).

Stace, Clive, *New Flora of the British Isles* (Cambridge University Press, 2010).

Stevens, John, *Discovering Wild Plant Names* (Shire, 1973).

Streeter, David, *Collins Flower Guide* (Collins, 2009).

Summerhayes, V. S., *Wild Orchids of Britain* (Collins, 1951).

Tanner, Heather, and Tanner, Robin, *Woodland Plants* (Garton, 1981).

Thomas, Jeremy, and Lewington, Richard, *The Butterflies of Britain and Ireland* (British Wildlife Publishing, 2010).

Walters, Max, and Raven, John, *Mountain Flowers* (Collins, 1956).

Wright, John, *The River Cottage Hedgerow Handbook* (Bloomsbury, 2010).

About the Author & the Photographer

Sarah Raven is a broadcaster, teacher and writer. She has written and presented the BBC2 series *Bees, Butterflies and Blooms* on the vital importance of pollinators to our health, wealth and happiness. She runs her own cookery and gardening school at Perch Hill in East Sussex and is the author of *The Cutting Garden, Sarah Raven's Garden Cookbook* (which won the Guild of Food Writers' Cookery Book of the Year Award in 2008), *Sarah Raven's Food for Friends & Family* and *Sarah Raven's Complete Christmas*.

Jonathan Buckley has been collaborating with Sarah Raven for fifteen years. His work has been widely published in books, magazines and newspapers worldwide. His awards have included the Garden Media Guild Garden Photographer of the Year, Features Photographer of the Year and Single Image of the Year.

Acknowledgements

First, thank you to my great friends Alexandra Chaldecott and Kate Hubbard, who urged me to write a pocket handbook on wild flowers, which somehow became the book that you are now holding in your hands.

It has been a massive team effort with a lot of different people involved. Jonathan and I were advised about and guided to good spots to find plants by many botanists and wild-flower lovers throughout the British Isles. Wardens and staff from Wildlife Trusts, the Woodland Trust and National Trust properties throughout the country provided us with invaluable on-the-ground information as to what was looking good at what time, and where we might find the best plants. Huge thanks to all of them.

Sue Nottingham at Plantlife, as well as Tim Pankhurst, a Breckland specialist, and Ben Sweeney, the warden at their Ranscombe Farm Reserve, were incredibly generous with their time and information. We had an exciting and rewarding few days with Mary Angela Keane in the Burren, Andy Byfield on the Lizard, Helen Hays and Rosanna James in Yorkshire, George Macleod and Johanne Ferguson, from Scottish National Heritage, in the Hebrides, and Gordon French, from the Rahoy Hill Reserve, in Morvern. Peter Gay also guided us round all the most fantastic wild-flower sites in east Kent.

Thanks, too, to Pip Morrison and Zam Baring in Hampshire, Carol Klein in Devon, Michael and Kitty Ann and Ben Cole in Sussex, John Leigh-Pemberton and Phil Williams in Kent, Peter Lawson in Morvern and Mike Adams near Tenbury Wells. For companionship on botanising trips, thanks to Jane Raven, Flora McDonnell and Andy Vernon, as well as all the helpful anonymous strangers who went out of their way to show us things when we met them on plant hunts. There was a man in a wood in Wiltshire who led us to Solomon's-seal, a lady walking her dog who showed us swathes of Field Pansy, and many others.

There are two people on whom I relied from beginning to end in creating this book. The botanist Andy Byfield read every word and checked every photograph to make sure we were not making any terrible misidentifications or botanical howlers. Huge, heartfelt thanks to him. Alfred Gay has worked indefatigably as my research assistant, reviewing much of the literature and providing me with invaluable science-based notes on all the flowers. I could not have done this book without him.

Thanks, too, to my agents Caroline Michel and Alexandra Henderson for all their support. At Bloomsbury, I'd love to thank Richard Atkinson for his inspiring understanding of what a book like this could be and should be. Natalie Hunt has done a monumental job, gathering all the strands of this book together and tying them down. Peter Dawson at Grade Design put together the book in the most ingenious way, so that the words had plenty of space yet there was still room for large numbers of pictures. Rachael Oakden, the copyeditor of this huge and complicated manuscript, worked so sensitively and meticulously. Sincere thanks also to Xa Shaw Stewart, Penny Edwards, Katie Bond, Alice Shortland, Peter Barnes, John Wright, Anne Askwith and Vicki Robinson.

Finally, enormous thanks to Adam, my husband, for his great patience with this book. Through the winter and spring, he sat on many evenings and let me read out the plant biographies I'd written that day, helping me hone and improve them. And to Jonathan Buckley, my tireless companion and creator of the inspiring photographs that make this book what it is.

First published in Great Britain 2011
This edition published in 2012

Text copyright © 2011 by Sarah Raven
Photography © 2011 by Jonathan Buckley,
except photographs listed opposite.
Illustrations © 2011 by John Wright

The moral right of the author has been asserted.

Bloomsbury Publishing Plc, 50 Bedford Square, London WC1B 3DP
Bloomsbury Publishing, London, New Delhi, New York and Sydney

A CIP catalogue record for this book is available from the
British Library

ISBN 978 1 4088 3375 9

10 9 8 7 6 5 4 3 2 1

Photography: Jonathan Buckley
Design: Peter Dawson with Louise Evans, www.gradedesign.com
Illustrations: John Wright
Index: Vicki Robinson

The text of this book is set in Minion.
Printed in China by C&C Offset Printing Co., Ltd

www.bloomsbury.com/sarahraven
www.sarahraven.com
www.jonathanbuckley.com

Picture credits

p.2 left © gartenfoto.eu/Martin Schröder; p.17 left © Geoff Kidd/
Science Photo Library; p.89 left © Biopix: J. C. Schou; p.92 right
© GAP Photos/Sharon Pearson; p.101 right © GAP Photos/J. S. Sira;
p.107 right © Florapix/Alamy; p.115 left © GAP Photos/Gary Smith;
p.151 left © GAP Photos/Dianna Jazwinski; p.159 left © Maurice
Nimmo/Science Photo Library; p.160 left © Organica/Alamy;
p.190 right © GAP Photos/Gary Smith; p.203 left © GAP Photos/
Sabina Ruber; p.204 right © GAP Photos/Janet Johnson; p.213
© Wikimedia Commons; p.214 left © GAP Photos/Dianna
Jazwinski; p.239 right © Georg Slickers/ Wikimedia Commons;
p.245 left © GAP Photos/Janet Johnson; p.247 right © John Miller/
www.photolibrary.com; p.249 left © Bob Gibbons/Science Photo
Library; p.256 left © Bob Gibbons/Science Photo Library; p.260
right © Bruno Petriglia/Science Photo Library; p.265 left © Jörg
Hempel/Wikimedia Commons; p.288 right © D. W. Howes/Science
Photo Library; p.296 left © Howard Rice/www.photolibrary.com;
p.300 left © www.aphotoflora.com; p.301 left © Howard Rice/
www.photolibrary.com; p.302 right © Sarah Raven; p.313 left
© Bob Gibbons/Science Photo Library; p.348 right © Science Photo
Library/Alamy; p.349 right © Wildlife GmbH/Alamy; p.351 left
© Mark Turner/www.photolibrary.com; p.363 left © www.
aphotoflora.com; p.363 right © Schulz/F1 Online/www.
photolibrary.com; p.367 right © Paroli Galperti/www.photolibrary.
com; p.369 right © GAP Photos/Dave Zubraski; p.406 right © GAP
Photos/Dianna Jazwinski; p.420 left © GAP Photos/Graham Strong;
p.423 left © Bob Gibbons/Science Photo Library; p.449 bottom right
© Sarah Raven; p.498 right © Sarah Raven.